MW01195574

Òrìṣà Devotion as World Religion

Òrìṣà Devotion as World Religion

The Globalization of Yorùbá Religious Culture

Edited by

Jacob K. Olupona

and

Terry Rey

THE UNIVERSITY OF WISCONSIN PRESS

This book was published with the support of
Temple University and the University of California, Davis.

The University of Wisconsin Press
1930 Monroe Street, 3rd floor
Madison, Wisconsin 53711-2059

www.wisc.edu/wisconsinpress/

3 Henrietta Street
London WC2E 8LU, England

Library of Congress Cataloging-in-Publication Data
Òrìṣà devotion as world religion : the globalization of Yorùbá religious
culture / edited by Jacob K. Olupona and Terry Rey.
p. cm.
Includes bibliographical references and index.
ISBN 0-299-22460-0 (cloth : alk. paper)—ISBN 0-299-22464-3 (pbk. : alk. paper)
1. Orishas. 2. Gods, Yoruba. 3. Yoruba (African people)—Religion.
I. Olupona, Jacob Obafemi Kehinde. II. Rey, Terry.
BL2480.Y60755   2007
299.6'8333—dc22   2007012910

This book is dedicated to
Professor John Pemberton III

and to the memories of

Professor Cornelius O. Adepegba,
Professor Ikulomi Djisovi Eason,
Professor Christopher T. Gray,
Babatunde Olatunji, and
Connie Francès Rey.

Contents

Acknowledgments

It requires a great deal of time, effort, and, of course, money to unite several dozen scholars from four continents for a three-day conference, and then to create a book out of, and worthy of, their efforts. The December 1999 event at Miami's Florida International University (FIU), "From Local to Global: Rethinking Yorùbá Religion for the Next Millennium," which served as foundation and inspiration for this book, was made possible thanks to a generous grant from the Ford Foundation, for which we particularly thank Dr. Constance Buchanan. The FIU College of Arts and Science, African–New World Studies Program, and Department of Religious Studies also provided substantial support, and we thank accordingly and respectively Dean Arthur Herriott and Professors Carole Boyce Davies and Nathan Katz. Several other scholars at FIU supported the conference in various ways, from chairing panels to promoting the event through their contacts, and likewise we express our sincere gratitude to them: Professors Ginette Ba-Curry, Isabel Castellanos, Christopher T. Gray, Christine Gudorf, Codjo Ochode, and Jean Muteba Rahier.

Local leaders of the òrìṣà community provided us with invaluable and greatly appreciated assistance and advice, especially Ọba Ernesto Pichardo, Ọba Miguel "Wille" Ramos, Chief Adedoja Aluko, and Adeyela Albury. Graduate students from our African and Caribbean religions seminars at FIU in 1999 helped out in ways too numerous to recount here (from formatting the conference program to finding a taxi big enough to bring Olatunji's drums from the airport!); thanks thus to Chanelle Rose, Patricia Sprinkle, and Erin Leigh Weston. For her tireless, knowledgeable, and pacifying collaboration throughout the entire sometimes maddening affair, we heartily say to our dear friend Iyalòrìṣà Maria de Oxala: *Muito Obrigado!!!* And finally—here especially we feel that we speak for everyone who attended the 1999 conference—we profoundly appreciate the critical contributions of Professors Charles Long and Michele Foster, who carefully listened to all forty-three presentations and offered their provocative summary insights during the closing panel.

Our evenings in Miami were beautifully animated by òrìṣà-inspired creative arts, and the event would certainly have been far less enjoyable were it not for the splendid contributions of poets Eintou Pearl Springer from Trinidad, Miriam Alves from Brazil, and Ọba Adrían Castro from Miami. Charo Oquet, from the Dominican Republic, likewise delighted us with a slide presentation featuring some of her intriguing and colorful paintings and sculptures. And, of course, there were drums. Neri Torres's celebrated Ifé-Ilé Afro-Cuban Dance Ensemble danced the òrìṣàs to the drums of the ancestors, while later the legendary Babatunde Olatunji drummed àṣẹ *(ashe)* into us all. We are as edified as honored for having been graced by all of these artists' remarkable talents at FIU as the second millennium drew to a close.

As for the book itself, we sincerely thank everyone, from the contributing authors and our editors at the University of Wisconsin Press, especially Gwen Walker and Matt Levin, to our families and colleagues for their patience and support. We are also deeply indebted to Temple University and the University of California, Davis, for their financial support for the publication of this somewhat unwieldy book. Special thanks are also highly in order to Marilu Carter, who painstakingly proofread and extensively helped prepare the entire manuscript for publication. Thanks also to Professors Akin Ogundiran and James Sweet for their helpful commentaries on select chapters and to the anonymous reviewers who recommended our book for publication.

In sincerest appreciation, we dedicate *Óríṣá Devotion as World Religion* to Professor John Pemberton III for his wholesome friendship to Yorùbá people in Nigeria and abroad, for his exemplary and groundbreaking scholarship in Yorùbá arts and religion, and, more generally, for his inspirational love for Africa.

Finally, because in some very real (though however abstract) sense everything of worth that we do in life we do for, and thanks to, our elders and our ancestors, and because we who knew them and learned from them are all better human beings thereby, we dedicate our personal efforts in bringing this book to fruition to the memories of Babatunde Olatunji, to Professors Cornelius O. Adepegba, Ilukomi Djisovi Eason, and Christopher T. Gray, and to Connie Francès Rey, who despite her illness was of tremendous support and inspiration during the conference. Àṣẹ!

Òrìṣà Devotion as World Religion

Introduction

JACOB K. OLUPONA AND TERRY REY

I got high john in my pocket,
Got mud on my shoes,
Walked all the way from Ilé-Ifè,
I'm gonna spread the news.
—Cassandra Wilson, "Voodoo Reprise"

In Detroit, an African American woman visits a *babaláwo* (diviner), who reads Nigerian *ikin* (oil-palm nuts) to advise her on marriage prospects. In Miami, crowds of Cuban-Americans dance for the goddess Yemayá to the animating rhythms of a *bàtá* (drum) ceremony at the Church of the Lukumí Babalu Aye. In Brooklyn, a Puerto Rican cabdriver makes his sunrise *ẹbọ* (sacrificial) offerings at the shrine of Ògún in his apartment before another day's work. In Trinidad, local men draped in red scarves sacrifice a goat for Ṣàngó to protect their homes and crops as a hurricane approaches. In southern Nigeria, masqueraders lead the annual Odun Egúngún procession to honor the ancestors. The differences between these religious events are no greater than those between a Greek Orthodox monk in contemplation on Mt. Athos and a poor farmer taking up snakes at a Pentecostal revival in Jolo, Tennessee. Just as the monk and the farmer are both embodiments of Christianity, so are the above-listed *òrìṣà* devotees all embodiments of Yorùbá religious culture, which, like Christianity, should now be considered a world religion.

3

The Yorùbá-speaking peoples of West Africa have cultural roots more than two thousand years deep, thus being one of the oldest identifiable ethnic groups of the African continent (Pemberton 1995: 535). In contemporary Africa's most populated country, Nigeria, their concentration is greatest. Including the several million others who reside in Benin, Togo, and Sierra Leone, the total Yorùbá population in West Africa is roughly 25 million (Abiodun 1987 as cited in Drewal 1992: 12). Descendants of Yorùbá victims of the transatlantic slave trade now live throughout the Americas, where Yorùbá religion, often in combination with elements of Native American, European, and/or other African religious cultures, is a taproot of African diasporic life.[1] In West Africa, meanwhile, where the Yorùbá have encountered Islam since the fourteenth century and mission Christianity and colonialism since the nineteenth (Peel 2000), indigenous religion has in large part shaped or filtered Islam and Christianity, which concomitantly have strongly influenced indigenous tradition. Manifest in Afro-Cuban Santería,[2] Afro-Brazilian Candomblé, Shango tradition in Trinidad, African American Yorùbá revivalism, and (to a lesser degree) Vodou in Haiti, New World Yorùbá religion likewise continues to refashion cultural and religious landscapes, as it has since the transatlantic slave trade. This phenomenon has long drawn the attention of anthropologists and historians. Ifá divination and the òrìṣà (spirits) have inspired poets, novelists, painters, sculptors, musicians, and dancers to creative genius throughout Africa and the African diaspora, just as biblical mythology and the saints have done for artists throughout the Christian world.

To explore all of this critically was the motive for our conference, "The Globalization of Yorùbá Religious Culture," held December 9–12, 1999, at Florida International University (FIU) in Miami, and represents the collective endeavor of this book. Thanks to the Department of Religious Studies, the African–New World Studies Program, various forms of assistance from other FIU entities,[3] and a generous grant from the Ford Foundation, scholars from four continents were able to gather to present their latest research and to discuss issues central to understanding Yorùbá religious culture. Both the conference and these resultant essays ride a twenty-year wave of widespread popular and scholarly interest in Yorùbá and Yorùbá-derived religious traditions, a "transnational," "diasporic," and "global" religious-cultural ensemble that we, the editors, call "Yorùbá religious culture."[4]

Globalization, World Religions, and Yorùbá Religious Culture

Ulrich Beck defines globalization as "a dialectical process . . . which creates transnational social links and spaces, revalues local cultures and promotes third cultures." In order to succeed, globalization requires three things: "(a) extension in space; (b) stability over time; and (c) social density of the transitional networks, relationships, and image-flows" (Beck 1999: 12). Regarding globalized Yorùbá religious culture: (a) its extension in space is concentrated mainly in West Africa, Brazil, the Caribbean, and the United States; (b) its stability over time is as old as Christianity's; and (c) the social density of its "transnational networks, relationships, and image-flows" is high, transcending and including dozens of "ethnic," "national," "transnational," and "diasporic" cultures and communities. As Kamari Clarke explains, this process in which a once local religious tradition in West Africa has become a veritable world religion is fraught with complexities:

> Globalization is producing culturally portable practices through which new forms of innovations are being legitimated in new localities using various forms of knowledge. Not only are these shifts enabling changes in techniques of legitimacy, but ontologies of modern identities are increasingly finding expression in sociohistorical imaginaries alongside biological forms of identity. These identities are deeply embedded in historically constituted strategies of power through which the movement of capital, people, and ideas have spread throughout the modern world. (Clarke 2004: 1)

Clearly, advances in technology and communications have abetted today's increasingly unrestrained flow of cultures, peoples, and ideas, such that the term "global village" is transformed from cliché into reality. Our globe becomes a "village," in effect, because geographic and now virtual space, with ever-increasing momentum, becomes "deterritorialized." Thus, across such deterritorialized space, in the twenty-first century our notion of what constitutes a "world religion" will radically change. If not, the concept itself will be rendered useless for describing little at all that is unique about certain religions as distinct from others.

The literature on religion and globalization frequently cites the work of Roland Robertson, who helped pioneer this important subfield of globalization studies.[5] Among his many poignant insights, Robertson has demonstrated that because of globalization "the pressure *to revitalize* societies has become a major feature of the modern world . . . [and] society as such experiences both internal and external pressures to define its vital cores." Thus "religion . . . is encouraged by this new circumstance" (Robertson 1989: 72).[6] In the case of Yorùbá religious culture, Ifá has served well over and again in diverse societies as a "vital core" that has allowed communities who serve the òrìṣà to revitalize themselves and their religion.[7]

Following Robertson, David Venter stresses that "globalization universalizes the particular (distinct national/individual identities) and particularizes the universal (global order/mankind)" (Venter 1999: 115). Thus, a particular "national" religious identity (Yorùbá), vis-à-vis the vital core of Ifá and the òrìṣà, becomes universal and revitalized in globalized Yorùbá religious culture. Or, as Peter Beyer puts it, globalization serves "to reorient a religious tradition towards the global whole and away from the particular culture with which that tradition identified itself in the past," which quite accurately reflects the unfolding of globalized Yorùbá religious culture (Beyer 1994: 10).

For Yorùbá tradition, the genesis of this revitalization process is to be located in Africa, where Islam and Christianity have long spearheaded globalization. In Africa, conversion to Islam and Christianity has been an entryway into a "global system" that revitalizes the "vital core" of Yorùbá religion. Throughout sub-Saharan Africa and especially in South Africa, African Independent Churches have Africanized Christianity and revitalized African identity by creating "inter-ethnic and transcultural associative networks" that are held together by "overarching symbols and doctrines" (Jules-Rosette 1989: 157). Bennetta Jules-Rosette's terms designate quite accurately globalized Yorùbá religion: an "inter-ethnic and transcultural associative network" (Nigerians, Cubans, African Americans, Trinidadians, etc.) united by "over-arching symbols and doctrines" (Ifá and the òrìṣà).

Notably, globalized Yorùbá religious culture represents an alternative modality in the contemporary landscape of globalization, wherein Western (and especially American) cultural, linguistic, economic, political, and religious forces take root and flourish in the farthest reaches of the globe.[8] Globalized Yorùbá religious culture is thus a prime example of what Peter Berger means by arguing that globalization "is neither uniform nor unchallenged": "It is differently received in different countries, and it is modified, adapted, and synthesized with local cultural traditions in many, often startlingly innovative ways. What is more, there are cultural movements, many of them religious, that originate outside the West and that have an impact on the West. These movements constitute alternative globalizations, opening up the intriguing possibility of alternative modernities" (Berger 2002: 8).

Historically, religions have become globalized[9] mainly through peoples' migration, missions, or conquest, some of them thereby becoming "world religions." Hinduism, Buddhism, Judaism, Christianity, and Islam have all spanned the globe in these three primary ways, which each effect and include conversion. Invariably the product of "first world" scholars and presses, world religions textbooks often also include chapters on Jainism, Sikhism, and Zoroastrianism, while woefully overgeneralizing and unsoundly grouping "primitive" (or "primal," "tribal" "oral," "nonliterate," or "basic") religions and offering the reader slender and derivative examples thereof from anthropological accounts of particular "tribal customs" of Africa (often of the Yorùbá), Native America, and/or the South Pacific. Such a demographic and geographic imbalance has virtually kept closed the entryway into the ranks of world religions and, because it gives the false impression of the putative world religions (and, in fact, all religions) being stagnant monoliths, renders the term itself anachronistic.[10] It is our contention that the term "world religion" is only salvageable (and can only move beyond its "East"/"West" centrism) through a critical rehabilitation in light of today's global religious landscape, and through an uprooting of the evolutionist premise of such Western typologies: such as "high" versus "low" religions, "scriptural" versus "primitive," "big traditions" versus "little traditions."[11]

Tomoko Masuzawa (2005: 4) argues that in spite of shifts in terminologies driven by concerns with political correctness, the very notion of "world religions" itself, and the ways in which it is used and taught, is structured by "some underlying logic silently at work in all variations":

> At its simplest and most transparent, this logic implies that the great civilizations of the past and present divide into two: venerable East on the one hand and progressive West on the other. . . . In contradistinction from both East and West, the tertiary group of minor religions has been considered lacking in history, or at least lacking in written history, hence its designation as preliterate. . . . On the strength of this assumption, these societies are relegated to a position in some sense before history or at the very beginning of history, hence primal.

What happens to the notion of "world religions," however, when a representative of the "tertiary" category, following this logic, spreads so widely and attracts millions more adherents than, say, Judaism, Sikhism, Jainism, or Zoroastrianism? This is precisely what has resulted with the globalization of Yorùbá religious culture, which forces the discipline of religious studies to carefully rethink or reconstruct its categories of analysis. For Masuzawa (2005: 328), in other words, our "historiography must always include historical analysis of our discourse itself."

So, rehabilitating the term "world religion" and freeing it from the obvious evolutionist bias of such typologies would likely expel certain demographically minor religions such as Jainism and Zoroastrianism (whose globalization largely has been limited to a handful of relatively insular immigrant communities) from the ranks of world religions and add other normally excluded traditions whose practitioners number into the tens of millions across several continents.[12] Such is especially the case with Yorùbá religious culture, whose central components of òrìṣà devotion and Ifá divination have crossed oceans and continents to take root and blossom in Santería, Candomblé, Shango, and African American Yorùbá revivalist movements. Still further afield, one scholar has reported a nascent Japanese movement that incorporates òrìṣà devotion, as Yorùbá religious culture also takes root in the Far East.

Òrìṣà Devotion as World Religion is thus overarchingly concerned with the relationship between globalization and an emerging world religion, and more generally with one of the richest religious streams of the African diaspora, which itself is clearly a central piece to the whole globalization puzzle. Thomas Tweed's (2006: 54) carefully constructed definition of religion will be useful for our readers (and for ourselves) to keep in mind while reading the chapters that follow: "Religions are confluences of organic cultural flows that intensify joy and confront suffering by drawing on human and suprahuman forces to make homes and cross boundaries." For all of the variation in forms of practice that Yorùbá religious culture demonstrates, it is nonetheless a "confluence" of diverse "cultural flows" unified in its appeal to "suprahuman forces" known as the òrìṣà and the Ifá oracle, which have enabled its practitioners to "make homes" and not only "cross boundaries" but also oceans.

Unlike most diaspora scholarship, which often focuses on identity and cultural retention, thereby failing to recognize the significance and importance of commodification in the emergence of diasporic cultures, many authors in this volume are centrally concerned with the implications of the commodification of knowledge about Yorùbá religion and culture in the Afro-Atlantic world and beyond. And, of course, the term "diaspora" is too limited for our purposes, for we are speaking of a global religious community whose membership is in part composed of individuals who cannot claim bio-hereditary membership in any Yorùbá or African diaspora. To borrow Arjun Appadurai's term, in a word, it is thus the religious dimension of the global Yorùbá "ethnoscape" that is the collective focus of this book.[13] Or, better yet, the global Yorùbá "religioscape."

Organization and Content

In our letter of invitation to conferees, we posed three questions as a framework for this project: (1) What are the dominant, normative, and essential components of Yorùbá religious culture's production of meaning? (2) What kinds of texts continue to legitimize Yorùbá religion in its local and global contexts?[14] (3) How are these texts validated, contested, and/or manipulated by the practitioners and other relevant agents and/or institutions? Of the more than forty papers delivered at the FIU conference, twenty-seven, most in revised and expanded form, make up *Òrìṣà Devotion as World Religion*. All of the scholars who presented papers at our conference were invited to contribute their essays to this book. Most accepted this invitation, and all of their contributions were accepted in kind. Several other presenters, for various reasons, opted not to contribute to this collection, including Oyeronke Oyewumi, whose influential argument regarding gender in Yorùbá culture is nonetheless discussed in the respective chapters by Rita Segato and J. Lorand Matory.

Before briefly introducing the chapters that follow, we wish to note that so much valuable conference discourse, as is usually the case at academic gatherings, was the product of informal discussions among participants and attendees and thus for the most part escapes the essays in this book. Also missing here is a record of the authoritative presentations delivered during the practitioners' panel by Oba Ernesto Pichardo, of Miami's Church of the Lukumi Babalu Aye; Iyalòrìṣà Maria de Oxala, from Bahia; Chief Adenibi S. Ajamu, of Òyótúnjí Village, South Carolina; and Chief Adedoja E. Aluko, a Miami-based African American *babaláwo*.

Yorùbá-inspired creative arts were powerfully represented at this landmark gathering. There were poetry recitals by Trinidad's Eintou Pearl Springer, Brazil's Miriam Alvez, and Miami *babaláwo* Adrian Castro; a slide presentation of the *òrìṣà*-inspired art of Dominican painter Charo Oquet; a dance recital by Neri Torres and her Ilé-Ifè Afro-Cuban Dance and Music Ensemble; and a masterful drum performance by Babatunde Olatunji. With an invocation, Miami-based *òrìṣà* priest (*ilari oba/ilari oriate*) and scholar Miguel "Willie" Ramos opened the entire gathering. Our sincere gratitude belongs to all of these people.

The impressive variety of thematic concerns represented here forces us to resort to two broad geographical categories in organizing this volume: "Africa" and "Beyond Africa." Whatever their geographic focus, numerous essays in this volume are pertinent to the liveliest debates at the 1999 conference, which were on the questions of legitimacy and gender. As Yorùbá religious culture becomes more heterogeneous, in part because of what Clarke (2004: 22) refers to as a "growing decentralization of knowledge production," a struggle over the legitimacy to represent the *òrìṣà* and interpret Ifá deepens for religious leaders, scholars, and "lay" practitioners alike. This struggle is raising many important questions, such as: How could an African American be taken seriously in her criticism of something about Yorùbá religious culture that the Yorùbá themselves do not recognize as a problem? What roles do homophobia and machismo play in the production and interpretation of Yorùbá religious thought and practice? Is there any merit to a Cuban Santero's claim that Yorùbá religious culture in its purest form is found today in Cuba and Miami but not in Nigeria, where exposure to Islam has weakened "tradition"? Or is there validity to Ọ̀yọ́túnjí Village's general theological position that Yorùbá-derived traditions in and from Cuba are somehow "contaminated" by Catholicism? Ultimately answers to these questions rely on answers to underlying epistemological questions such as: How is something "known" in Yorùbá religious culture? How is this knowledge transmitted, and what does it lose and/or gain in transcultural transmission? Who has the authority to represent this knowledge, and how is such legitimacy acquired and maintained?[15] What should the world most urgently learn from Yorùbá religious culture?

Part 1, "Yorùbá Religious Culture in Africa," comprises ten chapters, and part 2, "Yorùbá Religious Culture beyond Africa," comprises seventeen. The chapters begin with the conference keynote address, Wole Soyinka's compelling essay, "The Tolerant Gods." The chapters are followed by a postscript by John Pemberton III, and in recognition of his great contributions to Yorùbá studies, we dedicated our conference to him.

Part 1: Yorùbá Religious Culture in Africa

The keynote address is one of the highlights of any academic conference, and ours was especially dignified in this regard by a Nobel Laureate for Literature, Wole Soyinka. Soyinka's address, "The Tolerant Gods," is included in its entirety here as chapter 1. In his characteristically eloquent prose, Soyinka impresses upon us that the *òrìṣà* are a gift to humanity, being examples of how power and tolerance can blend harmoniously: "The accommodative spirit of the Yorùbá gods remains the eternal bequest to a world that is riven by the spirit of intolerance, of xenophobia and suspicion." Reflecting the beauty of the religion, which is itself as much as anything responsible for its appeal and hence its spread, Soyinka convincingly submits that this is a tradition that is capable of nothing less than the promotion of peace and the unity of humankind.

In chapter 2, "Who Was the First to Speak? Insights from Ifá Orature and Sculptural Repertoire," Rowland Abiodun reveals the meanings embedded in Ifá ritual paraphernalia, such as the *ikin* (sixteen palm-oil nuts), *ìrọ́kẹ́* (divining bell), and *osùn babaláwo* (a diviner's iron staff), firmly grounding his analysis in affirmation of the Èlà deity/principle that empowers both explication in Ifá and Yorùbá artistic expression. Abiodun convincingly argues that African art history in general must be grounded in African thought rather than Western intellectual typologies; more particularly, he shows that understanding Yorùbá art requires thorough knowledge of Ifá.

After thus answering the question "Who was the first to speak?" Abiodun concludes his essay with the equally important question, "In what tongue?" which is both the title and the subject of Ọlásopé O. Oyèláràn's subsequent paper in chapter 3. Oyèláràn demonstrates how Yorùbá religious culture has enjoyed "a secure means of . . . survival" in language, "the storehouse of our essence." Following an insightful analysis of several *odù* (sacred Ifá verses) that reflect language's "pivotal position in the Yorùbá cosmology and worldview," Oyèláràn asserts that "any strategy for a systematic intervention in the promotion of the Yorùbá culture on the global level will most likely expose it to misappropriation and unhappy misapprehension, *unless* language features instrumentally in such a strategy."

Olufemi Taiwo's philosophical exploration of Yorùbá religion in chapter 4, "Òrìṣà: A Prolegomenon to a Philosophy of Yorùbá Religion," rejects the historically problematic distinction between "traditional" Yorùbá religion, Islam, and Christianity. Instead, we should perceive of Yorùbá tradition as "a compendium of phenomena" that is inspired by a transcendent, "unsolvable mystery." In their quest to understand and establish harmony with this mystery, which would ultimately be revealed to them in Ifá and the *òrìṣà,* the Yorùbá arrived at several religious practices, such as *esin* (worship), *ẹbọ* (sacrifice, offerings, and propitiation), and *ni òrìṣà* (to have an *òrìṣà*). In effect, Taiwo has laid the groundwork for a rich phenomenological understanding of Yorùbá religious culture's past, present, future, and diversity.

The next three chapters in part 1 concern themselves with history. Those by Cornelius O. Adepegba (chapter 5, "Associated Place-Names and Sacred Icons of Seven Yorùbá Deities") and Flora *Edouwaye* S. Kaplan (chapter 6, " Twice-Told Tales: Yorùbá Religious and Cultural Hegemony in Benin, Nigeria") explore archaeological evidence and oral tradition to theorize the emergence of certain deities and the question of Yorùbá religious hegemony over Benin. The subsequent chapter by Sandra T. Barnes (chapter 7, "Meta-Cultural Processes and Ritual Realities in the Precolonial History of the Lagos Region") analyzes contemporary communal ritual in Yorùbáland to provide "a spatial map of historical memory." Both Adepegba and Kaplan are cautious of the "illogicality" of much oral tradition that problematizes the reconstruction of Yorùbá religious history. All the same, Adepegba deftly traces the origins and early geography of seven major *òrìṣà,* concluding significantly that belief in Olódùmarè predates their deification. Likewise avoiding the pitfalls of reconstructing history from oral sources, Kaplan critically challenges the long-standing assumption in Africanist scholarship that Benin originally derived its religious traditions from the Yorùbá.

The case of the 1983 ceremonial installation of the Olorogun Adodo (hereditary chief) in Lagos, as analyzed in chapter 7 by Barnes, reflects a cultural and religious flow in the opposite direction, as the new chief's "warrior ancestors came to Lagos from the Kingdom of Benin," and not vice-versa. This case thus supports Kaplan's argument. Barnes demonstrates how the procession route in this installation ceremony "represented a 'chapter' in the history of Lagos and revealed how one historical layer after another had been added to the community's constitution." Such a "meta-cultural" experience and production reflects the liberal flow of ideas and ritual practices that characterized West African religion on the eve of the transatlantic slave trade.

In chapter 8, "The Pathways of Ọ̀ṣun as Cultural Synergy," Diedre Badejo expounds upon the meanings and ways of the Yorùbá's most popular goddess, Ọ̀ṣun, the *òrìṣà* of rivers. As "healer, diviner, and warrior whose transmutability of form and substance canonize a 'dialogical' view in Yorùbá thought," for Badejo, Ọ̀ṣun's cult and mythology reveal how "essential to Yorùbá thought is its 'dialogical' view of perpetuity and mutability." This sense is nowhere more palpable than in Yorùbá's encounter with Islam, for, as H. O. Danmolé explains in chapter 9, "Religious Encounter in Southwestern Nigeria: The Domestication of Islam among the Yorùbá," Yorùbá traditional religion "continues to express itself in the practice of Islam." Effectively this means that Islam has for centuries been "domesticated" by indigenous religion in West Africa, in much the same way as has, more recently, Christianity. Both of these originally exogenous religions have undergone and continue to undergo a thorough process of commodification with indigenous Yorùbá religion.

Surely one of the strongest points of agreement among Islam, Christianity, and traditional Yorùbá religion—apart from a shared belief in the divine origin of creation—is the great value that each tradition places on spiritually grounded human character. In each case, moreover, this is rooted in a fundamental concern for some kind of higher good and moral imperative. Barry Hallen further elucidates in chapter 10, "Yorùbá Moral Epistemology as the Basis for a Cross-Cultural Ethics," the complexity and range of such ultimate values in Yorùbá religious culture by explaining the interplay between "epistemic, moral, and aesthetic values" that constitutes this religious culture's very cohesion. Ultimately, Yorùbá's high estimation of "coolness" in human character is the measure of both beauty and truth. Notes Hallen, here the Yorùbá have offered humanity a "noble, inspiring, challenging" way of ascertaining "what should and should not be involved in one's being and becoming an admirable human being."

Together, the essays in part 1 concern the origins, modes of expression, and flexibility of Yorùbá religious culture in West Africa. One of the central teachings of this section is that Ifá—and especially its generator of words and all other forms of human creativity, the deity/principle

Èlà—is the ultimate expression of Yorùbá religious culture, and that human cognizance of this expression relies upon language. This religious-cultural expression's worldwide spread (i.e., its globalization) further relies on a prophetic metaphor of human duty, or moral imperative, to be of truthful and of cool character to realize the ultimate good that the Supreme Being intends for humanity on earth.

Part 2: Yorùbá Religious Culture beyond Africa

Beyond Africa, Yorùbá religious culture is a major influence on religion in the Americas, on Islamic pilgrimage to Mecca, and, much less, even on European Christianity. The seventeen essays in this section take us from West Africa's Yorùbáland to Haiti, Cuba, Brazil, New York, Miami, South Carolina, Great Britain, Germany, and elsewhere in a collective demonstration of the impressive variety of shapes and forms that Yorùbá traditions have taken outside of the Mother Continent. Along the way, the authors show us that for Yorùbá religious culture, the globalization process is more complex than it might at first appear.

It is equally important to see that this process actually began in Africa long before the transatlantic slave trade, as Olabiyi Babalola Yai reminds us in chapter 11, "Yorùbá Religion and Globalization: Some Reflections." Yai outlines "three stages and modalities in the globalization of Yorùbá religious traditions, namely West African, Atlantic, and post-Atlantic." Because attention to this important historical reality is lacking in much scholarly discourse on the modern African diaspora, we should recognize with Yai that "Yorùbá religion [first] became global by sharing its òrìṣà with the immediate, West African neighbors of the people who have come to be collectively designated as Yorùbá." Deities in precolonial West Africa belonged to no single ethnic group but through their centuries-old "pendulum movement" became the common property and cultural production of several peoples, such as the Yorùbá, Igbo, and Fon.

Such pendular cultural diffusion in Africa prior to and during the arrival of enslaved Africans in the Americas demands a "revisionist" or "African-centric" approach to Afro-Atlantic history, as advocated by Paul Lovejoy: "An 'African-centered' focus, in contrast to the one centered in Europe or the Americas, reveals the often neglected and misunderstood impact of the African background upon the societies of

the Americas and hence the relationship of slavery to modernity itself"
(Lovejoy 2000: 1–2). Such a revisionist approach to the globalization of
Yorùbá religious culture would thus show with Yai that by the time of
the transatlantic slave trade spirits such as Ògún, Elegba, and Odùduwà
had long been "both Fon and Yorùbá, issues of origin and nationality
being of little interest to practitioners, even as they may preoccupy many
academics."

Revisionist or other, so much scholarship of African diasporic religion focuses on indigenous African "survivals" in the Americas, whereas
Afe Adogame in chapter 12, "New Paths into an Old Forest: Aládurà
Christianity in Europe," reminds us that Yorùbá Christianity is also a
significant *African* agent in the globalization of Yorùbá religious culture
in Europe. Established by Yorùbá Christians, Aládurà churches have
secured strong footholds throughout West Africa and in Europe and as
such are contributing to the present transformation of world Christianity.
As J. D. Y. Peel (2000: 1) writes: "The large scale adoption of Christianity has been one of the master themes of modern African history; and as
the third millennium beckons, it may well prove to be of world historical
significance too, contributing to a decisive shift in Christianity's geopolitical placement, from North to South." Since Yorùbá's encounter with
Christianity is a "noteworthy segment of this process," and since Yorùbá
Christianity (like Yorùbá Islam as seen in Danmolé's essay in chapter 9)
is integral to Yorùbá religious culture, this process contributes significantly to its globalization. To adopt Lamin Sanneh's (2001: 115) terminology, traditional Yorùbá "ways of thought and patterns of life" served
"as the functioning frame for Christianity" and Islam in Yorùbáland.

In the early decades of the twentieth century, around the time that
an African American Pentecostal movement was being planted in
Los Angeles the seeds of revival that would in one century transform
world Christianity, a group of independent African churches in Nigeria
emerged around various charismatic leaders, which effectively opened
a new and important stream for the globalization of Yorùbá religious
culture.[16] Today Aládurà churches count millions of members in West
Africa and thousands more in Europe. Adogame explores "their vitality,
their dynamism . . . and great capacity for incorporating change" behind
the spread of Aládurà Christianity in Great Britain and several other
European countries. In a remarkable twist to the globalization saga in
the religious field, Aládurà Christians "have been embarking on a missionary task to propagate their religious message to a wider world." This

Africanized expression of Christianity not only provides West African immigrants a sense of home in the diaspora but also becomes an important element of Europe's Christian landscape, providing a wide variety of social services for the downtrodden of all ethnic groups. It is thus not surprising that Aládurà churches attract many European converts and offer joint services with local European churches.

Taken together, the chapters by Yai and Adogame underscore the great complexities to the spread of Yorùbá religious culture in its myriad forms—complexities that are as deep today as they were during the era of the transatlantic slave trade. Laënnec Hurbon provides further indication of this in chapter 13, "Globalization and the Evolution of Haitian Vodou," with attention paid to the changes that globalization has wrought since the Second World War in the Haitian religious field, especially through the impact of North American Pentecostalism. Like the focus of most of the essays in this section Hurbon's focus is thus on the "post-Atlantic" (to use Yai's terminology) phase of the globalization of Yorùbá religious culture. Hurbon explains that post-Duvalier Vodou has become more visible in Haiti's public sphere, which has allowed for some marked changes in the religion. For instance, there are Vodou "churches" in Port-au-Prince that now feature weekly Sunday "worship" services that include the typically Pentecostal components of sermon, witnessing, faith-healing, and speaking in tongues. This is surely one of the most striking developments in Haitian Vodou since the nineteenth century—that a *lwa,* or an erstwhile *òrìṣà,* such as Ogou, might possess a devotee in a ritual space that looks everything like an urban storefront Pentecostal church. As Mercedes Sandoval in chapter 18 (discussed below) believes will be the case with Santería, in the future Hurbon sees Vodou becoming more heterogeneous, though drawing from its rich spirit of resistance to ultimately thwart any attempts to "normalize" or "unify" the religion in Haiti and abroad.

Being very much a "nodal point" for African religious globalization in the Americas, it is no surprise that Haiti would greatly inspire Oba Oseijeman Adefunmi I, the African American founder of both the Yorùbá Temple in New York and Ọ̀yọ́túnjí Village in South Carolina, arguably the most significant Yorùbá revivalist movement in the United States. As Ikulomi Djisovi Eason (chapter 14, "Historicizing Ifá Culture in Ọ̀yọ́túnjí African Village") and Tracey E. Hucks (chapter 17, discussed below) explain, Adefunmi had traveled to Haiti to study Vodou and returned to establish in New York a Vodou temple in 1957, well over a decade before founding Òyótúnjí Village in South Carolina. While Eason compares Òyótúnjí Village with the mythic history of the origins of Ilé-Ifè, Kamari Clarke, in chapter 15, "Ritual Change and the Changing Canon: Divinatory Legitimization of Yorùbá Ancestral Roots in Òyótúnjí African Village," is concerned with the function of divination rituals in the creation of "traditional Yorùbá imaginaries" in the Òyótúnjí experience. Using several rich case studies, Clarke ably demonstrates "how microlevels of personal ritual enable people to imagine themselves as part of a community that is culturally different from their own" and "how people employ these religious techniques in conjunction with larger cultural and economic frameworks to produce larger transnational movements of Yorùbá practitioners claiming cultural descent to Africa."

No single American has contributed more to the growth of òrìṣà devotion in the United States than Adefunmi, the late king of Òyótúnjí Village. That Adefunmi was initiated into the religion in Cuba in 1959, and that his earlier temples in New York initially relied heavily on Cuban priests to perform initiations (Capone 2006: 135), is reflective of the central role that Cuban òrìṣà devotion has played in the establishment and growth of the religion in the United States, especially in New York and Miami. In chapter 16, "The Dynamic Influence of Cubans, Puerto Ricans, and African Americans in the Growth of Ocha in New York City," Marta Moreno Vega traces the early development of New York's La Regla de Ocha, or Santería, the most voluminous stream of Afro-Cuban religion. Initially, La Regla made an impact in the city beginning in the 1930s. Vega's chapter is an important step toward understanding the unifying role of Puerto Ricans, Cubans, and African Americans in developing "new possibilities in the growth of African spiritual consciousness" in New York, and by extension throughout the United States.

Tracey Hucks's essay, chapter 17, "From Cuban Santería to African Yorùbá: Evolutions in African American Òrìṣà History, 1959–1970," sheds additional light on the spread of Yorùbá religion from Cuba to Harlem and throughout the United States during the crucial historical period of 1959 to 1970. It is important to understand this spread, she argues, as located within the African American struggle against oppression, for the "African American story within the Yorùbá tradition is one of deliberate agency and choice continuously mediated by symbolic interpretations of the continent of Africa, racialized notions of self-identity, and religious encounters with Spanish-speaking Caribbean communities."

The essays by Eason, Clarke, Vega, and Hucks thus illustrate the major influence of Santería on the spread of Yorùbá religion in the United States and permit us to call Afro-Cuban religion one of the richest streams down which Yorùbá religious culture has become globalized. In colonial Cuba, this stream was fed by Catholic-sanctioned *cabildos* that grouped Africans of common ethnic origin and thereby facilitated communal ceremony. After the *cabildos,* it may be that the Castro Revolution of 1959 has been the most catalytic sociopolitical influence on the development of Santería. As demonstrated by Mercedes Cros Sandoval in chapter 18, "Santería in the Twenty-first Century," the Revolution would result in a remarkable change in Santería's racial and class composition, as white Cuban elites turned to the religion by the thousands to secure their *cubanidad* in the Miami exilic experience. Meanwhile, converts from other Hispanic immigrant groups are further diversifying the ethnic tapestry of the religion. Sandoval attributes Santería's remarkable growth in the United States to the protection offered by the *òrìṣà* to those negotiating the "uprootedness" of the immigration experience, and by providing for its members, through divination, initiation, and the use of magico-religious ritual paraphernalia, a veritable "mental health delivery system."

Agreeing with the basic premise of Sandoval's assessment, Juan J. Sosa concludes in chapter 19, "La Santería: An Integrating, Mythological Worldview in a Disintegrating Society," that for Cubans in Miami, Santería "becomes a guiding social mechanism, which brings emphasis on past heritages and historical roots, allowing for some form of identity," much like Yorùbá religion had functioned for enslaved Africans throughout the colonial New World. Using a rich theoretical paradigm influenced by Victor Turner, Clifford Geertz, and Peter Berger, Sosa demonstrates the powerful function of symbols to be essential to Santería's spread. Santería's "dominant symbols" (Ochun, Chango, and Babalu-aye) place Yorùbá religious culture at the very center of popular Cuban American Catholicism in syncretized form, respectively as the Virgin of Caridad del Cobre, Cuba's patron saint, San Lazaro, and Santa Barbara.

Like Santería, the Afro-Brazilian religion Candomblé represents a major stream for globalized Yorùbá religious culture. In both cases, music and dance express and thereby maintain the meaning of dominant symbols such as Shango. This notion is cogently articulated by José Flávio Pessoa de Barros, who discusses Brazil's sacred Shango music in chapter 20, "Myth, Memory, and History: Brazil's Sacred Music of Shango," illustrating how music is one of the keys to Brazil's memories of Africa and its identity as the largest national community in the modern African diaspora. In his careful analysis of chants sung around this *òrìṣà's* bonfire, Pessoa de Barros reveals the source of Shango's elevated place in the Candomblé pantheon: as "Shango unaffected by death" he is "chief of earth."

In a groundbreaking essay (chapter 21, "Yorùbá Sacred Songs in the New World"), José Jorge de Carvalho traces the lineage of Recife's most important Xango house, Sitio of Agua Fria, to a Yorùbá priestess in the nineteenth century. Within a few generations of her death, command of the Yorùbá language was lost to the community, opening up new avenues of mythopoetics in the Recife Yorùbá corpus that has been preserved over the years in sacred chants committed to memory among priests. Having worked with this corpus for more than twenty-five years, Carvalho demonstrates the central place of such chants in "the extraordinary resilience of the Yorùbá diaspora religious community" and lays a solid foundation for the comparative analysis of Yorùbá mythopoetry from sources throughout the New World, such as Cuba, Trinidad, and New York City.

One of the essential components of and explanations for the spread of Yorùbá religion is its provision of meaning. In whatever form, Yorùbá religious culture is ultimately a worldview that explains to its practitioner the meaning of life and how to live and die accordingly. According to Reginaldo Prandi, in chapter 22, "Axexê Funeral Rites in Brazil's Òrìṣà Religion: Constitution, Significance, and Tendencies," Candomblé in Brazil is a combination of mostly Yorùbá traditions consisting of "ritual aspects and concepts of humanity and the world, including attitudes toward life and death. These concepts explain and guide the fundamental rites of initiation, especially the most significant, the funeral rites called *axexê (àjèjé).*" Yet one of the costs of the rapid spread of Yorùbá religious culture the world over, notes Prandi, is a loss of the essential initiation-dependent meaning of the *axexê,* especially in Sao Paolo and Rio de Janeiro, where Prandi has observed the recent proliferation of thousands of *òrìṣà* "houses," many of which are founded and led by dubiously trained priests who nonetheless claim authority.

With the advent of the Internet, questions of representational authority in Yorùbá religious culture have become even muddier, especially in the United States. In the year leading up to the Miami conference, we received several e-mails from *òrìṣà* devotees demanding that their *baba-láwo* or "godfathers" be invited to present papers or receive our homage. One went so far as to threaten that if his *ọba* from Los Angeles were not brought to the event, there would be tragic consequences! This e-mail also linked us to the *ọba's* colorful Web site. George Edward Brandon is following such contentious exchanges among the neo-Yorùbá community on the Internet, noting that with over "160 Web sites devoted to one aspect or another of Yorùbá religion," it would appear that "the *orisha* have begun to colonize cyberspace." In chapter 23, "From Oral to Digital: Rethinking the Transmission of Tradition in Yorùbá Religion," Brandon traces the complex history of the production of oral and literary texts in Yorùbá and Yorùbá-derived religion to contextualize and theorize the meaning of cyberspace and the rise therein of "cyber-elders" in Yorùbá religious culture and the forceful role that the Internet is beginning to play in its globalization.

Joseph M. Murphy likewise critically analyzes the impact of the Internet on the spread of òrìṣà traditions in chapter 24, "Òrìṣà Traditions and the Internet Diaspora." Because "new patterns of devotion to them [the *òrìṣà*] have been developing beyond any single person or house's ability to quantify or sanction them," unprecedented and at times undesirable changes are occurring in the religion. For one example, the Internet tends to anthropomorphize the *òrìṣà*, thus removing the spirits "from the ceremonial context where the *òrìṣà* have traditionally 'lived.'" One serious implication of this is the detachment of the *òrìṣà* from "stones and herbs so fundamental to traditional *òrìṣà* devotion."

One of the most heated debates at the Florida International University conference concerned the meaning of gender in Yorùbá religious culture. The tenor of this debate is well reflected in Rita Laura Segato's essay (chapter 25, "Gender, Politics, and Hybridism in the Transnationalization of Yorùbá Culture"). Segato engages the analyses of Oyewumi Oyeronke, who argues that gender distinctions were unknown in Yorùbá culture before the colonial era, and J. Lorand Matory, who disagrees strongly with Oyewumi's argument. Segato weaves her own rich experience as an ethnographer of Yorùbá traditions in Brazil into this debate, demonstrating, among other important insights, that the "complex gender system" working "in the traditional Yorùbá religious polis was one of the pillars . . . of the solid expansion of Yorùbá religion and cosmology in Brazil, and from Brazil to other countries."

Both the conference discourse and the voluminous e-mail correspondence surrounding the event made it clear that many practitioners only trust the work of initiate scholars. There was also revealed a tendency among practitioners and even some academics to favor the opinions and insights of native Yorùbá scholars over and above those of non-Yorùbá scholars. In chapter 26, "Is There Gender in Yorùbá Culture?" J. Lorand Matory challenges any facile acceptance of scholarly portrayals of gender in Yorùbá religious culture that may result from such prejudice. Drawing from a rich assortment of ritualistic and linguistic examples throughout the Yorùbá-Atlantic world, Matory argues that gender distinctions are quite rigid in Yorùbá culture, thus challenging claims that Yorùbá religious culture is "flexible" and "tolerant." For Matory, this entire dispute is part of a larger contest for authority between Africa and its diaspora.

Reflecting on over thirty years of study of Yorùbá religion in Nigeria, John Pemberton III happily reports that his "own experience has not been one that has suffered such a dichotomy," being instead an "intellectual and spiritual sojourn" of "respectful dialogue." Initially drawn by "the remarkable artistry of the Yorùbá people" in the early 1970s, Pemberton has long engaged in fruitful collaborations with Yorùbá priests, artists, and scholars of religion and has written some of the field's most important texts. We are thus most honored that his postscript concludes this book.

In the end, thanks to the outstanding scholarship of the contributors to this volume, *Òrìṣà Devotion as World Religion* contains important lessons about who was the first to speak Yorùbá religious culture and in what language; about the ultimate goodness and coolness that Yorùbá religion offers the world; and about how the multicultural, multilingual, multilayered traditions and expressions of individuals and communities who govern their lives according to Ifá and in harmony with the òrìṣà have indeed helped Yorùbá become one of the world's great religions. To some observers such as Soyinka, this amounts to an offering that Yorùbá religious culture places on the altar of humanity: "Òrìṣà is the antithesis of tyranny and dictatorship—what greater gift than this tolerance, this accommodation, can humanity demand from the world of spirit?" As in virtually all "world religions," we are taught here that the gods have done their part—the rest is up to us. To the extent that we fail to keep up our half of this cosmological bargain, even the most tolerant gods may legitimate the horrors of injustice, brutality, and exploitation. Why this occurs and how this most tragic of human tendencies can be averted in our rapidly globalizing world are questions that, far from being merely academic concerns, loom large and belie the existential question as to whether Yorùbá or any other religious culture will actually see the next millennium.

Notes

1. Although we cannot know with any precision the number of Yorùbá victims of the transatlantic slave trade, since most contemporary records indicate port of origin and often erroneously group varied ethnic groups under generic headings, Eltis (2003) has developed methodologies that suggest "Yoruba speakers made up less than 9 percent of Africans carried to the New World," over two-thirds of them to St. Domingue, Cuba, and Bahia. For other useful discussions of ethnic demographics among African victims of the transatlantic slave trade, see Curtin 1969; Lovejoy 1982, 1989, and 2003; Eltis 2001; and Eltis et al. 2000.

2. We respectfully recognize that many practitioners of Yorùbá-derived religions in Cuba and the United States prefer "Lukumí" or "Regla de Ocha" to "Santería" as the name for their religion. For the sake of brevity, we nonetheless group them all under the title "Santería" in this introduction.

3. Besides support from the Department of Religious Studies and the African–New World Studies Program, funding for the conference was also received from the FIU College of Arts and Sciences, the Center for Transnational and Comparative Global Studies, the Latin American and Caribbean Studies Center, and the Asian Studies Program.

4. We agree with Olufemi Taiwo's caution in his essay in this volume that the term "African Traditional Religion" (or "Yorùbá Traditional Religion") "is conceptually problematic, perhaps vacuous . . . [since] the liturgies, icons, etc., of much that is identified as 'African Traditional Religion' have not only changed, their representations show that they have been importing foreign bodies and assimilating same." J. D. Y. Peel reflects Taiwo's concern in writing of the impact of Christian missions on the Yorùbá in the nineteenth century, at a time when "Yorùbá traditional religion was less precisely that than part of communal furniture, an omnipresent facility which nearly everyone turned to for protection and empowerment" (Peel 2000: 13). By "Yorùbà religious culture" we mean then more this "communal furniture" that is now global than any putatively pure, pre-contact indigenous Yorùbá traditional religion. As such, Yorùbá expressions of Christianity and Islam are included in the term "Yorùbà religious culture," whose foundation and thrust remain nonetheless, at least in spirit, Ifá, and the òrìsà.

5. See in particular Hammond 1985; Beckford and Luckman 1989; Buhlmann 1990; Robertson and Garret 1991; Bruce 1992; Lechner 1992; Beyer 1994; Ahmed and Donnan 1994; Poewe 1994; Kurtz 1995; Van der Veer 1996; Berger 1999; Haynes 1999; Stackhouse and Paris 2000; Esposito and Watson 2000; Bayes and Tohidi 2001; Peterson, Vasquez, and Williams 2001; Coleman 2001; Hopkins et al. 2001; Wolffe 2002; Prebis and Bauman 2002; Mohammadi 2002; Center on Religion and Democracy 2002; Reid 2003; Jenkins 2003; and Juergensmeyer 2003.

6. See also Robertson and Chirico 1985.

7. As Peter Beyer (1994: 3) explains, "the global system . . . encourages the creation and revitalization of particular identities as a way of gaining control over systemic power. It is in the context of this last feature that religion plays one of its significant roles in the development, elaboration, and problematization of the global system."

8. On the complexities of this process in Brazil that are beyond the scope of the present essay, see Matory 2005, and in the United States see Clarke 2003 and Capone 2006. On methodological issues in the study of the globalization of Yorùbá culture in general, also beyond the present essay's scope, see Childs and Falola 2004.

9. By "globalized" we mean quite simply "become global."

10. Some recent world religions textbooks offer brief comment on the effects of globalization on religion. For example, with perhaps a measure of exaggeration, Robert Ellwood and Barbara McGraw (1999: 2) claim: "In today's pluralism and world community, almost any faith from anywhere is a presence and option throughout the world." They do not, however, go so far as to say this would make all religions world religions; neither do they offer a definition of what precisely a "world religion" is. Michael Molloy (1999: 457) offers this reflection: "We cannot help but wonder how this cultural unification will affect religion. So far, most of the world's religions have remained fairly separate traditions—even those that have spread to different countries and cultures. But globalism may make it impossible for separate religions to remain separate. . . . Globalism will also challenge parochialism and thus will contest any incomplete visions of reality offered by traditional religions."

11. "Perhaps the best known explicit typology was brought to life by Weber and elaborated by his followers as the great and the little traditions. Because these categories were grounded in an evolutionary perspective, the tendency when the two types of systems were studied in the same frame of reference— and here is where the legacy persists—to give the great traditions [i.e., 'the world religions'], such as Islam or Christianity, a central position and the little traditions a peripheral ones. . . . When these attributes are compared, global ideologies are seen to influence; little ideologies, to respond" (Barnes 1989: 21).

12. "More than 70 million African and New World peoples participate in, or

are closely familiar with, religious systems that include Ògún, and this number is increasing rather than declining" (Barnes 1989: 1). Surely, the worldwide total of òrìṣà devotees has increased considerably since Barnes's estimate in the introduction to her landmark volume on the global expansion of devotion to Ògún, the òrìṣà of iron and most things closely associate with metals, like warfare and some dimensions of farming. For a similar volume that focuses instead on global variations in devotion to Òṣun, the òrìṣà of fresh waters and feminine power, see Murphy and Sanford 2001.

13. "By ethnoscape, I mean the landscape of persons who constitute the shifting world in which we live: tourists, immigrants, refugees, exiles, guest workers, and other moving groups and individuals constitute an essential feature of the world and appear to affect the politics of (and between) nations to a hitherto unprecedented degree" (Appadurai 1996: 33).

14. By "texts," we of course mean primarily oral texts, or "orature."

15. Beyer (1994: 83) opines that for religion struggles over authoritative representation are a natural byproduct of globalization: "The problem of religious influence arises only when religion tries to encompass too many lives that are manifestly 'about' different things."

16. For an excellent discussion of the rise of Pentecostalism, see Cox 1995. It is noteworthy that the early twentieth century was also the period in African and world religious history that saw the emergence of the Kimbanguist Church in Congo, which like Aládurà has enjoyed tremendous success in Europe as well. See MacGaffey 1983 and Asch 1983. In South Africa, Zionist churches were emerging in the 1920s and 1930s, around the very time, moreover, that Ethiopianism gave birth to the Rastafarian movement in Jamaica. See, respectively, Sundkler 1961 and Barrett 1988. On the Aládurà movement, see Peel 1968.

References

Abiodun, Rowland. 1987. "The Future of African Studies: An African Perspective." In *African Art Studies: The State of the Discipline*. Papers presented at a symposium organized by the National Museum of Art, Smithsonian Institution, 63–89. Washington, DC: National Museum of Art.

Ahmed, Akbar S., and Hastings Donnan, eds. 1994. *Islam, Globalization and Postmodernity*. London: Routledge.

Appadurai, Arjun. 1996. *Modernity at Large: Cultural Dimensions of Globalization*. Minneapolis: University of Minnesota Press.

Asch, Susan. 1983. *L'Eglise du Prophète Simon Kimbangu: Des ses origines a son rôle actuel au Zaïre*. Paris: Karthala.

Barnes, Sandra T., ed. 1989. *Africa's Ògún: Old World and New*. Bloomington: Indiana University Press.

Barrett, Leonard E. 1988. *The Rastafarians*. Boston: Beacon.

Bayes, Jane H., and Nayereh Esfahlani Tohidi, eds. 2001. *Globalization, Gender, and Religion: The Politics of Women's Rights in Catholic and Muslim Contexts*. New York: Palgrave.

Beck, Ulrich. 1999. *What Is Globalization?* Oxford: Polity.

Beckford, James A., and Thomas Luckman, eds. 1989. *The Changing Face of Religion*. London: Sage.

Berger, Peter L., ed. 1999. *The Desecularization of the World: Resurgent Religion and World Politics*. Washington, DC: Ethics and Public Policy Center.

———. 2002. "Globalization and Religion." *Hedgehog Review* 4, no. 2: 7–20.

Beyer, Peter. 1994. *Religion and Globalization*. London: Sage.

Bruce, Steve, ed. 1992. *Religion and Modernization: Sociologists and Historians Debate the Secularization Thesis*. Oxford: Clarendon.

Buhlmann, Walbert. 1990. *With Eyes to See: Church and World in the Third Millennium*. New York: Hyperion.

Capone, Stefania. 2006. *Les yoruba du nouveau monde: Religion, ethnicité et nationalisme noir aux Etats-Unis*. Paris: Karthala.

Center on Religion and Democracy, ed. 2002. "Religion and Globalization." Special issue, *Hedgehog Review* 4, no. 2.

Childs, Matt D., and Toyin Falola. 2004. "The Yoruba Diaspora in the Atlantic World: Methodology and Research." In *The Yoruba Diaspora in the Atlantic World*, ed. Toyin Falola and Matt D. Childs, 1–14. Bloomington: Indiana University Press.

Clarke, Kamari Maxine. 2004. *Mapping Yorùbá Networks: Power and Agency in the Making of Transnational Communities*. Durham, NC: Duke University Press.

Coleman, Simon. 2001. *The Globalisation of Charismatic Christianity*. New York: Cambridge University Press.

Cox, Harvey. 1995. *Fire from Heaven: The Rise of Pentecostal Spirituality and the Reshaping of Religion in the Twenty-first Century*. Reading, MA: Addison-Wesley.

Curtin, Philip D. 1969. *The Transatlantic Slave Trade: A Census*. Madison: University of Wisconsin Press.

Drewal, Margaret Thompson. 1992. *Yorùbá Ritual: Performers, Play, Agency*. Bloomington: Indiana University Press.

Ellwood, Robert S., and Barbara A. McGraw. 1999. *Many People, Many Faiths: Women and Men in the World Religions*. 6th ed. Upper Saddle River, NJ: Prentice Hall.

Eltis, David. 2001. "The Volume and Structure of the Transatlantic Slave Trade: A Reassessment." *William and Mary Quarterly* 58, no. 1: 17–46.

———. 2003. "The Diaspora of Yoruba Speakers, 1650–1865." In *The Yoruba Diaspora in the Atlantic World,* ed. Toyin Falola and Matt D. Childs, 17–39. Bloomington: Indiana University Press.

Eltis, David, et al. 2000. *The Transatlantic Slave Trade: A Database on CD-ROM.* Book & CD-ROM ed. New York: Cambridge University Press.

Esposito, John L., and Michael Watson, eds. 2000. *Religion and Global Order.* Cardiff: University of Wales Press.

Hammond, Phillip E., ed. 1985. *The Sacred in a Secular Age: Toward the Revision in the Scientific Study of Religion.* Berkeley: University of California Press.

Haynes, Jeffrey, ed. 1999. *Religion, Globalization, and Political Culture in the Third World.* New York: Palgrave.

Hopkins, Dwight N., et al., eds. 2001. *Religions/Globalizations: Theories and Cases.* Durham, NC: Duke University Press.

Jenkins, Philip. 2003. *The Next Christendom: The Coming of Global Christianity.* New York: Oxford University Press.

Juergensmeyer, Mark, ed. 2003. *Global Religions: An Introduction.* New York: Oxford University Press.

Jules-Rosette, Bennetta. 1989. "The Sacred in African New Religions." In *The Changing Face of Religion,* ed. James A. Beckford and Thomas Luckman, 147–62. London: Sage.

Kurtz, Lester. 1995. *Gods in the Global Village: The World's Religions in Sociological Perspective.* Thousand Oaks, CA: Pine Forge/Sage.

Lechner, Frank J., ed. 1992. "The Sociology of Roland Robertson: A Symposium." Special issue, *Journal for the Scientific Study of Religion* 31, no. 2.

Lovejoy, Paul E. 1982. "The Volume of the Atlantic Slave Trade: A Synthesis." *Journal of African History* 23, no. 4: 473–501.

———. 1989. "The Impact of the Atlantic Slave Trade on Africa: A Review of the Literature." *Journal of African History* 30, no. 3: 365–94.

———. 2000. "Identifying Enslaved Africans in the African Diaspora." In *Identity in the Shadow of Slavery,* ed. Paul E. Lovejoy, 1–29. London: Continuum.

———. 2003. "The Yoruba Factor in the Trans-Atlantic Slave Trade." In *The Yoruba Diaspora in the Atlantic World,* ed. Toyin Falola and Matt D. Childs, 40–55. Bloomington: Indiana University Press.

MacGaffey, Wyatt. 1983. *Modern Kongo Prophets.* Bloomington: Indiana University Press.

Masuzawa, Tomoko. 2005. *The Invention of World Religions; or, How European Universalism Was Preserved in the Language of Pluralism.* Chicago: University of Chicago Press.

Matory, J. Lorand. 2005. *Black Atlantic Religion: Tradition, Transnationalism, and Matriarchy in the Afro-Brazilian Candomble*. Princeton, NJ: Princeton University Press.

Mohammadi, Ali, ed. 2002. *Islam Encountering Globalisation*. London: Routledge.

Molloy, Michael. 1999. *Experiencing the World's Religions: Tradition, Challenge, and Change*. Mountain View, CA: Mayfield.

Murphy, Joseph M., and Mei-Mei Sanford. 2001. *Ọ̀ṣun across the Waters: A Yorùbá Goddess in Africa and the Americas*. Bloomington: Indiana University Press.

Peel, J. D. Y. 1968. *Aladura: A Religious Movement among the Yoruba*. Oxford University Press.

———. 2000. *Religious Encounter and the Making of the Yorùbá*. Bloomington: Indiana University Press.

Pemberton, John, III. 1995. "Yorùbá Religion." In *The Encyclopedia of Religion,* vol. 15–16, ed. Mircea Eliade, 535–38. New York: Simon and Schuster.

Peterson, Anna, Manuel Vasquez, and Phillip J. Williams. 2001. *Christianity, Social Change and Globalization in the Americas*. New Brunswick, NJ: Rutgers University Press.

Poewe, Karla, ed. 1994. *Charismatic Christianity as Global Culture*. Columbia: University of South Carolina Press.

Prebis, Charles S., and Martin Bauman, eds. 2002. *Westward Dharma: Buddhism beyond Asia*. Berkeley: University of California Press.

Reid, Jennifer, ed. 2003. *Religion and Global Culture: New Terrain in the Study of Religion and the Work of Charles Long*. Lanham, MD: Lexington Books.

Robertson, Roland. 1989. "A New Perspective on Religion and Secularization in the Global Context." In *Secularization and Fundamentalism Reconsidered: Religion and the Political Order,* vol. 3, ed. Jeffrey K. Hadden and Anson Shupe, 63–77. New York: Paragon.

Robertson, Roland, and JoAnn Chirico. 1985. "Humanity, Globalization, and Worldwide Religious Resurgence: A Theoretical Exploration." *Sociological Analysis* 46, no. 3: 219–42.

Robertson, Roland, and William. R. Garret, eds. 1991. *Religion and Global Order*. New York: Paragon.

Sanneh, Lamin. 2001. "The African Transformation of Christianity: Comparative Reflections on Ethnicity and Religious Mobilization in Africa." In *Religions/Globalizations: Theories and Cases,* ed. Dwight N. Hopkins et al., 105–34. Durham, NC: Duke University Press.

Stackhouse, Max L., and Peter Paris, eds. 2000. *God and Globalization*. Vol. 2: *Religion and the Powers of the Common Life*. Philadelphia: Trinity Press International.

Sundkler, Bengt. 1961. *Bantu Prophets in South Africa*. London: Oxford University Press.

Tweed, Thomas A. 2006. *Crossing and Dwelling: A Theory of Religion*. Cambridge, MA: Harvard University Press.

Van der Veer, Peter. 1996. *Conversion to Modernity: The Globalization of Christianity (Zones of Religion)*. London: Routledge.

Venter, David. 1999. "Globalization and the Cultural Effects of the World-Economy in a Semiperiphery: The Emergence of African Indigenous Churches in South Africa." *Journal of World-Systems Research* 5, no. 1: 104–26.

Wolffe, John, ed. 2002. *Global Religious Movements in Regional Contexts*. London: Ashgate.

I

Yorùbá Religious Culture in Africa

1

The Tolerant Gods

WOLE SOYINKA

I shall begin by commenting that this gathering of minds on the eve of the millennium [Conference on the Globalization of Yorùbá Religious Culture, held in December 1999], to explore the Yorùbá world, one that I hope proves to be a quest beyond a mere academic exercise, was extremely timely. By that comment, I do not wish to contribute to the triumphalist hijacking of Time by one specific religion—the judeochristian. Fortunately for my cultural peace of mind, however, I believe that any recognizable watershed of human history, and even a mere calendar notation, deserves to be seized upon and made to serve even those whose mores and cultures maintain their suspicious distance from the genesis and cultural implications of such an epoch—if only as a motivation for their own internal stock-taking, and the relationship of their history to the other world in celebration. You will find, for instance, that many christians today follow, if only partially, the annual moslem discipline of fasting; they see in it an opportunity to embark on an internal spiritual dialogue, or reflection, through a mortification of the flesh, an exercise that is made easier when it takes place within the supportive context of the extended family of faiths. Mind you, it must be conceded that, for some, it is the ritual breaking of the fast at dusk with its sybaritic dimensions that offers the greatest attraction and fills their hours of self-privation with the anticipation of compensatory excess—don't take my word for it, just ask some of my christian acquaintances why they put on so much weight during the moslem season of Ramadan!

Still, the lesson holds. The millennium is, for the majority, an occasion for the Great Global Party; nonetheless, it cannot fail to trigger, for some of us, a reassessment of some of the great ideas that have dominated the world till now and, in the process, compel us to revisit those that, comparatively speaking, have either fallen or been pushed to the wayside, as if they have been nothing more than fleeting aberrations in the course of human development. Even if such ideas or systems of beliefs have totally vanished, the sense of the "passing of an era" and the threshold of a new one compel us to reconsider whether or not, in a moment of carelessness or globalization intoxication, some grains that once constituted the basis of our nourishment have not indeed been permitted to fly off with the chaff.

Those of us who insist on a belief in the unity, indeed, the indivisibility of the human community, no matter how buffeted such a concept has been within this century, especially by the anti-human excesses of ideology, religion, and doctrines of separatism such as racism, social darwinism, or apartheid, must consider ourselves fortunate if we happen to be heirs to certain systems of beliefs that have survived those overweening themes that appear to have successfully divided up or still contest the world among themselves. Let us name some of these: communism and capitalism, christianity and islam—plus their expansionist organs old and new in the struggle for a shifting world order—the Crusade and the Jihad, fascism and democracy, the judeo-christian Euro-American world and Arabo-Islamic consortiums, etc., plus all their extended families, aggressive offshoots, and client relations—and which, despite demonstrable and glaring errors that prove so costly to humanity itself and constantly disorganize communities, continue to arrogate to themselves the monopoly of Truth and Perfection. This mentality of binary conceptualization of a world order much, much older than many people bother to recollect makes it easy, on the one hand, to simplify "the Other," to belittle or vaporize it. On the other hand, it actually serves an ironic and contrary purpose. Even while remaining an instrument of the original hegemonic project, it eliminates, through a mere wave of the hand or aversion of the eyes, the existence of pluralistic actualities both in ideas and in human organizations, and thus saves up energy for the final onslaught between only two monoliths. To make this concrete: in the struggle between the (communist) East and (capitalist) West, was there ever much of a "worthy opponent" status accorded to any other ideological alternatives? No! Every concept of human organization outside these two was something primitive, inchoate, an aberration, a rudimentary form of one or the other, or a needless distraction.

Exceptions are few and far between. Traverse human history at any moment from antiquity to the present, and you will encounter this pattern of collaboration between the most powerful contending systems: let us join hands to take care of these minnows so we can then roam the ocean at will, devoid of minor irritants—you take the West side of the longitude and we take the East. This has been the pragmatic motivation of numerous historic pacts and treaties in both major and minor keys, from the European wars of possession of the sixteenth and seventeenth centuries and the opening up of the New World to the life-and-death struggle of capitalism and communism that has ended in a pyrrhic victory for one. In the process, alternative models and options in the creation of a just community of man are ridiculed, vilified, crushed, or simply rendered unworkable. Let us, in this connection, always call to mind the lessons of the Hitler-Stalin pact, which remains the most notorious and most chastening political symbol of the collaborationist nature of seemingly incompatible mega-themes within this century.

In the religious sector, the exemplar for this is no less uncompromising. Respect between two "world religions" but contempt or invisibility for all others. One example: the religion of islam accepts one other, judaism (and its gigantesque offspring, christianity) as a partner-rival—the absolute limits of its tolerance—since all others are regarded as offences against the Supreme Deity. Proselytization by its arch-rival is, however, rigidly forbidden, punishable by death in some nations. And conversion is equally fatal, being regarded as the capital crime of apostasy. As for the followers of all other faiths, they are obliged to convert or face permanent social exclusion, harassment, and even, in the case of members of the baha'i faith—death. The christians—roman catholics or protestant—for their part routinely relegate hinduism, buddhism, etc., to a framework of oriental quaintness, certainly not to be considered as belonging to the family of faiths with an equal status. Let us constantly recall that it is within this hegemonic context, the union, not really of opposites but of *opposants* for the destruction of minor contenders, that our exploration of the Yorùbá world is taking place.

That world—let us begin where it all begins, within human consciousness—that world repudiates the exclusivist tendency, as is demonstrable in its most fundamental aspect—the induction of a new living entity into the world and its dedication to the spiritual custody of unseen forces. A child is born. Quite early in its life, as early as the parents discern in this new organism traces of personality, those rudimentary characteristics that will some day coalesce into what will become known as character—*ìwà*—this newcomer is taken to the *babaláwo*—the priest of divination—who adds his tutored observations to the signs that have already been remarked by parents and relations. Sometimes, the *babaláwo* will take the child through the actual divination process. Mostly, however, it is his shrewd eyes, extensive experience, and honed intuition that decide for him—this, he observes, is a child of Òṣun, or this is a child of Ṣàngó, or Ọbàtálá. It does not matter that neither parent is a follower of any such deity, or that no one in the entire household or in the history of the family has ever been an initiate of the god—the child, it is accepted, brings his or her own *orí* into the world. It is futile to attempt to change it or to impose one on him or her.

Yet even this allotment of the child's spiritual aura is not definitive, nor is it exclusive. Some other life passage—a series of setbacks, a display of talent, creative or leadership precocity, or indeed some further revelation of earlier hidden traits such as a tendency toward clairvoyance, or simply the child's habit of enigmatic utterances—may lead the *babaláwo* to conclude that a different guardian deity is indicated for the child, or an additional one. And thus, a new deity is admitted into the household. There is no friction, no hostility. All gods, the Yorùbá understand, are manifestations of universal phenomena of which humanity is also a part. Ifá is replete with *odù*—those verses that are at once morality tales, historic vignettes as they are filled with curative prescriptions, verses that narrate at the same time the experiences of both mortals and immortals for whom Ifá divined, advised, and who either chose to obey or ignore Ifá. The skeptics are neither penalized nor hounded by any supernatural forces. The narratives indicate that they simply go their way.

Of course, Ifá is not without its own tendency toward a little self-promotion, and so we find that Ifá is also filled with verses that speak of the headstrong and cynics who merely fall deeper and deeper into misfortunes, until they return to the original path already mapped out by Ọ̀rúnmìlà. There is a crucial difference, however. It is never Ọ̀rúnmìlà, the divination god of Ifá, or any agent of his who is responsible for their misfortunes—no, it is their *orí,* destiny, the portion that they brought with them into the world, that very definition of their being that Ifá merely diagnosed before leaving them to their own devices, to their own choices. Nor is it, for instance, the resentment or vengeance of one rejected deity that proceeds to take up his or her own cause by assailing the luckless head of the unwilling acolyte—the gods remain totally indifferent toward whoever does or does not follow them or acknowledge their place in mortal decisions. The priest of Ifá never presumes to take up cudgels on behalf of the slighted deity. No excommunication is pronounced; a *fatwa* is unheard of.

The gods are paradigms of existence. Monotheism is thus only an attempted summation of such paradigms. Within it, all the inevitable variety and contradictions of human thought and physical phenomena, concepts of which are personified by the multiple deities, aspire to harmonization, representing the ideal to which humanity itself, as a unity, can hope to aspire. We find, therefore, that Revelation as Infallibility is a repugnant concept in Yorùbá religion—how can you reveal as infallible the aspects of what are in themselves only the projected ideal of human striving! If the source of such striving—the mortal vessel—is fallible, then its vision, its revelation of ultimate possibilities, must be constantly open to question, to testing, by the elected human receptacle and other human vessels to which such revelations are transmitted. By the same proceeding, the notion of "apostasy" is inconceivable in Yorùbá religion, that alleged crime of mortal damnation—in the eye of some acclaimed world religions—where the only guaranteed cure is execution, preferably by the supposedly salvationist means of stoning to death.

It was an unfortunate accident that Religion and Theology were ever linked with philosophy, a paradoxical coupling, since philosophy means a love of—and, consequently, a search for, indeed a passion for—truth. I say paradoxical because the experience of our world has been the very opposite. The dominant religions of the world and their theologies as received in present day have meant, not the search for or the love of, but the sanctification and consolidation—at whatever cost, including massacres and mayhem—of mere propositions of Truth, declared Immutable Revelation. It has meant the manipulation of Truth, the elevation of mere Texts to Dogma and Absolutes, be those Texts named Scriptures or Catechisms. This failure to see transmitted Texts, with all their all-too-human adumbrations, as no more than signposts, as parables that may lead the mind toward deeper quarrying into the human condition, its contradictions and bouts of illumination, a reexamination of the phenomena of Nature, of human history and human strivings, of the building of Community—it is this failure that has led to the substitution of dogma for a living, dynamic spirituality. And this is where the Yorùbá deities have an important message to transmit to the world.

There is an urgency about this, as the world is increasingly taken over by the most virulent manifestations of dogmatic adhesion, the nurturing terrain of which even tends to undermine my earlier attribution of such eruptions to Textual or Scriptural authority. In many of these instances, the defenders of the Text have never even seen the Text or are incapable of reading them, yet they swear by them and indeed presume to act on them. The explanation for this, of course, is the power of orality. The interpreters of text—even when read upside down—establish a hypnotic hold on the innate spiritual yearnings of their captive, often illiterate community. Their word is law, and where they claim to interpret the Word, their renditions of liturgy and catechisms take on an extra dimension of divinational authority over their adherents. Yorùbá "scriptural" renditions reduce this danger of subservience by making the people of Ifá key participants in the processes of divination, taking them through a route where the prognostic verses are selected in succession, intoned, and come to rest only when the suppliant recognizes a parallel of his or her predicament in the invocations of the priest. As for the actual worship of the òrìṣà, their liturgy does not pursue the path of separation between priest and laity, but the very effacement of distances, a communal celebration of the collective, direct intimacy between the gods and their followers.

If the sole achievement of our voyage into the world of the òrìṣà is to open a few eyes and ears to the subtle habit of denigration of African spirituality through the habit of elision, we would have contributed significantly to the ability of the world of knowledge to commence a serious critique of itself. I began by commenting that this voyage is timely, and, of course, that reference was addressed to a global context, the calendar notation that happens to have been universally adopted but remains a religious milestone on a road that is anything but universal. There is, however, a far more specific timing on my mind, one that relates to a hundred million people and is filled with retrogressive portents not only for the nation immediately under reference, Nigeria, which happens to be home to the largest Yorùbá population in the world. This timing serves urgent notice on all other African nations. For recently, in the northern, largely islamic part of Nigeria, a state called Zamfara took the unprecedented step of declaring itself a moslem state within the acknowledged pluralistic faiths of the peoples of that nation.

So far, so troubling. At the same time, however, a two-part series by an academic from Africa, exiled for many years in these parts, was published at this very sensitive moment in the media of that troubled nation, extolling the virtues of this particular religion, islam, especially in the areas of secularist practice and tolerance. This article, exhumed from a different context where it had appeared some time before, offered a comparative account of the West's, and christianity's, claims to such virtues. I offer it here a useful instance of that intellectual binary con trick that I referred to earlier, one that forecloses—by deliberate omission—any parameters that can be evoked from other spiritual worldviews, especially those of the autochthonous religions over which the two foreign contenders have spread their empires. Now, let me make it quite clear—I need to, since this is an academic who is notorious for playing fast and loose with facts—so, for all it is worth, let me state very clearly that I am not about to take issue with his claims; no, not in this essay. True or false, it is of no interest whatever to me. Indeed, in the interest of the avoidance of all distraction, I wish to agree with him, just for the sake of argument, that islam is indeed in every way superior to all religions that the world has ever known, that it is the most tolerant and is imbued with a secularist understanding that puts all other religions to shame. That leaves me free, I hope, to narrow down the cause of my umbrage simply to—its timing.

Now, of course, the comparative histories, sociologies, and moral attributes—including the abyss between precept and practice—of any religion are always legitimate areas of sociocultural discourse, a permanent terrain of exploration for journals of ideas. And so, of course, by all means, let us, again and again, take a terse, rigorous look at the claims of those religious ideas that have stamped their character on world civilization, the Western nations especially and their secular impositions. It is a long way from the United States of America to Nigeria, however, and I find myself puzzled by the timing of such an exercise at the very moment when that nation is threatened with disintegration on account of the action of one state that has taken the unilateral step of declaring itself a theocracy within a secular totality. Let me advance my contention by quoting a portion of a lecture that I delivered in Nigeria on this very theme, in response to what multitudes of Nigerians—christians, moslems, and traditional worshippers alike—regard as an assault on the cohesion of the Nigerian nation entity. I introduced my listeners to the existence of religious plurality in the United States, of which many of them remain unaware.

The religion of islam, especially, has proved the salvation of an ever-increasing number of African Americans, to the extent that many in that country even tend these days to identify islam as yet another spiritual value that especially defines the identity of the African American. No one can deny islam's claim to the second largest number of adherents among the religions practiced today in the United States. Islamic communities have sprung up all over that largely christian society. They run their own newspapers, schools, clinics, crèches, operate large, successful businesses, and are guided by the principles of *sharia*—from dress codes to marital conduct, and processes of arbitration in the community enclaves of which the mosque is the center. It is not unimaginable, therefore, that a governor may be elected in a largely black community who is a member of what is known as the Nation of Islam—so let us imagine that such an event takes place in the state of Illinois sometime within the next decade. I ask all men and women of reason—is it right, is it just or acceptable, that such a governor proceed to declare that the entire state of Illinois would henceforth be administered by the laws of the *sharia*?

It would not matter if the form of *sharia* being proposed within that renegade state were the most benevolent of its kind within the multiple versions of islam that are practiced over the world. It is only of interest for us to note that the governor of Zamfara state, northern Nigeria, has declared his intent to segregate schools, offices, and all public institutions by sex, to demarcate public transport and other utilities into rigid sectors by sex, that he has already decreed what forms of dress would be permitted for women in public places, plus a number of other measures that are anathema to other religions within the borders of the nation to which Zamfara belongs, a nation that has never been, and whose constitution does not permit the establishment of, a theocratic state. Is it only of incidental interest that the chairman of one of the local governments of that state, taking the official establishment of theocracy as his cue, has given an ultimatum to all female public employees within his local government to get married within three months—be they spinsters, widows, or merely celibate by choice—or else! Frankly I do not think that the average Nigerian gives a hoot for the historic fact that (and here I quote from that essay of supposed illumination) "Jewish scholars rose to high positions in Muslim Spain," or that "during the Ottoman empire, Christians sometimes attained high political office," as witness the reign of Sulaiman (1520–1566) or Selim III (1789–1807); whereas, by contrast, "Can we imagine an American presidential candidate confessing on *Larry King Live,* 'Incidentally, my wife is a Shiite Muslim'?"

An immensely impressive sequence of open-minded exemplars! What the average Nigerian would be interested to learn from this historian is how African traditional religions, from their own authoritative worldview, respond to the order given by a local government chieftain—in 1999—that all spinsters must marry within three months or face the wrath of the *sharia*! That women who have known virtual equality with men must now be relegated to a second-class citizen status. Or that felons would be dehumanized by public flogging or amputation of limbs.

Ralph Ellison captured the predicament of the black man in the United States in his acclaimed classic *The Invisible Man,* providing the world a bitter portrayal of the plight of millions of humanity who were rendered invisible by the arrogance of race within their own nation. I believe that it is time to speak of the Invisible Faiths and to highlight the many subtle tactics that are utilized to render them invisible. Whatever was the immediate purpose of those series, devoted at such a time to the comparative virtues of two alien religions, one immediate effect is to relegate to non-existence the anterior religions of that contested terrain. It leads the unwary reader to a perception—buttressed by centuries of indoctrination by the dichotomizing agents of the hegemonic project—of religious choices on our own soil being restricted to the demarcated territories of islam and christianity. But Zamfara, like many other parts of the so-called moslem or christian parts of Nigeria, also consists of other religious faiths, those pre-christian and pre-islamic faiths that are so wishfully dismissed as mere vestigial and inconsequential paganism. The Jukums, the Tivs, the Biroms of Northern Nigeria continue to follow (sometimes side by side with islam or christianity) the religions of their ancestors. At the moment, therefore, that a state opts to become a theocracy, it is only just that we are also permitted to consider what are the pronouncements of existing traditional religions on the establishment of a theocratic state on such a terrain. To such a question, the answer is clear: Abomination!

I limit myself for now, with merely reiterating that before islam or christianity invaded and subverted our worldviews, before the experience of enslavement at the hands of both Arabs and Europeans, the African world did evolve its own spiritual accommodation with the unknown, did evolve its own socioeconomic systems, its cohering systems of social relationships, and reproduced its own material existence within an integrated worldview, that those systems are still very much with us and have indeed affected both liturgy and practice of alien religions even to the extent of rendering them docile and domesticated. Thus, whenever, in contemporary times, the aggressive face of one or the other of these world religions is manifested, our recourse is primarily to the strengths of those unextinguished virtues of our antecedent faiths, the loftiest of which will be found to be expressed in such attitudes as tolerance—the genuine, not the nominal, rhetorical, or selective kind, not tolerance as an academic exercise of exterior comparisons, but one that is demonstrable by the very histories of our deities, their travails, errors, and acts of reparation, as recorded in their mythologies, and their adaptability to the dynamic changes of the world.

A periodic visitation to the world of the Yorùbá—or indeed to any of the "invisible" worldviews—must be deemed a contemporary necessity for millions of Africans, including the non-Yorùbá, the non-christian, non-moslem, as well as christians and moslems, for whom this will surely serve as a catalyst for a systematic assessment of their own cultures and values. Now, of course, I remain unaware if Ifá was consulted at any time since this conference was conceived of years ago, and even if it was, I am unaware that Ọ̀rúnmìlà was requested to cast for an appropriate date for it. Ifá does move in mysterious ways, however, his wonders to perform. One of the main organizers of the conference happens to be a Yorùbá, and one thoroughly versed in the mysteries of the Yorùbá world, so we do not really know how the spirit did move him. Thanks to our ancestral guardian spirits, we are enabled to remind ourselves and the world that it is not necessarily the self-promoting theologies that hold the monopoly of Truth, Justice, or Tolerance. I reiterate, and dare contradiction from any spiritual contender: Òrìṣà is the voice, the very embodiment of Tolerance. Not for one moment, of course, do I suggest that the faith that is òrìṣà claims monopoly on the virtues of tolerance—on the contrary. We simply urge those who attempt to promote the intolerance of one religion on African soil, in a modern African nation, through the route of proclaiming its *comparative* tolerance—real or imagined, provable or merely speculative—in relation to another alien faith, to be far less zealous in such a gratuitous exercise and to recognize, to begin with, the demonstrable tolerance, both in act and in precepts, of the anterior world of any people. The Yorùbá understanding of the nature of Truth is indeed echoed by the Vedic texts from yet another ancient world, the Indian, which declares: "Wise is the one who recognizes that Truth is One and one only, but wiser still the one who accepts that Truth is called by many names, and approached from myriad routes."

The accommodative spirit of the Yorùbá gods remains the eternal bequest to a world that is riven by the spirit of intolerance, of xenophobia and suspicion. This tolerance—if we may spend a little time on the nature of the gods themselves—this tolerance is not limited to the domestic front or to internal regulations only. The Foreign Affairs department—and that is not so whimsical a designation in a career that has entailed, in such poignant and universal dimensions, strategies for relating to external spiritual zones and evolving strategies of accommodation and survival—the Foreign Affairs department has shown itself equally adaptable to the incursion of foreign experiences. To understand the instructional value of this in relation to other religions, one has only to recollect that, for some religions, even today, the interpretation of their scriptures in relation to human inventiveness is toward foreclosure, so that modern innovations in the technological and cultural fields are simply never permitted. We may choose to call these fundamentalist sects, but authority for the exclusionist approach to new phenomena is always extracted from their Scriptures—the Bible, the Koran, or the Torah. By contrast, the corpus of Ifá, which we may consider the closest to any aggregation of spiritual findings of the Yorùbá that are usually termed scriptures or catechism—Ifá emphasizes for us the perpetual elasticity of knowledge. Ifá's tenets are governed by a frank acknowledgement of the fact that the definition of Truth is a goal that is constantly being sought by humanity, that existence itself is a passage to Ultimate Truth, and that claimants to possession of the definitiveness of knowledge are, in fact, the greatest obstacles to the attainment of Truth. Acceptance of the elastic nature of knowledge remains Ifá's abiding virtue, a lesson that is implanted in the Yorùbá mind by the infinitely expansible nature of the gods themselves.

Examine the attributes of Ṣàngó, for instance—what was this deity at the time of his adoption by Yorùbá society? The god of lightning. Following from this principle, Ṣàngó's portfolio becomes extended to include a scientific discovery and application—electricity. Michael Faraday was not born in the land of the Yorùbá, and certainly the autochthones of that land were not aware of the fact that he first succeeded in establishing the principles of electricity by harnessing lightning charges through a kite and running them down to a receptor. Nevertheless, when electricity came to Yorùbáland, it was immediately added to the portfolio of this god Ṣàngó. We dare not forget, by the way, that the priests of Ṣàngó were not above profiting from human disaster and attributing lightning strikes to the ire of the god who singled out malefactors for punishment. Nowhere in the world has the priesthood ever been devoid of opportunism, especially for economic advantage. What we wish to elicit from the relationship of the Yorùbá pantheon to both natural and human-engineered phenomena is simply the ethos of responsiveness, of a refusal to exclude experience for the sake of the pristinism of dogma or usage. For the Yorùbá, on encountering the taming and control of electricity, there was hardly any surprise. Ṣàngó was merely domesticating its power for the benefit and progress of humanity.

Or take Ògún, the god of iron, an especially remarkable case that goes beyond an adjustment of portfolios to technological progress. We all know of Ògún, of course—the god of iron, protector of the forge, and embodiment of the lyric arts. The mastery of iron and the evolution of metallurgy remain one of the crucial phases of human development; hence the especial notation that is given to the Iron Age as a quantum leap in the progression of civilization. There is no question that the formal investment of Ògún in Yorùbá consciousness is coterminous with the development or encounter with the arts of metallurgy. So significant is the assessment of such a step in the technological evolution that nothing less than the cooption of the entire Yorùbá world of deities and their relationship with mortal beings would satisfy Ògún's epiphany. It was as if the Yorùbá, encountering the virtues of metallic ore, its paradoxical character of durability and malleability, its symbolism and utility as alloy, read in it the explication of the potential integration of disparate elements of all nature phenomena. The myth of Ògún goes thus:

> The gods, who in any case were products of a primordial unity—as narrated in the myth of Atunda who shattered the original godhead into what we may now read as a principle of one-in-plurality and plurality-in-one—were beset by a yearning to unite with that portion of their original essence that had been flung across the primordial void, the

fragment of an original unity that became the primogenitor of mortals. Yearning for a recovery of the original unified essence, they decided to undertake the perilous journey across the void.

(In other readings, we do encounter a version in which the Supreme Deity had created the world of mortals, left them to their devices, and then one day invited his fellow deities to accompany him on a visit to see how that world was faring. My suspicion is that this is a corruption of the original myth, and that it smacks too much of the christian myth in which the Supreme Deity descends to earth in the body of his son, gets killed, and thereby atones for the sins of the world).

No matter what version we choose to adopt, however, the heart of the Ògún myth is this: when the gods began their journey for a reunion with the mortal realm, they found their progress impeded by a void that, during the aeons of time of separation, had become impenetrable. One after the other they tried to hack their way through the primordial growth, but all efforts were in vain.

It was then that Ògún rose and pledged to penetrate this chthonic outgrowth. He plunged into this seething chaos and extracted from within it the only element that would guarantee its defeat. That element was iron ore. From iron ore, Ògún forged the mystic tool and wielded it to hack a path for other gods to follow. It was this feat that earned Ògún a place as one of the seven principal deities of the Yorùbá pantheon, and one to whom belongs the pioneering urge—one of his praise-songs goes thus: *he who goes forth where other gods have turned*. On arriving in the land of the mortals, all the deities, like our well-endowed tourists, went their different ways, each one encountering a different adventure. Ògún ended up at Ire, where the people adopted him as theirs. He led them into battle, where, his sight clouded by an over-indulgence in palm wine, he mistakenly slew foe and friend alike. Even so, he was offered the crown of Ire but declined it, preferring to retreat into the hills, where he mourned his day of error, cultivating a farm patch and converting his terrible discovery to peaceful use. Do we see here why the Yorùbá would in no way be over-excited by the moral lessons of the horrors of atomic energy, followed by its peaceful conversion? Today, Ògún is guardian deity of all workers in metal—the truck driver, the engineer, the air pilot or astronaut. All human adventure is prefigured—symbolically—in the history of the Yorùbá deities. Thus, there is no surprise, no inhibition created from scientific encounters. Some new phenomenon, friendly or hostile, is encountered, and from within the armory of Ifá and the accommodative narratives of the gods, an understanding is extracted.

We begin to understand now why it was so logical that the Yorùbá deities should have survived in the New World, across the Atlantic, while most other religions and cultures atrophied and died. Encountering the roman catholic saints in the worship of their intolerant masters, these slaves who were already steeped in the universality of phenomena saw the saints as no more than channels and symbols of the spiritual quest and repository of the glimmerings of Ultimate Truth. They were intercessors to Supreme Godhead, bridges between the living and the ancestor world. If the plantation owners were hostile to any implantation of African spirituality on the soil of the Indies and the Americas, the solution was handy—co-opt the roman catholic deities into the service of Yorùbá deities; then genuflect before them.

Very much the same strategy was adopted in the secular arena, I recall, during one of our intermittent political crises in western Nigeria, home to the Yorùbá, when a somewhat ruthless political party, enjoying the advantage of incumbency, proceeded to coerce the populace into declaring allegiance to its candidates. The symbol of that party was the Hand—an image surely prone to positive interpretations. That government, however, had reckoned without the subversive ingenuity of its opponents, which consisted of nearly the entirety of the Yorùbá region over which it ruled. Compelled to display the symbol of the hand on their hats, vests, in business offices, and even in homes as proof of their allegiance to a detested government, the electorate of the then western region of Nigeria merely added a small lyrical phrase to the traditional repertoire of greetings and song, a message that was transmitted through a particular hand gesture that everyone soon learned to read as *ọwọ́ l' orí, oo r' ínuu mi*. Translated, it states simply: it is only my hand that you see, but not my mind—you have no clue as to my ultimate intentions. And, of course, when election time finally came, a seemingly cowed populace handed the regime its most memorable defeat. Yes, the slaves in Brazil, Cuba, and other South American plantations did bow to alien gods, but the liturgies that they intoned were very much the liturgies of their authentic spirituality.

The process went much further; it proceeded beyond internalization of spiritual allegiance and embarked on an appropriation of the christian symbols, and this, unquestionably, was a response to the insistence of the slave masters that their slaves display visible signs of their conversion, that they mount the iconic presence of the saints even within their paltry domestic spaces. So the slaves displayed the images of the saints but addressed them in the parallel names of their own deities—St. Lazarus/Ṣọ̀pọ̀ná, St. Anthony/Ògún, Our Lady of the Candles/Ọ̀ṣun, etc. And here is the point: this never constituted a spiritual dilemma, since the system of the gods has always been one of complementarities, of affinities, and of expansion—but of the non-aggressive kind. The deities could subsume themselves within these alien personages and eventually take them over. One cinematic illustration of this suggests itself—those films of alien body snatchers where the creatures from outer space insert their beings into the carapace of earthlings, eventually dominate, not only the human forms but the environment and culture, insert themselves into crevices of landscape and social actualities, and can only be flushed out with the aid of weed killers, flame throwers, gamma rays, or quicklime. The difference, of course, is that the African deities were made of sterner yet more malleable stuff—the principle of alloys. Always generous in encounters with alien "earthlings," they accommodated, blended, and eventually triumphed.

The key word, of course, is tolerance—and this I do wish to impress on our brothers and sisters of the Diaspora. Tolerance means humility, not daring to presume that one has found the ultimate answer to Truth, or daring to claim that only through one's intuitions will be found the sole gateway to Truth. All the major religions, the so-called world religions that are built on such claims, have inflicted competitive agonies on humanity since the beginning of time. It is time that we called such religions to their own altars of repentance.

There are religions in the world that point the way to the harmonization of faiths; it is the loss of the world that many of them are little known, their unassuming, ancient wisdoms being superstructurally dwarfed by the—admittedly—often awe-inspiring monuments on the world's landscape—cathedrals, mosques, temples, and shrines, and indeed by the challenging paradoxes of their exegeses—I say "paradoxes" because they are no more than intellectual constructs on foundations of the unproven and unprovable. The disquisitions—just to take one single but mesmerizing aspect of christian theology—on Transubstantiation alone since the textualization of christianity will fill an average university library. But these all-consuming debates and formal encyclicals are constructed on what we may term a proliferating autogeny within a hermetic realm—what is at the core of arguments need not be true; it is sufficient that the layers upon layers of dialectical constructs fit snugly on top of one another; there need not be any substance at the core. And when one examines the ancient manuscripts, the lovingly illuminated manuscripts especially of the so-called Dark and Middle Ages, when those artistic minded monks had nothing else to do during the long dark nights of winter seasons—daylight saving time not being thought of at that time—and had only the saints and angels as outlets for expressing their love for humanity, those manuscripts strike us today with awe and admiration and, of course, reinforce the beliefs of multitudes. So do the buddhist Sutras, the hindu Vedas, the prayer scrolls in buddhist temples, or the ancient texts of the Holy Koran.

Those very seductions that are the outward embellishments of these religions are also recognizable as competitive attributes of the secular world, especially those that are raised to ideological ascendancies. The monumental achievements of either fascism or communism, the splendor and pageantry that trumpeted their existence, the arts, architecture, and ideological treatises still attract or repel us. Their aesthetic virtues may not amount to much—witness the architectural horrors of the Third Reich or communist regimes!—but the sheer grandiose scale of their conception and execution continue to astound, yet neither ideology has presented the world with any lasting truths. Even thus must we view the existence of cathedrals and mosques, of temples and shrines, even as we feast our eyes on their illuminated scriptures, are enraptured by their spiritually elevating music, and imbibe the mystery of their rituals. Not one of these, or any religion known to humanity, can affirm, in any testable way, the eternal verities of whatever Truths they proclaim.

By contrast, apart from its own philosophical literature, and apart from that short-lived bemusing experimentation—arts, festivals of reason, architecture—from the French Revolution, Humanism, for its part, has no ostentatious monuments or rituals that testify to any ineradicable virtues. Its monuments exist, of course; they are visible everywhere in the advances of humanity in the arts and sciences, in the mundane handiwork of man and the constant enhancement of his productive capability and his environment, but these are never labeled as such. The great symphonies, the classic sculptures from the Yorùbá to the Arawaks, the successful orbiters and the failed Mars Lander are the monuments of humanism, though they are never mounted on a plinth labeled Humanism. But despite the absence of such nominal appropriation, we find that

Humanism does enjoy, at the very least, some element of lip service paid to its tenets by all religions. Indeed, these religions appear to fall over one another in attempting to ground their concerns in the elevation of humankind, just as the failed, contending ideologies attempted to root their principles in the primacy of humane values—egalitarianism, end of exploitation, universal brotherhood, etc. What we must pursue, therefore, is not a competitive, bruising arena for the claims of ideology or religion, but an open marketplace of both ideas and faith. Here, then, without any ambiguity is where Ifá, the divine body of precepts, proves itself one of the great humanistic tracts in the realm of religion. As quest, as the principle of spiritual enquiry, Ifá exemplifies this field of accommodation in one of its *odù,* the prognostic verses of Ọ̀rúnmìlà, the *odù* of IKADI:

B'ọ́mọdé bá nṣawo ògbójú, bí ó bá ko ògbó awo lọ́nà, kio o gba a l'ójú. Bí ó bá ko àgbà ìṣègùn, kí ó jẹ ẹ n'íyà lọpọ̀lọpọ̀. Bí ó bá burinburin tí ó rí àgbà àlùfa níbití ó ńfi orí k'alẹ̀, ki o d'oju rẹ dé 'bẹ. A da a f'àwọn aláigbọràn tii wípé: Kò sí ẹnití o lè mú wọn. Ee ti ri? Ẹyín kó mọ̀ pé: Àjẹpẹ́ aiyé kò sí f'ọ́mọ tí ó na Ògbó awo. Àtẹlẹpẹ́ kò wà fuń àwọn tí nna àgbà ìṣègùn. Ọmọ ti nna àgbà àlùfa níbi tí ó gbé ńkírun, ikú ara rẹ̀ ló nwá. Wàràwàrà mà ni ikú ìdin, wàràwàrà.

[The brash youth meets an ancient babaláwo and strikes him. He meets an old herbalist and humiliates him. He runs into a venerable moslem priest kneeling in prayer and knocks him to the ground. Ifá divined for such insolent ones who boasted that they were beyond correction. Is that so indeed? Don't you know that a youth who strikes a priest of Ifá will not partake of this world for long? Premature is the death of the youth who strikes the devout imam at his devotions. Speedily comes the death of maggots, speedily.]

Now bear in mind that islam invaded the black world and subverted its traditions and religions, sometimes violently and contemptuously. It rivaled the latter aggressor, christianity, in violence for violence, contempt for contempt. Both of them proven iconoclasts, yet, what wisdom does this largely superceded and humiliated religion of the òrìṣà prescribe for its own adherents? Tolerance, it enjoins, tolerance! You humiliate the moslem priest, warns Ifá, and you will die the death of maggots.

The òrìṣà do not proselytize. They are content to be, or to be regarded as, non-existent. We need not embrace the òrìṣà, however, to profit from the profound wisdoms that can be extracted from Ifá. Our self-vaunting repositories of exclusive spiritual truths can learn from this ancient, unassuming faith of our forebears. Ifá preaches tolerance. Ifá takes issue with any religion or faith that denies tolerance a place in its worship, and this is why, in another *odù,* you will encounter a sterner, critical face of Ifá turned against the same religion of islam. Ifá embodies the principle of the constant spiritual quest, one to which the notion of apostasy—and this we must continue to stress—the attachment of mortal sin to the act of religious conversion, is simply unthinkable. How could it be otherwise when the Source of knowledge, Ọ̀rúnmìlà, the mouthpiece of the Supreme Deity who directs the feet of the seeker toward a spiritual mentor or guardian deity, is not granted the cloak of infallibility even within Ifá, the very source of his wisdom? The Supreme òrìṣà, or Ultimate Godhead—Òrìṣà-Ńlá, who is also known as Olódùmarè—is nothing like the christians' "jealous god," but the òrìṣà are nonetheless the true embodiment of that christian dictum: Seek, and ye shall find.

It is the profound humanism of the òrìṣà that recommends it to a world in need of the elimination of conflict, since the main source of conflict between nations and among peoples is to be found as much in the struggle for economic resources as in the tendency toward the domination of ideas, be these secular or theological. Recalling the warning of W. E. B. Du Bois at the end of the nineteenth century, that the main issue of the twentieth century would be one of the color line, it is more than justifiable to suggest that the main issue of the twenty-first century, of the third millennium, will be one of religion; such is the all-consuming intensity with which the fanatic strain attempts to overwhelm our world. Yet the problem does not really lie with christianity, or with islam, judaism or hinduism, etc., but with the irredentist strain that appears to have afflicted these world religions, unlike the world of the òrìṣà. Let all these religions therefore pause and ask themselves, why is it that the worship of òrìṣà has never, in all these centuries, spawned an irredentist strain? The answer lies, of course, in the profound humanism of the òrìṣà.

Òrìṣà, being profoundly humanist, separates the regulation of community from communion with the spirit, even while maintaining a mythological structure that weaves together both the living community and the unseen world. But that world of the spirit does not assume any competitive posture whatever over the pragmatic claims of this world. *B' énìa kò sí, imalẹ̀ ò lè wà* (If humanity were not, the deities would not be). And very much in the same frame of apportionment is the seeming paradox that although every mortal is believed to have brought his own *orí,* or portion, destiny, into the world, that same view of existence declares: *ọwọ́ ara ẹni l' a fi ńtuń t' ara ẹni ṣe* (Within one's own hands lies the potential of directing one's destiny.)

My final word comes from the already mentioned address that I delivered in Nigeria in admonition of those theocratic politicians who are resolved to set our world on fire, and it is urgently directed at those meddlesome closet clerics who provide pretentious, spuriously objectivized academic covering fire for the incursion of prejudice, creating smokescreens to divert our attention from issues of life and death, issues of human dignity, mutual tolerance, and mutual respect, blithely ignoring the relegation of one half of humanity—the female—to subservience and social degradation through the selective interpretation of some of the scriptures they champion. Our counter-propositions arise as much from the glaring failures of the worldviews they have chosen to promote as models of perfection, or as liberalized exemplars, as from our knowledge of the tolerance amplitude of religions and worldviews that existed before the advent of these newly aggressive faiths.

Between fanaticism and Community, we choose Community, and òrìṣà is community. Community is the basic unit, the common denominator and definition of humanity—this is the lesson of the òrìṣà. And in the strategies for regulating and preserving community, the òrìṣà have ceded the right of choice to humanity and to the deductions of its intelligence—not to intuitions and their interpretations by any self-serving priesthood. Even the collective manifestation of faith is constantly selective and exclusive, unlike the secular order that necessarily embraces all—this Ifá recognizes, and this it is that nerves us to say, go to the òrìṣà and be wise. Religion, or profession of faith, cannot serve as the common ground for human co-existence except, of course, by the adoption of coercion as a principle and, thus, the manifestation of its corollary, hypocrisy, an outward conformism that is dictated by fear, by a desire for preferment, or, indeed, the need for physical survival. In the end, the product is conflict and the destruction of cultures. Let this be understood by the closet champions of theocracies where religion and dictatorship meet and embrace. Let us resolve to say to them: you will not bring our world even close to the edge of combustion. The essence of òrìṣà is the antithesis of tyranny and dictatorship—what greater gift than this tolerance, this accommodation, can humanity demand from the world of the spirit?

And thus, for all seekers after the peace of true community, and the space of serenity that enables the quest after Truth, we urge yet again the simple path that was traveled from the soil of the Yorùbá across the hostile oceans to the edge of the world in the Americas—Go to the òrìṣà, learn from the òrìṣà, and be wise.

2

Who Was the First to Speak?

Insights from Ifá Orature and Sculptural Repertoire

ROWLAND ABIODUN

Ta ló kọ́ wí?
Èlà ló kọ́ wí.
Ta ló kọ́ sọ?
Èlà ló kọ́ sọ.
Ta ni à ńpè ní Èlà?
Hòọ̀ tó rò náà
Ni à ńpè ní Èlà.

[Who was the first to speak?
Èlà was the first to speak.
Who was the first to communicate?
Èlà was the first to communicate.
Who is this Èlà?
It is the Hòọ̀, which descended,
That we call Èlà.]

—Pa David Adeniji, personal communication, 1980

"Who was the first to speak?" And, "In whose tongue?" It was Èlà, the òrìṣà who spoke through verbal, visual, and the performing arts and illuminated the highly energy-charged, restless, and heavenly constituents of Ọ̀rọ̀—the embodiment of wisdom, knowledge, and understanding. Since the Yorùbá are a traditionally nonwriting society, the arts became immediately important as efficient means of preserving culture and aesthetic values, recording history, and providing an indispensable body of information for healing physical and human problems.

Èlà is the explicatory principle within the Ifá divination system. Èlà

51

supports the notion that the arts may be used to study and interpret complex traditional religious thought patterns and aesthetics in Yorùbá culture. Artistic forms, therefore, can be examined, not only as objects of art but also as metaphors in their essential and traditionally perceived roles. In this role, art helps to raise consciousness above and beyond the physical and into the spiritual realm for the vivid realization of seemingly abstract ideas. This kind of examination represents a slight shift away from the conventional "art history" approach—an approach that often interprets African art solely on formal analysis and de-emphasizes culturally relevant concepts of art and African thought systems (Abiodun, 1990).

Focusing on a few objects of Ifá art, I demonstrate that without familiarity with Yorùbá orature, particularly the Ifá literary corpus, it would be difficult to fully understand Yorùbá art. Similarly, the study of Yorùbá oral tradition is greatly enhanced by the study of the visual arts in which the literary concepts are concretized.

The Ifá verse quoted above recognizes Èlà—in Ifá divination system—as the first authoritative source of communication at the dawn of creation. It was Olódùmarè, the Supreme Being who created Hòò-rò (or Òrò, the contracted form of Hòò-rò) that descended from òrun, the otherworld. Òrò is a combination of heavily charged life forces composed of ogbón (wisdom), ìmò (knowledge), and òye (understanding). It was not, however, until Òrò's descent on earth, when it became Èlà, that its contents could be used to solve human problems. Hence, the Yorùbá draw on the axiom Èlà l'Òrò (Èlà relieves Òrò of its mystical and enigmatic character; that is, Èlà makes Òrò more understandable).

The name Èlà derives from the verb là, which means to split open, as in Ó là á (He split it open). Other equally relevant meanings of là include wealthy, as in Okùnrin ná à là (The man is wealthy), to survive, as in Omo na á là (The baby survived), and to be civilized, as in Ojú rè là (He is civilized). All of the above meanings of là are essential to the understanding of Èlà, who speaks through òwe (proverbs), which can apply metaphorically to the communicative properties of àrokò (sculpture, dance, drama, song, chanting, poetry) and incantations similar to ofò, ògèdè, àyájó, èpè, odù, and èsà, as well as to many other metaphoric forms used extensively in ritual contexts.

In Yorùbá intellectual discourse, òwe and Èlà are intertwined in their meaning and function. Pa òwe which literally means "to crack òwe" (the proverb), is related to Èlà, which is "that which splits, illuminates, or educates" in that both are recognized educational tools in Yorùbá culture. In the following saying, *òwe* becomes the metaphor of the act of communication and elucidation:

> Òwe l'ẹsin ọ̀rọ̀
> Bí ọ̀rọ̀ bá sọnù
> Òwe la á fi í wáa.

> [*Òwe* are the horses of Ọ̀rọ̀ (lit. communication, but idiomatically
>   "something that is a subject of concern or action")
> When Ọ̀rọ̀ is lost (elusive),
> *Òwe* is summoned to find (illuminate) it.]

The connections between *òwe* and Ẹ̀là are even more intriguing when, in Ifá literary corpus, we are reminded that *òwe* is the language of communication: "*Bí òwe, bí òwe ni Ifá ńsọ̀rọ̀*, Like *òwe* (proverbs), like *òwe* (proverbs) are the pronouncements of Ifá" (Owomoyela, 2005: 113). *Òwe* is chosen as the mode of communication because of its profundity, indirectness, and subtlety. According to a Yorùbá axiom, "*Bí òwe kò bá jọ òwe, a kì í pa á*, if *òwe* does not apply to a situation, one does not use it" (159). Irrespective of the chosen medium of communication, be it verbal, visual, or performing, considerable skill and talent are required to master their explicatory and aesthetic dimensions.

Functioning as art, and existing as a metaphor, *òwe* lends itself to an almost unlimited range of interpretations and applications as a pedagogic tool in traditional education, in settling disputes, finding solutions to difficult problems, and in concretizing abstract and religious concepts in Yorùbá culture. In its role as art, *òwe* acquires aesthetic properties to fulfill effectively its functions as the provider of valuable insights into Yorùbá metaphysical systems, myths, and lore. I illustrate these points by discussing a few objects from the Ifá sculptural repertoire.

Ikin

Ikin, the sixteen oil-palm nuts (*Elais guineensis idolatrica*) of Ifá divination, are the most important objects in the Ifá instrumental repertoire. Most *babaláwo* (Ifá priests, literally, "father of secrets") possess at least one set of *ikin* for their divination practices. Usually very dark in color or even black, the natural patina of the palm-kernel nuts is enhanced by frequent handling that renders them smooth and shiny with age.

Aesthetically, this shiny blackness is considered so pleasing in Yorùbá culture that dark-complexioned children are named Adúbiifá, black as (the *ikin* of) Ifá. The Ifá literary corpus reports that before ascending to *òrun* (the otherworld, abode of ancestors), Òrúnmìlà (patron deity of Ifá) handed down *ikin* to his children. From that moment on, *ikin* ceased to be ordinary palm-kernel nuts. To Ifá priests and supplicants, *ikin* became sacred objects through which wisdom, knowledge, and understanding were transmitted to gods (òrìṣà) and humans. In Yorùbá culture, we are warned against trivializing the *ikin:* "*Ẹniti ó bá fi ojú èkùrọ́ wo Òrún-mìlà, Ifá á pa á*" (Whoever thinks that Òrúnmìlà is no more than just palm-kernel nuts, Ifá will kill such a person). When Ifá priests praise Òrúnmìlà as "*Ikú dúdú àtẹ̀wọ́*" (black death in the palm), the unpredictability of the divination outcome of the *ikin* is acknowledged.

The blackness of the *ikin* symbolizes the infinite knowledge and wisdom of Ifá, its deep and esoteric nature, properly called *awo* among *babaláwo* (Ifá priests). The blackness of *ikin* is a metaphor for the ambivalence—a mixture of fear and indispensability—with which the *ikin* is held in awe. While the ritual significance of other divination objects is indisputable, none, except the *òpẹ̀lẹ̀* (divining chain), which is considered a poor substitute for palm-kernel nuts, approaches *ikin* in ritual importance. Ifá orature is unequivocal with respect to this notion: for all the good things you want on earth (the *ikin*), is the one to whom the request must be made (Abímbọ́lá 1968: 39, translation mine).

Ọpọ́n-Ifá

Elsewhere, the Ifá texts say: "*Ilẹ̀ ni mo tẹ̀tẹ̀tẹ̀tẹ̀, kí ńtó t' ọpọ́n,* It was on the ground that I first printed divination marks, before I started using the Ifá tray" (Abímbọ́lá 1968: 43). Divining on the ground is often the case when Ifá priests travel long distances away from home or when their services are required in extraordinary circumstances, such as war. It is common to find diviner apprentices practicing divination marks on the ground before they graduate and before they can afford to commission an *ọpọ́n*-Ifá (Ifá tray) with which to begin their professional careers.

An accomplished carver, Fáṣìkù, the Aláayè (the traditional ruler) of Ìkẹ̀rin, claims he has carved more than two hundred *ọpọ́n*-Ifá. He explains the meaning of *ọpọ́n* as *ohun tí a fi pọń Ifá lé* (that which is designed to flatter and honor Ifá) (Abiodun, 1975: 436). The *oríkì* (citation

The border of this *ọpọ́n*-Ifá honors Ọ̀rúnmìlà. It displays animal and coil motifs with the face of Ọ̀rìṣà Èṣù, guardian of the ritual way, at the top of the tray. At the beginning of a divination session, the Ifá diviner will draw a crossroads pattern on the surface as a sign that this is a place of meeting between human concerns and spiritual powers.

Ọpọ́n-Ifá (divination tray), wood. 1999.19.a,b. Yorùbá, Nigeria. Mead Art Museum, Amherst College, Amherst, Massachusetts. The Barry D. Maurer (Class of 1959) Collection of African art purchased with Amherst College Discretionary Fund and funds from H. Axel Schupf (Class of 1957).

poetry) that honors Ifá actually functions more or less in this manner as well, in which case we may consider the *ọpọ́n* as a form of visual "salute" to Ifá. As in *oríkì*, its verbal counterpart, *ọpọ́n*-Ifá may range from a simple to an extremely sophisticated and comprehensive visual salute, sometimes identifying important characters in Ifá divination. Empowered by such verbal and visual salutes, Ifá divination is ready for action.

Almost literally, Ifá is charged or loaded (*kì*, implied in the term *oríkì*), as when a gun is loaded (*kì ìbọn*), and the Ifá priest can expect a prompt response to questions posed by clients. Most *ọpọ́n* vary in richness of design and iconographic detail, dictated by such factors as the skill and creativity of the artist as well as by the fee Ifá priests are willing to pay for an *ọpọ́n*.

The pre-eminence of the basic geometric forms of *ọpọ́n*-Ifá alludes to Ifá as *Ògẹ́gẹ́-a- gbáyé-gún*, that is, "perfection, primeval order—the regulative principle of the universe." An important word here is *gún*, meaning "to straighten, settle, or resolve"—all of which underscore Ifá's crucial role in healing various diseases and in normalizing abnormal situations. Thus, Ifá's *oríkì* includes *a-jẹ́-ju-oògùn* (the culmination of medicine), although *oògùn* (medicine) is the specialty of Òsanyìn, the deity (òrìsà) of herbs and medicine. Because of this re-creative function of Ifá, the carver eliminates any suggestions of malformation and crookedness from the basic shape of the *ọpọ́n*-Ifá. The central open space on the divining tray, called *ìta-ọ̀run* (the spiritual realm, the otherworldly space), is kept free of any designs. Only camwood dust (*ìyẹròsùn*) may cover the surface of the *ọpọ́n*. Its specific function is to serve as a kind of screen or open space on which Ifá priests may make appropriate *odù*-Ifá marks as dictated by the outcome of the divination process using the *ikin*.

As a rule, all *ọpọ́n*-Ifá must carry a symbolic representation of Èṣù, also known as Osetura, on their borders to acknowledge Èṣù's inescapable impact in the earthly and spiritual realms of activity. Characterized in Ifá divination poetry as "*A ṣòtún-ṣòsì-láì ní tìjú*, One who belongs to two opposing camps without feeling any shame," Èṣù is the òrìsà most crucial to the maintenance of the precarious balance between malevolent and benevolent powers of the universe. He is the major link between Òṣun—his mother, who happens to represent the power of "our mothers"—and the sixteen major òrìsà, all male, who were sent to the world at the time of Creation. In Èṣù's role as power broker, it is virtually impossible for any òrìsà to accomplish anything without propitiating him. Positioning his stylized symbolic face on the border of the *ọpọ́n* situates Èṣù metaphorically between the physical world and the otherworld of spiritual beings. This position calls attention to Èṣù's influence in the two worlds, as well as his needed cooperation in ensuring a trouble-free divination session. Furthermore, Èṣù's *àṣẹ* (catalytic life force and sanction) is always necessary in making Ifá's utterances and predictions come to pass.

Ìróké

By gently tapping its pointed end against the *ọpọ́n*, the priest uses the *ìróké*, or divining tapper, to invoke Ọ̀rúnmìlà during divination. With a clapper or bell at its open end, the *ìróké* is usually carved in ivory and sometimes seen in brass or wood. The tappers range between twenty and sixty centimeters in length. Typically, they have three major parts: a plain, pointed end separated from the (usual) equestrian figure in the lower section by a middle section often carved as a human head or a kneeling female nude figure holding her breasts.

The task of choosing a good *orí*, the inner spiritual head or destiny in heaven, is rather difficult since all *orí* are conical in shape and look exactly alike. The Yorùbá solution to this dilemma is to represent the kneeling female figure holding her breasts in the *ìróké*. Sometimes the design is abbreviated, and merely the head is represented. The female intervenes on behalf of humanity to ensure the selection of good *orí*, which must be chosen and "received kneeling down," *àkúnlẹ̀gbà*. The kneeling male figure is not as powerful or as sacred as the female figure, who indicates the kneeling called *ìkúnlẹ̀-abiyamọ*, "the-kneeling-of-the-pains-at-childbirth." Linked to the greatest act of reverence that humans give to the òrìṣà are the special qualities and status of women as those through whom all have come into the world. However, perhaps a more specific symbolic value here of the kneeling female is that she represents the very moment the selection of a person's *orí* occurs.

Generally translated as "destiny" but closer to a metaphysical concept embodying one's past, present, and future, the *orí* is here symbolized by the uppermost segment of the *ìróké*. This plain, conical part sits on top of a naturalistically rendered human head in such a way that its owner cannot see it. Thus, a psychological distinction is created symbolically between *orí òde* (the visible head) and *orí inú* (the inner head), an invisible counterpart symbolizing one's destiny, conveyed by the simple, abstract, conical form. The placement of the *orí inú* directly on the *orí òde* recalls the Yorùbá myth in which human destiny is supposed to become wholly part of the individual, once chosen before birth in *ọrun* (the otherworld). This arrangement, whereby the *orí inú* sits above the *orí òde,* is called *àyànmọ́* (that which is affixed to one). This portion of the *ìróké,* therefore, is regarded as the most important section—its form is not only constant but also self-sufficient and suitable for use in divination ritual (Abiodun, 1987).

Though usually carved in ivory, this *ìrókè* Ifá (divination tapper) is in wood. It consists of a figure with elaborate headdress astride a horse, holding a horse-tail fly-whisk. At the beginning of Ifá divination process, the Ifá diviner gently taps the *ìrókè* against the edge of the *ọpọ́n* and recites the *oríkì* of Ọ̀rúnmìlà, the òrìṣà of Ifá divination, asking it to reveal the contents of the supplicant's *orí* (spiritual head and destiny).

Ìrókè Ifá (Ifá divination tapper), wood. 1999.3. Yorùbá, Nigeria. Mead Art Museum, Amherst College, Amherst, Massachusetts. Gift of the Estate of Barry D. Maurer (Class of 1959).

When the upper segments are viewed together, they recall a traditional Yorùbá myth dealing with Àjàlá, the great molder of *orí* in *òrún*. The choosing of the *orí* is the most important event in the life and the creation of a human before birth. Humanity is thereby represented by a female figure because of her effectiveness in the act of honoring, soothing, and cooling the gods, influencing their decisions to favor human beings. Her position, *ìkúnlè-abiyamọ* (the kneeling posture suggestive of a woman experiencing the pains of childbirth), is the most appropriate way to salute the òrìṣà, who are called *Àkúnlèbọ* (those who must be worshiped kneeling down). Nudity among Yorùbá adults is not considered normal except on very rare occasions, such as when a person is communicating with the Creator or taking an oath on a very important issue. Similarly, a woman holding her breasts is considered to be performing a sacred act.

The third segment of the *ìrọ́kẹ́* appears to be presenting the desires of the supplicant in tangible terms. Thus, an equestrian, for example, may be interpreted as the fulfillment of a prayer to become successful socially and economically, while repeating the theme of a kneeling woman could be an expression of gratitude for one's *orí*.

In the Ifá literary corpus, the cost of purchasing an *ìrọ́kẹ́* was reported to be about 1,400 cowries, an extremely high price in the "cowry" era economy. The use of the elephant tusk was limited to the elites of high rank, such as the *ọba* (traditional rulers), important chiefs, and priests. *Ìrọ́kẹ́*, no doubt, indicate the prestige enjoyed by the Ifá priest who has now attained an enhanced economic status. An Ifá poem offers some insight on this status.

> A díá fún Ọ̀rúnmìlà,
> Ifá ńbẹ láàárín ọ̀tá mẹ́ta.
> Erin, ẹfọ̀n, ati irá. . . .
> Ìgbà tí Ọ̀rúnmìlà rúbọ tán,
> Láìsàìsàn, erin kú.
> Ọ̀rúnmìlà ní kí wọn o yọ eyín in rẹ̀ wá.
> Òun ni Ọ̀rúnmìlà fi ṣe ìrọ́kẹ́. . . .
> Erin ló kú,
> A méyín rẹ̀ gbẹke;
> Efọ̀n ló kú,
> A m'áwọ ọ rẹ̀ to pòólò;
> Ọ̀gbògbò irá ló kú,
> A mú'wo o rẹ̀ kùn lósùn gburu gburu; . . .
> Ògèdèǹgbé nIfá ó f'ọtá awo se.

[Ifá divination was performed for Ọ̀rúnmìlà
When he was surrounded by three enemies
The elephant, the bush-cow, and *irá* . . .
Ọ̀rúnmìlà performed sacrifice
The elephant died without falling sick at all.
Ọ̀rúnmìlà then commanded that its tusks should be removed,
And with it, he carved *ìrọ́kẹ́* . . .
When the elephant died,
We used its tusks to carve delicate objects.
When the bush-cow died,
We used its hide to make *pòólò*.
When the young *irá* died,
We took its horns and rubbed them thoroughly with camwood (*Baphia
    nitida*) ointment. . . .
Ifá will pull down his priest's enemies flat to the ground.]

Abímbọ́lá 1977: 113

Because Ifá speaks in *òwe*, we may read this poem as a celebration of
Ọ̀rúnmìlà's victory over his enemies, one of whom may have been the
ọba (paramount ruler) who is traditionally entitled to use elephant ivory
tusk as a status symbol. Very fittingly, therefore, Ifá, the victor in what
appears to be a kind of power rivalry, is hailed "*Gbọlajokòo, ọmọ ọ̀kínkín
tí í mérin ń fọn*, offspring of the two tusks that make the elephant's trum-
pet," to indicate that his priests do, in fact, have rights and privileges
comparable to those of the *ọba*.

Agere-Ifá

The richness of design, the intricate style, and the artistic creativity
displayed in the execution of some *agere*-Ifá more than justifies its
high price, which, in the Ifá literary corpus, was put at 3,200 cowries
(Abímbọ́lá, 1968: 26). The *agere*'s significance is heightened dramatically because it houses *ikin*, which symbolize Ọ̀rúnmìlà's presence
on earth and in all divination sessions. Thus, the *agere* is more than a
container or bowl for holding the *ikin:* it symbolizes the "temple" of
Ọ̀rúnmìlà.

Caryatidic in structure, most *agere* consist of a bowl and a pedestal representing humans and animals in action; they are usually carved
or fashioned from a single piece of ivory, wood, metal, or any chosen
medium. They vary in size and design, but many fall between ten and

Agere Ifá, a container with lid, carved in wood, ivory, or cast in metal, is used to store the sixteen sacred palm nuts (*ikin* Ifá) of divination. More than a container, this *agere* Ifá depicts Ifá as a way of finding aid for life's struggles: at center an Ifá priest sits before the Ifá tray (*ọpọ́n*-Ifá), surrounded by his wives.

Agere Ifá, wood. 1999.17. Yorùbá, Nigeria. Mead Art Museum, Amherst College, Amherst, Massachusetts. The Barry D. Maurer (Class of 1959) Collection of African art purchased with Amherst College Discretionary Fund and funds from H. Axel Schupf (Class of 1957).

thirty-five centimeters in height. Ifá priests and their clients contribute to the iconographic and aesthetic content of *agere* sculpture—a practice that often leads to personalized motifs or icons that carry deeper meanings for the client and priest who commission them. It must be noted that the clientele cut across gender, social, and economic classes. They include paramount rulers, artists, warriors, farmers, and traders; in Ifá

The base of this *agere* Ifá depicts a hunter/warrior sitting astride his horse, accompanied by sword and gun bearers as an image of power and prestige. The lid depicts a bird grasping a shrieking lizard. The motifs here depict Ifá as a way of finding aid for life's struggles.

Agere Ifá, wood. 1999.18.a. Yorùbá, Nigeria. Mead Art Museum, Amherst College, Amherst, Massachusetts. The Barry D. Maurer (Class of 1959) Collection of African art purchased with Amherst College Discretionary Fund and funds from H. Axel Schupf (Class of 1957).

orature, the list of clientele even extends to include all òrìṣà, flora, fauna, and, indeed, everything that exists.

Jubilation and the giving of praise to Ifá and his priests, the *babaláwo,* mark the successful outcome of many consultations of Ifá. Thus, most figures that form the pedestal of the *agere* are usually depicted in a celebratory mood. They dance, make music, ride on horseback, or celebrate in a great variety of ways (Abiodun, 2000). The following con-cluding lines from an Ifá poem represent a typical way of describing this high moment of celebration.

> Ijó ni ńjo
> Ayọ̀ ni ńyọ
> O ńyin àwọn awo rẹ̀,
> Àwọn awoo rẹ̀ ńyin Ifá
> Ó ya ẹnu kótó,
> Orín awo ló bọ́ sí ì lẹ́nu
> Ẹsẹ̀ tí ó nà,
> Ijó fà à.
> Agogo ní Ìpóró,
> Àràn ní Ìkijà,
> Ọ̀pá kugúkugù lójúdè Ìṣẹrímogbe.

> [He started to dance,
> He started to rejoice,
> He started to praise his Ifá priests
> While his Ifá priests praised Ifá,
> As he opened his mouth,
> The song of Ifá priests was what he uttered forth.
> As he stretched his legs,
> Dance caught them.
> Gongs sounded in Ìpóró.
> *Àràn* were beaten in Ikija.
> Drumsticks made melody in Ìṣẹrímogbe.]
> Abímbọ́lá 1976: 53

Ọ̀pá ọ̀rẹ̀rẹ̀, ọ̀pá ọ̀ṣoòrò, or osùn babaláwo

The *ọ̀pá ọ̀rẹ̀rẹ̀, ọ̀pá ọ̀ṣoòrò,* or *osùn babaláwo* is an iron staff that can be carried by the *babaláwo* or stuck into the ground at important gather-ings or occasions involving the presence of Ifá priests. In normal cir-cumstances, the staff stands in one corner of the walls of the priest's residence. Usually between 85 and 142 centimeters tall, one or two birds, standing on a flat disk, top the staff. Two sets of four slender conical bells are welded to the staff at different levels. The bird or birds atop the staff represent *ẹyẹkàn* (the lone or one bird), referring to the pigeon sacred to Ifá priests, who domesticate most pigeons. Unlike the

The *ọ̀pá ọ̀rẹ̀rẹ̀, ọ̀pá ọ̀ṣoòrò,* or *osùn babaláwo* is an iron staff carried vertically by an Ifá priest at important gatherings or occasions involving the presence of Ifá priests. When not in use, the staff stands in one corner of the Ifá priest's house. The staff is ritually important in the implementation of Ọ̀rúnmìlà's orders.

Ọ̀pá ọ̀rẹ̀rẹ̀, ọ̀pá ọ̀ṣoòrò, or *osùn babaláwo* (Ifá priest's staff), iron. 1999.189. Yorùbá, Nigeria. Mead Art Museum, Amherst College, Amherst, Massachusetts. The Barry D. Maurer (Class of 1959) Collection of African art purchased with Amherst College Discretionary Fund and funds from H. Axel Schupf (Class of 1959).

birds on the Ọ̀sanyìn staff, which are believed to represent witches or the malevolent powers of the world (*àwọn ẹyẹlẹ*), the *ẹyẹkàn*, which is also hermaphroditic, represents a more constructive and positive power of implementation. In Yorùbá myth, the first pigeon, *ẹyẹoko*, lived and remained childless for a long time until it consulted Ifá and performed ritual sacrifices. Thereafter, it produced two offspring. From that time, it became known as *ẹyẹ-ilé* (pronounced *ẹyẹlé*), "bird of the home," and was domesticated. In Ifá divination poetry, we hear how this staff brings prosperity to clients who ask for Ifá's guidance and who comply with Ifá's injunctions. In other instances, the staff is used in effecting physical healing, as shown in the following verse:

> The cultivator of a new farmland usually stands high on heaps.
> It was divined for Ọ̀rúnmìlà who was to receive the healing staff from *òrun* and proceed to the earth.
> On his way, Ọ̀rúnmìlà met a cripple and asked, "What made you so crooked?"
> Ọ̀rúnmìlà touched him with the healing staff,
> And immediately the cripple was made straight.
>
> Lijadu 1972: 71

Èjìogbè, the *odù*-Ifá (chapter of Ifá literary corpus) from which the stories about *ẹyẹlé* and the power of the *osùn* staff are derived, is regarded as the first, the most important, and the "father" of all *odù*-Ifá.

Beads

The wearing or use of beaded objects is considered an indication of being well dressed and aesthetically pleasing in Yorùbá culture. It rises above any garment in importance and more than compensates for the absence of any conventional fabric. A Yorùbá proverb conveys this notion quite succinctly: "*Ẹniti ó so ìlẹ̀kẹ̀ parí aṣọ*, persons who adorn themselves with beads have done the ultimate in self-beautifying" (i.e., dressing) (Owomoyela, 2005: 258). In the context of Ifá, they allude to the *babaláwo*'s high political status and socioeconomic success in Yorùbá society. In Ifá literature, all the icons of the *babaláwo* are beaded, conferring great significance: the *babaláwo*'s *ìkùtè*-Ifá (the Ifá priest's scepter), *adé babaláwo* (the Ifá priest's crown), *àpo jèrùgbé* (the Ifá priest's satchel), *ìkólàbá* Ifá (Ifá priest's shoulder piece), *ìkúnpá* Ifá (the

The diviner carries divination instruments such as *ọpọ́n*-Ifá, *ikin*-Ifá, *òpèlè* (divination chain), *ìrọ́kè*-Ifá, and gifts in this beaded bag (*apo* Ifá). The bag's flap displays an abstract rendering of a face that commonly appears on kings' crowns and dance panels of òrìṣà devotees with prominent eyes to indicate that through Ifá divination one may discern that which is not ordinarily visible.

Apo Ifá (beaded bag), beads, leather, cloth. 1999.20. Yorùbá, Nigeria. Mead Art Museum, Amherst College, Amherst, Massachusetts. The Barry D. Maurer (Class of 1959) Collection of African art purchased with Amherst College Discretionary Fund and funds from H. Axel Schupf (Class of 1957).

Ifá priest's arm band), *òdìgbe* Ifá (the casket for Ifá), and *ìrùkèrè* Ifá (the horse-tail fly-whisk).

Let us consider, for instance, *ìrùkèrè* Ifá, the beaded horsetail fly-whisk carried by Ifá priests. Other than the *ǫba* (paramount rulers in Yorùbáland), only Ifá priests ceremonially may use *ìrùkèrè* as a symbol of their priesthood status. A verse from an *àyájǫ́* (incantation) confirms this category:

> Bí babaláwo méjì bá pàdé
> Wǫn a ṣe ìrùkèrè wǫn yeturu yeturu

Fabunmi 1972: 67

> [Whenever two Ifá priests meet,
> They wave their horsetail fly-whisk in salutation.]

author's translation

From another Yorùbá incantation, we get even further insight into the socioeconomic significance of the *ìrùkèrè* for Ifá priests and its metaphorical allusion to their status, as we know it today.

> Ó díá ko kúkúǹdùkú tíí solójà isu,
> Òun ìrùkèrè tíí ṣǫmǫ Olókun Sèníadé
> Wǫ́n ní bó bá yẹ'rùkèrè tán, tó dẹ'rùkèrè l'órùn,
> Ó d'ẹni à-gbé-jó, ó d'ẹni à-gbà-yèwò.
> À-gbé-jó là á gbé'rù ẹṣin,
> À-gbà-yèwò ní tì'rùkèrè

Fabunmi 1972: 67

> [It was divined for *kúkúǹdùkú* (sweet potato) who is the king of yams
> And the horsetail that was the child of Olókun Sèníadé (God the
>   Creator)
> It was predicted that by the horsetail had become famous and
>   prosperous,
> He would become the focus of attention.
> We dance carrying the horsetail.
> We inspect the horsetail in admiration.]

author's translation

Ifá priests are Yorùbá intellectuals who go in search of knowledge, wisdom, and understanding—the main reason they are respected and honored by their clients and the community at large. The acknowledgment of their success, even by the priesthood, is captured graphically in these lines from the Ifá literary corpus:

Mo ní ẹṣin la o má gùn ṣawo
Ẹṣin la ó ma á gùn ṣawo o
Ẹṣin la ó ma á gùn ṣawo

[I (Ọ̀rúnmìlà) hereby declare that henceforth we (Ifá priests) will ride
on horseback as diviners.
We will ride on horseback as diviners.
We will ride on horseback as diviners.]

Abímbọ́lá 1968: 22

Thus far, I have tried to demonstrate an often overlooked observation that Claude Lévi-Strauss hinted at more than forty years ago, namely, "As theories go, the Yorùbá seem to have been able to throw more light than ethnologists on the spirit of institutions and rules, which in their society, as in many others, are of an intellectual and deliberate character" (Lévi-Strauss 1966: 133). Yet, too many Africanist scholars of Yorùbá culture still favor the current and more fashionable Western-derived "-isms" in their studies and analysis. Too few are willing to grant Yorùbá concepts de jure, equal and reciprocal elucidatory value as theoretical alternatives to Western paradigms, as Barry Hallen aptly noted in "A Philosopher's Approach to Traditional Culture" (1975: 259–72). To make meaningful progress in Yorùbá studies, not only must the Yorùbá thought system be guaranteed a place, but its full potential must also be explored. My experience in the study of Yorùbá art and culture leads me to believe that much of what has been labeled "local," or Yorùbá epistemologies, are immediately relevant to settling disputes and finding solutions to difficult situations in Africa and beyond.

References

Abímbọ́lá, Wande. 1968. *Ijinle Ohun Enu Ifá, Apa Kinni*. Glasgow: Collins.
———. 1976. *Ifá: An Exposition of Ifá Literary Corpus*. Ibadan: Oxford University Press.
———. 1977. *Ifá Divination Poetry*. New York: Nok.
Abiodun, Rowland. 1975. "Ifá Art Objects: An Interpretation Based on Oral Tradition." In *Yorùbá Oral Tradition*, ed. Wande Abímbọ́lá. Ilé-Ifè: University of Ifè.

————. 1987. "Verbal and Visual Metaphors: Mythical Allusions in Yorùbá Ritualistic Art of Ori." *Word and Image: A Journal of Verbal/Visual Enquiry* 3, no. 3: 252–78.

————. 1990. "The Future of African Art Studies: An African Perspective." In *African Art Studies: The State of the Discipline.* Washington, DC: National Museum of African Art, Smithsonian Institution.

————. 2000. "Riding the Horse of Praise: The Mounted Figure Motif in Ifá Divination Sculpture." In *Insight and Artistry in African Divination,* ed. John Pemberton III. Washington, DC: Smithsonian Institution Press.

Fabunmi, M. A. (Chief). 1972. *Ayajo: Ijinle Ohun Ife.* Ibadan: Onibon-Oje Press.

Hallen, Barry. 1975. "A Philosopher's Approach to Traditional Cultures." *Theoria to Theory* 9: 259–72.

Lévi-Strauss, Claude. 1966. *The Savage Mind.* Chicago: University of Chicago Press.

Lijadu, E. M. 1972. *Òrúnmìlà.* Ado-Ekiti, Nigeria: Standard Press.

Owomoyela, O. 2005. *Yorùbá Proverbs.* Lincoln: University of Nebraska Press.

3

In What Tongue?

ỌLÁSOPÉ O. OYÈLÁRÀN

The visibility of Yorùbá culture in the Americas in the twenty-first century is increasing as the world evolves into one global village. Driven by the information technology shrinking our globe, sudden changes present opportunities and challenges that we may ignore only at the risk of compromising the prospects that the vista of globalization dangles before us. Thus, this conference assumed tremendous strategic importance as we moved into the final year of the twentieth century, hoping that the conference proceedings would produce strategies that we would pursue for tangible results to encourage the spread of Yorùbá religious culture.

The commitment to pursue tangible results in this kind of gathering, which was not an assembly of mere dilettantes, persuaded me to raise the question that serves as my title, namely, "In what tongue?"

The conscious history of the emergence of the Yorùbá as the emblem of the Africanization of the Americas offers us a lesson about strategies we must adopt to stimulate qualitative growth and the influence of the Yorùbá culture. This lesson comes from the fact that although Africans could carry no material objects on the middle passage, two things survived the gruesome passage with them: native knowledge and language.

"Native knowledge," which some would describe as "cultural know-how," enabled survivors to generate modes of existence related to those left behind. The inalienable medium of expression for the creative genius of the survivors and, perhaps, a secure means of their survival was language. Language informed all creolized forms of African expression in the Americas, from jazz to capoeira, which have given the Americas their distinctive cultural characteristics.

The origin of language in general, or of the Yorùbá language in particular, does not concern me. I am satisfied that language is the only distinctive human attribute. It is the uniquely human faculty, a cognitive system with its expressive form for which culture and its superstructure of thought, worldview, and the psychosocial specificity of a people exhaustively serve as reference. Without re-opening the Sapir-Whorfian "language and culture" debate, which appears to have been put to rest, it seems that it is still by no means self-evident that each language is uniquely suitable for representing the intuition and the creative genius of its native speakers and their distinguishing culture, where "culture" is conceived in its most comprehensive acceptation. Thus, it is not self-evident why the Yorùbá language will less efficaciously *re*-present American culture than American English does. Or why the hymn "*Gloria in Excelsis*" or "*Adeste Fideles*" packs greater validity in Latin even for English-mother-tongue Christians compared to "Glory in the Highest" or "O Come All Ye Faithful."

I propose, in what follows, that language occupies a pivotal position in the Yorùbá cosmology and worldview. Unless the Yorùbá scholars avail ourselves of opportunities that arise in the twenty-first century to promote all aspects of the Yorùbá culture through the instrumentality of language, we shall compromise the very objectives that we hold dear to our cause. First, I borrow Awo Fatóògùn's voice, as I have done before (Oyèláràn 1988), to let Òrúnmìlà speak to us about the centrality of language to, at least, an expression of and about the Yorùbá world. Then, I offer one or two illustrations of why language matters to our cause. I end by suggesting at least one strategy, which we may adopt with cost effectiveness and with much gain.

Èdè (Language/Speech; Speech/Language)

The Odù, Book of Ifá, which informs us about the centrality of Èdè, is the Àmúlù Odù "Ogbèdí" below:

A í ì bọ Ògún láìlọ́tí
A í ì bọ òrìṣà láìlóbì
A í ì bọ Ṣàngó láìlórógbó
A í ì bọfá láìlópọ̀lọpọ̀ eku àtẹja
Ló dífá fún Ọ̀rúnmìlà
Njọ́ tí òun Ọ̀sanyìn ń bá awo
Tí wọn ń wáḍìí Ayé òun Ọrùn
Lọ sí Ọ̀dọ̀ Èdè
Tí í ṣe Òjíṣẹ́ Olódùmarè
Njẹ́ ẹ bá mi dúpẹ́ lọ́wọ́ Ìbọrú
Njẹ́ ẹ bá mi dúpẹ́ lọ́wọ́ Ìbọyè
Njẹ́ ẹ bá mi dúpẹ́ lọ́wọ́ Ìbọṣíṣẹ
Àwọn ni ò jẹ́ kílé baba ó ḍìgbòrò
Ẹ bá mi dúpẹ́ lọ́wọ́ Sísàómáajẹ́
Ẹ bá mi dúpẹ́ lọ́wọ́ Àìsàómáajẹ́
Ẹ bá mi dúpẹ́ lọ́wọ́ Sààsààlabẹẹ́rarí

A yin Sísàómáajẹ́ o
Gbogbo ìsèdè
Àìsàómáajẹ́ o
Gbogbo ìsèdè
Gbogbo ẹ̀, gbògbò ẹ̀, kó máa jẹ́ o
Gbogbo ẹ̀, gbògbò ẹ̀

[We never worship or supplicate egúngún without spirits[1]
We never supplicate òrìṣà without the kola nut[2]
One never supplicates Ṣàngó without the Garcia Kola[3]
We never supplicate Ifá without an abundant supply of land and sea
    creatures[4]
Divined and allotted for Ọ̀rúnmìlà[5]
On the occasion when he and Ọ̀sanyìn[6] joined to seek to penetrate the
    mysteries
When they seek the *logos* of both Ayé and Ọrùn[7]
Going to Èdè
The mouthpiece[8] of Olódùmarè
Reason for appreciating Efficacy-acts-of-worship-as-prescribed[9]
Reason for appreciating Success/survival-acts-of
    worship-as-prescribed
Reason for appreciating
    Effectiveness-born-of-gestures-of-worship-as-prescribed
They are the ones who join forces to ensure that the domain of their
    progenitor does not go to wilderness
Appreciate with me Effectiveness-of-all-asserted-as-prescribed

Appreciate with me Potency-of-prescription-waiting-to-be-asserted
Appreciate with me Effectiveness-of- rasing-razor-adorning-Orí[10]

Praise be to Effectiveness-of-all-asserted-as-prescribed
All ye endowed with articulate speech
Praise Potency-of-prescription-waiting-to-be-asserted
All ye endowed with articulate speech
That all, all asserted as prescribed have effective power
All, say "all."

This Odù narrates the story of Ọ̀rúnmìlà and Ọ̀sanyìn, who seek to acquire and know the accounts of and explanation for all things. They approach Olódùmarè, the Prime Mover, to ask about the totality of the *logos,* the essence of things corporeal and noncorporeal, perceptual or conceptual, all objects of consciousness and of thought. The two set out. When they reach the threshold of the precinct of Ọ̀run, the frontier of Ayé (the realm of phenomena) and Ọ̀run (the beyond), it is Èdè (Language/Speech), the Gatekeeper and Mouthpiece of Olódùmarè whom they meet and with whom they have to deal.

Ọ̀rúnmìlà and Ọ̀sanyìn open up their minds to Èdè. Èdè assures them that he, and only he, is the one they have come to consult. He tells them that it is from him that they will find everything they seek to know. So, Ọ̀rúnmìlà and Ọ̀sanyìn settle down to a life with Èdè. Èdè systematically reveals to them the essence and account of things one by one, teaching them the mystery of each.

At the completion of the first twenty-five years of their living with Èdè, Ọ̀sanyìn cut out, saying that he had acquired enough. He insists that, as for him alone, he is returning to the earth.

Another twenty-five years roll by, Ọ̀rúnmìlà has patiently acquired unfathomable information about the world of phenomena and the beyond. He himself now rises and heads back to the earth. Halfway to the earth, behold a human settlement out of nowhere! "Impossible! Unreal! How and when did a human settlement get here? Did we see any such thing here on our way out?"

Ọ̀rúnmìlà asks to be led to the ruler of this human settlement. As he comes into sight, as Ọ̀sanyìn catches sight of him, he (Ọ̀sanyìn) clasps him in a flying grab-hold, saying, "On to the earth! Oh, the misery of loneliness all these days on end that I have languished here by myself, not daring to go onto the earth alone!" Thus, both of them set out, *pregnant* with oceans of information and knowledge.

As they catch sight of their homes, each can't believe his eyes for the splendor of his abode. It is as if they had not left home for a single day. And so, they break into dancing and rejoicing. Ọ̀rúnmìlà thanks his own offspring Ìbọrú, Ìbọyè, and Ìbọ̀ṣíṣẹ̀. In a similar fashion, Ọ̀sanyìn thanks Sísàómáajẹ́, Àìsàómáajẹ́, and Sàásàálabẹ́ẹ́rarí, his three offspring; for it is they who have maintained and enhanced with splendor their abodes in the absence of their progenitors.

Both Ọ̀rúnmìlà and Ọ̀sanyìn break into a chant as they dance and sing:

> A í ì bọ Ogún láìlọ́tí
> A í ì bọ̀rìṣà láìlóbì
> A í ì bọ Ṣàngó láìlórógbó
> A í ì bọfá láìlọ́pọ̀lọpọ̀ eku àtẹja
> Ló dífá fún Ọ̀rúnmìlà
>
> Njọ́ tí òun Ọ̀sanyìn ń bá awo
> Tí wọn ń wádìí Ayé òun Ọ̀run
> Lọ sí Ọdọ̀ Èdè
> Tí í ṣe Òjíṣẹ́ Olódùmarè
>
> Njẹ́ ẹ bá mi dúpẹ́ lọ́wọ́ Ìbọrú
> Njẹ́ ẹ bá mi dúpẹ́ lọ́wọ́ Ìbọyè
> Njẹ́ ẹ bá mi dúpẹ́ lọ́wọ́ Ìbọ̀ṣíṣẹ̀
> Àwọn ni ò jẹ́ kílé baba ó dìgbòrò
>
> Ẹ bá mi dúpẹ́ lọ́wọ́ Sísàómáajẹ́
> Ẹ bá mi dúpẹ́ lọ́wọ́ Àìsàómáajẹ́
> Ẹ bá mi dúpẹ́ lọ́wọ́ Sàásàálabẹ́ẹ́rarí
> A yin Sísàómáajẹ́ o
> Gbogbo ìsèdè
> Àìsàómáajẹ́ o
> Gbogbo ìsèdè
> Gbogbo ẹ̀, gbògbò ẹ̀, kó máa jẹ́ o
> Gbogbo ẹ̀, gbògbò ẹ̀

Òtúá-Rosùn

Another Odù, Òtúá-rosùn, complements Ogbèdí about the centrality of language in the Yorùbá worldview. Briefly, Òtúá-rosùn narrates the mystery of Èdè as the effective generative feminine alter-ego of Olófin whose essence is *mind,* unrestricted by matter, time, or space.

Èdè is the most intimate of the three wives of Olófin. Olófin ends up defying the murderous nihilism of his two other wives who conspire and do in Èdè in his absence. Olófin transforms himself by incorporating into his own body the essence and attributes of Èdè. Olófin, in effect, becomes physically a hermaphrodite and essentially Olófin/Èdè.

Odù Ogbèdí and Òtúá-rosùn establish the centrality of language in Yorùbá cosmology. Ogbèdí, for one, is unequivocal about language as humans' most efficacious access to knowledge. Both Òrúnmìlà and Òsanyìn, among the òrìṣà, serve as tropes par excellence for the critical role of language in defining our humanity. Òrúnmìlà is the custodian of information about all things, while Ifá is Òrúnmìlà's medium, the totality of the language textual materials, the vehicle for and repository of information by means of which humans tap into Òrúnmìlà's accounts of all things past, present, and future, all objects of consciousness. The message through Ifá is usually in the form of Ìbọ; hence, Ifá's three sons, Ìbọrú, Ìbọyè, and Ìbọṣíṣẹ, personify efficiency and effectiveness in the transfer of information.

Òsanyìn, on the other hand, is the custodian for the subset of information and knowledge about human environment, including all flora and fauna, and about the Àṣẹ, the effective life force, that they pack. Notice also that, by virtue of the symbolic personalities of Òsanyìn's three children, humans can tap into the effective life force in man's environment, in general, and that which inheres in herbs and animal parts, in particular. But we can tap into these life forces *only* through articulate language and by means of exact assertion in spoken words: prayer, incantation, *oríkì* (as in *à ń kì í, à ń sà á*), and other forms of supplication.

Implications

Language, therefore, is the storehouse of our essence. The Yorùbá language, by the same token, occupies a position of strategic importance for our objectives in this conference, the globalization of the Yorùbá religious culture. We are called upon to tap into this storehouse with patience, industry, and eternal presence of the mind.

Significantly for us, the Yorùbá language has evolved through time and space and will continue to do so. This evolution of the Yorùbá language reflects the heterodoxy that David Apter (1992) has so authoritatively espoused for the Yorùbá sociopolitical history. It also reflects the *xenophilia,* which makes the metaphoric four hundred and one òrìṣà in the Yorùbá pantheon interpretable. In essence, as we have observed elsewhere, the odd "one" after the four hundred suggests that at any one point in time and space, the population of òrìṣà in the Yorùbá pantheon is finite; but there is the ever present possibility of accretion to that number by one. Historically, the mode in which the Yorùbá pantheon incorporates peoples and other cultures encountered—it does not assimilate—is by making room for the people's sources of renewal and regeneration of values in the Yorùbá system. Thus, Yorùbá integrates the people's òrìṣà into its own pantheon. To the same end, òrìṣà in the Yorùbá pantheon may acquire aliases to take care of new experiences, new life obligations by the people. Thus, it is not surprising that seven Ògún are acknowledged. and that we have as many Òrìṣà-Ńlá as there may have arisen heterodoxies that elected to subscribe to the divinity (cf. Pierre Fatumbi Verger 1986).

The expansion, growth, and development in the Americas and elsewhere in the African diaspora of the Yorùbá religious culture and other aspects of the Yorùbá civilization continue to evolve in ways that reflect the culture's pristine xenophilia and heterodoxy. This is so in Brazil, Cuba, Grenada, Haiti, Panama, Puerto Rico, Sierra Leone, St. Lucia, Trinidad and Tobago, and Venezuela, as in the United States of America. Nor does the Yorùbá culture remain static in the homeland. As evidence of these quasi-autonomous[11] developments, we witness differences in the character and population of the Yorùbá pantheon from one manifestation to another, also differences in the organization of the comity of òrìṣà in these pantheons.

With respect to texts and language, the recent compilation of multivolume texts of literary corpora of Ifá in Brazil, Cuba, and Nigeria record these autonomous developments. Dictionaries and special purpose wordlists have appeared and continue to appear, reflecting these autonomous growths and developments. Other creative expressions of the Yorùbá culture everywhere tell the same story. Most tellingly, the language of discourse about the Yorùbá culture in the homeland and in the diaspora registers the developments attendant on the expansion of the culture. This is why any strategy for a systematic intervention in the promotion of the Yorùbá culture on the global level will most likely expose it to misappropriation and unhappy misapprehension, *unless* language features instrumentally in such a strategy.

The autonomous developments to which we have just made allusion challenge us to ensure that communication remains unfettered where it has been established within the community described by the globalization of the Yorùbá culture. Where the line of communication needs to be opened, any further delay will fail to take advantage of the opportunities offered by the forces of globalization. The need for communication and mutual intelligibility within this emerging Yorùbá far-flung community dictates that we enlist the instrumentality of language in whatever strategies we adopt.

Illustrations

Consider the following few lines that open "Ògúndá Méjì" about Orí (Abímbọ́lá 1976: 118ff.). Since *orí* is a crucial construct in the Yorùbá worldview, one would like to see the discourse about it become both current and accessible throughout the Yorùbá global community. How do we ensure that this occurs, so that we do not require that an *awo*, an exegete, will always have to set out from his base from West Africa and make a round for the sole purpose of explicating the opening gambit of the following verses of the Odù wherever the discourse turns on Orí?

> Ẹbìtì, ẹ̀gbàkè ní í yẹ'dí pẹ́ẹ́
> A díá fún Orísẹ̀ẹ́kú, ọmọ Ògún;
> A bù fún Orílèémèrè, ọmọ Ìja;
> A díá fún Afùwàpẹ́, ọmọ Òrúnmìlà

> [It is a snare of the foothill, which strikes suddenly.
> Ifá divination was performed for Orísẹ̀ẹ́kú, the son of Ògún;
> Ifá divination was performed for Orílèémèrè the son of Ìja;
> Ifá divination was performed for Afùwàpẹ́ offspring of Òrúnmìlà]

These few lines present us with three levels of language use that, together, put a formidable barrier in the way of an enthusiast who has no exposure to the Yorùbá language of the homeland. On the first level is the literal reference of each of the salient terms: *Ẹbìtì, ẹ̀gbàkè, Orísẹ̀ẹ́kú, Orílèémèrè, Afùwàpẹ́*. On the second level, the reader must construct the contextual and metaphorical meaning of the terms severally and collectively. Alas, it is only the third level, the level of structure, that the function of lines such as these three in the opening gambit of the Odù is made available to the reader in chapter 3, "The Structure of Ẹsẹ Ifá" (45f.) of the source text of the above excerpt.

The point here has nothing to do with the undeniable merit of the text from which this illustration is taken or the incomparable scholarship of its author. It suggests, rather, that where the reader has acquired a modicum of a second language learner's intuition about the Yorùbá language, he or she should, at least, be able to surmise that *Èbìtì* is not just any snare; that all the three terms, *Orísẹ̀ẹ́kú, Orílèémèrè,* and *Afùwàpẹ́,* are compounds of elementary lexical items, in addition to Orí. Thus, the reader will harvest plausible components, such as: *ìsẹ́* or *ìsẹ́ẹ́kú, kú; ní, èmèrè; fù, wà/ìwà, pẹ́,* the cultural meaning of each of which adds to the elucidation of the allusion on which the Odù anchors this discourse on "Orí and free choice" in the Yorùbá worldview. The reader would, to that extent, appreciate the Yorùbá culture's insistence on "free choice" that calls for keen awareness and, therefore, accountability in all things and under all circumstances.

Our second illustration is taken from "In Praise of Artistry" (Pemberton 1994), introduction to part 2: "The Interplay of the Arts in Yorùba Culture" (Abiodun, Drewal, and Pemberton 1994):

> Ayonyéké, oyún ò yokùnrin, óye Olufadi
> Óye àre àgbà bá won mú tà n'Irè
> 20 Ọmọ ejíbojó, ará Ìlágbède
> Ìrèmògún ti gbódù nÌrè
> Ìjà lÒgún jà ó rè 'Rẹsà
> Kíní ṣe lé Ògún lágbẹ̀dẹ
> Ìrèmògún, ará Yónyẹ́kẹ́
>
> 25 Àjílé kò yọkùrin
> Ó ye Olúfadi
> Ọmọ eji tó n lọlá, ará Ìlágbẹ̀dẹ

[Oye Olufadi [a title], Obesity does not befit a man.
The senior chieftaincy title was sold to them at Ire.
Son of those who came early [whose ancestors were early settlers].
    Natives of Ìlágbède [home of blacksmiths].
Ìrèmògún consulted Odu at Ire.
It was a quarrel that took Ògún to Irêsa
What has happened to the Ògún house of the blacksmiths?
Iremogun, native of the town where people are well fed.

It is not good for a man to wake up in the morning and remain at home,
But it is appropriate for Olúfadi to do it [for he is a carver].
Son of those who prosper from little.]

Again, the following observations have nothing to do with the Yorùbá language competence of or with the superior work by the author of the source of this excerpt; nor with native intuition of the mother-tongue speakers on whose judgment the author might have relied. Rather, it concerns the kind of meaning that the reader alien to the Yorùbá language or to the context of the enactment of the passage is being led to construct from the text.

First, consider óye *Olufadi* (line 18) and Óye àre àgbà (19), on one hand, and *Ó yẹ* Olúfadi (line 26), on the other. The orthography and translations for both suggest different constructions. However, when you consider the phrases that precede both expressions, both phrases under discussion look like orthographic variants of the same statement, namely, that "on the contrary, the unexpected, i.e., pregnancy, looks well on Olúfadi," where *ye* is nothing other than the predicate *yẹ,* "to fit," "to look well on," and *ó* in the third person singular referential clitic *ó.*

Thus lines (18) and (19) must be emended to read as (18') and (19')

> Àyóñyẹ́ké, oyún ò yọkùnrin, ó yẹ Olufadi
> Ó yẹ àrè àgbà bá wọn mú tà nírè
>
> [Oye Olufadi [a title], Obesity does not befit a man.
> It is the itinerant elder who competes with them at Ire.]

Now, consider the terms *oyún* (18), Àjílé (25), *ejíbojó* (20), and *ejí* (27). First, from the translation of line (25), the first word of that line should be Àjílé, with the high tone on the last syllable. If correct, then Àjílé is a feminine personal *oríkì,* which a male would not normally bear, unless, as in the probable case of Olúfadi, the male sports a distinguishing physical or behavioral feature normally identified with a woman. Secondly, the item "*eji*" in lines (20) and (27) normally has the meaning "rain." This writer's own mother, for example, is *ọmọ ọn eji; eji* being her family "totem." Thus, *ejíbojọ́* may have the reading "the-rain-overwhelms-the-day," or if the full expression *ejíbọjọ́jẹ́,* "the-rain-mars-the-day." Line (27) should, therefore, probably read as follows, in order to make it interpretable:

> Ọmọ Eji-tó-n-lọ́lá, ará Ìlágbẹ̀dẹ
>
> [Offspring of rain-is enough-to-make-me-act-honored/privileged,
>   person from Ìlágbẹ̀dẹ]

In addition to works such as those from which the above excerpts have been taken, specialized materials such as one may encounter in Pierre

Fatumbi Verger's *Ewé* (1995) and others are being generated in the language of the homeland, even as we speak. We risk a pernicious demet-
aphorization of the Yorùbá phenomenon the globalization of which
appears is progressing as we speak. Literalization and aberrant construction of meaning will result and compromise an exciting reorientation to
human awareness, if we do not enlist access to the Yorùbá language as it
is used in every locale which generates these materials.

When we turn to texts and lexicons generated in the Americas such
as those by Maureen Warner-Lewis (1991, 1996; Trinidad), John Mason
(1992; Cuba and the United States), Lydia Cabrera (1957; Cuba) and
Rogelio Furé (1986; Cuba), Robert A. Voeks's *Sacred Leaves of Candomblé* (1997; Brazil), to usages in creative works by culture bearers in
the diaspora such as Nicolas Guillen and Kamau Braithwaite, we again
risk relegating the ultimate impulse, end, and sources of these works
to oblivion if we fail to put in place modalities to ensure that they become accretions to Yorùbá heritage and the fountainhead of its creative
renewal.

I wish to restate the proposal that motivates this chapter. To do so,
I wish to invite readers to borrow and expand David Apter's notion of
the "Yorùbá society" to include all lands and climes markedly touched
by the globalization of the Yorùbá civilization. Apter (1992: 228 n8)
insists:

> By "Yoruba society" I mean an abstract field of social relations and rep-
> resentations which underlie empirical variations in specific kingdoms
> and communities and which inform Yoruba conceptions of their com-
> mon ethnic identity and social life.

This compels us to adopt modalities that guarantee a regenerative potential for those commonalties that will continue to drive the globalization
of the Yorùbá culture and worldview.

Proposal

The foregoing does not call for an academy *à la française* to serve as the
watchdog for the purity of the Yorùbá language.

First, we need to cultivate the consciousness that the texts that we
manipulate should not remain repositories of esoteric knowledge and
quaint antiquarianism fit for the archives only. If we fail in this, given

the dizzying changes driven by the information technology, we are within one generation of losing the impetus that brought us together in Miami, Florida.

Second, our cause challenges us to create linkages among institutions on both sides of the Atlantic such as will guarantee the conducive atmosphere for individuals within and throughout the new "Yorùba society" to engage in productive exchanges and communication with minimal impediments.

A systematic attention to language should constitute an important element in and of these linkages.

By "institutions," I do not mean Euro-American Institution of Higher Learning. In addition to these, the so-called nonformal institutions that have incubated much of what we celebrate today, those institutions, which have produced intellectuals such as Awo Fatóògùn and informed monumental works such as Pierre Fatumbi Verger's, must be counted and courted along with apparatuses of state.

In the end, all individuals and all such institutions must be committed to the promotion of the means of understanding just what we "commit" to texts, whether oral, written, or electronically stored, and which we pass on to other lands and intend for the purpose of socializing generations to come. If we do this, the Yorùbá leaven will work to regenerate humanity as we believe it can.

Abọ̀ ọ̀ mi rè é. Ẹ kú ìkàlè ọ. (This ends my presentation. Thank you for your attentiveness.)

Notes

1. *Ọtí* usually refers to alcoholic distillates or brews. This is why we use spirits or alcoholic beverages as a near equivalent.

2. *Obì* is *cola acuminata,* indigenous to equatorial rain forest. For supplication, it must have at least three lobes. One may, therefore, not use *cola nitida* indigenous to the Gonja (Futa Jalon) region of West Africa.

3. Orógbó is *Garcia Kola Heckel Guttiferae,* sacred to Ṣàngó, the òrìṣà of energy and electricity.

4. Birds, mammalia, or fish may be used as sacrificial animals. *Eku àtẹja* are literally rodents and fish.

5. Ọ̀rúnmìlà is the òrìṣà custodian of information, and, therefore, mediator of knowledge. Ifá is the extensive corpora of texts of the compendium of

information that contains the body of esoteric knowledge, from which Ọ̀rúnmìlà distills counsels to the supplicants through experts, *babaláwo,* referred to in conventional literature as diviners.

6. Ọ̀sanyìn is the òrìṣà, the custodian of information about and knowledge of flora and fauna; and for that reason, of and about the healing herbs and animal parts.

7. *Ayé* refers to the realm of human experience and of phenomena; *ọ̀run* is the supernatural realm identified with the Primer Mover and the realm metaphysical populated by spirits.

8. *Òjíṣẹ́* is one who delivers or executes a commission. He gives articulate expression to what Olódùmarè, who is all *mind,* conceives.

9. Ìbọrú, Ìbọyè, and Ìbọṣíṣẹ are the three offspring of Ọ̀rúnmìlà. Sísàómáajẹ́, Àìsàómáajẹ́, and Sàásàálabẹ́erarí are offspring of Ọ̀sanyìn. Both mythic intellectual adventurers would leave their offspring at home as they set out, without looking back.

10. *Orí* embodies a concept that compels a sensitive apprehension of the subtleties of the Yorùbá worldview and, therefore, of the Yorùbá language. On the *odù,* which informs on *orí,* see "Orí and Man's Choice of Destiny" (Abímbọ́lá 1976: 113–49), in which Abímbọ́lá painstakingly portrays *orí* functionally as the mythic otherness responsible for and vigilantly safeguarding the wholesomeness of the individual's essence, provided that the individual remains assiduous about deserving Orí's vigilance. See also Rowland Abiodun's "Verbal and Visual Metaphors: Mythical Allusions in Yorùba Ritualistic Art of Orí" (1987) and Henry John Drewal, John Pemberton III, and Rowland Abiodun (1989: 26–33), *"Orí Inú" :* "Inner Head and the Concept of Individuality."

The metaphor in this line takes us from human physical head, adorned with minimal risk of injury only by the razor that is dangerously sharp, to the effectiveness of prescriptions that must be followed with precision of oral assertion, however precarious.

11. The term "autonomous" is used to mean driven by dynamics peculiar to each subcultural manifestation.

References

Abímbọ́lá, Wande. 1976. *Ifá: An Exposition of Ifá Literary Corpus.* Ibadan: Oxford University Press.

Abiodun, Rowland. 1987. "Verbal and Visual Metaphors: Mythical Allusions in Yorùba Ritualistic Art of Orí." *Words and Image: A Journal of Verbal/Visual Inquiry* 3, no. 3: 252–70.

Abiodun, Rowland, Henry J. Drewal, and John Pemberton III, eds. 1994. *The Yoruba Artist*. Washington, DC: Smithsonian Institution Press.

Apter, David. 1992. *Black Critics and Kings: The Hermeneutics of Power in Yoruba Society*. Chicago: University of Chicago Press.

Cabrera, Lydia. 1957. *Anagó: Vocabulario lucumí (el Yoruba wue se habla en Cuba)*. Miami: Colección del Chicherekú.

Drewal, Henry John, and John Pemberton III, with Rowland Abiodun. 1989. *Yorùba: Nine Centuries of African Art and Thought*. New York: Center for African Art.

Furé, Rogelio Martinez. 1985. *Poesia Anonima Africana*. La Havana: Editoria Arte y Literatura.

————. 1986. "Patakin: Littérature sacrée de Cuba." In *Cultures africaines*. UNESCO, CC-86/WS/24.

Mason, John. 1992. *Orin Òrìṣà, Songs for Selected Heads*. Brooklyn, N.Y.: Yorùba Theological Archministry.

Oyèláràn, Olasope. 1988. "Ìtàn Ìdàgbàsókè Ẹkọ́ Ìmọ̀ Edè Yorùbá Láti Ìbẹ̀rẹ̀rẹ̀ Pẹ̀pẹ̀." In *Yorùba: A Language in Transition*. Yaba, Lagos: J. F. Ọdunjọ Memorial Lectures.

Verger, Pierre Fatumbi. 1986. "Liste de divinités africaines au Brèsil et leurs lieux d'origine." In *Cultures africaines*. UNESCO, CC-86/WS/24.

————. 1995. *Ewé: The Use of Plants in Yorùbá Society*. São Paulo: Editora Schwarcz.

Voeks, Robert A. 1997. *Sacred Leaves of Candomblé, AFRICAN Magic, Medicine and Religion in Brazil*. Austin: University of Texas Press.

Warner-Lewis, Maureen. 1991. *Guinea's Other Sun: The African Dynamic in Trinidad Culture*. Dover, Del.: Majority Press.

————. 1996. *Trinidad Yorùba: From Mother Tongue to Memory*. Tuscaloosa: University of Alabama Press.

4

Òrìṣà

A Prolegomenon to a Philosophy of Yorùbá Religion

OLUFEMI TAIWO

Were this chapter being written in Yorùbá, might it be necessary to argue for the existence of Yorùbá Religion? On one hand, yes, because Yorùbá intellectuals might engage in the philosophical exercise of exploring the intricacies of the concept of religion, of its different conceptions, of the task of examining its genealogy, establishing the boundaries of what is and what is not, properly speaking, religious phenomenon, and so on, even as they do so in Yorùbá.

On the other hand, many of us, myself included, engage with this question in part because, at some point in our evolution as scholars, we have come across denials that hardly any religion is indigenous to Africa. These denials have motivated the proliferation of works that either refute them or try to show that even though there is religion that is indigenous to Africa, it is so different that it deserves a name all by itself: hence the appellation "African Traditional Religion." It is the equivalent in religion of "African Traditional Thought," the erstwhile discredited name of African Philosophy. Such is the depth of the lack of self-confidence among African scholars that for so long they felt that African equivalents or empirical analogues of their disciplines must forever be marked by inferiority and banished to existence in the "traditional" forest.

The notion of "African Traditional Religion" ought to be rejected, for it could only have come out of an attitude that still reels from hesitation about its own heritage. In some cases, it has served to keep the discourse about African Religions from attaining a sophisticated philosophical level. In this essay, I take a different tack.

First, I suggest that the appellation "African Traditional Religion" is conceptually problematic, perhaps vacuous. Bolaji Ìdòwú's (1973) effort to offer a definition of the concept is by far the most sophisticated. But even then, Ìdòwú's efforts fail to dispel the problems attached to the notion of "African Traditional Religion." When we say "traditional," what do we mean? If we mean that it is "indigenous," that is, "of native derivation," why don't we just say that? In that case, "traditional religion" would refer to that religion that does not owe its original birth to a source outside of the place where it is found. The problem is that when this is what we mean, in some parts of Africa, say Ethiopia or Egypt, Christianity *is* an indigenous religion. But I suspect that those who speak of "Traditional Religion" mean by it more than the fact of its origination. They wish to affirm that "traditional" refers to something more than the source of the phenomenon of which they speak. Sometimes "traditional" is contrasted with "modern." Usually, the contrast involved is between "Traditional Religion" and Christianity, which is adjudged "modern." But in this case "modern" is used interchangeably with "European." This is no less problematic.[1]

Christianity is not always an import in many parts of Africa. Additionally, when the contrast is so drawn, the boundaries of "traditional" are so wide as to include everything from the beginning of Time in many African countries to when the first Europeans set foot in Africa. If that is the case, then both Islam and Christianity are "traditional religions." Finally, "traditional" is intended to gesture toward some pristine African religion and other practices that have not been touched by the many alien historical movements of which Africa and its peoples have been victims and, less often, beneficiaries. This covers the gamut from Islam to Christianity, European-inflected modernity to the Baha'i Movement. If such a characterization were meant to designate some unchanging or slowly but imperceptibly changing compendia of practices and attitudes, then it would be necessarily false because we have evidence that the liturgies, icons, etc., of much that is identified as "African Traditional Religion" have not only changed, but their representations show that they have been importing foreign bodies and assimilating same.

The motivation behind the search for "African Traditional Religion" can be traced to the need felt by African scholars to refute the denial by others that Africa had religion. I contend that this need no longer exists and that to continue to operate as if we still must justify the existence of philosophy, religion, nay, anything in Africa is to continue to confer on racism a dignity that it has never deserved. More importantly, given that the entire discourse may not make any sense were we to conduct it in an African language—for example, Yorùbá—it is time that we abandoned latter-day versions of Ìdòwú's brilliant but nonetheless outwardly oriented, nationalist defense of the existence and integrity of "African Traditional Religion." Hence, in the rest of this discussion, I talk about African Religion or, more specifically, Yorùbá Religion. I use the modifier "Yorùbá" to refer to those religious practices, institutions, and attitudes that do not owe their original inspiration to extraneous or exogenous sources. And "Religion" is not used in the singular because I believe that there is only one religion that all or most Yorùbá subscribe to. I use it only in the sense of the generic noun that encompasses phenomena of a certain type that share all those characteristics, some of them described below, that we usually associate with "religion." Needless to say, given what was said above, an encyclopedic discussion of Yorùbá Religion *must* include such subtopics as Christianity, Islam, and whatever other religious practices of exotic provenance as they have come to be adapted in strikingly original ways by Yorùbá practitioners and religious innovators. This, I believe, is the path that holds the most promise of analysis that is as historically accurate as it is philosophically astute. It is the dearth of this sort of analysis and the necessity for some deck clearing that has led me to present this as a mere Prolegomenon.

At the base of much of the discourse about African empirical analogues of concepts such as religion, philosophy, and literature is what I call the cult of difference, under which for a phenomenon to be properly "African" it must be so radically different from other species of the same genus that our ability to identify it as an instance of its genus is impaired, perhaps lost. Thus, whether in the pioneering works of Ìdòwú[2] and John S. Mbiti (1999), or in the subsequent literature that has developed under their inspiration,[3] the overarching goal always is to show that African Traditional Religion is *different* from other types of religion. But therein lies the problem. I do not want to suggest that there is no difference between African Religion, traditional or otherwise, and other religions. If nothing else, we distinguish it from others by the qualifier "African." Nevertheless, in focusing on African religion in its difference from others of its type, we lose sight of what it shares in common with other religions, which enable us to identify it as an instance of the general type that we call "religion." Because we tend to absolutize difference, we do not see that almost all the characteristics that we ascribe to African Traditional Religion, especially in its most sophisticated presentation by Ìdòwú, are shared with other religions from other parts of the world. Ancestor worship is shared in common with many Asian religions. Belief in spirits characterizes ancient Greek religion and indigenous Native American religion. Ìdòwú took great pains to draw parallels between belief in multiple deities and the proliferation of saints in the Catholic Church. Thus, once we distance ourselves from the cult of difference, we find that some of the identifying features that are supposed to be peculiar to African Traditional Religion are not so at all. That leaves us with the modifier "African."

In the rest of this discussion, "African" will be the only modifier that we shall deploy, and we do this solely to talk about specific religious traditions that do not owe their origins to points outside of Africa. Otherwise, contrary to common practice, including Ìdòwú's, we start from an explication of the concept of "religion" and proceed to show how it is instantiated in an African culture, that is, Yorùbá. For unless there is a stunning reversal of the relation between a concept and its instantiations, African, nay, American, or Cuban, or any other religion must, in at least minimal sense, be an instantiation of the general type, "religion." In other words, in so far as it is the case that African Religion is merely a specific type of religion, it is more important to examine it as a religion rather than as African. This does not necessarily commit one to affirming a univocal meaning for the concept of "religion." It only means that even though there are many conceptions of religion, there must be sufficient family resemblances among the disparate phenomena that we put under that single appellation to justify our lumping them together. That is, as a concept, "religion" must have some identifiable boundaries that enable us to distinguish its particulars and their individuals from those of, say, oenology.

In what follows, I specify, in some rough approximation, the boundaries of religion by contrasting my discussion with that of Ìdòwú. Then

I proceed to seek the empirical analogues of the conceptual elucidations in Yorùbá life and show how the perennial questions of the philosophy of religion are posed in Yorùbá religion. I contend that such questions must constitute the meat and potatoes of any serious analyses, philosophical and other, of Yorùbá religion.

According to Bolaji Ìdòwú (1973: 75):

> Religion results from man's spontaneous awareness of, and spontaneous reaction to, his immediate awareness of a Living Power, "Wholly Other" and infinitely greater than himself; a Power mysterious because unseen, yet a present and urgent reality, seeking to bring man into communion with Himself. This awareness includes that of something reaching out from the depths of man's being for close communion with, and vital relationship to, this Power as a source of real life.

> Man thus realizes from the beginning that he has a dual nature: his commonplace life is here on earth; but there is a living Being to whom he is linked by reason of his essential personality. In short, man is so [constituted and] conditioned that he must be dependent upon God if his life is to be real, full, and harmonious. His life is really worthwhile only in accordance as it is controlled and sustained by God.

> Religion in its essence is the means by which God as Spirit and man's essential self communicate. It is something resulting from the relationship which God established from the beginning of (human) life between himself and man.

I propose now to examine Ìdòwú's characterization of religion because in it we find the antecedents of the style of writing and thinking that has continued to dominate the discourse of African religions as alluded to above. If we are to accept Ìdòwú's composite definition, then religion is essentially about the relation between humans and God. After all, the immediate genesis of religion is to be found in humans' "spontaneous awareness of, and spontaneous reaction to, [their] immediate awareness of a Living Power, 'Wholly Other' and infinitely greater than [themselves]." It is this same Living Power that is variously represented in the definition as "mysterious because unseen" and "a present and urgent Reality."

Ìdòwú's definition is problematic. In the first place, it places beyond the pale of religion any set of phenomena that does not have the idea of "God," monotheistically construed, at its core. In other words, where there is no "God," there is no religion, in Ìdòwú's understanding. As is common knowledge, we have sets of practices that are ordinarily adjudged "religions" but that do not center on the idea of "God." Examples include Hinduism and Buddhism, two of the world's major religions. Nor will it make sense within the universe of meaning presupposed by these two religions that the lives of their adherents are "controlled and sustained by God" or that their adherents owe their original creation to "God." Might we suggest that this simple fact escaped Ìdòwú's purview? I think it would be wrong to do so. The source of the problem may lie somewhere else.

The principal thrust of Ìdòwú's *African Traditional Religion: A Definition* is aimed at refuting some of the libels that had been heaped upon African religious phenomena, the sheer denial that they amount to a religion or that even when they seem to mimic religious attributes, they represent the most primitive instances of religion, properly conceived. Some of the points on which African religions were denied religious integrity or membership in the universe of religions include the following. At the top of the list of defects is the allegation of the persistence of polytheism in them. Needless to say, this charge comes out of a prior privileging of monotheism such that any set of phenomena that is not founded on the one God is, prima facie, an ineligible candidate for admission to religion status.

Closely related to this defect is another: the infinite changeability of African gods. In some African cultures, there is considerable shopping around for efficacious and efficient gods, gods that will deliver whatever it is that their devotees desire to have, be it longevity, good health, children, wealth, or just sheer survival. Those who deny the integrity of African religions because of these two defects trace them to what they regard as the primitive state of the African mind. The proliferation of gods and the phenomenon of shopping among them for desired results are supposedly reflective of a mind that lacks the idea of a self that is separate from its needs and, additionally, is without knowledge of "an absolute Being, an Other and a Higher than his individual Self" (Hegel 1956: 93). For, were the African conscious of "an absolute Being," she would not dare put such a being in competition with another—such an outcome bespeaks a less than absolute Being *ex definitione*. And, by the same token, there cannot be more than one absolute Being. The assumption here is that if this being is less than absolute, then it will not possess the quality of being higher than any other, including human, beings.[4] Meanwhile, as Hegel (93) insisted, "religion begins with the consciousness that there is something higher than man." Therefore, a people who do not evince the consciousness of "a Higher than [their] individual [Selves]" cannot be said to possess a religion. Once this initial premise is granted, others follow inexorably.

Africans, it is said, engage in ancestor worship and spirit worship. Those ancestors that are worshipped cover the entire gamut from those who are newly passed away to those who had gone on in remote antiquity. Africans are also alleged to indulge in magic and witchcraft, which both arise from their belief that they have the power to impart life to inanimate objects and, for that reason, play god themselves. Finally, Africans are held not to make a distinction between their gods and the icons with which the gods are represented. It is as if the icons are one with the gods that they are meant to symbolize, an attitude with which the misnomer "fetish" is associated.

The conclusion that is drawn from the preceding premises is that Africans are without a genuine idea of *transcendence,* the idea that there is some reality beyond that which we apprehend with the aid of our physical senses or our understanding. One can make the case that this charge is false because if indeed Africans do what has been reported, especially ancestor worship or spirit worship, it cannot be the case that they think that the objects of their worshipful exertions are *immediately* apprehensible either through their physical senses or their understanding. But the critics will not accept this as proof that Africans may indeed not be guilty as charged. They retort that it may not be enough to have a notion of transcendence, it must extend to the idea of a *Mysterium,* a reality that is not only not *immediately apprehensible* but, more importantly, by its very nature, can never be fully grasped by even the best of our facilities. That is, the reality concerned must be ineffable.[5] Somehow this brings us back to the notion of the monotheistic God of Christianity, the cultural arm of the imperial movement that cast doubt on the existence of any African genius, religious or otherwise, in the first place. In the Christian faith, it is this Mysterium that it is the object of Theology to unearth, to render comprehensible, however inadequately, to mortal humanity. For deniers of the integrity of African religions, Africans supposedly lack any *Theos* to the revelation of whose *Logos* Philosophy is dedicated. They do not possess a *Mysterium,* they lack *transcendence,* and are without a *Theos* whose *Logos* they might have constituted a theology to reveal.

I have spent considerable time showing that what is at issue in the denial of status to African religions is whether or not they mimic the dominant monotheistic religion—Christianity—in the name of which the original denial was issued. The far-reaching but pernicious influence of the mindset that glorifies monotheism of a certain variety needs to be exposed because, until we rid ourselves of its hold, we are likely to continue to engage in discourse that obscures the best that African religions have to offer the world. I would like to submit that Ìdòwú and other African scholars of religion have not problematized this paradigm and have, therefore, continued to write as if monotheism is an essential part of religion and that any body of phenomena that lacks at its vortex some idea of a supreme being, the variant of Hegel's "absolute being," cannot be religion.

On closer analysis, it can be shown that many other religious traditions in the world, including some pre-Christian ones in Europe, exhibit all the characteristic features that are adjudged afflictions in the African situation. We speak of the Greek pantheon.[6] No one has for that reason denied that the Greeks had religion. Catholicism, Roman and Eastern Orthodox, is suffused with ancestor equivalents, saints, and innumerable icons. Nor can one seek to minimize the importance of the ancestors in Judaism. The propitiation of spirits, of ancestors and others, or their iconic representations, is to be found in various Asian religions. Unfortunately, we continue to legitimize the privileging of monotheism, and this explains the overarching effort directed at proving that the African not only was aware of the supreme being in her indigenous milieu but was also engaged in worshipping the same.[7] I would like to argue that the consequence is the distortion of, for example, Yorùbá religion, to fit the model of Christianity in Ìdòwú's hands.[8] The explanation for this distortion is to be found in the fact that Ìdòwú's is an instance of the nationalist response to the imperialist denial of African religion, a response that regularly takes the form of finding the equivalents in Yorùbá—nay, all African—life of Christian features beginning with the idea of a "Supreme Being." What needs to be done instead is to challenge and repudiate pedigree arguments of the sort that deny that African religions are religions. We should quit the business of showing that the only way we can be is if we were like our detractors.

In the rest of this essay, I follow a different path. As I indicated in the introduction, instead of focusing on what makes African religions peculiarly African, I am concerned with showing their character as an instance of the concept "religion." In that case, I dwell on what the specific African religion I am looking at, Yorùbá Religion, shares in common with others of its kind. The idea is that, once we leave behind the defensive nationalist problematic of "African Traditional Religion," we can begin to generate the kinds of discourse that will yield new insights into the complexity of indigenous African religious practices.

One final caveat: the Yorùbá Religion I examine here is that religion whose roots are endogenous to the Yorùbá nation. That is, we cannot trace its origins to any source outside of the Yorùbá nation. This means that its narratives will reflect these origins, and that to wherever in the world it is transported, the integrity of this core will not be challenged. Wherever it migrates, its practitioners will evince striking convergences in their liturgies, rituals, and representations.[9] But this does not mean that there are no Yorùbá religions that are of alien provenance or that those that are endogenous to the culture might not have over time gathered alien accretions. It is only their indigeneity that is of moment here as a marker of their difference within the wider world of religious types. We must now turn to delineating the contours of this religion.

We have argued that religion does not require an acknowledgment of or commitment to monotheism. As we also pointed out, laboring under the burden of the mistaken judgment that every religion must eventually wend its way to the Supreme Being, many scholars of African religion end up distorting their subject matter. I would not like to be misunderstood. I do not wish to suggest that there are no African religions of indigenous provenance that tend toward monotheism. I am merely arguing that their status as religions is entirely unaffected by whether they incorporate several gods, recognize only one, or subscribe to none at all. Once we undermine the contention that religion is synonymous with monotheism, we have not thereby disposed of the necessity to account for the nature of religion.

Given the complexity of religion and the incredible variety of disparate phenomena that are usually subsumed under the idea, it stands to reason that one cannot capture it in any simple definition. However much appeal a simple definition may have for us, it is not likely to hold much theoretical or explanatory power. Hence, I propose instead to look at religion from the standpoint of the many practices that are often placed under its rubric.

Every religion presupposes, at a minimum, a duality of existence. One half of the duality is the reality that is inhabited by the participants in the religion and that they apprehend with the aid of their regular faculties of cognition, principally the senses. But this is never accepted as the ultimate reality. That status is reserved for another reality that is other than, is beyond, transcends, and is adjudged superior to the world of the senses. It needs be pointed out that an acknowledgment of a reality beyond that which is accessible to the senses is not limited to religion. It is also a fundamental presupposition of science. Nor is it uncommon for poets, philosophers, and others to speak as if they too subscribe to the idea that there is a world beyond that of the senses. We thus need to come up with some sense of the differences between the religious variant of this presupposition of a world beyond that of the senses and that of, say, science.

Implicit in science is a further presupposition, that access to this other world is in principle possible and that we have indeed unwrapped some of it, the most recent example being the mapping of the human DNA, the basic building blocks of life. Religion, on the contrary, insists that this other reality is characterized by mystery the like of which we are never likely to unravel *in our human state* using our *human-inflected tools*. This is the crucial difference. For a fundamental presupposition of a religious outlook is the insufficiency of human nature and of its potencies and, conversely, the unavailing mystery of the world beyond, one that *transcends* the most sophisticated tools of cognition, analysis, understanding and description, that we may possess. For instance, given that we are finite and contingent beings—even our sheer existence is not marked by necessity—and the reality that we speak of is infinite and ultimate, it is a logical impossibility for us to seek to unravel the contours of this reality. This, I believe, is the source of the overwhelmingness that we attribute to this ultimate reality and of our tendency to abase ourselves in contemplating it. It terrifies us; it fills us with dread. Its contemplation induces in us an almost disabling anxiety, and such is the nature of this reality that in nearly every instance of religion, it is held that our language can never capture it fully or even for the most part. Hence, this reality is characterized by ineffability. Sometimes, it is assimilated to the idea of the Supreme Being of the monotheistic religions. At other times, it is distributed among the many gods of the polytheistic religions. At yet other times, it is to be found in the many practices, icons, and other paraphernalia of nontheistic religions. In some religions, it is coeval with a way of life that is ever *becoming* but is never attained *as long as* we remain encased in our limited, contingent, corruptible, and insufficient human form.

If what I have described above is true, or at least plausible, then religion is a compendium of phenomena belonging to a reality that *transcends* that which we inhabit and is inaccessible to our normal tools of cognition, analysis, understanding and description. This transcendent reality represents to our limited nature an unsolvable mystery but one that we need to make sense of our place in the world, our fate beyond it, and to calm our anxieties about it. In science, we seek to master, to control, and generally to bend this reality to our will. In religion, we submit to it; we abase ourselves before it; we seek to be admitted to its secrets in order thereby to participate in it so that existence in our primary world may be more livable, more tolerable. My point, then, is that African religions, whatever their specific contours may be, are, *qua* religions, no different from others. What we need to do is to identify the nature of transcendence that is at the heart of each religion and to come to some understanding, however inadequate, of the *Mysterium* that it presupposes.

From this point on, Yorùbá religion is the object of our focus. Again, let us go back for a moment to Ìdòwú's account of the structure of African Traditional Religion. He identified five constituent elements: (1) Belief in Olódùmarè, the Supreme Being; (2) Belief in divinities; (3) Belief in Spirits; (4) Ancestor Worship and; (5) Magic and Sorcery. This is where it is relevant to consider the problem raised in the opening paragraph of this essay. The choice of terms with which to describe African religious practices sometimes leads to misrepresentation and distortion of what is going on in the religion concerned. It may be the case that some African religions are faith-based and worship-centered in the manner described by Ìdòwú. But it is problematic to say that Yorùbá religion is faith-based and worship-centered. Kólápó Abímbólá has distinguished between what he terms *faith-based religions* and *practice-based religions.* As the name implies, adherents of faith-based religions anchor them on the profession of faith in whatever is the object of religious veneration. Christianity is a good, almost paradigmatic, example of this type of religion. Some variants of Islam may also serve as instances. I doubt that Hinduism or Buddhism can be appropriately characterized as faith-based religions. Abímbólá (2006) suggests that neither is Yorùbá religion. He identifies the latter as an instance of practice-based religion where the profession of faith and an attitude of belief are less important, perhaps irrelevant, than the doing, the performing of the tenets of the religion. Thus, Yorùbá religion is more akin to a way of life, in a way similar to Judaism, than to a worship-centered, faith-professing religion.

When Ìdòwú speaks of "Belief in Olódùmaré," he gives the impression that were we to ask the adherents of the religion to describe for us what their observances entail, their description would include some reference to faith or belief of the sort to which he alludes. This is where it becomes instructive to examine what adherents of Yorùbá religion might say. To begin with, it is highly unlikely that if we were speaking in Yorùbá, with a Yorùbá adherent, our inquiry would be structured around what our interlocutor does or does not believe in. That is, such an adherent might find it awkward, perhaps even incomprehensible, were we to ask the following when our goal is to ascertain what is the object of devotion in our interlocutor's religion: "Kínni ẹ gbàgbọ́?" (What do you believe?). Or "Kínni ẹ nígbàgbọ́ nínúu rẹ̀?" (In what do you believe or have faith?). These interrogatories make little sense in the language especially when what is being talked about is the *mysterium* that supplies the object of transcendence in Yorùbá religion.

We might turn around and ask the same question in a different way. For instance, we might ask: "Ẹ̀sìn wo ni tiyìn?" (What type or brand of worship do you follow?). Or "Òrìṣà wo lẹ̀yin ń bọ?" (What òrìṣà do you worship or propitiate or sacrifice to?). These questions hardly make any more sense. In Yorùbá religion, *ẹsìn* (worship, observance, following) is only one part of what adherence to the religion entails. The same can be said for the verb *bọ* (propitiate, sacrifice to, cultivate, serve). Neither usage captures the richness, complexity, and sheer diversity of the phenomena that characterize the practice of Yorùbá religion. Finally, when we ask what òrìṣà someone worships, we distort, because we are speaking in English, two elements of the relationship. First, as we already pointed out, worship is one activity, among a plethora, in which the adherent engages. Second, because we are overly concerned in Christianity-inflected English with finding one god or another, we easily assimilate the Yorùbá referent to a god and translate it accordingly. One can argue that the sclerotic reduction of a multidimensional relationship between òrìṣà and their adherents to a single relationship of worship and propitiation may have arisen from the derogatory epithet that Christians gave to Yorùbá religious adherents who were dubbed "abọrìṣà" (One who propitiates or worships òrìṣà).

We need to move away from some of the conundrums just identified. In order to do that, we now introduce a much-neglected insight from Ulli Beier (1975: 44), who writes:

The relationship between the Yoruba and his orisha is essentially different from the relationship of a Christian worshipper to his God.

The Christian demand for "faith" in God has no meaning in terms
of Yoruba Religion. A Yoruba never says "I believe" in orisha. One can
believe or disbelieve another man's story or excuse. But in a religious
context, the word cannot be used. It would in fact imply the possibility
of disbelief. In Yoruba the word, *igbagbo* (a believer) stands contemptuously for "Christian."[10]

In light of what I said at the beginning of this discussion, I would
like to suggest that the probability of distortion is increased once we are
forced to conduct the discourse of Yorùbá religion in a language unrelated to the original and insensitive to its nuances. The passage quoted
from Beier corroborates our earlier claim that Yorùbá religion is not a
faith-based one and that the relationship between those who belong to
it and the *mysterium* that is the object of their religious exertions, òrìṣà,
as well as the transcendent subject in it, does not mimic that between
Christians and God or Muslims and Allah.

How then might one describe the relationship between òrìṣà and their
followers? Again, I refer to another insight from Beier (1975: 44):

The relationship between a Yoruba and his orisha is expressed in the
complex multivalent verb *li* or *ni* that is contained in the word *olorisha*. Olorisha is usually translated into English with the approximation
"orisha worshipper," but strictly speaking, it could mean "One who *has*
orisha," "One who *is* orisha," or "One who *makes* orisha."

This insight is worthy of some serious analysis for, if Beier is correct,
then a lot of what is put under the rubric "African Traditional Religion"
hides much more than it reveals about the specific contours of, in this
instance, Yorùbá religion. To begin with, the different senses of the verb
ní point to the very complex relationships that subsist between òrìṣà and
their followers. "To *have òrìshà* expresses the simplest and most obvious relationship. Most people have simply inherited their òrìshà, and a
failure to serve him would result in dangerous *disorder,* the symptoms
of which could be disease or death in the family, failure in business and
so on" (Beier 1975: 44). This sense of *ní* has to do with a relationship of
possession, of ownership of the òrìṣà in question. But Beier's description here may mislead some into thinking that the relationship involved
is one of proprietary ownership. Such a reading can be quickly dispelled
by the fact that, although one may obtain the mistaken impression that

the Olórìṣà may do what he or she wishes with his or her possession (after all, he or she "owns" the òrìṣà), nothing could be further from the truth. We find a close parallel in the way that Christians and Muslims alike claim to "have God or Allah." I do not think that when they utter this claim, they mean they have proprietary ownership of God or Allah. By the same token, the *ní* involved in *olórìṣà* connotes the relation that is entailed when someone says: "He or she *has* God or whatever on his or her side." In the case of olórìṣà, having òrìṣà means that òrìṣà is a presence in her family, and it will do service in all the ways that the *mysterium* we spoke of earlier is understood and expected to operate. Should anyone doubt that this is the most plausible meaning of the verbal phrase "to have òrìṣà," consider the fact that the inheritor of an òrìṣà is duty bound to commit to the service of the òrìṣà should the latter pick her or him to be its priest.[11] If this is true, then it remains true that "to have òrìṣà" may actually be more akin to being inherited by òrìṣà rather than the other way around.

The second sense of *ní* òrìṣà is that captured in the statement that "One *is* òrìṣà." This is one of the most misunderstood aspects of the relationship between òrìṣà and olórìṣà. One might suggest that it is the claim that one can *be* òrìṣà that has led many, including African scholars, into the erroneous belief that Africans believe that they are superior to their gods and that they can summon the latter to service at their whim. Again, the truth is to be found in the opposite direction.

> To *be orisha* is an equally correct translation of the word *olorisha*. The worshipper offers his body as a vehicle to òrìshà, he allows the *orisha* "to mount his head," to ride him, and he strives to become *for brief moments,* the personification of the *orisha*.
>
> Only very few and very powerful priests could really represent the *orisha* all the time. But every *olorisha* must become the *orisha* some time. (Beier 1975: 44)

It is in the nature of every religion that those who adhere to them seek to become one with the *mysterium* that supplies the transcendent subject that defines their religion. In Christianity, for instance, whether it be Protestant or Catholic, Pentecostal or otherwise, when its adherents become one with Christ and, simultaneously, God, on Resurrection Day, the promise of eternal life is realized. If the Bible is correct, only very few human beings are destined for this eventuality. While that represents the ideal, it is unattainable as long as we are still in the flesh. That has never stopped Christians from doing their best to make themselves worthy of receiving the Spirit and, for those who become priests, receiving "the call." From time to time, Christians strive to experience this being-one-with-God even as they remain attached to their flesh. Through it all, they are called upon to let go of themselves, to open up and let the Holy Spirit "possess" them. This aspiration receives its most dramatic manifestation in the Pentecostal denominations, when their members speak in tongues, although Christians of all stripes always hope that they will at some point be worthy of "being Christ." Needless to say, were they to become permanently transmogrified, they would stop being humans; they will be God. But this option is not available in the flesh. So, they settle for the only one available: being Christ or Spirit occasionally and, even then, only *for brief moments*. It is now time to return to Beier's passage quoted above.

In the passage, *olórìṣà* refers to one who offers his or her body as a vehicle to òrìṣà, who allows the òrìṣà "to mount his head," and so on. As we already pointed out, for the *olórìṣà* to become permanently the personification of the òrìṣà is for her to become òrìṣà. Thus, the best that the *olórìṣà* can hope for and actually needs to experience is to become, for brief moments, the personification of the òrìṣà. In those instances of Yorùbá religion where possession occurs, at the time when the *olórìṣà* is possessed, he or she, for that brief moment, and it must necessarily be brief, *is* òrìṣà. In that state, he or she is a participant in that *mysterium* that defines the religion, and he or she is taken out of the circle of mortal humans, is free from finitude and unshackled from all limits imposed by the human form. His or her voice, movement, and the like are adjudged those of the òrìṣà and are marked by the authority of the òrìṣà by whom he or she has been possessed. Even the very powerful priests cannot "really represent the òrìṣà all the time" unless by that one means that they make it their business *always* to strive to personify the òrìṣà. Were they permanently to personify an òrìṣà, they would make the transition from being priests to being òrìṣà themselves. Indeed this helps us to make better sense of how one becomes òrìṣà in Yorùbá religion. The closer one is to entering into that world beyond that accessible to our conventional human cognitive faculties, the more òrìṣà-like one becomes; and once one crosses the threshold such that one can be regarded as having taken permanent abode in that other world, one has thereby made a complete transition to being òrìṣà. It is no wonder that death is always a required minimum for one to qualify to become òrìṣà. I have never heard of an òrìṣà who is at the same time embodied.[12] By the same token, it is not everyone who dies who becomes an òrìṣà, or at least an important one. Additionally, given what has been said so far in this section, no physical object, human and material, can ever fully "house" òrìṣà. òrìṣà always go beyond their content. There are implications for our understanding of the place of icons, shrines, and other paraphernalia in Yorùbá religion. I cannot delve into those implications here.

Finally, the third sense of olórìṣà refers to "*making* òrìṣà." There are different forms of making òrìṣà. Worship is one form of making òrìṣà. Other forms include "*pípè*" (calling, invoking)," "*kíkọ*" (singing)," "*kíkí*" (saluting, greeting, hailing)," or "*kíkì*" (chanting or evoking *oríkì*)" of òrìṣà. Yet another form is seeking to establish the òrìṣà's wishes through divination. Finally, there is the offering at regular intervals of *ẹbọ* (sacrifice) determined by the specific attributes of each òrìṣà.[13] The ways of making òrìṣà are not exhausted by these modes. Others include the creation of icons to represent òrìṣà, the construction of shrines, the observance of myriad taboos, the creation of ritual cuisines, up to and including rules regarding interpersonal interaction in society and sexual behavior.

We can now draw some inferences from the preceding discussion. The idea of òrìṣà is not merely central to Yorùbá religion: it is Yorùbá religion. This point is apt to be misunderstood by many. Yorùbá religion is not about òrìṣà worship. We have already seen why that is a misnomer. Yorùbá religion is about making, appeasing, performing, dancing, enacting, worshipping, propitiating, invoking, feeding, seeking to understand òrìṣà and a lot more. It is the "a lot more" that has been missing from the discussion of Yorùbá religion so far. The reason that I insist that òrìṣà *is* Yorùbá religion is because, however we look at it, there is not an instance of the religion, at least the variety that we are interested in here, that does not ultimately revolve around or involve some relationship or another with òrìṣà in its innumerable concatenations. From Ṣàngó to Ayélála, from Ọ̀rúnmìlà to Ọbàtálá, from Olóde to Orí, they are one and all, where religion is concerned, òrìṣà. Thus, a serious philosophy of Yorùbá religion must grapple with the concept of òrìṣà and its theoretical implications.

What, after all, is òrìṣà? Let us proceed from a very important manifestation of Yorùbá religion that is often misnamed "ancestor worship." The process of ancestor making is instructive for our understanding of forms of transcendence prevalent in Yorùbá religion. To start with, it is

not everyone who is dead that is venerated as an ancestor. The conditions for becoming an ancestor can be quite strict. One must have died a
good death. So those who died "before their time," that is, young, cannot
become ancestors.[14] Those who die of unnatural causes, for example,
suicide, or of unexplained pestilences hardly ever are eligible for ancestor status. Eligibility for ancestor status is enhanced for those who lived
out their allotted time on earth, that is, till very ripe old age, and could
not be said to have reincarnated or to have remained within the realm of
those who might be candidates for reincarnation, and so on.

Above all, the passing into ancestorship is related to the way that
death is understood and processed in Yorùbá societies. Although the culture provides for reincarnation, there is an acknowledgment that death
marks a signal transformation, a termination of one form of being and
the commencement of another in the spirit world. There are many ways
in which the finality of death is intimated in Yorùbá culture as expressed
in the language. In funeral obsequies, the following dirge is often sung:

> Ó di gbére
> Ó dàrìnnàkò
> Ó dojú àlá
> Ó doko ẹlẹ́bọ.

> [It is only at the end of time
> Only in chance encounters
> Only in dreams
> Only when we offer sacrifices
> (Are we ever going to meet the deceased again).]

In the dirge, there is an awareness that the deceased who might have
departed only moments ago would never be seen again in the ordinary
way; that encounters between them and the living would never again
occur in *immediate* ways but only in *mediated* contexts: in dreams, in
those situations in which we, the living, do double takes because total
strangers look eerily like and somehow remind us of our dear departed;
in situations where we summon their spirits through the medium of sacrifices, of offerings designed to propitiate or invoke their spirits. The
upshot of the preceding is that the dead, or at least some of them, become part of that world to which human beings, *as living beings,* cannot have a direct, immediate access: they have now transited into and
have become members of a *transcendent* reality. They may become re-
embodied at the time of *Egúngún* festivals when living human beings

possess and are possessed by the spirit of the departed that the *Egúngún* supposedly incarnate.[15] Similar processes are at work in òrìṣà making. However completely a living being may appear to embody an element of the transcendent reality that is the defining feature of every religion, it is understood in Yorùbá philosophy that this embodiment can only be temporary, only for brief moments, and that *as long as we remain in our human frame,* we can only approximate but *never* become gods. This is what separates òrìṣà, even the lowliest among them, from mere mortals, even those mortals who are permitted a fleeting participation in the ways of being characteristic of òrìṣà. The fact that òrìṣà are beyond the bounds of Time and not subject to the limitations of space and the additional fact of the recognition of these characteristics in Yorùbá religion might explain the ease with which Yorùbá was adapted to the cause of Christian evangelization beginning in the nineteenth century. But this recognition of transcendence and the acknowledgment of a *mysterium* do not mean that there is no difference between its occurrence in Yorùbá religion and that of, say, Christianity. Wole Soyinka (1976: 143–44) has articulated this difference with characteristic perspicacity. He bears quoting at length:

> For the Yorùbá, the gods are the final measure of eternity, as humans are of earthly transience. To think, because of this, that the Yorùbá mind reaches intuitively towards absorption in godlike essence is to misunderstand the principle of religious rites, and to misread, as many have done, the significance of religious possession. Past, present and future being so pertinently conceived and woven into the Yorùbá worldview, the element of eternity which is the gods' prerogative does not have the same quality of remoteness or exclusiveness which it has in Christian or Buddhist culture. The belief of the Yorùbá in the contemporaneous existence within his daily experience of these aspects of time has long been recognized but again misinterpreted. It is no abstraction.

One way to construe Soyinka's point is to see in it a warning to all who are wont to see in the fact that the Yorùbá do not treat transcendence as an abstraction, nor consider the eternity of the gods as a sign of their absolute severance from the human realm, a failure on their part to see that their gods are, ultimately, superior to the living. Similarly, that adherents of Yorùbá religion do "strive to become *for brief moments,* the personification of the òrìṣà" and, on occasion, do succeed does not mean that they think, believe, or even act as if they, the living humans, *are* gods. The same can be said of their views of the icons with which they represent their gods and the objects that they generally venerate in the worship, propitiation, and celebration of their deities. The proximity of the gods to the quotidian experiences of their adherents and their location sometimes in the same spaces in which their adherents live do not at any time translate into an abolition of the chasm between gods and humans. The persistence of this chasm is presaged in the deep caution that, were one to treat the dead as if they were nothing more than one's erstwhile innocuous neighbor merely recently deceased, one would be rudely reminded of his or her inferiority when he or she is disrobed by the newly minted resident of the spirit realm. This is sheer recognition that, even at a most minimal level, the occurrence of physical death, the dead are definitively on the other side of the chasm that separates humans from gods. Again, Soyinka (1976: 144) puts it best:

> And yet the Yorùbá does not for that reason fail to distinguish between himself and the deities, between himself and the ancestors, between the unborn and his reality, or discard his awareness of the essential gulf that lies between one area of existence and another. This gulf is what must be constantly diminished by the sacrifices, the rituals, the ceremonies of appeasement to those cosmic powers which lie guardian to the gulf. Spiritually, the primordial disquiet of the Yorùbá psyche may be expressed as the existence in collective memory of a primal severance in transitional ether, whose first effective defiance is symbolized in the myth of the gods' descent to earth and the battle with immense chaotic growth which had sealed off reunion with man.

This recognition of the persistence of a chasm, of reality sundered in infinite ways, and of human inability to cognize all of it within the limits imposed by the finitude of our being is the source from which Yorùbá religion emanates. The continuing effort to make sense of the chasm, the aspiration to abridge it, and the keen awareness of the immensity of the task, perhaps its unattainability in the final analysis, all represent foundational elements of all religions, and Yorùbá religion is no exception. The specificity of the Yorùbá version is traceable to the peculiarities of Yorùbá historical experience and cultural genius. This is what allows us to speak, even if tentatively, of "Yorùbá Religion," which, to separate it from other instances of Yorùbá religion that are of external provenance, for example, Christianity, I suggest we must simply style "òrìṣà." If we must anglicize it, all we need do is follow the conventions established for referencing other indigenously derived religions in other parts of the world such as Judaism, Buddhism, Confucianism, Shintoism, or Hinduism. Hence my suggestion that rather than the vacuous concept of African Traditional Religion, we should substitute: *Oriṣaism.* One clear implication of this suggestion is that we abandon the homogenizing excesses of African Traditional Religion discourse. We embrace instead the reality of diversity in African Religions and take care to recognize each tradition in its specificity. If it turns out that what I have described herein is unique to Yorùbá religion, it will not make it any less African; if other African-derived religions are like it, it will not make it any more or peculiarly African. The facile resort to unwarranted, perhaps false, generalization must be resisted.

From what we have said so far, one cannot speak of Yorùbá religion without ultimately coming to some engagement or another with òrìṣà and its innumerable ramifications. Whether in worshipping, propitiating, performing, making, praising, singing, chanting, saluting, invoking, evoking, calling, and whatever else may be done, at the core of Yorùbá religious phenomena are òrìṣà and our relation to them. So, in adopting this nomenclature, we would be losing nothing. In fact, we'd be advancing understanding. Concomitantly, we can begin to offer robust analyses of the idea of transcendence, *mysterium,* the issue of the relationship between humans and gods, of the role and efficacy of sacrifice, the place of ritual, not to mention òrìṣà-inspired art, music, liturgies, fashion, cuisine, and sexual behavior. I hope that I have provided a solid prolegomenon for these tasks and that others more competent than I may build on it for the advancement of our knowledge of òrìṣà.

Notes

This is the written and updated version of a contribution to the Conference on the Globalization of Yorùbá Religious Culture held at Florida International University, Miami, Florida, December 9–12, 1999. I am grateful to Professor Jacob Olupona for extending to me the original invitation to attend the conference and Professor Terry Rey, his co-organizer. I completed the writing of the draft during my tenure as a Ford Foundation Visiting Postdoctoral Fellow at the Carter G. Woodson Institute for Afro-American and African Studies as part of its Center for Advanced Studies of Race, Ethnicity, and Society in Africa and the Atlantic World in the 2000–2001 academic year. This final version has benefited immensely from comments by Professor Barry Hallen; I cannot thank him enough.

1. See Jacob K. Olupona, introduction to Olupona 2000, and Fisher 1998, especially p. 7.

2. In addition to *African Traditional Religion: A Definition,* we may also cite Ìdòwú's earlier *Olódùmarè: God in Yorùbá Belief.*

3. For example, see Awolalu 1979 and Olupona 1991. For criticism, see Abímbólá 2001 and Bewaji 1998.

4. Those who are familiar with the ontological argument for the existence of God can easily recognize the pedigree of this argument.

5. See, generally, Otto 1950. For those who are familiar with Otto's work, its influence on Ìdòwú's characterization of Religion and of African Traditional Religion is unmistakable.

6. For some instructive parallels between Greek and Yorùbá religions, see Harrison 1991.

7. For even older attempts of this sort, see Schön and Crowther 1970.

8. See especially Ìdòwú's discussion of Olódùmarè's attributes in chapter 5 of *Olódùmarè.*

9. Interestingly, the same grid might work, too, for Yorùbá inflections of alien-derived religions. One is reminded here of the convergence of ritual observations of overseas branches of, for instance, Aládurà Christianity.

10. I have not altered the original usages in Beier's text to preserve authorial integrity.

11. There are different methods by which to establish this in Yorùbá culture. Sometimes there are signs to be read by the experts. The most common is through divination.

12. Even the Aláàfin of Òyó who used to be considered one of the most fearsome of Yorùbá Ọba and whose cognomen includes reference to his being next only to òrìṣà is not immune to this limitation. Although he may mimic òrìṣà in some of his ritual functions as the Aláàfin, in his embodied state he could not be more than second to òrìṣà: he could not be òrìṣà.

13. See, generally, Beier 1975: 44–45.

14. Exceptions will include those who die in supreme acts of self-sacrifice for the good of the community, e.g., Olúorogbo.

15. Loosely translated, *Egúngún* festival marks the time of the year when departed spirits come to visit, masked of course, with the living.

References

Abímbólá, Kólápó. 2001. "Spirituality and Applied Ethics: An African Perspective." *West Africa Review* 3, no. 1. Retrieved June 28, 2006, from: http://

www.africaresource.com/war/v013.1/abimbola.hrm. Available February 20, 2007, at: http://www.africaresource.com/war/vol3.1/abimbola.htm.

———. 2006. *Yorùbá Culture: A Philosophical Account*. Birmingham: Ìrókò Academic Publishers.

Awolalu, J. Ômôÿade. 1979. *Yorùbá Beliefs and Sacrificial Rites*. London: Longman, 1979.

Beier, Ulli. 1975. *The Return of the Gods: The Sacred Art of Susanne Wenger*. Cambridge: Cambridge University Press.

Bewaji, John A. I. 1998. "Olódùmarè: God in Yorùbá Belief and the Theistic Problem of Evil." *African Studies Quarterly* 2, no. 1. Retrieved June 30, 2006, from: http://www.africa.ufl.edu/asq/v2/v2ia1.htm. Available February 20, 2007, at: http://web.africa.ufl.edu/asq/v2/v2i1a1.htm.

Fisher, Robert B. 1998. *West African Religious Traditions*. Maryknoll, N.Y.: Orbis.

Harrison, Jane Ellen. 1991. *Prolegomena to the Study of Greek Religion*. Princeton: Princeton University Press.

Hegel, G. W. F. 1956. *The Philosophy of History*. New York: Dover.

Ìdòwú, E. Bolaji. 1973. *African Traditional Religion: A Definition*. Maryknoll, N.Y.: Orbis.

———. 1994 (1962). *Olódùmarè: God in Yorùbá Belief*. Memorial ed. New York: WAZOBIA.

Mbiti, John S. 1999 (1969). *African Religions and Philosophy*. Nairobi: East African Publishing House.

Olupona, Jacob K., ed. 1991. *African Traditional Religions in Contemporary Society*. New York: Paragon House.

———, ed. 2000. *African Spirituality: Forms, Meanings and Expressions*. New York: Crossroad.

Otto, Rudolf. 1950 (1917). *The Idea of the Holy*. Trans. John W. Harvey. Oxford: Oxford University Press.

Schön, James Frederick, and Samuel Ajayi Crowther. 1970. *Journals*. London: Frank Cass.

Soyinka, Wole. 1976. *Myth, Literature and the African World*. Cambridge: Cambridge University Press.

5

Associated Place-Names and Sacred Icons of Seven Yorùbá Deities

Historicity in Yorùbá Religious Traditions

CORNELIUS O. ADEPEGBA

Validation of Historical Events

The oral traditions of the Yorùbá offer a rich source of information concerning religious beliefs, particularly those steeped in an historical context. Yorùbá traditions are preserved primarily in the oral form of everyday language—myth, proverbs, maxims, *oríkì* (praise songs to the deities), and Ifá divination poetry. In the living culture and in the memory of elders, many oral forms are readily available today, some of which interested scholars from various disciplines have recorded and compiled in written form.

Compared to oral forms, archaeological data and material culture offer rather limited validation and sources of information of religious beliefs because relevant archaeological finds have been undertaken only in a few sites in contemporary Nigeria, and where undertaken, archaeologists have focused on disciplines other than religious epistemology. The notable excavations of Iwo Eleru, Ilé-Ifè, Old Ọ̀yọ́, Esie, and Ifè-Ijumu were undertaken not for religious considerations but in the inadvertent discovery of religious artifacts or general historical interest. Some archaeological sites in Nigeria today, which religious tradition associates with particular deities, are located in or near present-day communities. However, not all deities are identifiable with present-day place-names or sites, and a good number of deities are not associated with any particular geographical place-names.

Using oral traditions as primary sources of data to reconstruct the Yorùbá religious past cannot but pose uncertainty. Problems of contradiction and illogicality of events and their sequences must be expected. To begin with, there is a cultural blend of historical reality with the post-deification conceptualization of deities. In general, it appears that the Yorùbá imagination provides for the blending of myth with historical events and personages.

Èjìogbè is the name of a chapter of Ifá poetry. It is a primary source of the most revered Ifá divination poems in which the humanity of the deities is stressed unequivocally. Ifá, the God of Divination, is said to emphasize that Yorùbá deities, including himself, were originally humans who displayed extraordinary wisdom, skill, or power. Some Yorùbá proverbs reveal an association between gods and humans as reflected in the sayings of Ifá: *"Ẹni ó gbọ́n mà l' òrìṣà,* One who is wise is a deity," and *"Ẹni ó gbọ́n ni ẹ jẹ́ á máa bọ,* One who is wise is one who should be worshipped" (Sowande 1965). Thus, even a proverb may indicate a "historical" as well as mythical duality of Yorùbá deities, in addition to their supernatural attributes. They are believed to have existed in heaven with the Supreme God, Olódùmarè, before he sent them to the world to right its wrongs and to solve human problems.

According to the myth, one of the gods, Ọbàtálá, the god of creation, was involved in creating the world, but he is believed to be in charge expressly of creating human beings. Although Ọbàtálá often failed in his creations because he frequently became inebriated along the way to the world, he was the god whom the Supreme Being, Olódùmarè, first sent to create the earth upon the waters. The creation of earth on the waters occurred before the generally accepted legendary Father of the Yorùbá, Odùduwà, was sent to create the world. Despite this apparent contradiction between Olódùmarè and Odùduwà, Yorùbá deities eventually carried out God's instruction flawlessly, and the Yorùbá came to believe firmly that Ọbàtálá was responsible for human creation. The Yorùbá invariably attribute deformity to Ọbàtálá, referring to individuals who suffer deformity—albino, hunchbacked, disfigured, or disabled—as the people of Ọbàtálá or god's people, *eni òrìṣà*. Deformities were thought to be caused by Ọbàtálá's intoxicated condition that prevented him from recognizing defects and blemishes.

According to legend, the Yorùbá say that all deities descended to the world in at least thirteen "batches," each batch consisting of fifteen to seventeen deities (Adeoye 1985: 29–35). The deities descended from heaven by holding onto ropes, *won ro*. Invariably the gods are immortal; toward the ends of their lives, they change form into natural phenomena of the landscape, such as hills, outcrops, or rivers, as in the case of two female deities, Ọ̀ṣun and Yemọja. Some gods descended directly into the ground, as in the case of Òrìṣà-Oko, god of agricultural prosperity. Even Ifá is said to have vanished as he ascended into heaven.

Thus, the immortality of Ṣàngó, the king of Ọ̀yọ́ who committed suicide, is concealed within his name, Kòso (he who cannot be hung), the place-name for the site of his ignoble death. Kòso refers indirectly to an event, as a way of concealing the actual mortality of Ṣàngó, thereby protecting his devotees from any shame if Ṣàngó were to die ignobly. A common saying attests to the eternal deities, "Ayé ni 'molè gbò sí" (In the world, deities live long).

Suggested by the thirteen batches in which they descended to earth, some myths about certain deities contradict the sequential arrival of deities to the world. Initially, the males among the deities believed that only males were capable of the status of godhood. Ọ̀ṣun, a prominent deity who happened to be female, was rejected from their misogynous fold until she upset their supernatural exploits. Ultimately, however, Ifá, the god of divination, intervened on her behalf and counseled the male deities to consult with Ọ̀ṣun in whatever projects they planned in order to prevent her from thwarting their efforts.

There is some controversy over the nature of Ṣàngó, God of Thunder. Who was he, actually? On a cultural historical level, Ṣàngó appears to have been one of the kings of Ọ̀yọ́ based on archaeological and material culture associated with him that exist only in the Ọ̀yọ́ area where Ṣàngó is most actively worshipped. On a mythical level, it is claimed that a primordial "Ṣàngó" existed before the reign of the popular King Ṣàngó of Ifè (Adeoye 1985: 287, 289). It seems that King Ṣàngó is sometimes projected into the past to elevate him to the status or age of other deities.

Various accounts of affairs among the deities in divinatory consultation or matrimony suggest that deities were understood to be living human beings. Various versions of Ifá poetry narrate how most deities consulted Ifá for advice before they came to the world or later after they encountered problems in the world. There are legendary conjugal liaisons between well-known deities, but apparently their status as gods offered little immunity from the marital indiscretions of their human counterparts. Ọbàtálá married Yemòó; their daughter married Òrìṣà-Oko, god of agriculture and prosperity. Ọ̀ṣun married Ọ̀rúnmìlà (Ifá); she divorced Ifá to marry Ṣàngó. Ṣàngó wooed Ọya away from Ògún, and Ṣàngó in addition married Yemọja.

However, there seems to be some consensus on the number of deities, which are said to be four hundred and one, although not all four hundred and one are listed convincingly in any one source. Ọbàtálá is called by thirty-nine names, depending on the community in which he is worshipped. Besides, not all deities appear in human form. Some, like the earth or *ilẹ̀,* or the *ìrókò* tree, are certainly deified in forms of nature (Adeoye 1985: 356–60, 404–8).

Not all mythology surrounding a Yorùbá deity, therefore, can be expected to throw light on the historical character of Yorùbá religious traditions. I focus here only on principal Yorùbá deities who appeared clearly in human form and who enjoyed widespread popularity among many devotees before the advent of Islam and Christianity.

Seven major deities in the Yorùbá pantheon are discussed: (1) Ògún, god of iron; (2) Ifá, god of wisdom and divination; (3) Ọbàtálá, god of creation; (4) Òrìṣà-Oko, god of agricultural prosperity or wealth; (5) Ọ̀ṣun, goddess of the source; (6) Ṣàngó, god of thunder and lightning; and (7) Ṣàngó's wife, Ọya, goddess of wind and tempest. The worship of Ògún, Ifá, and Ọbàtálá cut across all Yorùbá subgroups and even spread beyond the Yorùbá, especially in the case of Ògún and Ifá. Òrìṣà-Oko was widely worshipped among the Ọ̀yọ́, Ègbá, and Ìjẹ̀bú. Ọ̀ṣun was well known among the Yàgbà, Ìgbómìnà, Èkìtì, Ìjèsà, and Ọ̀yọ́. The Ọ̀yọ́, among whom Ṣàngó and Ọya were especially popular, represent the largest subsection of the Yorùbá people. In the following section, each of the seven major Yorùbá deities is introduced briefly.

Sacred Places and Material Culture Associated with Yorùbá Deities

Ògún, God of Iron

As Sandra Barnes rightly put it, "Ògún is popularly known as the god of hunting, iron, and warfare," and today, "the realm has expanded to include many new elements from modern technology to highway safety—any event involving metal, danger, or transportation" (1989: 2) The worship of Ògún, god of iron, has, by extension, spread to professions, trades, and activities involving the production and use of iron implements. His appellation "Ògún, Baba Irin" (Ògún, father of iron) emphasizes this association, while another appellation, "Mogún Ìrè, Ọmọ a-bu-ilè-se owó" (Mogún Ìrè, Child of One who-takes-the-earth-to-make money), associates him with the smelting of iron. Traditionally, Ògún is associated with no other metal. Although the Yorùbá distinguish brass and lead from iron, they associate lead and brass with Ọbàtálá and Ọ̀sun. Consequently, iron smelters, blacksmiths, hunters, warriors, scarifiers, and barbers especially revere Ògún, whose sacred symbols of worship were tools traditionally fashioned primarily from iron.

Generally, the Yorùbá revere Ògún as capable of supernatural powers far beyond ordinary miracles, as they plead to him for precaution and safety against bloody accidents. Ògún can even prevent death involved in using metal implements—knives, hunting tools, weapons of war, cutlasses, spearheads, swords, and guns—as well as present-day dangers of death or accident by motor vehicles. Ògún is believed to be fierce and capable of controlling, preventing, or, out of anger, inflicting mishaps in using iron objects on or around individual persons. Consequently, even today the Yorùbá may fear taking an oath sworn in the name of Ògún.

Ògún is the communal deity of some towns, notably Òndó and Ilésà. He is said especially to have founded Ìrè, Isundùrin, Ìwòyà, and Sakí. However, two places are popularly alluded to as his native towns—Ìrè, an Ekiti town, and Sakí, an Òkè Oogùn town. Yet, references to explain these place-names as his native homes are more controversial than consensual.

Ògún is usually referred to as Ògún Onírè, a title that in itself can be interpreted in two ways: Ògún, the traditional ruler of Ìrè, or Ògún the Deity, the Ruler of Ìrè. An opposing claim says that Sakí town—not Ìrè town—was Ògún's original home. According to Samuel Ojo, the deity Ògún was a member of the Odùduwà party, which was the founder's immigrant party that first entered the land of the Yorùbá from Sakí (Bada 1977: 7). As a regent to Odùduwà in old age, Ògún is said to have settled in the town of Sakí before he visited Ìrè. This claim differs apparently from the rival claim only in sequence of the deity's residence in the two towns.

Traditional references to Sakí say, "Ògún kò ro 'kin, abide kò ro bàbá" (Ògún never carved ivory; he never worked in copper). Although emphasizing Ògún's connection to ironworking, these claims might also suggest that Ògún, as referred to in the two traditions, was not one or the same person. It is possible that Ògún was a generic name for smiths, forgers, or coppersmiths, as most Yorùbá names originate from complete sentences that can be shortened either to subjects or predicates. That was how Ògúndáhùnsi, the name of the founder of Ìrè Town, was shortened to Ògún (Barnes 1989: 8). With respect to the two towns, Sakí and Ìrè, it is therefore likely that references to Ògún are actually references to various followers of the deity and not to Ògún himself.

Archaeological Evidence in Material Culture

In West Africa, the oldest documented human remains were found in the Yorùbá region of Ìwó-Elérú in southwestern Nigeria. Recent archaeological research shows that humans were living specifically in Ìwó-Elérú as early as 9,000 B.C.E. and perhaps earlier at Ugwuelle-Uturu (Okigwe) in southeastern Nigeria (Shaw and Daniels 1984: 7–100). However, West Africa's oldest ironworking site is located in Nok, represented by sophisticated terra cotta sculptures from between 500 B.C.E. and 200 C.E. Nok lies north of the Benue River in what is now Kaduna State, just north of traditional Yorùbá districts. Worship of the god Ògún, therefore, may have been introduced to the Yorùbá along with the introduction of ironworking technology from beyond their empires. Moreover, evidence for this theory is consistent with the use of the dog as the animal that was customarily sacrificed to Ògún. The dog is used mainly for hunting. Thus, its use as the principal sacrifice to the deity suggests the introduction of the worship of Ògún to the Yorùbá during an era when hunting was a primary economy. This theory is supported further because farmers, who were greater in number than hunters and, therefore, likely to consume more iron than hunters, are not as strongly identified with Ògún. Likewise, Yorùbá woven textile arts associated with Ògún, which are said to be palm fronds, suggest a period earlier than the introduction of cotton cloth textiles. Speaking of the spread of the *ìjálá* chants as a traditional art form in commemorating Ògún, Adeboye Bàbálolá, a scholar known for his study of Yorùbá *ìjálá* oral poetry, stresses a probable cause as the itinerant life of Ògún (Bàbálolá 1989: 149).[1] It is likely that the worship of the deity predated Yorùbá urbanization, and thus the present-day place-names associated with Ògún may not have existed at the time the deity was introduced early in Yorùbá culture.

Ifá (Ọ̀rúnmìlà), God of Wisdom and Divination

Ifá is a kind of divinity in whom there is no ambiguity. He is an omniscient deity who knows the past, the present, and the future, and therefore he can advise on any situation in life. Hence, he is known as the god of wisdom and divination.

Information on Ifá abounds in oral traditions. His physique and complexion, as well as places in which he sojourned, are indicated, particularly in his praise names. He was known to be short and very black; he lived in a particular quarter of Ilé-Ifè. He is called Ọkùnrin kúkúrú Òkè Ìtaṣẹ̀ (the short man of Ìtaṣẹ̀) and Ọkùnrin dúdú Òkè Ìgẹ̀tí (the black-complexioned man of Ìgẹ̀tì). Even today, a person with very dark skin is referred to as adúbíifá (He who is as black as Ifá). Òkè Ìtaṣẹ̀ is located at the center of Ilé-Ifè, while Òkè Ìgẹ̀tì is located on the outskirts of Ifè toward Ilésà. Ifá is also associated with Adó and Ọ̀wọ̀ in the following lines from his praise poetry:

> Ifá pẹ̀lẹ́ o, Ọkùnrin kúkúrú ile Adó
> Ọ̀rúnmìlà pẹ̀lé, Erinmi Òde Ọ̀wọ̀
> Baba Ọlọ́wọ̀, Arara gejegeje.

> [Greetings, Ifá, Short Man of Adó
> Greetings, Ọ̀rúnmìlà, oh Mighty Hippopotamus[2] of Ọ̀wọ̀
> Greetings, Father of adorned and glorious Ọlọ́wọ̀.]

It seems unlikely that Ifá resided permanently in a particular place, but rather he led an itinerant life. Nor is it likely that Ifá is associated with any particular food because most Yorùbá foods are acceptable to him as sacrifice. Palm kernels of a special type represent his symbol of worship, as well as a tool of his priesthood divinatory. No mention is commonly made of his clothes. However, one of his praise names refers to Ifá as Egúngún Olú-Ifè, Ti i sán màrìwò pako (Masquerade of Olú-Ifè, Ruler of Ifè, He who wraps the fronds of raffia palm around). From this and a line in his other praise names, "Ọmọ a sò lódò ya màrìwò ọpe" (Child of he who stops at the river to cut palm fronds), we know that Ifá is associated with palm fronds, and it seems plausible that he, similar to Ògún, used to wear intricately designed palm fronds before the introduction of cloth textiles. Similar to Ògún, Ifá seems to have come from outside the Yorùbá Empire. Samuel Johnson referred to Ifá as a man of Nupe called Sètílù (Johnson 1921: 26–39). Ifá, which is also the word for the process of divination, is not exclusive to the Yorùbá. The Ìgbò, Edo, and Ebirra refer to divination by similar names, and although Egyptologists have not corroborated it, the word "Ifá" is rumored to mean wisdom in ancient Egyptian (Adeoye 1985: 174). Ifá divination, therefore, may have been introduced from the outside, similar to imported concepts of ironworking, and the era of the first Ifá diviner of the Yorùbá may not be very far from the era of Ògún.

Ọbàtálá, God of Creation

Ọbàtálá appears to be foremost of the Yorùbá pantheon. He is known by his other names, Òrìṣà-Nlá and Òrìṣà-Àlà, including the name Òrìṣà, the Yorùbá word for "lord" or "god." Ọbàtálá is also referred to as an *obá* or king. As indicated earlier, he is god of creation and is still believed to be the creator of humans and the god who in the beginning helped Supreme God, Olódùmarè, to create other deities. Although Ọbàtálá is capable of solving most problems of human welfare in securing well-being and freedom from disease, he is especially associated with childbirth because he is the great sculptor who molds the human form.

Ọbàtálá is said to be the founding king of Iranje; his origins may also be traced to Ifè, the sacred ancestral home of the Yorùbá. It was said that he married Yemòó, who is worshipped jointly with him by his priests in the same shrine and after whom Ìta Yemòó, the name of a district in Ilé-Ifè, is still called. He did not just establish Iranje; he watched it grow into a town and went on to found Iranje-oko, the Rural Iranje. However, his founding of Iranje has not been ascertained. It was most likely one of the settlements that eventually grew together to become Ifè because most Yorùbá cities and towns grew from clusters of villages. They were originally small settlements before coalescing into greater urban centers, and Ifè was no exception.

According to Yorùbá mythology, Ilé-Ifè was, and is, the center of the universe, the primary urban center where the Yorùbá first established the monarchy. That Ọbàtálá is referred to as a king indicates that he must have founded a kind of monarchy. Use of the term "monarchy" most likely implies that the claim has some basis in history, since Ọbàtálá was known as the first deity sent by the Supreme God, Olódùmarè, to create the world. Ọbàtálá's failure to do so "because he got drunk along the way," seems to imply that he failed to complete the building of Ifè into a city-state before another ruler, Odùduwà, or Odùduwà's dynasty, came into power. The epoch of Ọbàtálá, therefore, may have marked the beginning of urbanization of the Yorùbá. The fact that Ọbàtálá is worshipped as the titular deity, although under various names of many later towns, signifies the importance of his symbols of worship in establishing cities and towns.

Traditionally, Ọbàtálá's devotees wear white robes and clothes, embellished with bangles of lead, all which are said to come from the deity Ọbàtálá. Evidence of the woven white cloth produced in the epoch of Ọbàtálá is corroborated by the following lines from his praises:

Ọbàtálá ní asọ nílé
Ó rin ìhòhò wọ balùwẹ̀
Ó ní asọ, ó da àkíṣà bo ara
Ẹni tí kò bá ní asọ funfun
Kí ó má ba wa dé ojúbọ Òrìṣà
Nítorí pé asọ tí ó bá funfun
Ni àwa fi í sògo ní ilé wa
Asọ funfun kì i tí láé-láé

[Ọbàtálá has clothes at home.
He walks naked to the bath place.
He has clothes but covers himself with rags.
He who has no white clothes
does not follow us to the shrine of Òrìṣà Ọbàtálá.
Because white clothing
is a source of great pride in our house.
White clothing never fades.][3]

The association of Ọbàtálá with white cloth situates him within the Yorùbá epoch of a more advanced technological age than the epoch of Ògún or Ifá, who are associated with the earlier technology of intricately woven palm frond designs. Divination with cowries or ẹẹ̀rìndínlógún is traced traditionally to the goddess Òṣun. It is said that her first husband, Ifá or Ọ̀rúnmìlà, taught her. Nevertheless, more realistically, according to one myth, it seems that Ọbàtálá started the practice of using sacred cowries as evidenced by the cognomen for Ọbàtálá, "Ọbàtálá Efuru ri owó eyo mú se awo" (he who uses cowries to divinate), since divination with cowries itself is very common and well accepted as auspicious.

Òrìṣà-Oko, God of Agricultural Prosperity or Wealth

Òrìṣà-Oko, also known as Ajangele, is the god of agricultural prosperity or wealth. Òrìṣà-Oko and Ọbàtálá—otherwise known as Òrìṣà-Nlá,

Òrìṣà-Ògíyán, and Òrìṣà Olúfón—are Yorùbá deities whose names include the word *òrìṣà,* the Yorùbá term for god, gods, or deity. The various compound parts of the name are invariably adjectives to honor the Òrìṣà; hence, *òrìṣà-oko* means "god of the rural estate or province." To the Yorùbá, a city or town indicates their home, and any place beyond that indicates rural land or countryside. The name *oko* signifies the Yorùbá practice of differentiating between urban and rural abodes. Similarly, the legend of Ọbàtálá says that he founded two Iranjes, the Iranje-Ilé or Ode Iranje (home), and the Iranje-oko (rural province).

The god Òrìṣà-Oko started his life in Ifè-Ooyè (Adeoye 1985: 271) as a hunter and a fisher, who one day rescued, and subsequently married, the drowning daughter of Ọbàtálá and Yemòó. After his marriage, Òrìṣà-Oko became notoriously wealthy, and the people of Ifè started to malign him, spreading rumors that he had no resources of his own. Scandalously, they said that Òrìṣà-Oko was merely living off the fortunes of his parents-in-law. Nothing seems to summarize his disgrace more aptly as the ridicule sung in his praise songs:

> Òrìṣà-Oko ko gbin bara ti o fi n jẹ ẹ̀gúsí
> Ọlá àna rẹ̀ ní njẹ̀
> A jẹ ọsinsin má ro gbèṣè
>
> [Òrìṣà-Oko plants no melon; yet he eats its seeds (*ẹ̀gúsí).*
> He lives on the fortunes of his parents-in-law.
> He gulps down the delectable *ẹ̀gúsí* soup with no thought of family obligation.]

Ẹ̀gúsí soup is invariably used in making a sacrifice to Òrìṣà-Oko. According to the story, when Òrìṣà-Oko heard the slurs against him, he was highly insulted. He wondered what he could do to stand on his own to regain his good reputation. He consulted Ifá for advice, who told him to leave the town for a place where he would see a sign of certain birds. He traveled until he reached present-day Ìráwò, where he encountered the signs. Òrìṣà-Oko settled there, becoming prosperous and famous. He was worshipped and had numerous disciples. Eventually, it was there he miraculously entered "into the ground" (Òrìṣà-oko *wọ ilẹ̀ ní* Ìráwò, Òrìṣà-Oko descended into the ground at Ìráwò), which became a popular saying, using the well-liked metaphor of miraculous immortality.

Òrìṣà-Oko is associated with another city, Iwere, where he was praised as Ara Iwere, *Ajangele, agbalagba* Òrìṣà-Ìráwò. Iwere and Ìráwò are the names of two small towns in the Upper Oogún areas of the northwestern Yorùbá. Archaeological explorations have not been carried out in these areas, nor have the Yorùbá considered these sites to be of great historical significance. The sacred symbols for Òrìṣà-Oko include white chalk (*efun*) and cowries similar to Ọbàtálá's sacred cowries. However, Ọbàtálá's cowries designate divinatory significance, so they are not strung together. The *arere* or *ilarere* (cowries) of Òrìṣà-Oko are strung together as necklaces worn by his (male) devotees for adornment, not divination.

A strong taboo is associated with Òrìṣà-Oko that forbids the eating of the new yam. Devotees of Òrìṣà-Oko must not consume "new" yams until the time of the annual festival to Òrìṣà-Oko when yams are maturing.[4] His devotees, similar to those of Ọbàtálá, should also refrain from wearing the masquerade costume, as enjoined in this *ìjálá* chant:

> Èmi kò tètè mòpé Ọbàtálá ki i ru èkú.
> Egúngún Ijaola bu si yaara Òrìṣà-oko
>
> [Only just lately, I realized that Ọbàtálá wears no masquerade.
> The masquerade of Ijaola was defiled in Òrìṣà-Oko's room.]
> Adeoye 1985: 274

The legendary two deities, who refrain from wearing the masquerade, can be understood in an historical context of alienation with the Ìgbò, who frequently harassed the Yorùbá people of early Ifè by disguising themselves in terrifying straw regalia to masquerade as spirits to instill fear of the gods. Once, the Ìgbò went before Mọrèmi, a beautiful woman of Ifè, who uncovered their masquerade. Mọrèmi voluntarily appeared to give herself up as a captive to the Ìgbò and married the Ìgbò king, whose treachery she soon exposed; she ran back to Ifè to reveal the Ìgbò betrayal of her people. Masquerading is associated with malevolent spirits; thus, avoiding the masquerade signifies the desire of Òrìṣà-Oko and Ọbàtálá to be human, as those without deceit.

Ọ̀ṣun, Goddess of the Source

Ọ̀ṣun signifies a "great source" or "that which runs" as in moving water, as in *orísùn,* the source of a river, a people, or of children. Ọ̀ṣun is perceived as the eternal sustaining source of life itself. As indicated earlier, Goddess Ọ̀ṣun was the first female to be deified. The epic Ifá divination poetry, in which her deification is proclaimed, declares that Ose-Tura (Adeoye 1985: 203–45), the Goddess Ọ̀ṣun, sent forth her avengers, her lieutenants—Boribori *awo* (the Mystery-Maker of Iragberi); Egba *awo* (the Mystery-Maker of Ilukan); Ese *awo* (the Mystery-Maker of Ijebu Epe); and Atonu and their Mystery-Makers in Ikire Ilé. She sent them forth to inflict punishment on her assailants, but other deities were incapable of defending these assailants. God, through Ifá, advised the other deities to reckon with Òṣun's power if they wanted to succeed in helping people solve their problems.

As already indicated, Òṣun first married Ifá (Òrúnmìlà), and during their marriage, Òrúnmìlà bestowed upon her sixteen cowries (*ẹẹrìndín-lógún*) to perform divination as popularly claimed. Nevertheless, despite her daring deeds, Òṣun failed to bear a child for Òrúnmìlà. Out of deep shame and sorrow for her barrenness, she divorced Òrúnmìlà to marry Ṣàngó.

Although Òṣun was barren at first, she became a deity who was intensely associated with successful childbearing. After a reluctant consultation with Òrúnmìlà and the necessary sacrifice she was asked to make, she bore a child of her own and miraculously brought children to other barren women. Later, she helped women to care for their children who were sick.

Today, some communities, such as Òsogbo and Ìpolé, are referred to as "owning" Òṣun. However, these communities are most likely the places where Òṣun was actively worshipped after her deification. According to the traditional origin of Òsogbo town, its founder, Laaro, happened to fell a tree near the river named after Òṣun, which flows by the town. Moaning in distress that her dye pots had been smashed, the alarmed voice of a goddess was heard coming forth from the river, and since then, the people of the town have taken Òṣun as their titular deity.

A praise song refers to Òṣun as Ìjèsà, somehow associating Òṣun with Ìpolé. However, the only place where Òṣun may have been historically connected is Ìjùmú, which is not a town but a district of the northwestern Yorùbá. Since the late Stone Age, archaeological evidence has established the existence of continuous settlement there. Archaeological reconnaissance and excavations have taken place at the rock shelters at Itaakpa and Oluwaju and at the stone axe factory at Òkè dagba, as well as the ironworking site of Addo. Archaeological evidence from these sites revealed that settlement continued in the area from about 300 B.C.E. to its present-day recently abandoned villages (Oyèláràn 1998: 65–79).

Very esteemed among Òṣun's sacred symbols of reverence are brass bangles, brass fans, and carved combs (see Badejo 1996). In the northeastern periphery of the Yorùbá lands, archaeological excavations at the village of Esie uncovered a carved comb interpreted as belonging to Ọ̀ṣun.[5] Esie is just a stone's throw away from another town called Òró (literally, a space where people stand). Professor Wande Abímbọ́lá described the place-name Ọ̀rọ̀ as derived from the description of the great authority of Ọ̀ṣun.[6] As related by Ope Onabajo, an archeologist at Obafemi Awolowo University, Ilé-Ifè, a proverb indicates Ọ̀ṣun's charisma evidenced by the many guests in her house: "*Òró la ro ní ilé Ọ̀ṣun, ilé Ọ̀ṣun kò gbènìyàn,* There is standing room only, and no one could sit in Ọ̀ṣun's house. Ọ̀ṣun's house could contain no more people" (personal communication, 1999). Similar to Ọbàtálá, Ọ̀ṣun is associated with the revered white fabric, displayed as part of her shrine and as the customary clothing of her disciples.

Ṣàngó, God of Thunder and Lightning

Ṣàngó is the fearsome god of thunder and lightning. Sacred artifacts associated with his shrine and worship offer evidence that indeed there was a king of Old Ọ̀yọ́ of this name. The shrine's artifacts, the leather wallet, *lábá,* and the gourd rattle, *ṣẹ́ẹ́ré,* are well-known products of the Ọ̀yọ́ Yorùbá. *Gbègìrì* soup, with which Ṣàngó is associated and worshipped, is prepared and eaten only by the Ọ̀yọ́ Yorùbá, and his drum, the *bale,* is unique to them. However, other symbols of worship—the *ẹdùn,* the new Stone Age axe, and *orógbó* that is cut and cast before him—may not belong to the same era or domain of the Ọ̀yọ́ Yorùbá. These symbols may have been added during a later age.

The Stone Age axe is said to be the instrument with which Ṣàngó kills humans during a thunderstorm. After any death by lightning, the victims must not be buried until the chief priest of Ṣàngó unearths the stone axe in a lavish ceremony, paid for by the relatives of the victims. It is believed that the death and the unearthing of the stone axe occur mysteriously. Perhaps the power to attract thunder or lightning to kill people was harnessed by someone before Ṣàngó, and that person is probably confused with Ṣàngó. The *orógbó* nut is grown in the southern forests, but since it is marketed northward, together with kola nuts also grown in southern forests, they must have been popular articles of trade to the Ọ̀yọ́ regions.

Ṣàngó was a powerful medicine healer, and thus he is praised as *Ewélérè* (the herb or traditional medicine is profitable), as in *ewégbèmí* (the herb has profited me) (Adeoye 1985: 28, 302). Ṣàngó is even said to be wicked, and this wickedness led in due time to his defeat by one of his lieutenants and to Ṣàngó's eventual suicide. Another praise name for Ṣàngó is Árékùjayé (*a ru ékù j' ayé*) (he who carries on a masquerade in order to enjoy life). Incidentally, the masquerade of *egúngún* is a phenomenon associated with Ọ̀yọ́.

Ọya, Goddess of Wind and Tempests

The stories of Ọya are fraught with ambiguity. Ọya is popularly envisioned as the wife of Ṣàngó, and this alliance is the reason for her deification (Adeoye 1985: 303–6). While they were still in heaven, she is said to have married Ògún directly before descending into the world, where she became known by the name Àràká. After they were married for a while, she began to sneak away from home secretly from time to time to meet the members of her *ẹgbẹ̀* (heavenly society). When Ògún could no longer stand her absence, he beat her; and thus she left Ògún and went to marry Ṣàngó. Her interest in her own culture still continued, as well as her desire to meet with her society, as she wanted eventually to separate from Ṣàngó.

Another version of the legend says that after separating from Ṣàngó, Ọya remarried. During a hunting expedition, Olukosi Epe, said to be a fine hunter, spied Ọya in a masquerade costume crowned with buffalo horns. Ọya used to wear the costume anytime she wanted to sneak away to meet her heavenly peers. Her usual practice was to stash the costume before the rendezvous, and it was at this very moment that the hunter spied her. Later, Olukosi Epe removed the costume from its hiding place and took it home. Ọya, seeing the hunter's footprints, tracked the hunter to his home and eventually married him.

However, one day, when Ọya's husband was away from home, his jealous senior wife referred to Ọya's secret. The senior wife insulted Ọya by saying that Ọya's costume was hidden somewhere. Ọya became enraged: "*Maa je maa mu, awo re nbe l' aka!* (Eat and drink! Make merry! Your (true) self is inside the granary—it will soon be revealed!)." Today, the Yorùbá still indicate sarcasm with this saying that originated from the mythical insult. In frenzy, Ọya collected her costume from its secreted place, killed the senior wife, and attempted to kill her husband. Nevertheless, Ọya failed to do away with him. She therefore commanded her children that she should be consulted and worshipped using buffalo horns. Suddenly, like a goddess, she vanished from sight. The place from which she disappeared is popularly said to be Ira, a town of the northern Yorùbá.

Despite various legends, Oya continues to be associated popularly with Ṣàngó, and her buffalo horn symbols, white stone axes, and cloth wallet referred to as *lábá,* similar to the leather wallet of Ṣàngó, are kept lovingly in the shrine together with the sacred symbols of Ṣàngó. The dazzling beads, *kele,* worn around the neck of her disciples, are similar to those worn by the priests of Ṣàngó. Also notable is Oya's penchant for the masquerade, a favorite of Ṣàngó's.

Historical Analysis

Based on legend, poetry, proverbs, and myth surrounding these seven deities, Yorùbá religious traditions can be divided into three epochs using associated place-names, sacred objects, and popular or implied signifiers of time lines. Deification appears to follow primary epochs characterized by three probable contingencies: (1) the itinerant teaching of exogenous skills, (2) sedentary provisions for the well-being of people, and (3) a deity's use of terror to intimidate humans. Deifications of Ògún and Ifá seem to have fallen in the first epoch. Deifications of Obàtálá, Òrìṣà-Oko, and Òṣun fall in the second epoch, while those of Ṣàngó and Oya fall in the third.

Deifications of Ògún and Ifá derive from an age when outside ideas, skills, and knowledge were introduced to the Yorùbá. The two deities were itinerant, proffering their skills from place to place. Since many West African neighbors of the Yorùbá enjoy the same deities, it is most likely that the first persons who introduced the skills with which the deities are associated—ironworking and divination—to the Yorùbá were the people deified and given the names of the deities they brought with their trades or skills.

We know from archaeology that ironworking began in Nok on the plateau of northern Nigeria in the second century C.E., and the spread of it to the Yorùbá could not be much later than this time. A date from the ninth century C.E. has been obtained from an ironworking site at Ìjùmú of the northeastern Yorùbá (Oyèláràn 1998: 65–79). The worship of Ògún must have begun among the Yorùbá before urbanization. The association of Ògún with any present-day towns therefore must have started after his deification. The Ògúns mentioned in respect to the two places may refer to his later priests.

As indicated earlier, associating the dog as his sacrificial animal strongly indicates that Ògún's deification took place at a hunting stage of the culture. Moreover, Ògún and Ifá are associated with woven palm or raffia frond design, a material culture and art form that date them at a time before the Yorùbá adopted the later technology of woven cotton cloth. Narrow strips of cotton cloth represent weaving that is more recent. West Africans, including the Yorùbá, produce both broad and narrow woven cloth. Even today in the general region of the Congo, exquisite designs in woven raffia are still produced. Hence, Sieber is of the view that West Africans, too, may have woven with raffia before they began weaving with cotton. Akinwumi (personal communication, 1999) confirms this to be true among the Yorùbá. Woven palm (raffia fronds) as material for clothing must have preceded the production of cotton cloth. The introduction of ironworking, too, must have been perceived as a momentous technological leap in an environment overwhelmed by dense forests and dangerous animals, while divination, if only temporarily, lessened the onset of such anxiety. While Ògún was adored for protecting his followers from harm, Ifá was adored for granting them general welfare.

There came an epoch in Yorùbá history in which deities were sanctified more for the general well-being of the Yorùbá people than for any particular fear of their wrath. This was the great epoch of Ọbàtálá, Òrìṣà-Oko, and Ọṣun. Òrìṣà-Ńlá is noted more for bestowing successful childbirth than any other benevolence, since Ọbàtálá appears to have been deified for producing wholesome, healthy children.

In the epic poetry of Ifá divination, Òbàrà Ofún, the Òrìṣà Ọbàtálá created deformed individuals—albino, hunchback, and lame—but he immediately became alarmed and inquired about what was terribly wrong. Ọbàtálá was told to do as the Ifá divination poetry suggests:

> Mo mọ̀ Ọ̀bàrà, mo mọ̀ Ofú
> Bẹẹ ni kò yémi
> Àwọn ló dí Ifá fún Òrìṣà
> Tí nṣ'ọnà tí kò gún mó
> Wọ́n ní ẹbọ ni ki o ṣe
> Njẹ́ ta lówá ṣe ọnà ọmọ mí fun mi?
> Òrìṣà ló ṣe ọnà t'ọna gún
> Ọ̀ṣàṣọnà ọmọ mi Ọ̀ṣàṣọnà

[I know Ọbàrà, as well as Ofún.
Yet, I do not understand.
Thus, goes the prediction for Òrìṣà Ọbàtálá.
who was heartbroken at turning out such dreadful forms,
He was asked to make sacrifice, and thus he did.
Who then creates my child for me?
It is Òrìṣà who creates the most pleasing form.
Oh, my blessed child.][7]

Today, the epic poetry of Ifá divination is still popular and deemed appropriate for those who suffer difficulty in conceiving children. The child born after such difficulty is usually named Òṣàṣọnà, and the second part of the verse consists of praises to the Creator God, who, therefore, ensures the birth of perfectly formed children.

Often disciples of Òrìṣà-Oko, the deity of agricultural plenty and wealth, are given names beginning with "Òsó" or "So," symbolizing medicine or abundance. To have *oso* of anything, whether it is a crop or money, is to have the power or medicine to induce prosperity. The disciples now pray to Òrìṣà-Oko for other blessings, but the power for which he must have been deified is strongly related to his power in the provision of plenty.

In her case, Ọṣun appears noted for granting safe childbirth and healthy children. According to Ògúndase and relevant Ifá divination poetry, Ọṣun, as earlier related, was barren in her early life, even up to the time when she married Ṣàngó, her second husband. She was heartbroken and was forced to return shamefully to Ifá, her first husband, for divinatory consultation. Ifá told her she could never conceive a child unless she kept company with other barren women. She was told to make sacrifice and to take a sign to God in heaven. Thus, she obeyed and returned to have a child at the same time with other barren women. Later, the children were falling sick, and these women went to Ifá for advice. They had to be told to be grateful to Ọṣun for bearing children and to ask her for the medicines to cure their ailing children. They were told to ask Ọṣun to cure their ailing children, using the following adoration:

Ólàkàkà fi àpòró
A dífá fún Arídẹ̀gbẹ̀
Ti i ṣe ọmọ Èṣemòwé
Arí idẹ wẹ́rẹ́ wẹ́rẹ́ rẹ ọmọ
Lójọ́ tí kò sí ọmọ tuntun

Tí Ọ̀ṣun wá be Ọ̀rúnmìlà
Tí Ifá sọ fún Ọ̀ṣun pé
Kò lè dá ọmọ tiẹ̀ bí
Olódùmarè yoo da ọ̀pọ̀ ọmọ wẹẹrẹ
Sí àgbáyé fún ọ̀pọ̀lọpọ̀ àgàn
Ọ̀ṣun wá nké pé
Bí orí kan bá sunwọ̀n
Áran igba orí
Kí orí Olúsùnwòn kí o ràn oun
Ọ̀ṣun kaa sai bímọ sí ayé
Orí Olúsùnwòn yoó ran Ọ̀ṣun

[He who hangs his shoulder bag theatrically,
Who performs divination for Arídẹ̀gbẹ̀
The child of Èṣemọ̀wé
He who has brass bangles to delight children
When there was no new child
When Ọ̀ṣun went to plead with Ọ̀rúnmìlà (Ifá)
and Ifá told Ọ̀ṣun
that she could not have a child alone
God will send many children
to the world to help many barren women
Ọ̀ṣun then began to cry for joy.
If one head (person) becomes fortunate
Fortune will spread to two hundred heads (persons)
May the fortunate head spread to her.
Ọ̀ṣun will be blessed with children in her life,
the head of the fortunate will spread to Ọ̀ṣun.][8]

Commonly, young children everywhere suffer cuts and bruises in their enthusiasm for play, and even today the Yorùbá continue to rub a child's brass bangle, the symbol of Ọ̀ṣun, with the juice of a particular herb to promote healing.[9]

Divination is more or less the diagnostic aspect of traditional medicine. Of these three deities—Ọbàtálá, Òrìṣà-Oko, and Ọ̀ṣun—only two, Ọbàtálá and Ọ̀ṣun, are known for healing and sustaining life. Ọbàtálá and Ọ̀ṣun are associated with divination using cowries, òrìṣà or *ẹẹrìndín-lógún,* performed with simplified divinatory poetry of Ifá. Using the unembellished poetic form seems to be an attempt to indigenize the exotic, more complex Ifá poetry. The devotion of these deities to the people's well-being of their times does not seem to have been forgotten. Rather, the deities seem to have enjoyed a sedentary life or stayed in their local places for consultation. Ọbàtálá is referred to as "a joko ma ni ipekun, ipekun ni ipekun Òrìṣà" (he who sits without limit, his limit is that of the god [Ọbàtálá]). Òrìṣà-Oko is strictly attached to Ìráwò while Ọ̀ṣun's crowded house has been referred to in its full meaning by the name Òró, a town of the north-central Yorùbá. The multitude of people swarming to Ọ̀ṣun indicates her esteem and the extent to which people used to flock to her for consultation.

Although the three deities—Ọbàtálá, Òrìṣà-Oko, and Ọ̀ṣun—are associated with cowry divination, cowries are not of West African origin, and thus they cannot be used reliably in dating the epochs of Yorùbá gods. West Africa first received cowries from the Indian Ocean through North Africa, and later through the West African coast after contact with European traders (Eyo 1979: 42, 43). However, the brass associated with Ọ̀ṣun is likely contemporaneous with the metal sculpture of Ifè from the thirteenth through the sixteenth century C.E.

Around the fifteenth century, during the reign of Ṣàngó, the Third Aláàfin or traditional sovereign, old Ọ̀yọ́ was established. Thus, Ṣàngó most probably reigned as a king during the sixteenth century, after the epoch of Ọ̀ṣun. As already indicated, Ṣàngó was an overbearing ruler, and although he himself seems not to have decreed that he should be deified, his supporters imposed his cult after his worldly rule. Ọya, his wife, decreed to her children that she be worshipped before she departed. Although devotees of Ọ̀ṣun and Ṣàngó now pray to them for all sorts of blessings and for general protection, their powers seem to have begun more out of coercion and intimidation than from gentle persuasion. Incidentally, Ọ̀ṣun and Ṣàngó are associated with masquerading, camouflaged as dreaded spirits. The use of masquerading to mask identity was disastrously dealt with in the early history of Ifè as contained in the myth of Mọrèmi, a moral tale seeming to discourage antisocial behavior. The religious behavior of the Yorùbá, from their early urbanization to the time of Ọ̀ṣun, was encouraged primarily to promote the well-being of the people. Thus, we can assume that a deity with Ṣàngó's attributes would not have been accepted during the earlier period of Yorùbá religious history. The era of Ṣàngó and Ọ̀ṣun seems to have ushered in the worship of the ancestral masquerades in Yorùbá religious tradition. Therefore, we can theorize that it must have been from the Ọ̀yọ́ Epoch that masquerading spread to other Yorùbá subcultures.

Conclusion

Certainly, before the proliferation of many deities, the Yorùbá must have believed in Olódùmarè, the Supreme Being. Based on the life and post-deification attributes of the seven deities discussed, there is no doubt about the historicity of Yorùbá religious traditions. However, the ambiguity in reconstructing the Yorùbá religious past abounds in the uncertainties about the humanity of many deities. Yorùbá òrìṣà (deities), particularly, could have been deified during various epochs as settlers encountered or settled near certain regions of popularity with particular òrìṣà. Certainly, some deities may have even existed before the three epochs indicated above.

Notes

1. Bàbálolá received his education in Nigeria, Ghana, and Cambridge, England (Ph.D., University of London). He taught at the Institute of African Studies, University of Ife, and the University of Lagos. His work in *Content and Form of Yoruba Ìjálá* (1966) is an annotated anthology of *ìjálá* poems from hunters' songs. His writings are among the best recent scholastic efforts to safeguard African oral traditions. "Bàbálolá, S. Adeboye," *Encyclopædia Britannica,* 2006, Encyclopædia Britannica Premium Service, retrieved June 19, 2006, from http://www.britannica.com/eb/article-9011587.

2. Ifá is symbolized in Òwò as the hippopotamus, indicating Ifá's exceptional power and strength.

3. Adeoye 1985: 113.

4. In southern Nigeria, the New Yam Festival is an annual cultural celebration signifying the beginning of the harvest season, which occurs after the rainy season between the end of June and the beginning of September when the root crop is ready to harvest.

5. Some 800 steatite (soft stone or soapstone) statues were also discovered near the village of Esie. Although their date is uncertain, they precede discovery by the forebears of the current inhabitants, who moved to the region in the nineteenth century. Representing a single large collection, the realistic sculptures represent men and women generally seated on stools and occasionally kneeling. The figurines sometimes play musical instruments, hold machetes, or have their hands on their knees. The highly elaborate hairstyles, necklaces, and bracelets are rendered with great accuracy, Statues range from 14 cm to more than

1 meter. Retrieved May 16, 2006, from http://icom.museum/redlist/afrique/
english/page03.htm.

6. Wande Abímbọ́lá has taught African languages, literatures, religions, and
thought systems in various Nigerian and U.S. universities. He is a practitioner
of an African indigenous religion of the Yorùbá people, practiced also in the
African diaspora, including Brazil, Cuba, and Trinidad and Tobago, where an
Act of Parliament (1981) raised the Yorùbá Religion to the status of an official
religion. Abímbọ́lá is a high priest of the Yorùbá Religion, initiated as a *babaláwo,* a diviner, a storyteller, a counselor, and medicine healer. In 1981, all the
babaláwo of West Africa installed him as Awise Agbaye (Spokesperson of Ifá
and Yorùbá Religion in the World). Neither Christian nor Muslim, he is one of
millions of Yorùbá who keep the religion of their ancestors rather than convert
to Christianity or Islam.

7. Adepegba 1992: 1–6.

8. Adeoye 1985: 207.

9. I have mentioned this in Adepegba 2001.

References

Adeoye, C. L. 1985. *Igbagbo ati Esin Yorùbá.* Ibadan: Evans Brothers (Nigeria
Publishers) Limited.

Adepegba, Cornelius O. 1992. "Ona: The Concept of Ila among the Yorùbá."
Nigerian Field 57: 1–6.

———. 2001. "Ọ̀ṣun and Brass: An Insight into Yorùbá Religious Symbol-
ogy." In *Ọ̀ṣun across Waters: A Yorùbá Goddess in Africa and the Americas,* ed. Joseph M. Murphy and Mei-Mei Sanford, 102–12. Bloomington:
Indiana University Press.

Bàbálolá, S. Adeboye. 1966. *Content and Form of Yoruba Ìjálá.* Oxford:
Clarendon.

———. 1989. "A Portrait of Ògún as Reflected in Ìjálá Chants." In *Africa's
Ògún: Old World and New,* ed. Sandra Barnes, 147–72. Bloomington: Indiana University Press.

Bada, S. O. 1977. *History of Saki.* N.p.

Badejọ, Diedre. 1996. *Osun Sèègèsí: The Elegant Deity of Wealth Power and
Femininity.* Trenton and Asmara: Africa World Press.

Barnes, Sandra. 1989. "Introduction: The Many Faces of Ogun." In *Africa's
Ogun: Old World and New,* ed. Sandra Barnes, 1–26. Bloomington: Indiana
University Press.

Eyo, Ekpo. 1979. *Nigeria and the Evolution of Money.* Lagos: Central Bank of
Nigeria.

Johnson, Samuel. 1921. *The History of the Yorùbás*. Lagos: C.M.S.

Oyèláràn, Philip A. 1998. "Early Settlements and Archaeological Sequence of Northeast Yorùbáland." *African Archaeological Review* 15, no. 1: 65–79.

Shaw, T., and S. G. H. Daniells. 1984. "Excavations at Iwo-Eleru, Ondo State, Nigeria." *West African Journal of Archaeology* 14: 7–100.

Sowande, Sowande, ed. 1965. *Awon Asayan Odu Mimo Ifa: Akojopo Kinni*. Ibadan: ARSADA.

6

Twice-Told Tales

Yorùbá Religious and Cultural Hegemony in Benin, Nigeria

FLORA *EDOUWAYE* S. KAPLAN

Oft-told tales of Yorùbá origins of Benin traditions central to their identity have been repeated and published so often that they have come to be
regarded as true by most Africanist scholars. But are they? The Benin
themselves deny (though some now accept) the Yorùbá origins of their
dynastic kingship and of their royal bronze and brass casting technology.
Some oral traditions both resemble and contradict each other in the two
cultures. Given the scarcity of early historical sources, the limited hard
evidence of archaeology, and the largely out-of-context Benin art corpus, the twentieth-century cultural and religious ascendancy granted the
Yorùbá over Benin is all the more remarkable. In this chapter, I revisit
the Ife/Benin canon by drawing on my intensive ethnographic fieldwork
over two decades and by considering relevant Yorùbá and Benin oral
tradition in the light of their histories, religious beliefs, artistic practices, and cultural differences.[1] I find accepted Yorùbá hegemony is best
understood as a modern phenomenon rooted in mid- to late nineteenth-
century British intervention in West Africa, the slave trade, conquest
and colonial rule, as well as early global export of Yorùbá religion and

128

culture. This essay raises questions about who writes "history," when, for whom, and in what contexts. And it suggests why some tales told by two different ethnic groups are privileged—the one over the other.

Introduction

Western sources and written histories have granted Yorùbá religion and oral tradition hegemony over Benin.[2] This chapter proposes Yorùbá hegemony is best understood in the contexts of the slave trade, internal ethnic conflicts, and nineteenth- to early twentieth-century British colonial rule in Nigeria. The Benin traded slaves in small numbers from the first Portuguese contacts at the end of the fifteenth century, but they did not become a major source. Their preference was to keep captives for themselves. Slave trade with the West later peaked in the late sixteenth to early eighteenth century, increasing internal ethnic conflicts in West Africa to meet the demands in Europe and the Americas. Yorùbá raids in the mid-eighteenth century and their wars of the late eighteenth to early nineteenth centuries contributed to the supply of slaves and to the rise of Lagos as a port for their export (Drewal, Pemberton, and Abiodun 1989: 13; Law 1983: 343, 345, 347–48). Slaves carried their indigenous religious beliefs and practices with them along the lower Guinea Coast of West Africa and to other parts of Africa, Europe, the Americas, and the Caribbean. In the African diaspora, Yorùbá religious beliefs and practices came to be synonymous with "African religion" in local developments in conjunction with other religious traditions and in different, global historical contexts.

The British accepted and multidisciplinary Africanist scholars repeated the mantra that Benin's venerable Second Dynasty of sacred kings and their art of tin-bronze and leaded-brass casting were introduced from Ife by the Yorùbá. Most Benin people deny (though some now accept) these assertions of Ife primacy in their venerable religious, political, and cultural heritage. The Benin version of its origins, however, has gone virtually unrecorded and is ignored in most modern writings of "history" in southwestern Nigeria. In the course of deepening ethnographic research, I came to question the canon; and eventually Oba Erediauwa himself told me the story of the founding of Benin's Second Dynasty. It reverses the prevailing Ife-Benin canon. The critical section quoted below was presented by Benin Oba Erediauwa (1979–present) at the University of Ibadan Conference, "The Evolution of Traditional Rulership in Nigeria" (1984: 8–10, 11–18, 42–32, 48–49):

> We in Benin believe, and there are historical landmarks for such belief, that the person whom the Yorubas call Ododuwa was the fugitive Prince Ekaladerhan, son of the last Ogiso of Benin by name Ogiso Owodo; he found his way to what is now Ile-Ife after gaining freedom from his executioners and wandering for years through the forests. (13)

The Benin say it was none other than the royal heir, Prince Ekaladerhan, who had become Odùduwà, a king at Ilé-Ifè, who was finally persuaded by a search party of chiefs from Benin "to send his son Oranmiyan to rule," but his "stay in Benin was brief" (Erediauwa 1984: 12). Nonetheless, it was Oranmiyan's son from his union with a Benin woman who became Oba Eweka I, the founder of Benin's present Second Dynasty. Oranmiyan himself, it is said, was later sent by his father, Ododuwa (Odùduwà; born the Benin Prince Ekaladerhan), "to rule over Oyo where he became the first Aláàfin from where he ruled over Ife after the demise of Ododuwa" (14).

Oba Erediauwa gave this lecture at Ibadan, the largest Yorùbá city in Nigeria; and he delivered it at the University of Ibadan, long the nation's premier institution of higher learning and the fount from which flowed much modern historical research and publications. It is significant the Oba of Benin chose the University of Ibadan to publicly assert Benin's rightful place in the history of rulership in southern Nigeria (Erediauwa 1984: 8–10, 11–18, 42–43, 48–49). Today, the perennially fractious Yorùbá agree on the spiritual primacy of the Oni and the city of Ilé-Ifè, the latter thought to be the place where the world originated. But in the Benin order of things, the Oba takes precedence over his "brothers," the Yorùbá rulers at Ife and Oyo.[3]

Benin and the Yorùbá: Some Historical Background

At Ibadan, Oba Erediauwa called attention to the long traditional history at both ends, between Benin and Lagos, "relating to the origin of what is now Lagos, its ruler, and its connection with Benin" (Erediauwa 1984: 14). He noted many historians accept this connection, which he traced to Oba Orhogbua (ca. A.D. 1550–1578), a warring Benin Oba,

Oba Erediauwa. Official portrait, 1979. Royal Court of Benin, Nigeria. Photography by
S. O. Alonge. Collection, Flora *Edouwaye* S. Kaplan, New York.

who established early ascendancy over Lagos—and gave Lagos its first ruler, whom the Yorùbá call Ashipa. The Benin designation Aisikpa is used "to commemorate the Oba's many years sojourn at Eko . . . a contraction of the Benin phrase, '*Aisikpa-hienvborre,*' ('people do not desert their home-land')" (Erediauwa 1984: 18). The first man to hold that title was the administrator left at Eko by Oba Orhogbua to represent Benin interests and forward tribute. "'Eko' is a Benin word that means [war] 'camp'" (14–15); and it is still the traditional Benin name for Lagos. "'*Ashipa*' has been retained as a senior traditional chieftaincy title while his descendants now retain the modern name of 'Oba of Lagos'" (18). Each Oba of Lagos who ascended to the throne in the past was given something sent to him by the Oba of Benin, and it was kept in his palace. Present-day Obas of Lagos still acknowledge the Benin origin of their throne, although the earlier exchanges and tribute are no longer given (personal communication, Oba Erediauwa, September 24, 2001).

In his 1984 Ibadan lecture, Oba Erediauwa noted that oral tradition in both Benin and Lagos confirms Benin's early military ascendancy in the area. Apart from Lagos, Benin also had strong links, especially in court arts and customs, with Owo and Uhe (the latter a Benin name now associated with Ife). Owo ivory carvers in centuries past produced works for the Benin court, and Benin influence is still reflected in Owo court titles and regalia. There is a tradition in both places that the sixteenth Olówò of Owo, Osogboye, as crown prince, was sent by his father to be trained at the court of Benin. It is said he learned the art of warfare there, later managing to become independent of Benin. Both Chief Jacob U. Egharevba, the Benin historian, and his counterpart in Owo, Chief M. B. Ashara, agree Owo was "for periods of time under the suzerainty of the Obas of Benin" (Abiodun 1989: 240; Egharevba 1968: 34).

Apart from Owo, other notable Yorùbá kingdoms flourished and figured prominently and then declined over the last five hundred years, but all of them were connected only by loosely held and shifting alliances. Some, like Ijebu had fortifications in the fifteenth and sixteenth centuries and engaged in long-distance trade, but they rarely controlled very large areas for long. Even Oyo, the largest and most powerful Yorùbá kingdom to emerge, and whose first Aláàfin is acknowledged to be Oranmiyan, the son of Odùduwà, did not become a single, centralized state capable of ruling over all or most of Yorùbáland. No such single state is known to have emerged among the Yorùbá, either before or after

European contact. And there is no Yorùbá oral tradition or kingdom that lays claim to having conquered Benin in the last five hundred years.

Yorùbá kingdoms, polities, and communities were markedly competitive through the centuries, within and among themselves, in trading and power relations. They engaged in constant warring and raiding with other Yorùbá communities and with other ethnic groups. The Yorùbá religious pantheon reflects this competition and diversity in the multiplicity of deities and rituals that are elaborated at different localities, in addition to a widespread belief in a high god. There are also many versions of shared oral traditions, many local histories, and numerous dialects of Yorùbá language. When Oyo, the greatest Yorùbá kingdom of them all, collapsed in the early nineteenth century, what unity was achieved soon fell into disarray. In the vacuum of power left by Oyo's dramatic decline—escalating warfare in the region opened the way for British colonial intervention at Lagos.

The Yorùbá and Benin: Responses to Colonial Contacts

In Lagos, a bloody dynastic struggle erupted in the mid-nineteenth century between the Yorùbá Oba Akitoye and his nephew, Kosoko. Their power struggle provided the British an opportunity to intervene in 1851 (Fage 1969: 141). The British entered the conflict on the side of Akitoye, who had promised them to end the lucrative Yorùbá slave trade. Their support led to Kosoko's decisive defeat. In the wake of this victory, the British consul's influence was extended to include Lagos, thereby providing access to inland trade. Ten years later in 1861, the British annexed Lagos as a Crown colony; and the consul made Lagos a center of commerce, missionary activity, and expanding colonial rule throughout southern Nigeria.

I include Lagos in considering the Ife/Benin canon because of its historic relationship with Benin, its several roles over time, and its impact in southwestern Nigeria as a center of British colonial administration. Lagos also played an important role in foreign trade because of its navigable harbor and in the transport of slaves so instrumental in the globalization of Yorùbá religion. As a Crown colony, the port of Lagos also became an increasingly cosmopolitan center of influence, especially with the end of slavery abroad when many Africans returned "home" to Nigeria from Sierra Leone, Brazil, and England.

Outside of Lagos, most Yorùbá cities, towns, and villages continued to function as separate entities with their own dialects, deities, rituals, and masquerades. Those polities ruled by Obas who claimed the right to wear a beaded crown traced their ancestry to Ododuwa (Odùduwà) and to Ife. That tradition was extended by the British, who recognized many more "crowns" from Ife than originally existed (Pemberton and Afolayan 1996: 2). "Crowns" continued to proliferate from colonial days into the mid- to late twentieth century and up to the present day.

Many factors already mentioned—political, economic, social, cultural, and religious—contributed to the rising importance of the Yorùbá under the British. Not least among them were control of the port at Lagos and the sheer numbers of Yorùbá living in dispersed settlements. The Yorùbá were then and are today one of Nigeria's largest ethnic groups. They number more than 20 million in a national population of over 100 million in Nigeria, Africa's most populous country. The Benin (Edo-speaking peoples) number about 2–3 million but are still regarded by other ethnic groups, including the Yorùbá, with a mixture of fear and respect for guarding their traditions. Both the Benin and the Yorùbá are members of the (formerly) Kwa language group, now the South Central Niger Congo group of languages (Ruhlen 1991). However, their languages are mutually unintelligible, and each has many dialects—functions of time and the separation of the groups.

Whereas the Yorùbá language was a lingua franca of trade along the West African coast, the Benin deliberately discouraged the use of their language by others, including those who paid tribute to them. Benin's aggressive stance and exclusionary external relations over time kept their numbers relatively small and their identity intact. Nonetheless, the influence and impact of Benin culture was deeply felt and is manifested in court titles, regalia, art, and iconography across southern Nigeria. At the time of first European contacts in late fifteenth century and thereafter, Benin was and remained until 1897 an independent, hierarchical, ranked, and centralized state. Both before and after the fifteenth century, despite internal disputes, Benin remained politically centered and socially unified by the leadership and worship of a single Oba, at Benin City, who combined religious and secular power in his sacred person.

Benin City, unlike Lagos, was the heart of a distant inland kingdom, deep in the dense rainforest and difficult to reach overland. It was located away from a good port, leaving trade and outside communication to be conducted via the creeks and coastal lagoons. Overland travel was along narrow paths through tropical undergrowth and "mists" that had long claimed the lives of many European traders and seamen. In 1897 Richard Burton, an ambitious British consul, impatient to wrest control of inland trade from the Benin Oba, countenanced the uninvited visit of a British diplomatic party. Led by Acting Consul Captain James Phillips in Burton's absence while on leave, the unwelcome party was ambushed and killed before they could reach Benin City.

Only two British men escaped death to tell the tale. In his book *The Benin Massacre* (1898), Captain Boisragon described the hardships he and his companion, Mr. Locke, suffered as they made their way to the coast through the dense rainforest in 1897. Afterward, Boisragon spent time recovering on the coast, where the British were preparing a major naval expedition against Benin City. He tells of a message that was sent up to the Benin Oba by the British, asking if any white men were still alive after the massacre. The Oba's answer came back, "'None,' and as proof of it he sent back two rings that had belonged to poor old Crawford." Boisragon only heard "the other gruesome story about poor Mr. Gordon's finger and rings" from reading the English papers on the ship taking him home (1898: 159). Stories of mutilations and human sacrifice in Benin inflamed the British public.

To retaliate for the ambush of the Phillips party—and not incidentally to seize control from the Oba of trade inland and on the creeks and rivers—the British launched a massive military assault they titled "The Punitive Expedition." In heavy hand-to-hand fighting that lasted five days in Benin City, British marines and other personnel were killed and wounded. The heavy British cannon fire and artillery finally succeeded against the spears, antiquated guns, and bows and arrows of the Benin warriors. The aftermath was predictable. A number of important chiefs were executed, and a "trial" of Oba Ovonramwen ended with his exile to Old Calabar in eastern Nigeria.

Over the next twenty years active and passive Benin resistance to British colonial rule continued in the region. The prolonged Benin resistance, their ambush of the Phillips' diplomatic party, and the distressing casualties and deaths inflicted in the fighting of 1897 did little to endear the Benin to the British. The Benin elite, unlike the Yorùbá, initially also rejected the missionary education offered to their sons. Nor did the Benin people accept the legitimacy of the puppet chiefs chosen by the British to rule in place of the Oba. In 1914, after the demise of the exiled

Oba Ovonramwen in the east, the British found it expedient to restore his
rightful heir to the throne, Oba Eweka II (1914–33).

Unlike the Benin, the Yorùbá fought primarily among themselves.
In order to regain his throne from his nephew, Kosoko, the deposed Oba
of Lagos, Akitoye had welcomed British intervention and assistance in
1851. In the wake of British pacification of the area following their intervention, independent Yorùbá rule in the region was ended. Afterward,
the people in Lagos eagerly seized the new possibilities opened for trade
and accumulation of wealth. Apart from trade, the Yorùbá seized new
opportunities for education, schools, written Yorùbá, and English literacy that became the bases for other kinds of elites. As a result, the
Yorùbá benefited economically and socially. They gained good will and
the "ear" of the British and used their proximity to further advantage.
Among the benefits that accrued to the Yorùbá in Lagos and elsewhere
was the favor they found with British missionaries and the opportunity
to "tell" and write (as well as rewrite) their own history and that of others. In this, the Yorùbá resembled other former tributary groups, such
as the western Igbo, the Igala, the northern Edo, and others who were
formerly subject to Benin. They retold tales of Benin in new ways in
order to gain power and to redress the wrongs they felt they had suffered
under Benin rule (Okpewho 1998: xii, 12). The Yorùbá differed from
some other groups in the mid- to late nineteenth century in being center
stage via Lagos, declared a British Crown colony (1851) in Nigeria, a
new global and colonial arena.

The Yorùbá since then have assumed religious and cultural hegemony over Benin, whose suzerainty in southern Nigeria from the sixteenth century to late nineteenth century remained undisputed, and whose
military prowess and cultural impact are acknowledged by many ethnic
groups to this day. For five centuries, through changing fortunes, Benin
had remained a powerful and independent kingdom. Still, Benin tales
of their own dynastic origins and artistic casting traditions have been
replaced by Yorùbá twice-told tales. Possibly, the Yorùbá have it right,
but do they? Very possibly the Benin have it right, or have they simply
inverted the tale of kingship origin and casting to suit themselves? And
perhaps they both have it wrong, and their origins and respective monar-
chial traditions lie elsewhere? The answers to these and other questions
await renewed systematic archaeology in the region, along with continuing historic and ethnographic research. The rise of Yorùbá hegemony in
southern Nigeria may be found, in part, in the punitive British response

to Benin's resistance to colonial expansion. Other answers, in part, are to be found in Yorùbá proximity to the British and a more subtle style of accommodation, as well as Yorùbá conversions to Christianity under British colonial rule.

Reconsidering the Canon: The Ife-Benin Relationship

In his groundbreaking critique of the Ife-Benin relationship, Alan Ryder noted there were actually very few fifteenth- and early sixteenth-century Portuguese written sources that formed the basis of most of what has been written about Yorùbá hegemony vis-à-vis Benin. Moreover, he pointed out there was no suggested Benin dynastic relationship with Ife until *after* British occupation of Benin in 1897 (Ryder 1965: 25; emphasis mine). Like Ryder, other historians in the first half of the twentieth century were unaware of any documentary record of Ife before the midnineteenth century in Nigeria.[4] In his review, Ryder focused on historic documents along with some artistic issues. He concluded the origins of Benin kingship and artistic casting traditions probably emerged not at Ife but in the Nupe-Igala area at the confluence of the Niger and Benue rivers (37). Babatunde Lawal reached a similar conclusion a bit later in reviewing a wide range of competing but inconclusive theories regarding art and relations among the Benin, Ife, Nupe, Igala, Idah, Owo, and Oyo. He also found no hard evidence for Fraser's suggestion (1975) that some Nupe bronzes could be attributed to Owo. Lawal, like Ryder, concluded the Ogane's kingdom was probably somewhere in the area of the Niger-Benue confluence (1977: 210). Ryder and Lawal were also in agreement that the Oni of modern Ife was probably *not* the reported "Ogane" (ruler) to whom Benin was said to have paid tribute. The Ogane's kingdom to the north and east of Benin City has still to be located (Ife lies to the west).

Thus, the current Ife-Benin canon that gives precedence to the Yorùbá rests largely on an early Portuguese report that—some 300 years later— came to be identified with the modern city of Ilé-Ifè, and the Oni of Ife with the Ogane, the ruler of a still unknown kingdom in antiquity. The early Portuguese sources never made any connections between the two places or the two rulers. The Ife-Benin canon emerges with the spread of Christianity and the writing of Yorùbá history as told to British missionaries and scholars (Smith 1988: 16, 125–26).

It was only in the mid-twentieth century with archaeology conducted at Ife and related sites that Ilé Ifè was found to be in active use as a ceremonial center up to the fifteenth century. Today most contemporary Yorùbá accept Ilé-Ifè as a sacred site, but many Yorùbá still do not view the modern Ilé-Ifè as the original Ife (Lawal: 1977). Lawal noted references to seven different Ifès in *Odu Ifa,* the sacred Yorùbá divination verses, with modern Ilé-Ifè being the last. He noted as well the importance of the middle Niger-Benue area in early Yorùbá history (1977: 210).

The Benin proper (those residing in its eternal capital city of Benin) have no "migration myth." They believe they came directly from the spirit world to earth at the time of creation—to where they are now and have ever been. However, some Yorùbá groups (and most are concentrated in the west) have a migration myth that "*Ododuwa,* the mythical ancestor [at Ife] arrived from far away in the east" (Ajayi 1964: 1). Benin does indeed lie to the east of Ilé-Ifè; and beyond is the confluence of the Niger and Benue rivers.

Art as Evidence: "Messengers from Ife"

Duarte Pacheco Pereira, who made four visits to Benin between the end of the fifteenth century and the beginning of the sixteenth century, is cited by Ryder and other scholars among the early Portuguese sources (Ryder 1965: 25; Thornton 1988: 352–53). João Affonso D'Aveiro is another. In 1485, he reported a powerful ruler to the north and east of Benin. The "Ogane" would send a brass staff, a "hat," and a pectoral cross to confirm the new Oba of Benin (Ryder 1965: 26). This news excited the Portuguese imagination, leading them to believe the Ogane might be a Christian, possibly Prester John (Smith 1988: 16–17). This news and evidence offered in support of it are reexamined here: "Prince Ogane sent them a staff and a headpiece, fashioned like a *Spanish helmet,* made all of shining brass, in place of a scepter and crown. He also sent a cross, of the same brass, and shaped like those worn by the Commendadores, to be worn round the neck like something religious and holy" (Ryder 1965: 26; emphasis mine).

But the Benin "ambassador" who reportedly told D'Aveiro about the above confirmation gifts never saw the Ogane, who was hidden, "like some sacred object," behind silk curtains, leaving no clues to his identity. After D'Aveiro's fifteenth-century report, the Ogane's "confirmation" gifts are not mentioned again until much later in the early to mid-twentieth century.

In the twentieth century a group of eight cast bronze Benin standing figures were interpreted as bearing the Ogane's gifts and became known as "messengers from Ife."[5] These bronzes were briefly discussed in light of the Ife-Benin canon by Ryder (1965), Lawal (1977), and Willett (1967). They are reconsidered in this chapter, and a different interpretation of these "messengers" is offered based on their distinctive features.

"Messenger" figures are among the largest bronze cast sculptures (tin-bronze and leaded brass) in the Benin corpus of art. They are among an overall corpus of more than two thousand works of art looted from the Oba's Palace in 1897 by the British. Each messenger figure stands nearly two feet high, a measure of their importance. Stylistically, they date from the sixteenth to nineteenth centuries; none are attributed to the fifteenth century or earlier. They are alike in pose, distinctive features, and dress. All the messengers stand facing front, feet firmly planted and set apart, with their forearms raised at waist level and elbows bent at right angles. In his left hand, each messenger holds the blacksmith's hammer, the *avalaka*. In a clenched right hand (with the thumb pointing upward), the messenger carries either a "staff," or another object (missing in some examples). Possibly, something perishable or movable was placed in the now empty right hand: a staff, walking stick, or club of wood or iron. Their staffs, however, are *unlike* any found earlier in the palace. Their outlines closely resemble an oversize nail, a symbol of Ògún, the god of iron and war. Together, the hammer (*avalaka*), a nail, staple, and tongs are symbols of Ògún, working tools to be placed on his shrines. Miniature sets of Ògún's tools are also worn or carried as charms. They are sewn on the cloth worn by ritual priests and native surgeons as symbols of their power.

The pectoral cross and two bead necklaces worn around the neck of the messengers are also distinctive features. But the cross is neither a Latin cross, nor a Greek or Maltese cross (to which it bears some resemblance). It is an equal-sided "Benin cross." It symbolizes the four corners of the world if associated with Olokun, god of the waters and wealth; or it can symbolize the crossroads associated with Ògún. The latter refers to a place where witches gather, and where danger lurks: violence, accidents, unexpected illness, and injury (including modern

Standing Sculpture of Portuguese Soldier with Flintlock Gun and Other Weapons. Bronze, ca. mid-late sixteenth century. Royal Court of Benin, Nigeria. Collection, National Museum, Lagos. Photograph courtesy, © copyright of the National Commission for Museums and Monuments, Abuja, Nigeria.

traffic accidents). The equal-sided cross is a recurrent motif in Benin art and is not found in traditional Yorùbá art. The Christian cross of unequal lengths is found in association with worshippers and contemporary converts to Christianity among both the Benin and the Yorùbá.

The messengers all are richly dressed, wearing decorative wrappers tied Benin style, pulled up in a pommel on the left hip. The wrappers are incised with stylized geometric designs and heads of Portuguese (Europeans). Some messengers wear an elaborate fringed shirt; others are "topless," except for the pectoral cross and bead necklaces. It has been suggested these figures may represent an Ohensa, a Benin priest of the Aruosa Church. The Catholic churches founded by the Portuguese fathers in the sixteenth century are called Aruosa, "the Oba's church." Others have suggested the "messengers" may be members of the Ewua palace association (Ben-Amos 1995: 56). Still other scholars have suggested the "messengers" may be (Benin) court officials (Duchâteau 1994: 18, 77). The messengers all wear the same distinctive headgear: a kind of bowler hat, not at all like a Portuguese or Spanish medieval "helmet," which is peaked with a high crown. Their bowler hat has a low rounded crown decorated with two crosshatched bands (occasionally one) and a small narrow brim. In Benin this type of hat is made of woven or plaited plant fibers (the crosshatching reveals the medium). It is a kind of "straw" hat worn to shade a person's head from the sun.

Another distinctive feature of the messenger figures is their "cat's whiskers." These are facial cicatrices of three long lines that curve upward at the sides of the mouth and along the cheeks. The Benin people did not alter their faces or bodies to produce either true cicatrices (raised scars) on their faces or bodies and in the pattern shown on these sculptures. Free Benin men and women were "tattooed" with distinctive sets of flat, blade-like patterns on the chest and back. Only women were also tattooed on the face and around and below their navel. "Cat's whiskers" are identified with the Nupe-Igala area; and patterns of three or four curving lines are incised on some Ife period terra cotta heads, on Yorùbá carvings, and on living Yorùbá. In Benin art "cat's whiskers" and facial cicatrices represent foreigners, like those few bronze Benin trophy heads that have similar whiskers. Trophy heads without whiskers are identified as Ubuluku, a prideful local ruler who murdered Adesuwa, an intended bride of the Oba of Benin, after failing to seduce her (Kaplan 1991).

A group of rare Benin bronze plaques depicting battle scenes identify foreign rulers and soldiers from other ethnic groups by their facial

Standing Sculpture of "Trophy Messenger." Bronze, ca. mid-late sixteenth century. Royal Court of Benin, Nigeria. © Copyright the Trustees of the British Museum.

Battle Plaque. Bronze, ca. late sixteenth to seventeenth century. Royal Court of Benin, Nigeria. Plaque with Foreign Horseman being attacked by a Benin Soldier. © Copyright the Trustees of the British Museum.

Standing Sculpture of "Trophy Messenger." Bronze, ca. sixteenth to seventeenth century. Royal Court of Benin, Nigeria. The Metropolitan Museum of Art, gift of Mr. and
Mrs. Klaus G. Perls, 1991 (1991.17.32). Image © the Metropolitan Museum of Art.

scarification (four or five upward curving lines at the sides of their mouths)
(von Luschan 1968: 256–59; 382–87). These figures are on foot and
horseback, and shown being vanquished by Benin warriors. Horses have
long been associated with the north and the Nupe-Igala area. They have
reference to the fierce sixteenth-century Idah wars fought with Benin.

Standing Sculpture of "Trophy Messenger." Bronze, ca. eighteenth to nineteenth century. Royal Court of Benin, Nigeria. The Metropolitan Museum of Art, gift of Mr. and Mrs. Klaus G. Perls, 1991 (1991.17.30). Image © the Metropolitan Museum of Art.

Who then are these foreign "messenger" sculptures—and why are they represented in the Benin corpus? *If* they are not from Ife, bearing gifts from the Oni of Ife (né the Ogane) to a new Oba of Benin, why do they wear a Benin cross? Why do they wear a straw hat to shield them from the sun? What kind of staff do they carry? And why are no "confirmation gifts" found in the Benin corpus of art looted from the Palace in 1897? Why do the messengers carry a blacksmith's hammer, the *avalaka,* a symbol of Ògún, the god of iron and war? The totality of symbols and the messengers' distinctive features do not match the Ogane's stated "confirmation gifts" for the Oba of Benin. Nor do they fully support the identities posited by some scholars as priests, officials, or messengers from Ife. Their attributes fail to account for all or most of the recurrent and distinctive features of these standing sculptures. The totality of the messengers' distinctive features indicates the messengers are foreigners, non-Benin people, despite their rich Benin dress. In answer to these and other questions, I offer another interpretation.

The messenger sculptures are not messengers *from* Ife—but "trophy figures" who are messengers *to* a deity—in this case, Ògún. The messenger is indeed a foreigner, likely a war captive to be "used" and sent to Ògún with a message of thanks for success in war. The fine details of their cloth wrappers with motifs of Portuguese soldiers point stylistically to a sixteenth-century commemorative date—at least for some of the early figures. These and other details support the interpretation here of trophy figures or messengers with reference to important Benin wars fought in the north with Nupe-Igala peoples.

The practice of treating intended sacrificial victims with special favor, dressing them in fine clothing and ornaments, feeding them well, and indulging them to make them "happy" before dispatching them to a god or gods is well documented in other warrior cultures that practiced human sacrifice (Kaplan 1994). Certainly, casting formidable adversaries and the events associated with them to be remembered in bronze was common practice in Benin. Bronze casting in Benin was and *is* the recording of historic documents. Over the centuries, thousands of plaques, sculptures, and other objects were "archived" in the Oba's Palace up to 1897 (Kaplan 1991: 235). Important events and unusual objects are still recorded and remembered in this way. Historical events are also preserved by way of anecdote or adage (Erediauwa 1984: 17).

Art as Evidence: Ife and Benin Commemorative Heads

Ife and Benin art are characterized by naturalism but expressed in distinct and fully realized styles. Influence between them and from elsewhere is evident at times, such as in the facial whiskers of some terra cotta

Ife heads and in the facial striations of a few small Benin sculptures. Published analyses of the metal alloys used at Ife and Benin show their composition is different (Willett 1967, 1981). There is no oral tradition or other evidence of a casting tradition at Ife, and it is generally accepted the heads and sculptures found there were probably made elsewhere (where is not known) and brought to Ife. The reverse is true of Benin.

Traditionally, the head of a deceased Oba was cast in bronze after his yearlong funeral ceremonies were completed and his son was installed as the new Oba. The head commemorating his reign was placed on an ancestral altar in the palace. The head of the Íyóbá, the Queen Mother of Benin, was cast if she had passed away before her son came to the throne. If she was alive when her son was crowned, her head was cast after she died. The royal heads are considered formal "portraits" of specific rulers, according to Benin artistic conventions (Kaplan 1993b). Some attempts have been made to identify them in the succession (Dark 1975; Kaplan 1993b; Willett 1981). The queen mother heads were displayed on an altar in the palace and on her personal shrine at Uselu, outside of Benin City. Royal ancestral altars were decorated with other castings and carvings in ivory and wood to beautify them. These castings had reference to important events in an Oba's reign. They extolled his military victories, unique achievements, and innovations. Bells, cockerels, carved ivory tusks, figural sculptures, tableaux, large stone axes, and so forth are among the objects added to royal altars.

The Yorùbá have no comparable practice of casting heads after the fifteenth century. Some two dozen known, life-size heads cast in brass and copper and found at Ife are believed to be portraits of former rulers. Yorùbá scholars doubt they represent the Oni of Ife, rather possibly various officeholders. Given the superb quality of the Ife castings and the remarkable naturalism of the style, it has been suggested and widely accepted that these heads probably were the products of a single workshop that operated for a limited time. There is some speculation the Ife heads may have been used in "second burials" (Willett 1966). At excavated Ife-related sites, some small terra cotta heads have been identified as "queens" (women), but it is unclear who is represented in these Ife terra cottas. Only the queen mother and her attendants, not the Oba's wives, are represented in Benin court art.

Benin heads of kings and queen mothers lend themselves to ordering in a chronological sequence of changing styles from the sixteenth to late twentieth century. Over time, from the sixteenth century onward, the royal heads changed from simple, elegant life-size castings to become taller, thicker, larger, and heavier castings. A flanged base was added in the late eighteenth century and elaborated upon in the nineteenth century with miniature axes, frogs, human heads, trunks or hands holding leaves, and bound sacrificial captives displayed on the rims (Dark 1975).[6]

Among the Yorùbá Obas, from at least the nineteenth century on, tall multicolored beaded crowns have been used as prime symbols of kingship in the succession. The crowns are believed to be imbued with power. Each has long bead fringes that cascade over the face, obscuring the wearer and shielding others from his gaze. The reuse of a single crown belonging to a particular town or city in Yorùbáland emphasizes the office, rather than the individual officeholder. Its powers are renewed and strengthened with "medicines" each time. In Benin, the Oba uses only coral beads, and on various occasions, he wears different crowns belonging to earlier kings who are his ancestors. He also creates one (or more) of his own. Thus, the number and type of crowns are different in type of beads, style, and meaning in political organization and culture.

It is good at this point to put to rest another oft-told Yorùbá tale about the head of the Oba of Benin. The Yorùbá claim the Oba's head is sent to Ife for burial upon his demise. The Benin consider this statement extraordinary, without basis in oral tradition or living memory. It certainly did not happen from the mid-nineteenth century through the end of the twentieth century—a period in which four Obas passed away: Oba Adolo in 1888; Oba Ovonramwen in 1914; Oba Eweka II in 1933; and Oba Akenzua II in 1978. Reportedly, the Oba is buried standing upright, a custom very likely to include his head. When I asked chiefs at the royal court about this tale told by the Yorùbá, it was first greeted with laughter at the absurdity of such an idea. Then I was told with gravity—it would be an "abomination."

Art as Evidence: Ife and Benin Kings and Queens

Sculptures, emblematic of Ife and Benin art style, are briefly compared here. They are characterized by naturalism but realized in distinct styles. The first to be considered is a much-admired casting of a couple, described as a king and his queen (Ita Yemoo, circa A.D. early fourteenth to early fifteenth century). They stand side-by-side, facing front, wearing fine clothing, diadems on their heads, and heavy necklaces, and their

Standing Sculpture of Ife Ruler and Consort. Bronze. Ita Yemoo, Nigeria. ca. twelfth to fifteenth century. The intimacy and mutual interdependency shown in this fine sculpture of a man and woman (a king and his consort) reflects the political and social realities of Yorùbá society. It is unrelated to the ethos and culture of Benin society and art—in which no similar images of men and women together are found. The softer, rounder Yorùbá style is in marked contrast to the leaner, more restrained Benin works. Collection, National Museum, Ife. Photograph courtesy, © copyright of the National Commission for Museums and Monuments, Abuja, Nigeria.

arms and legs are laden with bead ornaments. The queen rests her right arm on his left forearm, while he deftly encircles her left ankle with his right leg. This overt touching and close physical linking of the pair, conveys intimacy and interdependence. Recent Yorùbá ethnographies recognize Yorùbá male/female political and social relationships as necessary and complementary (e.g., Abímbólá 1997; Kaplan 1993b; Matory 1994, 1997; Olupona 1991, 1997).

There are no comparable representations of male/female couples in Benin dynastic art. Overt complementary in male/female social, sexual, and economic, and political relationships is not part of the ethos and culture of Benin's royal court (Drewal 1989a; Kaplan 1993b, Matory 1994, 1997; and Olupona 1991, 1997). In Benin art as in public, any display of physical intimacy and touching between a man and a woman, husband and wife, king and queen or queen mother is not only absent; it would be regarded as inappropriate, even shocking.

When male and female figures appear together in Benin art, the couple is usually the Oba and his birth mother, the Íyóbá, queen mother of Benin. Two altarpieces, *aseberia,* in the Berlin Ethnographical Museum reveal how very different Benin male/female representations in art are from the Yorùbá. The two altarpieces (sixteenth and late eighteenth century) include the Íyóbá standing behind her son, but not touching him. She is accompanied by two attendants (sometimes male) and other young females in her male gender role as a senior chief (Kaplan 1993a, 1993b). She is shown as a small, stiff figure, her size indicating her subordinate position to him. When viewed from the front (the usual position of works placed on ancestral altars in the Palace and on shrines), the Íyóbá is barely visible. These altarpieces literally and symbolically illustrate her role is to "back" the Oba in his reign. The size differential and absence of physical contact between this couple stand in marked contrast to the entwined Ife royal pair from Ita Yemoo. The importance of the mother/son dyad is emphasized in Benin culture. Their close attachment *is* expressed—"Benin-style"—with emotion deeply felt, but understated. It is understood by the culture bearers in art as in life, by virtue of her physical presence and her close *proximity* to the Oba.

Telling Tales: Benin and Ife (Yorùbá) Creation Myths

The origin myths of Ife (Yorùbá) and Benin show marked differences in how they tell and account for the world's beginning, the behavior of

Standing Sculpture of Benin Oba (King) holding Symbols of Office and of Ògún, the God of Iron and War. Benin Kingdom Court Style. Edo people. Nigeria. Eighteenth to nineteenth century. Copper alloy. The oba stands stiffly in coral bead regalia and many ornaments. In his right hand is his sword of office, and in his left hand he carries a gong (a type made usually of iron) with menacing spokes. The overall impression is one of controlled power. It is unlike the more humanistic impression of Yorùbá sculptures of kings. Gift of Joseph H. Hirshhorn to the Smithsonian Institution in 1966. 85-19-12. Photograph by Franko Khoury. Courtesy National Museum of African Art, Smithsonian Institution.

deities and sacred kings, and the consequences they encounter on earth. The general outlines of their stories have similarities at this time, but the details and dynamics are quite different. Ife, according to Yorùbá myth, is the place where life and civilization began (Drewal 1989b: 45; Pemberton and Afolayan 1996: 28–29). There are many versions of the creation story, but the creator god, Olódùmarè, is a central feature in most of them. Olódùmarè appears in the following story that serves as a template for others in Yorùbáland. It is said the world was at first covered with water, so the divinity, Olódùmarè, descended on an iron chain from the spirit world. He took along a snail shell (or gourd) filled with earth, a cockerel (or five-toed chicken/bird), and a chameleon. Upon arrival, the deity poured the earth from the snail shell into the water, and the "bird" spread it, creating the land. The chameleon then walked warily and gently on it to test its firmness, after which the other deities arrived to establish human society (Drewal 1989b: 45). Creation continues when the sixteen sons of Obàtálá, a creator deity, spread out from Ife and founded many kingdoms whose rulers trace their origins to Ife, thereby claiming the right to wear a beaded crown. As noted earlier, the number of traditional "crowns" among the Yorùbá began to multiply in the colonial period and continues to do so, to this day (Pemberton and Afolayan 1996: 26).

In virtually all Yorùbá creation stories, there are fights among the deities from the start—for authority and the right to perform certain roles. The fights among the gods mirror those that were endemic among the Yorùbá on earth. They reflect the competitive character and decentralized nature of political and social organization among past (and present) Yorùbá. The sixteen sons of the creator god who dispersed after creation produced many progeny and scattered kingdoms throughout the "world." (Sixteen is an auspicious number among the Yorùbá.) Thus, from the beginning there are multiple and equal founders of competing kingdoms throughout Yorùbáland.

In some creation stories Obàtálá/Orisanla, the artist deity, molded humans out of clay. But that role was usurped by Odùduwà, after Obàtálá, who had drunk too much palm wine, started to create misshapen humans, such as hunchbacks and dwarfs, and finally fell asleep on the job. In some versions of this myth, Obàtálá/Orisanla is the original creator god with ultimate divine authority, and Odùduwà has political authority. In other versions, Obàtálá is the founder of the world, and Odùduwà is identified as a goddess. In still other versions, Odùduwà is held to be a powerful warrior king and god who came from elsewhere (the east, it is said) and first conquered, then assimilated with, the indigenous people at Ife who originally worshipped Obàtálá at Ilé-Ifè (Drewal 1989b: 45–46). The latter may hark back to the Benin story of Prince Ekaladerhan's wanderings until reaching the settlement that became Ife, and himself becoming Odùduwà, the first Oni of Ife.

The Benin creation story of its origins is still largely untold in the literature on Nigeria. Some reasons for this omission have already been suggested. The traditional story told by His Royal Highness, Omo N'Oba N'Edo Uku Akpolokpolo, Oba Erediauwa, in 1984 at the University of Ibadan went like this:

> This land of Edo is the origin of the world. It was founded by the first Oba of Benin who was the youngest son of the Supreme God. When the Supreme God decided to send his children to the world, He gave an option to each of them to choose what to take away. At that time (as the Holy Book came to confirm at a much later age) the universe was all water and no land. One of the children chose the sign for wealth; the other one took wisdom (or knowledge), another one chose medicine (mystical knowledge).
>
> When it came to the turn of the youngest child, there was apparently nothing left for him to choose; but after looking around the whole place, he saw a snail shell, which his senior brothers had over-looked because it was very dirty. He took that, broke it open only to find that it contained ordinary sand. The Father commended him for his intuition and told him that on getting to the world, he should empty the shell in any place of his choice and the place would be his. He emptied it in the area that is now Edo (Benin) and the whole place became land. His other brothers who had been hovering around for somewhere to rest then came round to request for a portion of land to settle on. These other brothers represent the three shades of "ebo" or "white men"—as we call them—who occupy the rest of the world. That is why one of the attributes of the Oba of Benin is that he owns land up to "evbo-ebo," meaning European country. And this is also why the earth features so prominently as part of our coronation rituals. (Erediauwa 1984: 9–10)

There are fewer versions of this myth than the Yorùbá creation stories. There is more consistency in the Benin story outline, the cast, and the details. Although Benin acknowledges a connection with Uhe (the name associated with "Ife," as they know it today), the link is through one of the Benin princes who founded the Second Dynasty, and not the world. Some distinctive Yorùbá features have crept into some Benin versions of creation and have been perpetuated even by serious scholars of Benin. In one purportedly "widely told myth," creation of the world, "as it is known to the Edo," begins when the high god sends his *three sons* into the world. After the others have chosen their gifts, the youngest son chooses a snail shell at the direction of *a bird (or a toucan)* that lives at the top of *a tree in the middle of the waters* (emphasis mine for probable Yorùbá borrowings). He then pours the sand from the snail shell to create land, and a *chameleon* walks on the sand to test the firmness of the earth. The place where the land emerged is said to be Agbon (today, an Igbo town to the east of Benin City). Agbon also is supposed to be the place where Òsànóbuà, the Benin high god, first came *down from the sky on a chain* and *demarcated the world* (Ben-Amos 1995).

Some Yorùbá features that appear in other Benin creation stories told to researchers are noticeably absent from the Oba's story.[7] They include descent from the spirit world on a chain; the descent of the high god to earth; also a bird, the chameleon who tests the land, and the number three. Features found in both Benin and Yorùbá stories are a number of sons who found the civilized world, a high god, use of a snail shell, pouring common sand to create earth, and descending into primal waters. Culturally distinct features (in Benin) are four sons, not three, the high god's sons' descent to earth, a boat, a choice of gifts, and a son of the high god (the youngest, the Oba of Benin), who founds the civilized world. There is no chain, bird, or chameleon.

The Benin origin myth and its variants account for the centrality and legitimacy of the religious and political order at the royal court in Benin City. The city is the place the world began. It is the center of power, the palace, and the Oba—through sometimes violent internal disputes, abuses of power, external regional and local challenges, as well as foreign contacts with the Western world for more than five hundred years. The Oba, the youngest son of Òsànóbuà, is given precedence over his "brothers," that is, other traditional rulers, at the world's creation. His primacy, authority, and centrality to the land and all those dwelling on it are established at the very beginning of the world. Without recourse to Freudian theory, shared features between the Yorùbá and Benin probably represent borrowings *both* ways as a result of being in long contact; they are probably not a result of one being the source for the other. Shared Ife-Benin features may also be rooted in older, still unidentified cultural layers that stretched across southern Nigeria (as has been proposed to account for the widespread and ancient worship of Ògún and a "sacred iron complex") (Barnes 1997: 1–2, 4).

Conclusions

The globalization of Yorùbá religion and culture accompanied the slave trade with European countries, especially in the eighteenth and nineteenth centuries, and continued to shape life and thought in the Diaspora. The declaration making Lagos a British Crown colony in 1851 was a result of earlier British intervention in fierce Yorùbá internal conflicts. At the same time, the advent of British colonial administration, which compromised Yorùbá independence, benefited them. It offered opportunities for material wealth, education, and literacy, and it spawned new elites in Lagos and elsewhere. A southern center of colonial power, the Yorùbá had access and the "ear" of missionaries and colonial administrators. It was only when Oba Akintoye was backed by the British that he then had the temerity to refuse to pay the tribute he traditionally owed to Benin (Ryder 1969: 242).

In the new colonial context, it seems the Yorùbá, like other ethnic groups formerly subject to the Benin, retold stories in a way more favorable to themselves (Okpewho 1998: ix–x, 1–3, 203). The Benin ambush of a "diplomatic" British party and the casualties and deaths suffered by the expeditionary forces to Benin City in 1897 was followed by Benin's intransigence that lasted up to 1920. The results were distrust and enmity on both sides. The bloody experience of the British in Benin led to a repressive colonial policy that was very different from the opportunities afforded the Yorùbá via the Crown colony at Lagos.

This chapter is, in part, a cautionary tale about privileging one culture's telling of another's tales. It reconsiders the Ife-Benin canon and reviews pertinent old and new evidence previously offered in support of it. The essay extends and reaffirms the cogent arguments of Ryder, who first questioned the canon (1965), along with Lawal and later Thornton (1988). Ethnographic research in Benin made reinterpreting figures of "messenger/royal officials" possible and gradually revealed lack of evidence for the Ogane's (né the Oni's) "confirmation gifts." Fieldwork, therefore, raises new questions here about the accepted claims of Ife's early hegemony over Benin. Rather, Benin "messengers" *from* Ife now appear as a kind of trophy figure, notable war captives, probably from

the Benin Nupe-Igala wars. They represent someone of real or fictive
high status to be remembered, who was dispatched as a "messenger"
with thanks *to* Ògún, the god of iron and war. Bronze trophy heads are
their counterparts.

There is no dispute that Owo, Oyo, and Lagos all came under the
suzerainty of the Benin Obas from time to time, over some five centuries. That unanimity on Benin's power should itself raise doubts about
accepting Yorùbá hegemony over Benin without further proof. There
is no oral tradition or historic evidence Benin was ever subject to Ife or
any other polity. The known exception is a fifteenth-century Portuguese
report of tribute paid by Benin to a still unknown kingdom.

Although Portuguese, Dutch, and other sources offer glimpses of
Benin City and countryside of old, their commercial purposes were of
brief duration and had political implications for all parties. Foreigners
were active agents of change but were given few chances to observe.
The movements of foreigners about the Benin capital city and their access to the Oba were severely restricted, from the fifteenth century up to
1897. Translators undoubtedly limited what foreigners knew and wrote
of what they saw and were told. Exchanges of information took place
between Europeans, Edo (Benin) speakers, and native speakers of other
African tonal languages and/or trade languages, linguae francae, such as
Yorùbá, that were in widespread use along the West African coast.

Christianity spread rapidly in Nigeria in the nineteenth century with
the establishment of colonial governance, foreign missionaries, and
trade—just as Islam had in Africa in earlier times in the north, east, and
parts of the south. Indigenous religions came under siege, especially
where human sacrifice was openly practiced, as it famously was in Benin (but continued secretly in Yorùbá land). European slave trade that
began slowly in the late fifteenth century with the Portuguese soon flourished along the Guinea Coast and across the seas. It carried along with
its human cargo indigenous religious beliefs and practices that took root
and flourished in the Diaspora. Globalization helped to reinvent Yorùbá
religion as a world phenomenon.

It may be that some twice-told tales of the Benin and the Yorùbá will
remain in circulation now and forever beyond our knowing with certainty if they are "true" or not.[8] But for each ethnic group the tales they
tell *are* true and should be so regarded and compared. Comparison raises
questions, informs our understanding of cultural history, and continues
to generate new research. Twice-told tales that reinvented Benin's he-

gemony were complicit with and inevitably complicated by the colonial experience, and are likely to remain so. They were surely changed by time and circumstance, by the secrecy that surrounds religious beliefs and practices—and by the tenacity and deliberate obfuscation characteristic of Benin culture—as well as the wiliness of the Yorùbá.

Notes

The keen interest and generous support of Oba Erediauwa Omo N'Oba N'Edo Uku Akpolokpolo have been the primary pillars of my research. The unique access he has granted me, his careful review and comments on several drafts, and the information he provided has enriched my knowledge of Benin culture and its historic relationships with other ethnic groups. I am grateful to him and to the palace chiefs he brought to consult with me.

I am grateful to Chief A. S. Guobadia for his careful answers to my questions and for facilitating the flow of information with the palace. He also provided additional information about his cousin, Chief Jacob U. Egharevba. I would be remiss if I did not acknowledge Prince Edun Akenzua, Enogie of Obazuwa-Iko, who generously gave of his fund of knowledge to this research. His was the first story of Prince Ekaladerhan to nourish my growing doubts about the accepted Ife-Benin canon. I wish to thank Priest O. Ebohon, who has been a valued friend and source of information on this and other areas of Benin religion and culture. I was the beneficiary of many discussions with Chief A. Y. Eke, and Prince Yemi Eweka, both of whom had an abiding interest in indigenous religion, enriching my understanding. Both having now passed away, they continue to be sorely missed. I most gratefully acknowledge the dozens of Benin people and Yorùbá friends in all walks of life who shared their stories with me.

1. Terms: "Benin" is used here in several ways depending on the context: the culture, the people (plural), the place. Benin City, capital of Edo State, is today part of the Federal Republic of Nigeria. The Edo proper (as Benin refer to themselves), those living in the city and surrounding environs, have been centered there spiritually and politically since medieval times. The city is the traditional heart of the kingdom and was the base of an empire. At its peak in the sixteenth and early seventeenth centuries, the Benin Empire reached across much of southern Nigeria, beyond the Niger River in the east and beyond Lagos in the west (unto the Republic of Benin, formerly Dahomey). Although Benin's size and power fluctuated over the centuries, its capital city remained the center of its religious, social, economic, and political life.

"Dynastic kingship" refers to what Egharevba termed a second dynasty of sacred Benin kings, or Obas (1968). His chronology begins with Oba Eweka I, son of Oranmiyan by a Benin woman, and followed the end of a more egalitarian period of "Ògísó" rulers. (He listed seventeen Ògísó, or "sky kings," including a few women.) Egharevba estimated the second dynasty began in the late twelfth century (ca. AD 1180). He based his chronology on elderly informants who were already adults at the time of the 1897 British conquest. The start date for his royal dynastic succession is necessarily arbitrary, but archaeological surveys of the Benin City walls, earth ramparts, and archaeological test pits and excavations at sites in and around Benin City in the 1950s to 1970s lent some support to Egharevba's "history" of events and the reigns of early Obas (Connah 1975; Darling 1984a, 1984b; Egharevba 1968). Despite scholars' tinkering with Egharevba's lists of kings, his work remains both a useful baseline and a heuristic device. More precise dating awaits the long delayed renewal of systematic archaeology in Benin, the region, and sites to the north, southwest, and east.

"Bronze" is used here to gloss Benin lost wax castings of tin-bronze and zinc-brass. Surprisingly, the testing of some metals has found bronze to precede brass casting in Benin (Connah 1975: 233). While many more objects need to be tested, some alloys show both brass and bronze occurred early in the Benin corpus. Bronze, a mixture of copper and tin, and brass, a mixture of copper and zinc, contain a number of other trace elements. Although some trace elements appear later in time, other trace elements yield mixed and inconclusive results. Evidently it was common practice in the past (as well as the present) for bronze casters to reuse old objects, those damaged and broken, and available scrap when casting, thus skewing the results (Dark 1975; Willett 1981). "Bronze," the term most widely used to describe Benin castings, is adopted here to avoid repetition and qualifying statements throughout this chapter, especially when the composition of most objects is unknown.

2. Only tales relevant to this chapter were compared from Benin and Yorùbá oral traditions.

3. Stylistically, four known standing "messenger" sculptures probably date to the sixteenth and early seventeenth centuries. Four others probably date later stylistically to the late eighteenth and early nineteenth centuries. The latter are heavier and have coarser details.

4. In support of the current Ife-Benin canon, it was asserted at the time of Oba Erediauwa's coronation (1979), "a popular recent version of Benin history has it that Eweka [I] was the great-grandson of *Owodo*," making Ife "the dynastic derivation of Benin, rather than, conventionally, the other way around" (Nevadomsky 1984: 41). The foregoing inverted tale was published in *African Arts* in 1984, the same year the Oba of Benin gave his public lecture on kingship origins at Ibadan University. But no reference to sources is given, nor is fact checking indicated by author or editors. It is remarkable to assert that the Oba of Benin—who read law at Cambridge University—would give a public lecture in

the largest Yorùbá city in Nigeria, based on what was described in *African Arts* as a "popular recent version of Benin history." The Oba was trained from childhood in Benin oral tradition. In preparation for the year-long funeral obsequies for his father, he was tutored by senior palace chiefs. Like many Benin people, Priest O. Ebohon protested the 1984 account of Benin's kingship origins, charging they were "falsified" in many respects. "The Benin," he had written, "do not subscribe to the believe [*sic*] that the Ododuwa, the father of Oranmiyan was a Yorùbá," but is [instead] the Benin Prince Ekaladerhan (Ebohon 1972: 5). Nonetheless, Benin's version of its own history is missing from most contemporary Africanist literature, and the Ife-Benin canon continues to be uncritically asserted. This chapter aims to encourage scholars to take note of the evidence and reconsider their views of the other half of the canon.

5. It is hardly surprising to *expect* or to *find* that different informants give differing versions of origin myths according to their ethnicity, status, education, experience, and motivation. Criteria such as quality of knowledge, consistency, and patterning are useful measures in evaluating informants. So, too, is a researcher's developing sensibilities to cultural fitness when interpreting and comparing information.

6. Egharevba's kings' list is adopted in this chapter from the third edition of his classic work *A Short History of Benin* (1968). What archaeology has been done, in and around Benin, and what historic documents and reports have been gathered thus far tend to support Egharevba's scheme. The origin of Benin's famed lost wax "bronze," the tin-bronze, zinc-brass casting tradition, has been attributed to Igueghae, a brass caster who is said to have come from Ife in the reign of Oba Oguola (about A.D. 1280). This story appears virtually everywhere in the literature by Benin scholars and others (Bradbury 1973; Ben-Amos 1995: 9, 25; Dark 1973; Egharevba 1968; Fagg 1963; Willett 1968, 1981; Willett, Torsney, and Ritchie 1994). But some scholars question the tale (such as Connah 1975: 233; Eisenhofer 1995; Kaplan 2000; Lawal 1977). The Benin themselves say Igueghae had been sent to Ife.

7. This study is based on interviews with more than forty informants at different social and economic levels of contemporary Benin society. They independently confirmed the tales told to me. My research included study of related objects in the Nigerian National Museums at Lagos, Ife, Owo, and Benin; and of information gathered on two trips to the archives at the University of Ibadan. From 1983 to 1985, I was a Fulbright associate professor, teaching in the Department of Sociology and Anthropology, University of Benin. I also held an appointment at the university's CenSCER (Centre for Social, Cultural, and Environmental Research). After 1985, my research continued on trips each year, some for extended periods that included two sabbaticals and several leaves from New York University through 2001, and most recently in 2006. My research is ongoing in Benin.

8. Chief Jacob Egharevba, Benin's first Western-style, self-taught, early twentieth-century indigenous historian, can be credited or blamed for accepting the Ife-Benin canon, according to the tales you favor. His view is rejected by royal court historians, knowledgeable Benin, and the Oba, categorically. Why and how he came to accept the canon is explored elsewhere in a forthcoming essay on Egharevba. His writings played an important role in perpetuating the Ife-Benin canon and influenced others.

Egharevba wrote: "Special royal regalia and other necessary insignia were sent to Eweka [I] at his coronation from Ife by his father" (1968: 8). And he specified the insignia as a helmet, a staff, and a pectoral cross. Unlike the story of dynastic origins told by Oba Erediauwa of Benin, Egharevba identified Oranmiyan (the father of Eweka I) as the son of Obalufon, the Oni of Ife, who came after Ododuwa (Odùduwà), the first Oni at Ife. In the several editions of his classic publication *A Brief History of Benin,* Egharevba writes of the story of Prince Ekaladerhan's banishment from Benin by his father, the Ògísó Owodo. Owodo was the last of the "sky kings" who ruled before the Second Dynasty. But as Oba Erediauwa made clear to me—in failing to connect Prince Ekaladerhan with Oranmiyan (his son, who fathered Oba Eweka I)—"Egharevba erred" (1984; personal communication, September 28, 2001).

References

Abímbọ́lá, Wande. 1997. "Images of Women in the Ifa Literary Corpus." In *Queens, Queen Mothers, Priestesses, and Power: Case Studies in African Gender,* ed. Flora Edouwaye S. Kaplan, 401–13. Annals of the New York Academy of Sciences 810. New York: New York Academy of Sciences.

Abiodun, Rowland. 1989. "The Kingdom of Owo." In *Yorùbá: Nine Centuries of African Art and Thought,* ed. Allen Wardwell, 91–115. New York: Center for African Art in association with Harry N. Abrams.

Ajayi, J. F. Ade, and Robert Smith. 1964. *Yorùbá Warfare in the Nineteenth Century.* London: Cambridge University Press.

Barnes, Sandra T. 1997. "The Many Faces of Ogun: Introduction to the First Edition." In *Africa's Ogun: Old World and New,* ed. Sandra T. Barnes. Bloomington: Indiana University Press.

Ben-Amos, Paula Girshick. 1995. *The Art of Benin.* Rev. ed. London: British Museum Press.

Boisragon, Captain Alan. 1898. *The Benin Massacre.* London: Methuen.

Bradbury, R. E. 1973. *Benin Studies.* London: Oxford University Press.

Connah, Graham. 1975. *The Archaeology of Benin: Excavations and Other Researches in and around Benin City, Nigeria.* Oxford: Clarendon Press.

Dark, Phillip J. C. 1975. "Benin Bronze Heads: Styles and Chronology." In

African Images: Essays in African Iconology, ed. Daniel F. McCall and Edna G. Bay, 25–103. Boston University Papers on Africa 6. New York: Africana.

Darling, P. J. 1984a. *Archaeology and History in Southern Nigeria: The Ancient Linear Earthworks of Benin and Ishan.* Part 1: *Fieldwork and Background Information.* Cambridge Monographs in African Archaeology 11. BAR International Series 215(i). Oxford: BAR.

———. 1984b. *Archaeology and History in Southern Nigeria: The Ancient Linear Earthworks of Benin and Ishan.* Part 2: *Ceramic and Other Specialist Studies.* Cambridge Monographs in African Archaeology 11. BAR International Series 215(ii). Oxford: BAR.

Drewal, Henry John. 1989a. "Art and Ethos of the Ijebu." In *Yorùbá: Nine Centuries of African Art and Thought,* ed. Allen Wardwell, 117–45. New York: Center for African Art in association with Harry N. Abrams.

———. 1989b. "Ife: Origins of Art and Civilization." In *Yorùbá: Nine Centuries of African Art and Thought,* ed. Allen Wardwell, 45–75. New York: Center for African Art in association with Harry N. Abrams.

Drewal, Henry John, John Pemberton III, and Rowland Abiodun. 1989. "The Yorùbá World." In *Yorùbá: Nine Centuries of African Art and Thought,* ed. Allen Wardwell, 13–43. New York: Center for African Art in association with Harry N. Abrams.

Duchâteau, Armand. 1994. *Benin: Royal Art of Africa.* Houston: Museum of Fine Arts.

Ebohon, Osemwegie. 1972. *Cultural Heritage of Benin.* Benin City: Midwest Newspapers Corporation.

Egharevba, Chief Dr. Jacob U. 1968 (1934). *A Short History of Benin.* Ibadan: Ibadan University Press.

Eisenhofer, Stefan. 1995. "The Origins of the Benin Kingship in the Works of Jacob Egharevba." *History in Africa: A Journal of Method* 22: 141–63.

Erediauwa, Omo N'Obo N'Edo, Uku Akpolokpolo, CFR Oba of Benin. 1984. "The Evolution of Traditional Rulership in Nigeria." Lecture delivered at the Conference on the Role of Traditional Rulers in the Governance of Nigeria, 11 September 1984. Ibadan: University of Ibadan, Institute of African Studies.

Fage, J. D. 1969. *A History of West Africa: An Introductory Survey.* Cambridge: Cambridge University Press.

Fagg, W. 1963. *Nigerian Images.* London: Lund Humphries.

Fraser, Douglas. 1975. "The Tsoede Bronzes and Owo Yorùbá Art." *African Arts* 8, no. 3: 30–35, 91.

Kaplan, Flora *Edouwaye* S. 1991. "Fragile Legacy: Photographs as Documents in Recovering Political and Cultural History at the Royal Court of Benin." *History in Africa* 18: 205–37.

————. 1993a. "Images of the Queen Mother in Benin Court Art." *African Arts* 26, no. 3: 55–63; 86–88.

————. 1993b. "'*Íyóbá*,' the Queen Mother of Benin: Images and Ambiguity in Gender and Sex Roles in Court Art." *Art History* 16, no. 3: 386–407.

————. 1994. *A Mexican Folk Pottery Tradition: Cognition and Style in Material Culture in the Valley of Puebla*. Carbondale: Southern Illinois University Press.

————. 2003. "Understanding Sacrifice and Sanctity in Benin Indigenous Religion: A Case Study." In *Beyond Primitivism: Indigenous Religious Traditions and Modernity*, ed. Jacob K. Olupona, 181–99. London: Routledge.

Law, Robin. 1983. "Trade and Politics behind the Slave Coast: The Lagoon Traffic and the Rise of Lagos, 1500–1800." *Journal of African History* 24: 321–48.

Lawal, Babatunde. 1977. "The Present State of Art Historical Research in Nigeria: Problems and Possibilities." *Journal of African History* 18, no. 2: 193–216.

Matory, J. Lorand. 1994. *Sex and the Empire That Is No More*. Minneapolis: University of Minnesota Press.

————. 1997. "The King's Male-Order Bride: The Modern Making of a Yorùbá Priest." In *Queens, Queen Mothers, Priestesses and Power: Case Studies in African Gender*, ed. Flora *Edouwaye* S. Kaplan, 381–400. Annals of the New York Academy of Sciences 810. New York: New York Academy of Sciences.

Nevadomsky, J. 1984. "Kingship Succession Rituals in Benin—2: The Big Things." *African Arts* 17, no. 2: 41–47, 90–91.

Okpewho, Isidore. 1998. *Once Upon a Kingdom: Myth Hegemony, and Identity*. Bloomington: Indiana University Press.

Olupona, Jacob K. 1991. *Religion and Kingship in a Nigerian Community: A Phenomenological Analysis of Ondo Yorùbá Festivals*. Studies in Comparative Religion 28. Stockholm: Almqvist & Wiskell International.

————. 1997. "Women's Rituals, Kingship, and Power among the Ondo-Yorùbá of Nigeria." In *Queens, Queen Mothers, Priestesses, and Power: Case Studies in African Gender*, ed. Flora *Edouwaye* S. Kaplan, 315–36. Annals of the New York Academy of Sciences 810. New York: New York Academy of Sciences.

Pemberton, John, III, and Funso Afolayan. 1996. *Yorùbá Sacred Kingship: A Power Like That of the Gods*. Washington, DC: Smithsonian Institution Press.

Ruhlen, Merritt. 1991 (1987). *A Guide to the World's Languages*. Vol. 1: *Classification*. Stanford: Stanford University Press.

Ryder, A. F. C. 1965. "A Reconsideration of the Ife-Benin Relationship." *Journal of African History* 6, no. 1: 25–37.

————. 1969. *Benin and the Europeans, 1485–1897*. New York: Humanities Press.

Smith, Robert. 1988. *Kingdoms of the Yorùbá*. Madison: University of Wisconsin Press.

Thornton, John K. 1988. "Traditions, Documents, and the Ife-Benin Relationship." *History in Africa* 15: 351–62.

von Luschan, Felix. 1968 (1919). *Die Altertümer von Benin*. New York: Hacker Art Books.

Willett, Frank. 1966. "On Funeral Effigies of Owo and Benin and the Interpretation of the Life-Size Bronze Heads from Ife, Nigeria." *Journal of Royal Anthropological Institute* 1: 34–45.

————. 1967. *Ife in the History of West African Sculpture*. London: Thames and Hudson.

————. 1968. "New Light on the Ife-Benin Relationship." *African Forum,* 3, 4, 4, 1: 28–43.

————. 1981. "The Analysis of Nigerian Copper Alloys Retrospect and Prospect." *Critica d'Arte Africana* 178: 35–49.

Willett, Frank, Ben Torsney, and Mark Ritchie. 1994. "Composition and Style: An Examination of the Benin 'Bronze' Heads." *African Arts* 27, no. 3: 61–101.

7

Meta-Cultural Processes and Ritual Realities in the Precolonial History of the Lagos Region

SANDRA T. BARNES

A long procession made its way through Isale Eko, the old quarter of Lagos Island, late on the afternoon of August 4, 1983. The procession was one part of the installation ceremony for the Olorogun Adodo, an hereditary chief whose warrior ancestors came to Lagos from the Kingdom of Benin.[1] The new chief was escorted along the city streets by the Eletu Odibo,[2] and they were followed by an entourage of hundreds of notables, family members, and well-wishers. The procession stopped at important landmarks and acknowledged famous historic figures and current titleholders in whose honor the Eletu Odibo and Olorogun Adodo performed the salute known as *ikanse* (alt: *ikikanse, kikan*).

Each stop along the procession route represented a "chapter" in the history of Lagos and revealed how one historical layer after another had been added to the community's constitution. The *ikanse* was a salute to the king of Benin, acknowledging the period, over several hundred years, when precolonial Lagos was a tributary of the ancient Kingdom of Benin. Even during this period, however, Lagos functioned in daily practice as a separate polity and in a broader way as one part of a politically and economically interdependent region. The identities of leading

164

citizens were constructed to exploit these two possibilities—local and regional—with both possibilities reflected in the procession for the Olorogun Adodo.

While the elder chief moved down the streets of the old city, he taught his new colleague how to execute the *ikanse,* and at the same time, he imparted knowledge germane to each salute. The procession was the new chief's official introduction to what was significant about the past, who should be remembered, why, and by virtue of what characteristics. These characteristics had much to say about one kind of knowledge—knowledge involving ritual beliefs and practices—that was transmitted in ancient times and why it was important throughout the Lagos region and far beyond it.

The goal of this chapter is to examine the 1983 procession because it provides a social and ritual stratigraphy of the community and a spatial map of historical memory.[3] There are two important things to be learned. The first is that Lagos was at the center of a large region in which there was a continuous flow of people during precolonial times (Law 1983). Trade, military, and marital alliances encouraged the movement of people and linked communities to one another. Membership in a community was defined by loyalty to its leaders but was not exclusive to a single polity. The places and people recognized along the procession route reflected this reality in that all of them or their forebears came from different localities, yet they were able to make a mark in the Lagos historical record.

The second consideration is that the procession route makes it possible to trace the importation of ritual knowledge into Lagos. Individuals or sites on the procession route were identified by their place of origin and by a shrine, deity, or some kind of esoteric knowledge they contributed to the Lagos community. In fact, in identifying an historically significant individual, ritually related information about that person often took precedence over information about a political, economic, or heroic contribution. People who came to Lagos carried shrines with them. They also introduced new secret societies, healing, or divination practices. It was essential to know and transmit information about unfamiliar ritual practices and beliefs since it was a form of cultural knowledge others did not have. Esoteric knowledge was a palpable passport to social acceptance and support in a new community. Just as importantly, it was a credential that reaffirmed an individual's identity and legitimacy when returning to the homeland. The circulation of people and goods in the

Lagos region was pervasive in precolonial times, but it was ritual knowledge and practice that gave people a sense of their own distinctive place in the world while at the same time bringing people together and providing them with a sense of belonging.

The Historical Context

Before turning to the procession, it is important to consider the centrality of Lagos in precolonial times and the circumstances that produced so compelling a ritual performance that it endured, albeit in continually altering forms, to the present. The coast along the Bight of Benin—the region from which many slaves were sent to the New World in the eighteenth and early nineteenth centuries—was laced with waterways. Creeks and lagoons running east and west and paralleling the coastline stretched hundreds of miles. They provided a near continuous inland waterway that facilitated the movement of people for trade, fishing, and warfare and acted as a vast and effective communications network. Several rivers also flowed from the north into these waterways, adding to the density of people, goods, and information that circulated into and out of the area.[4] The inland waterway extended for some four hundred miles from the River Volta (Ghana) to the Niger (Nigeria). Lagos was mainly active in that segment of the waterway between Allada (alt: Ardra) and Benin. Law described Allada as a natural breaking point in the water system, because nearby the east-west passageway was sometimes blocked by sand (1983: 321). For centuries, people living near these waterways engaged in social relationships, exchanged information, and blended language, culture, and history to the extent that regional meta-traditions emerged.

The Kingdom of Lagos was a tiny state in comparison to the interior monarchies of Ọ̀yọ́ or Ijebu, but it occupied a strategic location in the coastal region. One of the most important aspects in this respect was that Lagos residents controlled east-west inland water traffic thanks to their location at the mouth of a large lagoon that separated Lagos Island from the mainland and narrowed at the point where they were settled. Lagos harbor also provided the only permanent natural inlet from the Atlantic Ocean to the interior waterways, and therefore it attracted European traders and upcountry merchants hoping to do business with them. Harbor waters flowed into the lagoon behind Lagos Island, flooding it with saltwater fish in the dry season yet receding sufficiently in the rainy season for the lagoon then to be filled with freshwater fish from upcountry rivers. This meant Lagos was situated at one of the most diverse and protected inland fishing grounds on the coast. Landowning chieftaincy families whose properties fronted the lagoon controlled wharfs and fishing rights to the waters surrounding their wharfs (Payne 1894: 49; Ward-Price 1939: 8; Hill and Webb 1958: 320; Nigeria 1948). This was an ancient prerogative that was maintained to present times and that in the precolonial heyday of Lagos was, along with trade, a source of great wealth.[5]

Later, during the colonial period starting in 1861, Lagos retained its centrality as the eventual capital of what would become Nigeria and hub of the nation's economic activity. British administrators stripped ancient political institutions and their leaders of most powers, but they were not effective in curtailing their influence or their access to those with power. Contrary to the expectation that the traditional aristocracy would die out, it instead provided a transitional bridge between past and present for large segments of the population. Chieftaincy titles that had been passed down through families for centuries continued to serve as a mark of honor. Even up to the present, they provided recipients with a public platform from which to voice their and their followers' concerns, as well as a privileged position from which to seek favor in the allocation of local resources.[6]

The Procession

The ritual center of Old Lagos from the time of Benin's early occupation was Enu Owa Square, and it was here that the other titled descendants of the Lagos precolonial chiefs sat while the 1983 installation ceremony for Chief Olorogun Adodo unfolded. Secret aspects of the installation took place at the far side of the square inside the *ekpebi* (alt: *iledi*), a private capping room, controlled by the *apena,* a leader of the Oshugbo secret society. When the new chief and the installing official, Chief Eletu Odibo, left the *ekpebi,* the two men started their historical procession. Both men were clad in white loincloths, white caps of office, and royal coral beads, and in their left hands they carried *ofu* (medicines) wrapped in white cloth. Leading the way was the *ọba*'s (king's) representative, who carried the *ọ̀pá ọba,* a silver-topped scepter. Then came members

of the Eletu Odibo chieftaincy family, who carried the *ọ̀pá odiyon,* a
staff symbolizing the powers of Ifá divination that resided within their
descent group, and *lábá,* leather bags that held special paraphernalia
needed for the ritual.

First they acknowledged Chief Eletu Iwashe[7] (1 in table 7.1), who sat
apart from the other chiefs as a mark of honor and as a way of emphasizing his symbolic role as representative of the Ọba of Benin and caretaker
of two shrines: Oju Odiyon (alt: Ojodun) and Erinkina.[8] The number
in parentheses following Chief Eletu Iwashe's name corresponds to a
number in table 7.1 (below), which lists notables, shrines, deities, and
their origins that were recognized along the procession route. Both of the
shrines attached to the Eletu Iwashe were brought to Lagos from Benin
centuries earlier and placed in the square to protect the community. At
Enu Owa Square the feet of the Olorogun Adodo were ceremonially
washed beneath a towering akoko tree,[9] after which the two men and
their entourages walked back and forth three times along the main thor-
oughfare fronting the square. They walked briefly in the direction of Oju
Olobun (2 in table 7.1), a tree shrine controlled by the Eletu Odibo family and also brought from Benin, and then they turned back to pay homage to Oju Olokun (3 in table 7.1), a shrine for the deity of the sea. They
continued on to salute Oju Ajagbili (4 in table 7.1), a secret shrine whose
origin and controlling authority were not publicly revealed although
private accounts agreed that its powers were awesome, even frighten-
ing. Finally, they passed by the palaces and shrines of the Obanikoro (5
in table 7.1) and Ashogbon (6 in table 7.1) chieftaincy families.

At each site the two men performed the *ikanse* salute to the Ọba of
Benin by rubbing their hands together with palms fully open, stretching
the right arm forward over the left, swinging it in a circle three times,
and concluding with the arm fully raised and fist clenched in front of
the body. At some sites the *ikanse* included a recitation of the names
of significant ancestral figures who, as the Eletu Odibo stressed, were
important national figures,[10] by which he meant ancestors who figured
in the affairs of the entire kingdom and not those of a specific chiefly
family.[11] There were four classes of family members: (1) *olóyè:* chiefs
who were the titled heads of a chieftaincy family; (2) *ọmọye:* members
of a chieftaincy family as determined by biological descent; (3) *ibigas*
and *arotas,* slaves; and (4) *alábàágbé* and *asaforigi,* sojourners or refugees who, by their own volition, sought protection of a chief but were
not enslaved.[12]

Table 7.1. People, Places, Shrines, and Deities Recognized as Part of the Lagos Chieftaincy Installation Ceremony

Title or Name of Notable	Notable's Place of Origin	Shrine, Deity, or Secret Society Controlled/Owned by Notable
1. Eletu Iwashe	Benin	Oju Odiyon and Erinkina
2. Eletu Odibo	Benin	Oju Olobun and Akoko Tree
3. Onilegbale	Benin/Ijebu	Olokun and Iworo
4. *	*	Ajagbili
5. Obanikoro	Idoluwo Ile	Eje Pillar
6. Ashogbon	Benin	Akala Secret Society
7. Oniru	Keta/Volga River	Olokun**
8. Olumegbon	Eti-Osa/Aja/Lekki	Alele
9. Onisemo	Ilaro	Orona
10. Modile	Orile Oko/Abeokuta	Ejiwa and Riri
11. Oluwa	Iwa/Badagry	Elegba
12. Onisiwo	Porto Novo/Egun	Sangbeto
13. Eletu Ijebu	Ijebu/Ikorodu	Oshugbo Secret Society
14. Egbe	Apa	Akala Secret Society
15. Faji	Mahin	Iroko Tree***
16. Onimole	Ijebu	Ojuewa
17. Opeluwa	Awori	Oju Olosa/Elegba
18. Ọba (king)	Benin/Ijebu	Oju Olosa/Eshu
19. Olorogun Adodo	Benin/Arogbo	Onijegi and Alarogbo

Additional Ancestors Mentioned

20. Akinsemoyin	Benin/Apa	
21. Aromire	Indigenous	Iroko Tree
22. Erelú Kuti (queen mother)	Ijebu	Iga Kadan
23. Olugbani (king's wife)	Ijebu	Ologede
24. Ologun Kutere	Benin/Ijebu	

Notes:
* Secret.
** There were two Olokun shrines, both ocean deities, but with different origins and ritual practices.
*** There were two Iroko tree shrines, each with different origins and practices.

The Olorogun Adodo, having returned to Enu Owa Square, was next presented to previously installed chiefs who wore their white caps of office and were seated at the side of the square in a row according to seniority.[13] Each chief, as shown in table 7.1, was the descendant of an ancestor who had come to Lagos from another community, an ancestor who had brought shrines and deities that were remembered and in many cases still used, and who had made a sufficiently significant contribution to the Lagos community to receive an hereditary title that was still in existence. The Olorogun Adodo also saluted the erelú, the only female titleholder of the Oshugbo secret society, who represented the society at the ceremony and sat slightly apart from the white cap chiefs. Nearby was the palace of Chief Eletu Ijebu (13 in table 7.1), whose ancestors brought Oshugbo to the island. Chiefs and other notables held Oshugbo meetings at the Eletu Ijebu's palace, and still hold them, to discuss community affairs and provide a check on royal power.[14]

Representatives of Lagos war chiefs, wearing colored felt hats as their symbol of office, sat in front of a mosque further along the procession route.[15] They were Chief Egbe (14 in table 7.1), whose ancestor came to Lagos to protect Ọba Akinsemoyin (20) in the mid-eighteenth century, and Chief Faji (15 in table 7.1), whose ancestor aided an Ọba by financing his military endeavors. The Faji title was reserved only for women. The first Chief Faji was from an area located in today's Republic of Benin; she and her descendants were leaders of a Lagos market and market shrine located at the base of an Ìrókò tree.

The chiefs, who had been sitting at Enu Owa Square and the mosque, and their retinues joined the procession at this point, and it grew larger as it progressed toward additional historic sites. The chiefs recited the *ikanse* at the Ojuewa (alt: Oju Yewa, Iyewa) (16 in table 7.1), a shrine for an ancestral mother or mothers of Lagos kings. This shrine was guarded by the Onimole, who held a nonchiefly title, and was believed to have come from an Ijebu area northeast of Lagos. They also saluted the Oju Olosa (17 and 18 in table 7.1)—a shrine dedicated to the deity of lagoons and located at the wharf alongside the Lagos lagoon. This was the shrine where, once a year, the *ọba* dipped his toe in the water as a gesture of goodwill to the landowning Chief Opeluwa, who stood on the opposite shore of the lagoon and simultaneously dipped his toe in the water.[16] Chief Opeluwa's Awori forebears were indigenous to the area immediately west of Lagos, and the family maintained a large arena dedicated to the trickster deity Elegba (17 in table 7.1). Chief Opeluwa's arena was attended once a year by Lagos *idejo* (landowning) chiefs who held a two- to three-day ceremony there to mark their solidarity as landowners. Finally, the chiefs offered a salute inside the gate of the *ọba*'s palace grounds to the royal shrine dedicated to the trickster deity Eshu (18 in table 7.1). It was no accident that both Eshu and Elegba were acknowledged in the procession's two concluding tributes. Eshu was the name used for this deity by people east of Lagos as far as Benin, and Elegba (alt: Legba, Elegbara) was the name used for the same deity by people west of Lagos. The annual ritual performed by the *ọba* and Chief Opeluwa beside the Lagos lagoon symbolized the coming together of east and west and the centrality of Lagos in effecting that process.

The procession ended after the new Olorogun Adodo paid his respects to the Eshu deity in the royal compound. He entered the palace to receive the *ọba*'s blessing, partake of ritual foods, and dance to *igbe*, Awori drums indigenous to the western part of the Lagos area, played and sung to by women.[17]

Layers of History

Many layers of migration transformed Lagos at various points in its history. Lagos of the Benin period was a different place from the Lagos that experienced a large influx of Ijebu settlers at a later time. Historical influences, as revealed in the installation procession, came from different directions and left rich deposits of cultural material embedded in the community's ceremonial life. The installation did not display nor could it have displayed all of the influences that went into the melting pot that was Old Lagos. Yet, the ritual contained numerous representations that to the untrained eye could be construed as individually unique but if experienced from the perspective of those with some recognition of historical context were indicative of collective processes or personal achievements that contributed in remarkable ways to the development of civic life. Some of the knowledge they introduced into the community left indelible imprints on the historical record. Some of the practices they effected had the power to change public institutions.

Of the many contributions made from the outside, the three that are briefly described below transformed the social landscape of precolonial Lagos in significant ways. Just as importantly all three contributions were clearly represented in the capping ritual of 1983.

The Ado Period

Oral traditions from Benin tell of conquering and colonizing the Island of Lagos during a period documented as beginning in the sixteenth century and continuing into the nineteenth century by which time its control was becoming negligible (Aderibigbe 1975: 15; Egharevba 1960: 30; Ryder 1969: 73–74). Numerous reminders of this period were embedded in the ceremonial life of Lagos, including the *ikanse* salute to Benin's ruler and the special placement of the Eletu Iwashe at Enu Owa Square as a way of recognizing the former overlordship of Benin and its importance in building the Lagos community.

Benin extended its military and trading presence along the water corridor westward from Benin City as far as Allada by about 1530, and it appears that step-by-step it established staging, provisioning, and rest camps along the route. Qba Orhogbua of Benin is believed to have occupied the Island of Lagos around 1550 and to have established a military base from which he could march further west in search of trade, especially with European merchants. According to Lagos traditions, all that the Bini warriors found on the Island was a fishing camp inhabited by Aromire (21 in table 7.1), whose descendants remained in their original homestead near the lagoon but gave a nearby pepper farm to the Bini; the descendants of the Aromire settlement eventually became one of the Lagos chieftaincy families. Meanwhile, the Benin ruler waged war on people who rebelled against his authority in the immediate interior of Lagos but departed when he learned of a coup against him at home. He left behind Benin authorities to govern the camp (Egharevba 1960: 30–31; Jones 1983: 24; Ryder 1969: 73–74; Talbot 1926: 79–82).

Benin's dominance was pervasive in 1603 when a German surgeon, aboard a Dutch merchant ship, visited Lagos and described it as a large frontier town surrounded by a strong fence and inhabited by "none but soldiers and four military commanders, who behave in a very stately manner" (Jones 1983: 40). Each day the commanders came together as a court, and each day two envoys were charged with taking their decisions back to their ruler in Benin—a common practice in towns under Benin in this period. Lagos, the surgeon wrote, attracted many traders who brought their wares by water and land (40–41). A Dutch source of the seventeenth century indicated the king of Benin could mobilize from twenty thousand to one hundred thousand men and move contingents of them through the waterways between Benin, Lagos, and further westward in war canoes built to hold from fifty to one hundred armed soldiers each (Dapper 1960: 129). Descendants of these early Benin military commanders—including administrative chiefs with *eletu*[18] in their titles, such as Eletu Iwashe (1 in table 7.1) and Eletu Odibo (2 in table 7.1), and several military leaders, such as Ashogbon (6 in table 7.1) and Olorogun Adodo (19 in table 7.1)—maintained the tradition of recognizing their former ruler through the centuries at the installations of Lagos chiefs by performing the *ikanse* at shrines their ancestors brought to this new home.[19]

Benin's enduring contribution to Lagos governance was an institutional arrangement via which the first administrators came together as a council and governed Lagos as a colony. This institution came to be known as *osega*.[20] By the early nineteenth century, *osega* had evolved into a ceremonious meeting of Lagos chiefs. At an earlier time, the government of Lagos also had evolved into an independent monarchy with its own kingship. It was at this ruler's palace that the *osega* met regularly. *Osega* was devoted to proposing and debating policy that had community-wide ramifications. In all but the death penalty, which could be wielded by the *ọba* without consultation, the chiefs involved themselves in communal affairs. Before discussions at each meeting, which were held ideally every seventeen days, sacrifices were performed and afterward the members dined together and were entertained by the ruler.[21] As for Lagos kings whose ancestors had come from Benin, only a few names could be recalled, and thus they were known collectively as Ọba Ado.[22]

It is unclear when rights to sit on this highest decision-making body were extended beyond the Benin administrative elite to a wider body of leaders, but heads of village settlements and other powerful supporters of the Lagos *ọba* eventually began to attend *osega* meetings. Certainly this had occurred by the 1760s, when chiefs whose oral traditions did not claim Benin origin indicate they were brought into the community and given titles during a marked period of growth. The accretion of the small surrounding settlements was an important source of growth in the chiefly ranks (Agiri and Barnes 1987: 23–25). Over the years, the nature of Lagos ties with client villages surrounding the island varied from complete domination and overlordship to an almost co-equal relationship in which a village maintained autonomy in internal matters.[23] Chiefly appointments were also made on the basis of wealth, expertise in warfare, esoteric knowledge, or various combinations of these and other desirable qualities.[24] Attendance at the *osega* signaled that the chiefs or headmen of villages and their inhabitants would be loyal to the Lagos ọba and provide certain types of support, especially in military affairs, in return for which they would be protected from attacks and favored in commerce.[25] Given the centrality of Lagos and the advantages it offered, many notables cultivated relationships through this venue, even going so far, in the case of some village headmen, as to cede elements of their sovereignty but to gain through the *osega* a voice in local governance.

Western Alliances

The balance of power shifted dramatically during the second half of the eighteenth century when Akinsemoyin (20 in table 7.1) became ọba of Lagos. The divided seating arrangement for chiefs at the installation ceremony, with white cap chiefs seated at Enu Owa Square and warrior chiefs seated along the procession route but away from the square, was the physical reminder of this shift. Akinsemoyin's succession to the throne, circa 1760 (Law 1983: 344), marked a new era for the King-dom of Lagos in two respects. He managed to strengthen the power of the monarch and weaken that of pre-existing chiefs (Cole 1975: 15), and he introduced economic arrangements that provided Lagos with a much larger share of the Atlantic trade than it had experienced up to that point.[26] The changes came about because Akinsemoyin assumed of-fice with the backing of powerful military forces that were not linked to Benin in the east and were not represented up to that time in the *osega*. Instead, they were linked to rulers in the west where European traders were more active at the time. Benin was still the ratifying authority for Lagos rulers, and Akinsemoyin appears to have observed this conven-tion, but it did not prevent him from gaining control of Lagos through a show of force and establishing himself on the throne.

Strategic alliances were central to military operations in precolonial political life (Barnes 1997), and Akinsemoyin reinforced them by ap-pointing outside supporters to chiefly offices and bringing them into the Lagos polity. Communities within the Lagos region were allied with one another in a myriad of overlapping and sometimes conflicting ar-rangements, all designed to protect or enhance the interests of those in power. The alliance with the ruling family of Apa provided Ọba Ak-insemoyin of Lagos with sufficient military strength and workforce to gain the throne. The alliance was effected partly through Akinsemoyin's mother, who was a member of the Apa royal family and had been given in marriage to Akinsemoyin's father. As a reward for helping him gain the throne, Akinsemoyin gave one of the Apa warriors who accompanied him to Lagos his daughter in marriage, a place to settle near the royal palace, and a chieftaincy title. He was Chief Egbe (14 in table 7.1) whose successor was one of the two *abagbon* (warrior) chiefs—both from the west—who was waiting at the mosque in order to join the procession for Olorogun Adodo in 1983.[27]

Chief Egbe represented a new kind of chief. His placement—along with other chiefs of the warrior class at the 1983 ceremony—was a symbolic reminder that Akinsemoyin had appointed military chiefs who were not previously part of the administrative class of Benin-descended nobility, were not acting on behalf of Benin, were not constrained by local familial or factional ties, and therefore were not drawn into crosscutting relationships that might be at odds with those of the ruler. Instead, because the new warrior chiefs were appointed and given land and royal wives by the *oba,* they were entirely dependent upon him for their privileged positions in the community. These chiefs were outsiders who were not tied to the pre-existing system of governance. They added a fresh dimension to the structure of authority by greatly strengthening the power of the ruler who—whatever the pre-existing members of *osega* might decide—could independently enforce his will on the community and protect himself in the process.[28]

The warrior chiefs from Apa were not the only militarily oriented outsiders Akinsemoyin imported into the community. From an Egba-speaking area to the northwest of Lagos came another immigrant whose technologies of warfare so impressed Akinsemoyin that he too was welcomed with a chieftaincy title, a princess for a wife, and a plot of land for his palace; he introduced two important shrines and a secret society that attracted other leading citizens of the town. He was Chief Modile (10 in table 7.1) whose heir had joined the ranks of those who welcomed Olorogun Adodo in 1983. The first Chief Modile's fame rested more on the psychological prowess his weapons and charms provided Lagos soldiers than on his own military retinue, and therefore he became a personal *ogalade,* priest-chief to the *oba.* Nonetheless he, too, was dependent on the ruler for his position in the community and therefore was loyal to Akinsemoyin's regime.[29]

Akinsemoyin also established numerous economic alliances while cultivating his maternal ties in Apa and the nearby settlement of Badagry, another coastal town in the west. While in this area he spent time with European merchants—who were not active in Lagos but who taught him the ins and outs of the Atlantic trade. Commercial opportunities at the time were fading for Portuguese traders in the nearby coastal towns of Allada and Whydah, and Akinsemoyin was successful in encouraging them to establish permanent trading centers in Lagos.[30] This then attracted a wave of western immigrants who were intent on following European trade as it moved eastward to Lagos.

Akinsemoyin brought a number of outstanding Awori and Egba[31] notables from surrounding settlements into the chiefly ranks during this period of economic expansion.[32] The Awori, like Chief Opeluwa (17 in table 7.1), lived in rural settlements immediately surrounding the western and northwestern areas of Lagos Island. From further west came a wave of Aja-speaking peoples known colloquially to Lagosians as Egun. Many of them, from Apa, Allada, and other coastal areas of today's Republic of Benin, were probably in the region of Lagos much earlier for fishing and salt-making purposes. The ancestral area of Chief Onisiwo (12 in table 7.1) was Porto Novo, an Aja area. His family's holdings stretched from Lagos westward along the coast and incorporated numerous Egun fisherfolk who had lived in the area for generations, simultaneously maintaining social ties to their homelands and economic ties to Lagos.[33] No chief came from as far west as Chief Oniru (7 in table 7.1), whose ancestors were ocean-going seamen who came to Lagos Island from Keta in the Volta River estuary to operate the canoes that ferried people and goods between Lagos Island and European ships anchored offshore. Along with their commercial acumen, each of these chieftaincy families introduced new elements of cultural knowledge—linguistic, artistic, cosmological—into the cultural matrix of the growing city.[34]

By the end of his regime, Akinsemoyin had established a new layer of nobility in his home community: big men and women who were commercially experienced and helped bring about an era of economic opportunity and affluence, and military officials who enforced the ruler's policies and protected those he favored. The two types of notables clearly reinforced one another. Both were beholden to Akinsemoyin for whatever advantages they enjoyed, for once he assumed the highest office of the kingdom they could not advance their own interests without advancing his. Akinsemoyin made bold changes in the structure of government—changes that directly promoted his agendas and diminished those of the previously entrenched power holders—and as

a result he was remembered as an autocratic ruler.[35] Akinsemoyin also
was disdained for not sharing his wealth. An *oriki* (praise name) for the
Akinsemoyin family was *Ọmọ Adajo ba owo je,* "The offspring of he
who fixed a date for squandering money."

The Ijebu Dynasty

Still another transformation in Lagos governance came at the end of the
eighteenth century following the reign of Akinsemoyin. Although the
evidence is not direct, it could be seen as a reaction to Akinsemoyin's
strong-arm tactics. It involved a prolonged period of dominance by Ijebu
and their descendants who came to the city from the northeast. There
were numerous Ijebu-inspired contributions to the community's sociocultural repertoire, but two of them, both political in nature, changed
the face of the community. Both were represented in the installation
proceedings of 1983 and both by women. One was the Ojuewa shrine
dedicated to one or several Ijebu ancestral mothers of the royal family
and to whom tribute was paid by the processing chiefs. The other was
the Oshugbo Secret Society, whose only female officeholder, the *erelú,*
sat with the white cap chiefs at Enu Owa Square.

The first transformation was the establishment of a new royal dynasty, reflecting the vital interests of neighboring Ijebu peoples in
commerce—Ijebu-manufactured cloth being a central commodity—
and the role of women in supporting this particular niche in the Lagos
market. The dynastic transition was a complex affair involving Erelú
Kuti (22 in table 7.1), a princess whose Ijebu mother had brought great
wealth to Lagos through her connections with upcountry traders. Erelú
Kuti was the sister of Akinsemoyin, and she, too, helped him establish
a strong foothold in Lagos by agreeing to marry a famous Ifá divination
priest who was an alien client in some way attached to the household
of the Aromire family and who appeared to have great influence at that
time. The marriage gave Akinsemoyin another ally within the kingdom
itself, and this appeared to have been a critical addition to the coalition
he was building. The word *critical* should be stressed because Erelú Kuti
acquired extraordinary power for agreeing to the marriage in that, after
Akinsemoyin's death, succession to the throne shifted to her own child
from the Ifá priest and away from her brother Akinsemoyin's offspring.
In this way Erelú Kuti's son, Ologun Kutere (24 in table 7.1), became
the next *ọba,* and to this day the Ologun Kutere branch of the ruling

family—a family with strong Ijebu ancestral ties, and one that facilitated regional trade relationships—has occupied the Lagos throne.[36]

Erelú Kuti and her mother, Olugbani (23 in table 7.1), were sufficiently influential to have established an Ijebu-dominated quarter in the old city where annual rituals are still performed at shrines maintained in their honor.[37] The Ojuewa shrine (16 in table 7.1) dedicated to mothers of Lagos' ọbas is of Ijebu origin, and it is the place where the processing chiefs and the ọba himself acknowledge these women's contributions to the city's development.

The second transformation involved the introduction of an Oshugbo Secret Society into Lagos. This move was designed to rebalance the structure of authority by placing checks on the power of the ọba. The Oshugbo society was long known in the kingdom of Ijebu as a society where nobles, elders, and influential members of a community met in secret to debate and critique policy, censure rulers who defied public conventions, and mobilize and solidify collective action in economic undertakings. The strength of the society lay in its ability to unify the influential members of a community and draw them into close relationships among themselves. By achieving solidarity in their decisions and subsequent actions they were not dependent on the ruler, but instead made the ruler dependent on their good will if he wished to remain in power.[38]

Oshugbo appears to have been established in Lagos by a group of immigrant residents from the area and town of Ikorodu, located directly across the lagoon and slightly northeast of Lagos. Ikorodu was a key location in that its residents could facilitate or disrupt a significant amount of north-south trade between Lagos and other Ijebu towns and between Lagos and many communities attached to Ọyọ. The sponsors of Oshugbo had established residences on Lagos Island to facilitate trade and fishing opportunities and to house large numbers of temporary visitors from Ijebu communities. Subsequently Chief Eletu Ijebu (13 in table 7.1), believed to have been from Ikorodu, was appointed caretaker of the Oshugbo society and *eletu* of Ijebu migrants.[39] The Erelú Oshugbo, whose title was not related to that of the Erelú Kuti, joined the chiefs at Enu Owa Square in 1983, two centuries after Oshugbo was established, and in so doing symbolized the Ijebu role in establishing an institution that would provide the chiefs with a powerful, alternative way of having a say in governing the community.

Regional Ties

Each place of origin recognized in the Lagos ceremony represented a link in an extensive network of relationships that had been established throughout the region. As indicated, trade was a major element in the local economy, and business connections extended to every corner of the area. Early in its history, Lagos was known as a source of cloth, and later it continued to supply large quantities of handwoven cloth, slaves, ivory, and eventually palm oil products to European traders. Many of these products were obtained in the hinterland. Local economic strength rested on fish, locally produced salt, oil, and raffia palm products such as baskets and mats, all of which could be traded upcountry in return for products unavailable and in demand in coastal regions or by Europeans. Numerous chieftaincies were established or linked to upcountry settlements as a way of enhancing these trade opportunities (Cole 1975: 25–26; Losi 1967: 13; Law 1983).

Marital alliances also were pervasive. Obas and chiefs exchanged daughters in order to establish in-law relationships that obliged one another to provide assistance in commercial and military endeavors or to provide refuge during times of civil strife. Genealogies were peppered with names of women from outside communities who married into Lagos families. From the male point of view, propitious marriages provided an entry into an outside community where one could seek advice, protection, or economic help. From the female point of view, marital alliances presented numerous opportunities, not the least of which were chances to broker communications between two communities. Marrying-out provided a woman with the ability to trade or act as a trade agent between several communities, and Olugbani, mentioned above, a maternal ancestor of the current Lagos ruling descent group, was one of the most successful of these women in Lagos history (Barnes 1997: 13–15). Olugbani was involved in trade between her Ijebu homeland and commercial interests in Lagos in the mid-eighteenth century through two relatives whom she accepted as brothers and hosted on their trading trips. One was in contact with Ọ̀yọ́ and provided a trading link between that powerful kingdom and Lagos. The other brought goods, especially cloth, from Ijebu settlements to be sold to European merchants. No outsider, as Olugbani demonstrated, could reside in a community unless he or she were sponsored in business dealings by a chief or notable person in a royal or chiefly family.[40]

Protection was central to regional alliances. Between 1816 and 1853 alone there were eight civil wars and coups d'état in the Kingdom of Lagos resulting in the exile of six rulers or claimants to the throne (Barnes 1997: 5). Five took refuge in the homelands of the wives of their fathers—usually their mothers—or other maternal kin such as spouses or in-laws. The homelands of these women included Badagry, Apa, and Whydah in the west; Ijebu and Epe in the east; and Abeokuta to the north. In some cases, they or their relatives helped Lagos leaders arrange counterattacks, as was the case with Akinsemoyin and the ancestor of Chief Egbe (14 in table 7.1). The reverse also took place, with refugees arriving in Lagos seeking and receiving the help of in-laws or trade partners, as with the Onisemo (9 in table 7.1). Needless to say, these ties had long-term effects, with political alliances being used to arrange other marriages or trade relationships and vice versa. Those who brokered external relationships were able to build a large clientele, which gave them the kind of leverage and notoriety throughout the region that could be turned into considerable advantage in building power bases, some of which were sufficient to warrant chiefly office (Barnes 1990: 252–54).

Ritual Knowledge and Practice

The role of ritual was central to the process of creating, establishing, and perpetuating a historical persona in Old Lagos. It was not by chance that the Eletu Odibo and Olorogun Adodo paid homage to leading figures by recalling their relationship to sacred elements–rituals, shrines, or particular deities. It was customary, as mentioned, to take deities and shrines to a new community when one moved. Slaves brought them to Lagos and established them within the family compounds where they served; some of these ritual sites still function and are identified with their founders. A good husband was expected to give wives who came from another settlement a special place to establish their deity's shrines and slaves to help propitiate them.[41] Part of an individual's identity rested on having a relationship to a specific supernatural figure or a ritual group surrounding one or a group of deities, and it was incumbent on parents to socialize children into their ritual groups because knowing the correct observances was the way people proved they were rightful members of a family or home community (Barnes 1990: 255–59).

Chief Onisemo (9 in table 7.1), for example, stressed his allegiance to Orona, a deified heroic founding figure from his hometown, Ilaro.

His family maintained a Lagos shrine for Orona, called Oromina, to which people from Ilaro were welcomed.[42] It was not a coincidence that this chief also was an official in a large market near his palace where Ilaro people came to trade. Chief Onisemo had earlier in this century re-established connections to Ilaro after contact was lost for several generations. He sent three delegations to his ancestral homeland to discuss his intentions; then he returned and established his credentials by reciting his knowledge of Oromina and its first priest, Edu. Thereafter Chief Onisemo returned to Ilaro to celebrate the Oromina festival each year, and interaction between the two places became more vigorous.[43]

Ritual knowledge served as a kind of symbolic capital, valuable because it was a form of accumulation that could be converted to other uses (Bourdieu 1977: 179). Mastering it had multiple benefits beyond obvious economic and political advantages. Ritual knowledge enhanced an individual's status and established authority. A person who controlled a shrine or deity had a monopoly over knowing how to appease or activate a particular supernatural power and controlled a way to bring ideological and psychic support to bear on people's most pressing concerns. Only the owner of a deity or shrine had the requisite knowledge to lead others in invoking the mystical properties that needed to be appeased or released, and thus only he or she could be perceived as its appropriate authority. Ritual authorities—alien or indigenous—were among Lagos society's acknowledged leaders, the priestly *ogalade* class of chiefs being just one example.

For that matter, to be a chief, any chief, was to be a ritual authority. The two could not be separated since *ashe,* the notion of power itself, and the practices of all authority figures were simultaneously sacred and secular. No line could be drawn between them. To reach an acceptable judicial decision was as dependent on a proper divination or sacrifice as it was on mastery of customary legal principles. Control of ritual knowledge and practice, as much as mastery of pragmatic leadership skills, was integrated into a leader's expected persona, which meant these realms of human expression and experience were central to achieving success in civic life and participating in public affairs.

Conclusion

There was a continuous flow of people in the coastal region between Allada (and even as far as the Volta River) and the Kingdom of Benin in the precolonial era from the sixteenth through the nineteenth centuries. No one was immune from the possibility of moving from one community to another and learning new languages, traditions, and social conventions. Communities were linguistically and culturally diverse, contrary to accounts that often characterized localities of this region and time period as relatively monocultural and static. There were close ties among settlements; they were interdependent and linked together through a vast network of trade, military, and social alliances. Membership in a community was not exclusive to one place; rather, it could be exercised in several places.

In the heterogeneous region between Allada and Benin before the imposition of colonial rule, knowledge was exchanged and transported from one place to another. Ritual knowledge provided an idiom through which individuals established their place in the world. Ritual allegiances served as individual identity markers—unique for each person and based on the circumstances of his or her origins. Simultaneously ritual knowledge constituted belonging in the sense that the supernatural practices and ideas expressed through ritual bound people together who shared common origins and similar perceptions of existential phenomena.[44] This separated one group of people from another. At the same time, however, it was every group's goal to incorporate symbolic elements of their own ritual corpus into the civic ceremonial cycles of the communities in which they lived. By so doing, they signaled that they belonged to the wider society, and that they were part of—indeed members of—a functioning community. Yet their incorporation into the Lagos community did not deprive them of another kind of identity—the identity linked to their origins.

Rituals of installation were the activity, par excellence, that brought all parts of the old Lagos settlement together and distinguished it as a collectivity of diverse peoples. The incantations associated with the *ikanse* represented the Lagos nation, as the Eletu Odibo described it. Each landmark and each ancestral figure that was acknowledged by the participants in the installation procession could be identified by a separate homeland and by ritual practices that had been incorporated from an outside place. Together these were the parts that defined the whole. There could be no nation without these parts.

Taking account of this diversity and its significance in the past has broad implications. In a region where movement was deeply ingrained in the social fabric of the times, ritual beliefs and practices were essential to the arrangements that fostered opportunities for protection and economic survival. Esoteric knowledge was a mark of identification. It oriented people so that when they moved they remained connected to their most basic beliefs and sources of assistance. Ritual knowledge and ritual practices were critical elements in the precolonial history of the West African coastal region described here, and it was through ritual, the ritual of a chief's installation, that these critical aspects of Lagos tradition were preserved and represented.

Notes

1. The man who was installed as the Olorogun Adodo was Teslim Idowu Olorunlolewe Junid-Eko. Chief Ishola Bajulaiye Jiyabi II, the Eletu Odibo of Lagos, asked me to attend this event and to record and take notes on it. He briefed me before and after it was held in 1983 (IX: 120–26; IX: 135–41; X: 65–79) and again in 1984 (I: 6–11, 20–23). In addition, I made a tape recording of his description of this and other installation ceremonies (Misc: DD).

Earlier descriptions of installation customs provided by Lagos leaders and chiefs were recorded by Ward-Price (1933) and as part of the "Yoruba Historical Scheme (Western Region)" (1957). Notes from the latter were taken by Chief Ajani Olujare, research associate, who was accompanied by Dr. Peter Morton-Williams, anthropologist. The notes (mimeo) were given to me courtesy of Chief Olujare.

Much of the information from the 1983 installation ceremony is taken from texts of interviews that I conducted in 1983, 1984, and 1986. The texts of these interviews can be found in my research notebooks according to the date they were conducted and the following code: Roman numerals refer to a Notebook; Arabic numerals refer to page numbers in that Notebook. Thus (II: 11–12) is Notebook number II, pages 11 and 12. Transcriptions of tape recordings and unpublished texts are in my "Miscellaneous" file, coded according to a letter system, e.g. Misc: A through: Z, and Misc AA through ZZ.

2. The Eletu Odibo is known as the prime minister of Lagos; he is charged with installing the *ọba* (king) and all administrative chiefs.

3. Research for this article was conducted in 1983, 1984, and 1986–87 with the support of a Basic Research Grant from the National Endowment for the Humanities, a Fulbright Research Fellowship, a grant from the American Philosophical Society, and the Institute of African Studies, University of Ibadan, where I was a research associate. All of this support is deeply appreciated. I also wish to thank Steven Feierman for his insightful critique of an earlier draft of this essay.

4. For the centrality of Lagos in this water system, see Webb (1958) and Hill and Webb (1958: 319–22).

5. Interviews with Madam Asimowu Gogo Ajikobi, Alhaja Nimota Ajala, and Madam Simbiatu Akinbiyi, 27/6/86 (Misc: A). These market women quoted songs that acclaimed the wealth of historic fishermen and women fish traders of Lagos. The interviews were conducted and recorded by my research assistant, Prince Oladimeji Ajikobi, grandson of Madam Ajikobi.

6. The contemporary roles and benefits of chiefship are examined more fully in Barnes (1996: 19–40).

7. All sources of information pertaining to individuals or shrines mentioned in the text and listed numerically in Table 1 are provided in note 12.

8. The Erinkina shrine housed numerous smaller shrines.

9. The *akoko* was itself a shrine under the control of the Eletu Odibo chieftaincy family.

10. Interview on tape, Eletu Odibo, 25/6/84 (Misc. DD).

11. Chieftaincy families (also known as houses) were local descent groups and other members that formed whole quarters or compounds of the old city. A titled chief was the properly installed head of each chieftaincy family. Virtually all members of the Lagos community, in precolonial times, were connected in some way to a chieftaincy or royal family. Family members were expected to give loyalty to the head of their family and keep peace in the community. In return, members had rights to protection, adjudication, occupational choice, use of land or fishing rights, and shelter.

12. Sources of information pertaining to individuals or shrines recognized during the installation ceremony and important ancestors mentioned in the text are as follows:

1. Eletu Iwashe. Interviews Chief Badmus Olayimika Agoro, Eletu Iwashe of Lagos, 3/7/84 (I: 44–45) and Eletu Odibo (V: 26–28).

2. Eletu Odibo. Interviews 26/5/86 (V: 26–28) and 22/6/84 (I: 14); Eletu Odibo of Lagos, Chieftaincy Declaration, Ministry of Local Government and Chieftaincy Affairs, Lagos State (II: 69–73); "The History of Olobun Shrine Ritual Tree," manuscript prepared by Eletu Odibo, 1983 (Misc: B). Folami 1982: 108–10.

3. Onilegbale/Oju Olokun Iworo. Interviews Prince Tajudeen Oluyole Olusi, 22/5/86 (V: 12), Olawole Jeboda, Abore Olokun (Priest of the Olokun shrine), 14/7/84 (III: 19–24), 4/7/86 (VII: 65–68), Eleta Odibo, 26/5/86 (V: 28), and Onilegbale, 8/7/86 (VII: 81). The Olokun shrine was controlled by Chief Onilegbale, a member of the royal family and descendant of Erelú Kuti (22) who bore two sons, one of whom, Ologun Kutere, became *ọba,* and the other, Shokun, was given the Onilegbale title to compensate for not becoming *ọba.* The Abore Olokun

was responsible to the Onilegbale for maintaining the shrine. Iworo is a family shrine.

4. Ajagbili. Lagos City Council Chieftaincy Committee Hearings, 23/3/86, Files of the Lagos State Ministry of Local Government and Chieftaincy Affairs (VII: 2). Interview Abore Olokun 12/7/86 (VIII: 7) and interview on tape, Eletu Odibo, 25/6/84 (Misc. DD).

5. Obanikoro. Interview Eletu Odibo 19/7/83 (IX: 120–21); Ward-Price (1933: 44, 52–54).

6. Ashogbon. Interviews Eletu Odibo 19/7/83 (IX: 121), 26/5/86 (V: 26), Prince Olusi 22/5/86 (V: 17), and Chief Egbe 7/7/84 (I: 59–60).

7. Oniru. Interview at Oniru Chieftaincy Family Meeting of 12 elders, 3/4/86 (IV: 74-75). Interviews Prince Olusi 22/5/86 (V: 11), Eletu Odibo 26/5/86 (V: 28–32), Abore Olokun 18/6/86 (VI: 23), and Chief Lateef Adekunle Alli, Otun Maiyegun, and Baba Oja of Lagos (honorary titles), 4/6/86 (V: 82).

8. Olumegbon. Interviews Chief L. Y. Kalefo II, Olumegbon of Lagos, 22/4/86 (IV: 102- 3) and 26/4/86 (IV: 112–13).

9. Onisemo. Interviews Chief Tawaliu Adisa, Onisemo of Lagos, 8/7/84 (I: 63–65) and Chief E. O. Olatunji, Ilaro, 21/5/86 (V: 5–10).

10. Modile. Interviews Chief Adam A. R. Lawal Odu II, Modile of Lagos, 22/3/86 (IV: 18–21) and 26/3/86 (IV: 46–49); Unpublished Text (Misc: J).

11 Oluwa. Interview Chief Sulaiman B. A. Oluwa, Isikalu II, Oluwa of Lagos, 26/6/84 (I: 24–32).

12. Onisiwo. Interview Chief Yinusa Ayeni, Onisiwo of Lagos, and Alhaji A. B. L. Onisiwo 2/6/86 (V: 63–67); Unpublished Text (Misc: I).

13. Eletu Ijebu. Interviews Chief Abudu Wahabi Akinola Matimoju, Eletu Ijebu of Lagos, 23/4/86 (IV: 104–5), 28/4/86 (IV: 115–18), and 5/5/86 (IV: 136–37); Unpublished Text (Misc: K).

14. Egbe. Interview Chief Egbe, 7/7/84 (I: 57–62).

15. Faji. Interviews Chief Alhaja Ayoka Shasore, Faji of Lagos, 8/2/84 (I: 65–67), 9/7/84 (I: 75–76), and 25/3/86 (IV: 35–40). The Ìrókò tree—a shrine sacred to the Faji Chieftaincy family—was located in Faji Market.

16. Onimole. Interviews Eletu Odibo 12/7/84 (III: 5) and 5/3/83 (IX: 17); Minutes of the Lagos City Council Chieftaincy Committee, 18/11/1975 and 2/3/1976 (VII: 1–2).

17. Opeluwa. Interviews Chief Opeluwa 7/5/86 (IV: 144–47), 26/6/86 (VI: 104–8), and Chief Egbe 29/4/86 (IV: 120).

18. Qba. Interview Abore Olokun 9/7/86 (VII: 83–89).

19. Olorogun Adodo. Interview Chief Olorogun Adodo, 8/7/84 (I: 73–74) and Unpublished Manuscript (Misc: I). There is some evidence that the

founding ancestor of the Olorogun Adodo chieftaincy family moved step-wise from Benin to Arogbo, near Warri, and then Lagos.

20. Akinsemoyin. Interviews Chief Egbe 7/7/84 (I: 57–62) and 29/4/86 (IV: 119–23), Interview Prince Olusi 22/5/86, Law 1983: 343–48, Lagos 1978a, 1978b.

21. Aromire. Aderibigbe 1975: 1–8, and Interview Prince Abdul Lasisi Ajayi Ojora 14/6/86 (V: 115). The Aromire Ìrókò tree was maintained as a refuge and dedicated to preserving peace in the town. It stood in Enu Owa Square but was cut down. The tree, or the site where the tree once stood, was sometimes saluted during installation ceremonies.

22. Erelú Kuti. A brief unpublished history of Olugbani and Erelú Kuti was written by Chief Aziz B. Akinlagun, Onilegbale of Lagos (Misc: Onilegbale Papers A). Interviews Chief Onilegbale 14/3/86 (IV: 8–9) and 9/4/86 (IV: 84), Chief Comfort O. Maja, Erelú Kuti of Lagos, 24/3/86 (IV: 27–28), Prince Ojora 5/7/86 (VII: 76–77), and Eletu Odibo 22/6/84 (I: 12–13). See also Folami 1982: 115–16.

23. Olugbani. See Erelú Kuti sources above.

24. Ologun Kutere. Folami 1982: 22–23; Losi 1967 (1914): 14–16, and Interview Prince Olusi 22/5/86 (V: 11–15).

13. Seniority was calculated according to the date on which a chief performed the *iwúyè*, a second and more expensive installation ritual than the capping ceremony (which is the ceremony discussed in this essay). The *iwúyè* was not as ritually elaborate as capping, but it required more elaborate entertainment and clothing. A chief usually waited for months or a year after the first capping to collect enough money to perform the *iwúyè*.

The first installation, known as the capping ceremony, or *ijoye,* was rarely referred to by this latter Yorùbá name. It was the capping ceremony that contained a secret ritual during which an ordinary man was transformed from commoner to chief. This rebirth was symbolized by a distinctive white cap worn only by Lagos chiefs. Once capped, all chiefs were considered to be legitimate titleholders.

14. Interviews Chief Salawu Adisa Disu Egbe Okonu III, Egbe of Lagos, 29/4/86 (IV: 124–25) and Prince Olusi 27/5/86 (V: 32–41).

15. Although they were hereditary titleholders, war chiefs did not wear white caps. They were capped with felt hats (fez-shaped) that were then covered with black top hats at the *iwúyè*. The two kinds of headwear—white caps and top hats—symbolized different kinds of power among chiefs. White cap chiefs derived or wielded power from being administrators, priests, or landowners. Their interests were often independent of those of the ruler. Warrior chiefs derived power from their ability and mandate to protect and defend the *oba,* and thus their interests were dependent on and coincided with those of the ruler.

16. Interviews Abore Olokun 21/6/86 (VI: 58–59) and Chief Egbe 24/3/86 (IV: 33–34).

17. Interview Eletu Odibo 4/8/83 (X: 72–74).

18. *Eletu* was defined as an "owner, director, commander; someone who controlled; someone who was higher in status than leader." Interview Eletu Odibo, 21/6/84 (I: 7).

19. The Eletu Ijebu (13) did not originate in Benin, but because he was considered an administrator of Ijebu peoples, he was given a Bini title. Several warrior chiefs whose origins were traced to Benin did not have the administrative designation *eletu* in their titles; however, their ancestral association with Benin meant they were assigned to the administrative class of chiefs, known as *akarigbere*.

20. *Ose* + *iga* = regular meeting [at the] palace. Although we know Lagos administrators met regularly from the earliest days of Benin's overlordship, we do not know when the name *osega* actually came into use.

21. Robertson 1819: 289–90. Interviews Prince Olusi 27/5/86 (V: 39–41), 28/6/86 (VII: 15–17) and Chief Onilegbale 3/3/86 (IV: 71).

22. Ado = Edo. Edo is a term given to the language and people of Benin (also known as Bini).

23. See Cole (1975: 24–26) for a discussion of the relationships among Lagos chiefs and surrounding villages.

24. Lagos chiefs were formally assigned to four categories during the colonial period as a way of distinguishing how their ancestors came to power and therefore how the government should treat them. The four classes were: *akarigbere,* administrators; *idejo,* landowners; *ogalade,* priests; and *abagbon,* warriors.

25. Aderibigbe 1975: 9; Interviews Prince Olusi 28/6/86 (VII: 15–21) and Chief Onilegbale 3/3/86 (IV: 71).

26. Interview Prince Olusi 22/5/86 (V: 11–12); Law 1983: 343–48.

27. Aderibigbe 1975: 11; Payne 1894: 1–2; Lagos State 1975, 1978a, 1978b; Interview Chief Egbe 7/7/84 (I: 57–62).

28. Interview Prince Olusi 4/4/86 (IV: 80)

29. Interviews Chief Adam A. R. Lawal Odu II, Modile of Lagos, 22/3/86 (IV: 18–21) and 26/3/86 (IV: 46–49); Unpublished Text (Misc: J).

30. Lagos State 1978b: 19/9/1978.

31. Awori and Egba were Yorùbá-speaking subgroups.

32. Interview Chief Egbe 29/4/86 (IV: 119–23); Typescript by Prince Olusi (Olusi Papers #A);

33. I wish to thank Chief Onisiwo and the elders of the Onisiwo Chieftaincy family for taking me by boat to interview headmen and visit Onisiwo family villages located on the banks of creeks west of Lagos. They included Tarkwa, Tomaro, Ebute Oko, Abagbo, Agala I, Agala II, and Sagbo Koju (VI: 88–95).

34. Interview at Oniru Chieftaincy Family Meeting of 12 elders, 3/4/86 (IV: 74–75). Interviews Prince Olusi 22/5/86 (V: 11), Eletu Odibo 26/5/86 (V: 28–32), Abore Olokun 18/6/86 (VI: 23), and Chief Alli, Otun Maiyegun of Lagos (honorary title) 4/6/86 (V: 82).

35. Interview Abore Olokun 9/7/86 (VII: 91).

36. Interviews Prince Olusi 22/6/86 (VI: 67) and Prince Ojora 5/7/86 (VII: 77).

37. A Kekeku Festival was held on 20 April 1987 to pay homage to Princess Erelú Kuti at the Oju Egun shrine in her former palace, Iga Kadan. See note 5 (22 in table 7.1).

38. Interviews Eletu Ijebu 28/4/86 (IV: 124–25), Chief Egbe 29/4/86 (IV: 124–25), Chiefs Alli and A. O. Shonubi 8/5/86 (VI: 155), and Prince Olusi 27/5/86 (V: 34–35).

39. Interview Eletu Ijebu 28/4/86 (IV: 116–17).

40. Osanyin 1982: 413. Interviews Prince Ojora 5/7/86 (VII: 76), Chief Onilegbale 14/3/86 (IV: 8–9), Chief Lasisi Akinyemi, Bajulu of Lagos, 7/5/86 (IV: 150–51), and Chief Onilegbale 14/3/86 (IV: 10).

41. Interview Chief Onilegbale 8/7/86 (VII: 82) and Church Missionary Society (Birmingham University) CA2/087, 1854, Rev. White. I thank J. D. Y. Peel for drawing my attention to this document. See also Barber (1981: 732) for a contemporary account of wives bringing new deities into family compounds in a Yorùbá town.

42. The Oromina shrine was situated in what is known today as Pedro Village.

43. Interviews Chief Tawaliu Adisa, Onisemo of Lagos, 8/7/84 (I: 63–65) and Chief E. O. Olatunji, Ilaro, 21/5/86 (V: 5–10).

44. As Prince Olusi put it, "Most worshipers, as soon as they got to Lagos . . . tried to get to co-religionists," 13/7/86 (VIII: 17). See also Interviews Prince Ojora 5/6/86 (V: 89–90) and 5/7/86 (VII: 75).

References

Aderibigbe, A. B. 1975. "Early History of Lagos to about 1850." In *Lagos: The Development of an African City,* ed. A. B. Aderibigbe, 1–26. Nigeria: Longman.

Agiri, B. A., and Sandra T. Barnes. 1987. "Lagos before 1603." In *History of the Peoples of Lagos State,* ed. A. Adefuye, B. Agiri and J. Osuntokun, 18–32. Lagos: Lantern Books.

Barber, Karin. 1981. "How Man Makes God in West Africa: Yoruba Attitudes towards the Orisa." *Africa* 51, no. 3: 724–44.

Barnes, Sandra T. 1990. "Ritual, Power, and Outside Knowledge." *Journal of Religion in Africa* 20, no. 3: 248–68.

————. 1996. "Political Ritual and the Public Sphere in Contemporary West Africa." In *The Politics of Cultural Performance,* ed. D. Parkin, L. Caplan, and H. Fisher, 19–40. Oxford: Berghahn Books.

————. 1997. "Gender and the Politics of Support and Protection in Pre-Colonial West Africa." In *Queens, Queen Mothers, Priestesses, and Power: Case Studies in African Gender,* ed. Flora E. Kaplan, 1–18. New York: New York Academy of Sciences.

Bourdieu, Pierre. 1977 (1972). *Outline of a Theory of Practice.* Cambridge: Cambridge University Press.

Cole, Patrick. 1975. *Modern and Traditional Elites in the Politics of Lagos.* Cambridge: Cambridge University Press.

Dapper, Olfert. 1960 (1688). "Benin at the Height of Power." In *Nigerian Perspectives: An Historical Anthology,* ed. T. Hodgkin, 122–30. London: Oxford University Press. French ed., *Description de l'Afrique,* 308–13, Amsterdam, 1686. Dutch ed., 1668.

Egharevba, Jacob. 1960 (1934). *A Short History of Benin.* Ibadan: Ibadan University Press.

Folami, Takiu. 1982. *A History of Lagos, Nigeria: The Shaping of an African City.* Smithtown, N.Y.: Exposition Press.

Hill, M. B., and J. E. Webb. 1958. "The Ecology of Lagos Lagoon. II: The Topography and Physical Features of Lagos Harbour and Lagos Lagoon." *Philosophical Transactions of the Royal Society of London,* series B, vol. 241, 319–33.

Jones, Adam, trans. 1983. "Andreas Joshua Ulsheimer's Voyage of 1603–1604." In *German Sources for West African History, 1599–1669,* 18–43. Wiesbaden: Franz Steiner Verlag.

Lagos State. 1975. "Inquiry into the Obaship of Lagos Conducted by the Standing Tribunal of Inquiry into the Declarations Regulating the Selection of Obas and Recognised Chiefs in Lagos State." Council Chambers, City Hall.

————. 1978a. "Inquiry into the Akinsemoyin Ruling House as Affecting the Ọba of Lagos Chieftaincy Title . . ." Council Chambers, City Hall (courtesy of Chief Egbe).

————. 1978b. "Report of the Inquiry into the Obaship of Lagos Conducted by the Standing Tribunal of Inquiry into the Declaration Regulating Selection of Obas and Recognised Chiefs in Lagos State on the Akinsemoyin Ruling House." Council Chambers, City Hall (courtesy of Prince Olusi).

Law, Robin. 1983. "Trade and the Politics behind the Slave Coast: The Lagoon Traffic and the Rise of Lagos, 1500–1800." *Journal of African History* 24: 321–38.

Losi, John B. 1967 (1914). *History of Lagos*. Lagos: African Education Press.

Nigeria, Government of. 1948. "Report on Fisheries Investigations." Lagos: Government Printer.

Osanyin, Bode. 1982. "A Cross-road of History, Legend and Myth: The Case of the Origin of Adamuorisa." In *The Masquerade in Nigerian History and Culture,* ed. Nwanna Mzewunwa, 410–59. Proceedings of a Workshop Sponsored by the School of Humanities, University of Port Harcourt, Nigeria, Sept. 7–14, 1980. Port Harcourt : Printed by the University of Port Harcourt Press for the University of Port Harcourt Publications Committee.

Payne, John Augustus Otunba. 1894. *Payne's Lagos and West African Almanack and Diary for 1894.* London: J. S. Phillips.

Robertson, G. A. 1819. *Notes on Africa.* London: Sherwood, Neely, and Jones.

Ryder, A. F. C. 1969. *Benin and the Europeans, 1485–1897.* New York: Humanities Press.

Talbot, P. Amaury. 1926. *The Peoples of Southern Nigeria.* Vol. 1: *Historical Notes.* London: Oxford University Press.

Ward-Price, H. L. 1933. *The House of Docemo: Full Proceedings of an Inquiry into the Method of Selection of a Head to the House of Docemo.* Comp. Isaac B. Thomas. Lagos: Tika-Tore Press.

———. 1939. *Land Tenure in the Yoruba Provinces.* Lagos: Government Printer.

Webb, J. E. 1958. "The Ecology of Lagos Lagoon. I: The Lagoons of the Guinea Coast." *Philosophical Transactions of the Royal Society of London,* series B., vol. 241, 307–18.

8

The Pathways of Ọ̀ṣun as Cultural Synergy

DIEDRE L. BADEJO

The corpus of Yorùbá mythology is a complex metonymic system that serves as a method for the preservation and retrieval of Yorùbá cultural history, ideology, and epistemology (Yai 1994). Embedded in this system through a tapestry of interweaving narratives are clues to a collective cultural self-image and objective individual codes and ideals. Part of the cultural self-image, as Professor Olábiyi Yai points out, forms a generative cultural synergy that is transmitted regionally, globally, and artistically. Implicit in its embedded mythical systems and synergy are keys to Yorùbá ethos and its "dialogic" cultural change. Yorùbá mythical narratives frame the sociocultural notions of continuity and synergy that both preserve social adaptability and cultural fluidity. In short, essential to Yorùbá thought is its "dialogical" view of perpetuity and mutability. The architecture of Yorùbá, cultural resilience seems to withstand social disintegration while embracing infinite change. Similarly, Abiodun affirms the complex prism of meaning in Yorùbá thought as he explores the aesthetics and meaning of Orí as ritualistic art (Abiodun 1987). I argue that the complex ways of knowing Ọ̀ṣun through the metonymic system of her orature, rituals, iconography, and fine and performing arts indicate a cultural architecture that rests upon a foundation of longevity, suppleness, and synergy. Ultimately, this essay speaks to Ọ̀ṣun's paths as knowledge keeper and propagator, mother and warrior, wife and confidante, healer and protector, divine and woman being.

Knowing the Pathways of Ọ̀ṣun

According to Ifá oracular texts, Ọ̀ṣun is the only female deity present at the creation of the world, *ayé* (Badejo 1986). In Osetura, a major chapter of *Odù*-Ifá and occasional cognomen for Èṣù-Elegbara, Olódù-marè confers the leadership of the *àjẹ́* as well as the authority to give or withhold children on Ọ̀ṣun. As leader of the *àjẹ́* and giver of children, Ọ̀ṣun preserves human life and watches over the covenants of the *àjẹ́*, or powerful beings. An *àjẹ́* herself, she is the one among the four hundred and one òrìṣà in the Yorùbá pantheon. Occasionally referred to as the seventeenth òrìṣà, Ọ̀ṣun is also the one who stands between the two hundred òrìṣà on the left (*osi*) and the two hundred òrìṣà on the right (*otun*) (Abiodun 1989). With her perfectly carved beaded comb, Ọ̀ṣun Sèègèsí Òlòyá-íyùn, she parts the pathways that lead from the world of the unborn (*òrun*) to the world of the living (*ayé*). According to some of her songs, she is also *eégun*, an ancestor to those who answer her call and to those who seek her. She is seer and confidante, knowledgeable in the vagaries of life itself, a defender of humanity who witnesses the power of both constructive and destructive forces in the poly-dimensional world of the Yorùbá. In her manifestations, she is both divine and human, and as such, she shares in the pleasures and pain of both forms of being. Ọ̀ṣun is healer, diviner, and warrior whose transmutability of form and substance canonize a "dialogical" view in Yorùbá thought. Her evanescence serves as a key to understanding Ọ̀ṣun as a metonym of living energy (*àṣẹ*) and cultural synergy (*àjẹ́*) in the long history of humanity, deity, and the universality of change. She is Yéyé, the Good Mother, the universal womb, mysterious and awesome in its potentiality. Ọ̀ṣun presides over her world, *ayé*, and her children, *ọmọde*, both good and bad.

Orature of Ọ̀ṣun

As part of the Yorùbá oracular corpus, Ọ̀ṣun's oral literature shares its beauty and linguistic complexity with a cornucopia of Yorùbá verbal/visual and artistic performance traditions. Ọ̀ṣun's images represent a centralizing woman-presence positioned at the vortex of creation as well as life itself. Her *oríkì*, Ọ̀ṣun Sèègèsí Òlòyá-íyùn, is a critical motif that idealizes her primary position among the principal òrìṣà in the pantheon. It alludes to her as owner of the womb wherein the secret pathways and knowledge of human life resides. That secret life, I would suggest, mirrors the *awò* that exists in conjunction with her power as an *àjẹ́,* an awesome combination that serves as a metonym for her guardianship over the birth and destiny of human beings. As Yéyé, the Good Mother, she protects the life she gives, often employing her powers as *àjẹ́* to do so. Her physical presence is envisioned as a "robust woman" whose very body speaks to sensuality, quintessential motherhood, and prowess.

Often praised, Ọ̀ṣun's sensuality finds expression in several Odù Ifá and *oríkì* Ọ̀ṣun in Yorùbá orature. References to her passion for oils, bathing, clothes, and beautification along with references to brass, swords, calabashes, and agbo pots lead those familiar with Yorùbá cultural and aesthetic acumen to evoke images and meaning of Ọ̀ṣun in diverse environments. The Odù Ifá refers to her as the one who carves the pathways of human destiny with her perfectly carved beaded comb, a complex symbol of her feminine prowess, her patronage of the arts, her desire for perfection, and her sense of beauty. As a river, she is the one whose body handles the soft beauty of grass and the hard edginess of stone with equal ease and grace (Abiodun 1989). Even in elusive passages where she remains unnamed, interconnecting images and narratives make her presence known. She is identified with the numbers five (*aárùún*), sixteen (*meríndinlogun*), and seventeen (*metadinlogun*) and with parrot feathers, birds, cowries, cool waters, and honey.

Wande Abímbólá's (1975) article "Ìwàpèlè: The Concept of Good Character in Ifá Literary Corpus" and Rowland Abiodun's (1975) article "Ifá Art Objects: An Interpretation Based on Oral Traditions" illustrate how Ọ̀ṣun's presence is intuited in the Odù Ifá referenced in both articles. Although it is not the intention of either author to discuss Ọ̀ṣun, her presence in the subtext of the articles emphasizes confluences of Yorùbá culture. Abímbólá's article espouses the "concept of good character," Ìwàpèlè, an essential feature of the living human being. We learn that Ìwà was the beloved wife of Ọ̀rúnmìlà, the òrìṣà of wisdom and knowledge, who stands next to Olódùmarè as witness to creation (Eleri Ipin). In a different *odù,* Ìwà's place among the wives of Ọ̀rúnmìlà varies from first to third in an unspecified position. Although she is always associated with good character, like many òrìṣà, Ìwà has her frailties.

Several *odù* Ifá state that Ọ̀rúnmìlà is advised to take good care of her so that he will always prosper. He does so for some time, but then he slacks off. Consequently, Ìwà leaves Ọ̀rúnmìlà because he neglects, abuses, curses her, and breaks her taboos. In all cases, his life becomes miserable without Ìwà, and Ọ̀rúnmìlà must seek the counsel of other *babaláwo,* perform sacrifice, and begin a journey to locate her and bring her home. He completes all of these tasks, except the last, with varying degrees of success. We are told that she returns to her father's house, often Olódù-marè, after she has visited several kingdoms through which Ọ̀rúnmìlà must now travel. Consistent in each *Odù* Ifá is the narrative that Ìwà refuses to return home with Ọ̀rúnmìlà. Abimbola cites a minor odù, *ogbè alárá,* as the source for this *"pa ìtan"* as does Eleburuibon (1994) in his work, *Apetebii: The Wife of Orunmila.* Ìdòwú (1962) cites Ogbè Ègúndá from which he draws the following proverb: *"Eni l'ori rere ti kò n' íwà l'o màá b'ori rè jé*—However happy a person's destiny may be, if he has no character, it is (lack of) character that will ruin his destiny."

With such an emphasis on character, *ìwà,* one must ask what is an underlying discourse on character and destiny as represented by the òrìṣà Ìwà and Ọ̀ṣun? What can we glean from their interaction with other wives of Ọ̀rúnmìlà such as Odù? How do we interpret the essence of Ọ̀ṣun, as òrìṣà, *eniyan,* and *eégun?* What is the context for discerning the pathways of Ọ̀ṣun, as co-wife of Ìwà and Odù, and are those pathways mutually exclusive, transmutable, or, like one's *orí,* part of a greater whole? In short, what does Ọ̀ṣun represent, what do her pathways sig-nify, and what does her ability to part the pathways of humanity mean?

I would argue that her cosmogenic signature is the active principle by which human beings get on with the business of living. By that I mean that Ọ̀ṣun along with the other òrìṣà propose a spectrum of divine within rather than the divine unreachable and outside of the self. As one of her cognomens suggests, Ọ̀ṣun is Ìyálóde, mother of the outsides that is the marketplace of the world. Known for her business acumen, Ọ̀ṣun is an active principle of human engagement and exchange with *ayé,* the world. These attributes suggest that the relationship between Ìwà (char-acter) and Ọ̀ṣun (pathway to destiny) seals a core ideological premise in Yorùbá thought; that character determines the outcome of one's destiny as revealed through Odù, another wife of Ọ̀rúnmìlà. This triumvirate of Ọ̀rúnmìlà's wives underscores one of Ọ̀ṣun's major pathways as the guardian mother who knows the secret challenge contained in each indi-vidual (*orí*) human being that is born. Indeed, if Ọ̀rúnmìlà is the father of secrets, then Ọ̀ṣun is the mother of those secrets; hence her charge to set new human beings aright on their individual path at birth.

How intriguing, especially when we consider that in some Odù Ifá, Ọ̀rúnmìlà and Ọ̀ṣun parent Osetura, a major *Odù* Ifá and cognate for Èṣù-Elegbara, the guardian of the crossroads, keeper of the *àṣẹ* (life force) and inspector of each *ẹbọ* (sacrifice). Abiodun recounts the birth of Osetura in his article on "Women in Yorùbá Religious Images." Here, we find an esoteric confirmation of Ọ̀ṣun's place in Yorùbá creation and of her role as mother and the keeper of the *àṣẹ*. In this *odù*, we are informed that all *odù* derive from Ọ̀ṣun.

Woman in Yorùbá Religious Images

It was divined for the sixteen Odù
Who were coming from heaven to earth
A woman was the seventeenth of them.
When they got to earth,
They cleared the grove for Opa,
Opa was there.
They prepared a grove for Eegun,
They made a home for Eegun.
But they did not do anything for Ọ̀ṣun.
Nicknamed "Sèègèsí, the owner of the beaded comb."
So, she decided to wait and see
How they would carry out their mission successfully;
So, Ọ̀ṣun sat and watched.
Beginning with Eji-Ogbè and Oyeku meji,
Iwori meji, Odi meji, Irosun Meji
Owonrin meji, Òbàrà meji, Okanran meji,
Ògúnda, Osa, Orangun meji and so on,
They all decided not to countenance Ọ̀ṣun in their mission,
She, too, kept mute,
And carried on her rightful duty,
Which is hair plaiting.
She had a comb.
They never knew she was a witch
When they were coming from heaven.
God chose all good things.
He also chose their keeper,
And this was woman;

All women are witches.
And because all other Odù left Ọ̀ṣun out,
Nothing they did was straight.
They went to Eegun's grove and said,
"Eegun, let things be straight,
It is you who straightens the four corners of the world,
Let all be straight."
They went to Adagba Ojomu
Which is called Òró,
"You are the only one who frightens Death and Sickness.
Please help drive them away."
Healing failed to take place;
Instead, sickness deteriorated.
They went to Ose and begged him
To let the rain fall.
Rain did not fall.
Then they went to Ọ̀ṣun
Ọ̀ṣun received them warmly,
And entertained them.
But shame would not let them confide in Ọ̀ṣun,
Whom they had ignored.
They then headed for heaven
And made straight for Olódùmarè,
Who asked why they came?
They said it was about their mission on earth.
When they left heaven,
And arrived on earth,
All things went well;
Then later, things turned for the worse,
Nothing was successful.
And Olódùmarè asked,
"How many of you are there?"
They answered, "Sixteen."
He also asked,
"When you were leaving heaven, how many were you?"
They answered, "Seventeen."
And Olódùmarè said, "You are all intriguers.
That one you left behind,
If you do not bring her here,
Your problem will not be solved.
If you continue this way,
You will always fail."

They then went to Òṣun,
The woman with the beaded comb.
And said, "We have been to the Creator and He said,
After admitting that they never knew that all Odù derived from Òṣun.
That our suffering would continue
If we failed to recognize and obey Òṣun."
When they got to the earth,
All the remaining Odù wanted to pacify and please Òṣun,
But Òṣun would not go out with them,
Unless the baby she was expecting
Would go out with them.
Òṣun, however, indicated that if the baby she was expecting,
Turned out to be male,
This male child
Would go out with them.
But if the baby turned out to be female,
She (Òṣun) would have nothing to do with them.
She said she knew of all they (Odù) have eaten and enjoyed;
Particularly all the heads of dog and he-goat they ate.
As Òṣun was about to curse them all, Ose covered her mouth.
The remaining Odù started praying
That Òṣun might deliver a male child.
They then started begging her.
When Òṣun delivered,
She had a baby boy
Whom they named Ose-Tura.

Abiodun 1975

Several spiritual pathways of Òṣun appear in this Odù Ifá, some of which find correspondence as well as contradiction within the physical realm. Although the Odù ignore her at first, Òṣun is accorded a place among the divine objects of communication in the sacred grove, *òró* (word), *òpá* (staff), and *eégun* (ancestor spirit). Yet the Odù disregard her to their peril. Òṣun continues her business of hair plaiting silently and even entertains them without their confidence. When none of their plans work, the Odù consult Olódùmarè, who warns them to include Òṣun in their deliberations. She refuses to join them but promises to send her son, Osetura (Èṣù-Elegbara), to do so. At the moment when she would have cursed (*òfò*) them all, Òse, the fifth Odù in the *Meríndinlogun* divination system, covers her mouth. Consequently, when Òse appears in the *Meríndinlogun* casting, it is Òṣun who is speaking, thus triangulating her presence with the number five. Clearly, she is the source and means of communication between *òrun* and *ayé*. The *ese* Ifá mnemonically recalls that Osetura speaks for Èṣù-Elegbara, narrating his genealogy and signature as Ose speaks for Ọṣun. It suggests that Èṣù's guardianship of the crossroads is tied to Ose's heroic act of covering Ọṣun's mouth before she curses her peers and adversaries. Although the offence is committed against her, the Odù are spared her wrath by Èṣù's birth. Named partly in honor of Ose, Èṣù measures the *ẹbọ* signifying restitution to Ọṣun for their insult and disregard. Where they deny Ọṣun nourishment, the birth of her son redresses the injustice. Is this Odù, Osetura, suggesting that it is the progeny who care for the mothers as Èṣù cares for Ọṣun?

Although Ọṣun is Aje and owner of the beaded comb, she demonstrates patience, an indication of her character (Iwa-pele), as she observes their arrogance and lack of character. Similarly, she presides over the covenant of both malevolent and benevolent forces that are constantly stirring the pot of human affairs. In silence, she watches activities of both humanity and divinity alike, waiting like a Good Mother, to assist them when they so desire by appealing to her properly. Unquestionably, Ọṣun's maternal pathway is a dominant characteristic reflected variously in her roles as warrior, lover, friend, and confidante (Badejo 1996). Consider the following refrain from another more extensive *Odù* Ifá.

> Yemese o pa 'ni loni!
> O pa 'gun ra!
> Ọṣun Apara pa 'gun ra loni!
> O pa 'gun ra!
> Ọṣun Apara pa 'gun ra loni o!
> O pa 'gun ra!
>
> [Yemese killed for total destruction today!
> She waged a war for destruction;
> Ọṣun Apara waged war for destruction today!
> She waged a war for destruction;
> Ọṣun Apara waged war for destruction today!
> She waged a war for destruction.]
>
> Eleburiubon 1989

During several interviews, Yemi Eleburuibon, a Babaláwo and Ògún devotee, recited several Odù Ifá including this one where Ọṣun manifests as male energy taking on a warrior modality. In some of these manifestations, she presents as female and in others as male. In both cases, her bellicosity emerges in defense of a town and its people. In a

Yorùbá worldview where gender is associative, roles become transmutable irrespective of biological design. In the Odù Ifá Ereti Alao, Ọ̀ṣun is captured with other members of Osogbo Township and led away from their home. The frightened townspeople abuse her because she refuses to raise her sword against their enemies. She continues to tell the captives that they must be patient until the right time; however, they continue to abuse her and to grumble and complain. Nonetheless, she waits patiently until they reach a particular place before she reaches inside of herself and unsheathes a sword to cut down their captors. She advises the astonished townspeople that when she falls down to become a river, that they must follow the flow of her river if they are to return to their original township. This act of "falling down" to become a river path signals her leadership of Osogbo Township, and the call to its people to emulate her path as warrior and transmutable being. It is also a call to become a devotee, to follow her spiritual path as conserver of human life and culture. The seeming contradiction between being warrior and devotee dissolves in Ọ̀ṣun's cool waters of amelioration and healing.

In contrast to this warrior image, Ọ̀ṣun is also peacemaker. She entices Ògún, the òrìṣà of war and iron, to re-engage with the community of beings, just as she playfully captures the town of women who revolt against the men (Bascom 1980). Here, her honey-sweet words and sensuality persuade the errant òrìṣà and womenfolk to re-engage themselves in the marketplace of life; for the forges and the bellows will not work without Ògún's fiery essence, and life cannot continue without the regenerative powers of women. These *pa ìtàn,* or narratives, illustrate that one of Ọ̀ṣun's functions in Yorùbá thought is to mediate dialogical discourse. Her cosmogenic metonym, ultimately, stresses balance, orchestrates the vagaries of life, and places sacrifice at the crossroads of restitution, cleansing, and healing. Images of *ẹyẹlé* (birds) on Osanyin's staff or the Opa Oba or the Adé Oba signify the key spiritual position that Ọ̀ṣun holds while alluding to her own prowess as healer, ruler, and *àjẹ́*. Ọ̀ṣun's pathways simultaneously encompass the generative kinesis of worldly existence and the potency of human and divine synergy.

The Synergy of Yorùbá

As the owner of the universal womb, Ọ̀ṣun is the metaphor and dialectic of Yorùbá thought. Her dynamic energies activate the principles of human and divine existence in swirling ebb and flow among multiple layers of being. She mediates constructive and destructive impulses with patience, ease, and grace. She is an ultimate female with the potential to unleash devastating male energies of destruction. Òṣun is metaphorically the epitome of secrecy and the source of knowledge. In her most profound essence, she completes the cycle of life as both ancestor and mother, acknowledging the interrelatedness of birth and death. With respect to the Irunmole, they derive the art of divination from her in the form of the *Meríndinlogun* through which she also consults and speaks. Her synergy embraces the artfulness of life and the dynamic art of engagement embraces the energy of life itself.

In several *oríkì,* Òṣun's synergistic images signify the fusion of diverse energies that encompass her persona. An excerpt from Ijo Òrúnmìlà summarizes Yorùbá perspectives about women—as well as about knowledge, secrecy, and power (Ijo Orunmila n.d.).

> Òṣun, oyeye ni mo . . .
> O wa yanrin wayanrin kowo si . . .
> Obinrin gbona, okunrin nsa . . .
> Òṣun abura-olu . . .
>
> Ogbadagbada loyan . . .
> Oye ni mo, eni ide kii su . . .
> Gbadamugoadamu obinrin ko se gbamu . . .
> Ore Yéyé o . . .
> Onikii, amo-awo maro . . .
> Yéyé Onikii, obálódò . . .
> Otutu nitee . . .
> Iya ti ko leegun, ti ko leje . . .
>
> [Òṣun, who is full of understanding,
> Who digs sand and buries money there.
> Woman who seizes the road and causes men to flee,
> Òṣun, River that the king cannot exhaust . . .
>
> One who does things without being questioned,
> One who has large, full-bodied breasts,
> One with fresh palm leaves, who never tires of wearing brass.
> Enormous, powerful woman who cannot be subdued.
> Most gracious Mother,
> Onikii, who knows the secret of cults but never discloses.
> Gracious mother, Queen of the Mighty River,
> One who has a cool, fresh throne,
> Mother, who has neither bone nor blood . . .]

Like the Ifá corpus and the *Meríndinlogun* system themselves, Ọ̀ṣun's synergy resides at the crossroads, vibrating intensely with a unity of opposites found in her *oríkì* and her Odù. This dialogical thought underlies notions of mutability and transmutability of Yorùbá thought from its ancient past to its diverse present and its global future. This Yorùbá dialogical worldview speaks its authority and generative identity pulsating from its African source throughout a complex global manifestation. Because of its metonymic vigor, Ọ̀ṣun's pathways are well traveled by those who engage her nuanced deeds, words, iconography, and taboos. Once inside the flow of her river, Ọ̀ṣun's cool synergistic vision sweetly and wisely guides a multitude of pathways for human beings to choose to follow.

References

Abímbólá, Wande. 1975. "Ìwàpèlè: The Concept of Good Character in Ifá Literary Corpus." In *Yorùbá Oral Tradition,* ed. Wande Abímbólá, 389–420. Ilé-Ifè, Nigeria: Department of African Languages and Literatures.

Abiodun, Rowland. 1975. "Ifá Art Objects: An Interpretation Based on Oral Traditions." In *Yorùbá Oral Tradition,* ed. Wande Abímbólá, 421–69. Ilé-Ifè, Nigeria: Department of African Languages and Literatures.

———. 1987. "Verbal and Visual Metaphors: Mythical Allusions in Yorùbá Ritualistic Art of Ori." *Word and Image: A Journal of Verbal/Visual Inquiry* 3, no. 3: 252–70.

———. 1989. "Women in Yorùbá Religious Images." *African Languages and Cultures* 2, no. 1: 1–18.

Badejo, Diedre. 1996. *Ọ̀ṣun Sèègèsí: The Elegant Deity of Wealth, Power, and Femininity.* Trenton, N.J., and Asmara: Africa World Press, 1996.

Bascom, William. 1980. *Sixteen Cowries: Yorùbá Divination from Africa to the New World.* Bloomington: Indiana University Press.

Eleburuibon, Ifayemi. 1994. *Apetebii: The Wife of Ọ̀rúnmìlà.* Brooklyn, NY: Athelia Henrietta Press.

Ijo Ọ̀rúnmìlà. "Ara Ifa: Ijo Orunmila." http://ayodele_falade.tripod.com. Accessed June 30, 2006.

Yai, Babalola Olabiyi. 1994. "In Praise of Metonymy: The Concepts of 'Tradition' and 'Creativity' in the Transmission of Yorùbá Artistry over Time and Space." In *The Yorùbá Artist: New Theoretical Perspectives on African Arts,* ed. Rowland Abiodun, Henry Drewal, and John Pemberton III, 107–17. Washington, DC: Smithsonian Institution Press.

9

Religious Encounter in Southwestern Nigeria

The Domestication of Islam among the Yorùbá

H. O. DANMOLÉ

During the past three centuries, the indigenous religion of the Yorùbá has encountered two other world religions—namely, Islam and Christianity. These encounters have led to religious change among the Yorùbá as the two acquired religions have become dominant religions. However, despite their dominance, traditional Yorùbá religion has shown resilience as it continues to express itself in the practice of Islam and Christianity in Yorùbáland. This resilience persists because Yorùbá religion is embedded in the daily life of the Yorùbá people (Idowu 1962: 5). The encounter of Yorùbá religion with Islam and Christianity has produced religious diffusion because believers tend to take in or synthesize the values of one religion with another (Fadipe 1970: 317). This synthesis of values explains the domestication of these two extrinsic religions by the Yorùbá.

This chapter examines the encounter of Yorùbá religion and Islam. It posits that the early history of religion in Yorùbáland paved the way for the accommodation of Yorùbá politico-religious values in the practice of Islam by Yorùbá Muslims. I contend that the participation of Yorùbá Muslims in traditional festivals originating in traditional Yorùbá religion contributes to the domestication of Islam. However, this participation cannot be regarded as violating the tenets of Islam because traditional festivals have become symbols of unity rather than religious worship for various Yorùbá communities. In exploring the theme of Islam's domestication among the Yorùbá, the chapter proffers that the use of kola nut (*cola acuminata*) in wedding ceremonies among Yorùbá Muslims originated from the importance the traditional Yorùbá society attaches to the nut. Furthermore, the exploitation of Yorùbá storytelling techniques in Yorùbá Islamic songs is argued as a veritable example of incorporating Yorùbá values into the propagation of Islam. The chapter highlights continued controversy generated by Yorùbá Muslims who domesticated Islam.

Early Encounters: Islam and Yorùbá Religion

Studies on Islam among the Yorùbá of southwestern Nigeria have not yet been able to determine the date of entry of the religion into the area. Nevertheless, there is sufficient evidence to believe that the religion spread to Yorùbáland in the closing years of the eighteenth century. Adopting a new religion in an environment in which the entire populace practiced Yorùbá religion meant that the early converts were few, and they had to practice Islam in secret. Those who practiced Islam in its early days in Yorùbáland were reportedly foreign to the area. However, by the middle of the nineteenth century, the religion had spread to the nooks and crannies of the area (Gbadamosi 1978: 4–5).

The spread of Islam in Yorùbáland has attracted adequate attention from scholars, and thus no repetition is necessary here. Nevertheless, it is important for our study to examine briefly the development of Islam in the area with a view to comprehending the interaction between Islam and Yorùbá religion. Islam spread to the Yorùbá through the northern frontiers because of extensive trading contacts with Hausa Muslim traders and itinerant Islamic preachers from Hausaland, in what today is northern Nigeria. Some of these traders and Islamic preachers stayed behind in Yorùbáland with the sole aim of converting the Yorùbá to Islam. Apart from that, Islam took root in the coastal areas of Yorùbáland such as Lagos, Epe, and Badagry, as well as through trade connections with the other parts of West Africa. Reportedly, before the end of the eighteenth century, Yorùbá Muslims had become harbingers of the religion to other areas beyond the borders of modern southwestern Nigeria (Parrinder 1967: 33).

Perhaps the most important element in the development of Islam among the Yorùbá in the nineteenth century was the success of the Sokoto jihad in the second decade of the century. This jihad led to the founding of a caliphate covering a large area of Hausaland and extending to Ilorin on the northern Yorùbá border. One can reliably assert that from this period onward, the development of Islam among the Yorùbá was in the hands of Ilorin Muslims, who as traders and preachers, visited and became permanent residents in many Yorùbá towns (Danmolé 1982: 25–26). The fact that most of them spoke Yorùbá as their mother tongue helped in their bid to gain converts. Indeed, by the end of the first half of the nineteenth century, Islam was a force with which the Yorùbá had to reckon.

The progress of Islam in this area can be measured in terms of the attitude of both practitioners of Yorùbá religion and Muslim preachers toward the religion. To attract more converts, the situation may have called for Islamic preachers to condone some practices that were unacceptable in Islam. In Ibadan in 1855, a Muslim preacher was reported to have said that Muslims should accommodate some form of Yorùbá religious rites in their practice of Islam because Muslims were not strong numerically (Ajayi 1965: 20). Thus, the way and manner of the spread of Islam in the area where local customs were adapted to Islam contributed not only toward increasing the population of Muslims but also toward domesticating Islam among the Yorùbá.

During the second half of the nineteenth century, Islam had become so great a social and political force that it could no longer go unnoticed by Ifá diviners. It must be emphasized that Ifá was, and still is, an essential element of Yorùbá religion. To guide them in resolving very important issues today, adherents of Yorùbá religion continue to consult Ifá, whether the occasion is the birth of new baby or the selection of a traditional ruler (Abimbola 1976: 10). Nevertheless, rather than show hostility towards Islam because of its competition with Yorùbá religion, it would appear that Ifá diviners adapted their Ifá corpus to suit the new religion. The adaptation of Islam into the Ifá corpus is perhaps consistent with the suggestion of Walter E. A. van Beek and Thomas D. Blakely (1994: 16) that African religions often adopt extrinsic influences and essential elements into their religious systems.

As Gbadamosi (1978: 68–69) has shown, Ifá diviners predicted that many Yorùbá people would be born as Muslims, including leading personalities such as Prince Momodu Lamuye, who later became the Oluwo of Iwo in the 1860s. So also were the rulers of Ede and Ikirun. Indeed, the development of Islam particularly in these parts of Yorùbáland can partly be explained in terms of predestined Muslims. Certainly, the traditional rulers who were predestined Muslims promoted the cause of Islam in their domains. Their being Muslims attracted a large number of the traditional elite and their followers to Islam. Apart from those who converted from Yorùbá religion to Islam, there were those members of the traditional elite in places like Lagos and Ijebu-Ode who had earlier accepted Christianity but who later became Muslims because the religion had become fashionable with the chiefly class in the society.

The example of Ọba Momodu Lamuye in Iwo in the 1860s throws a great light on how Yorùbá traditional rulers whose duties included the protection of Yorùbá religion and culture accommodated Islamic practices within their palaces. As the Ọba, Lamuye had many religious rites to perform particularly during the *egúngún* and other festivals that were not acceptable in Islam. However, it is reported that a compromise was struck whereby he would stick to his religion while at the same time he rendered necessary assistance to other palace officials in the performance of their Yorùbá religious rites (Gbadamosi 1977: 91). Although this arrangement was perhaps workable during his reign, it does not appear that this tight division of labor because of Islam endured for a long time. This is because there are many *ọbas* and palace officials in present-day Yorùbáland who profess Islam but still participate in what would be regarded as forbidden in traditional Islam. Indeed, many Yorùbá religious rites are performed today more as symbolic gestures rather than strict religious belief because of the dominance of Islam and Christianity among the Yorùbá. This, however, is not to say that some adherents of Yorùbá religion see these rites as symbolic.

Islam among the Yorùbá during the twentieth century has been developing *parri passu* with increasing domestication of the religion. Because of this early history described above, Muslims may have adapted politico-religious titles of the Yorùbá in their various organizational structures in Yorùbáland. Notwithstanding the title Parakoyi, which was used very early for leaders of Muslim communities among the Yorùbá, various Muslim communities coined titles such as Balogun Adini (commander of religion) and Basorun Adini (protector of religion) to suit their particular environment. This is what Laitin (1986: 41) identifies as a push toward the "Yorùbácization" of Islam. Modern Muslim organizations that were founded to propagate Islam in various parts of Yorùbáland joined in honoring their members with these titles. Indeed, it is now common to honor rich Yorùbá Muslims who have contributed to the promotion of Islam in Yorùbáland with such honorific titles.[1]

Muslims in Yorùbáland attach great importance to these titles because of the honor and respect that such titles confer on the holders in the society. Yet, attempts by many rich Muslims to obtain such honorific titles often led to intrigues among Yorùbá Muslims. For instance, the crises of the Lagos Muslim community between 1915 and 1947 were fuelled partly by contestants for these positions. Besides, in a place like Lagos where Muslims have been active in local politics as far back as the middle of the nineteenth century, these politico-religious titles have been transformed into town-wide titles, recognized and conferred by the Ọba of Lagos. Titles such as Balogun Adini and Basorun Adini were created in the second half of the nineteenth century and have become Balogun and Basorun of Lagos, respectively (Danmolé 1987: 291). These titles have been held so far by members of the Lagos Muslim community.

Local and Global: Accommodation and Appropriation by Islam and Yorùbá Religion

There are many Muslim societies in the world, but Islam as a universal religion is one (Ahmed 1988: 58). This perhaps explains why some Muslim societies are influenced by certain cultural or religious ceremonies that had been grounded in some communities before the advent of Islam. Among the Yorùbá, the ọba was at the apex of Yorùbá traditional administration before the imposition of colonial rule. He was regarded as a divine ruler whose duty was to protect the religion and customs of his people. In modern times, the role of the ọba is no more than that of the custodian of Yorùbá religion and culture. Apparently, because of the traditional role of the Yorùbá ọba in the society, his selection and installation involve a variety of Yorùbá religious ceremonies that vary from one Yorùbá community to the other.

Yet, many ọba in Yorùbáland today profess Islam. However, in spite of their being Muslim, they were actively involved in the elaborate Yorùbá religious rites during the process of their installation as ọba of their respective towns. Their involvement in these religious rites according to the doctrines of Islam is *shirk* (associating other deities with God) and may not be accepted in another Muslim community—for example, among Hausa Muslims. This can easily be explained. First, Islam reached the Hausa much earlier than Yorùbá. It permeated Hausa society before the jihad of the nineteenth century in Hausaland. Second, this jihad renewed the status of Islam to the extent that is now not easy to differentiate between Hausa culture and Islamic values in the area.[2]

However, to the *ọba* and many Muslim communities in Yorùbáland, these religious rites are meant to fulfill their cultural responsibilities. As far as they are concerned, Yorùbá religious rites cannot be equated with worshipping another God.[3] Rather, they are only following the traditions of their ancestors. In addition, it is generally believed that if an *ọba* does not perform these religious rites before ascending the throne, because he is a Muslim or a Christian, his reign may be marked by several natural disasters. Moreover, the installation ceremony of a Yorùbá Muslim *ọba* is usually completed with special services in mosques devoted to praying for peace and prosperity during the reign of the *ọba*.

Traditional Festivals

Related to the installation of Yorùbá Muslim *ọba* are their roles in traditional festivals. There is hardly any Yorùbá community without one or more traditional festivals. These festivals have their origins in Yorùbá religion and, as rightly observed by Ogunba (1991: 51), they partly serve to re-enact the establishment of various Yorùbá communities. These festivals have within them the observance of Yorùbá religious rites, such as propitiation to the gods or visits to shrines. Some of the festivals are Oke'badan in Ibadan, Mọremi in Offa, and Ọ̀ṣun in Osogbo, to mention just a few. It is now common to find many Yorùbá, including Muslims, heading for their towns whenever these festivals are to begin. The festivals have increasingly become a source of ethnic identity for various Yorùbá groups. Because of the new role that these festivals perform, Yorùbá Muslims do participate actively in their organization and celebration. Muslim participation in these festivals introduces some element of domestication to the practice of Islam by Yorùbá Muslims, although conservative Muslims among the Yorùbá often raise eyebrows against the participation of Muslims in these festivals.

Several reasons can be proffered for the participation of Muslims in festivals whose aspects seem inconsistent with the teachings of Islam. First, Muslims who participate perceive these festivals as cultural festivals that must not be allowed to go extinct because of religion. Second, many Muslims use the festivals as opportunity to discuss other political and social issues affecting their community. Third, the social and political positions of many Yorùbá Muslims in Yorùbá society often dictate their functions in these festivals. Two examples are sufficient to illustrate this point. The Òṣun festival is an annual event in Osogbo. The chief priest and custodian of the festival is the Ataoja of Osogbo, Ọba Iyiola Oyewale Matanmi, who is regarded as an ardent Muslim. He had performed the holy pilgrimage to Mecca (Ogungbile 1998: 131). In the opinion of Ọba Matanmi, despite the elaborate Yorùbá religious rites, the festival was not for the worship of Òṣun per se, but to celebrate the "birthday of Osogbo-Oroki Asala" and re-enact the practices of their forebears. However, he admitted that several of Òṣun's devotees attended.[4]

Similar to Òṣun Osogbo, the chief guest during the Mọremi Festival in Offa is the Oloffa of Offa, Ọba Mustafa Olawore Ariwajoye, who is a Muslim. The festival consists of several religious rites and a visit to the Mọremi shrine in the town. Olupona (1991: 32) has rightly noted that some traditional festivals are often meant to honor ancestors of some Yorùbá communities. The Mọremi Festival in Offa falls into this category because it is meant to remember the role of the legendary Mọremi in the foundation of the town. Consequently, its celebration goes beyond religious affiliations. Oral evidence from Offa indicates that Muslims always join them in the celebration of this festival because it is also perceived as a unifying force for the people of Offa.[5] The participation of an ọba in traditional festivals is a significant gesture among the Yorùbá because his authority is based on traditions and not on his being a Muslim or a Christian. Therefore, he must identify with the traditional aspirations of his people. Apart from that, these festivals offer the ọba the opportunity to renew constantly the primordial allegiance between him and his people.

Just as Yorùbá festivals became a source of ethnic identity for several Yorùbá groups, the celebration of the Islamic festival of Eid-al-Kabir (the great feast), or Odun Ileya, has become a source of convergence for Yorùbá communities with large Muslim populations. The festival is celebrated with pomp and pageantry in towns such as Iwo, Epe, and Ijebu-Ode. Eid-al-Kabir is the most important feast in the Islamic calendar and the climax of the pilgrimage at Mecca (Glassé 1989: 178). For Muslims who do not perform the pilgrimage, those who could afford to do so donate to the poor and mark the feast with a congregational prayer and the slaughter of rams. In Nigeria, the federal government usually declares two public holidays to celebrate this festival.[6]

Among the Yorùbá of Ijebu Ode, a third day is added called Ojude Ọba (a special day for the Ọba). A ceremony takes place every year on this day when Muslims and non-Muslims go to the Awujale's palace, singing and dancing with the principal chiefs of the town and riding on horses to pay homage to the Awujale, no matter his religious affiliation. What is important is that he sits on the throne throughout the length of the ceremony to receive his people. According to Abdul (1967: 85), different age groups of Muslims and non-Muslims in specially tailored dresses dance around the town. Recent evidence collected from Ijebu-Ode suggests that the ceremony must have derived from Muslim chiefs and their followers in the town, who during the earlier part of this century used the opportunity provided by the festival to demonstrate their continued loyalty to the Awujale. However, with increasing modernization and the provision of public holidays for Muslim festivals, many people from Ijebu-Ode who work and trade in other towns such as Lagos, Abeokuta, and Ibadan come home to take part in the celebration.[7] Consequently, over the years the festival has acquired new meaning. It has ceased to be a purely Muslim affair as it now embraces features of local traditions.

In Islam, the office of the imam is an important one. The imam leads prayers and is expected to be well versed in the Qur'an and Islamic jurisprudence. An imam must possess other qualities as well, but our attention here is to the appropriation by Yorùbá Muslims of the Yorùbá traditional system of hereditary succession to political and religious offices to select or elect the chief imam of their mosques.[8] The traditional Islamic way of electing or appointing an imam is to choose the most learned person from the congregation, but this is not the common practice among the Yorùbá. Succession to the office of the imam, most especially chief imams of central mosques in Yorùbáland, is hereditary and confined to certain families. In Epe, the selection of iman is rotated among different quarters of the town. In Ọ̀yọ́, the office of the chief imam is rotated between the Ajokidero and Ogunbado families.[9] In Lagos, only the Nolla and Ibrahim families have so far produced chief imams for the central mosque.[10]

The appointment of imam is a telling example of domestication of Islam among the Yorùbá. The explanation for this development can be traced to the development of Islam in each Yorùbá town. Generally, there was no properly laid-down procedure, and as soon as a Muslim community was formed, a person considered to be learned or one of the preachers was appointed imam. After his death, he was always succeeded by his deputy, and in turn, the son of the first imam would become deputy of the new imam. Imams were chosen from the families of previous imams because they were considered to be the most learned in various Yorùbá communities. It then became an established convention and has now turned into a tradition among Yorùbá Muslims. Because of increasing enlightenment among Yorùbá Muslims about their religion, the practice of selecting imams from certain families began to generate controversy and division among Muslims in the last few decades, yet, the practice is adhered to.

The office of the chief imam has become a position that is sanctioned by the congregation alone and also by the traditional ruler of each town irrespective of his religious affiliation. Indeed, a newly appointed imam must pay homage to the traditional ruler as a sign of respect to the traditional political head of the town. However, some Muslim traditional rulers did try to exercise some influence in the appointment of imams (Gbadamosi 1972: 236). In Òyó Town, the appointment of a new chief imam after the demise of the incumbent reportedly was delayed by the Aláàfin Oba Lamidi Adeyemi because members of the Ajokidero family, who should produce the next chief imam, very vocally opposed the Aláàfin during the crisis between members of Oro cult and Muslims in the town. However, the appointment of imams by hereditary succession is not practiced by modern Muslim organizations such as the Ansar-Uddeen Society of Nigeria, Anwar-Ul-Islam Society of Nigeria, and many other Muslim societies.

Cultural adaptability is a recurring feature of Islam's encounter with Yorùbá religion. Almost every aspect of the social life of Yorùbá Muslims is affected by Yorùbá culture and traditions. Just as celibacy is forbidden in Yorùbá traditional society, it has no place in Islam.[11] Therefore, to both religions, marriage is an important milestone in the life of every person. Consequently, there are established processes involved in marriage ceremonies in the two religions. But one important aspect of the ceremony that merits our attention here is the use of kola nut (*cola acuminata*) in this ceremony among Yorùbá Muslims. The kola nut in the Yorùbá cosmos symbolizes, among other things, love, a bond of unity, strong covenant, communality, and acceptability. It is used in supplication, as a refreshment, and in entertaining guests. In essence, the kola nut plays a vital role in Yorùbá cultural life.

The cultural import of the kola nut among the Yorùbá would seem to have been adapted to marriage among Yorùbá Muslims. During a wedding ceremony, the Yorùbá Muslim family of the groom gives kola nuts, one of the essential items, to the parents and relatives of the bride as a gesture of love. This gift is not compulsory in Islam, but a Yorùbá Muslim marriage would not be complete if kola nuts were omitted in the voluntary gifts from the family of the groom to the bride. This symbolic gesture deserves some comment. Although such a gift is not un-Islamic, in areas where kola nuts are uncommon, Muslims rarely indulge in this practice. Despite the indigenous nature of the kola nut to Yorùbáland,[12] its use by Yorùbá Muslims appears to have been popularized by itinerant Muslim traders who were in the forefront of the spread of Islam among the Yorùbá in the nineteenth century (Agiri 1972: 49–55). Moreover, the use of kola nuts by Yorùbá Muslims demonstrates the resilient nature of Yorùbá cultural traditions. Furthermore, the use of kola nuts in Islamic ceremonies among the Yorùbá is not confined to marriage alone; for example, there is the breaking and distribution of kola nuts at Muslim naming ceremonies. Although traditional Yorùbá society uses kola nuts in such ceremonies for prayers, they are only served as refreshments among Muslims after naming the child.

Apart from using kola nuts as refreshments during the naming ceremony of a Muslim child, the encounter of Islam with Yorùbá religion is reflected in the names given to children. Essentially, the naming ceremony of a Yorùbá Muslim is Islamic in that other aspects of the Yorùbá traditional naming ceremony are not practiced by Yorùbá Muslims. However, the names given to the child are concrete elements of domestication of Islam among the Yorùbá. This is because Yorùbá Muslims have not abandoned all Yorùbá values that are important in naming their children, including the socioeconomic conditions of the parents of the child at the time of birth and the circumstances surrounding the birth of the child. Thus, a Yorùbá Muslim gives his child a combination of Islamic and Yorùbá names.[13] It is common to add one name as *oríkì* of the child.[14] However, as Oseni (1981: 26) has shown, the giving of names depicting family occupations and religious cults has waned among Yorùbá Muslims.

In addition to the influence of weddings and naming ceremonies, it is not out of place to touch on an aspect of burial among Yorùbá Muslims, which seems to derive from Yorùbá culture. The grave of the departed among the Yorùbá is a place to which attention is always turned for prayer and blessing in times of tribulation. To that extent, the grave is a sacred place among the Yorùbá. The Yorùbá dig their graves within the household of the departed, possibly the living room or bedroom. However, among Yorùbá Muslims, particularly in towns that have no cemeteries, the dead relative is usually buried in front of family houses. But among Yorùbá Muslims of Ilorin, dead relatives are buried at the back of the house.

Far more frequently, Yorùbá Muslims now decorate their graves with fanciful Islamic symbols, like slate (*wala*) used by Muslim children studying the Qur'an in local Qur'anic schools (*ile kewu*). They decorate their graves with Islamic writings, especially quotations from the Qur'an. At the Muslim cemetery in Lagos, it is now fashionable for prosperous Muslims to display their wealth by decorating the graves of their departed ones. Decoration of graves is not entirely forbidden in Islam. However, the decoration of graves among Yorùbá Muslims perhaps goes beyond mere Islamic inscriptions. Doi (1971: 14) reported that a Muslim grave in Oru, near Ijebu-Ode, displayed the statue of the dead Muslim in praying posture. The human figure, of course, is unacceptable in Islam. Indeed, the decoration of graves is uncommon among Muslims in other parts of Nigeria.

It is perhaps necessary to draw attention in our study of domestication of Islam among the Yorùbá to songs and music of Yorùbá Muslims. It is instructive to note that there is a difference of opinion among Muslim scholars regarding the appropriateness of songs and music in Islam (al-Faruqi and al-Qaradawi 1994: 1). However, one can safely say that most Muslim scholars encourage songs that give praise to God. Islamic songs and music have been a driving force in the spread of Islam among the Yorùbá since the nineteenth century. Through a synthesis or adaptation of some musical instruments, reportedly from Arab musical culture, such as *goje* with Yorùbá traditional music, new musical genres have been produced among Yorùbá Muslims (Euba 1971: 179).

These genres include *were, waqa,* and *seli.* This category of music is rendered during religious occasions. Until recently, during the month of Ramadan in the early hours of the morning in many Yorùbá towns, men rendered *were* songs to awaken Muslims so that they could prepare for their fast (Euba 1971: 177). Women's religious groups sing *seli,* especially during wedding ceremonies, and both men and women sing *waqa* in many Islamic gatherings. Other Yorùbá musical genres contain heavy doses of Islamic influence and can now be regarded as popular Yorùbá music (Omibiyi-Obidike 1979: 51). They are *sakara, apala,* and, recently, *fuji.*

A more recent development among Yorùbá Muslims is the emergence of professional musicians who specialize in *waqa* songs. *Waqa* songs have been receiving wide publicity for some time now as response to the conversion of young Muslim boys and girls to Christianity through modern gospel music. Indeed, with a view to making *waqa* songs appeal to large numbers of people, Muslims and non-Muslims alike, *waqa* songs are provided with music that has instrumental accompaniments featuring musical instruments generally associated with popular music, including guitar, keyboard, and percussion.

What is perhaps more important with regard to domestication of Islam in this musical genre is the use of Yorùbá storytelling techniques, such as those derived from the musical dramatic genre of *àló. Àló* is an aspect of Yorùbá folklore, similar to such tales anywhere in the world, that helps to educate the society, most especially the younger generation (Bascom 1965: 293). For example, the popular Yorùbá folktale narrative of Ayegbajeje is incorporated into a *waqa* song admonishing the affluent and popular members of the society to adopt a sensible lifestyle, which is the hallmark of wisdom.[15] The *waqa* ends with another Yorùbá wise saying: "Excessive expression of joy fractures the limbs of the frog." There are many of such stories and sayings in different *waqa* songs. Thus, these essentially Islamic songs sometimes exploit Yorùbá values to preach Islamic religious messages. Apart from that, under the guise of Islamic religious songs, *waqa* musicians may broadcast their commentary on current political and economic issues in Nigeria.

Reactions to Domestication

Many controversies and conflicts between Muslims and adherents of Yorùbá religion occurred during the second half of the 1900s. The most heinous was the Apalara episode of 1953. The causes of these conflicts range from continued competition for adherents to lack of sensitivity to each other's religion. However, our main concern is with the controversies traceable to adaptation by Yorùbá Muslims of certain aspects of Yorùbá traditional religion and values. Without doubt, these adaptations by Muslims have remained a veritable source of conflict among Yorùbá Muslims today. This is not to contend that without these cultural adaptations stemming from the encounter of Yorùbá religion with Islam, Islam among the Yorùbá would have been free from intrigue and tension, which are part of every human organization. The historical development of Islam among the Yorùbá contributed to the manner of the practice of the religion by Yorùbá Muslims.

Attention has been drawn to the use of Yorùbá politico-religious titles by Yorùbá Muslims in their organizations. The struggle to acquire these titles by many Yorùbá Muslims increased tension and generated intrigue among Yorùbá Muslims. Indeed, rivalry for these titles contributed in part to divisions within the Lagos Muslim community. At Epe, the Muslim community split in two after 1945 over the conflict for the title *Eketa Adini*. Tension and envy competing for these titles generated in many Muslim Yorùbá communities are subjects of soap operas on television and Yorùbá video films.[16] Yet, it has become a common practice among Yorùbá Muslims to create these titles most especially for raising funds.

Participation of Muslims in Yorùbá traditional festivals is another source of conflict, not only among Yorùbá Muslims but also between Muslims and non-Muslims. Participation in festivals such as Oke'badan is not acceptable to some Yorùbá Muslims who believe that to participate in such festivals is tantamount to moving away from the Islamic doctrine of the unity of God. In the 1960s, the Bandele movement in Ibadan preached against such Muslims (Doi 1969). In their sermons at open-air lectures and in the electronic media, Muslim preachers relentlessly try to convince devotees to cease taking part in Yorùbá festivals. Although Islamic ministers have not gone beyond constant condemnation of Muslims who participate in the festivals, there have been instances where exchanges between celebrants of these festivals and some Muslims almost degenerated into an affray. During the 1970s and 1980s, clashes were reported in Ibadan between Muslim followers of an Islamic preacher, Alhaji Azeez Ajagbemokeferi, and celebrants of traditional festivals such as Oloolu in Ibadan.

Swift action by the Aláàfin of Ọ̀yọ́, Ọba Lamidi Adeyemi, appears to have prevented open confrontation between Muslims and members of the Oro cult in Ọ̀yọ́. A graphic detail of what almost led to the confrontation is necessary here to understand the state of Yorùbá religion. The *oro* festival is an annual event in the traditional calendar of Ọ̀yọ́ town, celebrated in many Yorùbá towns.[17] The Yorùbá celebrate this festival for many reasons, such as the protection of their towns from evil or disaster, the provision of security in terms of safety of life and property, and honoring a deceased member of the cult (Daramola and Jeje 1995: 269–71). In Ọ̀yọ́, the festival lasts seven days during which time many religious rites are performed. One of the seven days is declared *ọjọ ìṣéde* (a day of curfew), a day on which members of the Oro cult are the only people who could carry their celebration from the Jabata area of the town to the palace of the Aláàfin.

In 1995, *ọjọ ìṣéde* occurred on a Friday. Muslims who opposed the celebration of the *oro* festival congregated in the mosque, defying the curfew imposed by members of the Oro cult. In his dual capacity as the custodian of traditional religious rites and as a Muslim, the Aláàfin did not want a situation in which members of the Oro cult would clash openly with the Muslims congregating in the mosque. Therefore, the Aláàfin ordered Muslims to disperse from the mosque. This action by the Aláàfin attracted condemnation by Muslims in Ọ̀yọ́ and across Yorùbáland. A leading Islamic magazine, *Al-Madinah,* interpreted the Aláàfin's action to mean support for the members of the Oro cult, while a popular *ewi* exponent and Muslim leader, Moshood Adepoju, produced audiocassettes that traded insults on the person of the Aláàfin. These audiocassettes were made available for sale to the public. The Aláàfin justified his action in a radio interview by reminding his critics that he is a Muslim. In as much as the Aláàfin's action displeased Muslims, he recognized the fact that he must maintain a delicate balance between what he considered as Yorùbá tradition and Islamic tradition. Despite criticism, some members of the Oro cult or any traditional cult in Ọ̀yọ́ and other parts of Yorùbáland do profess Islam.

Apparently responding to the condemnation of the Ọ̀ṣun Festival by some Osogbo Muslim leaders, celebrants sang songs offensive to Muslims as Muslims were praying in the mosque during the 1997 Festival of Ọ̀ṣun. As Ogungbile (1998: 136) shows, one song insisted that there was nothing wrong in participating in the festival while at the same time professing Islam. In Offa, many townspeople desired to reconstruct the Mọremi Shrine, which led to grave controversy between Muslims and those who clamored for repairing the shrine. Christians who continued to see the shrine as a symbol of "idol worship" fueled the altercation.

Indeed, Muslims wanted to relocate the shrine because of its proximity to the central mosque while others argued for the total destruction of the shrine.

Because Islam was domesticated, controversy and conflict among Yorùbá Muslims were not restricted to Muslims participating in traditional festivals and restoration of shrines. During the first half of the 1900s, succession to the chief imam's office generated conflict, mainly because the office became a hereditary one. Controversy arose because some Muslims genuinely opposed succession to the office based on heredity, which went against the Islamic ideal. Others opposed hereditary succession emanating from dislike of a particular candidate for the position rather than the principle of choosing the community's most learned scholars. This was the case in Lagos in 1919 when a section of the Muslim community rejected the candidate from the Buraimo (Ibrahim) family (Danmolé 1987: 298). Several archival records point to these controversies in Lagos, Epe, Iseyin, and other Yorùbá towns. Some of these controversies required many years to resolve.

Conclusion

Early encounters between Islam and Yorùbá religion would seem perhaps to facilitate the process of domesticating the practice of Yorùbá religion. During initial contacts between the two religions, Islam needed more converts, which meant that Muslims had to accommodate some local customs that inevitably became part of Islamic practice among Yorùbá Muslims. Indeed, Yorùbá religion in the form of Ifá was instrumental in domesticating Islam among the Yorùbá. Through Ifá divination, many Yorùbá felt "predestined" to become Muslims. Some Yorùbá Muslims included royalty who later became traditional rulers and promoted the cause of Islam in their cities and towns. Consequently, some Yorùbá palaces became meeting points of both Islam and Yorùbá religion. This joint usage in turn served to accentuate the degree of accommodation and adaptation between Islam and Yorùbá religion. In the attempt to evolve an enduring organizational structure, Yorùbá Muslims fell back on Yorùbá traditional political religious nomenclature for their office holders and confined the position of imam to certain families rotating in a hereditary fashion.

It has been suggested that Yorùbá Muslim *ọba* perform complex re-

ligious rites during their installation ceremonies and their roles in annual traditional festivals. These rites and roles may indicate the grip that
Yorùbá religion has on Yorùbá society—despite the prevalence of Islam
and Christianity among the Yorùbá. Without doubt, these religious rites
and the celebration of traditional festivals have changed in meaning over
time. Most Yorùbá Muslims and Christians who participate in them no
longer perceive these rites and festivals as religious worship but as an
annual renewal of their *cultural heritage*. In many Yorùbá towns in various parts of Nigeria, many, including Muslims, now commonly use the
opportunity provided by celebrating traditional festivals to call attention
to the social and economic needs of their communities.

It is important, however, to emphasize that many Yorùbá Muslims
reject the incursion of Yorùbá values into Islam. For instance, many
Yorùbá Muslims vehemently oppose the appointment or election of
an imam through hereditary succession. Apart from that, some Yorùbá
Muslims, who clamor for the practice of Islam in its pristine form, also
reject the participation of Yorùbá Muslims in Yorùbá cultural celebrations. Still, Yorùbá religious values that are embraced in Islam and that
have become part of Islamic practices among the southwestern Nigerian Yorùbá continue to be part of the religious practice of Yorùbá
Muslims.

Notes

1. Such rich Muslims include the late Chief Moshood Abiola, Alhaji Wahab
Folawiyo, and Alhaji Azeez Ansekola Alao.

2. For details of Islam in Hausaland and the nineteenth-century jihad there,
see Balogun 1980; Hiskett 1984; and Usman 1979.

3. Information collected by the author from the Soun of Ogbomoso, Oba
Jimoh Oladunni Oyewumi, Ajagungbade, September 19, 1999.

4. See the collection of Ọṣun Osogbo festival brochures for 1991, 1993,
1995, and 1996 in the library at University of Ilorin.

5. Alhaji Moshood Ekundayo, interview with the author, Ilorin, September
15, 1999.

6. It is now a common practice by the federal government of Nigeria to
declare two days of public holidays for the celebration of Muslim and Christian
festivals.

7. Lateef Onafeko, interview with the author, Ijebu-Ode, September 3,
1999.

8. An imam must be just, all his senses must be functioning properly, and he must not have lost any part of his body. For further details, see Levy 1969: 285.

9. I am very grateful to Professor R. O. Lasisi, Department of History, University of Ilorin, for this information.

10. Al-haji Issa Esilokun, interview with the author, Lagos, August 27, 1999.

11. For marriage in Islam, see Qur'an, *sura* 4, verse 3. The importance that Islam attaches to marriage can be seen in the following sayings of Prophet Muhammad: "When anyone demands your daughter in marriage, and you are pleased with his disposition and his faith, then give her to him, for if you do not so, then there will be strife and contention in the world." "A woman ripe in years shall have her consent asked in marriage, and if she remains silent, her silence is her consent and if she refuses, she shall not be married by force." And: "All young men who have arrived at the age of puberty should marry, for marriage prevents sins. He who cannot should fast." *Mishkatu '1-Masabih,* Book 8, as cited in Hughes 1885: 313–14.

12. Agiri notes that there are two types of kola nuts. One type is *cola nifida.* The trees were common in the forested areas of the Ivory Coast and modern Ghana, but they were introduced to the Nigerian region through long-distance trade in the nineteenth century. The first type is called *obi gbanja* among the Yorùbá. The second type is *cola acuminata.* The trees were found in the forested regions, i.e., southwestern and southeastern Nigeria. The nuts are called *obi abata* by the Yorùbá.

13. For instance, the names of a Yorùbá Muslim child can be as follows: Yusuf Bamidele Akangbe or Rsheedat Olubumni Aduke.

14. On *oríkì,* see Ayorinde 1973.

15. The story of Ayegbajeje goes thus: Ayegbajeje was a rich and famous man in the olden days. But he squandered his riches until he became very poor. He then eked out a living as a laborer. Consequently, everyone maligned and ridiculed him. This was too much for Ayegbajeje to bear, and he thought it was better for him to die. He set out to look for death. On seeing Mr. Death (personification by the author), Ayegbajeje narrated the travails of his life. Mr. Death asked him, "What should we do?" Ayegbajeje answered that Death should put an end to his life. Mr. Death then said to him, "I do not kill any one. It is only joy that kills. If you want to die, go to him." Ayegbajeje set out to look for Mr. Joy. On reaching him, Mr. Joy asked of his mission. Ayegbajeje narrated his story to Mr. Joy who then gave him plenty of money and other valuables. Ayegbajeje rejected the offer, saying that all he wanted was to die. Mr. Joy then retorted, "He who had no money and no wives in his household would not die in peace." Ayegbajeje accepted the money and a beautiful woman as a wife. He resumed his life of merrymaking, became a property owner, and continued to enjoy life

excessively. He had forgotten what took him to Mr. Joy and about his wish to die. After becoming rich again, he had a story building and wanted to perform a house-warming ceremony. News of Ayegbajeje's house-warming ceremony was everywhere. There was happiness on the horizon. He then thought about how great he was and decided to ride a horse during the house-warming ceremony so that the news would spread far and wide. As he climbed upon the horse, he jumped up, falling disastrously on his head. Mr. Death immediately appeared to him and asked, "How was it?" Ayegbajeje began to beg Mr. Death not to end his life. Mr. Death then said to him, "I told you that joy kills everyone," and then he took Ayegbajeje's life.

16. One of such Yorùbá home video films is titled *Iya Adini*.

17. In recent times, there have been bloody clashes between members of the Oro cult and Hausa Muslims in Sagamu, Ogun State, southwestern Nigeria. These escalated into ethnic clashes between Yorùbá and Hausas, and many lives were lost.

References

Abdul, Musa O. 1967. "Islam in Ijebu-Ode." M.A. thesis, McGill University.

Abimbola, Wande. 1976. *Ifa: An Exposition of Ifa Literary Corpus*. Ibadan: Oxford University Press.

Agiri, B. A. 1972. "Kola in Western Nigeria, 1850–1950: A History of the Cultivation of *cola nitida* in Egba-Owode, Ijebu-Remo, Iwo and Ota Areas." Ph.D. diss., University of Wisconsin–Madison.

Ahmed, Akbar S. 1988. *Toward Islamic Anthropology: Definition, Dogma and Directions*. Herndon, VA: International Institute of Islamic Thought.

Ajayi, Jacob F. A. 1965. *The Christian Missions in Nigeria, 1841–1891*. London: Longman.

al-Faruqi, Lois Lamaya, and Yusuf al-Qaradawi. 1994. *Music: An Islamic Perspective*. Minna, Nigeria: Islamic Education Trust.

Ayorinde, J. A. 1973. "Oriki." In *Sources of Yorùbá History*, ed. S. O. Biobaku, 63–76. London: Oxford University Press.

Balogun, S. A. 1980. "History of Islam up to 1800." In *Groundwork of Nigerian History*, ed. Obaro Ikime. Ibadan: Heinemann.

Bascom, William. 1965. "Four Functions of Folklore." In *The Study of Folklore*, ed. Alan Dundes, 277–98. Englewood Cliffs, NJ: Prentice Hall.

Danmolé, H. O. 1982. "The Growth of Islamic Learning in Ilorin in the Nineteenth Century." *Religions: A Journal of the Nigerian Association for the Study of Religions* 6/7: 14–35.

———. 1987. "The Crisis of the Lagos Muslim Community, 1915–1947." In

History of the Peoples of Lagos State, ed. Ade Adefuye et al. Lagos: Lantern Books.

Daramola, O., and A. Jeje. 1995. *Awon Asa ati Orisa Ile Yorùbá.* Ibadan: Onibon-Oje Press.

Doi, A. R. 1969. "The Bandele Movement in Yorùbáland." *Orita: Ibadan Journal of Religious Studies* 3, no. 2: 101–18.

————. 1971. "An Aspect of Islamic Syncretism in Yorùbáland." *Orita: Ibadan Journal of Religious Studies* 5, no. 1: 36–45.

Euba, Akin. 1971. "Islamic Musical Culture among the Yorùbá: A Preliminary Survey." In *Essays on Music and History in Africa,* ed. K. P. Wachsmann, 171–81. Evanston, IL: Northwestern University Press.

Fadipe, Nathaniel A. 1970 (1939). *The Sociology of the Yorùbá.* Ibadan: Ibadan University Press.

Gbadamosi, T. G. O. 1972. "The *Imamate* Question among Yorùbá Muslims." *Journal of the Nigerian Historical Association* 6, no. 2: 229–37.

————. 1977. "'Odu Imale': Islam in Ifa Divination and the Case of Predestined Muslims." *Journal of the Historical Society of Nigeria* 8, no. 4: 77–93.

————. 1978. *The Growth of Islam among the Yorùbá, 1841–1908.* London: Longman.

Glassé, Cyril. 1989. *The Concise Encyclopedia of Islam.* London: Stacey International.

Hiskett, Mervyn. 1984. *Development of Islam in West Africa.* London: Longman.

Hughes, Thomas Patrick. 1885. *A Dictionary of Islam: Being a Cyclopedia of Doctrines, Rites, Ceremonies and Customs, Together with the Technical and Theological Terms, of the Muslim Religion.* London: W. H. Allen.

Idowu, E. Bolaji. 1962. *Olodumare: God in Yorùbá Belief.* London: Longman.

Laitin, David D. 1986. *Hegemony and Culture: Politics and Religious Change among the Yorùbá.* Chicago: University of Chicago Press.

Levy, Reuben. 1969. *The Social Structure of Islam.* Cambridge: Cambridge University Press.

Ogunba, Oyin. 1991. "Hegemonic Festivals in Yorùbáland." *Ife: Annals of the Institute of Cultural Studies.* Ile-Ife: Obafemi Awolowo University.

Ogungbile, D. O. 1998. "Islam and Cultural Identity in Nigeria: The Osogbo-Yorùbá Experience." *Orita: Ibadan Journal of Religious Studies* 20, no. 1–2: 125–37.

Olupona, Jacob K. 1991. "Contemporary Religious Terrain." In *Religion and Society in Nigeria,* ed. Jacob K. Olupona and Toyin Falola. Ibadan: Spectrum Books.

Omibiyi-Obidike, M. A. 1979. "Islam Influence on Yorùbá Music." *Africa Notes* 8, no. 2: 37–54.

Oseni, Zacharaiyau I. 1981 (1950). *A Guide to Muslim Names*. Lagos: Islamic Publication Bureau.

Parrinder, Edward Geoffrey. 1967. *The Story of Ketu: An Ancient Yorùbá Kingdom*. Ibadan: Ibadan University Press.

Usman, Yusufu Bala, ed. 1979. *Studies in the History of the Sokoto Caliphate*. Sokoto, Nigeria: Sokoto State History Bureau.

van Beek, Walter E. A., and Thomas D. Blakely. 1994. Introduction to *Religion in Africa,* ed. Thomas D. Blakely, Walter E. A. van Beek, and Dennis L. Thompson, 1–20. London: James Curry.

10

Yorùbá Moral Epistemology as the Basis for a Cross-Cultural Ethics

BARRY HALLEN

When it was first intimated to me that I might be invited to contribute to a volume devoted to Yorùbá *religious* culture, I must confess that I hesitated. For my published work devoted to the study of Yorùbá culture has been explicitly—some might say too explicitly—secularly oriented. There is a reason for this, and if I am to justify this essay, I think I must say something about it.

I have never denied the importance of the religious dimension to Yorùbá life and thought. In fact, I have more or less embraced the paradigm or model portraying the continuities between the so-called natural and supernatural outlined by Wole Soyinka in his *Myth, Literature, and the African World* (1990). However, some years back, when I first expressed a professional interest in African and, in particular, Yorùbá thought and philosophy, the relevant published literature, in large measure a product of Western scholarship (Bascom 1969), seemed to focus so emphatically upon comparatively "supernatural" elements of the culture that I, given my admitted biases as an analytically and empirically minded (Western-trained) philosopher, could not help but wonder about those more prosaic dimensions to Yorùbá thought that might not be *so* importantly, intimately, or directly linked with the "supernatural."

From another, though complementary, point of view I suppose I was also indirectly posing the question, "What does it mean to be an optimal human being in the context of Yorùbá culture—more specifically that part of the culture that is not explicitly concerned with the spiritual dimension to human existence?" That relevant body of literature to which I have just referred seemed to link everything to being "traditional." Moreover, "traditional" Yorùbá culture was usually introduced via an overture outlining the elaborate and intricate pantheon of deities or òrìṣà, and a first movement describing the various rituals, rites, or festivals carried out or performed by human beings with reference to them. On the level of more specifically *human* being, a prominent role was assigned to the *orí* or destiny (also sometimes described as an òrìṣà) of the individual and the reliance upon divination, Ifá in particular, as a spiritual source of guidance during a person's lifetime (Abimbola 1976).

In texts that assessed the combined import of all these spiritual influences upon human behavior, a conclusion regularly implied and, again, linked to the word "traditional," was that this was not a cultural or intellectual context where there could be a significant role for initiative when it came to individual, independent, reflective, or critical action or thought. Because, in effect, so much was prescribed or proscribed *for* the individual that it did indeed make good sense to invoke some sort of "tribalized" model of the cellularly organic variety.

What intrigued me the most about this now deservedly controversial and contested portrait of African culture was the comparatively unimportant roles it assigned to *individualized* initiative, to *individualized* thinking, and to an *individual's* moral responsibility and rights when it came to his or her *self*-consciously identifying and embracing a set of moral values or, to borrow a phrase from Rowland Abiodun (1990), to the "art" of being human in ordinary, everyday life. By saying this, I am not in the least denying the relatively greater importance of the community in Yorùbá culture. I am only asking what is involved in being an individual in such a social and cultural context.

Epistemology, or the theory of knowledge, is the area of philosophy concerned, among other things, with the criteria recommended for distinguishing more from less reliable information. The more reliable is what people usually regard as *knowledge*. The less reliable is regarded as *belief* or, at worst, information that fails to satisfy even minimal criteria of reliability and is therefore labeled *untrue* or *false*. The approach to philosophy in and of Africa that I happen to follow is best known as ordinary language philosophy (Hallen 2006). It suggests that if we study the way people in a given language culture *use* the words or terms in everyday speech in which we as philosophers happen to be interested, we will be able to identify the *criteria* that *govern* their usage and, by extrapolation from those criteria, their relevance to certain philosophical topics or problems.

In 1986 I published a little book with my Nigerian colleague, Olubi Sodipo, as co-author entitled *Knowledge, Belief, and Witchcraft: Analytic Experiments in African Philosophy* (1997). In it we attempted to outline the criteria governing usage of the terms in the Yorùbá language conventionally translated into English as "knowledge" and "belief." What became clear from our analyses was that the meanings of these terms, the criteria that defined their correct usage in Yorùbá, were *not* the same as their supposed English-language equivalents. The biggest difference stemmed from the fact that "knowledge," in Yorùbá, was conventionally restricted to information arising from firsthand experience. This would mean that on the level of everyday experience the things of which the individual person is entitled to be most certain are things they have seen or witnessed for themselves. Information that is received in a secondhand manner—from other people, for example—is placed in another category approximating to the English-language "belief" and therefore is regarded as something that is not, strictly speaking, certain or true. In this essay I suggest that it may be helpful to use these Yorùbá epistemological priorities as a wedge or key or vantage point from which to better appreciate the reasons why Yorùbá culture places a high premium upon certain moral and associated aesthetic values (Hallen 2000).

When Yorùbá describe an individual as "truthful," a good deal more is involved than merely the assessment of moral character. Describing a person in this way means that the statements made, the information conveyed, by that person to others can be relied upon and used as if "true," for whatever essential or mundane purposes it may be needed. Some scholars have used orality to "type" a particular kind of mentality, which generally compares less favorably in analytic intellectual terms with its literate Western equivalent. The present discussion seeks to circumvent that increasingly controversial debate. The claim that, in "traditional"

Yorùbá culture propositional knowledge—secondhand information—preponderantly comes out of mouths is here an empirical observation rather than a theoretically weighted premise.

In an intellectual context where printed books and written script may not be taken for granted, the most obvious alternative *is* for secondhand information to issue from someone's mouth. And if this is the case, it is understandable that passing judgment upon such information's reliability or its likelihood of being "true," purely on instrumental or pragmatic grounds, involves *assessing the moral character* of the individuals who are its source, out of whose mouths it issues. For the information that comes out of those persons' mouths may then be shared-out and used by others who are trying to solve problems or to arrive at an understanding that is more than individual or personal.

In a significantly oral culture, one might therefore expect that special importance would be attached to how carefully individuals "hear" or "listen to" or observe what is going on around them, and the perspicuity underlying what they "say." Certainly, elocution and phrasing one's remarks in an intelligible manner are matters of importance to the Yorùbá. But that is not sufficient to explain the emphasis placed upon speaking *well* and hearing *well* as *values*.

People in Western societies have become concerned about exercising control over the media. In a significantly oral culture, the media are mouths. Doing these things *well* involves setting "broadcasting standards" for those mouths. "Speaking well" and "hearing well" may be euphemistically popularized in Nigerian English-language usage as not to "tell lies." However, not to "tell lies" means to tell the truth about what you really do have firsthand experience of, what you have only heard about secondhand, and what you have no information about at all. "Speaking well" and "hearing well" are not, then, *moral* values in the conventional Western sense. They are as much *epistemological virtues* because of their instrumental value for ensuring the accuracy and reliability of information.

"Hearing well," in fact, means being a careful observer, with the emphasis decidedly upon individual cognition, upon understanding what really is going on, rather than simply maintaining an attentive demeanor. "Speaking well" means that one should reflect thoroughly about a problem or situation to speak in a perceptive manner before opening one's mouth. This is what is important rather than merely elocution or, as we used to sometimes say in Nigeria, "blowing grammar."

With this linking of the epistemological and the moral in Yorùbá discourse, we move a step closer to value theory. If what a statement means and is taken to mean by others also depends upon which individual's mouth it is coming out of, then a speaker's reputation, a speaker's moral character *as defined by others,* becomes one prominent consideration to the epistemological rating—the reliability—attributed to the speaker's propositional knowledge. Reciprocally the reliability of the statements made by an individual, in principle on any subject, may become firsthand evidence of the individual's moral character. Nowhere is this clearer than in the case of the liar. Imagine what the life of a person might become if no information he or she volunteered would be received as reliable. A person's credibility as both speaker and actor, as witness and reporter, of his or her own or another's experience would become suspect.

The emphasis placed by the Yorùbá upon "patience" as a value was, I believe, first commented upon in Western scholarship by Robert Farris Thompson. Thompson linked the importance of patience to a person's being "cool" in his account of a Yorùbá aesthetic. One reason for the cool being an important value in Yorùbá culture was said to be its connection with dignity and kingliness. "Yorùbá, in brief, assume that someone who *embodies* command, coolness, and character is someone extremely beautiful and like unto a god" (Thompson 1971, p. 5; my emphasis).

However, an *external* patient demeanor or appearance should arise from an *internal* patience that is grounded in cognition. This suggests that its importance as a behavioral criterion is more epistemic than aesthetic. A "cool" temperament, the patient person, is far more likely to listen to and observe carefully what is happening and to speak with apperception and aplomb. In other words, that patience is perceived as a moral or aesthetic value associated with certain forms of appearance is grounded upon the objective benefits that derive from it as an epistemic virtue. A mind distinguished by patience, especially in difficult or problematic situations, informs a consciousness that maintains self-control and optimal communication with itself and its environment.

If it is indeed the case that in Yorùbá discourse certain epistemic values underlie and inform certain ethical values in an impressively systematic and coherent manner, then this may be seen to complement the manner in which a similar relationship seems to hold between moral and aesthetic values. For the transition between the "true" and the "good" then becomes analogous to that between the "good" and the "beautiful."

From an empirical or behavioral rather than an introspective point of view, one consequence of the importance attached to firsthand experience is that a person's (verbal and nonverbal) behavior—what they "say" and what they "do" in your presence—is regarded as firsthand evidence of their moral character: "Handsome is as handsome does," to invoke an old Western aphorism. The extreme caution and care with which secondhand information is received and evaluated—for example, about what a person is supposed to have said or done (which, after all, includes even gossip)—is a testament to Yorùbá prudence about human fallibility.

The Yorùbá term most frequently rendered into English as "handsome" or as "beauty" is *ẹwà*. Its most common usage is with regard to persons, to human beings. However, *ẹwà* or beauty as purely physical is rated superficial and relatively unimportant by comparison with *ẹwà* as good character, as *moral* beauty. This means that a person who, physically, would not conventionally be regarded as beautiful or handsome may still receive the highest aesthetic accolades because of their good moral character. In addition, this suggests that the underlying notion of "inner" beauty is more than metaphorical. In fact, it takes on the character of a *moral* attribute. In such cases it would therefore be appropriate to speak of a "beauty of moral character" or of a "beautiful moral character." To retrace the circle of interrelated epistemological, moral, and aesthetic values from a negative point of view, having a reputation for ugly or bad behavior (on an aesthetic basis) is linked to a person's being irresponsible (on a moral basis) and therefore not a source of reliable information (on an epistemological basis).

After reaching this point in the writing of my text, I still felt that some more explicit point of connection with or relevance to Yorùbá religion was lacking. In other words, is there a more explicitly Yorùbá *religious* reservoir that one might tap or look to for further confirmation (or, more pessimistically, denial) of these as value priorities? One obvious possibility would seem to be the numerous stories, tales, or myths about Yorùbá deities (or òrìṣà) and heroic figures.

Initially, I confess, I was tempted to summarize a few such tales that would serve that purpose here. But upon further reflection that seemed too superficial a tactic, too much of an ad hoc approach—to use as confirmatory evidence *one* example of a deity telling an untruth and suffering the consequences, or of a deity not listening carefully enough to what was being said and the ensuing misfortunes to which this led, or of the heroic figure who did not appreciate the inner worth of a companion or mate and the tragic consequences that followed. So what I am prepared to say is that a more leisurely and comprehensive assessment of that literary corpus is something I have added to my agenda, with the hope that more careful study will enable me to gauge just how importantly these values are reflected in and by it.

That constitutes the main body of my text, but I would like to share a bit of contemporary history that is more obviously directly relevant to the topic of globalization. During these past years I have had the privilege of being professor of philosophy at Morehouse College, which is the premier four-year private liberal arts college in the United States explicitly committed to providing young African American men with a first-rate intellectual and moral education. Over the course of those years, I have taught this hypothetical outline of the interrelation of epistemic, moral, and aesthetic values to numerous classes of Morehouse students.

We all know of the so-called crisis mentality in contemporary American society and culture concerning the resuscitation of "family values" as opposed to self-interest, the prevalence of rampant materialism, and the anxieties associated with the ultimate meaninglessness and valuelessness of human life, and their tragic consequences. I cannot impress upon readers enough how positive the response of many men of Morehouse has been to this limited selection of Yorùbá values regarding what should and should not be involved in one's being and becoming an admirable human being. They do not receive this information as old-fashioned or foreign. They receive it as noble, inspiring, challenging—as something to make the individual proud of his or her African heritage and as worthy of emulation. If this is indeed the case, then, is there not a place for the *promotion,* the popular dissemination, as well as the further study, of such values outside as well as inside Yorùbá culture, given this increasingly transcultural and multicultural world with which we human beings are still trying to come to terms?

References

Abimbola, Kola. 2005. *Yorùbá Culture: A Philosophical Account.* Birmingham, UK: Ìrókò Academic Publishers.

Abimbola, Wande. 1976. *Ifá*. Oxford: Oxford University Press.

———. 1997. *Ifá Will Mend Our Broken World: Thoughts on Yorùbá Religion and Culture in African and the Diaspora*. Roxbury, MA: Aim Books.

Abiodun, Rowland. 1990. "The Future of African Art Studies: An African Perspective." In *African Art Studies: The State of the Discipline,* ed. National Museum of African Art, 63–89. Washington, DC: Smithsonian Institution Press.

Bascom, William. 1969. *The Yorùbá of Southwestern Nigeria*. New York: Holt, Rinehart and Winston.

Bewaji, J. A. I. 2004. "Ethics and Morality in Yorùbá Culture." In *A Companion to African Philosophy,* ed. Kwasi Wiredu, 396–403. Malden, MA, and Oxford: Blackwell.

Gbadegesin, Segun. 1991. "Individuality, Community and the Moral Order." In *African Philosophy,* 61–82. New York and Frankfurt: Peter Lang.

Hallen, Barry. 2000. *The Good, the Bad, and the Beautiful: Discourse about Values in Yorùbá Culture*. Bloomington: Indiana University Press.

———. 2002. *A Short History of African Philosophy*. Bloomington: Indiana University Press.

———. 2006. *African Philosophy: The Analytic Approach*. Trenton, NJ, and Asmara, Eritrea: African World Press.

Hallen, Barry, and J. Olubi Sodipo. 1997 (1986). *Knowledge, Belief, and Witchcraft: Analytic Experiments in African Philosophy*. London: Ethnographica Publishers. Reprint, with foreword by W. V. O. Quine and afterword by Barry Hallen, Stanford, CA: Stanford University Press.

Ìdòwú, E. Bolaji. 1962. *Olodumare: God in Yorùbá Belief*. London: Longman.

Soyinka, Wole. 1990. *Myth, Literature and the African World*. Cambridge: Cambridge University Press.

Táíwò, Olúfémi. 2004. "Ifá: An Account of a Divination System and Some Concluding Epistemological Questions." In *A Companion to African Philosophy,* ed. Kwasi Wiredu, 304–12. Malden, MA, and Oxford, UK: Blackwell.

Thompson, Robert Farris. 1971. *Black Gods and Kings*. Los Angeles: Museum and Laboratories of Ethnic Arts and Technology, University of California.

Wiredu, Kwasi. 1996. *Cultural Universals and Particulars: An African Perspective*. Bloomington: Indiana University Press.

II

Yorùbá Religious Culture
beyond Africa

11

Yorùbá Religion and Globalization

Some Reflections

OLABIYI BABALOLA YAI

Discourse on globalization is undergoing an inflation in academic and non-academic circles alike. Perhaps the combined effect of the consequences of a unipolar world imposed on humanity since the disappearance of the Soviet camp, coupled with fin de siècle or, indeed, fin de millénaire obsessions, provides the context, if not the explanation, for this inflation. The mere mention of the term "globalization" often triggers opposite reactions and Manichean judgments, especially among intellectuals of the so-called Third World, as is often the case with new critical concepts proposed by their peers or mentors in the First World, especially in the West. Globalization no doubt has its enthusiasts, its passionate advocates as well as its crucifiers and its discontents. The expression "global village," from which the notion of globalization is derived, is today one of the most used clichés in the humanities and social sciences. The metaphorical nucleus of the expression is so removed from the life experience of most of its users, who have never lived in a village, that, in a sense, it has acquired a metaphorical status. For most writers, the notion of a "global village" is a metaphor of a metaphor. Little wonder, therefore, if "globalization," which is its derivative and

233

putative elaboration, has become a locus for controversies. What cannot
be doubted is that so proteiform has so far been the general situation of
our globe in recent times that any analysis of cultural life in the context
of globalization should be conducted with prudence. These are times for
conjectures, not for peremptory vaticinations. This call for prudence,
however, is no synonym with laxism in the apprehension of things cultural. Our task, I would like to conjecture, is to forge such conceptual
tools as to enable us to think the most plausible scenarios or new configurations for Yorùbá religious traditions in an era of globalization.

In this regard, perhaps our first and foremost task is to examine the
very notion of globalization from an African perspective in order to
ensure that we are not ensnared in concepts that engender issues and
debates over which we have little control. The notion of globalization,
in much contemporary discourse involving the term, refers to the spectacular and all-pervading power of late, post–cold war capitalism, especially its ubiquitous presence in the realm of finance, owing to radical
changes in the communication technology and the variegated cultural
consequences triggered by these processes. However, there is a definite
geographical bias that inheres in this etymologically derived definition.
To be sure, the tentacular and spectacular aspects of globalization are
fundamental to its definition. But fixation on them will not help us understand our "African-being-in-the-world." For each individual, group,
or community will interpret globalization in terms of their respective
"globes" (worlds) and what is being globalized. And, we do know that
"world" has meant different things for different communities at different times and places. Hence, the need to complete the contemporary
spectacular-tentacular, ultimately geographical facets of the notion of
globalization by a dimension that calls for a historical elucidation of
current manifestations. In other words, there is an indispensable "history depth" dimension to globalization. Failure to envisage globalization
issues in this historico-geographical perspective will result in incomplete and superficial appraisals that would have us deserve the sentential
Yorùbá, "Awon le n wo, e o reegun."

At a seminar on "Globalization and Indigenous Cultures" in Tokyo
some years back, I told an amazed and incredulous Japanese audience
that we Africans have been very active in the globalization process before them. For, although we have been somehow forcefully precipitated
into the process through what Basil Davidson so aptly termed "the curse
of Columbus," that is, the Atlantic slave trade, Japan decided to open

itself to the capitalist West only in 1868, with the Meiji Restoration adopting a historico-geographical approach. I'd like to suggest three stages and modalities in the globalization of Yorùbá religious traditions, namely West African, Atlantic, and post-Atlantic. The three stages are briefly summarized in the next section.

Yorùbá religion became global by sharing its òrìṣà with the immediate, West African neighbors of the people who have come to be collectively designated as Yorùbá, and by adopting some of their deities. Thus, the Edo, Yagba, Itsekiri, Nupe, Ibariba, Igbo, Igala, Fon, Gun, Aja, Ewe, Akan, and so forth belong in the same religious global village as the Yorùbá. The case has been made for Ògún as the paradigmatic West African "globalizer" deity in Barnes (1989). But one could identify avatars of virtually any Yorùbá òrìṣà in the pantheon of the above-mentioned ethnic groups. The Yorùbá gave and freely took deities in this area. In the realm of religion, Akinjogbin's *ẹbí* social theory is certainly a historical fact (Akinjogbin 1967). Ṣàngó and Oya are as Nupe as they are Yorùbá. Nana Buukuu is most likely Akan in origin, before it was adopted by pre-Odùduwà Yorùbá and subsequently traveled throughout Yorùbáland. Odùduwà, Òrìṣà, Yéyé Mowo, Ògún, Elegba, Sanpanna, clearly Yorùbá òrìṣà, have become Fon deities or *vodun* under the following audibly recognizable names respectively: Duduwa, Lisa, Mawu, Gun, Legba, Sakpata. In their new locale, they are both Fon and Yorùbá, issues of origin and nationality being of little interest to practitioners, even as they may preoccupy academics. A case in point is precisely Sanpanna, who is believed in parts of Yorùbáland to be of Fon origin, while the Fon emphatically affirm its Yorùbáness by calling his devotees Anagonu, that is, Anago (Yorùbá citizens).

This apparent contradiction is indicative of a general trend in the area and can be explained as follows: the spread of Sanpanna, like that of many Yorùbá deities has undergone a pendular movement in the area. In all likelihood, Sanpanna must have become so popular and strong in the Fon area as to attract Yorùbá devotees who now come to Fonland to acquire a surplus of *àṣẹ* in this deity. In this back-and-forth movement of deities over a long period in the West African area, a place of rebirth can easily be mistaken as the original birthplace (Yai 1996).

The Yorùbá deity Òrúnmìlà, and its system of divination, Ifá, is arguably the most "globalized" indigenous religious tradition in West Africa. The deity and its system are known from Ìgbòland in the East to Eweland in the West. The linguistic evidence of the globalization of this aspect of Yorùbá religious tradition is undeniable, although it calls for urgent comparative studies. Yorùbá being the language in which Ọ̀rúnmìlà expresses himself through the Odù, Ifá priests had to learn the corpus in the original language. Yorùbá thus became the language of religious and intellectual discourse in the area (Sandoval 1956; Yai 1992). Conversely, many verses in various languages of the area occur in the Yorùbá corpus of *odù,* as is attested in most collected texts (Maupoil 1943; Abimbola 1968).

An important dimension of the globalization of Yorùbá religious traditions in West Africa is their first encounter with an Abrahamic religion, that is, Islam, through the trans-Saharan trade. Yorùbá intellectual tradition has deemed this encounter as fundamental to record its modalities and peripheries within a single Odù, namely Otua, which has come to be known as Odu Imale (Odu about Islam). Globalization here consisted not only in making Islam known to the Yorùbá but also in syncretizing it with Yorùbá religious traditions. It also consisted in absorbing aspects of the cultures of the people who brought Islam into Yorùbáland, namely the Mande, the Songhai, the Dendi, and the Hausa, and in making aspects of Yorùbá religious traditions known in the same cultural areas.

The Atlantic globalization of Yorùbá religious traditions as a consequence of the slave trade has enjoyed an extensive and intensive treatment from the pioneering works of Nina Rodrigues, Fernando Ortiz, Roger Bastide, Lydia Cabrera, and Pierre Verger, to those of younger generations of researchers, some of whom were present at the 1999 conference. We are all familiar with the literature on the topic, and no further elaboration is needed. Central to the debates through generations of scholars is the issue of syncretism.

The definition and treatment of this important phenomenon depends and will depend on the often unconscious or unconfessed bias and ideology of the writer, or on circumstantial situations. In an assessment of syncretism as a historical phenomenon, what cannot be denied, though, is the African initiative (Mason 1994). Agency, as a problématique, has received little serious attention from students of syncretism and did not result from equal contributions by Catholic thinkers and their African counterparts in the serenity of religious conclaves. The (unsung) theologians of Afro-Christian syncretism are diaspora African intellectuals, such as priestesses and priests in Brazil, Cuba, Haïti, Trinidad, and elsewhere who are usually recognized in their *ilé,* casa, and péristyles through religious lineage praise songs. Their invisibility in official anthropological literature is a serious scientific blind spot.

But, there is a hidden face of the globalization of Yorùbá religious traditions that needs to be more exposed: the encounter between Yorùbá religion and other African, mostly Central African, religious traditions, as well as with Native American religious traditions.

Because students of Yorùbá religious traditions in the Americas almost exclusively originated from the Judeo-Christian world, they have tended to "naturally" emphasize the mixture of some Yorùbá religious features with those of the religious traditions they are most familiar with—theirs.

However, what we know of the habitat and mode of socialization of slaves in the New World should incline us to believe that Yorùbá religion is likely to be first globalized with religious traditions of the Congo and Volta river basins. And it actually did. Deities that did not exist in Central Africa emerged in the Candomblé Angola in Brazil and are, on analysis, "translations" of Yorùbá òrìṣà into Kongo culture and idiom. Similarly, in what is described as the most "pure" or "authentic" Yorùbá religious house (Opo Afonja), Mae Aninha, a Yorùbá *iyalòrìṣà* of Gurunsi ancestry, introduced Gurunsi deities that are now part and parcel of the Brazilian Yorùbá pantheon. Trinidadian Shango is another globalization of Yorùbá religious traditions through a re-encounter with West African religious, mostly Fon and Ewe (Senah 1999).

An in-depth study of this Yorùbá-African syncretism is urgently needed as an important aspect of Yorùbá globalization. This, of course, will require a necessary *linguistic turn* in Yorùbá and African diaspora studies.

In order to conceptualize better and characterize the post-Atlantic stage of Yorùbá religious traditions, it is important to compare briefly the contexts of the stages that preceded it.

West Africans were the sole actors of the globalization of Yorùbá religious traditions in Africa. Even in the case of globalization through Yorùbá-Islam syncretism, non-Africans never came in physical contact with the Yorùbá. In addition, orality was the main medium of globalization, even as Islam remained the "religion of the book" and despite the emergence of a tiny group of Yorùbá literate scholars in Arabic (Abubakre 1986). Consequently, rituals prevailed on doctrine.

The Atlantic slave trade, triggered by capitalism, provided the context for what we term "Atlantic globalization of Yorùbá religious traditions." The main actors here are the Yorùbá, other Africans and, peripherally, European descendants of popular extraction. The existence of libretas in certain areas notwithstanding, orality remained the medium of globalization par excellence at this stage, too.

"Post-Atlantic" Globalization

In the last thirty years or so, Yorùbá religion has been experiencing a new form of internationalization that is currently dovetailing in modern globalization proper. The following historical events provide the background for this new internationalization-globalization:

- The appearance on the international scene of new independent nations in Africa, with the attendant interest in African cultures and the homeland-diaspora exchanges (cf. the "*Roots* syndrome" triggered by Alex Haley's book and film).
- The civil rights movement in the United States, black nationalism, and the search for an "authentic" African religion radically different from the three Abrahamic religions, all of which were historically implicated in the Atlantic or Trans-Saharan slave. In this regard, the creation of Oyotunji African village in South Carolina, with its restoration of features of the precolonial Yorùbá Kingdom, takes on a paradigmatic significance, even as, from the standpoint of Yorùbá philosophical traditions, its tenets rest on methodologically shaky grounds.
- Population dynamics in the Western hemisphere (from the Caribbean to the United States), especially the Mariel boatlift and the massive transfer of Cubans to Miami, with their religion, Santería.
- The emergence, among Yorùbá religion practitioners worldwide, of a new consciousness of the universality of the òrìṣà tradition coupled with the promotion of appropriate organizations.

The combined effects of all these events significantly widened the constituency of the òrìṣà tradition. We now have a much broader spectrum of worshippers of all races with tremendous diversity in educational background, cultural exposure, including, especially, exposure to Yorùbá and African culture, professional experience, and skills. For convenience, we can distinguish three broad categories or actors in the new political economy of Yorùbá religion:

1. Africans in the homeland. They still make up the bulk of òrìṣà worshippers. They live in villages, towns, and cities in Nigeria,

Benin Republic, Togo, and Sierra Leone. Most are hardly educated in the Western system of education and are vaguely, if at all, aware of the international dimensions of their religious traditions. A few intellectuals more or less integrated in the tradition act as brokers between this group and the two other groups. This is a nonhomogenous group consisting of Yorùbá cultural nationalists, cultural entrepreneurs, bona fide priests, *honoris causa* uninitiated and self-appointed priests, and even some charlatans.

2. Africans in the diaspora. They constitute the second largest group of worshippers, in villages, towns, and cities of Brazil, Cuba, Haiti, Trinidad, Puerto Rico, Venezuela, and the United States. They belong to the lower classes and lower middle classes of these countries.

3. Non-Africans. They make up the smallest group and live mostly in Brazil, Cuba, and the United States. They are a relatively small or large minority, depending on the country and the definition of whiteness, and usually belong to the upper middle classes of these countries.

The tripartite division is as simplistic as it is necessary for the purpose of a preliminary analysis of a relativity new and proteiform phenomenon. Each of the three identified groups is at once homogenous and heterogeneous. The three are also traversed by contradictions and affinities based on language, hidden or (un)official religion of the countries of origin or settlement, pervasiveness and age of the African religion in the culture, and, above all, class.

What needs to be emphasized is the increasing role of the òrìṣà "community" of the United States in the new political economy of the òrìṣà tradition, which seems to reflect the unipolar scheme of the ongoing economic globalization. The increasing pauperization of the *élites* in West Africa and some Latin American states has prompted òrìṣà worshippers or their often self-appointed representatives to target the United States as the new haven for the survival of the tradition. New axes are taking shape between Nigeria, Haiti, Cuba, and Brazil as one end of the pole and several U.S. cities as the other pole. Consciousness of this new globalization of the òrìṣà tradition has generated the need for coordination and standardization initiatives.

Proselytizing, dogma, and orthodoxy are not features of òrìṣà tradition. Therefore, there is no central organ of decision or diffusion of behavior, information, or religious knowledge. Mostly informal bridges have been built between the three arms identified above. The World Congress of Orisa Tradition and Culture, whose first meeting took place in Ilé-Ifè in 1981, has intermittently functioned as a coordinating entity.

As is to be expected, the òrìṣà tradition is being affected by consumerism and the new technologies of the information age. Books and pamphlets of the "do it yourself" or "teach yourself" type are being published about rituals by generally uninformed and unscrupulous people who know that the religion is marketable, particularly in the United States.

Films and videocassettes showing òrìṣà ceremonies and rituals are broadcast and commercialized, despite the disapproval and condemnation of such practices by the most authoritative priests. More important, òrìṣà is now on the Internet. Discussions and debates about ritual practices, myths, prayers, divination issues, medicinal plants and preparations, the "right way of doing things," and the "religiously correct" are being held daily on the Web (Doris 1996; Capone 1999; Argyriadis 1999).

This development brings with it new issues, new stakes, new challenges. It is certainly pregnant with new, perhaps unprecedented, forms of cultural and religious engagements and syncretism.

The first feature of the new situation is the disjunction of the three groups of actors and their radically unequal access to the information age instruments and process of globalization. They are situated at different points from the center of the globalization galaxy. Africans on the continent are at the periphery of globalization. Most òrìṣà practitioners have no access to television, an instrument that is taken for granted in the globalization galaxy center. They are not participants in the debates about their religion on the Internet, for these debates are limited to select members of groups 2 and 3. Yet, Africa is the matrix of the religion, and Yorùbáland is universally acknowledged as the source and ultimate reference for authenticity, knowledge, authority, credibility, and legitimacy. With respect to religious knowledge and authority, most practitioners would rank the three groups identified above in their order of occurrence (1, 2, and 3); the ranking would be reversed (3, 2, and 1) should access to information technology and integration in the new globalization process be the criteria. One is tempted to conjecture that òrìṣà tradition has its foot in Africa and its head in America. This formula could meaningfully be turned upside down, if "foot" and "head" are given the deep meaning of the Yorùbá concepts of *ese* and *ori*. And therein lie the paradox and predicament of globalization, the resolution of which it is hard to precisely predict at this initial stage of the process. Yet, it is necessary and possible to adumbrate the contours of a few possible scenarios, directions, and orientations of the globalization process.

But before doing so, a few words of clarification are in order with respect to the notion of religious knowledge in the òrìṣà tradition. Religious knowledge is acquired through initiation. In Africa, devotees used to go through several stages and levels in the initiation process, which could take several months or years of partial or total seclusion. Priests' and diviners' initiation processes are even longer and more rigorous. Since òrìṣà tradition is not a "religion of the book," an extensive corpus of oral texts including praises, myths, stories, invocations, prayers, incantations, divination texts and their exegeses and interpretations, medicinal recipes, and so forth must be memorized in Yorùbá. More important, there is an esoteric stage and dimension to the process referred to as deep knowledge. These texts are sacred, but *not* in the sense this term connotes in the scriptures of religions of the book like Islam, Judaism, and Christianity. An increasing number of devotees in groups 2 and 3 rely on booklets (libretas) for their initiation, mostly as a complement to the oral tradition. These booklets even become central references for some. This is truer in Cuba and its diaspora in the United States. More and more practitioners in the diaspora, especially in the third group, heavily rely on books written by anthropologists on the tradition, with the inevitable misunderstandings, mistranslations, and Eurocentricism. There is no place for esoteric knowledge in these new media. For practitioners in Africa as well as in the diaspora, book knowledge, not acquired through initiation by a master in the context of a sacred space, does *not* qualify as religious knowledge because it is devoid of *àṣẹ*. The information age technology being the ultimate product of the "Gutenberg Galaxy," globalization necessarily and gradually implies and imposes an orality versus scripturality divide in the world of the òrìṣà tradition, a divide that will inevitably trigger an insiders versus outsiders debate and chasm. The ultimate implications of the new challenges that writing and its technological consequences impose on Yorùbá religion as a religion based on oral traditions are as immense as to deserve a conference. Suffice it to indicate the increasing centrality of the book in the tradition will trigger modelizing effects from the Abrahamic religions that are "religions of the book" par excellence, with their doctrinaire and even dogmatic consequences. There is already an indication of this development in the emergence of "isms" in certain discourses and treatises (e.g., "*Ifism*," claimed to be based on Ifá).

Given this general picture, what does globalization, which seems irreversible, hold for the òrìṣà tradition? The second group, diaspora Africans, seem promised for a pivotal role in the process since its members, located as they are in the geographical, political, intellectual, and technological heart of the globalization process are, and will by necessity become increasingly, grounded in it, while being sentimentally and culturally connected with the continental African matrix. The extent to which this group will play its role with efficiency largely depends on the degree of involvement in the process of the black media in the United States.

If the òrìṣà tradition is globalized along the lines here delineated, there will be a boomerang effect on Africa itself. The tradition will acquire a new legitimacy, a new *lettres de noblesse* or credentials, a global, societal equivalent of the return of the repressed, or perhaps more in line with Yorùbá philosophy, a return of the prodigal son. One consequence of such a scenario is that the òrìṣà tradition will now openly resist, engage, and challenge Islam and Christianity in their missionary, fundamentalist, and intolerant versions. Most likely, this boomerang effect will force African practitioners to openly practice or revive a spirituality, which will address issues of poverty, identity, and environmental issues, and indeed to question the legitimacy of globalization by exposing its inconsistencies and paradoxes. This cannot be done without the absorption of some "global features" on the African continent. For instance, a great amount of standardization will have to be achieved in training, rituals, and other aspects Most likely, a churchlike organization will be adopted, with a congregation and a temple or shrine, with a priest catering to *all òrìṣà* in lieu of *one priest for one òrìṣà* as in the past. Yorùbá language will remain for a long time the sole language for rituals, but it will inevitably share with English, Spanish, and Portuguese the function of language of knowledge and instruction.

One of the paradoxes of globalization is that it encourages or produces standardization as it creates multipolarity. In the age of globalization, a likely picture will be the emergence of multipolar regulatory organizations and fora. Similarly, globalization promotes individuality in creativity. This means that it will beget not the end of religion as is generally feared and believed but the rise of new forms of spirituality and religiosity, with people experimenting with the features of various religious traditions, resulting in "quilt-like," personalized, and loosely organized religions, such as Inoue's "neo-syncretism" or "patchwork" (Inoue 1997: 89–90).

With the increasing visibility of the Yorùbá people in literature (Wole Soyinka, a Yorùbá writer, won the Nobel Prize in Literature in 1986, the first awarded to an African or, indeed, black person) and in the visual and performing arts (Fela Amkulapo Kuti, Sunny Ade, Lamidi Fakeye), the òrìṣà tradition will become a main ingredient in these new, individualized forms of syncretisms. In that respect, one likely effect of globalization on the òrìṣà traditions, especially outside the Atlantic world, will be the partial, selective appropriation of its elements by individuals or small groups in the concoction of new, personalized forms of religious lifestyles. For example, an òrìṣà, or some moral, behavioral, or aesthetic aspects of an òrìṣà that are appealing to an individual or a community, may be selected as the base component, the idiosyncratic worldview or doctrine of the individual or the group, along with other features taken from, say, Judaism, Hinduism, Buddhism, and Christianity, resulting in the formation of a new religion or a new sect. This is a likely scenario in the decades to come, particularly in the third of the three identified main actors in the Atlantic world, and, perhaps more so, among those outside it who have come in contact with the òrìṣà tradition primarily through books and the newest techniques of the information age, as opposed to the conventional initiation under the instruction and guidance of a master. Acquisition of segments of òrìṣà religion without the affective and "roots" dimension encourages detachment from other, related aspects of the tradition and the grand philosophy that determines and unites them, thereby paving the way for "patchwork" or "quilt-like" reformulations.

Could such "quilt-like," personalized religious practices still claim any legitimate filiation to the òrìṣà tradition? Theoretically, the answer can only be in the affirmative, since the òrìṣà tradition knows of no orthodoxy or orthopraxis. The predilection for a metonymic approach to innovation in the Yorùbá tradition reinforces this theoretical position. But this question raises problems, not at the theoretical realm, but in real life. Absence of an orthodoxy is certainly *not* synonymous with "anything goes." Indeed, what guarantees *both* this absence of orthodoxy *and* individual creativity in the tradition, with no known history of sectarianism, is the structure of initiation that privileges strong interpersonal relationships between priest and initiand in the transmission of religious

knowledge. The fact remains that new forms of globalization confront
the tradition with new, unprecedented situations and issues. Globalization brings cultures together and sets the context for their contact, but
is unable to stimulate deep, serious engagement between them, as it is
more a conquest over space than an apprehension of time depth. Time
is one of the worst enemies of modernity. Hannah Arendt's remark that
"we have histories without a common past, [which] threatens to render
all particular pasts irrelevant" is, unfortunately, adequately descriptive
of the cultural effects of modern globalization. The problem then is,
without a thorough engagement with its *deep knowledge* component can
religious groups that use some aspect of the òrìṣà tradition still lay legitimate claim to Yorùbáness? On the surface of it and from the point
of view of Yorùbá philosophical traditions, this interrogation is a false
problem. Historically, the Yorùbá have demonstrated that they are not
afraid of "otherness" and change. Logically, they should be indifferent
to claims of "Yorùbáness" from religious practices only remotely connected with theirs. However, perhaps it is too early to ask questions,
since we are witnessing an incipient stage of a potentially unprecedented
revolution.

Be that as it may, the minimal impact of the òrìṣà tradition in the era
of globalization will be to help usher in a new era of spirituality by re-
centering the attention of humankind around the following issues:

- the need for a new equilibrium among the components of our globe: nations and states; men and women; women, men, and children; elderly
  people and younger generations.
- the urgency for a new balance between human beings and other creatures,
  who are *not* at our service.
- the need for a new equilibrium between man and the supernatural world
  (òrìṣà, *kami*, etc.).

Finally, I must emphasize a missing factor, an unknown, in the various scenarios I have endeavored to foresee for the òrìṣà tradition in the
context of globalization, namely the specific role and contribution of
women. This factor can alter the scenarios in ways that are unpredict-
able. At this stage, it is unclear what position African women occupy,
what role they play and are likely to play in the globalization process.
If the past is anything to go by, African women's position, roles, and
initiatives in the globalization process will largely determine the future
of the òrìṣà tradition.

Historically, women have played a prominent role at *all* levels in Yorùbá religion. In the last four hundred years, their position has become *vital* because of the slave trade. From that period until today women have been at the forefront of religious maintenance and creativity in the African homeland, and more so in the African diaspora. The position of African women of the diaspora is even particularly critical in this respect, as they are closer to the decision centers of the globalization process. Much of the orientation of the òrìṣà tradition, much of the tenor of the new syncretisms, will largely depend on whether African women occupy the center of the process or are relegated to its periphery; whether they assertively make use of what Aimé Césaire called "the right to initiative" or whether, on the contrary, they remain passive consumers in an assigned place in the global chain of consumers; whether they creatively invent new forms of solidarity and understanding with women and also men of other religious traditions, in an effort to collectively visualize and promote more humane forms of coexistence that transcend the *homo economicus* dreams of material satisfaction, thereby aspiring to new forms of spirituality that are compatible and commensurable with true globalization, which cannot be synonymous with homogenization.

References

Abimbola, Wande. 1968. *Ijinle Ohun Enu Ifa*. Glasgow: Collins.

Abubakre, R. Deremi. 1986. *Linguistic and Non-Linguistic Aspects of Qur'an Translation into Yorùbá*. Studien zur Sprachwissenschaft 3. Hildesheim, Germany: Olms.

Akinjogbin, Adeagbo. 1967. *Dahomey and Its Neigbours, 1708–1818*. Cambridge: Cambridge University Press.

Argyriadis, Kali. 1999. "Une religion vivante: Pratiques culturelles havanaises." *L'Homme* 151: 21–46.

Barnes, Sandra, 1989. *Africa's Ogun: Old World and New*. Bloomington: Indiana University Press.

Capone, Stefania. 1999. "Les Dieux sur le Net: L'essor des religions d'origine africaine aux Etats-Unis." *L'Homme* 151: 47–74.

Davidson, Basil. 1994. *The Search for Africa: History, Culture, Politics*. New York: Times Books/Random House.

Doris, David T. 1996. "An Òrìṣà in the Land of Technology: The Internet and the Construction of Yorùbá Identities." Paper presented to the Eleventh Triennial Symposium on African Art, New Orleans, April 8–12.

Inoue, Nobutaka, ed. 1997. *Globalization and Indigenous Culture*. Fortieth anniversary memorial symposium, Kokugakuin University. Tokyo: Institute for Japanese Culture and Classics.

Mason, John. 1994. "Yorùbá-American Art: New Rivers to Explore." In *The Yorùbá Artist: New Theoretical Perspectives on African Art,* ed. Rowland Abiodun et al. Washington DC: Smithsonian Institution Press.

Maupoil, Bernard. 1943. *La Géomancie à l'ancienne Côte des Esclaves*. Paris: Institut d'Ethnologie de l'Université de Paris.

Patterson, Orlando. 1994. "Ecumenical America: Global Culture and the American Cosmos." *World Policy Journal* 11, no. 2: 103–17.

Sandoval, Alonso. 1956 (1627). *De Instauranda Aethiopium Salute: El mundo de esclavitud en las Américas*. Bogotá: Empresa Nacional de Publicaciones.

Senah, E. 1999. "Trinidad and the West African Nexus during the Nineteenth Century." Ph.D. diss., University of the West Indies, St Augustine, Trinidad.

Yai, Olabiyi Babalola, 1992. "Translatability: A Discussion." *Journal of Religion in Africa* 22, no. 2: 159–72.

———. 1994. "In Praise of Metonymy: The Concepts of "Tradition" and "Creativity in the Transmission of Yorùbá Artistry over Time and Space." In *The Yorùbá Artist: New Theoretical Perspectives on African Arts,* ed. Rowland Abiodun et al., 107–15. Washington, DC: Smithsonian Institution Press.

———. 1996. "African Concepts and Practice of the Nation and Their Implications in the Modern World." Paper presented at the University of Texas UNESCO Conference, "The African Diaspora and the New World," Austin, February 21–25.

12

Clearing New Paths into an Old Forest

Aládurà Christianity in Europe

AFE ADOGAME

European society, or at least a large segment of it, seems to be plagued by a sense of decline or deterioration of religion—perhaps religion has even received a death notice. This trend is particularly accurate in relation to church-oriented religiosity. In Africa, however, religion is enjoying a tremendous upsurge of vigor, vitality, and development. A remarkable proliferation of new religious movements—such as the Alá-durà—within and beyond Africa gives evidence of this expansion. The global process—involving increasing worldwide interconnections and exchanges, as well as movements of people, images, and commodities— has led to an increasing exodus of Africans beyond their continent. As they emigrate from Africa, Africans are carrying their religions and cultural identities with them. As usual, living in diverse cultural contexts encourages immigrants to reconstruct, organize, and identify "their religion" both for themselves and for the host society around them. Africans developed their own strategies and dynamics to exert some influence on their host societies.

This chapter examines the emergence and geographical expansion of the African Aládurà movements in Europe. It focuses on how religious

247

movements are creating a spiritual consciousness that attempts to assimilate notions of the global influence, while at the same time maintaining local identity. It shows to what extent they are appropriating new forms of communication technologies in information processing, dissemination, and evangelism, as well as in their self-assertion on the European religious terrain.

Who Are the Aládurà?

The term *Aládurà* derives from the Yorùbá words *ala-* (owner of) and *adura* (prayer) or *al adua,* which means literally owner or possessors of prayer, those who practice the act of prayer or, simply, the praying people. This concept was used conventionally to describe a group of churches emerging among the Yorùbá of western Nigeria after the 1920s. These movements are so called because of their penchant and proclivity for prayer, healing, prophecy, visions, dreams, and other charismatic activities. Churches that fall under this category include the following: Cherubim and Seraphim (C&S, 1925) Society, Christ Apostolic Church (CAC, 1930), Church of the Lord, Aládurà (CLA, 1930), and Celestial Church of Christ (CCC, 1947). Other churches described as Aládurà are the Evangelical Church of Yahweh (ECY, 1973), Church of the Seven Seals of God (CSSG, 1979) and the various appendages and splinter formations from these earlier movements. They are classified as indigenous religious forms, popularly known and referred to as African Initiated Churches (AICs). Even though these categories of churches emerged specifically within the Yorùbá cultural religious context, they have proliferated over the years, spreading beyond the Yorùbá to other parts of Nigeria, as well as to Africa, Europe, the United States, Asia, and other parts of the world. Today total membership, now international in outlook, is several million as they have founded and sought affiliation with local and international ecumenical bodies, such as the Christian Association of Nigeria (CAN), the Organization of African Indigenous Churches (OAIC), and the World Council of Churches (WCC).

Some scholars of African religions have often treated the Aládurà phenomenon as if it can be understood simply as a single whole. However, Aládurà churches are diverse in terms of the affinity and differences that characterize their belief systems and ritual structures. Previously, this tendency of treating the phenomenon as a single entity required emphasis on their common features, as well as their peculiarities. Although Aládurà churches share many features, each Aládurà church has its own religious dynamic. There are significant differences between groups, especially in their foundational histories, the charismatic personalities of their founders, their belief patterns, ritual structures, organizational policies, and geographical distribution.

Patterns of Emergence

Two historical categories can be traced to the emergence of Aládurà churches. The first category of churches emerged from within already existing conventional churches for religious, cultural, and political reasons. Thus, Mitchell (1970: 459) observed, though one-sidedly, that Aládurà movements "have in common their initial emergence as prayer groups in mission churches." Previously, the nucleus of these movements existed as "prayer or fellowship groups," "societies," or "bible study classes" before their expulsion or voluntary secession and schism from the parent body. The earliest group that emerged under this category was the Cherubim and Seraphim (C&S) Society. For several years it was an interdenominational society, "preaching faith in prayers and renouncing the devil and all his works—including the worship of idols, the use of *juju* and charms, and the fear of the power of the witches." Formalizing the society as a church in 1925 was a consequence of the intolerance of "orthodox" churches (see Omoyajowo 1982: 9). The Christ Apostolic Church (CAC) resulted from the fusion of the Precious Stone Society (PSS) or Diamond Society (prayer groups within the Anglican Church), the Nigerian Faith Tabernacle (NFT), and the Great Revival, the event of 1930 that served as an impetus toward unification. The triumvirate of Joseph Babalola, Isaac Akinyele, and David Odubanjo established the nucleus of the church, which commenced "unofficially" as a prayer group within the Anglican Church. A myriad of issues—doctrinal conflicts (i.e., questions of faith, divine healing, and infant baptism), personality clashes, administrative problems, persecution from the mainline churches—transformed the movement under various names until 1943 when it was formally registered (no. 147) as the "Christ Apostolic Church" under the Lands Perpetual Succession Ordinance of 1924 (see Adegboyega 1978; Orogun 1982; Oshun 1983). The Church of the Lord (Aládurà) emerged from within the mission church tradition, founded by Josiah Ositelu in 1930 following his suspension from the Anglican Church (where he served as catechist) primarily over conflict of doctrinal questions (Turner 1967; Peel 1968; Ositelu 2002).

Those who did not sever from any existing mainstream church or who faced no form of ejection represent the second category in the emergence of Aládurà churches. This group emerged independently through the charismatic initiative of a leader. A clear example is the Celestial Church of Christ (CCC), founded spontaneously around the life, visionary experience, and charismatic personality of Samuel Bilehou Oschoffa (a carpenter turned prophet) in 1947 (Adogame 1999). Although it could be argued that charismatic leadership is not exclusive to the CCC among the Aládurà fold. Joseph Babalola of the CAC, Josiah Ositelu of the CLA, and Moses Orimolade of the C&S are no doubt charismatic founders and leaders in their own rights. The distinction that needs to be made here is that these latter groups all severed ties from established churches as groups whereas the CCC did not sever any ties. In some ways this distinction becomes more evident especially in comparing their belief and ritual systems.

Aládurà Christianity in Europe: Its Inception

The introduction overseas of a brand of Christianity influenced by African culture can be said to have emerged only during the 1960s, first in Great Britain (UK) and afterward in continental Europe. The growing presence of the Aládurà movement has been noticed in the last four decades, for instance, with the establishment in London of the first branch of the CLA in 1964 and the CCC in 1967. Other Aládurà churches such as the CAC and the C&S followed later. From the early 1960s onward, the investiture of Aládurà churches in Europe was essentially the handiwork of Nigerian students abroad or wayfarers on business or official assignments—those who perhaps never intended to reside permanently abroad. When a few members of each group found themselves in one city or community, the initiative came for them to meet and worship together. As their membership increased, the group became more inter-ethnic, diverse, and international in outlook. It was the nucleus group of the respective churches who met for fellowship and Bible studies in private homes that later transformed itself into several branches scattered all over Europe today. Thus, branches of these churches have been established in parts of the United Kingdom, Germany, Austria, the Netherlands, Italy, France, Belgium, and Spain. It must be noted that some of these groups had already experienced schisms in their histories. Thus, for a particular group, there now exist some factions, which are represented on the European religious scene. A second category of Aládurà churches in diaspora are those that have emerged in Europe either by severing from an already existing church or because of the charismatic quality of a leader. An example of this is the Aládurà International Church in London led by Olu Abiola.

Social Composition

As a religious movement develops and expands, so does the tendency to incorporate people from varying ethnic and sociocultural backgrounds. Aládurà churches in Europe throw open "hands of fellowship" to people of all races and colors who have chosen to become members or those who are interested in visiting and participating in their worship services. Visitors are warmly welcomed and given recognition during Sunday services or other religious programs. At every service or program, visitors or those attending for the first time are duly identified and are introduced or made to do self-introductions. Special prayers are also enacted in their favor, and they are further enjoined to call again or join the fold. In some cases, they are provided with registration forms specially designed for new members or visitors to fill out and return to the ushers or officers in charge. They are expected, among other things, to supply their contact addresses for follow-up personal visits by members or through correspondence, as the case may be. One other recurring question in these questionnaire-type forms is why they have come to the church and how they came to know about the church or who introduced them. This is one of their strategies for recruiting new members and for evangelization. Male visitors are usually followed up with visits by male members or a team comprising males and females, while female visitors are visited by female members or a team of males and females.

A large section of African members of the church in Europe are not illiterates but elites of their countries who have been sent to the Western world as diplomats, businesspersons, missionaries, or students or those who have come on their own to seek the "golden fleece." The membership cuts across all different levels of society from civil servants, diplomats, businesspersons, women, and skilled and unskilled factory workers to students, the unemployed, and asylum (political or economic) seekers or refugees. In recent times asylum seekers and refugees from different parts of Africa have constituted the membership of most of these churches. The incessant political, religious, and socioeconomic crises and upheavals in some parts of Africa have exacerbated the migration and exodus of mostly able-bodied youths to these parts of the world. They usually have high expectations before their sojourn, but oftentimes, as soon as they arrive and meet the new realities, they become despondent and frustrated. They believe that the "land unknown" will, in all respects, be better than the "land of their birth." As a member of one of the African new religious movements once proclaimed:

> There is a Kingdom of Heaven and a Kingdom of Hell on earth. England is a United Kingdom. It is the Kingdom of Heaven! If we work, we have food. If we do not work, we can still have food. If we decide to stop working before we are very old, someone will look after us. This is also what it is like in the Kingdom of Heaven. We have read about people like Christopher Columbus and Mungo Park. These good people came from these parts of the world and traveled long distances to bring wealth to their countries.[1]

The earlier part of this statement seems to eulogize why members of this movement may prefer this new land to their original homes, and, in fact, this is a view that may be shared by other African immigrants. The last sentence may suggest the member's interest in accumulating wealth in the foreign land in which he finds himself and eventually sending it back to his home country.

The Aládurà membership in Europe cuts across ethnic precincts to include Africans (mostly West Africans), Afro-Caribbeans, Surinamese, and Europeans. However, their membership has remained predominantly African, with the Yorùbá forming the largest share. Other members come from non-Yorùbá ethnic groups in Nigeria and other countries such as Benin Republic, Ghana, Côte d'Ivoire, Togo, and Senegal. The white population depends largely on the European country in question. Overall, there seem to be more Austrians, English, and Germans. Their membership can be linked primarily to intermarriage or to casual, friendly relationships with black (African) members.

The Proliferation of Aládurà Christianity in Europe

In the last four decades, an increasing proliferation of the Aládurà phenomenon is being witnessed in Europe and elsewhere. Such expansion has been stimulated by factors such as increasing transnational migration, missions, improved transportation systems, politics, commerce, global marketing, tourism, and the creation and use of new forms of global communication networks. There has been an increase in the circulation of cultural meanings, objects, and identities in diffuse time-space (Macus 1995), that is, movements of capital, communications, and people across national or geographical borders. The physical existence of Africans in Europe as well as the European existence in Africa is a feature that has a history of many centuries behind it. More interestingly, in the last decades a remarkable upsurge in the number of African migrants in Europe and those seeking to live in different parts of Europe heralds a new phase in the history of African presence on the European soil. Such an unprecedented trend forms an integral part of the global phenomenon of international migration. This feature has been aggravated by incessant political upheavals and instability, human rights violations, dwindling economies, the quest for greener pastures, war, poverty, population explosion, delusion, and intermarriages, as well as the desire to reunite with families abroad. The factors accounting for this dimension are, in fact, legion.

Conspicuous features of African-initiated churches such as the Aládurà movement include their vitality, their dynamism, and their demonstration of a great capacity for incorporating change, such as that witnessed in the contemporary era due to shifts in global migration patterns. One remarkable fallout of the globalization process is the increasing "dispersal" of Africans beyond their continental context, thus moving them from a local to a global presence. Consequently, the bridging of the gap brought about several strategies through which religious interchanges were exerted on the worldwide religious landscape. In reference to African churches in diaspora, Ter Haar (1998a: 23) notes that "their spread overseas has involved these churches in international networks of relations to which they did not have access until the late twentieth century. There is now a two-way channel of communication between churches inside and outside Africa, whether they belong to the first or the second generation of African-initiated churches. This shows that Africa has become fully part of a global world in religious terms. The founding of African independent churches all over the world is a sure sign of this."

The Aládurà church movements have come up with initiatives toward joining or forming ecumenical links or ties (national, continental, intercontinental). Thus, we have, for instance, the Organization of African Indigenous Churches (OAIC), Council of Christian Communities of African Approach in Europe (CCCAAE), Cherubim and Seraphim Council of Churches in London, Churches Together in England (CTE), Churches' Commission for Racial Equality (CCRE), Council of African and Caribbean Churches (CACC), and the World Council of Churches (WCC). The adoption of such labels as "international," "worldwide," "global," or "world" in their nomenclatures indicates their religiously inspired and promising access to transnationalism and the wide variety of their international linkages. A few examples here are the Celestial Church of Christ Worldwide, the Church of the Lord—Aládurà Worldwide, Christ Apostolic Church Worldwide, and Aládurà International Church.

Increasing globalization trends have influenced new forms, motivations, and techniques of missionary activities in the contemporary period. This global interconnection has carried with it mission exchanges from one part of the world to another. The repackaging and exportation of Aládurà Christianity to other parts of the globe was realized not only through migration processes but also via missions. The respective Aládurà groups have been embarking on a missionary task to propagate their religious message to the wider world. Most of these churches have not only developed their own mission, evangelistic strategies, and dynamics but have charged themselves with the task of taking their vision beyond their immediate environment and context. Turner (1979: 291) aptly remarked on this when he said:

> Some of the African churches have a sense of mission towards us (*Europeans*)! They see how static and ineffective we are, and how little we share some of their own central convictions about prayer, fasting, healing, the power of the Spirit and the joy of worship. They ride on the crest of a religion that works. They share also in the new-found African convictions of having an important contribution to make to the nations of the world, especially in the realms of human relations and of the spiritual where we are increasingly desiccated and inadequate. One sign of the authenticity of their Christian faith is a desire to share their discoveries and open up to us again the dynamic of our mutual heritage.

This view has been largely corroborated by Rufus Ositelu (Primate, Church of the Lord—Aládurà Worldwide), one of the African Instituted Churches. Describing the mission of his church in Europe, he said,

> The mission of our church is to bring Christ to all nations particularly outside Africa so that they too may experience spiritual fulfillment in Christ Jesus. This is as revealed to our founding fathers an age of importation of the gospel or mission-reversed into the industrialized world from Africa . . . our church is making an attempt to restore life into the churches through Spirit filled worship sessions and in-depth studies of the word of God . . . our mission is to bring good news to all people in this land irrespective of race or colour and to present to them yet another form of worshipping in the beauty of His Holiness in spirit and in truth. (Ositelu 1998).[2]

The Aládurà movements have made significant inroads into the life and religious arena of some European churches. The influence exerted has resulted in joint worship services and programs as well as the exchange of pulpits. A closer understanding and mutual respect of one another's worldview has been engendered through this process. The liturgical revolution of the Aládurà movement and its characteristic musical pattern, dancing, drumming, and the display of charismatic propensity have drawn a lot of attention from Europeans. Some of these churches are increasingly taking up extra-religious functions such as social welfare programs within European society. Thus, their focus is on not only the spiritual wealth of members but also their social, material, and psychological well-being. Beyond their church vicinity, they have taken up tasks such as the regeneration and rehabilitation of drug-ridden youths in the society, the socially displaced, the underprivileged, refugees, asylum seekers, and so forth. In some European countries, some church authorities have stood as intermediaries, guarantors, and intermediaries between their members and the government, public and private agencies, especially in cases of employment, legal actions, social security issues, residence permits, visa approval, deportation orders, and law enforcement.

Over the years the Aládurà churches in Europe have grown to acquire immense properties and real estate. Erstwhile warehouses, abandoned church buildings, cinemas, and pubs have been acquired at huge financial costs. Some were procured outright while others were leased or rented for several years. Some churches have also acquired a fleet

of cars and buses, which are used by members for official church purposes or for commercial purposes as vehicle hires or rentals. Business
centers, lodging and accommodation, religious book centers, guidance
and counseling units, recreation centers, musical halls, video and audio-
cassette shops, and shopping malls are also owned by these churches.
Such activities no doubt have immense religious-economic import for
the churches as well as for the immediate environment and communities
in which they are located. This development suggests that some of these
churches have come of age in these new cultural environments.

The Aládurà churches in Europe today display a significant model of
African Christianity in the way they organize themselves, with features
emanating from both their European location as well as their African
heritage. Some of these groups have burgeoned owing to the unwel-
comeness experienced by African migrants in European churches and
their quest for spiritual satisfaction. Closely related to this is the phenomenon of xenophobia or racism at both individual and institutional
levels. Africans continue to experience exclusion and discrimination in
various forms all over Europe. This along with the impact of racism is
too conspicuous to be easily wished away as exceptions or aberrations.
As a leader of one of the African Initiated Churches[3] aptly observed:

> Another reality is that racist experiences are part of the daily lives of
> Africans and all Black people. We are talking of the experiences people
> endure because of their skin color. *Because they experience it at all
> times the church cannot help but address it,* even though it has been
> sometimes said that it is challenged with excessive force, whatever that
> means. But more importantly, when people have no peace or respect
> at work, when they are under pressure constantly, when they are under
> constant surveillance because they are distrusted, when they are con-
> stantly trying to find a reason for existing, constantly needing to reaf-
> firm their humanness, and they cannot find it because they are treated
> like less human wherever they go, when people are denied the best ser-
> vices, of homes, employment, career choices, when the society they
> live in constantly tells them they are irrational and primitive because
> of the worldviews they hold, when they look on history and the present
> predicament saps away their hope and ambitions, in the tension where
> they are always expected to become something other than who they are,
> and so on, there must be a place where they can say and sing, *"Now I
> am in my Father's house I can rest and enjoy His peace."* (Jehu-Appiah
> 1995)

Thus, members have found the Aládurà churches as "places to feel at home" and a "home away from home."[4] The churches have therefore become places where people can feel important and feel valued. When they are dancing, screaming, jumping, and rejoicing, they are expressing their humanity; they are expressing and celebrating their thanks to God. They are saying, "I thank God that He gave me the church where I can go and be myself and not be ashamed of it." Irrespective of the cultural background of members, a sense of belonging and community is rekindled in the church.

The Use of Media Technologies

Some of the Aládurà churches in diaspora are already using and appropriating new forms of media technologies in information processing and dissemination in their task of "fishing for men (and women)" and in their self-assertion on the European religious context. This involves the creation and use of computer Web sites, fax and electronic mail systems, audio- and videotapes, books, tracts, magazines, handbills, leaflets, and so on. An example from the Celestial Church of Christ Worldwide will suffice here.[5] The CCC seeks to create a global network using Internet Web sites and electronic mail.[6] In a release on December 15, 1997, announcing its (Riverdale site) presence on the Internet, it stated:

> Halleluyah!!! . . . Celestial Church of Christ now has a dominant presence on the World Wide Web. The main focus of this page is to present a unified and cohesive communication vehicle for Celestial Church as a whole, world-wide . . . As the web site evolve[s], we hope to use it as a vehicle to communicate news about Celestial Church of Christ on a global basis, both information geared toward Celestians and non-Celestians alike.

The UK site complemented the church's objective through its mission statement that states, in part: "To introduce CCC to the whole world . . . to bring all the parishes together by obtaining free e-mail addresses for interested parishes and contribute to the free flow of information in the church . . . to use the medium of the Internet as a vehicle to recruit new members."

A careful look at the full contents of these mission statements shows the intention of the church is manifold. First, the new media technology would help to bridge the communication gap between branches as well as between the church and the "outside world." Second, it would serve as a medium for educating members and nonmembers about the church. Complementarily, as a strategy toward evangelism, the medium would function "as a vehicle to recruit new members."

Alexander Bada succeeded Bilehou Oschoffa as pastor and overseer of the CCC Worldwide from 1987 until his demise in 2000.[7] Bada's intensification of revivals and evangelism was not limited to Nigeria (where the church is most popular), but he has extended them to the overseas parishes through his "annual pastoral tours." Such visits usually last from at least one week to several months, depending on the lined-up program of events (spiritual and administrative). In 1987, Pastor Bada, accompanied by an entourage of five members, embarked on a two-month (from 8 May to 9 July) tour of twenty-eight parishes in the overseas diocese.[8] Countries visited were the United Kingdom, Germany, Austria, France, and the United States. Originally the pastoral visit was expected to take place every two years, but because of the widespread nature of the church, its attendant problems (negotiations for new church buildings, settlement of intra-church disputes, discussions on registration, and proliferation of parishes), and the need to intensify evangelism, the pastor has embarked on more frequent (overseas) tours annually. More important, the annual pastoral visits to the overseas diocese have been necessitated by the need to conduct the anointment ritual for its members abroad.[9] Evangelistic strategies such as revivals, public lectures, and press interviews are increasingly utilized to register the church on the global religious map. Courtesy calls are also made on such tours to churches and other religious leaders in Germany, Britain, Austria, France, Belgium, and other parts of Europe where branches are located. The church leadership has participated in religious and public forum discussions through the electronic media.[10]

Conclusion

As noted earlier, Aládurà churches and other African religious movements are burgeoning not only on the European religious scene but also in other parts of the world. They have met with a myriad of impediments in their various attempts at "fishing for souls" and "making their voices" heard on the European religious soil. The problems encountered by these communities in different parts of Europe include language barriers, lack or paucity of space (accommodation), loud services (hostility of neighbors), transience of membership, and administrative matters—status of churches and legal status of church members. Other problems include cultural barriers, understanding of the host welfare system, finances, weather conditions, long duration of services, and the nature of some practices or tenets (i.e., prohibitions on alcohol and cigarette smoking). However, it appears that the Aládurà churches will continue to make inroads and sink their roots deeper and deeper into the European soil and elsewhere, so long as the uncertainties, anxieties, and vacuums created by prevailing global socioeconomic and political realities do not go away or at least seem to be mitigated. The taking up of extra-religious functions such as social welfare programs has been shown to be meaningful and relevant in contemporary European society where social workers, bureaucrats, and governments are engaged in a "tug of war" to reform failing welfare systems. The Aládurà churches are also serving as an abode of spiritual solace, especially for many political and economic asylum seekers and refugees in Europe. In these contexts, spiritual, physical, moral, psychological, and material support and assistance are extended to members and nonmembers alike.

Notes

1. See the full text of the testimony of a member of the Brotherhood of the Cross and Star in Kerridge 1995: 56.

2. Rev. Dr. Rufus Ositelu was formerly the overseer of all branches of the Church of the Lord-Aládurà in Europe and America. He is currently the primate of the Church of the Lord-Aládurà Worldwide.

3. Jerisdan Jehu-Appiah is a minister of the Musama Disco Christo Church (one of the African Instituted Churches) in London.

4. See Adogame 1998, 1999, 2000a, 2002a.

5. For a wider treatment of the CCC use of new forms of media technologies, see Adogame 1999.

6. See, for instance, the Web site addresses http://www.celestialchurch.com (operated by a parish in Riverdale, Maryland, USA) and http://www.celestial church.mcmail.com (accessed January 20, 1998) (administered from the UK). Their electronic mail addresses are webmaster@celestialchurch.com and celestialchurchofchrist@mcmail, respectively.

7. For details, see Adogame 1999.

8. Details of his activities at this singular visit are documented in Okunkola 1995: 77–84. In 1987, Bada embarked on pastoral visits to northern states in Nigeria—Kano, Kaduna, and Katsina.

9. Immigration laws and other harsh conditions in several overseas countries pose an impediment for many members who intend to participate in the annual anointment ritual at the international headquarters of the church in Lagos, Nigeria. In some cases only members who had valid resident permits in their "countries of sojourn" and who could afford the exorbitant airfares were able to attend the ritual. To alleviate this hardship and bridge the existing communication gap, Pastor Bada enacted the annual anointment ritual in the overseas diocese with the assistance of the then Superior Evangelist Ajose, the general overseer of the Overseas Diocese.

10. During the pastoral visit of Bada in 1975, the church was featured for thirty minutes on Radio 4 in Britain. The first baptismal rites in the UK were enacted by him at a stream at Kingdom-upon-Thames in Surrey. In 1987, the pastor was interviewed by the *West Africa Magazine* in North London, and he delivered a live sermon on the Sunday religious program on a Chicago local television station (courtesy of CCC Chicago Parish, June 21).

References

Adegboyega, Samuel G. 1978. *A Short History of the Apostolic Church in Nigeria*. Ibadan: Rosprint Press.

Adogame, Afe . 1998. "A Home Away from Home: The Proliferation of the Celestial Church of Christ (CCC) in Diaspora—Europe." *Exchange* 27, no. 2: 141–60.

———. 1999. *Celestial Church of Christ: The Politics of Cultural Identity in a West African Prophetic-Charismatic Movement*. Frankfurt am Main: Peter Lang.

———. 2000a. "Mission from Africa: The Case of the Celestial Church of Christ in Europe." *Zeitschrift für Missionswissenschaft und Religionswissenschaft* 84, no. 1: 29–44.

———. 2000b. "The Quest for Space in the Global Religious Marketplace: African Religions in Europe." *International Review of Mission* 89, no. 354: 400–409.

———. 2002a. "Engaged in the Task of 'Cleansing' the World: Aládurà Churches in Twentieth Century Europe." In *Transcontinental Links in the History of Non-Western Christianity*, vol. 6, ed. Klaus Koschorke, 73–86. Wiesbaden, Germany: Harrassowitz.

————. 2002b. "Traversing Local-Global Religious Terrain: African New Religious Movements in Europe." *Zeitschrift für Religionswissenschaft* 10: 33–49.

————. 2004. "Engaging the Rhetoric of Spiritual Warfare: The Public Face of Aládurà in Diaspora." *Journal of Religion in Africa* 34, no. 4: 493–522.

————. 2005a. "African Christian Communities in Diaspora." In *African Christianity: An African Story,* ed. Ogbu U. Kalu, 494–514. Pretoria: University of Pretoria.

————. 2005b. "African Instituted Churches in Europe: Continuity and Transformation." In *African Identities and World Christianity in the Twentieth Century,* ed. Klaus Koschorke, 225–44. Wiesbaden: Harrassowitz Verlag.

————. 2005c. "To Be or Not to Be? Politics of Belonging and African Christian Communities in Germany." In *Religion in the Context of African Migration,* ed. Afe Adogame and Cordula Weisskoeppel, 95–112. Bayreuth African Studies Series, no. 75. Bayreuth, Germany: Bayreuth African Studies, Universität Bayreuth.

Harris, Hermione. 2002. "The Cherubim and Seraphim: The Concept and Practice of Empowerment in an African Church in London." Ph.D. diss., University of London.

Hill, Clifford. 1971. *Black Churches: West Indian and African Sects in Britain.* London: Community and Race Relations Unit, British Council of Churches.

Jehu-Appiah, Jerisdan H. 1995. "An Overview of Indigenous African Churches in Britain: An Approach through the Historical Survey of African Pentecostalism." In *Report of the Proceedings between the World Council of Churches and African and African-Caribbean Church Leaders in Britain,* 30 November–2 December: 49–65.

Kerridge, Roy. 1995. *The Storm Is Passing Over: A Look at Black Churches in Britain.* London: Thames and Hudson.

Macus, G. 1995. "Ethnography In / Of the World System: The Emergence of Multi-Sited Ethnography." *Annual Review of Anthropology* 24: 95–117.

Mitchell, R. C. 1970. "Towards the Sociology of Religious Independency." *Journal of Religion in Africa* 3, no. 1: 2–20.

Okunlola, D. O. 1995. *Bada and the Great Commission.* Lagos.

Omoyajowo, Akinyele Joseph. 1978. "The Aládurà Churches in Nigeria since Independence." In *Christianity in Independent Africa,* ed. Edward W. Fashole-Luke et al., 96–110. Bloomington: Indiana University Press.

————. 1982. *Cherubim and Seraphim: The History of an African Independent Church.* New York: NOK.

Orogun, J. B. 1982. *A Short History on the Founding of Christ Apostolic Church of Nigeria and Its Expansion to All Parts of Nigeria.* Lagos: CAC.

Oshun, C. O. 1983. "Nigeria's Pentecostalism: Dynamics and Adaptability." *Religions* 8: 40–59.

Ositelu, Rufus. 1998. "The Church of the Lord—(Aládurà), Hamburg—Altona." Paper read at Werkstattgespräche zur Bedentung der Afrikanischen religiosen Diaspora in Deutschland, Missionsakademie, University of Hamburg, September 9–11.

————. 1999. "Aládurà—Kirche—Afrikaner bei uns." *Zeitschrift fur Missionswissenschaft und Religionswissenschaft* 83, no. 2: 169–76.

————. 2002. *African Instituted Churches*. Munster: Lit Verlag.

Parris, G. A., ed. 1996. "Sharing the Struggles and Hopes of African People in Europe." WCC-URM, CBWCP. Malaga, Spain.

Peel, J. D. Y. 1968. *Aládurà: A Religious Movement among the Yoruba*. London: Oxford University Press.

Simon, Benjamin. 2003. *Afrikanische Kirchen in Deutschland*. Frankfurt: Lembeck.

Ter Haar, Gerrie. 1998a. *Halfway to Paradise: African Christians in Europe*. Cardiff: Cardiff Academic Press, 1998.

————, ed. 1998b. *Strangers and Sojourners: Religious Communities in the Diaspora*. Leuven: Peeters.

Thompson, Jack. 1995. "African Independent Churches in Britain: An Introductory Survey." In *New Religions and the New Europe,* ed. Robert Towler, 224–31. Aarhus: Aarhus University Press.

Turner, Harold. W. 1967. *African Independent Church*. Vol. 1: *The Church of the Lord (Aládurà); vol. 2: The Life and Faith of the Church of the Lord (Aládurà)*. Oxford: Clarendon Press.

————. 1979. *Religious Innovation in Africa: Collected Essays on New Religious Movements*. Boston: G. K. Hall.

13

Globalization and the Evolution of Haitian Vodou

LAËNNEC HURBON, TRANSLATED BY TERRY REY

Toward the end of the eighteenth century, Haiti became the first subjugated national community to mount a successful challenge to European colonial rule. In doing so, Haitians salvaged the original living culture of Vodou, an African religious system expanded and integrated with diverse European and indigenous American cultural elements. A thorough discussion of Vodou's current evolution in the context of modern globalization requires a comprehensive survey of its history, which began as a mode of cultural resistance against the effects of New World slavery. Far from representing a new phenomenon distinct from the era of Atlantic slavery, as some theorists would have us believe, contemporary globalization sits directly on the historical timeline as an extension of the age of colonization. In this essay, we highlight certain characteristics of contemporary globalization and ways in which it differs from an earlier phase of globalization that the transatlantic slave trade represents. More significantly, this extension sets the stage to demonstrate the effects of globalization on Haitian Vodou's present evolution, which is the focus of this essay.

Contradictions in Theories of Globalization

Because so many theories of contemporary globalization have been advanced recently, we are unable to enter squarely into the debate.[1] Instead, we briefly outline the more salient points of these theories in order to orient our central investigation of the effects of globalization on Haitian Vodou. Some theorists argue historically that globalization is a recent phenomenon brought on with the fall of the Berlin Wall, and that it has intensified with the advent of new means of electronic communication. Consequently, the world has been effectively transformed into a "global village," and vast stores of information are now readily accessible across the globe. According to this perspective, concepts of nation-state, national culture, national territory, and national sovereignty lose all theoretical relevance. They are thus rendered obsolete. Henceforth, civil society is transnationalized and no longer wholly distinguishable from the state, a concept that is itself more loosely framed today than ever.

Other theorists hold that the most crucial aspect of globalization is post–cold war capitalism's unbridled spread.[2] With the relative deterritorialization of nations, world resources are open to multinational corporate exploitation as never before. These corporations hold great influence over the foreign policies of the world powers. As a result, a "McDonald's fast-food culture" is spreading across the globe at the expense of local cuisine and culture. Analyses of this destructive influence, however, are somewhat inattentive to the contradictions of globalization. Such a global cultural hegemony is far from evident, in fact, and it is equally possible that contemporary globalization will result in a multipolar world precisely because of the weakening of national boundaries. In effect, the more one country accesses the latest information technologies, the more it is able to compete economically. Furthermore, the grievances of oppressed peoples can now find a new transnational space in which they can be expressed and heard. On the cultural level, the contradictions of globalization are even more pronounced. Given the neoliberal economic orientation that is very much the basis of contemporary globalization, numerous peripheral countries and regions will become increasingly marginalized. In such places, the lower classes will have less access than ever to education, health care, and means of communication—in a nutshell, to the basic means of human dignity. Furthermore, in such peripheral countries or regions we witness the severest environmental tragedies, because neoliberalism is by definition indifferent to the common good and aims to diminish as much as possible state control.

It is not surprising that globalization by the First World has thus been met with mass protest against its resultant "deculturation" and economic domination of the Third World. Many societies are now rallying in efforts to reinforce national culture and identity, to the extent of reinstating fundamentalism, racism, and ethnic cleansing. In reality, such phenomena are new only in appearance. As Immanuel Wallerstein (1991) demonstrates, the world economy has long developed through this very capitalist system by its practices of conquest, slavery, and colonialism. Beginning in the sixteenth century, the West's claim to have the ultimate and defining civilization wrought colonial domination, under whose legacy the world still lives today. The only true hope of moving beyond this situation is to recognize all nations as one, without distinctions of "race," religion, or nationality, all the while promoting universal democracy. However, regrettably, present political and economic realities are less conducive to the promotion of universal principles and more conducive to anarchy.

Could the case be made that these historical developments are irreversible and hold nothing but negative results for marginalized societies? Nothing is entirely certain, especially in light of certain social reactions to globalization that, in fact, lead to both a revitalization of traditional cultures and a re-appropriation of the resources of globalization toward maintaining cultural uniqueness among the marginalized.[3] It is interesting to recall that despite the transatlantic slave trade's politics of cultural amnesia, an African-derived cultural creativity of exceptional originality emerged in the Caribbean and the Americas. In what follows, we demonstrate that Haitian Vodou, a religion drawing significant inspiration from traditional "Yorùbá" religion and related traditions, is presently entering a new phase in the process of globalization—itself spawned by modern colonial conquest and transatlantic slave trade.

Effects of Globalization on Haitian Vodou

Until the 1930s and 1940s, Vodou was widely considered an amalgam of superstitions incompatible with anything called an orthodox "religion," having survived in large part thanks to an ongoing tradition of maroonage and self-alienation from the state. Vodou's existence and development depended upon the creativity of rural peasants in the Haitian mountains and plains. Following the period from Haitian independence in 1804 until the signing of a concordat between Haiti and the Vatican in 1860, Vodou was the victim of a series of campaigns of persecution. As of 1864, rumors of sorcery and cannibalism surrounded the practice of Vodou and drove the nation's power elite to attempt to eradicate a national shame that "relegated" the Haitian people to the status of "savages." In 1896, the Catholic clergy inaugurated and organized the first systematic "anti-superstition campaign," benefiting from the U.S. military occupation from 1915 to 1934, orchestrated under the pretext of bringing "civilization" to a "black" society prone to despotism and incapable of governing itself. With the assistance of the government, the next campaign occurred in 1941. In parishes throughout the nation, the Catholic Church preached its infamous *rejeté* sermon, forcing the faithful to repeat an oath denouncing Vodou, declaring this resilient African "defect" a satanic cult.[4]

Globalization was only indirectly responsible for the changes that would occur in the prevailing public attitude toward Vodou, because abandoning the inquisition against the religion was actually prerequisite to the emergence of Haiti's pro-democratic movement, and not vice versa. During the thirty-year Duvalier dictatorship from 1957 to 1986, Vodou was employed by the political regime as a means of ideological control over the country's uneducated poor. Although Vodou is now embraced as a source of authentic Haitian cultural expression, clearly it remains a still-dominated religion. Furthermore, it is still widely regarded as a cultural system emerging among the peasantry, a worldview corresponding to a way of life beset by underdevelopment and backwardness. Even to those who feign to defend the religion, Vodou represents an insular world opposed to modernity and progress. Thus, under a recent dictatorial regime, permits were still required to practice Vodou and were just as mandatory under nineteenth-century penal codes.

Not until the 1987 inauguration of the Haitian Constitution, with its concern for fundamental human rights, did the official persecution and exploitation of practitioners of Vodou decrease. Yet, in spite of subsequent gains in the freedom of worship, Vodou is rarely recognized as a religious tradition in Haiti. Nonetheless, after the 1987 Constitution, most significantly there has been a direct correspondence between the decriminalization of Vodou and the process of democratization. For the first time in Haitian history the historically marginalized, politically excluded peasant was recognized as a true citizen. We cannot, then, locate the central effects of globalization on Vodou in the process of democratization. These effects are far more longstanding and complex and require analysis in light of the integral place of Vodou in Haitian politics, economics, and social life.

The globalization process, at least in its present form, tends to transnationalize civil societies, whose needs and values are so increasingly diverse that they can no longer be understood merely in terms of nationhood (Beck 1997). Migration of people from marginalized societies to more developed nations is radically transforming the notions of territory (with borders becoming contingent), nation-state (the adoption of bi- or multinationality society is now common), and cultural identity (the adoption of multicultural identity traits is now virtually universal). In the case of Haiti, this process began early in the twentieth century with massive migrations of Haitans to Cuba and the Dominican Republic to work on sugar plantations. Moreover, the migration gained momentum in the 1970s and 1980s, as Haitian emigrants made their way in significant numbers to the United States, Canada, France, and other Caribbean islands of the Bahamas and Guadeloupe. By now, such waves of emigration have swept over 10 percent of Haitians to other lands, indicating a grave crisis reaching to the very foundation of Haitian society.

Whereas during what we have termed the first wave of globalization (colonial conquest) Vodou was necessarily an insular religion—largely a collection of clandestine, esoteric cults—twentieth-century migrations forced open the doors of the religion.[5] Furthermore, Haitians now found themselves able to openly declare Vodou as their religion, and this with impunity. Emerging from such declaration was a greater conviction that Vodou was both the true source and savior of Haitian cultural uniqueness. This phenomenon encouraged an impressive retreat by Vodou's adversaries and marked a new era of relative openness and acceptance for Haitian traditional religion. To outsiders, Vodou became a source of artistic inspiration for music, dance, and, especially, painting. In the United States, DeWitt Peters had already brought so-called primitive Haitian painting to acclaim, and it soon was in demand throughout the Caribbean and in Europe. In 1976 André Malraux conducted research on the Saint Soleil School, concluding that Haitian painting, anchored in the world of the Vodou spirits, was of universal significance.

However, the more the aesthetic dimension of Haitian Vodou was promoted and transnationalized, the more its truly religious dimension was overlooked and diluted. One could perhaps even speak today of a kind of watered-down version that serves as the religion's transnational gatekeeper. At risk is the erosion of Vodou's uniqueness, which also results from profits sought through the exploitation of the religion's extraordinary artistry. For example, numerous Vodouesque elements are now incorporated into the Catholic Mass in Haiti. Vatican II's promotion of *aggiornamento* has driven the Catholic clergy to introduce the drum, Vodou's central musical instrument, in Sunday services set to traditional Vodou rhythms. Furthermore, as liturgy is now said in Haitian Creole, and the Bible is translated into Haitian Creole, the Vodou worldview has managed to find a sense of place in the very language and liturgy of Christianity. In a way, Haiti's Catholic faithful consequently feel more at home in church than ever before.

In Baptist and Pentecostal forms of Haitian Protestantism, preachers seek especially to exploit the sometimes demanding nature of Vodouisant belief and practice toward gaining converts and promoting crusades against the country's traditional religion. It is beginning to appear that the more open and public that Vodou becomes, the more license Protestant pastors take in demanding that it be rejected. Moreover, although Pentecostalism is especially fervent in denouncing Vodou as "satanic," Pentecostalism nevertheless appropriates Vodou's most expressive forms of identity, such as interpretation of dreams, spirit possession, African-derived rhythms, or glossolalia (speaking in incomprehensible languages). For example, in the Haitian Pentecostal congregation known as the Celestial Army, ritual behavior of converts very closely resembles that found in a Vodou ceremony, despite the Celestial Army's stated mission to combat the forces of Satan in Vodou.[6] Not only does the Celestial Army borrow directly Vodou's rhythms and dances, but it also employs dream interpretation as a form of communication with spirits and ancestors and a means of healing, using the time-worn interpretations of Vodou priests.

In Haiti, Pentecostalism is gaining more converts daily than other religions, largely because it is especially adept at responding to the spiritual needs of the urban poor in Port-au-Prince and provincial cities. Driven from the countryside by increasingly scarce resources and a degraded environment, the growing class of urban poor are in a sense deterritorialized and left with but one hope for survival: to emigrate abroad. These are the forgotten victims of globalization, and yet interestingly, a significant segment of the middle class is swelling the ranks of the Pentecostal explosion. Similarly, over the past fifteen years, the Catholic Charismatic movement has drawn heavily from the Haitian middle class. The Charismatic renewal movement exhibits the same forms of worship and expression as Protestant Pentecostalism: the call for witnessing, dream interpretation, possession by the Holy Spirit, faith healing, and general ecstatic fervor.

Without pretending to elucidate further reasons for Pentecostalism's success, it is worthwhile to note that Vodou is losing some of its appeal insofar as it does not afford the deterritorialized individual the space to live autonomously. In migrating from rural Haiti, the Vodouisant is removed from family lineages that are closely aligned with the spirits, and hence removed from all debts owed the spirits and the dead. What now becomes important—over and above the need to overcome the daily struggles of life—is a greater inwardness of one's spiritual life that opens up a new kind of relationship with the divine. This new relationship is no longer based upon scrupulous respect for the forbidden, but on the transformation of one's moral sense. Thus, the powers of Vodou's religious specialists can only decrease, subtly though inevitably, breeding a sentiment of insecurity among practitioners of Vodou and a revitalization of their values.

As it unfolds, the process of globalization is fomenting uneasiness—even a crisis—in Haitian society. That Vodou has been afforded greater public space thanks to globalization is beyond doubt, but at the same time, it has been placed under certain pressures that mortgage its future and threaten to dilute its richness even further. At the same time, Protestant sects and the Catholic Church have formidable support structures in the forms of school systems, mass media, local development initiatives, and, above all, international connections. Faced with such realities, Vodou might seem like a religion on the wane. Yet, rather than attempt here to read the future, I now propose to explore some of ways in which Vodou reacts to these present ramifications of globalization.

Reactions of Vodou to Globalization

Following the ouster of the dynastic Duvalier regime in 1986, popular protest in Haiti took the form of *dechoukaj* (uprooting), which aimed to destroy anything physically associated with the dictatorship. Many

Vodou priests, accused of being members of the infamous paramilitary Ton Ton Macoutes, or simply accused of sorcery, became targets of rage. In an attempt to eradicate all sources of evil and misery in Haitian society, groups of protesters, stoked by vitriolic sermons denouncing the empire of Satan reigning in Haiti, lynched dozens of Vodou priests throughout the country. The need for organization and solidarity among regional Vodou fraternities toward the defense of the religion thus arose, and numerous artists and writers professed their support of a new pro-Vodou association called Zantray. As the wave of *dechoukaj* subsided, Vodou's now public stature became its greatest defense against future inquisitorial campaigns, and little by little the religion came to enjoy a greater level of acceptance in Haitian society.

Beginning in 1986, Vodou took Haiti's public stage with unprecedented vigor. Many private radio stations regularly scheduled programs of Vodou hymns, even in the absence of broadcast debates on the religion's influence on Haitian history and culture. As noted above, Vodou first gained public exposure in the middle of the twentieth century with the arrival of Haitian painting on the international scene. No less forceful today is the explosion of Vodou-inspired rock fusion groups, Haitian musicians who dub their genre *racine* (root). In concerts and during carnival, some *groupes-racines* go so far as to simulate Vodou temples (*ounfo*) and ceremonies on stage. One group, led by a Vodou priest named Azor, is one of Haiti's most popular carnival bands, using its chants to honor the spirits. Abnor, a Port-au-Prince Vodou priest of the Societé Grand Drap (Society of the Great Sheet), gives public concerts accompanied by his disciples in front of his temple. Haiti's most famous *groupe-racine,* Boukman Eksperyans, is dedicated to celebrating the memory of Boukman, the famous Vodou priest whose ceremony at Bois Caiman in 1791 sparked the insurrection that mushroomed into the Haitian Revolution. Such a cultural migration from the sacred to the profane space does not preclude trance, possession, and other ecstatic religious experiences from occurring in the streets and concert halls, events that no longer raise eyebrows in the public audience. Yet, it is likely that rather than witnessing reenactment or reinforcement of the sacred in Haitian Vodou, we are seeing the religion's emerging tendency toward secularization. Perhaps stemming from this cultural drama is an unwitting erosion of the true strength that the religion holds in the confines of the temple and the *lakou* (Vodou center composed of several lineage groups under the direction of a single religious leader).

Under contemporary globalization, two other reactions to Vodou demand our special (if only cursory) attention.[7] First, Vodou has appropriated elements from Catholicism, such as the liturgical calendar, saint cults, churches and chapels, and pilgrimage in the support of Vodou's beliefs and symbolic system. It is well known, for example, that Vodou has long adopted most of the important Catholic feast day celebrations, especially since the schism with the Vatican from 1804 to 1860. Thus, for example, the feast day of Notre Dame de Altagrâce in the Port-au-Prince neighborhood of Delmas corresponds to the celebration of Ezili Danto, one of the most popular Vodou spirits, whose stature approaches that of national mother goddess.[8] Danto also corresponds to Notre Dame du Perpetuel Secours, whom the Catholic Church declared Haiti's national patron saint. Annually, the number of faithful who make novenas for Altagrace grows, part of a general growth in devotion to sainthood also evident during the feast of Saint Claire in the Frères neighborhood that borders Petion-Ville. As far as Vodouisants are concerned, Claire is none other than Clermezine, or Saint Anne, Mother of the Virgin Mary, that is to say, Ezili Freda, goddess of love. The feast day of Saint Yves, likewise, draws countless pilgrims, who are as much in attendance to worship Gede, the Vodou spirit of death, whose faithful are especially visible throughout the country around All Saints and All Souls days each November.

We could expound at length detailing the assimilation of saints with Vodou spirits, but we focus instead on a small chapel in the Petion-Ville shantytown of Deshermittes. Although originally dedicated to the Virgin Mary, this chapel serves as a veritable shrine for Ezili Danto. In my careful study of the history of this chapel, I discovered that at some point the Catholic clergy abandoned it; they virtually surrendered to the enthusiastic assault by Vodouisants. In effect, the church surrendered the chapel to Vodou. In turn, many of the Deshermittes faithful came to believe that a miracle had occurred there. The Virgin Mary had appeared in Deshermittes in the form of a statue and asked that a chapel be built for her there for her veneration. The curate of Petion-Ville attempted to gain control over the escalating devotion to the "Queen of Deshermittes" by transporting the statue to the Church of St. Pierre, just up the hill. Nevertheless, according to popular belief, the statue miraculously transported itself back to Deshermittes! Subsequently, a local Vodou priestess and lay Catholic named Eloise declared herself the medium for the Virgin who had appeared in Deshermittes. She explained to me how she had a dream one night in 1975 in which she saw a black Virgin who was none other than Ezili Danto, demanding to be honored in Deshermittes. This inspired Eloise to compose a series of chants for Danto, and in time, numerous miracles were reported during prayers in the chapel—successful marital arrangements, employment, protection against evil, and revenge against enemies.

Ceremonies at Deshermittes take place late in the morning each Tuesday and Thursday, consisting of prayers and songs directed by some kind of a sexton standing before the altar, which supports a wooden statue of the Virgin. The faithful, mostly drawn from the lower class, fall into trance, and a few are possessed during hymns praising the Virgin Mary. Surrounding this chapel, which doubles as a temple for Ezili, are Danto's preferred food offerings. Several Vodou priestesses and priests are on hand to do readings, while outside the chapel are merchants offering a dizzying array of religious paraphernalia (medals, hymnals, candles, saint icons, etc.). Makeshift restaurants have also cropped up near the chapel, making Deshermittes a veritable *lakou*. The whole experience unfolds as if the temple were a site of Vodouisant pilgrimage on the level of the celebrated Saut-d'Eau, whose parish is dedicated to Notre Dame du Mont Carmel and who is identified with Ezili Freda, or of the feast of Saint-Jacques in la Plaine-du-Nord, which corresponds with the celebration of the great Yorùbá-related god of war, Ogou Ferray. The difference in the case of Deshermittes, however, is that here the Catholic Church no longer recognizes this Virgin as its own.

As practitioners of Vodou attempted to preserve its uniqueness and to carve out a greater public space to accommodate it, the movement began to institutionalize the religion. Beginning in 1998, under the auspices of the Ministry of Cults, the movement was formalized through a national commission, Commission Nationale pour la Structuration de Vodou, directed by Wesner Morency, an ex-seminarian-cum-Vodou priest. Among the commission's projects is the rendering of Vodou hymns and prayers into written form because, according to Morency, Vodou is suffering a state of decline. It is besieged in a competitive modern world imposed by Western globalization. Also vital to the religion's survival is the articulation of the universal nature of its God and his specific Haitian forms of incarnation. Clearly, Vodou stands to undergo significant transformation should the committee's influence be far reaching.

On several occasions I have attended Sunday ceremonies organized by Morency in the Bois-Verna neighborhood of central Port-au-Prince.

Immediately, I was struck by obvious attempts to make these ceremonies appear as much as possible like a "Vodou Mass," so to speak, altogether analogous to Catholic and even Protestant Sunday assembles. It was as if Vodou was being transformed into a "mainstream" religion, that is, a religion like Christianity itself. These Sunday Vodou ceremonies were held in a warehouse laid out like a Catholic chapel or a Protestant church. The celebrant used an incensory to mark the four cardinal points of traditional Vodou ritual that delineates sacred space. The main ceremony occurred as hymns were sung to glorify the Vodou spirits, only without the drums and possessions that are so central to ordinary Vodou ceremonies. The celebrant next went on to a reading of texts expounding upon Yorùbá or Fon mythology. The congregation was told that Vodou has a supreme God, Olohoun, who is distinct from the foreign God of Christianity.

In these ceremonies, the celebrant preached a sermon commenting on readings by the choir. Everyone was then invited to witness to, that is, to give testimony to, the good that the Vodou spirits had done in daily life. Overall, this community seemed oriented by a goal to revitalize Vodou and restore its purity in the face of additives from Vodouisant readers of the book *l'Ange conducteur,* along with extraneous Rosicrucian beliefs that border on magic. It was all about presenting what the celebrant referred to as "the truths of Vodou" or Vodou's "principles and rules," which were rooted in a respect for nature, the environment, and the earth, representing the way to social harmony in Haiti. He reminded us also that Vodou must contribute to national economic development and political life, and must never be excluded from these processes: "It [Vodou] must be present in every venue . . . and must come from the conscience of every Haitian so that they do not become traitors to the national soul."

To mark its third anniversary, the Commission Nationale pour la Structuration de Vodou published a statement in the newspaper *Le Nouvelliste* outlining specific objectives. Here we read that Vodou possesses a sacred text entitled *Code Vodou,* which contains the most essential spiritual wisdom for humankind, and especially for Haitians. The book explains the actions that the Supreme God, Olohoun, has taken on behalf of Haiti and, above all, how Haiti has become a "beacon" and a "turning badge of the world," thanks to the grace of Olohoun. "Olohoun created his people to establish a great civilization." Here we have a "Vodou Code" that not only pronounces doctrine but also prescribes modes of behavior to be adopted in a world that represents a menace to Vodou. Equally important are the code's measures that determine which true representatives of the religion can be distinguished from the multitude of charlatans claiming representational authority. In a word, the commission's main objective is to create an "institutional Vodou" geared "to protect" the religion, "guarantee its serene existence in the face of external aggressors," and above all ensure the dignity of its practitioners.[9]

We are thus witnessing the gradual emergence of a veritable "Vodou Church," a term that is actually employed in the commission's anniversary declaration. Paradoxically, the more vigorous this movement's effort to safeguard Vodou's original purity, the more it is influenced by Christian ecclesiological models. Beginning in 1986, certain Vodou priests similarly embarked on a campaign to eradicate any Catholic elements from the religion by offering in their temples all of the sacraments normally offered by the Catholic Church. What are we to make of this? To be sure, it remains difficult to make a sound prognosis for the future of Vodou. I would point out, nonetheless, that the transformation under discussion here is certainly taking place under, and hence is clearly influenced by, the pressures of globalization. Such transformations indicate a phenomenon of self-reliance in determining Vodou's public space in an effort to resist erosion, whether manifest in the expansion by appropriating chapels and other Catholic sacred space, by invading public space to obtain a visibility equal with other religions. This twofold approach is seen within the Commission Nationale pour la Structuration de Vodou, which aims to realize a modernized religion, complete with written scriptures and an institutional body, while at the same time claiming to be the true space of Haitian "authenticity."

What appears here to be a contradiction may in fact be symptomatic of a crisis affecting Haitian society. The increasing number of Protestant converts provides further testimony to this crisis, as especially seen in Pentecostal churches. As evidence of this crisis in Haiti, I would also point to the upsurge of belief in sorcery, which at times leads to the lynching of suspected witches. In one sense, globalization pits all religious systems against each other, openly competing for public space and provoking a revitalization of their values and sources of anxiety, such as fear of those who have the power of sorcery.[10] The individual feels increasingly obliged to choose from among a variety of belief systems in Haiti, indicating that religion no longer grows without self-criticism. A recent study by François Houtard and Ansèlme Remy on globalization

and Haitian culture demonstrates that today the country may be represented as a cultural configuration in which at least two critical changes
are taking place in the religious field: (1) Catholicism is progressively
losing its hegemonic power over Haitian society, much to the benefit of
Protestant expansion; and (2) Vodou is experiencing a general secularization, weakening its religious force, in part because of growth in the
popularity of Haitian arts (Houtard and Remy 2001: 114).[11]

Could it be that globalization will result ultimately in an attenuation
of those cultures that have little or no access to the powers of multinational corporations? To the contrary, it is just as possible—the entire process being, as it were, something like the ancient Italian gatekeeper deity,
Janus—that globalization may serve as the spearhead of Vodou's revalo-
rization through the collective memory of all Haitians (practitioners and
nonpractitioners alike), of all Caribbean peoples, and of all communities
of African descent in the Americas. Emerging as underground culture,
this collective memory should drive the quest for a deeper understanding
of Vodou as the order of the day. After all, the prejudice that marginalized Vodou was caused in part by the obscurity and esotericism long
surrounding the religion's beliefs and practices. Consequently, the more
the national educational system develops, the greater the opportunity to
engender respect for Vodou, as a general sense for religious tolerance
becomes the norm. Perhaps better still, the practice of Vodou would thus
become one of a series of "cultural rights," which are not perceived as
merely "a new category of human rights" but as stepping stones toward
fuller human rights, as Boris Martin (1999) argues.[12] Put otherwise, there
is no reason to expect contradictions between cultural and human rights.
Still, one must remain vigilant in the struggle against fundamentalism,
nationalism, and ethnocentricism. Therefore, the possibility of practicing
Vodou as a cultural right is consistent with the concept of democracy as a
universal good. In other words, it is precisely the process of democratization that, through its spirit of self-criticism, has made possible Vodou's
decriminalization and ensuing freed expression.

Conceiving of globalization as a process of colonial conquest of
the Americas that laid the foundation for Western global hegemony,
we are clearly reminded that Vodou—initially labeled "seditious" and
systematically forbidden by this emerging hegemony—has long proven
itself capable of adapting to the most difficult conditions. Thus, there
is a strong chance that in the face of globalization in its contemporary
form, Vodou will once again draw from its rich cognitive and symbolic

systems and offer Haitian culture the weapons of resistance to deculturation. Toward such an end, some of Vodou's deepest values, such as
environmental awareness, tolerance, solidarity, and respect for life, will
necessarily be stirred to offer Vodou's greatest gifts to humanity. At the
same time, those aspects of Vodou that turn the practitioner once again
toward the past must be brought into question. Recognition of human
rights and democracy—which must no longer be considered the export-
able property of the West—will favor such a constructively critical spirit
of Vodou's beliefs and practices and the very process of globalization,
wherever it violates the equality of nations and impedes the realization
of a truly universal democracy.

Notes

1. On globalization, among many publications, see Morin and Nair 1997,
which offers an excellent critical synthesis; Beck 1997; Giddens 1990.

2. See Wallerstein 1991.

3. On the effects of globalization, see Scheijack 1999. It would seem, according to Scheijack, among others, that increasingly certain countries are seeking to utilize the globalization process as a springboard for the revitalization of
their own cultures, despite the ambiguities implied by such an effort.

4. For an extensive discussion of the civil-versus-barbaric paradigm upon
which such Catholic inquisitorial practices in Haiti were based, see Hurbon
1988, 1999a, 1999b.

5. For a portrayal of Vodou in New York, see Brown 1991; on Vodou in
Montreal, see Augustin 1999.

6. On the Celestial Army, see Corten 1995, 2001.

7. This section of the essay draws on my fieldwork on Vodou, Catholicism,
and Pentecostalism in Haiti. Space limitations disallowed a thorough sociological interpretation of this data here, though hopefully my treatment in this essay
will give the reader a glimpse into the magnitude of the crisis facing not only
Haitian Vodou but the very foundation of Haitian culture.

8. Rey (1999) demonstrates the power of the cult of the Virgin Mary, who
corresponds to the Vodou goddess Ezili, in Haitian politics and society.

9. As in *Le Nouvelliste*, February 1, 2001.

10. Brodwin's (1996) detailed analysis of therapeutic approaches in each of
Haiti's three main religions demonstrates how peasants in daily life negotiate
religious competition.

11. Houtard and Remy (2001) make a compelling analysis of the relationship between symbolic and analytical thought in Haitian culture. Houtard and

Remy argue that Vodou may still become a source of resistance to the cultural uniformization effected by globalization, while at the same time demonstrating much of Haitian society is slowly shifting from "the traditional" to a modernist culture.

12. See also Abou 1992.

References

Abou, Selim. 1992. *Cultures et droits de l'homme*. Paris: Hachette.

Augustin, Joseph. 1999. *Le vodou liberateur*. Montreal: Tanboula.

Beck, Ulrich. 1997. *Was ist Globalisierung? Irrtumer des Globalismus—Antoworten aur Globalisierung*. Frankfurt: Suhrkamp.

———. 2000. *What Is Globalization?* Cambridge, UK: Polity Press.

Brodwin, Paul. 1996. *Medicine and Morality in Haiti: The Contest for Healing Power*. New York: Cambridge University Press.

Brown, Karen McCarthy. 1991. *Mama Lola: A Vodou Priestess in Brooklyn*. Berkeley: University of California Press.

Corten, Andre. 1995. "Un mouvement religieux rebelle en Haïti: L'Armée céleste." *Conjonction* 203: 53–62.

———. 2001. *Misère, religion et politique en Haïti*. Paris: Karthala.

Giddens, Anthony. 1990. *The Consequences of Modernity*. Stanford, CA: Stanford University Press.

Houtard, François, and Ansèlme Remy. 2001. *Haïti et la mondilaisation de la culture*. Paris: L'Harmattan.

Hurbon, Laënnec. 1988. *Le barbare imaginaire*. Port-au-Prince: Deschamps.

———. 1999a. "American Fantasy and Haitian Vodou." In *Sacred Arts of Haitian Vodou,* ed. Donald J. Cosentino, 181–97. Los Angeles: UCLA Fowler Museum of Cultural History; Hong Kong: South Sea International Press.

———. 1999b. "Haitian Vodou, Church, State, and Anthropology." *Anthropological Journal on European Cultures* 8, no.2: 27–38.

Martin, Boris. 1999. "Les droits culturels comme mode d'interprétation et de mis en œuvre des droits de l'homme." *M.A.U.S.S.* 13: 236–60.

Morin, Edgar, and Sami Nair. 1997. *Une politique de civilization*. Paris: Arlea 1997.

Rey, Terry. 1999. *Our Lady of Class Struggle: The Cult of the Virgin Mary in Haiti*. Trenton, NJ, and Asmara: Africa World Press.

Scheijack, Thomas, ed. 1999. *Menschenwerden im Kulturwandel*. Luzern: Exodus.

Wallerstein, Immanual. 1991. "L'Amerique et le monde, aujourd'hui, hier et demain." *Futur anterieur* 5: 31–64.

14

Historicizing Ifá Culture in Òyótúnjí African Village

IKULOMI DJISOVI EASON

In the far southeast corner of South Carolina, located between Charleston and Savannah in the forested coastal low country of Beaufort County, is the tiny hamlet of Sheldon. Near Sheldon is a twenty-seven-acre settlement, the Kingdom of Òyótúnjí African Village, established in 1970.

Any historicizing of South Carolina's Kingdom of Òyótúnjí, which is modeled after a Yorùbá village, must be set in the context of its ancient African Yorùbá motherland in southwest Nigeria, West Africa, and its traditional Yorùbá spiritual center, Ilé-Ifè. The Ilé-Ifè of Nigeria is an urban center occupied almost continuously since the first millennium C.E. It was most populous during the fourteenth and fifteenth centuries, and to the Yorùbá, Ilé-Ifè represents a holy city and the mythical center where the world was created.

Writing a history of his beloved Ilé-Ifè, Chief M. Ajayi Ifabumni observed that all Yorùbá historicity begins with Ilé-Ifè. His observation was based on the understanding that the Yorùbá Ifá deities, the Odu Ifè oracles, and the Ifá divination systems are the oldest repository of traditional Yorùbá religious and cultural history.

The ancient system of Ifá divination, of "knowing" and solving problems, seems to have appeared first in Ilé-Ifè and spread later throughout the Yorùbá diaspora of West Africa, the Americas, and other parts of the world. Ifabumni claimed that the Ifá canon had identified at least seven incarnations of Ilé-Ifè, whose names suggest periods in Ilé-Ifè history that occurred so long ago only the barest traces persist in today's Ifá verses. The sacred verses have been passed down orally by memory, generation to generation over the centuries.

To chronicle the antiquity of the kingdom of Ilé-Ifè, cultural historian and archaeologist Omotoso Eluyemi, who was director-general of Nigeria's National Commission for Museums and Monuments, developed the use of archaeological evidence to corroborate the oral historical legends of the Yorùbá. He set up a model of archaeological training at Ilé-Ifè in the cultural history mode, emphasizing the use of oral traditions to inform archaeological science and vice versa. After much research, Eluyemi found that Ilé-Ifè's early history occurred in three phases. With a multidisciplinary approach, evidence from archaeological digs, Ifá orature, and oral traditions pointed to the following three phases.

In the first phase, Ifè's ancient beginnings ended in a tremendous flood; in the second phase, survivors of the flood began anew in the same region. Over time, survivors and their descendants assembled themselves into thirteen to sixteen virtually autonomous family enclaves that worshipped the deity Obàtálá. Among the families, two leaders are remembered in the Ifá verses as Obawinrin and Agboniregun or Setilu alias Ifá/Òrúnmìlà. In the third phase, beginning around the fourteenth century C.E., these enclaves came together to fight off invading forces known as Odùduwà. When the invaders became victorious, they pressured the several aboriginal families to form a centralized kingdom under their rule. The political and cultural influence of the Odùduwà invaders persists to the present day.

The South Carolina Replica of Òyótúnjí African Village

In contrast to the ancient city of Ilé-Ifè, whose origins are so distant that they are difficult to date with specificity, the Òyótúnjí African Village in South Carolina's low country began only recently, in the 1970s. Its beginnings are traceable to a single African American—His Royal Highness Oba Efuntola Oseijeman Adelabu Adefunmi I, née Walter Eugene King (1928–2005). Oseijeman was the first African American ever to be initiated into the priesthood and initiation cult of any traditional African religion (spiritual system). His initiation paved the way for other African Americans to regain and practice traditional African beliefs lost during the transatlantic crossing and vicissitudes of American slavery.

Learning about Africa early in childhood, Oseijeman was enchanted by stories his parents told about the continent. He relished especially the family legend that his "great, great, great maternal grandmother [had been an] African . . . brought to America [before the American Revolution] while she was teething. . . . The quality of jewelry she had on [caused folk to speculate] that she must have been a chief's daughter" (Hunt 1979: 83). In later years, he recalled that as a child he had yearned to know more, feeling that his destiny was to awaken his African identity.

In the early 1950s, Oseijeman's curiosity took him to New York City, where he searched widely for information about Africa. He frequented jazz clubs, black theater, and the NAACP Youth Council and studied in the New York Public Library's Schomburg Center for Research in African Culture. He also learned about people of African descent in the diaspora by meeting and talking with Haitian and Cuban immigrants.

By 1956, Oseijeman had traveled to Europe, Egypt, and Haiti. After returning from Haiti, where he first encountered Voodoo religious culture, he established the Haitian Order of Dambada Hwedo in Greenwich Village. He studied Ghanaian history, and in 1957, the year of Ghana's independence from Great Britain, Oseijeman took the title *nana,* which means "chief" in the Akan language of Ghana. In 1959, Nana Oseijeman traveled with Christopher Oliana to Matanzas, Cuba, and became the first-known African American to be initiated into the Santería priesthood of Obàtálá.

Oseijeman returned to New York and organized the Shango Temple on East 125th Street, incorporating influences from Haitian religious traditions. Impressed with Yorùbá language and culture in Cuban Santería, he replaced the Akan title with the Yorùbá title *bàbá,* which means "father." He observed that Santería priests had altered Yorùbá traditions, which Cubans of African descent combined with Catholic rituals. He began to talk about "purifying" Santería, which to him meant removing whatever was alien to African culture. He began to surround himself with like-minded advocates and changed the name of Shango Temple to Yorùbá Temple. He became well known in Harlem as the "Voodoo Priest."

By the 1960s, Oseijeman assumed several nationalist cultural identities and helped to merge the uniquely African diaspora religious and cultural movements with the black cultural nationalist movement of African Americans in the United States. Amiri Baraka, the American writer of poetry, drama, essays, and music criticism, who was popularly known as LeRoi Jones and Imamu Amiri Baraka, was one of Oseijeman's associates during the 1960s and wrote about Oseijeman as a Black Nationalist. Oseijeman founded the African National Independence Party, affiliating it with the Yorùbá Temple. During a party rally in 1962, he announced, "By 1972, an African state—identifiable by its practice of African traditions—would emerge in the United States. The foundation of the state will be African, and it will be purely African in culture" (Baraka 1984: 205).

At that time, Oseijeman encouraged members of the party to wear traditional African clothes. As a Yorùbá Temple priest, he established *bembes* (communal drum ceremonies) honoring the African deities. This vibrant reclamation of African culture began to attract African Americans from other regions of the United States. Some were fascinated with his focus and integration of Yorùbá and diaspora religious traditions in the struggle for liberation.

Reading about New York's Yorùbá Temple movement in *Hep Magazine,* a Gary, Indiana, steel worker, who became known as Medahochi, went to New York to invite Baba Oseijeman to Gary to meet with a group of African Americans interested in what was taking place in New York. In 1964, Oseijeman and the renowned Santería priestess Mama Keke went to Gary and officiated over seven Afro-Cuban Eleke ceremonies. Afterward, the Yorùbá Temple in New York spread to areas in Gary and Chicago. In the late 1960s, Oseijeman sought to fulfill his 1962 prophecy that there would be an "African state" within the United States. He eventually moved to Savannah, Georgia, and from there to Paige Point Road in Sheldon, South Carolina, and in 1970 to Bray's Island Road. There he began to build models of Yorùbá temples to establish the Òyótúnjí African Village, initiating Yorùbá rites of passage for African Americans in the United States.

Although Cuban practitioners could very well have presided over initiation ceremonies, African American devotees at that time insisted that an authentic African American–inspired Yorùbá order needed to be established. Thus, Chief Elemosha Owolowo of New York, Akanke Omilade of Gary, Indiana, and Medahochi Omowale of Gary became

the first three initiates of Ọyọtúnjí African Village and the first generation of African American Yorùbá priests. They in turn recommended
others to preside over initiations, such as Efundeji, Edubi, now Chief
Ajamu, and the late Kpojito Omiyale Hwesihuno.

Since the 1950s, the passion of Efuntola Oseijeman Adelabu Adefunmi I for knowledge of African traditional religion and black cultural nationalism had continued to grow with each passing decade. In the
early 1970s, he acquired ten acres of land and a farmhouse and moved
the village to its present site in Sheldon, South Carolina, making it renowned as the Ọyọtúnjí African Village. In 1972, Oseijeman traveled
to Abeokuta, Nigeria, where he was initiated as a *babaláwo,* the highest
level of Yorùbá priesthood. Aware of the Village's Black Nationalist
beginnings, Mikelle Omari (1991) aptly observes that Ọyọtúnjí African
Village is the only African American community in the Americas that
has no links to the survival of slave cultures.

The 1970s ushered in the Ọyọtúnjí African American struggle for
authenticity and legitimacy, just as the Haitian Vodoun movement and
the Cuban and Caribbean Santería movements had been authenticated
in the New World. William Bascom (1979: iii) noted about the Village
in 1979 that "[w]hat is truly remarkable is . . . [Oseijeman's] success in
[re-]creating, with amazing accuracy, the culture of the Yorùbá of Nigeria." Oseijeman's first Ifá tutor in Ọyọtúnjí Village seems to have been a
Nigerian priest who was remembered as Ojo. In 1981, Oseijeman experienced an international epiphany after his pilgrimage to Ilé-Ifè. During
this encounter, the Ooni of Ilé-Ifè performed sacred ceremonies and rites
of passage making him an official and acknowledged representative of
the Ooni and Yorùbá *bale* or king of the town of Ọyọtúnjí. More than a
decade before his visit to Ilé-Ifè, Ọyọtúnjí villagers had performed their
own rites and ceremoniously elevated Oseijeman to the position of king
or *ọba.*

Today's Ọyọtúnjí Yorùbá realize that African American religion and
culture were formed over generations of post-enslaved Christian orientation and that a number of them are former Christians or have family
members who are Christian. Therefore, Ọba Oseijeman was meticulous
in trying to divest Ọyọtúnjí Village of enslaved religious influences
rooted in Catholicism, Baptist, and other Christian manifestations. Yet,
it may be that as former Christians, with a few former Black Muslims,
the Ọyọtúnjí Yorùbá undoubtedly can identify with Christian sentiments
because aspects of the Christian religion and culture resemble ancient Ifá

religious practices. There are, for example, many elements in common in biblical and Ifá traditions—proverbs, miracle narratives, mythology, rituals of sacrifice, death, and resurrection, to name a few.

Ọ̀yọ́túnjí African Village in South Carolina and Ilé-Ifè in Nigeria are linked with historical and ethnic diversity. Most African Americans in Ọ̀yọ́túnjí Village, and the United States in general, reflect an ethnic composition of West African, Native American, and European American ancestry. Ilé-Ifè, too, has a mixed population and remains politically controlled by the colonial hegemony established and maintained by the descendants of Odùduwà over the indigenous descendants of Òrúnmìlà/Ifá. Today, Ilé-Ifè includes many diverse Yorùbá traditional ethnic groups, Christians, Muslims, and Africans from other parts of Nigeria and other African countries, the diaspora, Europe, and Asia. Unlike Ilé-Ifè, South Carolina's Ọ̀yọ́túnjí Village consists predominantly of Ọ̀yọ́túnjí African American Yorùbá and their children. In this respect, Ọ̀yọ́túnjí Village may be more like the precolonial Odùduwà era when Ifá followers with like spiritual minds settled and maintained Ilé-Ifè—and whose center of Yorùbá tradition evolved around Ifá, versus the postcolonial Odùduwà era with it's political and anti-indigenous Ifá hegemony.

Reflected within the Holy Odu Ifá in Ilé-Ifè and in Ọ̀yọ́túnjí Village is the Yorùbá belief in a supreme ultimate reality that inhabits all existence, laws, and forces in the universe. Both the Ọ̀yọ́túnjí Village and the Yorùbá of Ilé-Ifè possess a strong sense of collective and individual destiny guided by Ifá—not limited to and inclusive of a universal human and unfolding history, which are central to both cultures. Yet, Ọ̀yọ́túnjí has not yet begun to document and contemplate its Holy Odu Ifá as a latter twentieth-century Yorùbá historical phenomenon, establishing its own literary form and mytho-historical canon that recounts its creation and evolutionary developments. Instead, it continues to recount Ilé-Ifè's Odu Ifá.

Whereas the Ilé-Ifè Ifá traditionalists are aware of radical reduction in the literary images in their Odu Ifá narratives, Ọ̀yọ́túnjí Village remains in the process of expending its energies in efforts to recover the post-Odùduwà era literary traditions and ceremonies and other aspects of colonial Yorùbá religious tradition and culture. Therefore, Ọ̀yọ́túnjí Village tends to accept shifting images within the present political Odu Ifá, often referring to them more as dualities without treating them as signs of radical historical and social change within Odu Ifá and other Yorùbá literature. It does not talk as the Ilé-Ifè Yorùbá do about changes in Ifá culture that took place with the arrival of a male-centered Odùduwà, who may have brought Islamic patriarchal influences with him and diminished roles of female Ifá priests and female universal forces. Òyótúnjí has a tendency to borrow from a colonial and a negatively redacted Ifá tradition, rather than the pre-Odùduwà and female-centered, indigenous Yorùbá tradition.

It would appear that at one time Òyótúnjí had adopted some sexist attitudes and practices from the Ifá priesthood in Ilé-Ifè, no doubt because the priests there had not engaged in the kind of historical investigation of Ifá Odu and culture that would lead to gender egalitarianism. In the early 1990s, pressure from the Òyótúnjí women would lead to a radical development in African American women being accepted into the Ifá priesthood. Traditionally, they had been restricted to the role of *apetibis*, female priests who are relegated to inferior roles in the Ifá priesthood and who do so much of the difficult work for initiations and other rituals within the movement. Ultimately, there was an ameliorating effect, which was documented in the 1993 publication of Oba Oseijeman's keynote address at the Shango Temple, Chicago, when he described Òyótúnjí's pilgrimage to the Republic of Benin or ancient Dahomey.

It was then that the first generation of Òyótúnjí female priests were welcomed into the Fa/Ifá priesthood in the Benin Republic. The fact that Òyótúnjí traveled to the Republic of Benin, and not to Ilé-Ifè, was interesting. The women of Òyótúnjí were initiated into the Fon Fa priesthood as equals to their male counterparts. The Republic of Benin seems to be more pre-Odùduwà centered and female friendly. Their Ifá system is referred to as Fa and linked to the Fon goddess Gbadu, the mother of the Fa Du/Ifá Odu, and goddess of the divination systems among the Fon in Benin. Ironically, although these people called themselves Fon, they also trace their ancestral origins back to the Yorùbá of Ilé-Ifè.

Despite knowing that formerly gender equity was more prevalent within the priesthood and lines of rulers, in the wake of both Odùduwà and British patriarchy, the present-day Awoni Chief Ifá priests of Ilé-Ifè persist in restricting women's roles in the Ifá priesthood. With Òyótúnjí Village better established, however, perhaps future generations will expend more time asking more questions with respect to documenting their own unique historiography of North American Ifá Yorùbá cultural traditions.

Who knows? Perhaps in the future, Òyótúnjí Village will decide in-

tentionally to reconstruct Odu Ifá in their village along the autochthonous (pre-Odùduwà) lines that may be more in tune with modernity than
those following on the heels of the Odùduwà conquest. At that point,
Ọ̀yọ́túnjí may lead Ilé-Ifè's Ifá priesthood beyond the confines of patriarchy, gender, and Yorùbá ethnic inequality.

Critical comments aside, Ọ̀yọ́túnjí African Village represents a val-
iant attempt to recover and adopt traditional Yorùbá Ifá culture, a recovery that has followed primarily as the Ọba and his chiefs (re)discovered
it in Santería and in books during the 1950s, 1960s, and 1970s. Carl
Hunt argues that there is a political inference to Ọ̀yọ́túnjí Village in
that it has a two-fold goal—to disparage racism and to repudiate conventional "anti-African identity" in the United States. Additionally, its
mission is to promote further awareness of culture and religious tradition stripped from the captured Yorùbá during the transatlantic slave
trade. Thus, Ọ̀yọ́túnjí African Village identifies its movement as a traditional Ifá culture originating in Ilé-Ifè, Nigeria. The more we know
about Ọ̀yọ́túnjí Village in Sheldon, South Carolina, and the Ifá diaspora
movements that have emerged in the twentieth and twenty-first centuries
in the Americas, the better we can understand their relationships.

References

Baraka, Amiri. 1984. *The Autobiography of LeRoi Jones/Amiri Baraka.* New
York: Freundlich Books.
Bascom, William. 1979. Introduction to *Ọ̀yọ́túnjí Village: The Yoruba Move-
ment in America,* by Carl Hunt, iii–vi. Washington, DC: University Press
of America.
Hunt, Carl M. 1979. *Ọ̀yọ́túnjí Village: The Yoruba Movement in America.*
Washington, DC: University Press of America.
Omari, Mikelle Smith. 1991. "Completing the Circle: Notes on African Art,
Society, and Religion in Oyotunji, South Carolina." *African Arts* 24, no.
3: 66.

15

Ritual Change and the Changing Canon

Divinatory Legitimization of Yorùbá Ancestral Roots in Ọ̀yọ́túnjí African Village

KAMARI MAXINE CLARKE

This essay examines how divination provides Yorùbá revivalist practitioners in the Americas with an institutional mechanism for producing new forms of practices. The formation of new practices has consequences for how we chart the legitimacy of Yorùbá traditions and how
we understand the mechanisms by which people reshape the nature of
daily practice. By shifting the terms of engagement from that of the "national" subject to the institutions of power through which agents produce
classificatory logics, I examine how particular formations for transcending the boundaries of the nation are concretized through divination as the
means of legitimizing race-based homeland attachments for Ọ̀yọ́túnjí
practitioners. Ultimately, I am interested in exploring the imaginary by
recognizing the existence of two levels of analysis in order to theorize
the production of new practices within institutions of religious ritual.
The first begins with the individual. I explore the techniques of personal
transformations that are deployed by black American practitioners as
they make direct connections with their African ancestors. Here I am interested in how micro-levels of personal ritual enable people to imagine
themselves as part of a community that is culturally different from their

own. On a broader level of analysis, I explore how people employ these religious techniques in conjunction with larger cultural and economic frameworks to produce larger transnational movements of Yorùbá practitioners claiming cultural descent to Africa.

In exploring the uses of personal ritual techniques set in relation to economic realities of global travel and exchange, I am also interested in the power of the state, its laws, or its codes of subjugation. I want to examine the role of knowledge and power—global and more circumscribed—in producing contradictory conditions of possibility through which people incorporate spiritual understandings while also mobilizing dominant meanings, even as they re-signify them for their purposes. In so doing, I reconceptualize the role of agents in shaping the basis by which sovereign power should be understood.

The first sphere of power exists within a particular ideological power through which agents code everyday life. It reflects an always unfinished articulation of subject formation and exists in relation to regimes of modernity, articulating within modern regimes of knowledge and power. Within this sphere, we see that individuals enforce a logic of practice from which the organizing principles of national citizenship circulate.

The second sphere is connected to the first but interacts with the ways in which individuals both incorporate and contest larger spheres of meaning production outside of their control. As a perpetually incomplete process, it characterizes individual agency within the transformative possibilities of shifting meanings. As we shall see, these forms of micro-processes and negotiation are productive of new sites of innovation and productive of incremental change. Ultimately, the relationship between the second sphere—globalizing forces, the state, colonial powers—and the first sphere—agents of change who are at once historical and contemporary—highlights the complexities of cultural production as it plays out in transnational spiritual divinatory techniques.

To this end, I focus on the re-Africanization of Yorùbá practices in the United States and the development of new divinatory practices within reorganized networks of power. These new practices are productive of new conceptions of belonging and these networks transcend the territorialized nation-state. As we shall see, it calls for a rethinking of place and belonging and a rearticulation of the ways that divinatory techniques can be used to deploy new forms of diasporic knowledge. In 2002 a keyword search on the World Wide Web using "Santería" or "Yoruba" and "divination" would pull up over seven thousand hits in which a range of transnational òrìṣà institutions could be called upon for obtaining online divinatory readings, information about the history and culture of Yorùbá peoples, the history of slavery, and adaptations of òrìṣà rituals by Africans in the Americas. Any approach to understanding globalization and the making of communities outside of popular modern determinations of homelands, therefore, must not only recognize the various geopolitical zones of interaction within which Yorùbá practices, but it must also examine the institutional mechanisms by which new forms of practices have continued to change.

The widening constituencies of changing Yorùbá òrìṣà practices can be classified within four significant groups: (1) òrìṣà practitioners principally in Nigeria and Benin as well as in various surrounding West African countries (although there is also a growing number in this category who are transatlantic òrìṣà intellectuals who travel between the West and Nigeria teaching Yorùbá cultural and ritual practices, most in this category tend not to be educated within Western traditions, are poorer than nonpractitioners, and claim òrìṣà worship as their religious faith); (2) òrìṣà, Santería, or Lukumi practitioners in the Americas who constitute the largest group of religious worshippers and can be found in urban and rural religions throughout Cuba, Haiti, Trinidad, Puerto Rico, Brazil, and the United States; (3) òrìṣà worshipers and Yorùbá revivalists or òrìṣà revivalists who are part of a relatively new (post-1960s) òrìṣà economy of practitioners who are interested in the return to a more orthodox traditional practice that is often inspired by racial (black) consciousness; (4) òrìṣà modernists, a relatively new (post-1980s) group of initiates, led by predominantly white American practitioners, who are part of a growing movement interested in the transcendence of racial belonging through the emphasis of ancestral lineage. These four groups constitute multiple networks of òrìṣà practitioners that have produced òrìṣà institutional practices throughout the Americas, and are having a critical effect on the invention of new òrìṣà institutional practices. For the purposes of this essay, I focus on the third group and analyze a particular group in a community called Òyótúnjí African Village in order to highlight the play of transnational power operative outside of the nation-state.

I explore the ways that Òyótúnjí practitioners produce interpretive variations and argue that the processes of enacting divinatory performances do not differ substantially from that of the Ifá canon characteristic of Nigerian Yorùbá religious traditions. As we shall see, the invention of a new form of divinatory ritual reading known as a roots reading enables practitioners to incorporate the form and structure of Ifá divination and the history of slavery and women's insubordination into new institutional forms. For if religious ritual is useful, it is because it creates relevant information consistent with both the past and changing daily circumstances.

Case Study: Divination in Ọ̀yọ́túnjí Village

Named after the once-powerful West African Ọ̀yọ́ Empire of the six-teenth to eighteenth centuries, Ọ̀yọ́túnjí is a Black Nationalist com-munity of African American religious converts who have reclaimed West Africa as their ancestral homeland in their Yorùbá practices. Most Ọ̀yọ́túnjí practitioners trace their origins to that of the descendants of the men and women taken from West African communities and exported to the Americas as slaves. As a result of the belief that they have a right to control the African territory that was their homeland, prior to European colonization, residents of Ọ̀yọ́túnjí Village, claiming diaspora connec-tions to the ancestral history of the Great Ọ̀yọ́ Empire of the Yorùbá people, have reclassified their community as an African Kingdom out-side of the territoriality of the Nigerian postcolonial state.

Founded in 1970, Ọ̀yọ́túnjí was at its political height by the late 1970s when it boasted a residential population of 191 residents. It was built to accommodate up to twenty-five housing compounds with a potential capacity of over 500 people by the mid-1980s; however, the institutional format of the community shifted, and the average population plummeted to 70 residents. Compared with past numbers, fewer revivalists than ever resided in Ọ̀yọ́túnjí in the 1990s.[1] Between the early 1980s to the late 1990s, increasing numbers of practitioners left the community for urban centers.[2] This outward migration laid the seeds for the spread of new in-stitutional forms of urban Yorùbá practices, and through the creation of rural-urban linkages throughout the United States new Yorùbá revivalist networks were forged.

Because of this added level of deterritorialized networking between Ọ̀yọ́túnjí and its satellite communities in urban centers, Ọ̀yọ́túnjí be-came more important than ever for practitioners to claim a network of shared Yorùbá revivalists. Through the regulation and standardization of revivalist rituals, dress codes, and routinized daily practices, a normative form of Yorùbá practice took shape in the late twentieth century; literary texts, books, and computer technologies were used as necessary tools for the teaching of and learning about traditionalist Yorùbá doctrine. These tenets of practice, formerly communicated and circulated within the once separatist Òyótúnjí community, were, in the 1980s and 1990s, reconstituted through the spread of new institutional forms of knowledge. With these new circulations of knowledge, the movement, estimated to exceed six to ten thousand adherents—spanning major urban and rural centers throughout the United States—reconstituted itself as Black Nationalist and as drawing its power from the symbolic prestige of the African past.

Divination as Transnational Knowledge Production

A range of anthropologists have studied the centrality of divinatory knowledge in the lives of individuals, demonstrating that divination provides a means by which individuals can understand their world and interpret their role in it (Bascom 1969a, 1969b, 1980; Abímbólá 1976, 1977; Akinnaso 1995). Divination is an interpretive mechanism by which agents interpret, consult, and hold symbolic power (Clarke 1997). Yet, even as divination involves the repetition of formal acts and utterances through which sacred knowledge is derived, it is a highly interpretive act, embedded in particular relations of power. Contemporary studies of the processes of interpretation have placed increasing attention on the value and power of divination as a ritual property as well as on the role that ritual processes play in making the past and present coterminous (Herzfeld 1992; Maddox 1993). However, they have paid less attention to the specific processes by which changing divinatory interpretations are both incorporated into the divinatory canon, thereby changing the canon itself. Even as ritual incantations are used by practitioners to render ritual practices legitimate, the sites of change from which meanings are produced emerge not from discontinuities in meanings but in the production of apparent continuities of ritual form.

Òyótúnjí Tradition: Divination and Social Change

Practitioners represent divination as an application of sacred knowledge. It operates as a mechanism through which canonical divinatory structures enable priests to transport information through the temporal past to detached spaces. For divinatory communication to be seen as efficacious, however, the process must involve the systematic repetition of ritual protocol. The specialized knowledge derived is enacted in the daily life of Ọ̀yọ́túnjí Village residents and is characterized by a performative language and a discourse of legitimization through which the diviner and client engage in creating the ritual process. Ritual practices are central to Yorùbá revivalist life. Not only do they offer practitioners the ability to control their fate and therefore empower themselves with transformative acts, but they also allow practitioners to promote an underground economy from which like-minded practitioners can form economic alliances. Praise-laced gossip and the differential size of clientele, along with the monetary gain, also create order as status through the respect achieved by the differentially successful diviners, who are already hierarchically structured in terms of age and, to some extent, gender. Diviners in Ọ̀yọ́túnjí tend to be the highest paid and respected because of their specialized knowledge and power of interpretation. The main sources of income for residents in Ọ̀yọ́túnjí range from ritual services such as divination and counseling to tourism and sales. Most practitioners who join the community strive to undergo the necessary ritual procedures so that they can become initiated in an òrìṣà cult and train to be a diviner.

Both initiated and uninitiated Yorùbá practitioners solicit the work of priests and priestesses to perform divinatory rituals. Among Ọ̀yọ́túnjí-affiliated Yorùbá practitioners there are two standard forms of divination readings: the most common and personal forms and the community-oriented rituals. If the divinatory interpretation is performed for an individual client, the priest's task is to pose a question or request and to interpret the encoded message. If the message is understood as negative, the priest must ascertain the type of sacrifices to remedy a client's condition. If the divinatory reading is employed to serve a public purpose, broader questions might be asked and more variables investigated. During such processes, after the invocations and opening questions are completed, the actual consultation through divination can begin.

In order to unpack the ritual efficacy of divinatory practices, it is necessary to understand the relationship of ritual practice vis-à-vis its cosmology and relation to power. When practitioners are initiated into òrìṣà cult groups, divinatory readings are conducted to communicate with both the òrìṣà gods and Olódùmarè. This process of communion with the gods is at the center of practitioners' obligations to a higher

authority, and the *odù* (verses) that are derived and interpreted form
the basis for personalized law of conduct. Revivalist practitioners derive meanings from divinatory packages of knowledge rules known
as readings. These readings are performed within the particularities of
those ritual codes deemed legitimate. These interpretations are written,
sometimes tape-recorded, and revisited as reminder of personal rules of
conduct. These rules shape personal obligations that bind practitioners
and provide the path to divinity (often referred to as "road") and a type
of specialized ritual knowledge based on the philosophies, training, and
epistemologies of religious specialists.

One of the highest forms of Yorùbá ritual initiation is the marriage
of a worshiper to one of the gods. This ritual process produces qualifications of priesthood into the world of òrìṣà worshippers and marks a
reconnection to the ancestors below and above the earth.[3] It involves
committing one's life to god forces, thereby entering the òrìṣà priesthood, and undergoing a series of ritual cleansings in which the old body
must die for the new body to emerge. The strength of these ceremonies
lies in their ability to link the past to the authority of god and to present
contemporary social contexts.

In many religious traditions, the nature of interpretive narratives
makes extreme diversity of interpretation problematic. Yet, unlike highly
textualized religions that depend on one sacred text from which social
codes are shaped, the power of prophetic messages in Yorùbá divination
is in the social insights and relevant social advice that are transmitted
through them. To look at essential forms of authority to understand how
interpretive determinants change and how they are legitimized is to begin with the assumption that the recognition of knowledge as legitimate
always involves critical processes of declaring the basis of authority.

In the case of Yorùbá divination, it is believed that through the course
of a given ritual, the priest channels the ancestors and therefore receives
insights about the past and guidance for the future. Through the transmission of oral predictions, the priest is thought to engage in symbolic
processes and as a qualified intermediary derives from divinatory acts
ancestral messages with which to link relevant social values to relevant
social conditions. The act of spiritual channeling, therefore, results in the
production of the prophetic message that is seen as being in the realm
of the transcendental. Seen thus, the relationship between the symbolic
and the social produces the conditions for structuring variations that are
regenerative and paradoxical.

Victor Turner's (1967) work on ritual, borrowing from Arnold Van Gennep's (1960) theory of rites of passage, led to a philosophy of change that was simultaneously about the dialectic of structure and anti-structure, producing a theory of ritual freedom within the conditions of constraint. By developing liminality as a passage of transmission—from one social status to another, one condition to another (Apter 1992)—Turner developed a modality through which to locate how ritual may provide a space for the articulation of ambiguity in which regeneration and renewal were possible within conditions of structural regulation. This dialectic of structure and anti-structure marked the paradox in Turner's work and is fruitful for thinking about the production of spaces of variation, their limits, and their exceptions. In the case of the Ọ̀yọ́túnjí divinatory mechanisms, national identities, temporal ordering of ancestral continuities, and racial meanings are being ritually remapped. In divinatory terms, new narratives are being legitimized in the context of superhuman power. As we shall see, when a divinatory ritual is performed and an interpretive analysis embarked upon, ties between hegemonic ritual structures are established and reproduced, and taxonomies in violation of particular forms of order are born. Thus, it is in this moment of religious trance—the embarkation of what Catherine Bell (1992) refers to as ritualization—that the divinity of the superhuman produces the site of exception, of difference, of erasure, where momentary change is possible. Ultimately, I build on Turner to demonstrate that liminality, predicated on what Andrew Apter (1992) referred to as a "negative dialectic," can be pushed further to characterize particular forms of social power—that of Giorgio Agamben's (1998) conception of states of exception—as an articulation of bare life, an existence that is included in democratic life through its exclusion. This realm of exclusion, this polluted state in need of redemption, is the sphere in which Yorùbá revivalists are engaged. And if we see the reordering of exclusion as the realm of the prophet, the taking up of the slavery of Africans, the people without history now marginalized and impoverished in the Americas, is productive because the diviner is operating outside of the legibility confines of not only the law but also the nation-state, thereby engaging in a form of transcendence that both reinforces and overturns the social order.

Using the example of the Yorùbá prophet in the person of the Ọba (divine king) of Ọ̀yọ́túnjí who claims to be able to use Ifá divination to trace the ancestry of all black Americans, we see that by attempting to address those outside of the reach of the sovereign, in the realm of exception, he engages in the power to suspend the reaches of sovereign pronouncements of citizenship and instead to recast forms of knowing the past with alternate knowledge technologies. As the ultimate authority, the Ọba uses ritual mechanisms to engage in the suspension of particular norms of knowing by which to produce exceptions. This suspension of the law through the empowerment of the exception and the negation of the intelligible is a site of agency where variation is possible and a site of power mobilized to produce new routinized forms of practice within different fields of logic. Seen thus, the exception may become the norm within particular fields of power, not just because he is already in command of community power, but because the discourses of redemption, which are engaging the moral authority of subversion of the racial hierarchy of scale that marginalized blackness in the first place, were able to achieve this only through the ordering of whiteness in paradoxical distinction between blackness and whiteness. The national and racial order being subverted in Ọ̀yọ́túnjí divinatory discourse is possible only through the suspension of the forms of institutionalization that initially created black marginalization. When this is done, the divinatory order and supernatural logics are called upon to produce a reordering. In this context, what circulates is a threshold of chaos, a domain of disorder in which new spatiotemporal limits are assigned and racially derived ancestral mapping is produced according to race and not citizenship. Agamben, speaking through Carl Schmitt (1927) has explained that this is made possible

> through the creation of a zone of indistinction between outside and inside, chaos, and the normal situation—the state of exception. To refer to something, a rule must both presuppose and yet still establish a relation with what is outside relation (the non-relational). The relation of exception thus simply expresses the originary formal structure of juridical relation. In this sense, the sovereign decision on the exception is the originary juridico-political structure on the basis of which what is excluded from it acquire their meaning . . . As such, the state of exception itself is thus, essentially unlocalizable (even if definite spatial-temporal limits can be assigned to it from time to time).

This articulation demonstrates that if the rule of determining citizenship and ancestral roots can be understood only in relation to a particular regime of authority, then the production of a new regime of logic, whether a supernatural regime or a regime that uses useful knowledge techniques, emerges outside of the authorial regime. It is the moral authority of Ọ̀yọ́túnji divinatory reclassification that carries human redemptive goals that make explicit the ways the exception—the racial Other—is intimately tied to the fundamental ordering of race. Therefore, the production of the two categories of extreme difference—whiteness and blackness—is already included in the whole. Where Agamben concludes that sovereignty is precisely what applies to the exception, the spaces of exception—which seem to appear outside the social order—are able to mobilize change precisely because it constitutes the antinomy of that order. Divinatory ritual, as a technique of redemption, can produce variation if the structures of legitimacy are in place, and the moral order can be mobilized to remap new inclusion, even if with different domains of knowledge.

Producing Spaces of Exception in Yorùbá Divination

There are six principle methods of Yorùbá divination in Nigeria (Akinnaso 1995: 237) that range from Ifá to *obì* divination. Among New World Yorùbá, four standard divinatory techniques and approaches are used. Yet, despite these differing techniques, the objectives involve communication with a higher power. Nevertheless, not everyone in Ọ̀yọ́túnjí is a diviner, and not everyone has equal participation in all divinatory rituals. There is a clear distinction between those individuals who are initiated into the priesthood and those who are not. Priestly initiates gain access to sophisticated divinatory practices, and their status in the community is imbued with the mystique of secrecy. Uninitiated practitioners interested in divinatory knowledge either consult a priestly initiate for divinatory knowledge or perform their own divinatory methods with a four-piece divinatory apparatus known as *obì*.

The *obì* approach allows non-initiates to pursue questions for which a "yes–no" response is adequate. The *obì* divinatory system is the most basic form of Yorùbá divination (for more see Gonzalez-Wippler 1992: 3; Mason 1992: 26–35). However, the *ẹ̀rìndínlógún* and Ifá forms of divination are only performed by initiated priests and are also seen as being more accurate; therefore, they have a higher knowledge-producing status. It is no accident, thus, that in Ọ̀yọ́túnjí Village, the *ọba* was for many years the central figure for performing exclusive rituals and for producing the authoritative word on various divinatory interpretations.

Between 1972 and 1988, the ọba of Ọ̀yọ́túnjí was the only Ifá priest, otherwise known as a *babaláwo,* performing Ifá divinatory readings.[4] The scarceness and complexity of stages of Ifá initiation and divinatory training contributed to its prominent status in Ọ̀yọ́túnjí. One could not easily become a *babaláwo* in Ọ̀yọ́túnjí since initiations into the Ifá cult were not conducted in Ọ̀yọ́túnjí Village until 1972 and were scarcely found in the United States. The initiations, however, have become more accessible in the early twenty-first century.

Ọ̀yọ́túnjí revivalist practitioners are not hierarchy neutral. For this gift, diviners are valued according to their status as priests. Social boundaries are deeply embedded in status and rank rather than conventional class distinctions. Their particular forms of specialized knowledge, their gender, access to archaic technology, political standing in the community, and reputation from general gossip and client feedback all contribute to their rank. Throughout the 1970s to the late 1980s, the unique status of the *ọba,* being the only *babaláwo* to conduct Ifá divination, contributed to a situation in which his services were always necessary components of all priest initiations in Ọ̀yọ́túnjí. By the late 1980s and early 1990s, as more Ọ̀yọ́túnjí priests traveled to Nigeria and Benin to pursue *Ìgbò odù* (the initiation procedure of obtaining a primary divinatory *odù* for Ifá), increasing numbers of residents became equipped to conduct the highest form of Yorùbá divination. It was not until the late 1990s when a group of five priests had traveled to Benin and Nigeria and pursued their own Ifá initiations that high-ranking chiefs could replace the *ọba' s* involvement.

Ifá divination is represented in Ọ̀yọ́túnjí Village as the most sophisticated and ancient form of divinatory knowledge. It is believed to have sustained its ancient and traditional form over longer periods than the other system, *ẹẹ̀rìndínlógún* (Brandon 1993: 142). *Ẹẹ̀rìndínlógún* divination is the most common form of divination among recently initiated priests in Ọ̀yọ́túnjí and throughout U.S.-affiliated and Santería communities. This approach is more inclusive in its potential for participation. Both women and men can function equally as *ẹẹ̀rìndínlógún* priests. This is not true for Ifá divination. Everyone does not have equal access to the Ifá priesthood. Although both women and men can undergo the preliminary stages of initiation, granting them tools to legitimately conduct Ifá divination, only men are permitted to pursue the secondary, more complex level of Ifá initiation in which they are said to go to *Ìgbò odù* to become *babaláwo.* The successful completion of an initiation in *Ìgbò odù* raises the initiate to the highest rank of priesthood—a *babaláwo*. Since the majority of prominent priests in Ọ̀yọ́túnjí are now *babaláwo,* much of the following will be based on my observations of Ifá divination.

Following genealogies of scholarship that connect Max Weber (1947, 1958, 1963) to Pierre Bourdieu (1990) to their contemporaries, I am not interested in privileging class in its traditional Marxian sense as an economically determined means of production. Thus, although most of the new clients who visited Ọ̀yọ́túnjí tended to be from lower middle-class to working-class families and ranged in age from their late twenties to late forties, classifications of class distinctions are complex and do not always fit neatly into traditional approaches to power, access, and privilege. I am interested in establishing particular material measurements of wealth and access that shape the relations of possibility by which status is measured. I approach class in relation to its intersections with not only income level, occupational skill, and education, but also consumption practices and social values in so far as they cross-cut status and prestige, gender and patriarchy, in particular fields of power. The ability of practitioners to enforce different meanings depends on both the basis from which claims are legitimated and the status of agents making those claims. Through an examination of the status and authority of diviners, I demonstrate how in particular hierarchies of institutional power particular types of agents employ certain types of knowledge. The age structure of the community, combined with the economic conditions that make ritual specialization a financially desirable opportunity, and the rules regulating qualifications are among the key factors that shape who can become apprentices and who can perform certain types of divinatory rituals. In this manner, I show how outcomes of involvement in divination enhance the hierarchy of priestly diviners.

Institutionalizing Readings: Types of Divination Readings

I have classified divination readings into two categories: (1) the standard individual reading (which incorporates the ancestral family) and (2) the civic society reading (which incorporates cult groups known as *ẹgbẹ́*). Different divinatory methods involving both *ẹẹ̀rìndínlógún* and Ifá are used for the standard individual reading. However, only Ifá readings are used for readings in civic contexts.

Individual readings are the most common in both Yorùbáland and the

Americas and are conducted between a client and a diviner. In Nigeria, they must take place in the presence of the client. In the United States, although in most cases the presence of the client is necessary, there are innovations in which absentee divinatory readings can be derived and communicated by telephone.[5] Nevertheless, the standard interaction is organized as a private consultation in which the priest functions as a conduit by which messages from the ancestors and òrìṣà are transmitted. In the pursuit of ritual interpretation, the priest interprets the configuration of the divinatory tools and is then expected to verbalize these interpretations for a client in the form of an oral message. Individual divination readings can also be a necessary part of social activities. Some examples of the creative incorporation of standard readings in American revivalist movements are the river reading, designed to ritualize the process of initiation of new Ọ̀yọ́túnjí residents, or the family reading, orò ìdílé, otherwise known as the roots reading.[6] Divinatory roots readings follow the same logic and format as both standard and civic readings, but their goal is to recover client ancestral histories. By tracing family lineage, determining kin occupations, and endowing the client with new Yorùbá names, it has a transformative purpose. It reproduces a canon of Yorùbá divinatory structure while reshaping the terms by which Yorùbá history is re-signified in new locations. With the goal of obtaining knowledge about Yorùbá or West African ancestors, the exchange of knowledge between the client and diviner is made possible through the ritualization of the Ifá canon.

Both forms of divinatory processes share the same methods but serve different functions. The most necessary form of divination for establishing a personal ancestral connection to West Africa is the roots reading. The highly individualized standard reading can be contrasted with the civic society reading. Although the two are structurally similar, the civic society reading is conducted for the purposes of group, not individual, instruction. In both Nigeria and Ọ̀yọ́túnjí Village, chief priests conduct these readings in an attempt to alert the leadership, the community, or the nation of the oracle's predictions. The various types of civic readings popular in Ọ̀yọ́túnjí range from the reading of the week, the reading of the month, the reading of the year, and the annual òrìṣà cult (ẹgbẹ́) readings.[7] Often civic readings are performed by a group of two or more priests from a designated cult group and occur in incrementally consistent periods.

The reading of the year is one such civic divinatory ritual and represents a set of predictions for the new year. Similarly, the readings of the week or of the year are conducted on a weekly basis in Ọ̀yọ́túnjí and represent practitioner attempts to collect and document authoritative translations of the Yorùbá past. Although delivered orally, and traditionally committed to memory, the production of these divination "readings" in the late twentieth to the early twenty-first century has shifted from the oral transmission of narratives to the translation of oral narratives to the written documentation of these predictions and postings in electronic mail and on the World Wide Web.

The priests who are called on to provide services are always compensated for their labor. In developing a client pool, the priest provides services for these individuals. The divinatory interpretation of mandatory follow-up ritual work deemed necessary by the gods for uninitiated nonpractitioners tends to generate additional income-producing possibilities for priestly practitioners. Most of the income earned from divination comes from nonresident, nonpriests who call or visit Ọ̀yọ́túnjí for that purpose. If uninitiated nonpractitioners or practitioner residents express interest in further exploring the remedies to conditions raised during the divination reading, they may establish a work relationship with a priestly intermediary who can agree to serve as their consultant or *olórìṣà* (òrìṣà guide or trainer).[8]

Up until the mid- to late 1960s in New York City, Santería-based divinatory techniques were incorporated by many Òrìṣà-Voodoo Yorùbá revivalists and provided adherents with the necessary tools to produce Yorùbá ritual knowledge about the past and to predict the future. Over time, Ọ̀yọ́túnjí-centered revivalists attempted to radically adapt their divinatory rituals in order to produce a new mechanism through which the ancestral past could be known. These ritual acts incorporated the logic of slavery and were made to perform the changing face of Òrìṣà-Voodoo. Through the development of ritual institutions, various rituals, such as divination readings, circulate as a form of producing knowledge about the past and future.[9] Yet with the increased centralization of authoritative divinatory texts and the emergence of a centralized authority, the institutionalized authority of divination became less personal and individualized and more bureaucratic. This process of transformation led to the routinization of particular forms of authority through which religious movements and their constituents create ways of arranging, structuring, and resolving disputes connected to how to come to terms with other competing claims to authority. That is, through the establishment of normative values and bundles of divinatory types, transnational Yorùbá revivalists tend to reproduce the social values in their world. Challenges to these norms, whether from external political institutions such as states or superior authorities, are often incorporated or routinized within the social norms of the everyday, or they are rejected. In the case of Yorùbá revivalism, the symbol of whiteness, Santería, and slavery are distinguished from signs of blackness and Africanness. The rules regarding who can belong and why, how rituals should be performed, and how people can redeem themselves or claim privileges of ritual action are connected to the routinization of authority for the purposes of self-preservation.

First Roots Reading: The Recanonization of Ifá Divination

This day resembled many other days in which visitors from various parts of the United States, England, and the Caribbean visited Òyótúnjí during its monthly three- to eleven-day festivals in search of divinatory advice or "new religious possibilities." During my year of fieldwork in Òyótúnjí, I recorded in excess of one hundred client divinatory readings performed by eight different priests in Òyótúnjí Village, and over the years I have read or listened to more than forty roots readings performed by the Qba of Òyótúnjí.

The overwhelming majority of clients tended to be African Americans who had converted to Yorùbá practices. Although some of these practitioners, in describing their need for a divination reading, claimed that they had converted to Yorùbá religious practices because they "couldn't live like Christians in racist America," most discussed their need for support and guidance during their period of personal transformation. As one client—a young dreadlocked man in his twenties whom I refer to as Adé Tölá—told me, "any kind of help will do in this hellhole called Àmëríkà." In discussing other reasons for converting to Yorùbá traditions, a small minority revealed that they were in search of clarity or "answers to explain the reasons for the enslavement of black people." An essential element of their conversion often involved a predisposition to reject Christianity and believe in something "African." Of the vast majority of the individuals who consulted Òyótúnjí practitioners over the course of March 1995 to March 1996, 69 percent (N = 111) eventually adopted or had already adopted Yorùbá "traditional" beliefs because they were disillusioned with what they identified as the eurocentrism of Christianity.

I sat and waited outside of the king of Ọyọtúnjí's palace gates for another client to begin her divination session. I was struck by how long we had to wait for each divinatory reading. I was intrigued by the seriousness with which they incorporated the new information. My new acquaintances did not appear to be bothered by the passing time. Both Adé Tölá and the second client, whom I refer to as Ôsúngbèmí, were prepared for a full weekend of ritual, communion, and personal transformation. After her divinatory ritual, Ôsúngbèmí was proud that her new Yorùbá name identified the Yorùbáland town in which the priest told her that her ancestors had lived over six hundred years ago. So proud was she that when I introduced myself to her, she was determined to remember the pronunciation of her new name and introduced herself, integrating the new name.

"Ôsúngbèmí Ajayi" she said as she contorted her face and nodded her head to the right side on every syllable.

"Nice to meet you," she continued with an outstretched hand and a big smile. The practice of quickly incorporating such "traditional" practices—new names, clothes, and greetings, is a common practice among many of the African American visitors with whom I met during my year in Ọyọtúnjí. For new practitioners the divinatory roots reading references the nostalgia of the past and provides guidance for the future. "If you know where you came from, then you'll know where you're going," Adé Tölá said to me a few days later. On this particular day the "where you're going" portion of Adé Tölá's statement was answered with a divinatory directive for him to reclaim "traditional" practices in order to redeem himself—a call that he had already begun to incorporate into his new African-centric lifestyle. This statement is particularly appropriate since it is in keeping with popular metaphors that form the basis for Ọyọtúnjí roots readings.

The first client, Adé Tölá, took his place on the mat. He sat down and then arose as he remembered that the standard protocol involved saluting the priest by lying in front of him with his body prostrate on the floor. As he lay there the priest responded, "Dìde," and motioned him to rise up.

"Thank you," replied Adé Tölá, inappropriately responding in English. "Ẹ káàbọ̀" (You are welcome), responded the priest in Yorùbá. After this preliminary exchange, the priest resumed his place on the divining mat, and the client sat across from him. The priest began with a melodious incantation with which he beckoned the gods and the ancestors to join them. As he spoke, he repeatedly dangled his *òpèlè* (divining chain) over the beaded cowry in front of him. He then asked Adé Tölá to place his money on the mat. The priest's voice cracked as he spoke. The money became the object with which the divining chain made contact.

The priest was dressed in a white cotton *agbádá* (traditional shirt) with matching pants. Necklaces embellished his neck, and rings decorated his fingers. His hair, with its white streaks, was combed back and braided at the end. His head was covered with a distinguished and flashy Yorùbá "traditional" hat known as a *fìlà*. As he chanted quickly in Yorùbá, offering invocations to the various Yorùbá deities, he continued to touch the money with the divining chain. This part of the ritual incantation is generally followed by a sequence in which the divining priest pays homage to religious and ancestral kin. As the priest methodologically lowered and elevated the divining chain (*òpèlè*), he chanted a meticulously constructed incantation. Even after he finished recalling all of the names by memory, revering a genealogy of gods, ancestors, Ọyọtúnjí, Cuban, and Nigerian priests, and places imbued with diaspora nostalgia, he continued to look at his *òpèlè*, posing questions to it in Yorùbá in an attempt to obtain a response. The response is possible through the priest's identification of the configuration of the *òpèlè*, known as the *odù*. There are a total of 256 *odù* configurations, and as the priest cast his chain down continuously, as if to throw dice and await the numeric configuration before him, he called out each *odù*, interpreting them as responses to each question posed. His assistant recorded all of them on a sheet of paper; and upon establishing the initial four *odù*, he studied the sheet of paper that had the *odù* configurations listed, one after the other.

The diviner studied the *odù* markings, occasionally muttering in English the story of a proverb (*odù* or verse) associated with one of the four *odù* before him. After careful consideration of the proverbs associated with all four *odù* and their meanings, he began the interpretation, as if he were translating the information for the client into English, prefacing each interpretation of the *odù* with the slow and pensive authorial claim, "Ifá says." The diviner began by claiming the sanctity of the interpretation as something ordained by the gods. He carefully selected his words, often combining his English sentences with Yorùbá, and declared, "Ifá says that your family was from a lineage of Yorùbá royalty who practiced Ifá worship during their reign. These clansfolk," he declared as if an insightful revelation, "lived in Ọ̀yọ́ and ruled there for centuries before evil individuals, commoners from a nearby town, deceived them and sold your family into transatlantic slavery . . . Ifá says that the redemption of the offspring of this kinship clan could be realized through the worship of the Yorùbá deities Ifá and Ọbàtálá," he added. He told Adé Tölá that his family was from a royal kinship lineage and that the factors leading to the sale of the family into transatlantic slavery were the result of the wrongdoing of others. The *odù* in the positive or *ìre* (prayer), as illustrated by the *odù Ogbè ̣́yé+ mo jalè*, is the component of the canon that the diviner referenced in order to designate Adé Tölá's family as emerging from a royal clan.[10] In this case, the reading is an *ìre* or positive reading and with such an "*ìre* blessing from the ancestors."

Attempting to establish a connection between New World identities and precolonial Yorùbá societies, the divining priest ritualized the incantations in Yorùbá in order to reference the institutional domain of Yorùbá power. The bodily movements performed by the priest also flagged repetitious mechanical rituals common among Yorùbá priests throughout southwestern Nigeria. Through the routinization of repetitive bodily movements and speech acts—acts that Foucault (1991) referred to as techniques of the self—the priest reinforced particular inscriptions of power and knowledge through which truth emerged within a structure of rules that are communicated according to a range of discursive forms. Through these techniques of the self, we see how agents deploy particular ritual acts to cultivate particular practices through which subjects constitute themselves as subjects, as well as contextual frameworks through which the particularities of truth are produced. The diviner, who is usually highly trained, is endowed with the license to interpret the divinatory apparatus for clients (Akinnaso 1995) and to narrativize solutions.

The production of legitimate narratives from which a sacred, ancient, and fixed source must be referenced is the duty of the diviner alone, and in this process the diviner is in command of diagnosing the problem and narrativizing the solution. The diviner's ability to enact a ritual environment and to link the *odù* to relevant interpretations of the past forms the basis for the production of divinatory authority. When I looked into the eyes of the diviner as he spoke in his slow and pensive mantra, I surmised that he saw himself as involved in a legitimate process of interpretation. To interpret the *odù*, not only was he employing his training, but he saw himself as being in a trance, which enabled him to communicate with the ancestors. In addition to his enactment of the divinatory ritual, the slow delivery of speech and his glazed eyes were important indicators that the interpretation of the *odù* emerged from an altered state. Anthropologists have long written about the authenticating dynamics that ritual-induced possession, often illustrated with altered speech (slow and pensive), has on the perceived legitimacy of ritual performances. In the midst of this, I attempted to interject my interests into the course of the interaction. However, I was cut off instead and forced to return to my role, already designated by the divining priest. This further reinforced the uneven relationship between the diviner and the client. These productions, shaped by determinations of truth as "natural" or truth as emergent from the heavens, are inextricably linked to the social, historical, and geographical worlds from which their meanings were constituted.

I turn now to various institutional zones within which the particularities of Yorùbá transnational connections are embedded and through which new meanings are spatially and temporally legitimized. Here, I demonstrate how ritual practices are fashioned and refined to render a useable past to those who travel there seeking assistance and the interpretative constructions of particular kinds of ancestral connections with West Africa. Thus, with linkages established, the power of ritual often lies in the personal authority generated by the subject who is revered—as one would revere a prophet or a saint.

The availability of academic texts describing divination practices during the colonial period in West Africa provides a critical canon for the interpretative process. Although the canons that otherwise direct and shape the authenticity, stability, and, hence legitimacy of the ritual are critical, the authority of the diviner—the one in command of diagnosing and narrativizing the solutions—is as central to the formation of the legitimacy of the ritual process as is the authority of the canonical history. The process of performance allows Òyótúnjí practitioners the means of narrating selected ancestral lineages; differentially affixing blame to past ancestors of those lineages is consistent with the gender and behavioral characteristics the diviner attributes to particular persons seeking their assistance.

Second Roots Reading

Like all the others, the priest's reading of my ancestral genealogy began with a standard incantation to the gods. As I approached the ritual space and sat on the mat across from the diviner, I began to tell the diviner about my project and why I was there, and I quickly realized that my unsolicited comments had no place in the diviner-client exchange. The priest's incantations and technique of identifying my family lineage was based on an authorial determination by which he consulted the oracle in Yorùbá—not me. This was followed by his request for a monetary payment from me. Once I had paid the requested amount, the diviner continued with his invocation.[11]

A presumption of "authority" on the part of the diviner is negotiated in the process of client-diviner interaction and is an important component of the ritual. Although clients may, indeed, question or challenge the interpretation offered to them and doubt the efficacy of the ritual or the qualifications of the diviner to exact his or her interpretations, the ritual is often measured by the client according to the extent to which the form and content of the ritual is in alignment with a dominant canonical structure (Akinnaso 1995: 244).

In an American-Yorùbá dialect, the diviner posed to the gods the necessary questions about my ancestral heredity. To obtain the answers he cast the *òpèlè* each time, deriving a new *odù* configuration. As he cast the chain, he called out the name of the *odù*, and his assistant recorded it on a piece of paper. Once completed, the diviner read the paper with the *odù* and took a few minutes to think about the interpretation. The diviner, puzzled by the meaning of the first configuration in relation to the last, had his assistant priest open the large text, entitled *Ifá Divination: Communication between Gods and Men in West Africa* (Bascom 1969a), that had been on the floor next to the divining tray and consulted the relevant interpretation of the first *odù*. After thinking about the meaning, in a slow and thoughtful—almost in a trance-like state—he interpreted the oracle, always looking at the paper before him:

> Ifá says this was a brilliant society of enormously psychic *babaláwo*. The rule and respect of Ifá was predominant in this clan, which lived in the environs of the capital city of Òyó. Ifá says this was a clan, which had produced numerous individuals of outstanding citizenship. They were the pride of their community. On the negative side, there were many females who tended to become very proud, arrogant, and out-of-control despite numerous warnings from their *babaláwo* husbands. Ifá says domineering women persisted in following their own minds, which ultimately brought a perversion in the destiny of the clan. Much *èbo* was done and though every one of half adult years held membership in

some cult, tragedy befell the clan in the form of numerous deaths and losses. The massive ẹbọ included the sacrifice of youthful members into the transatlantic slave trade. While these cruel sacrifices did redeem the clan's fortunes, it brought greater discipline to its female membership. Those sacrificed in their ocean-bound prisons sailed out of sight and were never to be heard from again.

The narrative referred to me as a black female, an apparently independently minded intellectual who emerged from an ancestral line that was once seen by town people as brilliant and that was gifted with both psychic powers and social respect. As communicated by the diviner, my ancient family did not emerge from royalty but from a noble and respectable background of gifted diviners who produced "individuals of outstanding citizenship"; they were the pride of their community. According to the priest's interpretation, a tragedy befell my ancestral kin, and although their babaláwo husbands served as innocent bystanders whose warnings went unheeded, the females contributed to the demise of my ancestral clan, which had the consequences of transatlantic enslavement.[12]

As represented by the diviner as emerging from Ifá, my family's nobility was described as being redeemed with the sacrifice of thousands of youth and adults who were held captive in slave ships and transported to the Americas. The lesson for my ancestral lineage, therefore, was that the women of the clan needed to exercise greater self-discipline. I was told that I could finalize the punishment of enslavement by resuming my family's ancestral worship and, as Ifá had instructed, "Revert to a Yorùbá way of life."

Ọ̀yọ́túnjí priests often highlight insubordination as a central cause of the enslavement of both men and women from Ọ̀yọ́ to the Americas. Its relevance is most profound in relation to the ways that women's roles are heavily regulated in accordance with what it means to be traditional, insubordinate, and harmonious. As can be seen in the majority of the roots readings, the priest identified that a wrong deed was committed either by a female, an egocentric individual, or an unruly kin member, and consequently a tragedy befell the entire community. Regardless of whether the client's family was the victim or perpetrator of enslavement, priests often foreground enslavement as a curse that insubordinate ancestors, especially females, brought upon their community members.

As seen in the diviner's interpretation of my odù, the occupation of my ancestral clan is similar to my current occupation. The Ọ̀yọ́túnjí divinatory interpretations that emerged from divinatory ritual sessions were informed by wider social and historical concerns specific to local responses of racism and attempts to reach a deeper understandings of how the past can be rectified in the present.

Literary texts play an important role in shaping and authorizing the diaspora interpretations of the canon. The referential use of William Bascom's text, for example, provided and continues to provide practitioners with literate documentation of the standard interpretations for *odù* Ifá. Many African Americans who were initiated by Cuban practitioners in the 1950s and 1960s relied on these English textual explanations of the practices in which they were initiated (see Bascom 1969a, 1969b, 1980). These texts provided both the translation and the explanations for how to conduct Ifá divination as well as how to procure ritual sacrifices, interpret proverbs, and construct incantations for Yorùbá ritual. In order to legitimize their contemporary knowledge about Yorùbá ritual, Ọyọtúnjí priests continue to rely to on the academic works of Nigerian cultural practices, the priesthood, initiation and divination rites, and the results of their own divinatory innovations. Nevertheless, because the divinatory canon, thus recovered, exists without long histories of New World precedents, Ọyọtúnjí villagers have a substantial degree of advantage from which to "narrativize" the past.

Ritualists, as intellectual producers, chart historical narratives and predict the future. They perform divination for clients and connect dislocated histories with U.S. realities. Understanding the politics of Yorùbá divinatory training, interpretation, and the transmission of knowledge about the Yorùbá canon are critical to understanding the complexities of status and authority that shape the ways that innovations are possible. An example of the processes of creative change can be seen by the ways that the diviner incorporated the canon into a new interpretation of my past. His interpretation began with a linear progression of my kinship origins, traceable along both paternal and maternal notions of racial descent. Through standard ritual mechanism that located race as a biological feature that passed down generation by generation according to a linear pattern, from one black ancestor to the next, he determined that my ancestors on the maternal side contributed to the tragedy of enslaving my ancestral kin.

In addition to the gendered implications of blame in his articulations of transatlantic slavery, implicit in these slavery narratives is the complicity of African kin in the enslavement of African Americas as well as the complicity of each person in participating in their enslavement. As the divinatory discourses demonstrate, because of their wrongdoing African men and women were the central agents who perpetrated the enslavement of their kin. The diviner explained that through the evils of their ancestors, contemporary black Americans still suffer from racism, poverty, and social marginalization—all consequences of the slave past.

Conducted in communities such as Ọ̀yọ́túnjí Village, divination provides the believer with the means of enacting personal prestige and power. Practitioner determinations for which rituals are seen as "appropriate" and which interpretations are seen as being accurate raise concerns about the grounds by which knowledge production is shaped. Although Nigerian diviners do not conduct roots readings as such, anthropologist Bascom (1969a: 37–39), in his examination of Yorùbá Ifá priests in Nigeria, documented more than sixty divinatory incantations and interpretations offered to the African gods by Nigerian Yorùbá diviners. These prayers also followed a standard sequence seen in New World divinatory performances but invoked the "gods from the heavens, fields and trees" to join them, never making reference to transatlantic slavery. Even with the variability of New World revivalist concerns, the improvised structure of divination is maintained as credible because it incorporates Yorùbá divinatory ritual structure and language, assumes communication with the gods, ancestors, and the diviner, and pulls from interpretive structures known to the well-studied practitioners.

In order to divine using the highest form known as Ifá divination, a priest must invoke the gods with chants, cast the divining chain, identify the specific configuration in which the divining pieces land, match its configuration with the associated *odù,* and interpret the *odù* for the client for whom the divination is being conducted. The key to interpretation is in matching the divining chain configuration to one of the 256 *odù* that exist. Its importance and authorizing power exists because each *odù* is seen as being a sacred message from the Yorùbá high God known as Ọrúnmìlà. Ultimately an *odù* represents ancient wisdom from the heavens. Each *odù* is identified by a two-word name that symbolizes specific characteristics, marking it as unique and enabling the diviner to connect to it a parable or verse known in Yorùbá as an *ẹsẹ*. Matching the *odù* with a characteristic and applying its meaning to the social life of the client enable variations to emerge as adaptations of—not deviations from—the Yorùbá canon.

As we have seen, the challenge of charting the production of new institutional forms of divinatory knowledge is in understanding the tenets of legitimacy upon which new narratives are imported into seemingly fixed forms. That is, canonical legitimacy depends on the perception of the reproduction of an authorial canon. And even as texts may appear fixed, priests incorporate new interpretations into fundamental tenets of the divinatory canon. For indeed, in Ọ̀yọ́túnjí, as in many Yorùbá divinatory settings, both performative language and ritual acts play a central role in ensuring the authority of the priest's ritual interpretations.

Third Roots Reading

The next client was Ôsúngbèmí. Her roots reading followed the same pattern of noble beginnings, trauma, and redemption. The priest described her family as people who provided "initiates into the cult of Ifá"—a noble and esteemed position. They were seen as intelligent and talented. However, the factors that led to the demise of her ancestors were different from the previous two examples. In her case, the sin was far more severe. The family's arrogance and their neglect of religious practices led to their tragedy, and issues of jealousy and disagreements led to "serious calamities in their households." Yet, the priest consoled her by suggesting that the transatlantic slave trade provided her with opportunities to make sacrifices to the gods on behalf of the female members of the household.

The diviner raised other concerns about the existence of sexual promiscuity. "Females are advised to proceed with care into polygamous households and to worship Ifá," he warned. This example of calamities that led to the rupture of this family emphasizes the notion of African responsibility for sending their families into slavery. Interestingly, all of those who were involved were in a clan of diviners and were not themselves actively involved in selling African bodies into slavery, but they encountered situations in which slave sellers victimized them. Again, the enslavement of the members of this family was represented by the diviner as a punishment, symbolically representing slavery as the result of West African wrongdoing.

The slavery narrative highlights the same dynamic in which African historical figures were seen as agents and genitors of the transatlantic slave trade. Here again, only redemption can bring about the possibility of social change. In other words, Yorùbá Nigerians, and by extension Ôyun Bemi, as agents of "wrongdoing," are able to correct past infractions through their reclamation of ancient traditions. According to the narratives circulated by Ọyọtúnjí diviners and practitioners, their "fall" from these traditions led to the prevalence of such destructive circumstances.

The diviner located the roots of this young female client, a first-year college student of Native American and black American parentage, in southwestern Nigeria. He did not identify her ancestral lineage as coming from her Cherokee grandmother's line, but from her African American father's line. In this case, she was told that her ancestors might have been Ìjêbú, Êgbá, or Nàgó. As I sat and listened to the way in which lineage was identified, I tried to ascertain whether Ôsúngbèmí was disturbed that her Native American ancestry was not included in the explanation of her ancestral lineage. I studied her facial expressions as the priest continued to talk about the confusion of the African women in her past. No mention was ever made of her Cherokee Indian grandmother, and this did not seem to matter to her. As the priest relayed his interpretation of her past, Ôsúngbèmí sat on the mat with her tape recorder running and her eyes closed, arms apart and up, and her palms cupped to the ceiling. Occasionally Ôsúngbèmí took notes, but she seemed to be more interested in experiencing the moment by helping the priest channel this information.

When Ôsúngbèmí and I were in the Beaufort Applebee's Bar and Grill restaurant later that afternoon, a middle-aged African American woman who noticed us in our "traditional" clothes approached us to ask if "we were from that village" and if it was true that "the Ọyọtúnjí king is a fake light-skinned man from Detroit." In the king's defense, Ôsúngbèmí responded angrily that it didn't matter that the Ọba was "born in Detroit—and who cares what shade his skin is?"

"He's black, isn't he?" she added rhetorically.

I eventually understood the transformative meaning that the divinatory ritual had for her. She revisited the topic as we returned to the car by telling me that it really bothered her that people "judge the authenticity of their ancestral practices based on skin color and shade. This light-skinned dark-skinned thing is messed up," she added by insisting that when the priest was conducting her roots reading, it did not matter to her that "he had been born and raised in Detroit." What mattered to her was that "he knew how to channel Ifá through the gods of Africa."

For Ôsúngbèmí, the performance of ritual was "real," and the obvious changes of descent patterning and New World adaptations were fine so long as the priest was acting through the guidance of Ifá. When I asked her how she knew that the diviner successfully used Ifá to contact the ancestors, she told me that she "felt the vibration" and that was why she kept the palms of her hands outstretched. Her sense of the authenticity of the ritual was based on both the feeling she encountered from being engaged in the ritual and the priest's ability to create a credible, moving environment of ritual performance. The priest's responsibilities for the environment included chants in Yorùbá, the divinatory equipment, the establishment of the *odù,* his references to those *odù,* and the use of a slow, pensive speech in his delivery. But also, Ôsúngbèmí entered the situation with a willingness to believe and a need to make changes in her life. Although disappointed with the news of her family's historical turmoil, so pleased was she with the follow-up redemptive strategies to engage in "intense worship of Ifá" that she not only paid the standard $100 fee but included an extra ten dollars in the bundle. I asked her why she paid more money than she was asked to. To that she replied, "He helped me explain my true African identity." She added, "No more slave master's name and no more shame. That's all I wanted, and that's what I got. One hundred dollars isn't enough [money] for that kind of satisfaction."

Redemption from the shame of a history associated with enslavement is indeed an important aspect of the process of reclaiming preslavery African traditions. A range of prescriptive redemptive follow-up rituals usually follows the predictions and advice of a divination reading. These follow-up activities provide clients with the possibility of redemption and often involve follow-up rituals, often involving prices that begin at $100 (head cleaning and sacrifices) and might escalate to $4,500 (initiation into the priesthood). The readings themselves, however, cost a basic fee of $40 to $100. In general, monetary exchange is a significant component of the ritual, but according to many of the clients that I interviewed, money was not seen as a satisfying way to reward someone with "psychic powers." Nonetheless, most agreed that diviners should be paid for their services.

Because individuals new to these traditional practices choose freely to engage in divination readings in order to elicit answers to questions beyond the ordinary range of human comprehension, it seemed clear that they already had a desire to accept the possibility that the divination can bear redemptive and transformative results. These potential clients are often willing to engage in the follow up rituals. For Ôsúngbèmí, the follow-up rituals would give her a chance to redeem her family's destiny. In her words, the family's wrongdoing from slavery "could be dealt with once and for all with Yorùbá initiation."

There remain three similarities between most of the Ọyọtúnjí diviner's roots readings. First, all three readings establish an ancestral connection with West Africa. Although relatively little has been written on Yorùbá history before the nineteenth century, and the pre-1800 period lacked literate documentation, various mythic representations of the Yorùbá past have been transmitted through divinatory verses and oral histories.

Another shared feature between the diviner's roots reading text is thematic. All readings developed out of an underlying concern about the tragedy (Akinnaso 1995: 253) of transatlantic slavery, thus reinforcing the capacity of the divinatory oracle to interpret the past and prophesize the future. In the case of these examples, all three clients were told about the historical components of the transatlantic slave trade. The diviner linked their contemporary social concerns with agreed-upon historical "facts" and strategies for redemption that put the diviner in the position to provide insights and relieve social suffering. The manipulation of genealogies of ancestry as expressed through ritual serves this purpose. For divinations become "readings," in both the ritual sense (i.e., "a roots reading"), and the literary interpretative sense—in accordance with which enslavement is no longer an event that "happens to" Africans as a consequence of eternal forces; it is the product of the internal morally inappropriate actions of specific ancestors. These actions, when properly understood by those who see themselves as the now differentially embodied continuities of these types of ancestors, can be corrected by a proper alignment with Yorùbá tradition as defined and practiced in Ọyọtúnjí. In relation to the success of what might otherwise be classified by outsiders as a "ludicrous derivation of the slave past," divination and the processes of incremental change that follows highlight the ways that new narratives are incorporated into otherwise "fixed" texts. In addition to these symbolic transformations of cause, blame, subordination, and control, diviners garner financial gains, and many are able to make a living with this version of Yorùbá ritual. Despite being identified as the descendants of more or less egregiously blameworthy ancestors, clients often leave divining sessions grateful for both the knowledge that connects them with their previously unknown pasts and the knowledge about how to go on in the future. Òyótúnjí residents' articulations of their slave past both intersect with models of knowledge transmission and push us to ask not new but different questions about the criteria by which we chart the processes of change in Yorùbá divination.

The third similarity between the divinatory narratives is the degree to which the priest engaged in the ritual process adapted a "traditional" Yorùbá rhetorical structure of the divinatory text. This stylistic adaptation is symbolic of the process by which themes, ideas, and events are adapted into divinatory texts and how the texts are in turn recontextualized to suit particular circumstances in space and time (Akinnaso 1995: 253). Many contemporary approaches to understanding how traditions are changed and how those changes are structured around authorial components of rituals demonstrate how even as traditions change in structure and form, they are not always identified by those who live in them as having changed at all (Bell 1992: 118; Akinnaso 1995). The notion of traditional practices sometimes persists as being fixed and unchanging, yet even some anthropologists who recognize that change exists still miss the ways in which authorial ritual institutions and figures in positions of power play prominent roles in producing historical and social alliances. In thinking of the national transformation of Yorùbá religious ritual, it is significant to understand these shifts in the context of hierarchies of relevant social relations and their reconfigurations within particular spaces.

The relationship between change and its consequences across transnational borders demonstrates that although identity is continually enacted through ritual, ritual is not only a site of identity formation but also a site for the reformulation and regulation of local practice within particular ideological economies. The relationship between the regulation of Yorùbá ritual and the reproduction of the Ifá divinatory canon raises additional questions concerning what space producers of Yorùbá divinatory knowledge take up in their appeal for inclusion in the Yorùbá canon and what the consequences of those new alliances are. Therefore, while divinatory roots readings function as a form of social redemption for Òyótúnjí practitioners, the mechanics of producing divinatory change depends on the incorporation of its innovations into pre-existing authoritative structures. It is through this form that new and appropriate meanings can emerge (Akinnaso 1995), and as such the divinatory reading becomes a map of particular religious alliance.

Despite the necessary performance of divinatory methodology or the substantive role of divinatory ritual production, most Yorùbá diviners are intent on locating the efficacy of the ritual as ancient and therefore "authentic." The relevance of thinking about change and innovation as a study about sovereign power is that the diviner's interpretations and his or her authority has to be produced. Thus, divinatory authority is created in the process (Akinnaso 1995: 254), and the status of the diviner, the basis for his or her knowledge, and the sites of variation are dependent on the personal and political histories of those involved. And yet, the Ifá canon can only be changed if practitioners recognize the form, structure, and meaning of the rituals as remaining intact. Once the appearance of fixity and authenticity is in place, creative variability, within particular relevant terms, is possible.

In contemporary ritual theory today, more is known about the role of religious ritual when we move beyond the strictly ritual function to how they incorporate contemporary diaspora concerns to create new transnational alliances. Social rules set ideals for behavior, establish norms of belonging, and reinforce power relations. These rules work through institutions and establish entitlements based on the practical logics of ritual norms, legal norms, and performative acts. As we see, it is not state rules but, instead, informal and formal nonstate norms that are institutionalized through social norms. The norms enable the development of de-territorial community networks that gain legitimacy within particular fields of logic and power. Designations of ancestral-racial inclusion follow historical fields of biology as subjectivity, and this is not because they are believed to be as such. It is because modern social order operates with requisite institutions, which structure qualifications of participation according to classifications of birth status—origins, gender, race, and so forth. As literature on modern capitalism indicates, individual distinctions were shaped by human differences through a discourse of state-enforced racial biology. The shift from biological difference to individual-centered narratives about roots, though a response to the intensification of global migration and an attempt to territorialize displacement, was also reflected in the work of markets—literary and divinatory—in capitalizing on the shift to territorial heritage. These roots readings are yet another institutional instrument through which global displacement is territorially placed.

Toward a Theory of Social Change

How should we approach an understanding of ritual change when the relevance of attachments to place, history, and bodily inscriptions seems to suggest limitless possibilities to creating the social imaginary? This essay breaks from theorizing religion as a function of larger hegemonic categories or as merely constructed categories within which agents create meanings. Instead, I examine the ways in which agents use racial and religious forms of classification to perform the task of alliance, erasure, and ideological forms of forgetting. In charting social change, we need to understand the ways in which imaginary is made into reality and how what may be seen in larger terms as an inauthentic form of unreality is a means by which new exclusions are enforced.

This essay demonstrates that even while categories are constructed and their meanings change incrementally over time, their alliance with larger institutional forces of power are what embed their legitimacy and are essential to the institutional regimes that maintain them. What is most striking about the interplay between constructivism and the categories that reproduce their existence is that the categories work within particular institutional spheres that shape how and why people act and the meanings—historical and otherwise—related to why they act. These categories are constituted by boundary-making processes that pervade questions about how social relations are both remembered and reconstituted in complex relations of power.

By asking how people use religious rituals to both remember and forget the past we see that not only does religion do critical ideological work, but it also reflects the historical and political conditions from which it emerged. Through the performance of Yorùbá ancestral rituals, practitioners transform ritual structures in order to re-signify particular social conditions as the basis for racial alliances.

In *How Societies Remember,* Paul Connerton suggested that distinctions between social memory and historical reconstruction must be made in order to identify evidence of interpretive legitimacy of social acts (1989: 3–4). He argued that though narratives of the past serve to legitimatize contemporary social order, these narratives are insufficient without being conveyed and sustained through routinized practices—what he called "performative acts." In considering the routinization of ritual as performative, such practices serve a transformative purpose. For even as particular inscriptions of power are ideologically reinforced, ritual innovations are possible within the institutional power of ritual practice. The focus of this essay is to examine the multiple ways in which individuals recast ancestral roots through the institutional legitimacy of religious ritual. These webs of power are foundational and frame the basis by which groups are granted privileges to claim particular roots and not others, to redefine some cultural alliances and not others. Òyótúnjí practitioners have important questions to ask. How are historically transnational explanations about the African past formed, maintained, and also legitimized? What signs and symbols govern membership, and how is membership expressed and realigned through ritual practice? And what privileges does membership grant? What does it take to transform hierarchies of membership? The ability to create traditional Yorùbá imaginaries is evident in the ways that Yorùbá revivalists use religious divinatory institutions to turn attention from the popular conceptualization of American life to ideals about the West African past.

Notes

This chapter was previously published as "Many Were Taken but Some Were Sent: The Remembering and Forgetting of Yoruba Group Membership" in *Mapping Yoruba Networks: Power and Agency in the Making of Transnational Communities*. Copyright, 2004, Duke University Press. All rights reserved. Used by permission of the publisher.

1. Many practitioners lived in Òyótúnjí at one time; others pursued ritual initiations there over a period. I conducted a population tabulation of residents every three months over a one-year period; during that period, the population shifted from 57 to 48 residents.

2. At one time, many of the early residents were able to supplement their household income with government assistance payments. However, in the late 1980s, the Òyótúnjí Ògbóni council outlawed federal and South Carolina state government assistance. This new law, as well as the growing power of the Crown, made it increasingly difficult for many practitioners to make an adequate living on their religious trade alone. Unable to make ends meet, and in need of more political agency, hundreds of practitioners moved to U.S. cities, forming Yorùbá satellite communities from which to continue their religious practices.

3. The priesthood ritual is also known in Santería circles as "making Ocha" or "going under" and means that one is marrying a god.

4. The term *babaláwo* is a Yorùbá word that refers to a male high priest of Ifá. Visitors and residents in Òyótúnjí interested in standard initiations would have to request the presence of a *babaláwo*.

5. Otherwise, it is known as divination by phone.

6. Unlike the other forms of divinatory rituals, clients tend to conduct only one roots reading in a lifetime. The diviner performs this ritual in order to provide the client with knowledge of his or her paternal or maternal lineage, the specific historical explanations of his or her family's preslavery status, and the major calamities that led to the enslavement of the client's ancestors. Most important, the roots reading ritualizes the transformation of the client from an individual whose preslavery past was unknown and whose name reflected the legacy of being designated as chattel to the diviner's assignment of a new Yorùbá name to an otherwise American identity. Through the divinatory process of the roots reading, the divining priest uncovers the client's past and designates a new Yorùbá name to mark the end of a sacrificial cycle.

7. There are twelve cult groups in Òyótúnjí; during different times in the year, each group organizes a festival to venerate the òrìsà that bears its name (e.g., the Òsun Festival every April is organized to celebrate the Òrìsà Òsun). Members of that cult group conduct a pre-festival reading (in order to ascertain the type of offerings that should accompany the festival celebrations) and a post-festival reading (in order to establish whether the offerings were well received by the venerated òrìsà). There are twelve cult groups, and with the direction of the divinatory interpretations, each group organizes one festival during a different month each year.

8. Initiated divining priests also have relationships with priestly mentors, but because they tend to have more training than the uninitiated, they require less guidance. These diviners usually perform services for residents for bartered goods or services.

9. One could argue that they are also packaged as intellectual property and sold as history-producing commodities.

10. My findings have confirmed that the majority of clients who participated in roots readings are told they come from noble and well-respected families of *Ifá* traditional worshippers. However, besides a few scattered examples of individuals (one out of fifteen roots readings), the majority of the people who are told that they emerge from royalty are those who are in the current king's family.

11. In 1995, all roots readings cost $100.

12. In the context of Yorùbá cultural influences, as they have been shaped by African-Atlantic triangular webs in particular trade routes, the most convincing historical evidence suggests that Yorùbá (Lucumí) captives were sold not to North American but to Caribbean and South American traders. However, Òyótúnjí Village revivalists' reclamation of Yorùbá ancestral membership does

not constitute a miscalculation of the history of Yorùbá slave routes. Rather, it is the disjuncture between historical routes of trade and the symbolic roots of racial descent that point out how in the adoption of Yorùbá practices in North America Yorùbá revivalists inscribe onto the past the complexities of the historical present.

Works Cited

Abímbólá, Wande. 1976. *Ifa: An Exposition of Ifa Literary Corpus.* Ibadan: Oxford University Press.

———.1977. *Ifa Divination Poetry.* New York: Nok.

Agamben, Giorgio. 1998. *Homo Sacer: Sovereign Power and Bare Life.* Trans. Daniel Heler-Roazen. Stanford, CA: Stanford University Press.

Akinnaso, F. Niyi. 1995. "Bourdieu and the Diviner: Knowledge and Symbolic Power in Yoruba Divination." In *The Pursuit of Certainty: Religious and Cultural Formulations,* ed. Wendy James, 234–58. London: Routledge.

Apter, Andrew. 1992. *Black Kings and Critics: The Hermeneutics of Power in Yoruba Society.* Chicago: University of Chicago Press.

Bascom, William. 1969a. *Ifa Divination: Communication between Gods and Men in West Africa.* Bloomington: Indiana University Press.

———. 1969b. *The Yoruba of Southwestern Nigeria.* New York: Holt, Rinehart, and Winston.

———. 1980. *Sixteen Cowries: Yoruba Divination from Africa to the New World.* Bloomington: Indiana University Press.

Bell, Catherine. 1992. *Ritual Theory, Ritual Practice.* New York: Oxford University Press.

Bourdieu, Pierre. 1990. *The Logic of Practice.* Stanford, CA: Stanford University Press.

Brandon, George. 1993. *Santeria from Africa to the New World: The Dead Sell Memories.* Bloomington: Indiana University Press.

Clarke, M. Kamari. 1997. "Genealogies of Reclaimed Nobility: The Geotemporality of Yoruba Belonging." Ph.D. diss., University of Michigan.

Connerton, Paul. 1989. *How Societies Remember.* Cambridge: Cambridge University Press.

Foucault, Michel. 1991. "Governmentality." In *The Foucault Effect: Studies in Governmentality,* ed. Graham Burchell, Colin Gordon, and Peter Miller, 87–104. London: Harvester Wheatsheaf.

Gonzalez-Wippler, Migene. 1992. *Powers of the Orishas: Santeria and the Worship of Saints.* New York: Original.

Herzfeld, Michael. 1992. *Social Production of Indifference: Exploring the Symbolic Roots of Western Bureaucracy.* New York: Berg.

Maddox, Gregory, ed. 1993. *African Nationalism and Revolution.* New York: Garland.

Mason, John. 1992. *Orin Orisa.* Brooklyn, NY: Yoruba Theological Archministry.

Schmitt, Carl. 1927 (1996). *The Concept of the Political.* Chicago: University of Chicago Press.

Turner, V. W. 1967. *The Forest of Symbols: Aspects of Ndembu Ritual.* Ithaca, NY: Cornell University Press.

———. 1969. *The Ritual Process: Structure and Anti-structure.* Chicago: Aldine.

Van Gennep, A. 1960 (1909). *The Rites of Passage.* London: Routledge & Kegan Paul.

Weber, Max. 1947. *The Theory of Social and Economic Organization.* New York: Oxford University Press.

———. 1958. *The Protestant Ethic and the Spirit of Capitalism.* New York: Charles Scribner's Sons.

———. 1963. *The Sociology of Religion.* Boston: Beacon Press.

16

The Dynamic Influence of Cubans, Puerto Ricans, and African Americans in the Growth of Ocha in New York City

MARTA MORENO VEGA

During the time of the slave trade, enslaved Africans and their descendants in Cuba developed the Yorùbá-based religion known as La Regla de Ocha, popularly known as Santería. Driven by plantation economies late into the nineteenth century, Cuban elites depended on the forced servitude of enslaved Africans and their descendants even after slavery was abolished. Cuban plantation owners tenaciously resisted pressure from the British to abolish slavery; thus, Cuba became one of the last countries in the Western Hemisphere to do so. Although a law was passed on July 29, 1880, to abolish enslavement in Cuba, the statute instituted an eight-year tutelage period for enslaved Africans that officially ended slavery in 1888 (Knight 1970: 177).

The unintended consequences of a continuous infusion of "Negros de Nación," Africans born on the continent, invigorated the memory of the sacred traditional African praxis for the existing population of enslaved and freed Africans in Cuba. Among the many and various ethnic groups brought to Cuba in the latter part of the nineteenth century were the Yorùbá people of West Africa. Historian John Thornton explains that although enslavers tried to diversify the "cargo" of their ships to deter rebellion, generally the Africans aboard represented ethnic groups from similar national groupings, which served to maintain cultural and linguistic bonds in the New World. Thornton notes:

> These circumstances operated to ensure that most slaves would have no shortage of people from their own nation with whom to communicate and perhaps to share elements of common culture. These groupings of slaves served as a base from which many elements of African culture could be shared, continued, and developed in America and perhaps even transmitted into the next generation. (Thornton 1992, 197)

Joseph M. Murphy attests to the fact that the Yorùbá in Cuba were able to maintain their sacred beliefs in the religious practices of Santería. "Like the candomblé of Bahia, Cuban Santería has its origins among the Yorùbá priests and priestesses of the òrìshàs who were enslaved at the close of the eighteenth and the first decades of the nineteenth centuries" (Murphy 1994: 81). Murphy further explains that Santería evolved as parallelisms developed among Yorùbá traditionalists with those of the Roman Catholic Church. Murphy describes the process:

> They developed multiple levels of discourse to organize their heteroge-neous religious experience, referring, in more public and secular con-texts, to the Yorùbá *òrìshàs* by the Spanish word *santos*. Alerted to the energetic devotions to these *santos* practiced by Afro-Cubans, out-siders labeled their religion *santería,* "the way of the saints." (Murphy 1994: 81)

In La Habana, Cuba, I interviewed one of the religion's elders, Ba-baláwo Elpidio Cardenas, who is called by the Yorùbá name Otura Sa. In 1999, he indicated that the name given by followers of the religion is La Regla de Ocha (the rule of the Òrìṣà). Cardenas explained how the followers preserved their religious practice as a system:

> When the Yorùbá slaves were brought to Cuba, they wanted to practice their religion. They honored their *ancestral* spirits and the gods and goddesses of Africa hidden from their Spanish oppressors. In order to practice their religion, the African priests and priestesses formed a coun-cil to decide how they could continue to worship their ancestral beliefs. Realizing that there were not enough traditional leaders to maintain the regional system of worship established in Africa, in which one òrìshà protected a geographic area or village, they decided to join all the òrìshà practices under one system, which they called *La Regla de Ocha.* They used Catholic saints with similar attributes to the òrìshàs to camouflage

their African divinities. They knew, as we know, that the òrìshàs are not Catholic saints. (Personal communication with the author)

The words of Cardenas resonate in the work of art historian Robert Farris Thompson, who described the diversity of African groups brought to the Americas:

> New World Yorùbá emerged from all this strife. Ketu Yorùbá men and women captured by the Dahomeans turned up in Haiti and Brazil, where to this day they are called by the Dahomean word *nago*. Oyo and other captives of the Fulani were brought to Cuba, Brazil, and the Caribbean, notably Trinidad. The Yorùbá of Cuba were called Lucumí. . . . A remarkable fusion of òrìshà, long separated by civil war and intra-Yorùbá migrations, took place in the New World. (Thompson 1984: 17)

The oral history of Cardenas and Thompson's documentation affirm the dynamic intercultural threads that came together to forge La Regla de Ocha in Cuba.

During my interview with Babaláwo Elpidio Cardenas, he further explained that the ability of the religion and devotees to adapt to new realities is the strength that makes this religion relevant in contemporary society and that has made it an international religion. According to Babaláwo Cardenas, La Regla de Ocha is an inclusive religion that respects and worships the forces of nature. According to him, African divinities have spread to all parts of the world; because of their universal Nature-based principles, people of all races and cultures practice their principles. Cardenas again echoed the studies of Thompson by suggesting that wherever Yorùbá and other ethnic groups were taken, they developed a receptive environment for the continuity of their beliefs. Thompson credits this to the organizing philosophic streams of creativity, imagination fostered by the ancient African principles that continued to link New World African cultures as well as attracting millions of European and Asian people to their cultural expressions (Thompson 1984: xiii–xiv).

The people of African descent shared and nurtured the growth of La Regla de Ocha, the ancient organizing spiritual principles that flourished in Cuba and eventually in New York City. Initiates and scholars concur that the founding father of La Regla de Ocha in New York was Babaláwo Pancho Mora. In 1981, I had the opportunity to interview Babaláwo Pancho Mora, who was called by the Yorùbá name Ifá Moroti, as I began preparing for and organizing the First International Conference of Orisha Tradition and Culture, which took place in Ilé-Ifè, Nigeria, in 1981 at the University of Ifè.

According to Mora, he was initiated in Cuba on January 27, 1944, as a priest of the oracle òrìṣà (Yorùbá divinity) Ifá. He first traveled to New York City in 1946, and on his second trip in 1950 decided to stay. Mora noted that his first spiritual clients were members of the Puerto Rican community. He explained that the Cuban community was small and mostly composed of Afro-Cuban musicians who sought his spiritual guidance. White Cubans, he noted, did not want to be identified with a religion that they regarded as "primitive." Nonetheless, he noted with a smile that when in trouble, white Cubans would visit his home late at night to receive the advice of the òrìṣàs. Mora made it clear that over time, the small community of Puerto Rican, Cuban, and African American *creyentes* had expanded in New York, creating an ethnically diverse following.

To date, little research has been done to understand the historical environment that created the receptive conditions for the growth of the religion in New York City. This chapter focuses on those individuals who helped create a receptive environment for the growth of La Regla de Ocha in New York City. In interviews with Mario Bauza, Pancho Mora, Graciela, Julito Collazo, Katherine Dunham, Mongo Santamaria, Mercedes Nobles, and Louis Bauzo, among others, it became evident that the history of many contributors who helped the religion grow has yet to be told. This chapter is the first in a series that will call the names of the unsung heroes who contributed to the flourishing of La Regla de Ocha.

Historical Context

The investigations of African American scholar W. E. B. Du Bois in the United States and anthropologist Fernando Ortiz in Cuba in the early 1900s provide a beginning point in understanding the dramatic spread of La Regla de Ocha. Links connecting these two scholars and their protégés provide the threads that document the work of musicians, traditional leaders, and scholars in fostering a receptive environment for the eventual growth of La Regla de Ocha in New York City. Many names that must be called often are not associated with the growth of this religion. This chapter seeks to remind us of the many people who contributed to the incubation of an Afro-Cuban religious consciousness; they are not generally acknowledged as contributors to the spread of the religion.

When we speak of La Regla de Ocha, we must call to mind the many names of our ancestors—W. E. B. Du Bois, Irene Diggs, Zora Neale Hurston, Willie "El Bolitero" (surname unknown), Arsenio Rodriguez, Mario Bauza, Frank "Machito" Grillo, Fernando Ortiz, Lydia Cabrera, Chano Pozo, Dizzy Gillespie, Chris Oliana, Julito Collazo, Miguelito Valdez, Tito Puente, Mongo Santamaria, Rogelio Martinez y La Sonora Mantancera, Celia Cruz, La Lupe, Pearl Primus, Oba Sergiman, Wilfredo Lam, Nilo Tandron, Melville Herskovits, and Pancho Mora. The names of pioneers and legends who continue to enrich the growth of La Regla de Ocha must also be recalled. The list includes, and is not limited to, Katherine Dunham, Xiomara Alfaro, Graciela Perez, Francisco Aguabella, Fela Mendez, John Mason, Stephanie Weaver, and Osaye Mchawi. These traditional leaders, artists, and scholars, although functioning in different realms of society, created a synergy that ultimately opened a safe, sacred space for the practice of the religion in New York City.

In 1903, W. E. B. Du Bois, author of *The Souls of Black Folk,* introduced "the model for the inter- or multi-disciplinary methodologies to be found in black studies departments today," according to historian Henry Louis Gates Jr. (Du Bois 1989: xiii). Du Bois documented the aesthetic threads that Africans in the United States retained from their African root cultures. Ortiz's extensive studies of the African-based traditions in Cuba were concurrent with the investigations of Du Bois and Herskovits. In 1906, Ortiz had published *Hampa Afrocubana, Los Negros Brujos, Apuntes para un Estudio de Etnografía Criminal,* a study associating Africanisms with criminality. Eventually Ortiz changed his perspective, acknowledging the intellectual value, strength, and contributions of African descendants to Cuba. The separate investigations of Du Bois and Ortiz were linked through the work of Du Bois's protégé, Ellen Irene Diggs, in 1944.

Ellen Irene Diggs, African American journalist and scholar, wrote her dissertation at La Universidad de La Habana on the contributions of Fernando Ortiz in the area of race and culture She acknowledged that the new anthropological investigations of pioneers such as Ortiz and Herskovits proved that Africans and their descendants were not inherently less intelligent, which was the popular belief at the time. Diggs stated in her postscript: "Recent trends of investigation have emphasized the study of primitive culture and have led to a wide realization of the essential likeness in the development of early human culture and emphasis on the fact that difference is no proof of race inferiority or cultural limitations" (1944:108).

In the late 1920s, anthropologist Melville Herskovits refined the field of African studies. Today his work would be defined as African diaspora studies. His work developed macro international research concepts that were being studied at the micro level by a small network of pioneering anthropologists in their respective countries. Fernando Ortiz in Cuba, Gonzalo Aguirre Beltrán in Mexico, and Nina Rodriques in Brazil were also investigating the cultures of Africans and their descendants in their geographical areas. Understanding the interconnections among African descendants attempting to retain their ancestral legacy, Herskovits introduced new concepts to define his findings that included cultural tenacity, retention, and reinterpretation.

Simultaneously, Ortiz in Cuba was introducing the concept of transculturalism to define the transformations of Africans and their descendants in Cuba. Important to the study of African diaspora cultures was that these pioneers eventually established institutions in which they were able to do comparative studies on African continuities in the Americas. These scholars were important catalysts nurturing generations of scholars and promulgators of African-based traditions. The dissertation and journalistic work of Ellen Irene Diggs provides an example.

Diggs dedicated her dissertation to Du Bois: "Al Doctor W. E. Burghardt Du Bois, filósofo, maestro, guía y amigo" (to Doctor W. E. Burghardt Du Bois, philosopher, teacher, guide and friend). The dissertation focused on the life and works of Ortiz; Du Bois wrote the introduction, entitled, "The Revelation of Saint Orgne the Damned." In a newspaper article written for the *Pittsburgh Courier* in 1944, Diggs discussed the creation of the International Institute for Afro-American Studies in Mexico and listed members including Herskovits, Alain Locke, Arthur Ramos, and Jorge A. Vivó. These connections between the scholars and journalist-scholars contributed to a circular sharing of information that evidently spread beyond academia to popular culture.

Connections—Melville Herskovits and Fernando Ortiz

The relationship between Fernando Ortiz and Melville Herskovits allowed them to recommend and refer exceptional students to each other, helping students expand upon their investigations. Herskovits referred

Katherine Dunham, a student of anthropology, to Ortiz when she decided to develop her comparative study of African religious dances and rituals in the Caribbean. Ortiz, in turn, introduced Dunham to traditional religious artists who eventually were included in her international touring dance company that presented her anthropological studies in staged musicals. In "Shango Suite," Dunham combined Haitian, Cuban, and Trinidadian elements of African-based traditions including chants, music, dance steps, and imagery of Vodou, Santería, and Shango belief systems.

Katherine Dunham

In an interview in the summer of 1994, Katherine Dunham indicated that even before traveling to Cuba, she met Afro-Cuban drummer initiates in La Regla de Ocha in 1937 and 1938 in New York City's West Village. Reminiscing, she noted, "I found Julio Mendez and LaRosa Estrada, star drummers of the Dunham Company, from 1937 and 1938, for the next fifty years or so" (Dunham unpublished autobiography: 1). This information indicates that practitioners were already active in New York City ten years before the arrival of Mora.

Katherine Dunham had already traveled to Haiti, Trinidad, Martinique, and Jamaica to record the rituals and ceremonies of African diaspora religions and practices. According to Dunham, the assistance of Herskovits enabled "doors to be opened" to her in the Caribbean. Dunham recalled, "It was with the letters from Melville Herskovits, head of the Department of Anthropology at Northwestern University, that I 'invaded' the Caribbean—Haiti, Jamaica, Martinique, Trinidad, passing lightly over the other islands, then Haiti again for the final stand for the real study" (Dunham 1969: 3).

In the editor's notes on *Island Possessed* by Katherine Dunham, the context of her work appears in brief.

> Katherine Dunham first went to Haiti in 1936 when she was granted a Rosenwald Fellowship to study primitive dance and ritual in the West Indies and Brazil. . . . She recognized patterns of culture and behavior, which are found in areas of the New World that were strongly influenced by the African slaves brought from the Old World. . . . She soon realized that the strongest influence, the unifying and vitalizing force, was vaudun, or voodoo, and she was initiated into the first class, or group, of vaudun, the lavé-tête. (Dunham 1969: 2)

Her own initiation into the Vodou religion in Haiti and the reinterpretation of the dances for the international public stage helped create a knowledge base of receptivity to African-derived creative expression globally. Another student who was pursuing her studies in this area was African American Zora Neale Hurston.

Zora Neale Hurston

In 1927, Zora Neal Hurston was investigating the folk practices of Voodoo in the southern United States. She traveled from Alabama to Florida and then to Louisiana collecting information on the traditional cultures of Africans. By 1929, Hurston began to establish links between African practices in the Caribbean and the United States. She traveled to the Bahamas in 1930 and went to Jamaica and Haiti in 1936, also returning to the Bahamas during this period. Historian Robert E. Hemenway explains, "She also began to see links between Afro-American and Afro-Caribbean folklore. She had met so many West Indians in the Miami area that she was sure 'their folklore definitely influences ours in South Florida'" (Hemenway 1977: 127). Both Hurston and Dunham concluded similarly that the spiritual practices of Africans and their descendants were the connecting link between the U.S. and Caribbean folklore.

Another important academic link was Hurston's association with W. E. B. Du Bois. Studying the introduction to Hurston's *Mules and Men,* historian Arnold Rampersad indicates that Hurston was one of Du Bois's "talented ten." Draping her Africanity as a "fabulous robe" in her writings, Hurston affirms the receptive environment that existed in the United States toward African spirituality:

> Hoodoo or Voodoo, as pronounced by the whites, is burning with a flame in America, with all the intensity of a suppressed religion. It has its thousands of secret adherents. It adapts itself like Christianity to its locale, reclaiming some of its borrowed characteristics to itself, such as fire-worship as signified in the Christian church by the altar and the candles and the belief in the power of water to sanctify as in baptism. Belief in magic is older than writing. So, nobody knows how it started. (Hurston 1990: 183)

The initiation of Hurston into the Hoodoo religion of New Orleans provided Herskovits with the material to make the following comparison.

"There is much in Hurston's descriptions of the initiations she experienced into various cult groups that can be referred to recurrent practices in West Africa, and in the Catholic New World countries where pagan beliefs of Africa have persisted" (Herskovits 1958: 248). The immersion of Hurston and Dunham into the religious practices they were researching made important contributions to the spread of African religions in New York City.

The Role of Traditional and Popular Musicians

Katherine Dunham's insistence on incorporating traditional sacred Afro-Cuban drummers into her company brought them to New York City and provided the opportunity for them to drum in secret sacred ceremonies in Spanish Harlem. Dunham included two drummers, Francisco Aguabella and Julito Collazo, who were integral to the growth of the religion in New York. The pioneering anthropologist Fernando Ortiz introduced Dunham to Aguabella and Collazo on her trip to Cuba. Soon after arriving in New York in 1954, they began to attend and play for religious ceremonies in Harlem. Collazo recalled that the first ceremony Aguabella and he attended was in the home of the policy numbers runner Willie "El Bolitero." Collazo noted that when Aguabella and he started singing the chants to the òrìṣàs in ancient Yorùbá, following their lead, everyone in the room turned around to celebrate their common knowledge of the songs. Willie, who was Puerto Rican, had been initiated into the religion in Cuba. His godmother in the religion was the sister of Pancho Mora, who was to become the first Afro-Cuban *babaláwo* in New York City. Playing congas at the ceremony, as a celebration to the Òrìṣà Shango, the musicians were the Afro-Cuban musicians Arsenio and Kiki Rodriguez. The brothers, sons of former enslaved Congo parents, were influential in introducing chants and music from this tradition into their music in Cuba during the 1940s and in New York City during the 1950s.

Afro-Cuba and African America Meet: Mario Bauza, Machito, Graciela Perez, Chano Pozo, and Dizzy Gillespie

Afro-Cuban and African American musicians were significant contributors to the expansion of La Regla de Ocha in New York. Probably the most important among them was Afro-Cuban master musician Mario Bauza, composer, arranger, and creator of Afro-Cuban jazz with his brother-in-law Machito (Frank Grillo). Bauza arrived in New York in 1930. His extraordinary talents quickly brought him to the attention of major orchestra leaders of the time, who incorporated him into their jazz orchestras. He played with Noble Sissle, Chick Webb, and Cab Calloway, among others. Bauza was instrumental in introducing Dizzy Gillespie's talents to Cab Calloway, thereby beginning Gillespie's rise to fame. Most important, Bauza introduced Gillespie to the complexities of Afro-Cuban rhythms.

By 1938, Gillespie expressed to Bauza the desire to incorporate a Cuban drummer into his musical group. In 1947, when he again made the request, Bauza introduced Gillespie to Chano Pozo. Pozo, an Afro-Cuban, was initiated in La Regla de Ocha. One of the first sacred drummers to play with a jazz group, Pozo introduced the multirhythmic drumming patterns and òrìṣà chants in the musical arrangements. Gillespie explained in *To Be or Not to Bop: Memoirs of Dizzy Gillespie* that Pozo was African, noting, "All of the Nañigo, the Santo, the Ararra, all these different sects, the African things in Cuba, he knew, and he was well versed" (Gillespie 1979: 319).

During the height of the Harlem Renaissance, Bauza lived in Harlem, relishing the world of African American jazz. By the early 1940s, with his brother-in-law Machito, he developed an orchestra named Machito and the Afro-Cubans. Concurrently, during this era, the collaboration of Gillespie and Pozo gave birth to Cubop while the collaboration of Machito and Bauza gave birth to Afro-Cuban Jazz. Interviews with Mario Bauza in 1990 and vocalist Graciela Perez, the sister of Machito, in 1999 confirmed their connections to Afro-Cuban traditional practice and music. According to Perez, her childhood memories were infused with recollections of African religious practices.

From Cuba to New York

In our interview, Graciela Perez shared that she and Machito had a paternal grandfather named Amelio, who traced his heritage to the Mandingo. Their maternal grandmother, who had been a slave named Mercedes, was purchased by a Spaniard who took her to Matanzas, which is recognized as one of the locations that protected and restructured the Yorùbá òrìṣà tradition into a Cuban òrìṣà system. As Perez shared her childhood memories, other connections began to emerge.

Perez noted that the midwife who delivered Machito was an African woman named Latuan. In my interviews with Julito Collazo in 1995, he explained how an African woman by the name of Ayai Latuan initiated his mother, Ebelia, into La Regla de Ocha. Ayai Latuan is credited with being a pioneer who established the òrìṣà tradition in the region of Regla. The system became known as La Regla de Ocha—the rule of the òrìṣà.

Graciela Perez further recalled how the home of Ebelia was a meeting place for musicians who eventually made their mark in New York, including Mongo Santamaria and Miguelito Valdes, whose music celebrated the òrìṣà, their attributes, and rhythms.

Recalling their early days in New York, she fondly remembered the first time Machito and his Afro-Cuban orchestra were broadcast in 1948 from Harlem's world-famous Apollo Theater. Also on the program were African American artists Billie Holiday and Dinah Washington. During the 1940s, vocalist Miguelito Valdes recorded with the Afro-Cubans in New York City. Later, the arrival of Arsenio Rodriguez and Mongo Santamaria helped spur the expansion of the religion by celebrating the songs and music of the òrìṣàs in their popular music.

Mario Bauza, Pancho Mora, and La Regla de Ocha

Bauza recalled for me during an interview how he would return to Cuba when he needed spiritual guidance. He would consult with the elder high priest Quintin Lecon, the godfather of Pancho Mora. Bauza described how he tried to encourage Lecon to travel to New York by explaining its growing religious community, but Lecon refused to travel there. Instead, on the advice of Bauza, he sent his representative, godson Pancho Mora, to New York. According to Graciela and Bauza, when Mora decided to remain in New York, he became the godfather of most of the Afro-Latin musicians, including Machito, Graciela, Mongo, and Bauza. Mora became one of the first priests to initiate and include African American practitioners in his religious family. The flourishing of La Regla de Ocha from the late 1940s to the mid-1960s is captured in the following quotation referring to Mora.

In 1964, he organized a drum ceremony for Shango at the old Casa Carmen in Harlem that attracted three thousand people, including Latin music stars Julito Collazo and Machito. As his reputation grew with his *ile,* he came to be called on to preside at initiations throughout the Hispanic world. Since the 1950s, he has been flown to nearly every South American and Caribbean country to be godfather to a new initiate. By his own estimate, he has some six thousand godchildren. (Murphy 1988: 50)

Wilfredo Lam and Fernando Ortiz

Important to the popularity of Afro-Cuban religious iconography in New York was the work of Afro-Chinese Cuban Wilfredo Lam, who attended religious ceremonies with Fernando Ortiz and Lydia Cabrera. The investigations and writings of Cabrera, a protégé of Ortiz, have served as important texts to initiates in New York on the history and practices of La Regla de Ocha.

As a child, his spiritual godmother, Mantonica Wilson, a Shango priestess, introduced Lam to the religion. Although, according to historian Julia P. Herzberg, Lam was not initiated, throughout his youth he was nurtured in the Yorùbá-based religion. Here again, Ortiz played an important role in nurturing and influencing Lam during adulthood. Herzberg observes, "When Lam returned to Cuba at the end of 1941, a small group of Cuban intellectuals was actively exploring Afro-Cuban history, folklore, literature, music and dance" (Herzberg, 1996: 164). Fernando Ortiz and his colleagues and protégés were at the center of the black studies and arts movement.

As a member of the surrealist movement, which was grounded in the spiritual world, Wilfredo Lam brought with him an Afro-Cuban worldview steeped in La Regla de Ocha (Herzberg 1996: 151). In 1942, New York City's major galleries exhibited Lam's work, which reflected the cosmology that was part of his Afro-Cuban cultural experience using the images that reflected the spirits and òrìṣàs. In describing Lam's work, Herzberg observed:

> The anthropomorphic nature of Afro-Cuban òrìshàs is a principal theme in any number of Lam's works in the 1940s. Two deities most often depicted are Ellegua [Elegua] and Ogun both of whom retained their primacy from the African to the Cuban context. (156)

In our interview, Dunham explained that Lam often attended the Boule Blanc events at her school. These events attracted artists including Ernesto Lecuona, Celia Cruz, Tito Puente, and others. Here again, we can trace the interconnecting threads that reflect the coming together of individuals interested in African traditions, particularly African religious themes. Lam's friendship with Ortiz and Cabrera clearly placed him in the circle of the intellectuals studying black cultures in Cuba, the Caribbean, and Latin America. Lam's childhood experiences, his attendance at rituals with Ortiz and Cabrera, coupled with the international influence of his work, helped to give rise to the international status of the òrìṣàs.

Mongo Santamaria

In an interview focused on the spread of La Regla de Ocha, Mongo Santamaria shared how he introduced Julito Collazo to Puerto Rican musician Tito Puente in the mid-1950s. He smiled as he recalled that many of New York's Latin orchestras had little knowledge of Afro-Cuban instruments such as the *chekere* and *bàtá* drums or the chants to the òrìṣàs. The introduction of Collazo and Aguabella to popular musicians such as Puente contributed to the expansion of the Latino musical rhythms. The fusion of Afro–Puerto Rican and Afro-Cuban musical idioms is evident in Puente's album *Top Percussion: Tito Puente*. Sacred drummers Julito Collazo and Francisco Aguabella played on the album, contributing songs that included "Obàtálá Yeza" (the Yorùbá òrìṣà of creation), as well as Mongo's "Eleguana" (song to Elegua, òrìṣà of the Crossroads).

Dunham and Ortiz Connect

Based on my research, the first *bàtá* drums were probably brought to New York by the Katherine Dunham Company. In a photograph taken of Dunham in Cuba in 1947, the legendary traditional drummer Jesus Perez is seen showing her a set of *bàtá* drums. According to Dunham, Fernando Ortiz introduced her to Perez, whom she commissioned to construct a set of *bàtá* drums for her company. The *bàtá* set is on exhibition in the Katherine Dunham Museum in East St. Louis.

After leaving the Dunham Company in 1954, Julito Collazo began to play with contemporary orchestras in New York. Mongo Santamaria shared how he and other musicians would go to the Dunham "School" after their "gigs" at the Palladium nightclub to jam with the Dunham musicians during rehearsals. During this time, Mongo indicated that he held a public celebration in 1956 to the Òrìṣà Shango at the Palladium. One of the featured dancers was Julito Collazo. In my interview with Graciela, she recalled how Katherine Dunham and members of her company would dance at the Palladium rehearsing their mambo dance choreography. The reverberation of expression among the artistic community, scholars, and traditional leaders of La Regla de Ocha in Cuba and New York developed into a surge of popularity that continued to re-energize and expand the growth of the religion. In 1955, the Dunham Company was featured in the Italian-produced feature movie *Mambo,* with Silvana Mangano, Shelley Winters, and Vittorio Gassman (Ponti 1954).

The opening scene of the movie featured Afro-Cuban vocalist Xiomara Alfaro chanting to the òrìṣàs accompanied by drummers Julito Collazo and Francisco Aguabella. Here again, the cross-cultural synthesis of artists functioning as popular performers using traditional ceremonies continued to blur the lines between the sacred and secular, thereby bringing international attention to La Regla de Ocha. According to Katherine Dunham, the filming was halted when Xiomara Alfaro became possessed by divinity during the filming. In the film, the sacred music of Afro-Cuba and popular rhythms of New York mambo came together under the direction of Dunham's choreography.

The Next Generation

As a younger generation of musicians grew out of the orchestras of Machito, Puente, Mongo, and Bauza, their desire to learn the rhythms to the divinities of Africa intensified. In an interview in 1995 with one of the most respected contemporary traditional drummers, Puerto Rican Louis Bauzo, he recalled that the books of Fernando Ortiz in the 1970s provided the texts, illustrations, and scores from which the new generation of drummers could learn. However, the unspoken rivalry between Cuban and Puerto Rican musicians provided little space for learning. Therefore, the Puerto Rican drummers decided to learn from the records of Mongo Santamaria and Tito Puente. Bauzo indicated that listening to Mongo's recordings and reading Fernando Ortiz's books allowed the Puerto Rican musicians to advance their studies.

During my interview with Mongo, he pulled out an album entitled *Katherine Dunham Presents the Singing Gods: Drum Rhythms of Haiti, Cuba and Brazil,* recorded in the early 1950s, featuring the work of Francisco Aguabella and Julito Collazo. The liner notes offer evidence of Dunham's pivotal role in the collaborative work:

> For a number of years Dunham has been a close personal friend and admirer of Fernando Ortiz, outstanding Cuban folklorist, anthropologist and writer. On one of her visits to Cuba, Miss Dunham saw Francisco Aguabella and Julito Collazo working in a group, which Fernando Ortiz had organized for the investigation and preservation of Cuban cult material. Francisco and Julito have become strongly integrated into the Dunham Company and are known to the capitals of the world for the subtlety and precision of their drumming and the intensity of their "santos" and nañigo songs.

Katherine Dunham's role in promoting African diaspora sacred songs, drumming, dances, and rituals is evident is this quotation from the liner notes of the album referring to the composition of her company.

> Another form of diffusion . . . Francisco from Cuba meets La Guerre from Haiti. They discuss the water-goddess, Yemanya, as she is known in their respective countries. In Brazil, after performances of the Teatro Republica, they go to all-night ceremonies and there exchange ideas with Tia Lucia, Aunt of our Brazilian drummer, Jairo. Forgotten African cult language is remembered, rhythms are refreshed.

African Spiritual Consciousness

The influence of the pioneers continues to inspire the growth of New York City's òrìṣà religion. A growing community of initiates influenced by the black and Latino power movements look to the religion as the foundation for cultural and spiritual identity. The environment created by traditional leaders, scholars, and musicians has forged multiple levels of understanding and exposure to La Regla de Ocha. The interconnections among many individuals established a strong foundation for its expansion and contributed to the upsurge of its popularity worldwide. The evolution of the òrìṣà religion from West Africa to the Americas has not been linear. Like a puzzle that is pieced together, the process is complex when bringing together individuals of varied interests who cross paths around a similar vision. Still, pieces must be identified to clarify the history and the development of La Regla de Ocha.

This chapter is the first in a series seeking to identify the interconnections among individuals who encouraged the growth of La Regla de Ocha in New York City. There is still much work to do in documenting the experiences that brought Puerto Ricans, Cubans, and African Americans together. Despite cultural clashes, they developed new possibilities for the growth of African spiritual consciousness. As we learn who they are, it is important that we call out their names and remember their pioneering contributions. Part of our work is to make certain that they are recognized as part of the rich history that explains the journey of the òrìṣà religion from West Africa to the Caribbean to New York.

Aché (May it be so).

Texts

Diggs, Ellen Irene. 1944. "Fernando Ortiz y Fernandez La Vida y La Obra." Ph.D. diss., La Universidad de la Habana.

Du Bois, W. E. B. 1989 (1903). *The Souls of Black Folk.* New York: Bantam.

Dunham, Katherine. 1969. *Island Possessed.* Chicago: University of Chicago Press. 1969.

————. N.d. "Mindfield." Unpublished manuscript.

Gillespie, Dizzy. 1979. *To Be or Not to Bop: Memoirs of Dizzy Gillespie.* New York: Doubleday.

Hemenway, Robert E. 1977. *Zora Neale Hurston: A Literary Biography.* Urbana: University of Illinois Press.

Herskovits, Melville J. 1958. *The Myth of the Negro Past.* Boston: Beacon Press.

————. 1966. *The New World Negro: Selected Papers in Afro-American Studies.* Ed. Frances S. Herskovits. Bloomington: Indiana University Press.

Herzberg, Julia P. 1996. "Rereading Lam." In *Santería Aesthetics in Contemporary Latin American Art,* ed. Arturo Lindsay, 149–60. Washington, DC: Smithsonian Institution Press.

Hurston, Zora Neale. 1990 (1935). *Mules and Men.* New York: Harper Perennial.

Knight, Franklin W. 1970. *Slave Society in Cuba in the Nineteenth Century.* Madison: University of Wisconsin Press.

Murphy, Joseph M. 1988. *Santería: African Spirits in America.* Boston: Beacon Press, 1988.

————. 1994. *Working the Spirit: Ceremonies of the African Diaspora.* Boston: Beacon Press.

Thompson, Robert Farris. 1984. *Flash of the Spirit: African and Afro-American Art and Philosophy.* New York: Vintage.

Thornton, John K. 1992. *Africa and Africans in the Making of the Atlantic World, 1400–1680.* New York: Cambridge University Press.

Vega, Marta Moreno. 1995. "Yorùbá Philosophy: Multiple Levels of Transformation and Understanding." Ph.D. diss., Temple University.

Sound Recordings

Dunham, Katherine. 2005 (1956). *Katherine Dunham Presents the Singing Gods: Drum Rhythms of Haiti, Cuba and Brazil.* Caney Records, SP.

Puente, Tito. 1977. *Top Percussion: Tito Puente.* Arcano Records.

Rodriquez, Arsenio. 1968. *Primitivo.* MAS Records.

Valdes, Miguelito. 1963. *Reunion: Miguelito Valdes with Machito and His Orchestra.* Tico 1098.

Films

Carlo, Ponti. 1995 (1954). *Mambo.* Paramount Pictures.

Blank, Les. 1995. *Sworn to the Drum: A Tribute to Francisco Aguabella.* Flower Films.

Vega, Marta Moreno, and Robert Shephard. 1992. *When the Spirits Dance Mambo: African Religions in Cuba.* Franklin H. Williams Caribbean Cultural Center/African Diasporic Institute.

17

From Cuban Santería to African Yorùbá

Evolutions in African American Òrìṣà History, 1959–1970

TRACEY E. HUCKS

In January 1969, North American blacks assembled for Friday evening *bembe* service at Yorùbá Temple in Harlem, New York. They gathered to honor the known òrìṣà divinities of ancient Yorùbáland and to pay homage to the ancestors of Africa and the Atlantic world. Adorned in African-styled garb, beaded *eleke* necklaces, and head coverings to protect their spiritual *orí,* the descendants of enslaved Africans in the United States venerated the ancestors of the transatlantic diaspora and commemorated the new African spirits they encountered nearly a de-cade earlier through cultural exchange with Caribbean-Latino immi-grants. Amid rhythms of drums, hand-held *sekeres,* and the pounding of wooden staffs by first-generation African American Ogboni elders, African American practitioner Baba Oseijeman Adefunmi commenced the ritual ceremony to the òrìṣà spirits with an offering of fruit and the sacrificial blood of a rooster. Ancestors of Africa and the African diaspora were recognized: *"Mojuba* (I salute you), Patrice Lumumba, Malcolm X, W. E. B. Du Bois, Harriet Tubman, Nat Turner, Langston Hughes, Jean-Jacques Dessalines, Marcus Garvey" (Goodman 1969: 32). The sacred songs of the deity filled the air of the temple and the streets of Harlem. African American practitioners danced the òrìṣà, creating a ritual drama that revisited ancient sacred myths. Ògún, the Yorùbá god of war and iron, was the honored deity for the Friday evening service. Holding Ògún's sacred emblem of a machete, one Yorùbá Temple member paid tribute in gesture and dance. Nearby, an Afro-Cuban participant listened intently to hallowed drum rhythms, believing Ògún's presence would be invoked only when his rhythms were played with exact precision. According to George Goodman's (1969: 33) account of this ceremony in "Harlem's Yorubas: A Search for Something to Believe In," African Americans in Harlem went "down the road to the past" as they ritually honored the newly discovered gods of Africa. For African Americans in the 1960s, this "road to the past" was a deliberate and decisive journey of cultural and religious reclamation. The Yorùbá tradition, as understood by its early African American practitioners, provided religious formation and structure to an existing nationalist vocabulary and offered spiritual citizenship to a world of African divinities and ancestors.

Background

The early history of the African American Yorùbá tradition in the United States is one closely aligned with Cuban migration. As early as the 1940s, Latinos migrating from the Caribbean commenced a process of transplantation, transformation, and expansion of Santería practices into U.S. urban locales. By the late 1950s, the Cuban Revolution had sparked a rapid influx of Cuban immigrants into major U.S. urban centers such as Miami and Tampa, Florida, and New York City. Stephen Gregory states that in less than ten years over fifty thousand Cuban immigrants had entered the United States, and along with many of them came the religio-cultural complex commonly referenced as Santo, Lucumi, Ocha, or Santería (Brandon 1993: 104; Gregory 1986: 55–56; Dixon 1988).[1]

Coinciding with the social history of Black Nationalist movements among African Americans, Cuban migration to North America greatly influenced the expansion of Santería among U.S.-born black Americans. Equally influencing black North American religious, cultural, and political consciousness during the late 1950s and early 1960s was the upsurge of independent nation-states on the African continent. As African Americans extended their diaspora solidarity and radicalism to include support for decolonization movements on the African continent, their racial and nationalist consciousness intensified and broadened.

The coupling of domestic Black Nationalism and transatlantic Pan-Africanism resulted in unique ideological responses to sundry social and racial tensions occurring within the United States. During the 1960s, Black Nationalist–born Americans responded to these racial and social tensions with various formulations of Anglo-cultural and religious rejectionism, anti-colonial ideologies, autonomous black nationhood, economic and political self-determination, racialized global citizenries, and strong affinities toward Africa as a single continental entity (Marable 1984: 59; Moses 1978: 17; Van Deburg 1992: 131). For African Americans, the religion of Santería complemented these ideologies and was positioned as an added prism for synthesizing radical concepts of race, religion, culture, nationalism, and Africa.

Steeped within a larger climate of Black Nationalism, black territorial separatism, and black racial consciousness, African Americans throughout the 1960s developed a distinct interpretation of Santería that mirrored their need for a sustained "African" identity in America. They willfully extracted what they identified as the "African" elements of Santería and re-appropriated these elements within their new developing consciousness of Africa. Moreover, they reconceptualized the complex Cuban hybrid of seemingly West African Yorùbá and Anglo-Catholic elements into what they understood at that time as a more authentic "African" religion based on pre-travel and textual paradigms gathered from literary sources. What emerged from this amalgamation was an alternative "African" religious tradition that enabled them to renegotiate the social and racial terrain of the United States by linking their local American identity to an older primordial moment in Africa. Ultimately, this emerging religious consciousness bestowed new agency, authenticity, and authority to North America's black citizens by offering a reference for identity that was both pre-Atlantic and pre-American.

In this essay, I analyze the historical trajectories of Black Nationalism, religious racialization, and literary text production as key elements in reconfiguring the complex layers of African American Yorùbá identity during the years 1959–70. As African Americans began to embrace Yorùbá-influenced traditions within this eleven-year period, they simultaneously engaged in a self-conscious and deliberate process of negotiating what it meant to be "African" within the geographical contours of the United States. In part, this meant forging a new history, a new aesthetic, a new culture, and a new territorial homeland that would mirror African American ideals of their distant ancestral Africa. Through their assertions of agency and authority, African Americans systematically shifted the religious origin and foci of Santería away from Cuba in the Caribbean toward Yorùbáland in West Africa as a conscious way of creating new standards of religio-cultural authenticity and meaning in North America. This interpretation of Yorùbá religion among black North Americans is thus best understood when analyzed within localized contexts of American social history, emergent Black Nationalist discourses, competing racial ideologies, literary and textual development, and African American agency and "self-determined legitimacy" (Long 1997: 26). Thus, scholarly frameworks concerned with issues of acculturation, survivals, Africanisms, adaptation, transmission, and continuity do not adequately yield a comprehensive understanding of the historical evolution of Yorùbá religion among African Americans during this period. Above all, this early African American story within the Yorùbá tradition is one of deliberate agency and choice continuously mediated by symbolic interpretations of the continent of Africa, racialized notions of self-identity, and religious encounters with Spanish-speaking Caribbean communities.

African Americans and Santería in Harlem, New York

Studies of the early history of African American Yorùbá commonly begin with Oseijeman Adefunmi, who is most often credited with the rapid transformation, institutionalization, and cultivation of Yorùbá religion among African Americans in the United States and is most noted as the founder and first ọba-king of Oyotunji African Village in South Carolina, a residential society dedicated to the practice of Yorùbá religion in 1970. Born Walter Eugene King in Detroit, Michigan, on October 15, 1928, Adefunmi was raised by parents who were heavily influenced by the teachings of Marcus Garvey and members of the United Negro Improvement Association. In short, Adefunmi's parents advocated Garvey's principles of racial uplift and his overall vision of economic and cultural redemption. They also shared in Garvey's broader plan for emigration to Africa and were both monetary contributors to his Black Star Line with plans of returning to Africa. Given his young age, Adefunmi was not a direct participant in the Garvey movement but admits that he was influenced both by his parents' convictions and by the neo-Garveyite movements in which he later participated in Harlem in the late 1950s and early 1960s.[2]

As a teenager, Adefunmi remembers asking his mother, "Who is the African God?" Prompting this question, he admits years later, was his disenchantment with the Christian church he attended and his increasing interest in Africa. As a youth, Adefunmi says he sought answers in several places to this profound question of an African God. He first sought an immediate answer from his mother, who simply told him that Africans had lost their God when they were brought to America during slavery. He then sought long-term answers from written texts on Africa such as those of noted historian J. A. Rogers, author of multiple historical volumes on Negro history and the "Our History" section of the *Pittsburgh Courier,* as well as other ethnographers of Africa. Finally, Adefunmi began a personal travel quest to find the "African God" that led him as a young man to Egypt, Haiti, and later Cuba. Africa was meaningful to African Americans during this time as a primordial point of reference rather than as a collection of distinct national units. Although it signified a source of cultural and religious inspiration, Adefunmi, like many of his contemporaries, had never engaged in extensive travel to sub-Saharan Africa. This did not come until several years later in the 1970s. However, as is evident in African American history, the religious implications of a figurative Africa far outweighed that of an actual experiential Africa. This pre-travel, pre-experiential, and largely textual Africa inspired a powerful quest to sustain social identity, cultural meaning, and institutional concepts.

The Order of Damballah Hwedo Ancestor Priests

Following a short trip to Haiti, Oseijeman Adefunmi's first organizational means of venerating what he understood as an African God occurred in 1956 when he established the Order of Damballah Hwedo Ancestor Priests in Greenwich Village, New York. It was a society built in honor of the Haitian Vodou divinity Damballah. For Adefunmi, Damballah was the snake god that connected African Americans to their African ancestors. The ideological premise of the organization rested firmly on the undeniable pronouncement that black North Americans were incontestably composed of African ancestry. However, in the absence of a structured approach to African religions, the emphasis on ancestors became a critical way of establishing the "African-ness" of American-born blacks.

The Order of Damballah Hwedo meshed various elements of African and African diaspora cultural practices into its rituals. Adefunmi constructed ritual space centered on a Ghanaian stool, a table that served as an altar, and a handmade replica of a Haitian Vodou flag with an image of the serpent Damballah. Ceremonies consisted of eclectic sacred rituals devised primarily from various written sources on Africa, and travel experiences in the diaspora. Ceremonies always included numerous public readings on diverse African cultures, often paying special attention to the more popularly known Yorùbá and Akan cultures (Métraux 1972: 361; Hunt 1979: 24; Herskovits 1967: 207–8). Weekly meetings for "Ancestor Priests" strictly excluded white participation.

Three years after the Order of Damballah Hwedo was established, an important event occurred that greatly influenced the organization's direction and leadership. During one of its Sunday meetings, an Afro-Cuban, Christopher Oliana, attended a ceremony at the Order of Damballah Hwedo. Knowledgeable of Cuban Santería, Adefunmi revealed that Oliana sympathized with their desire and efforts to re-create African religious cultures in America. However, Adefunmi stated, "At the same time, [Oliana], being much more familiar as a Cuban with the more *pure* African approach, criticized us as well as encouraged me, that if I really wanted *authentic* African religion, I should go to Cuba."[3]

According to Adefunmi, during a divination session performed by Christopher Oliana, it was revealed that Adefunmi needed to construct a sacred altar for the òrìṣà Shango. Oliana assured Adefunmi that the Catholic image of Santa Barbara would adequately suffice as a valid representation of Shango. For Oliana, there was no apparent contradiction that Santería's "purity" included Euro-Catholic influences and iconography. However, Adefunmi was attracted solely to the "Africanness" of the religion and challenged these Catholic elements as obvious expressions of European imposition and cultural domination. Adefunmi recalls his rising suspicions of Santería's Catholic inclusions and Oliana's advice:

Chris Oliana knew about *Santo*. He told me I should get into *Santo,* and he told me. . . . I should get a statue of St. Barbara. But, of course, at that time I was deeply involved in the Nationalist Movement of the 1960s.

So the mention of a thing called *santo* which, of course, translated into English means saint, [and for us] who are raised in the Protestant religion and have no knowledge of Catholicism, to tell you that you must get a statue of St. Barbara, a saint, means that you are going to become a Catholic. So, quite naturally I objected to this and refused to get involved with it and told him: "No, I'm interested in African [religion]." But he says: "Well, it is African!" I say: "How can it be African and you want me to get a statue of St. Barbara?" This is not an African name; this is not an African saint. And from the picture you showed me, this certainly is not an African lady. This is not an African god. This is a white woman!

Adefunmi added that in the end, Oliana "explained to me: this is just called *Santo*. This is a Spanish name. It's got an African name. The African name is *Ocha,* he explained. And all of the ceremony in it is all *purely* African. . . . It took me a year before Oliana clearly described to me that Santería had only a veneer of Christianity and that underneath it everything else was *purely* African" (Palmié 1995: 78). For Adefunmi and Oliana, as for many African American practitioners, *purity* and *authenticity* were not formally assigned fixed standards of measurement and quantification. *Purity* and *authenticity* instead occupied fluid ideological spheres. They often fluctuated within at least five major domains: social and geographical contexts, competing ethnic orthodoxies, inherited historical knowledge and local modes of authority, multiple claims of legitimacy, and exclusive citizenries. Above all, *purity* and *authenticity* are heuristic categories of analysis that are often shaped, negotiated, and reified with contested domains.

With the acceptance of Santería's authentic Africanness, in 1959 Adefunmi along with Oliana traveled to Cuba to undergo full initiation into the tradition. Arriving in Havana and eventually making their way to Matanzas, they met the priest who would conduct their initiations and become their godfather. Known by the name Sonagba, the priest proceeded, on August 26, 1959, to perform the necessary rites for initiation. Oliana would become a devotee of the deity Aganju, and Adefunmi would become initiated as a devotee to the deity Ọbàtálá. Speaking in the third person, Adefunmi reflects on this initiation process:

In the summer of 1959, . . . Serge [Eugene] King went to the island nation of Cuba because he had been told by his Afro-Cuban friend and guide that the Afro-Cubans had preserved the religions of several West African cultures. The most dominant of these West African cultures was that of the Lucumis, who were themselves, descendants of the ancient Yorùbá Kingdoms of Nigeria. When King arrived in Havana, he was driven to Matanzas, which is known as "little Africa" because of the intensity of the Lucumi, Dahomean, and Congolese religions preserved there. From that moment on, his great spiritual sojourn took him into a mysterious labyrinth of occult tunnels and corridors through which a man must pass in search of his Racial Soul. (Adefunmi 1988: 39)

Adefunmi inevitably interpreted his initiation as a foreshadowing of a larger symbolic return of African Americans to the gods of their ancestors and to the integrity of their Racial Soul. Africa and things African were understood by Adefunmi within a larger racialized discourse that served as a primary marker of group identity and membership and would later undergird the institutional creations of Shango Temple, Yorùbá Temple, and Oyotunji African Village.

Shango Temple (1959) and Yorùbá Temple (1960): The Racialization and Localization of Yorùbá Religion in North America

Upon their return from Cuba in 1959, the collaborative efforts of Oliana and Adefunmi brought forth Harlem's earliest public temple for the practice of òrìṣà traditions on the second floor of 71 East 125th Street, named Shango Temple. For Adefunmi, this newly adopted religion held great possibilities for African Americans. He believed that the religion, along with the institutional support of Shango Temple, would create a new lineage of African American òrìṣà priests in the United States. Oliana and Adefunmi performed basic ceremonies and rituals at Shango Temple but were unwilling, given their novice status, to perform full initiations. Those interested in obtaining initiation into the religion through Shango Temple were directed to Ascencíon Rodriguez Serrano, better known as "Sunta," who had migrated to New York City from Puerto Rico. Chronologically, Serrano was the first of the three to undergo full initiation into the religion, becoming a priestess of the òrìṣà Obatala in August 1958, preceding Oliana and Adefunmi by one year (Drewal and Mason 1998: 128). Although residents of the United States, each of these three early forerunners of the Yorùbá tradition was initiated on Cuban soil, reflecting the continued cross-fertilization and strong transnational ties that were in place at that time. In her study of Santería tradition in New

York City, Marta Vega states that Serrano received a divination reading during her initiation revealing that Serrano was destined to initiate black North Americans into the religion. Vega (1995: 137) notes that the early efforts of Serrano helped to break "down the barrier between the Latin and African American community" during the 1960s. She helped to assuage the linguistic, ethnic, and cultural obstructions that intermittently divided the African American and Latin Caribbean communities. By January 1960, the short-lived Shango Temple had evolved into Yorùbá Temple with a new location at 28 West 116th Street. African Americans were attracted to the new Yorùbá Temple, in part because of the work of Adefunmi and Oliana but also because of the tireless efforts of women such as Sunta Serrano, Mama Keke, and Queen Mother Moore, who helped to develop, enrich, and expand the temple's practices. Collectively, they were crucial figures in the early exposure of African Americans in the United States to Yorùbá-influenced traditions.

Yorùbá Temple also became an important vehicle for creating Great Benin Books, a publishing branch through which Adefunmi printed several written texts that he distributed under the African Library Series. The series consisted of several Temple publications written primarily by Adefunmi describing Yorùbá religion in light of history, theology, anthropology, culture, and polity. Within this small literary corpus, Adefunmi put forth his most extensive commentary on Yorùbá religion, his philosophy on racial origins, his treatise on polygamy, and his organizational understanding of the African world. These publications were primarily short books and pamphlets that were available for purchase at Yorùbá Temple and cost approximately one dollar each. Through these texts, Adefunmi provided African Americans with a new paradigm with which to negotiate race, religion, culture, and American society. Attempting to appeal to African Americans of a presumed racial nation, Adefunmi hoped to generate a print medium that would explain the philosophies of the Yorùbá Temple, Yorùbá religion, and African nationhood. These texts became central in the localization of Yorùbá religion among African Americans in the United States. More importantly, they provided African Americans with ancestral justification for a trans-American identity, a reconnection to the continent of Africa, and a rationalization for the collective return to African religion and culture.

Texts such as *The Gods of Africa* and *Tribal Origins of the African Americans* sought to outline the history of the Yorùbá people in Africa and the transmission of òrìṣà religion to the Americas. These texts described the theological tenets of the religion, introduced African Americans to the gods of Africa and their attributes, and stated the purpose of Yorùbá Temple and its new emerging priesthood. The texts also outlined a series of practices central to Yorùbá religion, including Adefunmi's description as the vital practice of ancestor veneration, in which he declared that "all civilized people worship their ancestors either through special memorial days, public statues, portraits in oils or photographs, and many other methods" and that the Yorùbá ancestors were venerated through elaborate masquerades, the maintenance of shrines, and the pouring of libations. According to Adefunmi, "in this way, the culture of the Yorùbá continues, for by keeping alive their memory, their traditions, dress, language, organizations, laws and customs, they preserve their total civilization" (Vega 1995: 12). Ancestral veneration would constitute a vital component of the religion because it offered African Americans a connection to ancestors beyond America. Within *The Gods of Africa,* African Americans were encouraged to create small ancestral shrines and altars in their homes. Containing offerings of fruit, flowers, water, and an *egúngún* ancestor figure, these private shrines would create an ancestral connection for African Americans that could be continually maintained and reinforced. Adefunmi's vision was that ancestor veneration would assist African Americans in the recovery of their own unique African culture in America.

Similar to *The Gods of Africa,* Adefunmi's *Tribal Origins of the African-Americans,* published in 1962, was a fervent explication of the religion of the Yorùbá and its African origins. It was an attempt to trace the historical origins of African Americans to Africa, to address the question of black self-identity, and to explore the question of African retentions in the United States. According to Adefunmi (1962: i), "there is no tragedy that has caused a deeper personal conflict in the mind and spirit of the black American than the question of his pre-American origins." Equipped with charts and a map entitled "Our Ancestral Land," Adefunmi sketched the historical origins of African Americans as far back as ancient Egypt and as immediate as the West Coast of Africa. He argued for a "natural continuity" and connection between African Americans and Africa. This connection, he argued, was violently severed through the transatlantic slave trade but could now be restored through the adoption of African religious and cultural traditions. Both Adefunmi's texts and the resources of Yorùbá Temple would now "begin the re-endowment of every African-born-in-America with confidence and appreciation of his origins and culture" and begin "laying the foundations of West African culture in America, beginning with the African religion of Orisha" (11).

As an indicator of collective social identity, race became an important and powerful unifying factor around which African Americans organized themselves in the 1950s and 1960s. African Americans envisioned themselves as a national racialized community possessing a single historical narrative. This racialized conception of community in America was linked to a broader understanding of a shared history that began in Africa. American social history during this time was filled with intense racial tension and institutional discrimination, which met with emphatic national responses by African Americans. Reflecting on immediate memories of legal segregation, African Americans questioned the possibility of full citizenship and reexamined issues of identity in light of an emerging "African" paradigm that was slowly invading African American consciousness. During this period, places such as Harlem, New York, became the major centers for African American cultural, political, and religious revitalization. African Americans formed black art societies, African music and dance associations, and countless black bookstores and cultural centers in order to disseminate this newfound "African" culture. It was out of the context of social, cultural, and political upheaval that Adefunmi formed Yorùbá Temple and engaged Yorùbá religion. For Adefunmi, race as a political and social category in America could neatly be incorporated into religious service to the Yorùbá gods. He believed that religion, culture, and politics were indistinguishable and that the activities of Yorùbá Temple would be reflective of this integrated philosophy.

> The reason I had gone into [Yorùbá] was based on my nationalist philosophy in which I had conceived the notion that it is through religion that a people preserve their culture . . . And so I was trying to figure out what is it that makes a people who they are and have a distinct tradition . . . and who is it that preserves it . . . I arrived at the conclusion that it is religion that really is a contingent of a people's culture.[4]

Adefunmi wanted to attract African Americans to Yorùbá Temple who held analogous philosophies of race, religion, and nationalism. With the establishment of Yorùbá Temple, Adefunmi localized his intensely racial and political interpretations of Black Nationalist philosophies, creating a complex web of religion, race, culture, and nationhood. These interpretations evolved into nuanced nationalist platforms of racial autonomy, self-reliance, and territorial nationhood.[5] He proposed a black religious nationalism that situated Africa as the pivotal hermeneutical paradigm upon which to craft and remake African American identity. Yorùbá Temple would function as the crucial religious institution for launching the Africanization of his newly acquired Santería tradition and would eventually become one of the central agents of Africanized religion and cultural production in Harlem.

During the 1960s, Yorùbá Temple was crucial in launching a deliberate Africanization of Santería and became one of the central agents and institutions of African religious and cultural production in Harlem. Its appeal extended across nationalist boundaries, permeating the wide religious and cultural ethos of Harlem. In his autobiography, poet and activist Amiri Baraka reflected on the influence of Yorùbá Temple in Harlem in the 1960s. According to Baraka (1995: 312):

> Some of us were very much influenced by the Yorùbás. When we first arrived in Harlem, Oseijeman's group was very political. They dressed as traditional West Africans from Nigeria, but upheld the right of black self-determination, declaring that Africans in Harlem must control it. Some of us were influenced by the Yorùbás because we could understand a connection we had with Africa and wanted to celebrate it.

For Baraka and other Harlem nationalists, Yorùbá Temple was a vehicle for engaging an African world in America. One of Yorùbá Temple's primary aims was to symbolically elevate Africa and African-styled culture to a place of standard origin and prominence within the U.S. òrìṣà tradition. The temple stood as an important attempt at African American autonomy, legitimacy, and institutional agency within the wider Yorùbá-influenced tradition. Its appeal was in its ability to make the cultural and religious forms of Yorùbá religion accessible and palatable to African American communities. Its leaders dispensed African names, sold African clothes, provided spiritual divination readings, and, most importantly, distributed written literature to the American community of Harlem informing them of their past in Africa. Gradually, the temple facilitated a new era of African American involvement within an emerging U.S. Yorùbá tradition. However, to some of Adefunmi's Cuban religious counterparts the establishment of Yorùbá Temple was increasingly perceived as an attempt to compromise the religious authority of the tradition. As a result, its presence in Harlem met with both ardent support and strong criticism.

Cooperation and Conflict: African Americans, Cubans, and the Struggle for Religious Orthodoxy and Authority

By the late 1960s, African Americans were attempting to create their own authentic space within a burgeoning Yorùbá tradition in the United States. Gradually shifting from a dependence on Cuban religious knowledge and ritual interpretation to a reliance on their own creative agency, African Americans raised much concern on the part of Cuban practitioners regarding the question of orthodoxy and authority within the religion. Although supportive in many ways, some Cuban practitioners looked on with great ambivalence as African Americans refashioned traditional Santería practices into their own ritual formulations that included adding names of prominent African American leaders in the litany of ancestral salutations, making African attire a standard ceremonial norm, and utilizing the public streets of Harlem as ritual space over and against private and clandestine places.

Consequently, authority, legitimacy, and autonomy within the larger Yorùbá tradition became critical issues for African Americans in the 1960s. The assertive agency and creative innovations that African Americans formulated within the tradition greatly reflected the complexities of Black Nationalist discourse with its ideological attachments to the continent of Africa and rigid racial concepts of identity. In response to this, Yorùbá Temple began to reorient the religion with a strong racial image, cultural style, and religious iconography mirroring conceptions of Africa. Steven Gregory, in his study "Santería in New York City," identifies this growing Africanization of Santería on the part of African Americans. According to Gregory (1986: 61–62), "members of the Temple rejected the association of the Yoruba orisha with Catholic saints, as well as other symbolic or terminological traces of Christianity within Afro-Cuban religious practice. An emphasis was placed on reconstituting 'pure' Yoruba religious traditions by going directly to West African sources. Ironically, these sources were often to be found in anthropological literature." Adefunmi confirms both the conscious ways in which African Americans in the 1960s sought to privilege the African origins of Yorùbá religion and the textual ways in which they gathered their perceptions. According to Adefunmi, the African Americans' refusal

> to continue the syncretism between the Orisha and the Roman Saints, which had been so necessary during the slave era, but which now they regarded as an anachronism, deeply frustrated and angered their Afro-Cuban mentors. Indeed, instead of purchasing prints and statues of the Roman Saints, the temple membership [was] encouraged to carve traditional Yorùbá images of the Orishas copied from the photographs in "African Art" publications. (VARRCRC 1981: 11)

In addition, members of Yorùbá Temple orthopraxically differed from Cuban practitioners in their commitment to practice the religion publicly rather than clandestinely. African Americans in Yorùbá Temple openly practiced the religion, paraded it through Harlem streets dressed in African attire accompanied by African drums, and publicly performed rituals under the gaze of the American media. Cuban elders such as Pancho Mora grew increasingly concerned about the public displays of the religion and sought to admonish Adefunmi about the possible repercussions. Adefunmi recalls,

> I remember Pancho telling me at one time, "You know all this show that you're doing is going to mess everything up. It's going to cause a lot of trouble for a lot of people, you know, because you know in this country this religion is regarded as witchcraft." He [Pancho] didn't like the idea at all that I was beginning to expose it. I had been on television and even radio talk shows, a lot of them heard it and they didn't like the things that I was saying on there.[6]

In addition to differences regarding ritual space and public displays of the religion, a final source of contestation between Latino and African American òrìṣà communities involved moments of prejudicial, discriminatory, and ethnocentric attitudes toward American-born blacks. According to Vega (1995: 136), "the racist attitudes of the Cuban and Puerto Rican communities were . . . manifested when African Americans began initiating into the Yorùbá tradition in New York City." Moreover, she adds, "The divisions between the African American and Latino communities, due to oppressive, racist attitudes [Latino] communities had internalized, were confronted as African Americans actively sought to incorporate the Orishas of Cuba . . . into the Black Power Revolution" (Vega 1995: 104). Although conflicted at times, the relationship between African American and Latino communities was never rigidly polarized;

periods of contention were readily met with moments of cooperation. In fact, many African Americans remain deeply indebted to the early Cuban community in Harlem. As African American Yorùbá practitioner Lloyd Weaver attests:

> Black Americans . . . had to find ways to make Orisha worship relative to them in ways that were not real concerns for their Cuban elders. We were interested in the religion as an alternative to western Christianity. Many of us had turned to Islam in this search—but others of us, wanted something that was more specifically ancestral. And having found it we were not as inclined, as had been the Cubans, to hide our religion. We staunchly refused to keep Christian artifacts in our shrines as disguises and could never begin to refer to Orishas as "saints" even though we totally respected and appreciated the fact that if the Cubans had not done these things, instructed by Orisha itself, we would not have authentic *ashe* [*àṣẹ*] of Orisha that is in our heads today.

Within this early decade, African American practitioners, including Adefunmi, were fully aware of the complex symbiotic relationship that existed between themselves and their Latino counterparts in òrìṣà. As an African American practitioner, Weaver captures the essence of these sentiments when he concludes, "Our respect for those Cuban priests of the Caribbean will never cease, nor will our gratitude" (Curry 1997: 160).

Conclusion

From 1959 to 1970, the hermeneutical transformation of Santería into Yorùbá by African Americans was a symbolic movement involving the assertion of religious self-agency while simultaneously attempting to negotiate multiple discourses of orthodoxy and authority. This historical transformation reshaped the diaspora boundaries of Yorùbá religion, creating room within the tradition for the unique social, ideological, and theological expressions of African Americans in the United States. The incorporation of Black Nationalism into the U.S. practice of Yorùbá religion created a two-way exchange that introduced religion into the Black Nationalist movement of the 1960s and introduced complex notions of race and nationalism into Yorùbá religion. The years 1959–1970 could also be conceivably read as oscillating moments of dissension and conflict between African American and transplanted Latino communities regarding the tradition's ritual and institutional practice. However, more nuanced readings of this period would represent both communities as attempting to devise their own concrete ways of generating religious meaning of the òrìṣà tradition within a shifting North American social context. Religious meaning was for both communities intricately linked to the content of their localized experiences within America and to the layers of interpretation they derived therein. However, for many African Americans, Black Nationalist discourses underscored the fervor with which they engaged the tradition. By 1970, this fervent ideological combination of Black Nationalism and Yorùbá religion became for Adefunmi the basis for the formation of Oyotunji African Village with its twofold purpose to adhere to the nationalist tenets of racial solidarity, black separatism, economic self-determination, and religio-cultural redemption as well as its purpose to create a space where Yorùbá traditions could be established and practiced as a religious, cultural, and societal norm (Hunt 1979: 53–55; Jordan 1994: 24; Drape 1991). For Adefunmi, Oyotunji African Village, as well as Shango and Yorùbá Temples, would help to facilitate a wider "African Restoration" movement among the people of the broader diaspora of Africa. Throughout his lifetime, his ultimate mission, efforts, and hopes were devoted to interrogating the complex meaning of the "African-born-in-America" and the ways in which Yorùbá religion could lend solidity and stability to this complicated identity.

Notes

1. Before 1959, minor traces of Santería were evident with the activities of Cuban *babaláwo* (diviner priest) Pancho Mora in New York City in the 1940s and with the early trailblazers of Afro-Cuban jazz such as Tito Puente, Julito Collazo, Chano Pozo, and Cal Tjader. However, unbeknownst to most, one of America's initial introductions to Santería came through popular media culture in the 1930s, to which Desi Arnaz later paid musical homage as the Yorùbá òrìṣà Babalu Aye on the sitcom *I Love Lucy*. For further details on early Santería in the United States, see Vega 1995: 86–93; Thompson 1994: 225–26.

2. Oseijeman Adefunmi, interview by author, tape recording, Ọ̀yọ́túnjí African Village, summer 1994.

3. Oseijeman Adefunmi, interview by author, tape recording, Ọ̀yọ́túnjí African Village, January 1996.

4. Ibid.

5. The Republic of New Africa was formed in 1968 as a nationalist orga-

nization committed to obtaining monetary reparations from the U.S. government and the acquisition of five states for the creation of a black homeland in America. Adefunmi served as the organization's minister of culture while simultaneously leading Yorùbá Temple (Van Deburg 1992: 148).

6. Oseijeman Adefunmi, interview by author, tape recording, Òyótúnjí African Village, January 1996.

References

Adefunmi, Oseijeman. 1962. *Tribal Origins of the African-Americans.* New York: Great Benin Books.

———. 1988. "Notes on the Return of the Gods of Africa and the Rising of Oyotunji." *Sagala: A Journal of Art and Ideas.* 38–43.

Baraka, Amiri. 1995 (1984). *The Autobiography of LeRoi Jones.* Chicago: Lawrence Hill Books.

Brandon, George. 1993. *Santeria from Africa to the New World: The Dead Sell Memories.* Bloomington: Indiana University Press.

Curry, Mary Cuthrell. 1997. *Making the Gods in New York: The Yoruba Religion in the African American Community.* New York: Garland.

Dixon, Heriberto. 1988. "Cuban-American Counterpoint: Black Cubans in the United States." *Dialectical Anthropology* 13: 227–39.

Drape, Joe. 1991. "African Village in the Carolinas: Home Is Where Yoruban Heart Is." *Atlanta Journal and Constitution,* April 23.

Drewal, Henry John, and John Mason. 1998. *Beads, Body and Soul: Art and Light in the Yoruba Universe.* Los Angeles: UCLA Fowler Museum of Cultural History.

Goodman, George. 1969. "Harlem's Yorubas: A Search for Something to Believe In." *Look* 33.

Gregory, Steven. 1986. "Santería in New York City: A Study in Cultural Resistance." Ph.D. diss., New School for Social Research.

Herskovits, Melville J. 1967. *Dahomey: An Ancient West African Kingdom.* Evanston, IL: Northwestern University Press.

Hunt, Carl. 1979. *Oyotunji Village: The Yoruba Movement in America.* Washington, DC: University Press of America.

Jordan, Milton. 1994. "African Kingdom in South Carolina." *Sepia,* June 26.

Long, Charles. 1997. "Perspectives for a Study of African-American Religion in the United States." In *African-American Religion: Interpretive Essays in History and Culture,* ed. Timothy Fulop and Albert Raboteau, 22–35. New York: Routledge.

Marable, Manning. 1984. *Race, Reform and Rebellion: The Second*

Reconstruction in Black America, 1945–1982. Jackson: University Press of Mississippi.

Métraux, Alfred. 1972. *Voodoo in Haiti*. New York: Schocken Books.

Moses, Wilson Jeremiah. 1978. *The Golden Age of Black Nationalism, 1850–1925*. New York: Oxford University Press.

Olatunle, Adetokunbo. 1976. "Oyotunji, South Carolina: Field Report." In *Black People and Their Culture: Selected Writings from the African Diaspora*, ed. Rosie Lee Hooks. Washington, DC: Smithsonian Institution Press.

Palmié, Stephan. 1995. "Against Syncretism: 'Africanizing' and 'Cubanizing' Discourses in North American *orisa* Worship." In *Counterworks: Managing the Diversity of Knowledge*, ed. Richard Fardon, 73–104. New York: Routledge.

Thompson, Robert Farris. 1994. "The Three Warriors: Atlantic Altars of Esu, Ogun, and Osoosi." In *The Yoruba Artist: New Theoretical Perspectives on African Arts*, ed. Rowland Abiodun, Henry Drewal, and John Pemberton III, 225–39. Washington, DC: Smithsonian Institution Press.

Van Deburg, William. 1992. *New Day in Babylon: The Black Power Movement and American Culture, 1965–1975*. Chicago: University of Chicago Press.

Vega, Marta Moreno. 1995. "Yoruba Philosophy: Multiple Levels of Transformation and Understanding." Ph.D. diss., Temple University.

Visual Arts Resource and Research Center Relating to the Caribbean (VARR-CRC). 1981. "The World Conference on Orisha, Ilé-Ifè, Nigeria, June 1–7, 1981: A Special Report." *Caribe* 5 (Fall/Winter): 1–14.

18

Santería in the Twenty-first Century

MERCEDES CROS SANDOVAL

The people of the Caribbean, as well as Central and South America, have experienced considerable movement of population over widespread areas. In many instances, these shifts in population are caused by sociopolitical upheaval, by changes from consumer to agricultural market crops, and, ultimately, by overpopulation. Moreover, inadequate distribution of resources has fostered negative effects by strengthening these social stressors. These conditions have overwhelmed the social value systems and the social institutions of culturally and ethnically heterogeneous peasants in small-town, rural societies. Political, social, and economic changes have encouraged unprecedented flight to cities and to other countries, especially to the United States. Migration has brought greater opportunities for social and economic mobility for some, and displacement, uprootedness, resentment, and alienation for others.

Migration and population displacement are certainly not new to these areas. During the last five centuries, the cultural traits of Amerindian, African, and European peoples of mostly Spanish, Portuguese, and French origins have intermingled. These processes produced a cultural

355

tapestry in which values such as authoritarianism, subjugation, mysticism, opportunism, and personalism have influenced the survival strategies of people experiencing abrupt cultural contact. With the merging of many different cultural traditions in a short period of time, cultural reinterpretation, syncretism, and, in many cases, transculturation have occurred. This context provided a rich environment for Santería to flourish and evolve, acquiring new religious significance at the threshold of the twenty-first century.[1]

Santería is the name of an Afro-Cuban religious system that shares historical and functional similarities with Afro-Brazilian Candomblé.[2] During pre-Revolutionary Cuba of the 1940s and 1950s, Santería enjoyed a significant, but limited, following. In many parts of the island, Santería was totally unknown. Moreover, it had a reputation for being a religion of "lower" class, primarily black, mulatto, and white uneducated people.[3] However, in the last forty years it has gained a greater following and visibility among Cubans on the island, regardless of their ethnic, social, and economic background. Santería demonstrated its efficacy by assisting people to ameliorate the shock and stress suffered while adapting to the new ways of the Revolution.[4]

Furthermore, outside of Cuba, during the last forty years Santería demonstrated its appeal to serve as a mediating institution for many Cubans exiled from their homeland, who suffer from stress caused by acculturation to the customs of a new country.[5] Currently, in the United States, Santería exerts a pull on individuals of non-Cuban extraction, such as Puerto Ricans, Nicaraguans, Venezuelans, Mexicans, Colombians, and other Hispanic Americans, who are also trying to adapt to American culture. African Americans are attracted to Santería for reasons of cultural identity.[6] Santería has gained a following in Latin America where Cuban exiles have settled. In these countries, as well as in the post-industrial society of the United States, Santería serves to lessen feelings of ambivalence, confusion, frustration, and lack of control caused by rapid change and culture shock. The characteristics of these new followers demonstrate that Santería is rapidly becoming a complex fusion of religious cultures. As a magic-based religious system, Santería is assisting its heterogeneous following to cope with the tensions of modernization, as well as the alienation experienced by immigrants and marginalized people who live in the shadows of a post-industrial milieu.

The Origins of Santería in Cuba

Santería originated with the religious beliefs and practices of Yorùbá-speaking slaves brought to Cuba primarily during the eighteenth and nineteenth centuries from the region of Nigeria, West Africa. At the end of the eighteenth century, and during the first half of the nineteenth century, Yorùbá-speaking people were brought to Cuba in large numbers. Experts agree that many high priests were among those who came as slaves. This factor accounts for the rich cultural-religious heritage of elaborate rituals, impressive mythology, and complex divination systems preserved in Cuba and other areas of the New World.[7]

Santería evolved as an Afro-Cuban religious system in which Yorùbá beliefs and rituals assimilated other African religious practices and incorporated, by means of associative processes, images, and dogma of Spanish Catholicism and European spiritualism. The highly heterogeneous and eclectic religious complex that developed in Santería is characterized by the worship of the òrìṣàs/*santos* (gods/saints).[8]

While acting as symbolic power brokers between the Supreme Being and humans, the òrìṣàs/*santos* exhibit emotions and other human qualities. Olódùmarè, the Supreme Being, has all of the sublime functions displayed by a creator God of more institutionalized religions—eternity, omnipotence, omniscience, omnipresence, mercifulness, and justice. He is perceived as too powerful and remote to respond to the base needs of mere mortals. Thus, humans depend on intermediaries, the òrìṣàs/*santos,* to intercede on their behalf, accessing for them the power and assistance of Olódùmarè. In most instances, òrìṣàs act with great independence from the Supreme Olódùmarè. Often, because of their quasi-human personalities, the òrìṣàs are motivated to sympathize more with humans than Olódùmarè would. Olódùmarè remains inaccessible to mortals as awe-inspiring sublime Presence.[9]

The òrìṣàs/*santos* personify the forces of nature. Yemayá is goddess of the sea. Changó is the god of thunder. Oshun is the goddess of the river. Some òrìṣàs own certain areas of the human body. If the *santos* became enraged, they may cause illness to particular areas of the human body. Conversely, when these areas are afflicted by disease, health can be restored if the *santo* is effectively propitiated. Other òrìṣàs and *santos* act as patrons and protectors of certain human economic activities; for example, Ògún is the patron of the smithy or smith who works in black metal.

In practicing Santería, humans need to know appropriate ways to propitiate the divinities to receive the benefits of protection and support in daily life. Thus, Santería is characterized by great reliance on consultations with the divinities by means of several divination systems. The devotee seeks a consultant to obtain advice to solve problems and resolve issues pertaining to health, worldly conflicts, and crisis. In addition, the òrìṣàs make their wishes known to the believers through dreams and trance possession states.

Santería has a rich mythology, an elaborate system of ritual, and a large core of *santeros/santeras,* priests and priestesses, who propitiate the òrìṣàs on behalf of their followers. However, there is no priestly class in charge of enforcing strict traditions or orthodox dogma. Thus, the practice of Santería varies according to the knowledge and preference of the individual priest and priestess, as well as the perceived needs of their followers. The *santeros* preside over ceremonies, as medicine men, soothsayers, and witch hunters. They are the keepers of the traditions, the trainers and initiators of individuals who enter the service of an òrìṣàs, either to become a priest or to obtain greater assistance and support.

The essence of diverse and elaborate rituals of Santería is validated by the special knowledge of how the ritual should be performed and which elements must be exhibited. The ritual is not upheld based on faith, intention, or authority bestowed upon the *santeros*—neither by the òrìṣàs nor by initiation. Thus, *santeros* are respected according to the esoteric knowledge they accumulate, by their demonstrated ability to perform the magic or metaphysical ritual, and by having initiated or having participated in the most complicated, uncommon, and mysterious ritual. It is important to have a godfather or godmother who is experienced. Seniority is very important in Santería performance. The *santeros* are bound to their godparents by virtually unbreakable bonds of respect and submission.[10] However, essentially because of the uprooting experienced by Cubans who left the island, current practices demonstrate that, after initiation, *santeros* and *santeras* enjoy greater independence than previous practice allowed.

The magical and ritual practice of Santería is motivated primarily to enhance the individual practitioner's feelings of security, protection, and power. The focus on personal protection was fostered by highly stressful conditions underlying confusion, identity crisis, and lack of control that slavery caused in the newly arrived Africans and later their descendants.

This highly individualistic religious practice can lead to considerable variety in conducting rituals aimed at results, some of which outsiders might consider antisocial or socially negative. Yet, insiders or practitioners consider such actions as ego-protective and ego-integrative. In this fashion, a ritual designed to obtain the attention of someone else's spouse, conducted to cause illness in an oppressive boss, or carried out to bring harm to the enemy of a client is perceived as protective rather than aggressive in nature.

Reverence to the spirits of the dead is an essential element of Santería. Yet, the uprooted Yorùbá religion in Cuba was unable to uphold successfully the integrity of the cult of the sacred ancestors. The extended family, which remained in Africa, was the essence of that cult, and the slaves lost extended families. However, remnants of this ritual of ancestral lineage are manifested in important, necessary solicitations and reverence to the ancestors' religious lineage of a *santero*. In others words, reverence and solicitation of the departed souls of a person's godfathers and grand-godfathers are necessary. Furthermore, during initiation, when devotees receive a particular òrìṣà, they receive the uncompromising protection of a deceased person. The soul of the deceased, when alive, was also a child, a protégée, of the òrìṣà/*santo* that one is receiving. In the New World, this deceased person does not have to be related to the living initiate by extended family or by religious lineage ties. Again, the emphasis in Santería remains on providing the individual with personal protection and power in whatever way is possible.

In the Yorùbá religion, the use of medicinal herbs and plants for magical and curative purposes is important.[11] Osain, the òrìṣà who has dominion over wild plants, has to be called upon when conducting any ritual. In many instances, contemporary access to modern medicine has detracted from the exclusive use of plants for curative purposes. Most *santeros* encourage clients to go to their doctors, follow instructions, and take prescribed medications.[12] Nevertheless, the use of flowers, herbs, twigs, and leaves continues to be an intrinsic part of every ceremony. Their curative powers as complements to the doctor's prescription are unquestioned, and their magical properties have not yet been challenged.[13]

Offerings and sacrifices are an integral part of the religious practices of Santería. The òrìṣàs/*santos* and spirits are offered specific cooked delicacies and special foods, the sacrificial blood of animals, fruit, and other gifts that they particularly enjoy. In most instances, offerings are

meant to establish a state of communion with supernatural entities, solicit a favor, or honor a deity on a specific important day. In these cases,
the believers partake of the offerings. On the other hand, when animals
are sacrificed and offered as scapegoats to placate an enraged òrìṣà/*santo*
or to undo a harm caused by witchcraft, the flesh of the animal cannot be
eaten. In these cases, the carcass must be disposed of according to ritual
procedures.

Santería beyond Cuba

During the past forty years, a great number of Santería practitioners
have abandoned the island of Cuba and brought their religious beliefs to
the communities in which they have settled. Outside of Cuba, Santería
has undergone significant changes.[14] Many of these changes happened
because of the unique circumstances in which the exiled practitioners
found themselves. Other changes resulted from Santería's adaptation to
the new needs of immigrant believers and to the new following it was
attracting.

One of the most important factors causing changes in Santería was
demographic. The Cuban population in exile was not representative of
the ethnic configuration of those remaining on the island. The number
of blacks who left Cuba in the 1960s and 1970s remained below the
incidence of the black population on the island. Thus, the religion of
the Yorùbá, brought to Cuba by African slaves, again was uprooted. A
syncretic, "Cubanized" version, once more displaced, was taken out of
the island by *santeros/santeras,* many of whom were of non-African descent. Consequently, in this diaspora, white *santeros/santeras* achieved
a preeminence that they would not have had, if the migratory situation
had been representative of the population remaining in Cuba.

The limited presence of a black constituency representing Santería in
exile has had a tremendous impact on its present state, in many instances
de-emphasizing previous important functions. For many Afro-Cubans,
for example, the religion of the òrìṣàs/*santos* is more than a religion; it
is the core of their ethnic identity. Consequently, the religion became an
integral part of their cultural history, something uniquely theirs, which
survived the long period of assimilation to the cultural patterns that dominated the island. In contributing to this function of identity formation,
Santería offered great ego-integrity value to Afro-Cubans. As such, it

provided its followers an important core group identity, as well as cultural and historical continuity. For others of non-African descent, this function was non-essential even though great benefit was provided by the religion.

Uprootedness, on the other hand, affected the *santeros/santeras* in a manner similar to that affecting other exiles, with widespread feelings of loss, ambivalence, lack of control, and frustration. In addition, for many of these priests and priestesses, departing from Cuba meant that they had to leave their social support networks of godfathers and godmothers behind as well as their sacred religious objects, which they were prohibited from bringing with them. Furthermore, many newly initiated *santeros/santeras,* still lacking sound knowledge of ritual and creed as well as magical "know how," felt impaired by the impossibility of continuing their esoteric training with their godparents in a structured fashion.

Esoteric training is extremely critical in a religion where the priests and priestesses are professionals of the supernatural. Based on their knowledge of the metaphysical and the magic, they must be able to efficiently tap into supernatural power sources outside of themselves on behalf of the believers. Consequently, if the *santero/santera* remains unknowledgeable or uninformed, the rituals performed can be rendered ineffective or, even worse, can bring great tragedy to the clients. Thus, many new *santeros/santeras* had to start or continue their practices with what they knew, even though there were some limitations to their knowledge of how to perform some important rituals. Thus, in adapting to this new situation, some rituals were changed in response to the circumstances of the migration and the pressures of the new environment.

Another important change was that many of the new *santeros/santeras,* looking for reliable sources of information, reached out to the academic literature concerning Santería and the Yorùbá religion. In Cuba, until the 1950s, this consultation would have been unnecessary— and could even have been considered by senior religious leaders almost sacrilegious since religious knowledge was acquired through observation and participation. It was also transmitted by the use of handwritten notebooks, prepared especially by the godfather for the godchild.

The study of academic literature opened a window to Africa, to the very roots of the religion they were practicing. This new situation also prompted many *santeros* to initiate contact and correspondence with both Cuban and African scholars. Some *santeros* went to Africa as pilgrims in search of greater meaning. Others went to validate their credentials by undergoing specific religious experiences and initiations in their cultural and religious homeland. Finally, there were those who went to Nigeria simply as interested tourists.

These circumstances created new opportunities for the practitioners who were becoming informed by the academic literature. In the United States, Puerto Rico, and elsewhere, *santeros/santeras* began to attend and participate in conferences about Santería and the Yorùbá religion. Accordingly, they began writing and publishing their own manuals, books, newspapers, and newsletters about Santería. They became part of a literary tradition while using it as a means to communicate, learn about, and expand the knowledge of Santería, the Yorùbá religion, and its practices. Some *santeros/santeras* have entered the world of academia as students writing dissertations about the religion, as curators for museum exhibits, as part-time lecturers, and as scholars with full-time academic appointments.[15]

Another change occurred in 1979 when the Castro government permitted former exiles to visit the island. Many *santeros/santeras* visited Cuba and have continued to do so for a variety of reasons: to renew contact with their godparents, to recover sacred paraphernalia left behind, or to participate in some ritual they need to experience or learn for use with followers. These visits strengthened the practice of Santería outside Cuba.

In 1980, when the Mariel boatlift occurred, many black Cubans were able to leave the island. Included among this new wave of exiles were many Santería priests and practitioners. At first, some complained about the conditions of Santería outside Cuba. They viewed the religion as having become materialistic and opportunistic in exile. Many also implied that they were more knowledgeable than the *santeros/santeras* practicing in exile. This "friendly confrontation" was not too different from the complaints of the newly arrived Cubans concerning how life in the United States had changed the exiles of the 1960s and how different their brand of Cubanía seemed to the new émigrés.

The Mariel boatlift provided an opportunity to contrast the culture of Cubans in exile since 1960 with that of those who had remained on the island and came in the boatlift. The lifestyles of both groups had dramatically departed from the cultural patterns shared in the Cuba of the 1950s. Change naturally occurs through the passing of time, especially between two groups that have taken separate paths. Mostly, however, changes were caused by the difference in adaptive strategies developed by the two distinct groups in markedly different contexts.[16] The exiled Cubans changed as a result of adjusting to the conditions prevalent in post-industrialized societies, while those staying on the island coped with adaptation to the drastic changes prevalent in a society undergoing a radical communist revolution and isolation from the outside world.

In the final analysis, the arrival of large numbers of *santeros,* during and after the Mariel boatlift, greatly enhanced the visibility of Santería outside Cuba. Numbers were added to the already growing communities of practitioners and followers. Also, practices were enriched with knowledge and information obtained and shared in the visits to Cuba by *santeros/santeras* and followers.

In addition, outside Cuba, where observation and research by the author has been possible, the function of Santería as a social and economic network and as a supportive complementary healthcare system is shown to have been enhanced. Devotees who regularly frequent the house of a *santero/santera* become part of an intimate, surrogate family that represents a significant substitute for estranged or absent extended families. This setting offers members an open-door policy and a realm of religious activities with great opportunities to socialize. The surrogate family offers the individual valuable assistance in job and apartment hunting and in solving the numerous problems and conflicts present in everyday life.

This augmented social support function of Santería has expanded into a viable mental health delivery system, which offers social support, counseling, and socialization opportunities to many people who are suffering from the many stressors that characterize acculturative, immigration, and de-culturative processes.[17] Thus, Santería, similar to many other religious organizations—Christian and otherwise—offers the believer a wide social network to buffer the trauma of migration. It provides people who feel alienated—who suffer from feelings of lack of control, from role confusion, or from having no meaningful social role—with a sense and experience of belonging and of importance, without requiring the strict moral restraints that many small evangelical churches demand.

Finally, the negative influence of the use and trade of illegal drugs in the larger society of the later part of the twentieth century has also affected this religion. Santería's emphasis on the individual's protection, coupled with its lack of emphasis on community welfare or its moral standards, is responsible for earning it a reputedly "amoral" posture.

Normally, Santería does not place any moral judgment on a person based on his professional activities, personal characteristics, or sexual orientation. For example, some drug dealers have joined Santería in hopes of obtaining supernatural protection from the authorities and from their enemies. Also, many homosexuals and people whose lifestyles do not conform to the dominant value orientation are initiated as priests, and they enjoy a wide following. This perceived moral ambivalence, in some instances, has damaged the reputation of Santería and its followers. However, it has not deterred the growth and spread of the religion.

Santería's Current Status: New Following and Recent Trends

As Cuban exiles settled in different parts of the United States and Latin America, knowledge of Santería became more widespread. Thus, Santería evolved from a religion practiced by mostly black Cuban believers to a religion with appeal to a larger following. It attracted adherents among Puerto Ricans, Venezuelans, Colombians, Mexicans, Dominicans, Nicaraguans, Ecuadorians, and other Latin Americans. It has also achieved a stronghold among American blacks, but for different reasons.

Many initiated African Americans find in Santería the divinities that their ancestors might have worshiped. Santería offers them a source of authentic ethnic (racial) identity, similar to that offered the African-Cuban population. In the early 1980s, while attending a Santería drum festival in Miami, I asked an African American woman if she experienced any dissonance having acquired knowledge of the Yorùbá religion through Cuban immigrants and participating in an African religious festival being celebrated by Cubans of European descent. Her response was revealing. "It is the way of the *orichas* that the Cubans were to be the ones to bring their religion to the United States. This might be the greatest contribution Cubans ever made to American culture." Later, as the conversation continued, she complained that white Cubans did not wear the "traditional" African garments to the festivals and that they wanted to serve Cuban food during celebrations.

To some African Americans, Santería represents a resilient link to Africa, to their roots. Even though they generally reject Catholic influences in Santería, they participate in its practices and join the ranks of the initiated.[18] After a while, some reject Santería as a Cuban experience, trying to re-create Yorùbá belief and practices. This new Yorùbá revisionism trend entails an exclusive Afro-centric stance in former Santería practices, as seen in the cult houses that African Americans attend and have founded in the United States.

Beyond Santería's appeal to Third World societies in Latin America, Santería has caught the attention of new followers. Kardecian spiritualist beliefs and practices, as well as the practice of *curanderismo,* enjoy widespread influence in Latin America and have facilitated the acceptance of Santería in Latin countries.[19] Santería has borrowed from the many practices and beliefs of spiritualists. Belief in the interference of the souls of the deceased in human affairs represents a common value. In addition, the widespread use of herbal remedies and esoteric magical practices of *curanderismo* makes its ritual elements comparable to Santería.

Although Santería's religious beliefs and health practices are situated outside mainstream society, it offers its devotees a complex code of beliefs, a rich mythology, diversified and symbolic religious paraphernalia, highly structured sets of rituals, and compelling music and dance, as well as a viable road to priesthood. The complexity and intricacy of Santería's magical practices, which require long training and experience, are to some extent equivalent to professional accreditation. This characteristic attracts and challenges people who may be marginalized, living in the shadows of a society that favors technocracy and materialism. Conversely, Santería offers charismatic, insightful, and aggressive individuals great economic opportunities, as well as positions of prominence as ceremonial leaders and counselors. Furthermore, the *santeros/santeras* are exempt from many restraints by which professionals and other religious practitioners have to abide, including the need for academic accreditation, and may enjoy tax-exempt status. Thus, Santería has opened a wider avenue for upward social and economic mobility by means of a populist priesthood. This avenue is especially meaningful for women (*santeras*), who are well accepted and represented in Santería's priestly class, except for the priesthood of Orúnla, the òrìṣà of divination.

Santería has enjoyed, as well as suffered from, media attention. Especially in the United States, television, newspapers, and popular magazines have played up the fascinating practice of Santería. Frequently reporting on or featuring stories about African drum festivals, complex divination systems, and trance possession, the media have brought notice to the unusual rituals and "bizarre" sacrifices of animals. The fairly common finding of carcasses of sacrificed animals in rivers or in the vicinity of railroad tracks, intersections, "sacred trees," and other sites has prompted the attention of informative, but often sensationalized, reporting.

In areas where such sightings take place, concerned neighbors, members of humane societies, and others seeking the protection of animal rights contact the local police. These interactions between the police and the *santeros* have brought frequent, though not positive, visibility to Santería. Everywhere that Cuban *santeros* and their followers have had such interactions, the press has been eager to cover it and to inform the public about these esoteric practices. A Hollywood movie, *The Believers,* featuring well-known actors Martin Sheen and Jimmy Smits, brought public attention to the practice of this religion—and even more negative publicity.[20]

Another projection of this trend toward sensationalism prompted *santeros* to bring their religious practices into the open in attempts to mainstream their beliefs and make them more open to public scrutiny. One such effort took place in Hialeah, Florida, where *santeros* opened a Lucumí Church. Unfortunately, this attempt precipitated an open confrontation between municipal authorities and members of the church, encouraged by community protest. The conflict was brought before the United States Supreme Court, and a decision was reached that was favorable to the advocates of Santería. The Court decided to support the right of any religious group to express religious practices and to uphold freedom of religious expression.[21]

Other *santeros* have opened *cabildos* and a variety of centers for students to study their religion, learn the Yorùbá language, and dispel fears about the practices of Santería.[22] Social and cultural activities are accentuated. Some *santeros* have organized "processions similar to the ones in Cuba," using cars to drive the religious images and the believers around one of the busiest streets of greater Miami.

Overall, Santería has become more visible than ever before. Scholars are developing and organizing conferences in which practitioners and experts from Africa and the Americas can share their knowledge and their experiences. *Santeros/santeras* are more than eager to participate and to share knowledge with scholars attracted to the religion of Santería and to those initiated in it.[23]

Conclusion

Inevitably and corresponding to the nature of cultural dynamics everywhere, the twentieth and the twenty-first centuries represent change in all social milieus, and the ancient African origins of Santería, its evolution in the New World, and its current expansion reflect its ever-changing nature. Today, often high-ranking elder and junior *santeros/santeras* still cling to the traditions and "know how" handed down to them by their godparents. They practice their religion inconspicuously, secretively, just as the first Yorùbá-speaking slaves did, and they shy away from the public and the media.

Some priests/priestesses now learn about their religion and its origins by research scholarship and academic discourse, corresponding with scholars, participating in conferences, and traveling to Nigeria. Other scholars are even attempting to "purify" aspects of Santería by rejecting and expunging elements that reflect Catholic influence. The goal of these scholars is to try to revitalize Santería by reinstating original Yorùbá practices that were lost in Cuba as the religion began to change under pressures of adaptation to that cultural and political milieu. Still other *santeros/santeras* are looking for acceptance or at least tolerance from the larger society through a variety of public relations initiatives.

For the religion of Santería to have survived and flourished as it has is truly noteworthy. Given its history as a religion practiced secretly and surreptitiously, initially by Africans under the most abject and severe conditions of slavery, and later, given its social position at the margins of mainstream culture, by a predominantly black but also mulatto and white underclass population of pre-Revolutionary Cuba, its flourishing presence in many parts of the New World today is all the more remarkable.

As Santería continues to adapt to new conditions of challenging social, political, and economic times, and as new directions are explored, this multifaceted religious system will continue to appeal to an even more heterogeneous following, a situation that will further impact Santería's beliefs and practices. The religious system of Santería will continue to appeal to those who, for whatever reason, experience unprecedented chaos and disruption in their lives, physical displacement, trauma, and other adverse situations of control and mastery. Many of the new followers will be among those who migrate, whether by choice or by force—people whose modus vivendi will be greatly affected by the pressures of assimilation to other cultures and to modern society.

Santería's appeal will continue among people who have been up-rooted, marginalized, or disillusioned by their experiences in more established societies. There will be followers among people who are not particularly interested in the afterlife but in the solutions of everyday problems, here and now; people who reach out to supernatural forces beyond the power of an individual to negotiate favor on behalf of their own needs. It is appropriate to predict that, if current social and political trends and their economic consequences continue, many more disciples will seek support in the refuge of Santería.

The religion of the Yorùbá, brought to Cuba by enslaved peoples from Africa, gained many followers among black Cubans of non-Yorùbá descent and among Cubans of non-African descent as well. Later, as large numbers of Cubans abandoned the island, Santería gained an even wider audience. Santería is now a new transformational religious phenomenon. It assists people of various cultural and ethnic backgrounds to adjust to apparent or actual nonsupportive conditions that they endure under complex, impersonal, materialistic, ever-changing, and frequently unscrupulous societies.

Notes

1. Santería represents a more contemporary term referring to complex African-Cuban religious forms. In earlier times, Santería was called Regla de Ocha or Regla Lucumi. Santería is also known as a religion in the Yorùbá language of origin, whose devotees in Cuba use Yorùbá terms such as *Bàbáòrìshàs* (father of the saints), *Iyaorichas* (mother of the saints), or *Moriches* (children of the saints).

2. Candomblé represents an African-Brazilian religious fusion of Yorùbá, Catholic, Amerindian, and Allan Kardec's spiritualist beliefs and practices.

3. For more information concerning Santería in Cuba see Cabrera 1971; Diaz Fabelo 1956, 1960; Ortiz 1987, 1959, and 1985. See also Lachatañeré 1938, 1942b; Sandoval 1975.

4. Sandoval 1986.

5. For more information concerning the changes experienced by the Yorùbá religion in Cuba, see Sandoval 1975. See also Sandoval 1979.

6. Sandoval 1995.

7. For a firsthand account of the cult of the òrìṣàs in Cuba, as it was practiced by the old *santeros* during the first half of the twentieth century, see Cabrera 1971.

8. Òrìṣà/*santo* or òrìṣàs/*santos*. Among many believers in Santería, the association between the Yorùbá òrìṣà and the Catholic *santo* is so close that they perceive them as manifestations of the same divinity. The believers who are more knowledgeable of the Lucumí religion see the òrìṣà as equivalent to but different from the *santo*. Among those believers with an Afro-centric stance, the association between the òrìṣà and the *santo* was a strategy. To them, the *santos* are seen as having been used by the early practitioners of the Yorùbá religion in Cuba as a mask to protect their belief in the African òrìṣà.

9. For more information, see Cabrera1971; Sandoval 1977.

10. Godfather, *santero,* and godmother, *santera,* are terms used to designate devotees in charge of training a novice or apprentice.

11. For more information concerning the use of magical and medicinal herbs in Santería, see Cabrera 1971.

12. Sandoval 1979.

13. Ibid.

14. Canet 1973; Julio Cortes 1971; Ramos 1982, 1988.

15. Ramos 2000.

16. For more information concerning differences in adaptive strategies among Cubans on the island and in the United States, see Sandoval 1986.

17. Sandoval 1979.

18. An African American of Cuban decent who has written about Yorùbá religion is John Mason. See Mason 1981, 1985.

19. *Curanderismo* is a Spanish word applied to the practices of healers who remain outside the medical orthodox health systems, regardless of whether or not they use the rituals and pharmacopoeia of Spanish Amerindian or African origins.

20. Murders committed in Matamoros, Mexico, in April 1989 by drug dealers who claimed they were members of a cult where human sacrifices were offered for protection elicited horrified national and international attention. Since the leader of the group had some knowledge of Santería and other Afro-Cuban religions, negative light was again cast on Santería.

21. The Lucumi Babalu Aye Church was opened in Hialeah, Miami-Dade County, Florida.

22. In Puerto Rico, the Centro de Estudios Y Culto Religioso Yorùbá, Inc., founded by Yrmino Valdes, was very active. In Miami, some *santeros* founded Cabildo Yorùbá Omo Orisha, Inc.

23. See Gonzalez-Wippler 1988. See also Murphy 1988.

References

Cabrera, Lydia. 1957. *Anagó: Vocabulario Lucumí*. Havana: Colección del Chicherekú en el exilio.

———. 1971 (1954). *El Monte*. Miami: Colección del Chicherekú.

———. 1974. *Yemayá y Ochún: Kariocha, Iyalorichas y Olorichas*. New York: Colección del Chicherekú en el exilio.

———. 1980. *Koeko Iyawó: Aprende novicia; Pequeño tratado de Regla Lucumí*. Miami: Colección del Chicherekú en el exilio.

Canet, Carlos. 1973. *Lucumí: Religión de los Yoruba en Cuba*. Miami: Air Publications Center.

Díaz Fabelo, Teodoro. 1956. *Lengua de Santeros: Guiné Gongorí*. Havana: n.p.

———. 1960. *Olorún*. Havana: Departamento de Folklore del Teatro Nacional de Cuba.

García Cortez, Julio. 1971. *El Santo*. Mexico City: Editorial Latino Americana, S.A.

Gonzalez-Wippler, Migene. 1988. *Rituals and Spells in Santeria*. New York: Original.

Lachatañeré, Rómulo. 1938. *Oh mío Yemayá*. Manzanillo, Cuba: Editorial El Arte.

———. 1939–42. "El Sistema Religioso de los Lucumis y Otras Influencias Africanas en Cuba." *Estudios Afrocubanos* 2 (1939), 3 (1939), 4 (1940), and 6 (1942a).

———. 1942b. *Manual de Santería*. Manzanillo, Cuba: Editorial Arte.

Mason, John. 1981. *Onde Fun Orisha: Food for the Gods*. Brooklyn, NY: Yoruba Theological Archministry.

———. 1985. *Four New World Religious Rituals*. Brooklyn, NY: Yoruba Theological Archministry.

Murphy, Joseph M. 1988. *Santeria: An African Religion in America*. Boston: Beacon Press.

Ortiz, Fernando. 1959. *La Africanía de la Música Folklórica de Cuba*. Havana: Ministerio de Educación, Dirección de Cultura.

———. 1985 (1951). *Los Bailes y el Teatro de los Negros en el Folklore de Cuba*. Havana: Editorial Letras Cubanas.

———. 1987 (1916). *Los Negros Esclavos*. Havana: Editorial de Ciencias Sociales.

Ramos, Miguel "Willie." 1982. *Ceremonia de Obaloaye*. Puerto Rico: Centro de Estudios y Culto Religioso Yoruba, Año 1.

———. 1988. *Seminario de Religion Yoruba: Santería and Eleda*. Miami: Cabildo Yoruba Omo Orisha.

————. 2000. "The Empire Beats On: Bàtá Drums and Hegemony in Nineteenth Century Cuba." M.A. thesis, Florida International University.

————. 2003. "La division de la Habana: Territorial Conflict and Cultural Hegemony in the Followers of Oyo Lukumí Religion, 1850s–1920s." *Cuban Studies* 34: 38–70.

Sandoval, Mercedes Cros. 1975. *La Religión Afrocubana.* Madrid: Editorial Playor.

————. 1977. "Afro-Cuban Concepts of Disease and Its Treatment in Miami." *Journal of Operational Psychiatry* 8, no. 2: 52–63.

————. 1979. "Santería as a Mental Health Care System." *Social Science and Medicine* 13, no. 2: 137–51.

————. 1983. "Santería." *Journal of the Florida Medical Association* 70, no. 8: 619–28.

————. 1986. *Mariel and Cuban National Identity.* Miami: Editorial Sibi.

————. 1995. "Afro-Cuban Religion in Perspective." In *Enigmatic Powers: Syncretism with African and Indigenous Peoples' Religions among Latinos,* ed. Anthony M. Stevens-Arroyo and Andrés I. Pérez Mena, 81–98. PARAL Studies 3. New York: Bildner Center Books.

19

La Santería

An Integrating, Mythological Worldview in a Disintegrating Society

JUAN J. SOSA

I have always described *la Santería,* as it is perceived outside of Cuba, as the "worship of African *orishas* under the appearance of Catholic saints, a result of transculturation and religious syncretism in various cultural groups of the Caribbean."[1] The following pages attempt to provide a theoretical framework for the transculturation of the Cuban population in Miami and the role Santería has played in that process beginning mostly after January 1, 1959. Such reflections surface out of my own anthropological background. The concept of syncretism, which some seem to disregard today or, like Brandon (1993: 157–75), to substitute for symbiosis, touches the very heart of my theological framework. As a teacher and a pastor, I have found syncretism to be a unique paradigm, perhaps the product of a *religious mestizaje* that presents itself as a composite of worldviews transformed into one that—from a religious perspective— does not liberate an individual to experience "God" but rather seems to confuse him or her.

Regardless of whether some agree or disagree with my theological appraisal of this religious phenomenon, this is not the moment to discuss it. The following pages merely mention the depth of my theological reflections on the subject of syncretism and its impact on Catholic theology and practice, which I take up more fully in another publication (Sosa 1999). I hope, however, that my analysis of the transculturation of Cubans in Miami, vis-à-vis the spread of Santería, will shed some light on this fascinating subject that touches the core of culture, philosophy, and religion across the Caribbean and Brazil.

In fact, an analysis of the process of transculturation has allowed us to perceive the complex developments of the Yorùbá religion as it moved from Nigeria to Cuba and now to South Florida.[2] If, for the Yorùbá of Southwestern Nigeria, religion provided an integrated mythological process in their everyday living, for the sons and daughters of the Yorùbá of Cuba, as well as for Santería's believers of present-day South Florida, religion as syncretism continues to facilitate that same process.

In this sense, religion becomes a representation of some part of objective reality with all its complexity, anguish, and hopes. For the Yorùbá, for the *lucumí* believers, and for the present-day followers of Santería, religion seems to explain profound relationships that preserve and re-enact narration and ritual about the origin of nature and the symbolism of objects and human beings. Moreover, it seems to facilitate integrated space and time to help people cope with disintegration, urbanization, departmentalization of human life, and personal dehumanization.

Within a Western world that seems to uphold Aristotelian categories above all others, the phenomenon of la Santería may represent an absurd and illogical option, even as a religious form. Imbued with Aristotle's law of contradiction, most members of our Western society either accept or do not accept events, phenomena, or the objectification of reality itself. For them, "things" either "are" or "are not." African mentality, among other non-Western styles of thinking, provides a different perspective than that maintained in the Greco-Roman legacy of our society. La Santería, even as a religious syncretism, can make sense to people who resist nontraditional forms of worship and who need to re-create a meaningful, traditional worldview in the midst of change and innovation. From this perspective, part of reality is expressed and symbolized—but a part that makes sense only to those who have internalized it and have assumed it. In the words of Berger and Luckmann (1966: 128): "What remains sociologically essential is the recognition that all symbolic universes and all legitimations are human products; their existence has its base in the lives of concrete individuals, and has no empirical status apart from these lives."

Before we assume to present an analysis of la Santería within the process of transculturation of Cubans in South Florida, let us discuss, though briefly, the nature of two essential concepts and social realities: religion and syncretism.

La Santería: Religion or Syncretism?

Clifford Geertz (1975) has helped us synthesize the role of religious symbolism within a cultural group's vision of society. He mentions two essential ingredients in any group's religious beliefs: the group's ethos and its worldview. For Geertz (126), a cultural group manifests its ethos in its moral, aesthetic, and evaluative elements, while the group's worldview encompasses its cognitive, existential aspects:

> Religious belief and ritual confront and mutually confirm one another; the ethos is made intellectually reasonable by being shown to represent a way of life implied by the actual state of affairs which the world view describes, and the world view is made emotionally acceptable by being presented as an image of an actual state of affairs of which such a way of life is an authentic expression.

Religious beliefs, therefore, are not found merely as abstractions. As Geertz (1975: 126) continues to explain, the meaning provided by a religious system can be stored only in symbols that find dramatization in ritual activity, namely, a re-enactment of a cultural group's ancestral mythology. Such symbols will dramatize positive and negative values within a given group's understanding of reality; in the dynamism of these opposite poles lies the resolution of a critical situation for the individual within the group. In this context, religion can become supportive of social values. In the words of Geertz (131):

> The force of religion in supporting social values rests, then, on the ability of its symbols to formulate a world in which those values, as well as the forces opposing their realization, are fundamental ingredients. It represents the power of the human imagination to construct an image of reality in which, to paraphrase Max Weber, events do not just happen

in a certain place, but they have meaning and only happen because of that meaning.

The need to recapture such meaning, for people undergoing rapid changes, becomes more apparent as key values of human life continue to be destroyed, as C. D. Keyes (1979: 11) explains, through cruel and deceptive language and the misuse of power. In bringing a people's ethos and worldview together, sacred symbolism in ritual action provides for the entire group an appearance of objectivity.

According to Geertz (1975: 90), religion is "a system of symbols which acts to establish powerful, pervasive, and long-lasting moods and motivations in men by formulating conceptions of a general order of existence and clothing these conceptions with such an aura of factuality that the moods and motivations seem uniquely realistic."

To simplify the elements of his definition, we shall select its key ingredients: as tangible, external models "for" and models "of" cultural patterns, symbols give meaning to social reality by "shaping themselves to it and by shaping it to themselves." This "shaping" induces in the believer a motivation to act in a certain way; likewise it stimulates him to fall into a certain mood. Geertz (1975: 97) provides us with a fine distinction: "[M]otivations are 'made meaningful' with reference to the ends toward which they are conceived to conduce, whereas moods are 'made meaningful' with reference to the conditions from which they are conceived to spring."

Such motivations and such a mood relate the believer to a sense of order, which lies beyond empirical reality itself. Faced with chaotic situations and experiences of disharmony within his own quest for harmony, the believer is confronted through religious symbolism by the need to move beyond "what is," the need to overcome suffering (which on most occasions appears as illness and death), and the need to overcome evil. Ultimately, he can clothe these conceptions with a perspective that is intrinsic to religion.

Distinct from a "common-sensible" perspective, whereby things are given, a scientific perspective, whereby things are questioned, or even an aesthetic perspective, whereby things are seen as appearances and not in themselves, the religious perspective facilitates a unique type of experience. From a narrow outlook on everyday life, the religious perspective moves the believer to a wider acceptance of "beyond-ness" through faith; from a feeling of detachment, it likewise provides a sense of commitment; and rather than an opportunity for analysis, it facilitates an "encounter." The dynamism of the process is best perceived through ritual. As Geertz (1975: 112) claims:

> For it is in ritual—that is, consecrated behavior—that this conviction that religious conceptions are veridical and that religious directives are sound are somehow generated. It is in some sort of ceremonial form— even if that form be hardly more than the recitation of a myth, the consultation of an oracle or the decoration of a grave—that the moods and motivations which sacred symbols induce in men and the general conceptions of the order of existence which they formulate for men meet and reinforce one another.

In this context, and although a believer cannot maintain himself consistently within this mood, his "religion," his religious system of ritual symbolism, "shapes" his vision and his relationship with others in the world. For this reason, one must look at each cultural expression of such religious symbolism within its own mythological origin and growth. Rather than providing a black-and-white approach, when describing such a process *in* a given culture, one must capture the varieties of perspectives and expressions that diverse groups of people manifest in themselves and in their relationship with others. We must quote Geertz (1975: 123) again:

> For an anthropologist, the importance of religion lies in its capacity to serve, for an individual or for a group, as a source of general, yet distinctive, conceptions of the world, the self, and the relations between them, on the one hand—its model "of" aspect—and of rooted, no less distinctive "mental" dispositions—its model "for" aspect—on the other. From these cultural functions flow, in turn, its social and psychological ones.

As Bastide (1971: 129) claims, religion has a tendency for being a living experience but not of being "alive," for it tends not to evolve. It tends to become anchored to the acting out of specific rituals that shape up the meaning of the group, although at times some innovations may take place.

The openness of religion to possible innovations, consequently, leaves its door open to syncretisms. Bastide (1971: 153–54) himself has analyzed the nature of syncretisms throughout his studies of Afro-Caribbean religious forms. For him, the blending of religions took place at different levels: syncretisms were more prominent among the Yorùbá and Bantus than the Dahomeyans; syncretisms become more pronounced away from rural areas and in the towns, where groups of blacks could function together in associations; syncretisms were more possible in what he terms "live" religions, in a process of adaptation, rather than in "preserved" religions, traditionally resistant to any innovations; and, lastly, syncretisms are more functional when parallels are established, as in the case of the Yorùbá òrìṣàs and the Catholic saints.[3]

Rather than spatial syncretisms, which remain on the plane of coexistence between disparate objects, the Yorùbá, for Bastide (1971: 156) brought about a syncretism between gods and saints to conceal their pagan ceremonies from European eyes and, in our opinion, to intensify a natural feeling that their ancestral mythology, their gods, had not abandoned them at this most critical stage of their life (as a group). In either case, the religion of the Yorùbá suffered this process of syncretism in space and time. Bastide (159) himself describes it:

> When we turn from the sphere of collective representation to that of ritual gesture, we find ourselves confronted with a heterogeneous mass of developments; the principal ones are outlined below. Moments in time, like objects in space, can form solid, clearly delimited points, unchanging in the nature of their syncretism. The Christian moment remains Christian, the African moment African; they come into juxtaposition solely as masses in space.

La Santería, as a magico-religious experience, appears before us as a religious syncretism rather than a natural religion. Although a few innovations have taken place in its nature, these have been the result of social changes undergone by slaves first, then their descendants, and lastly those who follow and have followed this religious syncretism and have brought it to the surface in South Florida.

As a syncretism, however, la Santería shares in the overall quest for meaning that moves beyond empirical reality and that may shape up the lives of its devotees when they are confronted with the problem of suffering and the problem of evil. It offers an avenue of commitment and a definite encounter with a "beyond-ness" not reachable by empirical evidence. It motivates people to act as their *santeros* prescribe that they should act, and to feel as their sessions inspire them to feel.

From these general considerations of the viability of religion and syncretism, as oriented by Geertz, Keyes, and Bastide, we may attempt to define or, better, describe la Santería *as the worship of African gods*

under the appearance of Catholic saints, a result of the transculturating
process of the Cuban people and the religious syncretism that resulted
from such a process. We turn our attention now to the relationship of la
Santería within the process of transculturation among Cubans in South
Florida.

La Santería and Cubans in South Florida

Our subsequent analysis will show the role of mythology and ritual symbolism within la Santería as one of the instruments of adaptation in the
transculturating process of Cubans in South Florida. It will consider the
model presented as the basis of Cuban integration into the mainstream of
American society and will capture the effect of this religious syncretism
vis-à-vis such a model. To facilitate such a process, let us recapture in
essence the nature of the model and the nature of the ethnographic data
on la Santería.

Cubans in South Florida have attempted to re-create the traditional
worldview that shaped their lives in history when confronted with rapid
social changes. Politically motivated to leave their land, Cubans have
reacted to a general attitude of assimilation, usually presented by a larger
and dominant cultural group, by integrating into that cultural group
without losing their roots, namely, by looking for a sense of identity
and renovating those institutions that provide basic, primordial ties of
a "relational" quality among the members of the group. Motivated, like
most cultural groups that face a larger, dominant group, by the need
to succeed economically and politically, Cubans seemed to have succeeded economically in South Florida despite the basic strains that they
felt at the beginning of their exile and that they continue to experience
at various levels: the strain to subsist economically as they themselves
perceive they should; the strain to overcome a disorder in their basic relationships to society, within their own families and as people in search
of prestige inside and outside of their own collectivity; and, the strain
brought about by a loss of a mythological worldview that shaped their
way of seeing reality in the past.

La Santería seems to provide, for some, a determinant ingredient
that intensifies relationships and lends itself to integrate the disintegrating worldview of Cubans. It seems to offer an avenue of economic

success and social prestige; but, above all, it represents a transitional, marginal stage that provides a sense of liberation in the midst of structural "oppression."

To remind us of the breakdown of la Santería, offered in previous reflections, let us present such a composite picture of elements in an outline form:

A. Mythology: collective representations proclaimed through a consistent oral tradition: *mayorales* and *tatas*
   1. Sacred place: *El Monte* (The Wilderness)
   2. Òrìṣàs: identification with ancestral world
      a) Olódùmarè: God Creator and a distant god, although for Nigerians even today, Olódùmarè is the one who grants favors from those who use the òrìṣàs as intercessors
      b) Òrìṣàs: intervening gods that must be appeased
      c) Reciprocal participation between gods and devotees
   3. Priesthood: *babalaos* and *santeros*
      a) Reiteration and continuation of oral tradition
      b) Establishment of personal contact and a relational encounter that provides a sense of security and ultimate power
      c) Facilitators of a longed-for encounter with the divinities themselves through ritual activity
B. Ritual activity and sacred symbolism
   1. Consultation process: cowry shells and/or palm nuts.
      a) *Despojos*
      b) *Rogación de cabeza*
      c) *Ebós* or animal sacrifices and food offerings
   2. Imposition of necklaces (*collares de fundamento*)
   3. Rite of initiation: separation, liminality, and incorporation
   4. Post-initiatory rites
      a) Handing on of the *bàtá* drums
      b) The three-month *ebó*
      c) Other taboos and norms that forbid contamination for the year of novitiate

In light of this information, we shall now proceed to view it within the general model of integration—the preferred model, by the way, for the Catholic Church in the United States. This model, we must remember, became a composite of three principal elements that appeared as guiding, though basic, principles: cultural diversity or differentiation as opposed to uniformity, selectivity as opposed to determinism, and liminality as opposed to social structure (as used by Turner). These three principles may provide the framework for a healthy process of integration in what are known today as "multicultural" communities.

La Santería and Diversity

One must note that cultural differentiation, or cultural diversity, has provided in the past a sense of history for cultural groups and has not necessarily led to conflict (Greeley 1971). In fact, in keeping with the dialectical style of Lévi-Strauss (1967), diversity within a cultural group and between different groups became a healthy quality; it provided for a healthy type of dynamism within social structures. In other words, the diversity of norms and standards (Glazer and Moynihan 1963) that cultural groups have brought to bear on society have become a way of dealing oneself into society (Greeley 1971) rather than a way of alienating oneself from it. From this perspective, Cubans in South Florida have made themselves different while integrating into the more dominant group that welcomed them into this land.

La Santería, within this concept of differentiation or diversity, has accentuated the need for diversity itself. La Santería has brought to the surface, through myth and ritual, a different folklore, a different style of music and dancing, a different kind of rhythm that, though predominantly African in origin, conveys the worldview of three different cultures.

Second, la Santería provides for its believers a sense of unity in the midst of such diversity, for it helps them identify the source of their power in the ancestral mythology, which has been preserved down through the centuries. Yorùbá mythology has found its place in the oral tradition of the Cuban people, first through the *mayorales* and *tatas* who, perhaps for different reasons, maintained the traditions of the Yorùbá religion.[4] It re-creates a sense of the wilderness in an urban, industrial setting as South Florida and begins to facilitate an "encounter" with the "beyond-ness" provided by the multiple divinities of the Yorùbá pantheon.

Third, at this mythological dimension as well, la Santería, by its existence, reminds Cubans in South Florida about the social adaptation of nineteenth-century slaves under an oppressive, though fairly tolerant, social structure. This mythological function continues to appear through the repeated intervention of *babalaos* and *santeros* in the decision-making process of their devotees. The overwhelming activity of these Santería priests involves the believers of the religion in the manipulation of two modern-day symbols: economics and social prestige. Believers can risk borrowing money from others in order to acquire the prestige that la Santería seems to offer to them in the midst of their crisis. Bastide (1971: 123) points to this process among the blacks of the Antilles: "Such people find much that they need in these sects the first place, an atmosphere of security, a protection against life's hazards, and also a chance to better themselves, in so far as they can mount from rank to rank in the priestly hierarchy. Finally, they enjoy a prestige status that they could never hope to attain in society at large."

I believe that this process continues to exist among South Florida Cubans attracted to la Santería for it facilitates for them an experience of death and resurrection, leaving old things behind and experiencing new life without a complete loss of heritage. In this fashion, la Santería shares in one of the most ancient and better-known mythological themes through its ritual activity.

From a strictly mythological perspective, then, la Santería shares in the quest for universal symbols that other primitive mythologies have manifested down through the centuries, as Joseph Campbell (1959: 61) claims. Whereas in the Yorùbá stage, previous to slavery in the New World, it served as a means to cross the widely recognized thresholds that face human beings from early infancy to death, in Cuba it served to bridge the social gap brought about by an unwilling condition of slavery, and in the United States it seems to aid in the crossing of a new threshold, especially that of social adaptability to a new situation.

From conversations with recent arrivals from Cuba through the Mariel exodus of 1980 and the *balsero* phenomenon (fleeing the island in rafts) of 1994 and beyond, we venture to speculate that la Santería has grown in Cuba in the same manner but as a way of resisting the new social order present on the island. Such possibility has appeared in the literature before, in the words of Campbell (1959: 130): "The elementary idea (*Elementargedanke*) is never itself directly figured in mythology, but always rendered by way of local ethnic ideas or forms (*Volkengedanke*), and these, as we now perceive, are locally conditioned and may reflect attitudes either of resistance or of assimilation."

In this context, while la Santería shares decisive elements of traditional mythology, as captured by Campbell (1959: 231)—creator god, intermediary divinities, objectification of symbols as sacred realities, preservation of rites of passage, maintenance of a priesthood which characterizes planting societies as distinct from hunting societies—the religious worldview of the Yorùbá-*lucumí* believers is open to creative forms of social adaptability to the degree that it is used to aid the believers to adjust to the social world around them. And from this analysis, as Campbell (1968: 4) claims once again, it may have the strength to become a creative mythology:

> In the context of traditional mythology, the symbols are presented in socially maintained rites, through which the individual is required to experience, or will pretend to have experienced, certain insights, sentiments, and commitments. In what I am calling "creative" mythology, on the other hand, this order is reversed: the individual has had an experience of his own, or order, horror, beauty, or even mere exhilaration, which he seeks to communicate through signs; and if his realization has been of a certain depth and import, his communication will have the value and office of living myth.

For Cubans both outside of the island and inside their country, la Santería has become a creative tool to overcome and manipulate an experience of terror and alienation brought about by the social order beginning with the triumph of the Revolution of 1959 and continued by the need for social adaptation as a result of the exile.

Particularly for Cubans in exile, la Santería may facilitate an experience of a transcendent reality and not just a narration of a transcendent presence. From the perspective of the 1960s, when Santería grew so rapidly among Cubans throughout the United States, a universal phenomenon seemed to have been in process: a resurgence of religion as a way of bridging the gap between industrial civilization and ultimate mystery. As the United States witnessed an explosion of "cults," Asian religions (i.e., Hare Krishna), and devil worshippers, la Santería found its place in this socioreligious revolutionary process that has not ceased, for it continues to be the source of reflection and speculation among philosophers, social scientists, and theologians alike.

As these movements have made a difference in American culture for the last two decades, la Santería has contributed with its diverse origins and developments to the multicultural setting of this country. La Santería has become a way of preserving cultural and historical identity with the past, and a way of transmitting such identity to younger generations, whose innate releasing mechanisms, as Campbell (1959: 44) writes, are open and subject to imprint in a more obvious way. Such was the strength of its growth in the 1970s, a growth manifested by the invention of *botánicas,* herb shops that sell a blend of religious articles and that are sponsored by active *santeros.* It was at this time that the hierarchy of the Catholic Church began to explore the growing phenomenon of la Santería as a syncretized religious form that jeopardized social adaptation of Cubans outside of Cuba by means of a church-related process.

The need to blend the historical and nonhistorical aspects of mythology and religion becomes apparent in the analysis of la Santería as a growing phenomenon in a new social order for the Cuban community. Local newspapers and television newscasts in Miami usually have researched the topic in search of sensationalism rather than objectivity. Although Santería did not assume the institutional role of organized religion until recently (i.e., the Church of Babalú-Ayé in Hialeah, Florida), its impact continues to be felt as people visit *santeros/santeras* for a few times only, or eventually choose, out of fear or personal crisis, to become a full-fledged member of the Yorùbá-*lucumí* religion. Joseph Campbell (1959: 263) once again can help us synthesize this process:

> In the religious lives of the "tough minded," too busy, or simply untalented majority of humankind, the historical factor preponderates. The whole reach of their experience is in the local, public domain and can be historically studied. In the spiritual crises and realizations of the "tender minded" personalities with mystical proclivities, however, it is the non-historical factor that preponderates, and for them the imagery of the local tradition—no matter how highly developed it may be—is merely a vehicle, more or less adequate, to render an experience sprung from beyond its reach, as an immediate impact.

La Santería and Selectivity

We had established that when cultural groups come in contact with each other, the less dominant group will tend to select those cultural traits from the more dominant one that do not clash with pre-existent traits or that have something in common with pre-existent traits (Herskovits 1958). In this context, changes in organization and in material culture— accidental changes—are made more readily than changes in personal habits and emotional attitudes—more substantial and personal, changes. Moreover, selectivity, as a guiding principle, provided these cultural groups with two dimensions: the dimension of economic or political interests and the dimension of affectivity.

If the mythology of la Santería is best appreciated as enhancing the "different" nature of Cubans in South Florida, its ritual activity will accentuate and enhance the "selective" dimension of this process of transculturation.

By re-creating a traditional worldview, which includes a distant god and intermediary gods who participate in the lives of its believers through ritual action, this religious syncretism has engaged itself in a selective process by which its basic traits have remained intact in a new social setting. Other ingredients have been modified, whereas drumming is an essential ingredient of Santería gatherings; drumming has been curtailed in South Florida for fear of negative public repercussions. Whereas initiation in the past included two weeks of separation from the community, the adjustment to one week has become necessary in highly urban, industrial centers, from which people cannot depart for a long period unless they are on vacation. Whereas money, as Lydia Cabrera (1974: 133–34) claims, represented an "instrumental" symbol in Cuba, in South Florida it has become a "dominant" symbol (i.e., initiation ceremonies in Cuba were priced at between $200 and $300—rather than the $5,000 or $7,000 mentioned before).

The selectivity in the adjustment of these traits, however, appeared in a negative manner by way of resistance on two different occasions. First, *santeros* of Miami vehemently opposed the suggestion made by a Cuban *santero* who visited Nigeria and who returned to South Florida advocating the need to disrobe all Catholic symbolism from Santería and the need to erect a Lucumí Church in the outskirts of Dade County with original African languages, rituals, and artists' representations. Second, *santeros* of Miami caused a great uproar in 1980 when a Nigerian *babalao,* while visiting Miami's priests, suggested that in Miami—as in Nigeria—women should be admitted to take part in the high priesthood of the religion.

Despite these adjustments in material organization and the resistance to change inherent, traditional elements of the "religion," la Santería facilitates in the rites a means of community definition. It allows for economic independence and the acquisition of prestige within its own collectivity, through which a neophyte, though submissive to his or her *santero/santera* at all times, becomes a senior in the religion in relationship to other neophytes who are initiated after him, no matter his role in society or his status within the family. (That is, if the child is initiated before his parents, he is a senior to his parents in the religion; the same hierarchy is maintained if the wife is initiated before the husband. Such a change demands a definite adjustment in family relationships for the members of a given family.) Only at the liminal stage, as noted below, are believers stripped of all status and exposed to an encounter with the core of the religious system that la Santería portrays.

This selective dimension of the process of integration, as Cubans have opted to live in South Florida, appears in la Santería, consequently, with that affective dimension that Patterson (1975), Bell (1975), and Greeley (1974) had pinpointed before. Through the consultation process and up to the initiation rite and the post-initiatory rites, la Santería re-creates that relational quality of affective ties that traditional societies preserve but that is lost in more departmentalized and disintegrated urban centers.

The consultation process provides the familial ties and the basis of a kinship relationship, which Cubans seem to lose in their process of initial adaptation to a new society. While the extended family of Cubans seems to disappear slowly as the years of the process of transculturation pass, the *santero*-client relationship provides the believer with immediate and personal attention. Besides the primordial worldview enacted by the mythology, the consultation process allows the believer to turn to someone else who can help him in the midst of social stress.

The pre-initiation rites, or the reception of the *collares de fundamento,* prepare the believer for his ultimate goal, complete communion with the divinities—without whom he cannot subsist in this new social setting. The initiation process, complex as it may appear, facilitates for him a sense of belonging to a functional mythology and to an ongoing group of people who gather occasionally for support. More than this sense of belonging to a group, the initiation rite provides the believer, as mentioned before, with prestige and subsequent seniority; in a world characterized by inequality, having undergone a radical social change that lowered him in the social scale, the rite of initiation raises the believer to a higher level of respect, perhaps not experienced since he left Cuba, where his social position was considered to be higher than in South Florida. This opportunity for seniority within his own collectivity is coupled with the opportunity to manipulate and bargain with the divinities themselves who are now familiar characters among his kinship relationships.

The prestige acquired by initiation into la Santería is worth all the post-initiation sacrifices and the maintenance of norms and disciplines that follow the neophyte for a whole year. As negative or positive sanctions, which call for punishment or reward, these norms intensify the mythology behind la Santería and must be seen within the various ritual *ebós* that, after initiation, the new member of Santería must make. As these sacrifices are made, more power becomes available to the neophyte through the acceptance of the *bàtá* (drums), the sacred stones (*otán iye-biyé*) and the preservation of these sacred symbols in a special room set apart at his home for the òrìṣàs, as Cabrera (1974: 131) specifies.

Intimacy with these divinities provides a sense of security as a means of continued manipulation for favors needed; it likewise instills great fear if norms and taboos are broken or accidentally modified. Although happiness and solutions to immediate crises characterize the reward aspect of these sanctions, the loss of *aché* (power) and the anger of the gods characterize the breaking of these rules. For la Santería, the òrìṣàs must always be kept happy, or they will turn against the believer. Underlying all these nuances of the year of novitiate, following initiation, requires that each neophyte be dressed completely in white for the duration of his novitiate; the use of such color reiterates for him in a selective manner the mythological theme of death and resurrection and offers him a constant reminder of his new beginnings. Through ritual activity, even if this includes a sense of awesome fear toward the divinities, Santería believers pursue a basic ethnic identity, which they mean to transmit to future generations as original as it has been preserved down through the centuries.

La Santería and Liminality

If, in general, the overall mythological worldview of la Santería facilitates a source of reference for cultural diversity, and if its ritual symbolic system provides a means of becoming selective and of preserving such a traditional worldview without drastic innovations, it is within the rites themselves, particularly at their liminal stage, that believers of la Santería begin to experience a sense of *communitas* as a reaction to an oppressed structural setting.

We have noted how mythology has offered a series of themes that are repeated in history and that seem to appear in the collective unconsciousness of all cultural groups (creation and destruction, death and resurrection, leaving the old aside and putting on a new self). Moreover, we have noted likewise that rites of passage facilitate the re-enactment of these themes in a dynamic process by which the individual, assisted by his cultural group, can assume a new responsibility in his own collectivity and in his relationship with others. From its minor rite of consultation to its major rite of initiation, la Santería seems to provide for believers a space and a time apart from everyday existence and in touch with a transcendental experience of reality.

Separated from his cultural milieu—in many occasions a difficult task due to the rapid growth of urban developments within and outside of Miami-Dade County—informed of his new role by members of the group (*santeros* and *santeras* present), and, eventually, incorporated into it through a final ritual, the neophyte appears to them at last as an almost new "creation." He has passed a threshold to enjoy the happiness of a new existence.

The very crossing of these thresholds, captured vividly by the universal literature of indigenous mythologies, provides a dialectical process: at every critical stage, at each life crisis, the human person becomes conscious that he must move beyond into a new stage in life; his first inclination is to resist such a journey, and, symbolically, he wishes to move back ("into his mother's womb") to that which has made him comfortable so far; incapable of regressing, however, he experiences the anguish of moving forward into a new situation; he "crosses the given threshold" soon to experience the joys of a new lifestyle and the group's acceptance of his new self.

In essence, rites of passage serve as aids in the crossing of the thresholds that human beings anticipate before, during, and at their life crises. In these various rites, religious symbolism usually predominates as the objectified intermediary between a transcendent reality and the culturally dynamic process undergone by both the individual and the group. Usually at this stage, symbols cease being representations of reality and, for the most part, become reality itself for those who participate in such a mythological worldview—a reality that has been set apart as sacred and untouchable.

La Santería provides an opportunity for symbolic participation through which its sacred symbols (stones, soup bowls [*soperas*], necklaces, and drums) cease being representations of the òrìṣàs; they become the òrìṣàs. At this stage of identification with symbols, the believers feel that they are in the company of the divinities and experience support while, simultaneously, prescribing themselves to norms and regulations necessary to keep the divinities in a state of gratification and not of anger. This process takes place as a liminal state in the believer not only within a given rite but also as an available, consistent condition to which he turns when in crisis.

Consequently, the dominant and instrumental symbolism provided by la Santería may confuse the objective researcher if he is to look for a clear distinction as the one provided by Turner's (1967) model. In terms of the syncretism as such, the three most "dominant" symbols of Cuban Santería are Our Lady of Charity (goddess Ochún), St. Barbara (warrior-god Changó), and St. Lazarus (identified with the fictional character of Luke's gospel and seen as Babalú-Ayé). Although the first symbol permeates throughout the entire Cuban nation, the latter two seem to prevail mostly in the eastern provinces of the island.

The dominant aspect of these symbols, nonetheless, becomes more evident through the vast crowds that attend the celebration of the days assigned by the Catholic Church to these characters of Catholic tradition. Such dominance likewise becomes apparent in the small altars raised by Cuban families outside or inside their homes as a sign of gratitude for favors granted or favors requested. However, dominant symbolism for Santería believers appears in the objectified representation of the sacred, through stones and necklaces, as mentioned above, that in other religious systems would be classified as instrumental symbols.

At this instrumental level, moreover, the use of herbs, and the distribution of prayers from la Santería, the selling of "potions" required for specific purposes and other syncretized symbolic representations continue to emerge in the lives of those whose dominant symbols employ the more attractive Catholic images and statues. Operationally, these symbolic representations are human-made but become pregnant with divine presence through the prayers of the *santeros* as well as through the non-objectified intervention of transcendent reality.

Although not all those involved in Santería reach the depth of involvement that full-fledged members reach in the various rites of this religious form, symbolic representations appear basically at work as mechanisms of support and protection from evil. In the words of Campbell (1959: 240): "The highest concern of all the mythologies, ceremonials, ethical systems, and social organizations of the agriculturally based societies has been that of suppressing the manifestations of individualism; and this has been generally achieved by compelling or persuading people to identify themselves not with their own interests, intuitions, or modes of experience, but with the archetypes of behavior and systems of sentiment developed and maintained in the public domain."

As a reaction to the prevalent individualism that characterizes the American style of life, the rites of la Santería provide a means of communitarian activity, which, although temporary, seems to help the individual involved overcome his sense of alienation and gives him a sense of belonging to an ethnic group that finds itself in a process of adaptation outside of its own sociocultural milieu.

La Santería, then, participates in the transculturation of Cubans in South Florida as a liminal stage, a mechanism of adaptation. At this stage, when symbols become more necessary, la Santería facilitates believers with a rhythmical pattern: (1) it allows them to begin to experience "spontaneous *communitas*" as a reaction to bureaucracy; (2) it divests them of attributes while holding them obedient to the authority figure, the *santero,* and on equal basis to the other members undergoing the process with them; and (3) there is an ongoing communication of *sacra,* sacred words and sacred knowledge that will keep the tradition alive.

Away from the critical situation, which has led him to the *santero* priest, the believer hopes to find meaning in the relational qualities that la Santería promises to facilitate for him. We would like to assume that what happens to an individual believer as he moves through a critical stage in his life and is supported by Santería mythology and rituals has happened to groups of believers—many Cubans of South Florida—who at various stages of their life turn to la Santería for an experience of liberation in the form of *communitas.* Whether they actually find such liberation and such *communitas,* as proposed by Turner (1969), is another issue.

Divested of all attributes, in such an individualistic society as the United States appears to be, the believer becomes one with others undergoing stages of *lucumí* initiation. Doctors, lawyers, factory workers, or university students come together in "sacred poverty" before the *santeros* to experience an elevation of status that is based on power and the manipulation of sacred divinities. Incapable of overcoming inequality in the current social structure, these believers can overcome it as they move to anti-structure and experience a transitional form of friendship, as Keyes (1979: 93) would propose: "Friendship based on the good not only resists value destruction, but it is also a source of happiness which makes base action and misery less likely than they would be without it, for once we have experienced the good it also leaves its mark." Whether such relational qualities perdure among Santería believers is another question; the fact remains, for transitional encounters with this religious system, these qualities may surface on the initial contacts and become the goal of many believers.

What is most consistent in this liminal process of la Santería—again, not only within a given rite, but also as a mechanism of social adaptation—is the communication of its *sacra*. After the year of novitiate, the believer may wish to continue to learn from his *santero/santera* more secrets of la Ocha: more detailed knowledge of the language as used in the rites, how to interpret the oracles, how to prepare *ebós,* or when they should be used, and so forth. The process is long, but it is worth the effort. In the economic scale, we reiterate, *santeros* and *santeras* have assumed a nonprofit position by expecting cash for their services, especially those that concern the rite of initiation, the most expensive of all. Outside of the economic perspective, the communication of Yorùbá *sacra* creates a certain mood that elicits a definite commitment from its believers, although fear of punishment appears consistently as a motivating factor for such a commitment.

As a good liminal model, the rite of initiation presents a perfect setting for the communication of *sacra*. In the process of one week, the believer is presented with intimate truths about his tradition, sometimes in a disproportionate, dramatic, and mysterious manner: from the tedious consultation of the oracles, in Lydia Cabrera's (1974: 179) terminology, the Itá, to being in touch with the blood of the animals sacrificed and being bathed at a special time, while witnessing shortly afterward the killing of animals in sacrifice. Ritual exhaustion usually accompanies such a traumatic week. Yet, the function of communication of *sacra* at the liminal stage has been carried out, as Turner (1967: 105) claims:

> From this standpoint, much of the grotesqueness and monstrosity of *liminal sacra* may be seen to be aimed not so much at terrorizing or bemusing neophytes into submission or out of their wits as at making them vividly and rapidly aware of what may be called the "factors" of their culture. . . . The communication of sacra and other forms of esoteric instruction involves three processes. . . . The first is the reduction of culture into recognized components or factors; the second is their recombination in fantastic or monstrous patterns and shapes; and the third is their recombination in ways that make sense with regard to the new state and status that the neophytes will enter.

Lastly, it may be argued that rather than liminal, la Santería presents a "marginal" quality, as previously distinguished by Turner (1974: 233). Although the marginal quality includes participation in two or more groups with different cultural norms or religious expressions, in la Santería such a distinction is not seen. Reality is syncretized, and the loss of temporary status, for instance, ultimately leads to the elevation of status within a new vision of reality. The economic sacrifices that many Cubans make to join the ranks of Santería neophytes bear witness to the integrating dimension of Santería mythology and rituals; rather than hoping for economic and political success in the American scene, while holding on to the traditionally Cuban style of life, these believers—in an apparent social dichotomy—find integration and unity in the religious form that la Santería provides for them. In la Santería they make an existential choice, conditioned by an ancestral mythology, which is filled with ritual symbolism that shapes up their present and, so they hope, their future as well.

Conclusions

We have established that as cultural groups come in contact with each other a dialectical process seems to emerge: choices of assimilation, "ghettoism," or integration become not only feasible but possible. As integration became the choice of Cubans who attempt to maintain their heritage in the midst of social change, we can view la Santería as one of the several functional mechanisms that re-creates the needed traditional worldview that prevents them from being lost in an anonymous social setting, the result of a highly bureaucratic industrial society. In this context, moreover, la Santería provides the necessary primordial ties that can aid individuals in given situations to define themselves as part of a group in a process of adaptation. In the midst of a disoriented social setting, la Santería becomes a guiding social mechanism that emphasizes past heritages and historical roots, allowing for some form of identity to take place.

Second, we have established that as cultural groups come in contact with each other, the diversity established by their unequal social, political, and economic norms may not necessarily lead the less dominant group into alienation or isolation; rather, it may become a way of coping with reality that may contribute, by its richness, to the total social picture at hand.

Since Cubans in South Florida have become a strongly economic cultural group with a dominant culture that aspires to political dominance, la Santería may serve them as a means of manipulating the economic life of its members and a possible avenue for prestige within its own collectivity, since it is virtually impossible in most cases to acquire such prestige outside of it. Similarly, la Santería may provide a means of definition in the attempt that Cubans make to "integrate" into American society without losing their own rich traditions. La Santería may become a way of asserting ethnic values and assisting Cubans in establishing themselves with institutions that provide primordial ties for relating effectively among themselves and with the rest of their social setting.

Third, we have established that as cultural groups encounter each other, the process of culture borrowing is selective. In fact, cultural traits are exchanged to the degree that they have something in common with, and do not cause conflict with, the pre-existing culture. Likewise, through this process of transculturation, changes in social organization and in material culture are made more readily than changes in personal habits and in emotional attitudes. From this perspective, and as a result of this principle of selectivity, a resistance to change the very core of this religious worldview has been made known publicly in special circumstances.

Although symbols and rites have changed gradually over the centuries, the essence of the rite is maintained and preserved for future generations. As a selective instrument, however, la Santería seems to bring answers to disintegrated institutions that have suffered changes through the process of transculturation; by reiterating a traditional worldview and selecting the best of its roots, la Santería wants to bring to families, civic gatherings, and even Church believers a sense of the sacred and an experience of mystery that has been lost in our present society.

Fourth, from the model offered by Victor Turner, we established that as cultural groups come in contact with each other, they may develop—as a group—a series of mechanisms of adaptation that may assist them in overcoming alienation and crisis. Deprived of primordial ties, they react to an oppressive structure and seek to form a *communitas*. This anti-structural dynamism may result in stages of adaptation referred to as liminal by Turner. Not only does la Santería provide for liminal stages in the life crises of individuals, whose cultural group undergoes drastic social changes, but it also becomes in itself a liminal stage in the social adaptation of Cubans in South Florida. Through a growing emphasis on ritual activity and the sacredness of Santería symbolic representations, Cubans resist assimilation into a foreign cultural milieu, re-enact basic, primordial ties with their roots, and relate personally to representations of transcendent reality "who" intercede for them in times of stress, and who will continue to assist them "if" they treat these representations accordingly by observing all the prescribed rituals and by keeping the expected norms.

As a liminal stage in social adaptation, la Santería fits likewise in the bicultural model presented by Szapocznik and Kurtines (1980: 144) that determines that the acculturation process tends to take place along two independent dimensions: "This acculturation/bicultural model further suggests that the most important variable influencing the individual's accommodation to the host culture is the amount of time a person has been exposed to the host culture, while the most important variable influencing the individual's retention of the characteristics of the culture of origin is the degree and availability of community support for the culture of origin."

Through devotees and *santeros* alike, la Santería seems to provide the occasional community support that individuals who become highly disoriented in a bicultural setting need for their own development in such a setting.

From the general considerations provided by the literature on indigenous and creative mythologies as well as the models on rites of passage, from the ethnographic data provided by past and present-day observances of Santería mythology and rituals, and from the analysis of such data in light of the anthropological criteria established earlier in this essay, we may conclude that la Santería is a magico-religious experience that seems to provide an integrated worldview wherein processes of differentiation and selectivity are at work. In essence, la Santería represents a liminal stage in the cultural adaptation of Cubans to a new social setting. As the worship of African gods as Catholic saints, la Santería fits in the current religious revival across the world and provides, likewise, an opportunity for the establishment of primordial ties and kinship relationships that can assist people at critical stages of their life. As a religious form, it continues to be a unifying factor that helps believers transcend alienation and suffering. In brief, by creating a mood that motivates believers to act in a certain fashion, it becomes a way of looking at reality.

Notes

1. This article, including this definition of la Santería, is mostly taken from chapter 3 of "La Santería: A Way of Looking at Reality," a thesis submitted in 1981 to the Faculty of the College of Social Science at Florida Atlantic University.

2. I visited Yorùbáland in 1997 and met with Catholic bishops, priests, and laity who consistently preach the Gospel to their own people, as well as with those who believe in the religion of their ancestors. I learned many things, four of which have been particularly interesting or enriched me personally and as a researcher. (1) In southwestern Nigeria, among the Yorùbá, traditional religion is not polytheistic. The òrìṣàs function as "messengers" of Olordumare [Olódùmarè], the God-Creator of all. (Victoria, the priestess of the temple of Ochún in Osogbo, consistently repeated this to me in our conversations.) (2) Among the Yorùbá, even those who have embraced Catholicism, the symbiosis or syncretism of Santería is not only absent but is unthinkable; this process is, indeed, a phenomenon of the Americas. (3) Among the Yorùbá, the concept of slavery is clear: although the *conquistadores* may have purchased African people to be sold as slaves, Yorùbá leaders also sold their own people, probably from the lower classes of the society of the times, to acquire more profitable goods. (4) Among the Yorùbá, prayer is significant and important, as displayed by the blind elderly priestess of Ochún who rested at the temple, to whom I was introduced as a Catholic priest; she immediately offered to pray over me and had me pray over her. At that moment, not only did I feel "ecumenical" but also "blessed."

3. Following is a list of òrìṣàs and their corresponding Catholic saints:

Agayu—St. Christopher
Aguema—St. Philomena
Baba—Our Lady of Mercy as a male instead of a female
Babalu-aye—Lazarus (the unforgettable character of Luke's gospel)
Los Bellis—the Twins, St. Cosmas and Damian
Chango—St. Barbara
Dada—Our Lady of the Rosary
Elefuro—St. Ann
Eleggua—Souls in Purgatory, St. Anthony, or *El Niño de Atocha*
Ellecosun—St. Lucy
Eshu—St. Michael the Archangel or the Devil
Igui—St. Christopher and in some places St. Luke
Iroco—The Immaculate Conception
Nana Burucu—Our Lady of Mount Carmel
Oba—*La Candelaria* in Havana and St. Catherine in the country
Obamoro—Jesus of Nazarene

Obatala—Our Lady of Mercy
Ochosi—St. Norbert
Ochun—Our Lady of Charity
Oggun—St. Peter and also St. John
Oke—St. John
Olordumare—God the Father
Olosi—The Devil
Ordua—San Manuel (St. Emmanuel)
Orguidai—St. Bartholomew
Orichaco—St. Isidore
Oya—St. Theresa or the popular advocation of Mary as *la Candelaria*
Ozacrinan—St. Joseph
Ozain—St. Raphael Ynle in Havana and St. Ambrose in the country
Ozun—St. John the Baptist
Unle—St. Julian
Yanza—St. Theresa and at times St. Beatrice
Yegua—St. Claire
Yemaya—Our Lady of *Regla.*

4. *Mayorales* were overseers of the work of the slaves on the plantation; they served as a liaison between the slaves and their masters and made sure the work was done. *Tatas* were the black nannies who took care of, and many times raised, the children of the slave owners. In most cases, they put the children to sleep with stories about the Yorùbá òrìṣàs. Both *mayorales* and *tatas* functioned as institutions in the transmission of Yorùbá beliefs to those whom they served.

References

Alzaga, Florinda. 1976. *Raíces del alma cubana.* Miami: Ediciones Universal.

Bach, Robert L. 1980a. "The New Cuban Immigrants Their Background and Prospects." *Monthly Labor Review* 103: 9–46.

———. 1980b. "Pre-Mariel Cuban Refugees and the Mariel Groups: A Comparative Review." Paper presented at the Conference on International Migration and Refugees the Caribbean and South Florida, Florida International University, Miami.

Bach Robert L., Jennifer B. Bach, and Timothy Triplett. 1980. *The Flotilla Entrants: Latest and Most Controversial.* Albany: State University of New York Press.

Bascom, William. 1969. *The Yorùbá of Southwestern Nigeria.* New York: Holt, Rinehart and Winston.

Bastide, Roger. 1971. *African Civilizations in the New World.* New York: Harper and Row.

Bell, Daniel. 1975. "Ethnicity and Social Change." In *Ethnicity, Theory and Experience,* ed. Nathan Glazer and Daniel F. Moynihan, 141–74. Cambridge, MA: Harvard University Press.

Berger, Peter. 1969. *A Rumor of Angels.* New York: Doubleday.

Berger, Peter L., and Thomas Luckmann. 1966. *The Social Construction of Reality: A Treatise in the Sociology of Knowledge.* New York: Doubleday,

Berry, John W. 1980. "Acculturation as Varieties of Adaptation." In *Acculturation: Theory, Models and Some New Findings,* ed. Amado M. Padilla, 9–25. Boulder, CO: Westview Press.

Brandon, George. 1993. *Santeria from Africa to the New World: The Dead Sell Memories.* Bloomington: Indiana University Press.

Cabrera, Lydia. 1970a. *Anagó: Vocabulario lucumí.* Miami: Colección del Chicherekú.

———. 1970b. *Otán Iyebiyé: Las piedras preciosas.* Miami: Colección del Chicherekú.

———. 1970c. *La sociedad secreta Abakuá.* Miami: Colección del Chicherekú.

———. 1971. *Ayapa's cuentos de jicotea.* Miami: Ediciones Universal.

———. 1974. *Yemayá y Ochún: Kariocha, iyalorichas y olorichas.* Madrid: Colección del Chicherekú.

Campbell, Joseph. 1959. *The Masks of God: Primitive Mythology.* New York: Penguin Books.

———. 1968. *The Masks of God: Creative Mythology.* New York: The Viking Press.

Clark, Juan. 1977. *Why? The Cuban Exodus: Background, Evolution and Impact in the U.S.A.* Miami: Union of Cubans in Exile.

Davidson, Basil. 1964. *The African Past.* Boston: Little, Brown.

Eliade, Mircea. 1957. *The Sacred and the Profane: The Meaning of Religion.* New York: Harper and Row.

———. 1958. *Patterns in Comparative Religion.* New York: Sheed and Ward.

Garcia Cortéz, Julio. 1971. *El santo: Secretos de la religión lucumí.* Miami: Editorial Universal.

Geertz, Clifford. 1975. *The Interpretation of Cultures.* New York: Basic Books.

Glazer, Nathan, and Daniel P. Moynihan. 1963. *Beyond the Melting Pot.* Cambridge, MA: MIT Press and Harvard University Press.

———, eds. 1975. *Ethnicity, Theory and Experience.* Cambridge, MA: Harvard University Press.

Gordon, Milton. 1975. "Toward a General Theory of Racial and Ethnic Group Relations." In *Ethnicity, Theory and Experience,* ed. Nathan Glazer and Daniel P. Moynihan, 84–110. Cambridge, MA: Harvard University Press.

Greeley, Andrew M. 1971. *Why Can't They Be Like Us?* New York: E. P. Dutton.

———. 1974. *Ethnicity in the United States.* New York: John Wiley and Sons.

Greeley, Andrew M., and Gregory Baum, eds. 1977. *Ethnicity.* New York: Seabury Press.

Greene, Juanita. 1971. "Cubans in Dade: 1 in 4 by 1975." *Miami Herald,* June 18.

Hanke, Lewis. 1951. *Bartolomé de las Casas: An Interpretation of His Life and Writings.* The Hague: Martinus Nijhoff.

Herskovits, Melville J. 1958. *Acculturation: The Study of Culture Contact.* Gloucester, MA: Peter Smith.

———. 1967. *Man and His Works.* New York: Alfred A. Knopf.

Horowitz, Donald L. 1975. "Ethnic Identity." In *Ethnicity, Theory and Experience,* ed. Nathan Glazer and Daniel P. Moynihan, 111–40 Cambridge, MA: Harvard University Press.

Ìdòwú, E. Bolaji. 1962. *Olódùmarè: God in Yorùbá Belief.* London: Longman.

Jahn, J. 1970. *Muntu: Las culturas de la Negritud.* Madrid: Ediciones Guadarrama.

Keyes, C. D. 1979. *Four Types of Value Destruction: A Search for the Good through an Ethical Analysis of Everyday Experience.* Washington, DC: University Press of America.

Kitagawa, Joseph M., and Charles H. Long, eds. 1969. *Myths and Symbols: Studies in Honor of Mircea Eliade.* Chicago: University of Chicago Press.

Klein, Herbert S. 1967. *Slavery in the Americas: A Comparative Study of Virginia and Cuba.* Chicago: University of Chicago Press.

Knight. Franklin W. 1970. *Slave Society in Cuba during the Nineteenth Century.* Madison: University of Wisconsin Press.

Leiseca, Juan J. 1926. *Historia de Cuba.* Havana: Montalvo, Cardenas.

Lévi-Strauss, Claude. 1963. *Structural Anthropology.* New York: Basic Books.

———. 1976. *Structural Anthropology.* Vol. 2. New York: Basic Books.

Linton, Ralph. 1963. *Acculturation in Seven American Indian Tribes.* Gloucester, MA: Peter Smith.

MacGaffey, Wyatt, and Clifford R. Barnett. 1962. *Twentieth Century Cuba.* New York: Anchor Books.

Malinowski, Bronislaw. 1948. *Magic, Science, and Religion.* New York: Doubleday.

Martínez, Rafael. 1979. "Afro-Cuban Santería among the Cuban-Americans in Dade County, Florida: A Psycho-Cultural Approach." M.A. thesis, University of Florida.

Mbiti, John S. 1969. *African Religions and Philosophy.* London: Heinemann.

McCoy, Clyde B., J. Bryan Page, and Diana H. Gonzalez. 1980. "Cuban and Other Latin Immigration to Florida." *Florida Outlook* 4, no. 2: 77–82.

Ortiz, Fernando. 1906. *Los negros brujos: El Hampa afro-cubana.* Madrid: Editora Americana.

———. 1951. *Los bailes y el teatro de los Negros en el folklore de Cuba.* Havana: Publicaciones del Ministerio de Educación.

———. 1965. *La Africanía de la música folklorica de Cuba.* Havana: Editora Universitaria.

Padilla, Amado, M. 1980. "The Role of Cultural Awareness and Ethnic Loyalty in Acculturation." In *Acculturation: Theory, Models and Some New Findings,* ed. Amado M. Padilla, 47–84. Boulder, CO; Westview Press.

Parrinder, Geoffrey. 1965. *Religion in Africa.* New York: Praeger.

Patterson, Orlando. 1975. "Context and Choice in Ethnic Allegiances: A Theoretical Framework and Caribbean Case Study." In *Ethnicity, Theory and Experience,* ed. Nathan Glazer and Daniel P. Moynihan, 305–49. Cambridge, MA: Harvard University Press.

Raggi, Carlos M. 1970. "Las estructuras sociales de Cuba en los fines de la etapa colonial." *Exilios Temática Cubana* 2: 63–80.

Russell, Rogelio Duocastella. 1977. "Anterrial Migrations as Agents of Social Change." In *Ethnicity,* ed. Andrew M. Greeley and Gregory Baum, 48–56. New York: John Wiley and Sons.

Rycroft, W. Stanley. 1968. *Religion and Faith in Latin America.* Philadelphia: Westminster Press.

Sandoval, Mercedes Cros. 1975. *La Religión Afrocubana.* Madrid: Playor.

Santovenia, Emeterio S., and Raul M. Shelton. 1965. *Cuba y su historia.* 3 vols. Miami: Rema Press.

Scott, Clarissa S. 1974. "Health and Healing Practices among Five Ethnic Groups in Miami, Florida." *Public Health Reports* 89: 534–41.

Smith, Robert Freeman, ed. 1965. *Background to Revolutions: The Development of Modern Cuba.* New York: Alfred A. Knopf.

Soler, Frank. 1971a. "Have You Visited a 'Botánica' or Sampled a Dish of Paella?" *Miami Herald,* June 15.

———. 1971b. "Here Is a Calendar of Festive Dates." *Miami Herald,* June 15.

Sosa, Juan J. 1974. "La Santería." In *Cuba Diáspora, annuario de la iglesia catholica,* 65–78. Miami: Revista Ideal.

———. 1999. *Sectas, cultos y sincretismos.* Miami: Editora Universal.

Szapockznik, José, and William Kurtines. 1980. "Acculturation, Biculturalism and Adjustment among Cuban-Americans." In *Acculturation: Theory, Models and Some New Findings,* ed. Amado M. Padilla, 139–57. Boulder, CO: Westview Press.

Testé, Ismael. 1969. *Historia eclesiástica de Cuba*. Burgos, Spain: El Monte Carmelo.

Turner, Victor. 1967. *The Forest of Symbols: Aspects of Ndembu Ritual*. Ithaca, NY: Cornell University Press.

———. 1969. *The Ritual Process*. Ithaca, NY: Cornell University Press.

———. 1974. *Dramas, Fields, and Metaphors*. Ithaca, NY: Cornell University Press.

Turner, Victor, and Edith Turner. 1978. *Image and Pilgrimage in Christian Culture*. New York: Columbia University Press.

van Gennep, Arnold. 1960. *The Rites of Passage*. Chicago: University of Chicago Press.

Wetli, Charles V., and Rafael Martínez. 1981. "Forensic Aspects of Santería: A Religious Cult of African Origin." *Journal of Forensic Sciences* 26: 32–38.

Wiedner, Donald L. 1962. *A History of Africa South of the Sahara*. New York: Random House.

Wolf, Eric. 1969. *Peasant Wars of the Twentieth Century*. New York: Harper and Row.

20

Myth, Memory, and History

Brazil's Sacred Music of Shango

JOSÉ FLÁVIO PESSOA DE BARROS,
TRANSLATED BY MARIA P. JUNQUEIRA

Coinciding with the five-hundredth anniversary of the "discovery" of Brazil by Europeans, this chapter considers the legacy of the different ethnicities that have contributed to the formation of Brazilian national identity. We focus here in particular on the indelible mark that the Yorùbá have made on this identity, and most especially on the influences of the *terreiro* communities collectively called Candomblé. Candomblé has constituted a privileged locus of maintenance of an Afro-Brazilian identity, contributing centrally to the preservation of the African memory in Brazil.

Candomblé is the result of the re-elaboration of diverse African cultures, the product of different affiliations, which actually has resulted in the existence of numerous forms of Candomblé: Angola, Congo, Efan, and so on. The form described in this chapter is mainly derived from the Yorùbá and Fon/Ewe cultural language groups, which originated in what is today Nigeria and Benin. A result of the synthesis of these ethnic groups and the Brazilian historical process, *Candomblé jeje-nago,* as it is called, is thus a religion of African origin, but it is specifically Brazilian and is composed of practitioners of all races. It transmits ancestral memory through rituals and chants, and its specific initiation methods and worldview inspire in its adepts a particular approach to understanding and living life.

The liturgical language utilized in the *terreiro* communities is an archaic form of Yorùbá, similar in a sense to the Latin used in the Tridentine Mass. Practitioners "know" the meaning of the songs and prayers, but not necessarily the signification of each word. Commonly we are told by adepts, "this is the language spoken by the *orishas.*"

It is in this ancestral language that all of the ritual Candomblé chants are sung, and this liturgical Yorùbá dialect constitutes an essential component of Candomblé and is critical for understanding its rituals. These chants and the rhythms that accompany them are thus integral to the preservation of the African memory in Brazil, and hence our focus. The majority of this musical production was researched in public ceremonies that follow the Candomblé liturgical calendar. The chants were then re-recorded, without instruments accompanying them, by religious specialists; then the chants were transcribed into Yorùbá and analyzed by linguists proficient in this language.

According to Berrague, the repertoire of the òrìṣà house "is numerically expressive and their symbolic content is at the same time functional, because the music has an important role in the maintenance of religious groups" (1976: 131). Analyzing the sacred musical pieces of the Ketu and Jeje nations during the 1970s, Berrague concluded that "the repertoire is traditional and seems to have endured very little change, although the characteristics of their execution were transformed somewhat in the last thirty years." He evaluated the transcriptions and recordings done by Herskovits and others in the 1950s and opined that these classical studies are quite limited since they cover only one segment of the repertoire: an "old, traditional style that is characterized by short melodic phrases, continuous repetition with trimming variations and a vocal style that has a high, hard and metallic quality in the vocal production."

Our analysis is of the "Fogueira de Xangô" (Shango's bonfire), a feast that celebrates this òrìṣà. We identify the different mythical and historical references preserved in the memory of the communities through their chants and their specific rhythms.

This ceremony can be divided in two distinct segments: First, a bonfire is lighted in Shango's homage outside of the *terreiro*. Second, dancing and singing the òrìṣàs' praises take place in the *barracão,* the central room of the temple that shelters, besides the audience, a space reserved for the ritual orchestra. The musical instruments also occupy a special place there, in recognition of their sacramental nature. They are generally separated from the area of the dance and the audience by small walls or, less often, by cords, which delineate a sacred space. This space is saluted by the visitors as they arrive and by the òrìṣàs and initiates throughout the Xirê.

A specialist called the *alabe,* one of the most respected positions in Candomblé, directs the orchestra. The title *alabe* can be divided in two categories. The *otun-alabe,* "the one of the right," is older in initiation and knowledge, and the *osi-alabe,* "the one on the left," is younger and less knowledgeable. An *osi-alabe* can only be promoted upon the death of an *otun-alabe.* Being an *alabe* involves leading the chants, teaching the ritual songs to the novices, caring for and tuning the instruments, and assuring their consecration. Only then, through the music they create, can the instruments establish the desired relationship between humans and deities.

In Candomblé, the ritual battery is composed of several percussion instruments: three drums, or *atabaques,* and two iron bells, the *agogo* and the *gan,* which are played with metal sticks.

The drums are of various sizes and specific names. The largest of them, with a low pitch, is called *run,* which in Yorùbá means "voice" or "grunt" (*ohùn, hùn*) (Cacciatore 1977: 222). At least one scholar argues for a Fon origin of this term, meaning blood or heart (Lacerda 1998: 7). Whether meaning "voice," "grunt," "blood," or "heart," the term essentially refers to the special character and heavy responsibilities that the instrument has in the religious context. It is responsible for the musical solo, for the variations in melody, and for invoking the gods. Striking it with a wooden stick and one of the hands generally produces the *run*'s deep sound. This drum is considered the "one that calls the òrìṣàs," making the sound that reaches "*òrun,*" or the land of the òrìṣàs and the ancestors.

It is the *rumpi,* smaller than the *run* and bigger than the *lé* (the third drum), that has the role of musical support or of maintaining the rhythm. The two, *rumpi* and *lé,* have the same function and are played with *aquidavis,* wooden sticks made from branches of the guava tree. These drums sustain a melodic line, composed of permanent repetition of a rhythmical model, for relatively long intervals. They create the space in which the *run* can freely improvise the musical variations that constitute the solo, giving support and sustaining the entire sacred musical piece.

The name *rumpi* is derived from the Yorùbá term *hùn* (grunt/roar) plus *pi,* meaning "immediately" (Cacciatore 1977: 222). The etymology of this name reflects the *rumpi*'s position in the orchestra and in the musical execution.

The term *lé* in the Ewe language means "small" and refers to the third drum's size (Cacciatore 1977: 160). The sound is considered of higher pitch than the *rumpi,* which is of moderate pitch compared to the *rumpi* and the *run*.

Sounds, Words, and Gestures in *Terreiro*-Based Rituals

In this world of sounds, the texts, spoken or sung—like the gestures, ritual objects, and symbols—transmit a mosaic of meaning, once introduced into different rituals. Together they reproduce the dynamic and memory of the group, reinforcing and integrating the basic values of the community, through the dramatization of the myths, dance, and the chants, in much the same way that elders' stories do.

Terreiro communities are, Verger writes, "the last places where the rules of protocol reign . . . the questions of etiquette, the order of elder-ship, the salutes, the kneeling are observed, discussed, and passionately criticized; in this world of hand kissing, of bowing, the different head inclinations, the hands slightly thrown in blessing gestures, amount to protocol as detailed and softly practiced as in the court of the Sun King," a reference to the most pompous of European monarchies. *Terreiro* rules of living are organized into age categories, which are largely delineated by initiations. Apprenticeship is a living practice that issues from an initiatory process, which is steeped in the oral transmission of knowledge. It is common, though, for the younger initiates to keep notebooks in which they write what they observe: the chants, prayers, and other secrets learned in the initiatory process; but although these observances are written down, they are kept absolutely secret.

In initiation, knowledge is transmitted from elders to initiates, usually young individuals who must first be accepted by the elders as able and respectful of the fundamental norms of the group. Knowledge "comes with time," as the elders say. Therefore, through a slow and thorough process wisdom is not only transmitted to the initiand but is also im-printed in the deepest part of his being (Cossard-Binon 1981: 139). It is very much a life-transforming rite of passage.

In the end, the initiate's efforts will engender ritual knowledge and the ability to enact rituals correctly; that is, to sing chants as memorized, to dance with precision, to respectfully salute the elders, and ultimately to live in harmony with the originally African spirits.

The word has a special place in Candomblé, possessing the power to animate life and stimulate the Ashe contained in nature. The intentions, petitions, and desired outcomes of religious practice should be verbalized. It is unthinkable to ask the òrìṣàs anything in silence. Petitions must be pronounced in a loud voice and chanted in the form of a prayer. "The speech should reproduce the back-and-forth pattern that is the essence of rhythm" (Bâ 1982: 186). Thus, in order for it to reach the gods, the word should be movement.

Like the word, sound is also essential to Candomblé ritual because it too brings forth the Ashe. With or without musical instruments, it has a special strength that is zealously guarded in memory.

The transmission of these texts (invocations, myths, chants) occurs in an unsystematic way and continues to nurture the initiate for life. Once this mnemonic process is stimulated, practitioners are capable, in a relatively short time, of reciting from memory long praises or chants. And although the original meaning of each word in Yorùbá has been lost, their "sense" persists, and thus the meaning of the chants is known to the Nago initiate, according to Welch (1980: 2).

Oral chants of praise have forms of presentation that vary according to the goals of the ritual in question: *oríkì*—invocations; *orins*—chants of praise; *àdúrà*—prayers; *ibá*—salutations; and *òfò*—chants directed toward herbs. During the *xirê,* or memorial rites, any combination of these different styles can be present, invoking, praising, and saluting the òrìṣàs and ancestors. It is as if the most intimate ritual gatherings of the community best inspire the retelling of stories of the òrìṣàs and the ancestors. At the same time, these narratives provide a recollective outline of Candomblé cosmology and honor those within earshot as worthy of partaking of such wisdom.

Initiates generally do not acquire true knowledge of Yorùbá language, which is only employed liturgically in ritual chants and prayers. Quotidian *terreiro* existence breeds understanding of Yorùbá names for ritual paraphernalia, words that originate in a religious language that Abimbolá calls ancient or fossilized imprinted in the memory of òrìṣà devotees everywhere (Abimbolá 1976).

Chants for the Òrìṣàs

Ritual chants have very specific characteristics derived from their musical origins and expressed in patterns of melodic and synchronous rhythms. Typically, chants are respondent tones carried by the soloist singer, the *alabe* or *iyatabexé*. Melodies in pentatonic scales are also typical aspects of these musical pieces, both in religious and folkloric music of African origin.

The *alabe* is initiated specifically for the function of orchestra leader. The term is derived from the Yorùbá language (Cacciatore 1977: 45), meaning *ala* (owner) and *agbè* (drum or gourd). In general, besides being a percussionist, he is also responsible for the liturgical chanting. The *alabe's* female correspondent, *iyatabexé* (*iyatabeshe*), only chants; women very rarely play drums in *terreiro* communities. The female title in Yorùbá means literally "the mother who makes the propitiatory supplications" (*ìyá*—mother; *té*—propitiates; *bè*—supplications). This title is reserved for women of special talents who generally possess many years of initiation in the *ogan* and *ekedi* category.

Alabe are initiated into priesthood in their specific functions and denominated *ogans,* learning the chants and rhythms (*toques*) during many years of apprenticeship. They are elevated to this position after an initiatory period that ends in a public presentation, where they demonstrate their artistic talent and religious knowledge. After the initiation, they receive a liturgical name that will identify them forever, a name that will be recognized warmly by the community as "fathers," who can give blessings to all and who are blessed too.

These priests/musicians are distinguished as the most illustrious members of the *terreiro* communities and have the prominent role of welcoming the òrìṣàs through their performance. Excellence in performance is rewarded by collections of monetary offerings made by congregants, who deposit money before the ritual orchestra. Visiting performers of especial talent forever remain in the memory of the *terreiro* and receive considerable gifts from host *terreiro* members.

The *run* drum, whose possession and music is solely the domain of the *alabe,* can only be passed on to another *alabe* when its owner becomes unable to perform. Such respect for seniority is also seen when the eldest determines the time of the feast and in the general generosity and obedience granted to elders.

The chant, or better the chorus chant, which is the way that the melodies are sung, obeys precise patterns in its execution. It can be presented in solo and then answered altogether, or in duo, when alternating in praying. In general, the chants are short strophes, easily memorized, with differentiated melody. The solo singer commands the execution and produces variations over the chanted theme. Embellishments on traditional rhythmic patterns are discouraged.

Musical instruments usually accompany the chants, but the prayers are sometimes sung a cappella. Their themes are ample and generally associated with the human fate and the glory of the gods and ancestors. In rare cases in which chants are recited without instrumental accompaniment, they normally take the place of prayers (àdúrà), laudations (oríkì), salutations (ibás), and enchantments (òfòs).

Existential issues such as life and death occupy a special place in the poetry of the sacred chants. These chants also speak of ancient civilizations, dynasties, sacred places, alliances and conflicts, and relations with nature, which are all seen as the privileged place of the religious experience. The music and poetry praise the gods and call the faithful to follow the models dramatized in the voice and dance.

The messages obey the musical sequence inscribed in the proper logic of the myths, being so intimately associated that their order cannot be altered. Their true meaning, woven throughout the entire performance, can be grasped only by hearing the chants in their entirety.

At times slight alterations are made in the meanings of the praising to the òrìṣàs and more rarely in the structure of its melody. The alterations in the poetry are, possibly, a result of the influence of Portuguese or willful embellishments by *terreiro* communities that distinguish the so-called nations. In any case, such variations are usually policed by the *alabe* (musical specialists), each with his own style of execution. This is not unique to the Brazilian case. Welch (1980: 3) noted similar alterations in Yorùbáland: "even in today's Nigeria, many texts lost their exact meaning and there are discrepancies between the executors from one area to another. Variables such as memory, feelings, and momentary circumstances affect any execution. The faithful knows that the praising is directed to a particular òrìṣà, because in the Nago practice the sequence is ritually prescribed."

Merian (1951: 98), analyzing the recordings done by Herskovits between 1941 and 1942 in Bahia, says that "the Ketu chants show African patterns . . . in such an intense way that it leaves no doubt between the relation of the Ketu style (Nago) and of the West African . . . the relation can not be controversial."

Berrague (1976: 131) brings up two hypotheses as to the differences encountered in Brazil and Africa. The first is that the recent Nigerian and Dahomean repertoires have undergone quite different evolutions than those of their Brazilian counterparts. The second is that a distinctly Bahian repertoire was produced locally and independently in Brazil.

We consider both of these hypotheses plausible. Candomblé must necessarily be conceived of as the result of an ongoing process of synthesis, hence the impossibility of finding a pure form in ritual musical expressions. The African and Brazilian contexts had markedly different influences in their historical formation, which without doubt caused alterations in the distinctive liturgical musical productions.

The cultural musical memory brought from these African regions by the Nago, made possible, we believe, the re-creation of other chants within the same patterns. We know at least one of them, which talks about a particular circumstance that happened in the *Ile Ya Naso* that we will discuss in a future publication.

Although the literal meaning of each African word could have been forgotten because the language was not utilized in daily, secular life in Brazil, their general significance persists in the memory of the *terreiro* communities. The melodies are part of an expressive cultural legacy that unites West Africa to Brazil and is one of the most significant aspects of the Brazilian musical production. Welch (1980: 4), recognizing the importance of this heritage, affirms: "A mental musical structure was preserved, within which the *nago* chants can be expressed, and can be in existence for at least fifteen generations in Bahia."

This production, more than talking about the antiquity of a culture, express a hidden face of five hundred years of history, a face that reveals itself in an expressive liturgy, that is celebrated in songs, and fully lived in the community of the *terreiros*.

The Specificity of the Rhythms

In West Africa, oral traditions have a strong connection to songs and instrumental music, especially to those produced by drums. Together, these amount to a vast repertoire that talks about the political and social life of the populations encountered there. The oral traditions are generally preserved via intergenerational transmission, and by professional singers and storytellers, who are the repositories of history and communal memory:

It was due to the intense and extensive presence of the oriki in the Yorùbá life—and due too, to the extraordinary variety of objects that this form submits to a poetical treatment—that *Bólánlé Awé* was able to use it as a source of historical information. Awé aligns himself, then, in the movement of the so-called oral history. He goes in a sure path. The British historiography, for example, often goes to popular ballads for their reconstruction and interpretation of certain eras. In addition, in Africa, the oral traditions are being used more and more in the efforts of historical reconstruction. The poetry (historical, religious, etc) forms one of the main fields of the African oral tradition. (Risério 1992: 38)

These traditional musicians, or *griots,* were historically of fundamental importance because they would activate the memory of a past, usually heroic and linked to paradigmatic figures of these societies. They previously had a greater social status, whereas today the role is not lucrative and therefore losing appeal. Very few young people are willing now, for instance, to commit to the apprenticeship of long poems (*orìkís*) and stories, or any of the other rather onerous demands that the profession makes.

The *orìkís* are poems whose multiple authors are unknown. They talk about attributes of people or òrìṣàs being praised or evoked, whose positive or negative aspects can be used as themes. Simple and melodious, they illuminate in a special way the Afro-Brazilian religious community, informing about the social organization, the belief system, and the oral history derived from Africa. Authors such as Berrague (1976: 131) revalidate the importance of music in this reconstruction of the past, giving a special place to religious music analyzed by this author in Bahia. Within the huge repertoire that he evaluated in the houses of *jeje-nago* origin, the chants to Shango were considered by him as the most traditional and closest to their African counterparts.

Four rhythms are the basis of the majority of the musical production dedicated to Shango.

Bàtá

Bàtá is a small Yorùbá drum, made of wood. Ramos (1934: 162) informs us, "In Bahia there are numerous types of drums, from the small *bàtás* to the big *ilus* and *bàtácotos* (war drums)." The *bàtá* is a drum of two membranes distended by cords, which "is used hanging from the player's neck and played in both sides" (Cacciatore 1977: 64). It is a repetitive rhythm, used mainly in rituals to Shango and played with the hands without the use of *aquidavis,* or wooden sticks. It is accompanied by chants and is sometimes used to praise other òrìṣàs. The term is of Yorùbá origin, meaning "drum" for the cults of Egun and Shango (Pessoa de Barros 1999: 66).

Although other authors talk about the presence of this drum in the Brazilian case, Verger (1997: 140) affirms, "The *bàtá* drums were not known in Brazil, although they still are in Cuba, but the rhythms played to Shango are the same. They are warlike and quick rhythms, called *tonibobé* and *alujá,* and are accompanied by the sound of the '*shere*' shaken at the same time."

Alujá

Alujá is quick sounding with war characteristics, dedicated to Shango. It means "perforation" or "hole" in Yorùbá. According to certain priests, it "is the hole that Shango opened in the earth, going into it, leaving the kingdom and becoming an orisha." Ramos (1934: 303) relates it to the dance done by Shango. In general, the dancer—in this case, the òrìṣà—also accompanied by beats of the *run* drum, tells in gestures of Shango's feats as a warrior and his attributes as the god of thunder capable of launching the thunderstone (*ẹdun-ààrà*) to earth. The dancer's gestures are also guided by the *alabe,* and each stronger sound corresponds to a larger gesture and a firmer step by the "Lord of Thunder." In this performance, dancer and musician are intimately linked in the recounting of these powerful myths.

The *alujá,* in general, follows three different timings during its execution. The first moment, slower than the other two, corresponds to the dance steps when the òrìṣà crosses the whole space of the *barracão.* Next, the drums gradually accelerate the rhythm, becoming more vibrant in unison with the dance steps. Finally, quicker still, the musical piece reaches its climax when Shango, in front of the orchestra of drums, "fights proudly with his '*oshe,*' and as the music accelerates, he makes a gesture of picking up an imaginary '*lábá*' (leather pouch) containing the thunderstones, which he throws to the earth" (Verger 1997: 140).

Tonibobé

Etymologically, *tonibobé* is a Yorùbá term that can be broken down as *tó*—"just"; *ni*—grammatical reinforcement; *bo*—"to adore";

bè—"supplicate, ask"; so in combination the meaning is "ask and adore with justice." Its special timing reminds one of the rhythms of a bolero, and so at times this dance is called the Bolero of Xangô (Pessoa de Barros 1999: 70).

The dance done by Shango in this rhythm has unique features. The feet go slowly, and the heel, with a stronger marking beat, accompanies the gestures of the hands at the level of the face of the dancer. The hands are closed, with the exception of the pointing finger, as they turn around themselves and repeatedly launch to the right, then to the left, and up, as if throwing something. In each hand gesture, one of the feet lifts, in a rhythmic way. In relation to this performance, it is said: "Shango is preparing the lightning with his fingers and then he throws the thunderstones up, so they fall all over."

It is interesting to note that this rhythm is done only with musical instruments; there is no text associated with it.

Kakaka-umbó or *Batá-coto*

The first term, *kakaka-umbó*, of Yorùbá origin, means *ka*—"embrace, involve" (the repetition is a reinforcement); *nbó*—"return, in circle; involve in circle." Its rigorous gestures consist of the hands closing progressively until the closed hand repeats several times the gesture of a pestle smashing.

The second term, *batá-coto*, is the name of a war drum of Yorùbá origin. These were mostly destroyed in the time known as the Revolt of the Males, in the nineteenth century. According to Carneiro (1935: 110), importing this drum has been prohibited since 1855, and to play it meant prison or even death. This rhythm, with its distinctive gestures, is performed in the dances of Shango and Ogiyan. We suspect that it was once associated with war dances (Pessoa de Barros 1999: 70).

The rhythm *kakaka-umbó*, with the dance described above, dramatizes the use of the pestle and is associated with Shango and Ogyian in a special way. Ogiyan does a war dance, usually in the ceremony called "the feast of the pestle," wherein balls of yam are offered and dedicated to this òrìṣà, considered the "king of war." The same meaning and gesture is performed in Shango's dance, which "destroys, [with] violent beating with his hands, his enemies."

Bonfire and the Circle of Shango

During the first phase of the celebrations dedicated to Shango—that is, during the rites performed near the bonfire, or the "òrìṣà of the fire," one of the titles given to the old Aláàfin of Oyo—prayers are chanted. There are many prayers dedicated to this òrìṣà; we analyze but one here:

> ba ìrú 1 'òkò
> ba ìrú 1 'òkò
> Ìyámasse kò wà ìrà oje
> Aganju k mã nj 1 kan
> Ãrá l'òkò láàyà
> Tóbi òrì à,
> ba run Ãrá ba oje

> [The king threw a stone.
> Ìyámasse dug at the foot of a big tree and found it.
> Aganju will shine, then, once more, thunder
> Threw a stone with force (courage).
> Great òrìṣà of the Orun (land of ancestors) watches.
> The king of thunders, at the foot of a tree (thunderstone).]

In this prayer Aganju, the Aláàfin of Oyo, is saluted as son of Ajaká and nephew of Shango. Ìyámasse, his mother, reveals to mortals the thunderstone symbol of his power, found at the foot of the big tree. The brightness of the lightning and the noise of the thunder remind Aganju, watcher over Orun, of the land of ancestors, his people, and believers.

The chanting goes on for a long time, and one by one, all the known names of Shango will be chanted. After Aganju, in this chant follows Ayra, then Baru, and others, twelve in total. One by one, all of the "kings of Oyo" are saluted.

After the prayers, the Alujá is usually played in specific rhythms for Shango, wherein the sound of the òrìṣà dancing is marked by clapping hands and the *shere* rhythms that demarcate the final part of this first ritual moment.

The "Roda de Xangô," however, occurs inside of the space called *barracão*. In general, some twenty chants are recited, whose order can vary in function of the different traditions of the community. From these, we will choose two from this beautiful, expressive repertoire.

Dàda má sukun
Dàda má sunkun mo
O feere feere Ó gbé 1 'aye
L'orun Bàbá kíní 1 ' n
n áa rí.

[Dàda, do not cry anymore.
In frank acceptance, he lives.
In the Heavens is the father
Who watches the road to protect us.]

The strong and repetitive rhythm of the *bàtá* salutes Dàda or Ajaká.
The dancers, facing the central pole that supports the roof, where the
crown of Shango is usually found, do a dance distinctly for this ceremony, the circle of Shango. This dance differs from those that precede
it in the continuous movement of the dancer's head, which turns repeatedly to the two sides of the shoulder, in an obvious expression of negation, which lasts through the chanting.

Verger (1987: 32), citing one of the Dàda myths, notes that this òrìṣà
founded the city of Ishele and was very rich. When he became king of
Oyo, he brought his wealth to his new kingdom, ever awaiting more provisions from his old town. Verger adds that "when Shango wants to possess one of his priests, people sing before: '*Dàda ma sukun mo*'—Dàda,
do not cry anymore." Dàda is, in effect, exhorted not to worry because
new riches will arrive soon. This chant emphasizes Ajaka's tolerance.
Ajaká is the peaceful *ọba,* the rich one, who many times acts as if he
does not see "the arrogant air of his older brother, Shango," who is much
given to disputes and discord. Further reflecting the community's faith
in his wisdom, kindness, and tolerance, this text also asks of the king to
watch over the less fortunate:

Báyànni gìdigìdi Báyànni
Báyànni gìdigìdi Báyànni
Báyànni adé Báyànni olà
Báyànni adé Báyànni owó

[Bayani (Ajaká) is strong
and very, very rich.
The crown of Bayani is honorable
and very rich.]

The crown of the honorable Bayani that is described in this chant is
said to belong to an Oba Ajaká, the third king of Oyo. The word *owó,*
meaning "money" or "wealth," refers to the great number of cowries

that cover this crown, which were once used as money. The word *owó* thus establishes a link between honor and wealth. Use of the superlative term *gìdigìdi*, referring to a strong and large animal, is exemplary of the common employment of wordplay in Yorùbá language. This association was made by a priest explaining to me the hymn's meaning by referring to the myth of Shango and the ram:

> The *oshe* of Shango, his *axe,* can have the format of the ram horns, because one day Shango fought with this animal, which is the one he prefers to eat . . . the reason for the fight no one knows . . . the ram was losing, went to his house and got the horns . . . then everything changed, Shango was beaten, and could not forget the humiliation . . . with a great roar he disappeared in the earth, becoming an *orisha,* but he still eats ram for its taste and because of his anger.

The ram, according to Verger (1999: 348), is an animal that distinguishes with precision the two different dynasties of Shango, rulers of the Oyo kingdom: the Shangos Tapa, represented by a mask in which it shows the ram, and the Mesi Shango, represented by the mounted figure of a horseman. Mesi Shango, according to the myths, originated from the Borgu, who lost their crown to the Tapa, who are of Nupe origin.

After the "Roda de Xangô," the ceremony continues, praising the "òrìṣà of the fire" with dances anchored in a repertoire of sometimes hundreds of chants. From this treasury we offer this one example:

> Aé aé ó gbè lé m
> nsó ojú m n,
> Aé aé ó gbè lé m
> nsó ojú m
> n ba olórí 1
> g ó ní yé
> ba olorí Ilú Àf njá dé o,
> aé aé ó b, rí ó,
> Aé aé ó b, rí ó,
> aé aé ó b, rí, Ò b,
> rí ó (ikú kójáàde-ó k tà bèrú).

> [Ae ae knows by sight his children,
> Ae ae he knows by sight his children,
> Chief of kings,
> fine and agreeable
> Chief of earth,
> he is Àfònjá that arrives,
> ae ae he exists,

I saw him,
ae ae he exists,
I saw,
I saw (he took death outside—he sells the cowards).]

Àfònjá was a general (*kakanfô*) of the Aláàfin Aolé. He fought in numerous battles and was considered a great military commander. Despite losing in battle, he was named governor of Ilorin for his feats, but he felt himself to be in disgrace with the *ọba*. Nonetheless, Àfònjá refused to commit suicide, as was traditionally required of losing generals: "The Aláàfin sends against him an army that lost, thanks to the support of the Peule of Malam Alimi. When he wanted to get rid of these embarrassing allies, totally destroyed . . . commits suicide then, becomes a peule emirate" (Ki-Zerbo 1972: 362).

This chant celebrates the "chief of earth" who punishes cowards who desert him in battle, selling them as slaves. For this, he is honored in Brazil as an òrìṣà, a Shango unaffected by death.

A Brief Conclusion

The memory of Shango in Brazil is indelibly inscribed in the Candomblé community, both in their system of symbols and in the chants and myths that inform and invigorate the lives of òrìṣà devotees. This communal mnemonic expression of the god of thunder is gives "form and content to this great abstraction that is identity, be it of a people, of a group or of a nation. Very few would oppose the idea that the access of the individuals to memory is a fundamental factor for cultural transmission, so, to the permanent re-foundation of a society" (Gondar 1997: 53).

References

Abimbolá, Wande. 1976. *The Yoruba Traditional Religion in Brazil: Problems and Prospects.* Ilé-Ifè: Department of African Language and Literature, University of Ifè.

Bâ, Amadou Hampâté. 1982. "A tradição viva." In *História geral da África,* ed. J. Ki-Zerbo, 181–218. Paris: UNESCO / Ática.

Beata de Yemonjá, Mãe. 1997. *Caroço de dendê, a sabedoria dos terreiros: Como Ialorixás e Babalorixás passam conhecimentos a seus filhos.* Rio de Janeiro: Pallas.

Berrague, G. 1976. "Correntes regionais e nacionais na música do Candomblé baiano." *Revista Afro-Ásia* 12. Centro de Estudos Afro-Orientais da Universidade Federal da Bahia, Salvador.

Cacciatore, O. G. 1977. *Dicionário de cultos afro-brasileiros*. Rio de Janeiro: Forense Universitária / SEEC—RJ.

Carneiro, Édison da Souza. 1935. "Xangô." In *Estudos Afro-Brasileiros: Trabalhos Apesentados ao Premeiro Congreso Afro-Brasileiro*, 139–45. Rio de Janeiro: Ed. Ariel.

Cossard-Binon. G. 1981. "A filha-de-santo." *Olóòrisá*. São Paulo, Ed. Ágora, 1981.

Gondar, Josaida. 1997. "O Esquecimento como crise do Social." In *Memória Social e Documento: Uuma abordagem interdisciplinar*, ed. A. Wehling, 51–62. Rio de Janeiro: UNIRIO.

Ki-Zerbo, J. 1972. *História da África Negra*. Vol. 1. Viseu, Portugal: Publicações Europa-América, Viseu.

Lacerda, Marcos Branda. 1998. *Drama e Fetiche: Vodum, Bumba Meu Boi e Samba no Benin*. Rio de Janeiro: FUNARTE / Centro Nacional de Folclore e Cultura Popular. Sound recording.

Merian, A. P. 1951. "Songs of the Afro-Brazilian Ketu-Cult: An Ethnomusicological Analysis." Ph.D. diss., Northwestern University.

Pereira da Costa, J. 1908. *Folclore Pernanbucano*. Recife, Brazil: RIHGB.

Pessoa de Barros, José Flávio. 1999. *O Banquete do Rei . . . Olubajé. Uma introdução à música sacra afro-brasileira*. Rio de Janeiro: UERJ/INTERCON.

Ramos, A. 1934. *As Culturas Negras no Novo Mundo*. São Paulo: Companhia Editora Nacional.

Risério, A. 1992. "De Oriquis." *Revista Afro-Ásia* 15. Salvador, Brazil: Centro de Estudos Afro-Orientais da Universidade Federal da Bahia, em coedição com a Edições Ianamá

Silva, Vagner Gonçalves da. 1995. *Os orixás da metrópole*. São Paulo: EDUSP.

Sodré, Muniz. 1988. *O terreiro e a cidade: A forma social negro-brasileira*. Petrópolis, Brazil: Vozes.

Valla, Victor. 2001. *Religião e cultura popular*. Rio de Janeiro: DP&A.

Verger, Pierre. 1987. *Carybé: Lendas africanas dos orixás*. São Paulo: Corrupio.

———. 1997. *Orixás—Deuses Iorubás na África e no Novo Mundo*. Salvador, Brazil: Corrupio.

———. 1999. *Notas sobre o culto aos orixás e voduns*. São Paulo: EDUSP.

Welch, D. Baille. 1980. "Um melótipo Iorubá / Nagô para os cantos religiosos da diáspora negra." *Ensaio e Pesquisa* 4. Salvador, Brazil: Centro de Estudos Afro-Orientais.

21

Yorùbá Sacred Songs in the New World

JOSÉ JORGE DE CARVALHO

Yorùbá Culture in the New World: A History of Repression and Resistance

Among so many aspects of the African memory preserved in the New World, certainly one of the most outstanding is the Yorùbá religious tradition, which was reconstituted in various countries and left its mark especially in the performing arts related to sacred rituals: drumming, dancing, and singing (Carvalho 1984, 2000). Although Yorùbá drumming and singing are fairly well known by researchers, another crucial area has remained quite alive but still quite enigmatic until today: the song texts, that is, the sacred poetry of Yorùbá divinities that is sung by adepts in festivals, sacrifices, and rituals of initiation.

The existence of those sacred texts in the Yorùbá language, preserved in Brazil, Cuba, Trinidad, and other parts of the New World, has been mentioned extensively in the literature on Afro-American religions since the end of the last century. In the case of Brazil, practically all the works written about these religious traditions (be it *candomblé, xangô, tambor-de-mina, batuque,* or other names they have in different parts of

416

the country) include, even if as mere illustration, one or two song texts in African languages.

In spite of this overwhelming presence, we have had up to now very little knowledge about the linguistic, musical, and literary value of the oral texts in Yorùbá preserved in Brazil, simply because, with the exception of a few examples taken from the *candomblé* of Bahia, researchers had not been able to present the translations of a wider or more coherent set of song lyrics and texts.

To clarify, *xangô* (Portuguese equivalent of the English Shango) is the name given in Recife to the traditional Afro-Brazilian religion, being fairly similar to the *candomblé* of Bahia. The Yorùbá are called Nago in Brazil, and the different styles of cults are referred to as Nations. Thus, in Recife, the Yorùbá cult is called Nago, while in Bahia the two Yorùbá Nations are known as Ketu and Ijesha; the Bahian Ketu is fairly similar to the Recifean Nago. Granted that, we should not confuse *xangô* (the religious community) with Shango, the god of thunder, one among the many deities worshiped by *xangô* members. Obviously, the cult received that name in Recife precisely because of the popularity of the god Shango (see Carvalho 1988, 1992, 1993, 2000, 2003, forthcoming).

Many scholars had stated emphatically, for decades, that the majority of the texts of Afro-Brazilian ritual songs showed a mixture of Yorùbá, Ewe, and Fon words together with words belonging to Bantu languages, such as Kikongo and Kimbundu; they found an answer for this by invoking the history of slavery. It is a well-known fact that slaves brought from various parts of the African coast converged in some ports and remained there grouped together, waiting to be taken to the New World. It was therefore believed that already a certain degree of cultural and linguistic mixing, or at least of loss of each one's own traditions, occurred during that period of waiting in the African trade ports. Whenever they arrived in Brazil, the slaves were redistributed with the explicit criteria of mixing ethnic groups. By preventing those who spoke the same language from staying close together, the chances of reorganization and of rebellion would be thus minimized. One of the consequences of this forced regrouping, from the point of view of the slaveholders (who desired to exert tight control over the slaves), would be the destruction of the specific cultural traditions, including the language, of each one of the nations living together under the regime of slavery. Influenced by this hypothesis, William Megenney (1989, 1992), among other scholars, has argued recently that there was a strong linguistic mixture in the song texts of the *candomblé* and the other forms of cult.

Opposed to this theory of cultural hybridity, Pierre Verger (1999) and Juana Elbein dos Santos (1976), among others, argued repeatedly that the songs, which circulate in the traditional *candomblés* of Bahia, have preserved many authentic and still comprehensible Yorùbá texts. Based on the edition of Yorùbá song texts from Recife, I can now be sure that the majority of the ritual texts sung in traditional *xangô* houses (many of which are sung in other parts of the country as well) have been preserved in an almost intact Yorùbá, despite some distortion in pronunciation and certain ambiguities or displacements of the standardized tones.

Granted then the arguments in favor of the linguistic unity of these texts, still another assumption, quite widespread and well formulated by Roger Bastide, among others, could finally be submitted to an empirical test. Without ever showing a translation of at least one single African ritual text preserved in Brazil, Roger Bastide stated, in his influential book *O Candomblé da Bahia* (1978), that the song texts explained, or complemented, the myths that were shown in possession dances and in gestures expressed by the practitioners during public festivals. A careful reading of the translations of song texts in praise of the gods performed in Recife, however, will lead us to conclude that not all of them convey messages that correspond directly to the choreographic or gestured language explored in ritual as they are codified in Brazil. This direct correspondence is true for only a small portion of song texts. In most cases, the text runs in a plane of philosophical, mystical, or proverbial meaning that links itself with the Yorùbá cosmology as a whole and not specifically with its ritual place inside *xangô* practices. In the case of the rituals for the *eguns* and for the *ori,* this relationship between the literal meaning of the texts and other gesticulated and choreographic conventions seems equally remote. Actually, only the spoken invocations and the songs for sacrificing animals show an overt homology with the performatic occasion of their enunciation.

Thus, the assumption, which seemed more plausible and attractive— and to a certain extent easier to suppose—is not what happens more frequently, at least in the case of *xangô*. And that is so because the nature of the poetical elements employed was not known, even superficially, nor was there knowledge of the conventions and the strictly literary potentials of these Yorùbá verbal formulae still performed in Brazil.

These Afro-Brazilian texts have really become enigmatic, discussed numerous times by diverse authors but never clearly understood. We can see this, for instance, in the work of Melville Herskovits, which has been extremely influential among our scholars. Despite his impressive scholarly output, only one of his publications presents translations of Afro-Brazilian texts: the record album, with explanatory notes, that he published together with Frances Herskovits for the Library of Congress in 1947 (*Folk Music of Brazil: Afro-Bahian Religious Songs*), in which six Yorùbá songs are translated. Here are the song texts transcribed in the explanatory notes for the album, with a "free translation," as he called it:

1. Ketu for Eshu
Ibarabo-o mojuba
Iba koshe omo deko
Elegbara
Ileba Eshu Lona
2. Odara kolori onejo
Sho-sho-sho abe
Kolori eni-ijo
3. Eshu tiriri
Bara obebe
Tiriri lona

[O great one, I pay obeisance
A young child does not confront
The powerful one;
To Elegba Eshu, who is on the road.
The good one, who has no head for dancing.
The stubborn knife
Has no head for dancing.
Eshu the awesome,
O powerful knife!
The Awesome one, on the road.]

The first song, for Eshu, is found, with slight variations, in the Nago corpus I edited from Recife:

Ìbà àgbà o, àgbà o, mo júbà, ìbà á she
Àgbò àgbò àgbò mo júbà ọmọdé kú ilé
Ìbà àgbò àgbò mo júbà Elegbàrá àgò l'onà
Ìbà àgbà àgbà o mo júbà—With respect, people, I bow to you, I beg
     your attention
Ìbà á shẹ—the request will be granted; that is: our prayers will succeed
Omodé kú ilé—Children, I wish you well at home [a sort of greeting
     formula]
Elegbàrá àgò l'ónà—Elegbàrá, clear the way.

Now, here is the same song as it is preserved in the repertoire of the Cuban Santería, edited by John Mason in his book *Orin Orisa:*

Ìbà rá goo àgò mo júbà
Ìbà rá goo àgò mo júbà
Ìbà rá goo àgò mo júbà
Ìbà rá goo àgò mo júbà

[Homage to the relative of the Club. Give way, I pay homage
omodé kóni ki shìbà go àgò mo júbà Elegbá Èshù lonà
Child who teaches the doctrine of paying homage to the club,
Make way, I pay homage to the Owner of Vital Force,
Èshù is the one who owns the road.]

                                                   Mason 1992: 61; his translation

And, to show the extraordinary resilience of the Yorùbá diaspora religious community, in spite of all the pressures to erase the collective memory during slavery and after, here is the same song as it is sung in Trinidad, presented by Maureen Warner-Lewis in her book *Yorùbá Songs of Trinidad:*

Èshù Bàrágbó o
Mo júbà
A ré, a ré
Èshù Bàrágbó o
Mo júbà
omodé korin
Mo júbà Rágbó o
Mo júbà Alábàrà
Èshù Bàrà o

[Eshu, Lord Aragbo
I pay homage to you
I am here, I have come
Eshu, Lord Aragbo
I pay homage to you
Your child has come to sing
I pay my respect to Aragbo
I pay my respects to the Powerful One
Eshu, Lord]

        Warner-Lewis 1994: 37; her translation

Finally, here is one variant of that same song as recorded in Oshupa, Benin, by Juana Elbein do Santos:

Ìbà Àgbò ó Àgbò mo júbà
Ìbà Ìbà
Bomodé nkorin a júbá Agbó ó
Àgbò mo júbà
Elegbà a Èshù ònà

[I present my humble respects, *Agbó,* for Your Elderliness;
I present my humble respects to *Agbó.*
I place myself under the authority of the eldest.
Children should not perform rites without presenting their humble
    respects to *Agbó.*
Agbó, here are my humble respects,
Èshù, Lord of Power and of the ways.]

Santos 1976: 195; her translation

I have also identified this same song in the repertoire of traditional
cult houses from Porto Alegre, in the extreme south of Brazil. Actually,
this song, as well as dozens of others I edited in *xangô,* can be found today in almost every state capital of Brazil because of growing expansion
of the *candomblé* model of Afro-Brazilian religion.

In order to confirm the kind of similarity between these three main
New World Yorùbá traditions, here is another song, dedicated to Ọya:

Ọya dé ariwo Ọyamẹsàn rorò j'ọkọ lọ
Ọya mà dé pariwo Ọya Digbi Ọgerọ j'ọkọ lọ
Ọya dé ariwo—Ọya has come; shout
ariwo—a shout or exclamation, as a response to the presence of the
    goddess
Ọyamẹsàn rorò j'ọkọ lọ—Ọyamẹsàn is tougher than a husband
Ọyamẹsàn—Nine Ọyas, literally; used as one of the names of Ọya
Ọya Digbi Ọgerọ—a praise name

Here is the same song in Trinidad:

Ọya dé
Mariwo
Îkàrá rorò jọkọ lọ

[Ọya has come
Children of the deity
Îkàrá is more fierce than her husband]

Warner-Lewis 1994: 65; her translation

And here is the song in Cuba:

Ọya dé ariwo. Ọya-n-sán l'órò ñòkòtò
The tearer arrives noisely.
The tearer who splits has a tradition of trousers
Ọya dé ariwo. O mẹ sán l'órò ñòkòtò
The tearer arrives noisely. Nine has a tradition of trousers.

Mason 1992: 324; his translation

A variant of the first verse in another Cuban song:

Ọya dé màrìwò ya

[The Tearer arrives, the palm-fronds tear]

Mason 1992: 328)

I managed to identify more than forty songs of the repertoire of the *xangôs,* which are the same ones recorded in Bahia by Melville and Frances Herskovits. Practically all of the Bahian songs come from the Ketu and Ijesha Nations of *candomblé,* which are the two religious styles closer to the Nago Nation in Recife. This repertoire has been kept alive as it is presented, with very few changes, in the new anthologies of *candomblé* songs organized by José Flávio Pessoa de Barros (1999 and 2000). Moreover, I could also identify at least fifty songs from Brazil (either from Recife or from Bahia) in the great anthology of Afro-Cuban religious music edited in the 1950s by Lydia Cabrera.

Another piece of evidence that the majority of these Afro-Bahian texts were unknown until very recently can be found in the monumental work of compilation of oral sources published by Pierre Verger, *Notes sur le culte des Orisa et Vodun* (1957). Throughout the six hundred pages of his book, the Bahian *candomblé* texts are shown in Yorùbá only. Very few of them appear translated, and some only partially, whereas the thousands of song texts and praise poems gathered in Nigeria and Benin are invariably presented with a literal translation. Why is that so? Are the Bahian texts deformed to a point beyond comprehensibility, so that translation is not possible anymore? Whatever the answer, the fact of the matter is that Pierre Verger did not discuss openly the issue of translation of the *candomblé* texts in his book. As to the *tambor de mina* of Maranhão, where the Ewe and Fon religious traditions were more strongly preserved, various researchers have confirmed the existence of a great corpus of song texts in Fon, but so far they have not been translated into Portuguese.

Texts from the *Xangôs* of Recife

In 1976, Rita Segato and I recorded the entire repertoire of the songs of the Nago Nation sung by a priest respected for his family origin, which goes back to the foundation of the local Yorùbá religious tradition. In 1977, during a second period of fieldwork, we taped once more the entire Nago repertoire, this time sung by a woman, Amara Reis Gomes, also connected to that traditional house and justly regarded in the community as one of the people with the greatest command of this repertoire. This second collection considerably widened the scope of the first one because of the number of songs registered for each one of the gods. Thus, for instance, the only time I was ever able to listen to a song for Ìròkò was during the special recording sessions we had with Amara Gomes. Apart from this song, all the songs collected in 1976 were repeated, and particularly the repertoires of Òsanyìn, Òrúnmìlà, Sàngó, and Oya were considerably expanded.

In 1980, we finally managed to get close to Malaquias Felipe da Costa, who displayed one of the best Yorùbá pronunciations of the city, a fact that later my Yorùbá friends in Belfast could confirm. We taped all the rituals of the Nago Nation in the oldest and most traditional cult house of Recife, known as the Sítio of Pai Adão (Father Adam's compound), located in the metropolitan area of the city.

In 1981, we returned to Queen's University, Belfast, after our fieldwork, to write our doctoral theses. There, we had the happy surprise of meeting a Yorùbá graduate colleague, Oluyemi Olaniyan, who gave himself, with extreme good will and extraordinary patience, to the task of listening to our numerous recordings of *xangô* music and, step by step, trying to translate the texts of the songs.

Despite the fact that these Yorùbá songs are performed in hundreds of cult houses in Recife, I feel quite confident stating that one of the few cult houses in the city where the Yorùbá language is still preserved to an intelligible point is the Sítio of Água Fria. Of course, there are still practitioners outside the Sítio who preserve satisfactorily the Yorùbá pronunciation, but their number is being reduced each year. Since the whole collection that is here presented is directly linked to this cult house and to its main priest, I trace briefly a profile of them.

The Sítio of Água Fria is one of the matrixes of the dominant Nation of Afro-Brazilian cult in Recife: the Nago Nation, which exhibits clear

similarities with the Ketu Nation of Bahia. For cult members of practically all the houses in the region, the Sítio represents the model of worship, from every point of view—in the sophistication of the rituals, in
the beauty of the music and dance, in the number of deities worshipped
(since deities are found in the Sítio that are not worshipped anywhere
else), in the spiritual power of possessions, all of this indicating a tradition that has been better preserved there than anywhere else. The house
was founded around 1870 by a Yorùbá woman called Ines Joaquina da
Costa (Ifá Tinuké), who brought with her to Brazil, when she came as an
adult, various deities, in the form of symbols, images, objects, and even
seeds, in order to plant a gigantic Ìrókò-Tree (African teak; *Chlorophora
Excelsa,* but also the *Ficus Doliaria* in Brazil), which exists until today,
and which is worshipped as the deity called Ìrókò. With her when she
came to Recife was another priest, called João Otolú, whose daughter,
Vicência (Fádáyìró), lived in the Sítio until 1984, when she died at the
age of ninety years old.

The house has always functioned as a base for a great community of
Africans and their descendants. With the death of Ifá Tinuké in 1916, the
leadership was transferred to Felipe Sabino da Costa (Ope Watàna), better known as Pai Adão (Father Adam), who was doubtlessly the greatest
personality in the history of the *xangô* cults. Among other talents, he
counted on great spiritual powers, a deep knowledge of the ritual, aesthetic, and mythological foundations of the tradition, having complete
command of the Yorùbá language. After his death in 1936, the Sítio
was led by another priestess, Juana Batista, who died in 1952. From that
year until 1972, a son of Pai Adão, José Romão da Costa (Ojo Okunrin),
was in charge of the house. With the death of José Romão in 1972, his
brother Malaquias Felipe da Costa (Oje Biyí) took the leadership, in
spite of certain periods of absence due to a conflict of inheritance with
his nephew, Manuel Nascimento Costa, son of José Romão.

Malaquias lived with his father from 1910, when he was born, until 1936, the year that Pai Adão died. From his father, he learned all
the immense repertoire of songs, the subtleties of the complex ritual
cycle, and the oracle of sixteen cowries, known in Brazil as *jogo de
búzios.* He did not learn, however, to speak the Yorùbá language, but
he managed to preserve admirably well the pronunciation of hundreds
of songs and invocations without knowing what they meant literally.
He used to say that Pai Adão was extremely severe in the teaching of
the Nago repertoire to his children and would shout at them whenever

they repeated wrongly the text of a song. Even if he was not the only person to learn with Pai Adão, Malaquias was endowed with a special gift for singing and pronouncing correctly the Yorùbá phonemes. From the recordings with Malaquias, Oluyemi Olaniyan was able to translate the greater part of the repertoires for Èshù, Orúnmìlà, Oshun, Yemoja, Shàngó, Oya, Òrìshànlá, egun, Ibori, washing of the head, and songs for the sacrifices.

One of the main transmitters of the present Yorùbá literary corpus, Amara Reis Gomes, was reared from childhood in the Sítio of Água Fria under the care of a woman called Odú Baeto, probably one of the last descendants of Africans in Recife who could speak Yorùbá. Like Malaquias, Amara was an exceptionally gifted singer, capable of animating festivals, offerings, and sacrifices. Apart from that, she was endowed with a great memory for the songs of the Nago Nation. Her major contribution for the corpus we edited was the vast repertoire of Osányìn, the only one translated entirely from the recordings I made with her. Of course, a considerable part of the lesser-known repertoire of the other òrìsàs translated here has come from Amara's tapes.

It is worth noting that the majority of texts collected by the São Paulo ethnographic mission of 1938 (undertaken at a time when police repression closed the *xangô* temples) were copied from notebooks owned by some cult members. Notebooks containing the lyrics of songs, as well as general information about *xangô* rituals, have become quite common in Recife. Except for the Sítio, we were able to confirm the existence of notebooks in all the cult houses we visited. It has even been established nowadays that those who have just finished their initiation organize a notebook with the basic information about the world of the òrìsàs, song texts included.

The Yorùbá language is certainly much better preserved in the oral tradition than in its written version in the notebooks, generally transcribed in Portuguese orthography by people with limited schooling in their own language. These notebooks function evidently as a secondary mnemonic device for devotees who live in constant contact with the cult life and who are able to sing the diverse repertoires of songs during rituals. In other words, most cult members sing them through the practice of reproducing as faithfully as possible what they have heard and not because of having memorized them based on what they wrote down in their notebooks. Maybe that is the reason why members talk about songs, and not about texts.

My reconstruction of the *xangô* history allows me to suppose that fifty years ago, by the time Pai Adão died, very few people (not more than a dozen, probably) were really capable of speaking fluent Yorùbá, or at least understanding it. From what I could infer, these few Yorùbá speakers had an attitude of arrogance and censorship toward the new cult leaders who were appearing in the local religious scene and who did not show the same satisfactory command of the language of their African ancestors. They first directed their criticism against the leaders and adepts of the Shamba Nation, who had arrived in the first decade of the century from Maceió, the capital of the neighboring state of Alagoas, and who apparently had a much poorer command of the Yorùbá language and of the singing tradition. We could confirm this because we also recorded the Shamba repertoire, and Olaniyan found the song texts to be in a highly distorted Yorùbá.

As this class of guardians of African orthodoxy disappeared, the symbolic practice of *xangô*s entered a more dynamic phase: the mythopoetic imagination of people was liberated from traditional constraints, and the meaning of songs started to be reinterpreted more freely. The words were then converted in a kind of kaleidoscope, a catalyst, or a locus of speech for emotions and visions experienced. Thus, new associations and mythical narratives could be developed, now adapted to a distinct form of life, typical of a spatial, temporal, and formal distance from the original source of the sacred Yorùbá repertoire.

It was exactly when knowledge of Yorùbá declined that the tradition of hermeneutics of sacred songs became richer. Beyond, therefore, the already worn-out opposition between purity and contamination, we can observe how the so-called decadent or distorted practice of a tradition can open a space for recombination and inventions of meaning for the texts, even if absolutely condemned by the immobilizing purist line of that tradition.

And it is precisely for this reason that I tried to build a polyphonic text, so that, together with the accuracy of the Yorùbá words of people such as Malaquias, other adepts, coming from less central initiative biographies, could display their talents as mythmakers, builders of symbolic bridges, certainly mistaken from the point of view of the orthodoxy but nonetheless creative and, who knows, ready to inspire new centralities whenever the Yorùbá standard of purity ceases to be exclusive.

Put another way, the anthology of Yorùbá song texts from Recife shows a literary corpus that survives outside its original linguistic province. It is inevitable, therefore, that mental operations taken to be irrational, Kabbalistic, even Lacanian in style (I am here thinking mainly of the issue of homophony, very common in Yorùbá but which occurs, in this case, also between Yorùbá and Portuguese) infiltrate themselves sometimes in the mere attempt at preserving and interpreting the repertoire. In other words, the corpus translated is entirely Yorùbá; on the other hand, the mythopoetics that transpires from it is not African, but Afro-Brazilian—or Afro-American, for that matter. As a matter of fact, these song texts, understood in their local context, can be defined as mid-Atlantic texts: although the articulation of signifiers upon which they were created sprung from a Nigerian historical experience, the fictional translations and the commentaries I was able to register belong to the Afro-Brazilian historical experience.

It is possible that there are singularities in the Afro-Brazilian style of preserving the sacred songs because of the specific historical constraint that people were not able to make up new songs; they could only repeat the ones they learned from their elders instead. This conservative attitude toward the texts might have influenced the resulting musical performance, perhaps conditioning them to emphasize aesthetic parameters different from those more commonly used among West Africans. For example, in Nigeria the practice of creating variations for the lyrics of the sacred songs is quite common; in Recife extemporization—or even mere attempts at individualizing the ritual-musical event—had to be channeled mainly through the melody, via the exploration of *melismas,* using secondary embellishments and adding extra vowels to the words. One consequence of this work of melodic creation within the Yorùbá text—and an unfortunate one, as far as our project of translation was concerned—was to complicate linguistic audition, to the point of often rendering it impossible for the translator to distinguish the constitutive phonemes of a particular word from those sounds that have been added on solely for aesthetic purposes. In other words, both the lyrics and the melodies were then distorted: melodies ignore textual incoherence, and texts are indifferent to melodic excesses.

Another great difficulty for the control of the correct uttering of texts—and one that makes the great capacity of *xangô* members toward preservation even more surprising—lies in the fact that not a single *xangô* adept of all those I knew was aware that Yorùbá is a tonal language! They simply did not seem able to conceive the radical difference of meaning that any group of phonemes can manifest when there is a change in the relationships between the tone in which it is pronounced.

Translating *Xangô* Texts

As I have already noted, I owe most of the translations to Oluyemi Olani-yan, a master in the art of *dùndún,* the Yorùbá talking drum, who was my colleague in the Ph.D. program in the anthropology of music under John Blacking at Queen's University. We worked on the collection of record-ings for eight months uninterrupted, in long and strenuous sessions of listening, choosing alternatives, and translating.

After Olaniyan's departure for Nigeria, I counted on the generous help of a Yorùbá couple who resided in Belfast at that time: Sunday Aderemi Aderemo and his wife, Idowu Aderemo. They offered to mark the tones in all the words of the anthology, and that task ended up in a total revision of all the texts translated by Olaniyan. Sunday and Idowu confirmed 90 percent of the deciphering and the semantic interpretation of Olaniyan; in all of those cases in which their interpretations disagreed with each other, I chose to include both versions. The Aderemos were able to decipher some twenty additional songs and invocations that had eluded Olaniyan's hearing.

Let me stress that the three translators are not necessarily devoted to Yorùbá traditional religion; it is possible, therefore, that certain more esoteric mythical or symbolic connections have escaped their under-standing, but I do believe that the major part of the material I showed them was understood and absorbed adequately. Luckily enough, Bolaji Campbell, who was a Ph.D. student at the University of Wisconsin–Madison in 1999 and who has specifically researched aesthetic aspects of the religion of the òrìṣàs, diligently tried his best to cover the areas of understanding obscure to Olaniyan and the Aderemos. Finally, in order to complement our general understanding of these texts, I conducted rather extensive research on the classical sources about the Yorùbá tradi-tional religion written in Western languages. Thus, the reader can appre-ciate how intact this tradition has been preserved in Brazil, as well as the degree of similarity, with these classical sources, of the interpretations formulated by the translators.

Evidently, as happens to all attempts at translating, one cannot guar-antee complete accuracy in the achievement. First, there are the difficult conditions of preservation of the original texts in Brazil. Second, we have the syntactic and semantic complexities arising from the Yorùbá language itself, such as its tonal character and its recurring mechanisms of union and fusion of radicals, which allow more than one manner of unmaking the process of composition of some words. Third, there is the strong polysemy intrinsic to this sacred tradition. And finally, it is relevant to remember that the translators belong to different groups inside the Yorùbá nation: Olaniyan is from Ibadan, Sunday and Idowu are from Ekiti, and Bolaji is from Ilé-Ifè. Who knows? This regional difference might explain why each one had a better understanding of some songs and not of others. Olabiyi Yai was struck by the homogeneity of the material translated and called my attention to a possible "Òyọ́centrism" on the part of Olaniyan: probably he felt comfortable translating only the texts from the Òyọ́ dialect of Yorùbá.

Recife, Cuba, Trinidad: Yorùbá Mythopoetics in the New World

Although my main objective has been to edit the Yorùbá corpus in Recife, another possible contribution of the translations is to set a firmer ground for comparative work between the various traditions within the Yorùbá diaspora. That is why I searched for the same song texts in the collections already published of the equivalent corpora for the òrìṣàs in Cuba and in Trinidad. In the case of Cuba, where there is a vast literature on the Yorùbá tradition, I decided to concentrate on a dialogue with the anthology prepared by John Mason, *Orin Orisha* (1992). Although living in New York, John Mason has compiled a convincing corpus of Yorùbá sacred songs belonging to the Cuban tradition. In the case of Trinidad, my reference has been the work of Maureen Warner-Lewis, especially her book *Yorùbá Songs of Trinidad* (1994). Based on these two works, we can now establish, without any doubt, that the same religious tradition came from some area of Yorùbáland and managed to be reproduced independently during slavery days in places as far from each other as Brazil, Cuba, and Trinidad. As far as I know, no historical link has ever been registered between the slaves in Brazil and in these two Caribbean islands. This leaves us to pursue a more realistic and fascinating hypothesis: priests, religious specialists, diviners, and musicians, taken from Nigeria and Benin to different parts of the New World in the nineteenth century, were able to reorganize the core elements of their religious traditions. After that first feat of reconstruction (obviously, without discarding the components of invention and reinterpretation), their descendants managed to preserve that corpus of song, myth, and poetry with such a will that people like Lydia Cabrera (1975), Argeliers León (1971), Rómulo Lachatañeré (1992), Fernando Ortiz (1950), John Mason (1992), Maureen Warner-Lewis (1994), Melville and Frances Herskovits (1947), Pierre Verger (1999), Juana Elbein dos Santos (1976), and myself (1993, forthcoming) were able to collect these texts more than one hundred years after they left Africa in the minds of those determined Yorùbá slaves.

My aim has been simply to open the avenues for comparison. I left out pieces of verses and fragments that are similar to Cuban ones. One aspect that can be developed later is the differences in the styles of constructing the same pieces in the three corpora. For instance, the Cuban model of song text is built around a sequence of small fragments of verses whose patterns are repeated while new elements are being introduced at the beginning of every repetition; on the other hand, the Recifean model favors a longer text with two sections, a first one, repeated entirely, and then a second one, repeated to allow the song to reach its climax. Apart from that, both *xangô* and *santería* show a clear sequence of song texts, corresponding closely to the ritual function of the piece. As to the Trinidadian corpus, on a first look, a song text seems to be organized in a way similar to the *xangô* one: long and with two sections. Unfortunately, the presentation of the Trinidad corpus in Warner-Lewis's book does not allow us to know how a complete sequence of songs (a *shire,* as it is called in Brazil, or an *orú* as it is called in Cuban *lukumí*) is worked out. But this—and many other questions—are now, more than ever, wide open for African Yorùbá scholars as well as for New World Yorùbá scholars.

Characteristics of *Xangô* Song Texts

Similar to what scholars of the Yorùbá literary tradition have already shown, the content of the texts and lyrics of songs is built upon an extremely concise and compressed idiom, one that just allows us to grasp its general meaning and that moves around an entirely poetic ambiance, with a great amount of musical sounds, alliterations, onomatopoeia, reiteration, and play on language tones. There are numerous proverbs, sayings, fixed expressions, spells, magical formulae, greeting formulae, comparisons—all frequently supported by metaphor, personification, and, above all, epithet.

Instead of undertaking a literary analysis of the *xangô* Yorùbá corpus, my purpose is to offer to various researchers—theologians, linguists, literary critics, writers, anthropologists, historians of religion—and practitioners of Afro-Brazilian religions, Africanists, specialists and practitioners of Afro-Cuban and Afro-Trinidadian religions, dilettantes of all sorts—the Yorùbá material with its corresponding Brazilian rereading and its variants found in Cuba and in Trinidad. Nonetheless, I feel the need to highlight a minimum of signs, which seem to me relevant for a richer reading of these texts. Following the typology put forward by Síkírù Sálámì (1991), one has to recognize, first of all, that not only are there *oríkì* (i. e., invocations or epithets) in the Recifean anthology, but also *ibás* (greetings), *àdúràs* (prayers, such as in some Òrúnmìlà texts), and, obviously, numerous *orin* (songs).

Of all the song types edited and translated, three repertoires seemed to me to be especially rich and original, in terms of the little information available about Yorùbá texts in Brazil: the songs for the *eguns,* for Osányìn, and for Orúnmìlà. The rather substantial collection of songs for the *eguns* not only helps to widen our knowledge about this fascinating aspect of traditional Yorùbá spirituality but also contributes mainly to correct a somewhat distorted view about the preservation of the *egun* cult in Brazil. Contrary to what has been stated in the literature so far, the cult to the Yorùbá ancestors does not exist exclusively in Salvador and Itaparica (cities in the state of Bahia); it can also be found in Recife. Although the spectacular apparition of the masquerades, as performed on the island of Itaparica, is not found in the *xangô* cults, a strong ritual tradition is kept quite alive there, vibrant enough to preserve a collection of songs, texts, and lyrics of such magnitude.

The Osányìn collection is certainly the most complex, from a hermeneutical point of view, for it condenses a maze of charms, spells, curses, magical prayers, and abstract and philosophical expressions. Moreover, since we are dealing here with sacred texts, I cannot restrain myself from suggesting a comparison, which will probably be taken as "out of the blue" by some people, but which becomes proper and feasible if we accept the possibility of a universal dimension of the spiritual experience: I mean to put together certain aspects of the repertoire of Osányìn and the Taoist view of the world. For example, the contrast established in a couple of songs between *tutu* and *iyeye* leaves reminds me clearly of the arguments of chapter 4 of the Book of Chuang Tzu (1968) on the advantages of uselessness: *tutu,* which is good to eat, lives a short life; whereas *iyeye* lives many years, exactly like the old twisted oak tree of the Chinese parable that was never cut down precisely because it failed to serve ordinary human needs.

Olaniyan himself was surprised by the excellent state of preservation of that entire sequence of Osányìn texts; he managed to translate all the texts, without exception, in their exact ritual order of performance. On the other hand, specialists on Bahian *candomblé* have mentioned very few elements of this symbolic complex of the god of leaves. In comparison, the song lyrics for the òrìṣàs, better known and more popular in Recife, showed a much higher degree of distortion, although they were much more widespread locally and regionally.

A few words on the repertoire of Ọ̀rúnmìlà. As in the case of the *eguns,* we can here revise a dominant assumption in the literature on Afro-Brazilian cults, namely that the Yorùbá religious culture was concentrated almost entirely in Bahia. Ọ̀rúnmìlà, worshipped in the Nago nation of Recife as the god of time and destiny, being the entity closer to Ọlọ́run, the Supreme God, is a deity who condenses an extremely rich set of myths and symbols, which can be inferred simply by a reading of his repertoire. However, as far as I know, nothing even similar to what is presented here has ever been registered in the ethnographies on Bahian *candomblé.* Besides, texts of Ọ̀rúnmìlà are particularly inspiring, as long as they express the more profound and transcendent religiosity of Ifá, and through them we have access to fragments of enigmatic oracular texts known as *odùs.*

As to the texts for the other deities, it is worth highlighting some epithets, such as the one of Èshù that says: "The-one-who-weeps-while-the-others-are-weeping"—a complete quality (and a surprising one for many people) expressed in one single word! The authors of these songs frequently use many typically religious concepts or sentiments. Exclamations of fear because of the presence of the deity are common in Oya and Òrìshànlá; sense of awe, for Òrìshànlá and Sàngó; violence and energy in the songs for Ògún; jubilation and a sort of childish attitude, for Yemoja, Òshún, and Ode; lightness and admiration in the brief verses for Òshùnmarè; and trembling and extreme respect, for the *eguns.* Finally, hierophanies, lyricism, moral lessons, paradoxes, mystical rapture, and poetry.

Some translations reinforce and confirm clearly the mythical-symbolic complex that circulates in Recife about these deities and these rituals. In other cases, however, the restitution of this tradition contradicts the African mythopoetics. The reader should remember, for instance, that in Nigeria, Yemoja is a goddess of the sweet waters (more precisely, of the Ògún River), and not of the sea, as in Brazil. Thus, the high frequency, in the lyrical texts dedicated to this deity so much worshiped among Brazilians, calls up images of aquatic environments and the fertility of the soil that produces maize and banana.

A comparison that seems appropriate, if we bear in mind the extremely difficult conditions of retrieving oral texts that have been taken out of their original linguistic community, would be with the so-called popular Latin, preserved with so much persistence in the prayers and songs of religious ceremonies and festivals typical of the so-called popular Catholicism in the interior of Brazil and in other parts of the New World. Could a Latinist understand and translate these Latin words, whose endings are certainly distorted after being repeated, sometimes for centuries, by people who ignore the language, without looking at their written, canonical version? Probably not.

Various factors pertaining specifically to the religious practice of Recifean *xangô,* and which were articulated in an efficacious manner, have contributed considerably to preserve these Yorùbá repertoires. First, there is an extremely rigid precept, linked to the worship of the god Osányìn, which makes whistling and humming inside a cult house totally forbidden. Consequently, anytime some one utters any text that belongs to this sacred repertoire, it has to be through singing, with music and lyrics together; such mnemonic devices are an effective way of safeguarding the texts that today's worshippers received from the elders who came directly from Africa. Moreover, since these texts are actually sung, the various musical factors, such as rhythm, measure, phrasing, and lyrics, work as aesthetic guardians of the literary text: pronunciation of the words is then incorporated as an additional musical element, turned into a musical stimulus that saves the exact text.

Finally, it is necessary to emphasize that there is a reasonable degree of phonetic compatibility between Yorùbá and Portuguese that makes it easier for a Portuguese speaker to memorize and reproduce a text recited or sung in Yorùbá compared to speakers of German, Dutch, or even French, for instance.

As regards the choice of words in the translations, my aim has been merely to offer to students of this tradition the mythical and literary potential of the Yorùbá material together with its Recifean (re)reading. I have taken relatively few liberties, just enough to convey its meaning in an English idiom as faithful and transparent as possible. I only allowed myself to point out the possibilities of alternative mythopoieses still to be explored in the future. The idea, however, is to help the assimilation of the mechanisms of juxtaposition of ideas, images, and expressions of Yorùbá poetics, so that, starting from them, readers can proceed to formulate their own poetic version of the English text.

I have called the translations of my Yorùbá colleagues literal translations. In those cases, however, where they chose to provide only a general idea of a song text they understood, instead of a word-for-word translation of its meaning, I have called their translation interpretive. As to the translations that were offered me by *xangô* adepts in Recife, I have named them fictional, because I am aware of the fact that they ignore the Yorùbá language; their translation is clearly a creation, that is, a new semantic arrangement based on mythic and symbolic elements of the Yorùbá tradition in Brazil. They are not false, in the sense of a radical linguistic positivism, but can accurately be said to be fictional, in so far as they cannot be directly related to the literal meaning of the original utterances. In some special cases, I was even able to show that the fictional translation went parallel to the corresponding literal translation, or the interpretive one; and this is strong evidence that *xangô* people knew the Yorùbá language not so long ago.

The fictional translations were not elicited intentionally, but they appeared in the context of interviews and discussions about rituals and deities. Sometimes, while commenting on a certain passage of a myth, the narrator would mention a particular song and "translate" its meaning, obviously applying it to the situation being discussed. The greater part of these native, or fictional, translations are concentrated around the repertoires of the more popular òrìsàs, that is, those who possess initiates and who are, for this very same reason, objects of more intense mythological projection on the part of cult members. On the other hand, about the repertoires of deities like Osányìn and Orúnmìlà, whose translated repertoires are much bigger than those of the others, paradoxically no fictional translation was ever offered to me.

Finally, these translations represent an event of significant histori-cal proportion, not only for Afro-Brazilian studies, but also for those of the African diaspora in the Americas as a whole. It is enough for the reader to consider the fact that many of those song texts have been around the literature of Afro-Brazilian cults, in a Portuguese translit-eration that renders them almost entirely unintelligible, since the first decades of the twentieth century. And there have been constant visits of specialists in African languages to Bahia, in search of preserved Africanisms, since the 1940s, without any of them showing material equivalent to this one. For all that, after almost one hundred years of the dissolution of the Yorùbá linguistic community in Brazil (and, for all we can guess, this community must have been considerably smaller in Recife than in Bahia), it seems a true miracle that the edition of such a corpus could be carried out at all. It is therefore cause for rejoicing, to give these extraordinary pieces of poetry and myth, both to the actual generations of Yorùbá living today in Africa and to their kinfolk liv-ing today in Brazil, Cuba, Trinidad, and other parts of the New World. Ashe o!

References

Barros, José Flávio Pessoa. 1999. *A Fogueira de Xangô . . . O Orixá do Fogo.* Rio de Janeiro: UERJ/Intercon.

———. 2000. *O Banquete do Rei . . . Olubajé.* Rio de Janeiro: Ao Livro Técnico.

Bastide, Roger. 1978. *O Candomblé da Bahia.* São Paulo: Companhia Editora Nacional.

Cabrera, Lydia. 1975. *El Monte.* Miami: Ediciones del Chichereku.

Carvalho, José Jorge. 1984. "Music of African Origin in Brazil." In *Africa in Latin America,* ed. Manuel Moreno Fraginals, 227–48. New York: Holmes & Meier.

———. 1988. "A Força da Nostalgia: A Concepção de Tempo Histórico nas Religiões Afro-Brasileiras Tradicionais." *Religião e Sociedade* 14, no.2: 36–61.

———. 1992. *Shango Cult in Recife, Brazil.* Caracas: Fundación de Etnomusi-cología y Folklore/CONAC/OAS.

———. 1993. *Cantos Sagrados do Xangô do Recife.* Brasília: Fundação Cul-tural Palmares.

———. 2000. "Afro-Brazilian Music and Rituals. Part I: From Traditional

Genres to the Beginnings of Samba." Duke–University of North Carolina Program in Latin American Studies, Working Paper Series 30.

———. 2006. "A Tradição Musical Iorubá no Brasil: Um Cristal que se Oculta e Revela." In *Músicas Africanas e Indígenas no Brasil,* ed. Rosângela Pereira de Tugny and Ruben Caixeta de Querioz, 265–92. Belo Horizonte: Editora da UFMG.

———. Forthcoming. *Yorùbá Mythopoetics in Brazil.* Madison: University of Wisconsin/African Library Institute.

Herskovits, Melville J. 1947. *Afro-Bahian Religious Songs.* Record album with notes. Washington, DC: Library of Congress.

Lachatañeré, Rómulo. 1992. *Oh, Mío Yemaya!* Havana: Editorial de Ciencias Sociales.

León, Argeliers. 1971. "Un Caso de Tradición Oral Escrita." *Islas* 13, nos. 2–3: 141–51.

Mason, John. 1992. *Orin Orisa: Songs for Selected Heads.* New York: Yorùbá Theological Archministry.

Megenney, William. 1989. "Sudanic/Bantu/Portuguese Syncretism in Selected Chants from Brazilian Umbanda and Candomblé." *Anthropos* 84, nos. 4–6: 363–83.

———. 1992. "West Africa in Brazil: The Case of Ewe-Yorùbá Syncretism." *Anthropos* 87, nos. 4–6: 459–74.

Ortiz, Fernando. 1950. *La Africanía de la Música Folklórica de Cuba.* Havana: Ministerio de Educación.

Salami, Sikiru. 1991. *Cânticos dos Orixás na África.* São Paulo: Editora Oduduwa.

Santos, Juana Elbein. 1976. *Os Nagô e a Morte.* Petrópolis, Brazil: Ed. Vozes.

Verger, Pierre. 1957. *Notes sur le Culte des Orisa et Vodun à Bahia: le Baie des touts les saints au Brésil et à la ancienne Côte des esclaves en Afrique.* Dakar: Mémoires de l'IFAN, no. 51.

Warner-Lewis, Maureen. 1996. *Yorùbá Songs of Trinidad.* London: Karnak House, 1994.

22

Axexê Funeral Rites in Brazil's Òrìṣà Religion

Constitution, Significance, and Tendencies

REGINALDO PRANDI,

TRANSLATED BY MARIA P. JUNQUEIRA

Candomblé, the religion of òrìṣàs of Brazil, reconstituted itself in the New World, largely from African religious traditions, especially of Yorùbá origin. These traditions consist of ritual aspects and concepts of humanity and the world, including attitudes toward life and death. These concepts explain and guide the fundamental rites of initiation, especially the most significant, the funeral rites called *axexê (àjèjé)*. With social changes in Brazil and the loss of many original African concepts, as well as the profound influence of Catholicism, African religious organizations of the diaspora remade themselves in a fragmented way. Great numbers of priests of Candomblé often lack information about particular rituals, especially the funeral service of *axexê*. In this chapter, after briefly describing the rituals of *axexê* and anthropological references, as well as the social conditions in which the service occurs, I try to explain certain changes and tendencies occurring in contemporary Candomblé, especially in the regions of São Paulo and Rio de Janeiro where the religion of òrìṣàs multiplied itself by thousands—thousands of houses of recent origin.

In diverse cultures, the religious concept of death is contained within

437

the concept of life; they are inseparable. The Yorùbá and other African groups, who provided the cultural basis for African-Brazilian religions, believe that life and death alternate in cycles in such a way that the dead return to the world of the living, reincarnated as a new member of the family. Several Yorùbá names express this return precisely, such as bestowing the name *babátúndé*, "father-comes-back."

There are two worlds in Yorùbá cosmology: (1) a natural world in which humankind lives in contact with nature or the world of the living, which is called *ayé;* and (2) a supernatural world where the òrìṣà, the deities and spirits, live. It is where all the dead go. This world is called *òrun*. When someone dies in the *ayé* world, his or her spirit, or a part of it, goes to *òrun,* from whence it returns to the *ayé* world, being born again. Ultimately, all humans—women, men, and children—go to the same world. The Yorùbá have no concept of punishment or reward after death; consequently, there are no notions of heaven, hell, or purgatory. Furthermore, there is no judgment after death, and the spirits return to life in the *ayé* as soon as they can, because the ideal world is the world of the living, where living is good.

Spirits of the illustrious dead, such as kings, heroes, famous priests, founders of cities, and lineages are praised in the *egúngún* festivals. During these festivals, such ancestors take up residence in the body of priests and masqueraders, enabling the ancestors to be among humans once more and to judge their faults, solve their disagreements, and arbitrate community matters. However, this role of the *egúnngún* ancestor as moral arbitrator and guarantor of social harmony unfortunately failed to be reproduced in Brazil. Although the *egúnngún* cult survived in Bahia in a few specialized *terreiros*, the *egúnngún* Candomblé of Itaparica Island (later present also in Salvador and São Paulo) is very distant from the daily practice of the òrìṣà Candomblé and practically absent in the ordinary life of the society. In other words, the *egúnngún* ancestor has completely lost its original African moral and social functions (Braga 1992). The Yorùbá religion in Brazil, throughout the òrìṣà *terreiros,* was transformed into something strictly ritualistic and devoid of ethics. The institutional components of value orientation and behavior control regarding the collective morality exercised by the African ancestral *egúnngún* are totally absent in the daily life of the believer in Brazil.

The Yorùbá notion of rebirth is sometimes extremely exaggerated in Brazil, where some spirits are born and quickly die, only for the pleasure of being able to be immediately reborn again. These are the so-called *àbíkú* (from the Yorùbá; literally, "born to die"), which explains in traditional Yorùbá culture the high level of child mortality. In general, the child is reborn in a succession of births from the uterus of the same mother. When a child is identified as *àbíkú*, numerous rituals are performed to prevent the child's premature death. Whereas the *egúnngún* society praises the masculine ancestors of the group (Babayemi 1980), another society of masqueraders, the *gèlèdé* society, celebrates the ancestral mothers, who oversee the care and health of children, including the *àbíkú* (Lawal 1996). However, *gèlèdé* festivals failed to survive in Brazil.

Professor Agenor Miranda Rocha, initiated in Candomblé in 1912, told me that in the beginning of the twentieth century, disputes caused the groups to separate, and the foundation of the Axé Opô Afonjá by Mãe Aninha Obá Bií, *iyalòrìṣà* of Professor Agenor, the initiative of the constitution of the *gèlèdé* society did not prevail. In addition, the essential concept of *àbíkú* did not survive entirely unchanged in integrity. The term began to designate, in many Candomblés, people who are considered hereditary initiates of certain òrìṣàs, thus having no need to be shaved, as do most initiates. The fragmentary way in which the African religion was reconstituted in Brazil after the transatlantic crossing clearly implies several changes in the concepts of life and death, changes that influenced the sense of certain ritual practices, which were deeply affected by their Catholic ritual counterparts.

Christian tradition teaches that the human being is composed of a material body and one indivisible spirit or soul. Yorùbá tradition teaches that a human is composed of the material body, or *ara,* which disintegrates on death and returns to nature. Moreover, the spiritual part of the human is composed of four unified elements or aspects, each with its own existence: (1) the vital breath or life itself, or *èmi;* (2) the personality destiny, or *orí;* (3) supernatural identity or identity of origin that links each person to nature, the personal òrìṣàs; and (4) the spirit itself, or *égún.* Each element needs to be integrated in a totality that makes up the living person, but after death, each element has a different destiny. Represented by the act of breathing, *èmi,* the vital breath that comes from Ọlọrun, leaves the physical body at the moment of death and returns to the collective mass that contains the generic and unending principle of life, or the vital cosmic force of the primordial god Olódùmarè-Ọlọrun. The *èmi* is never destroyed and is constantly being reused. The *orí,* as the head is called that contains the individuality and the destiny, disappears at death, because it is unique and personal. No one can inherit someone else's destiny. Each life will be different, even with reincarnation. Unlike the Christian notion of all souls deriving from the one and only God the Father, the individual òrìṣà defines the mythic origin of each person, as well as an individual's potential and limitations. The individual òrìṣà may be derived from a number of sources, and it returns at death to the collective òrìṣ̀à, of which it is a miniscule part.

Finally, containing the proper memory of the living in its passage through the *ayé,* which represents the identity, social, biographical, and existential link to the community, the spirit itself, the *égún,* goes to *òrun,* able then to return, reborn into the lineage, or midst, of its own ancestral biological family. When the *égún* is of someone famous or powerful, the living can praise her or his memory by invoking the *égún* at a shrine. Here a sacred pot is prepared for the *égún,* just as is generally done for òrìṣàs and other spiritual beings. Commonly, sacrifices and other offerings are made to the *égún* to integrate the lineage of family ancestry with the larger community. They represent the roots of that group and form the basis of collective identity.

In traditional Africa, days after the birth of a Yorùbá child, there is a ceremony in which a name is chosen for the newborn, when the *babaláwo* divines to find the origin of the child. The ceremony of divination will reveal if the child is a beloved one reincarnated. Yorùbá names always designate the mythic origin of the person, which may refer to their personal òrìṣà, determined by patriarchal line, to the condition of the birth, type of pregnancy, or sibling order—signifying, for instance, one born after twins or conditions such as *àbíkú.* From the moment of the naming ceremony, there are several rites of passage associated not only with social roles, such as adulthood and marriage, but also with the construction of the individual. Here the major moments of life passages and multiple components of the spirit are integrated. With death, these rituals are redone, so that each element reaches its destiny, rebuilding in this way, the balance only temporarily disrupted by death.

In Brazil, in Candomblé and other African-derived religious traditions, the death of an initiate requires the performance of specific funeral rites. Such rites are called *axexê (àsèsè, àjèjé)* in the Ketu nation; *tambor de choro* in the Mina-jeje and Mina-nago; and *sirrum* in both the Jeje-mahin and in Batuque; and *ntambi* or *mukundu* in the Angola nation. Generally speaking, these rites have two main objectives: (1) to undo the *igba ori,* which is done and praised in the *bori* ceremony *(ebòorí),* which precedes the praising of the personal òrìṣà; and (2) to undo the links with the personal òrìṣà to whom the deceased was devoted through initiation, which directly implies the breaking of the link with the entire *terreiro* community. Such a break also severs the *aye*, because the *igba* òrìṣà is physical and exists in the *aye* as a representation of its existence in *òrun* or the parallel world. Even the *abian*, the non-initiate persons who are beginning life in the *terreiro* and have done their *bori*, must have these ties severed, and thus their *igba orì* must be sent away, though obviously in a much simpler ceremony.

We can say that in the initiation sequence (*bori*, òrìṣà initiation, obligations at one, three, five years, *decá* in the seventh year, and subsequent obligations every seven years) a member of Candomblé, Xangô, Batuque, or Tambor de Mina embodies the deepening and amplification of religious ties, when new responsibilities and rights culminate and merge—such as *iyalorixá* (*iyálòrìsà*) or *babalorixá* (*bàbálòrìsà*), the *terreiro* community, òrìṣà children—with the larger complex of the religious community. Upon death, these chains have to be broken, thereby liberating the spirit, the *égún*, from the obligations to the world of the , including the religion. The funeral rites thus comprise the breaking of bonds and the liberation of the spiritual elements that constitute a human being. As more than a mere symbolic rupture, it is thus not surprising that in this ceremony the sacred objects of the dead are undone, broken, separated, and sent away.

The term *axexê*, which designates the funeral rites of the Candomblé of the Ketu nation and other variants of Yorùbá, Fon-Yorùbá, or Jejenago, as they are known, is probably a corruption of the Yorùbá word *àjèjé* (J. Santos 1976). In Yorùbá, the death of a hunter usually required the sacrifice of an antelope or other wild animal as part of the funeral rite. Part of the animal was eaten by relatives and friends of the deceased at a feast of homage, while other parts were taken to the forest and offered to the spirit of the dead hunter, together with the hunting tools of the hunter. This *ebó* was given the name of *àjèjé* (Abraham 1962: 38). The *axexê* that occurs in Brazilian Candomblé can be conceived of as a grand *ebó* or offering of sacrificed meat to the spirit of the dead, which is accompanied by various ritual objects.

Since Candomblé is a religion of possession, several deities participate actively in the funeral rites, especially those òrìṣàs associated with death and the dead, such as Oyá or Yansan, who here occupies a special place. Oyá is considered the òrìṣà in charge of taking the dead to Orun, and she is the patron of the *axexê*, according to a myth told by Mãe Stella Odé Kaiodé, *iyálòrìsà* of the Axé Opô Afonjá. This myth captures well the idea of the *axexê* as a ceremony of praise for the one who has passed:

> In the land of Ketu lived a hunter called Odulece.
> He was the leader of the hunters.
> He took as his daughter a girl born in Irá,
> Who, because of her smart and quick ways, was known as Oyá.
> Oyá soon became the favorite of the old hunter,
> Attaining a high place among her community.
> But one day, death took Odulece, leaving Oyá very sad.
> The young woman thought of a way to praise her adopted father.
> She gathered all the hunting tools of Odulece
> and wrapped herself in a cloth.
> She also prepared all the foods that he liked so much to savor.
> She danced and sang for seven days,
> Spreading everywhere her wind and her chant,
> Bringing all the hunters of the earth to that place.
> In the seventh night, followed by the hunters,
> Oyá went to the forest
> and left at the foot of a sacred tree
> the belongings of Odulece.
> At that moment, the bird "*agbé*" went on a sacred flight
>
> Olorun, who sees all,
> was touched by the gesture of Oyá-Yansan
> and gave her the power to guide the dead
> in their trip to the Orun.
> He transformed Odulece into an Òrìsà
> and Oyá into the mother of the sacred spaces.
> Since then, everyone who dies
> has his spirit taken to Orun by Oyá.
> Before though, one had to be praised by their loved ones
> in a feast with food, chanting, and dancing.
> Thus, the *axexê* ritual was born.
>
> M. Santos 1993: 91

The òrìṣàs Nana, Iyewa, Omolu, Oshumare, Ogun, and inevitably Oba all participate in the *axexê*. Conspicuously absent from this list is Shango, who, according to other myths, does not like the *égún*.

The sequence of *axexê* rituals begins immediately after death, when the priests handle the cadaver so that they can remove from its head the symbolic òrìṣà markings that had been implanted during initiation. Traditionally, these markings are implanted into the initiate's shaved head through the *osu,* a cone prepared by mashed *obi* and other ingredients and fixed through ritual incisions. The hair of this area is taken, and the head is washed with *amassi* (an herbal potion) and water. This washing of the head is a symbolic inversion of the first act of initiation, when the beads and the head of the new devotee are also washed by the *iyálòrìsà.* The liquid of the head washing is the first element that is part of the grand *ebó* of the dead person.

After the funeral, the *axexê* proper will start. This will vary from *terreiro* to *terreiro* and from nation to nation. It is more elaborate for powerful persons or high priests, and its size is often dictated by the material means of the family. Generally, the *axexê* unfolds in the opposite order of initiation proceedings. There are five stages: (1) music, chanting, and dance; (2) possession, with at least the presence of Oyá; (3) sacrifices and diverse offerings to the *égún* and the òrìṣàs ritually linked to the person, with Eshu being always the first to be praised and the one to take the *ebó,* obviously, and the ancestors praised by that group; (4) destruction of ritual objects of the dead person (*igbas,* beads, cloths, implements, etc.), although some could be inherited by a member of the group; and (5) the sending away of the "broken" sacred objects, together with the offerings and objects used during the ceremonies, such as the musical instruments specific for the occasion or mats.

At the end of the *axexê,* everything is sent away from the *terreiro* in a large basket, and no religious object belonging to the deceased is left in the temple. The deceased is no longer a member of that house, and only in the future can the deceased be incorporated into the community of famous ancestors and be consecrated and praised. At this moment, the *égún* is free to go. In the same way, the personal òrìṣà or òrìṣàs of this person are not "seated" (*igba* òrìṣà) anymore, so all the links are broken. The *orí* that died with its owner no longer exists in an *igba orí* (sacred vessel). If any object, or *igba,* is given away, it has a new owner, to whom the care and religious responsibility are transferred. Nothing belongs to the deceased anymore, and nothing binds her or him to the *terreiro.*

During the *axexê,* it is believed that the dead person can express her or his last wishes. Toward this end, the priest supervising the ritual uses the *meridilogun* (cowry shells) constantly. Therefore, before each of the deceased's religious objects is destroyed, the priest divines to determine which objects, if any, should stay with a close friend or relative. Generally, however, it is preferable that most objects be discarded. If the founder of that *terreiro* or another priest of comparable stature has died, it is customary to bequeath the *igbas* of his main òrìṣàs to the *terreiro,* which in turn is venerated by the community. Disputes over such *igbas* are not unheard of, sometimes escalating into gunfights and banditry.

The *axexê* occurs in two spaces of the *terreiro:* in an enclosed area, preferably a tent specifically constructed with sticks and foliage; and in the *barracão* (a large, central temple room). In the tent, which is off-limits to most, the ritual objects belonging to the deceased are broken and kept, and sacrifices for the òrìṣàs and the *égún* are performed. Dancing also takes place in the *barracão,* where members of the *terreiro,* relatives, and friends lodge over the duration of the funerary rites. The *barracão* also serves as the ritual dining hall, as participants partake of the sacrificial meats, with the portions most highly charged with *ashe* (vital force) being set apart for the ancestors, òrìṣàs, and *égúns.*

The deceased is represented in the *barracão* by an empty gourd, into which every person present adds coins. Immediately thereafter, each participant dances to the *égún,* which is a compulsory form of homage to the deceased and his or her òrìṣàs. Despite the many dances and chanting, the mood of the celebration is explicitly melancholic. The drums are made of ceramic pots that produce a smothered sound from the wicker fans that slap their mouth. Other musical instruments include two large calabashes, turned upside down in clay pots with water, which are struck with stick *aguidavis.* The celebrants use pieces of palm leaves (*màrìwò*), wrapped around their wrists, as a protection against any eventual wrath of the *égúns.* All of these instruments, in the end, will also be banished to the woods.

In a separate room, the dead priest is represented by new clay recipients, which in the future can be used to "seat" the spirit, as other famous ancestors, or they will be sent away. Influenced by Catholic ritual, which repeats its funeral masses in regular intervals, in many *terreiros* the rituals of *axexê* are repeated after a month, a year, and every seven years, especially regarding the death of a *bàbálòrìsà* or *iyálòrìsà.* The majority of initiates, though, do not enjoy even a single day of *axexê.* This is because of lack of interest by relatives, who many times do not themselves practice Candomblé, because of economic limitations of such expensive ceremonies, or because of the ineptitude of *terreiro* leaders. In many cases where no grand ceremony is performed, the *otás* (sacred stones of the *igbas*) are nonetheless sent away with some homily, and other objects are reused.

With today's ever-accelerating expansion of Candomblé, the *axexê* is disadvantaged compared with other ceremonies. This is especially true in São Paulo, where the religion is less than fifty years old, and there are few *terreiros* with priests and priestesses trained to conduct such sophisticated funeral rites. This disadvantage forces the São Paolo Candomblé community to employ the services of religious leaders who are unrelated to the *terreiro,* and they often charge high prices for funerary services. Recently, however, many Candomblé experts became professional priests who specialize in *axexê*. They are called in for the ceremony whenever an understaffed *terreiro* needs them. This demand, of course, leads to increased prices, which often, however, make the ritual impossible for poorer practitioners. Even when a high priest of the *terreiro* dies, it is difficult to celebrate the funeral rites, especially in situations when the death of the leader causes the closing of the house, usually because of disputes over the successor and related inheritance issues. It is important to recall that we can probably count on ten fingers the numbers of *terreiros* in all of Brazil who survived their founders. Generally, the family of a priest has no interest in holding the *axexê* and does not want to spend money or maintain the *terreiro*. Conversely, very few priests and priestesses, especially in São Paulo and Rio de Janeiro, are willing to perform any type of ceremony without being paid, even if the person interested in it is a member of the same *terreiro*. Many *bàbálòrìsà* and *iyálòrìsà* have their *terreiros* as a means of financial support, which causes the principles of market economy to take precedence over communal religious life.

Apparently, religious communities are increasingly lax in observing funeral rites. This is particularly striking in light of the high levels of energy and large amounts of money routinely spent on initiation rituals. It is as if death is declining in importance in these traditions. This decline is bringing about profound changes in the initiation process itself, whose philosophical and liturgical expression of death (and consequently of life) is considerably lightened. The original African concepts thus fade further into oblivion in Brazil, and, in turn, Candomblé will accommodate even more Catholicism, Kardecism, and Umbanda. This could even result in an entirely new religion. Indeed, this new religion is already manifesting itself in urban Brazil, and we may call it, pejoratively, Umbandomblé. In Umbandomblé, the *égúns,* who are certain ancestors of a specific community in the Yorùbá thought, are losing their African characteristics and becoming generic spirits, without linkage to any kinship lineage or *terreiro;* they simply appear in *terreiros* "to work" and assume the justifications of the Christian-Kardecist idea of practice and charity. Moreover, slowly but surely, African models of ancestry, kinship, and their concomitant rituals are being overwhelmed and lost. This new way of understanding life and death by a great number of Candomblé experts, especially the newer ones, constitutes a major reason for the lack of interest in the realization of *axexê* for all initiates. With this, certainly, the concepts and ideals of Umbanda gain ground, as Candomblé loses it. This trend runs directly counter to the Africanization movement and represents the opposite process of the "Umbandization" of Candomblé.[1] Without *axexê,* the initiation to the òrìṣà makes no sense, at least in terms of the African traditions that introduced òrìṣà devotion to Brazil. The cycle of life and death is no longer complete, and its mythical repetition, so fundamental to the African philosophy of existence, cannot realize itself.

Notes

1. Africanization is the process of retrieval of African traditions that began in the 1960s in houses of the Yorùbá or Nago nation. It involves the reappropriation of the Yorùbá language, the recuperation of mythology and rituals previously forgotten and altered in the diaspora, including oracular processes, and the rejection of syncretic Catholic practices and entities of non-Yorùbá origin, such as the *caboclos* (Prandi 1991, 1996). Mãe Stella Odé Kaiodé, *iyalorixá* of Axé Opô Afonjá, of Salvador, Bahia, has been one of the most outspoken leaders at the local and national levels in the struggle against Catholic syncretism, having clearly abandoned in the house she governs, at least formally, Catholic practices that elsewhere are usually are mixed with Candomblé thought and ritual.

References

Abraham, R. C. 1962. *Dictionary of Modern Yorùbá*. London: Hodder and Stoughton.
Babayemi, S. O. 1980. *Egúngún among the Oyo Yorùbá*. Ibadan: Oyo State Council for Arts and Culture.

Braga, Júlio. 1992. *Ancestralidade afro-brasileira: O culto de babá egum.* Salvador, Brazil: CEAO and Ianamá.

Lawal, Babatunde. 1996. *The Gèlèdé Spectacle: Art, Gender, and Social Harmony in an African Culture.* Seattle: University of Washington Press.

Prandi, Reginaldo. 1991. *Os Candomblés de São Paulo: A velha magia na metrópole nova.* São Paulo: Hucitec and Edusp.

————. 1996. *Herdeiras do axé: Ssociologia das religiões afro-brasileiras.* São Paulo: Hucitec.

Santos, Juana Elbein dos. 1976. *Os nàgó e a morte.* Petrópolis, Brazil: Vozes.

Santos, Maria Stella de Azevedo. 1993. *Meu tempo é agora.* São Paulo: Oduduwa.

23

From Oral to Digital

Rethinking the Transmission of Tradition in Yorùbá Religion

GEORGE EDWARD BRANDON

One evening when I was surfing the Internet, perusing Web sites devoted to òrìṣà, I encountered an interesting exchange. One devotee was criticizing the knowledge of another—neither appeared to be a priest—and the final hammer blow of the critique was that his opponent's knowledge of Santería was mostly derived from books. (Why this should even be a criticizm was not explained.) The wounded party's retort was that although he did read a lot of religious literature, the foundation and most important continuing source of his knowledge was his godparents, both of whom were illiterate Cubans. The argument or contest between the two was not so much about depth of knowledge as about authenticity, with illiteracy taken as the negative symbolic guarantor of it (the implied flip-side being oral transmission, or tradition). It is ironic that both the argument and the appeal to authenticity were taking place on an Internet newsgroup—as literate and text-laden a medium as you can imagine—by two people who were obviously comfortable and skilled in both reading and writing. Anyway, the irony, lost on them, was not lost on me and set me to thinking about what was actually at stake in this argument about the media of religious transmission and how we might use and think about it.

Mouth and Pen: Concerning the Metaphysics of Orality and Literacy

African religions are usually perceived as purely oral traditions. This perception occurs within a series of broad, pervasive, and powerful assumptions about the nature of the relationships between African and African American oral traditions and writing that privilege a particular idea of the oral. These assumptions are not restricted to literary and cultural studies of people of African descent but apply to all non-Western peoples who did not originate writing systems of a particular kind. Furthermore, the assumptions extend outside of academia and constitute a kind of metaphysical postulate in the philosophical anthropology of the West and, as such, have become cosmopolitan. This postulate not only puts speech and writing in opposition to each other; it opposes them in a specific way. Gayatri Spivak has summarized this opposition as exhibited by Jacques Derrida in the following pithy and accurate statement: "Western metaphysics opposed the general principle of speech, on the one hand, to writing in the narrowest sense on the other" (Spivak 1993: 98). This is certainly worth examining, and we can find examples of this pervasive metaphysic where we least expect them.

Pierre Verger, in the remarkable introductory chapter of his ethnobotanical monograph *Ewe,* is concerned with some of the same issues that concern us here. In this chapter of his study of Yorùbá herbalism, as it is practiced by Ifá diviners, he makes several comments contrasting oral tradition and literacy. Verger describes the verbal associations established between the name of a plant, the medicinal or magical action it is expected to carry out, and the *odú* Ifá under which the plant is classified by the *babaláwo*. These verbal links—associations between the names of things—are essential aids that help the diviners hang on to the knowledge transmitted by oral traditions believed to be the vehicle of the divine power on which the diviners and humanity as a whole depend. Verger feels compelled to comment: "This means that they consider the written word to be entirely ineffective, in order to have an effect and in order to act, words have to be spoken" (Verger 1995: 14). It is difficult to imagine either the meaningfulness or the relevance of a comment like this—made by Verger or by his informants—in a situation in which writing did not exist. In the background of this comment is not the situation of the ancient times in which Yorùbá herbalism and divination first developed but of the more modern situation in which many Nigerians read and write English, Arabic and also, alas, Yorùbá. Oddly enough, the concepts of orality and literacy are mutually constitutive. They arise together in situations where a writing system is introduced from outside, and they are shaped also in reference to a particular view of writing, one that views writing mainly as a medium for recording or substituting for speech. In a mutually defining moment, writing brings the concept of oral tradition into existence. To quote Walter Ong, "Without textualism, orality cannot even be identified" (Ong 1982: 169).

Verger goes on to describe the mechanisms by which verbal links are established. The *babaláwo*'s medical and divinatory knowledge are transmitted through short sentences based on the rhythm of breathing. Constant repetition transforms these short sentences into verbal stereotypes and then into easily accepted definitions. "This knowledge, verbally transmitted, is essentially a creative force, not just at an intellectual level but at the dynamic level of behavior. It is based more on reflex than reasoning, reflexes originated in the impulses that come from the background of Yorùbá society" (Verger 1995: 15).

What is verbalized is not the knowledge itself; that knowledge is vital and energetic rather than conceptual in nature, nonetheless, is still socially contextualized and very densely so if I understand Verger correctly. And when Verger speaks of reflex, he does not mean an automatic muscular action that takes place out of awareness, or rather, not only that kind of action, but rather a similar kind of trained and embodied cultural response of the total individual interacting with all the social, historical, and cultural forces that surround and constitute them. What Verger describes is a pathway from the corporeal to the conceptual, from reflex to rhythmic repetition, on to verbal stereotypes and then definition as a final artifact. This is essentially a process for the codification and storage of knowledge by means of training the body and mind in the association of verbal images and metaphors through speech practice, a process that is inherently poetic.

In a society with no means of graphically representing speech, words do not exist either experientially or socially if they are not spoken. Many other things exist, however. Concepts and conceptual distinctions may

exist whether verbalized or not; body movements and gestures, the placement of objects in space, and the demarcation of boundaries concretely
convey ideas and conventions; sensory information from seeing and
feeling animals and plants and interacting with other human beings—all
these form part of "background of Yorùbá society" from which Verger
traces the "reflex" at the base of the process he describes. Although
these elements are surely present and even significant for the process
he describes, none of them is speech. Instead they are either in effect
excluded from the picture entirely (a product of the Western metaphysic
cited by Spivak), or they are collapsed into a concept in which speech
becomes the general principle that represents them all and in which they
lose any independent claim to existence; they disappear entirely and
only the speech remains. On the other hand the speech/writing dichotomy requires that all graphic representation of concepts (i.e., writing
in the broad sense) or all graphic efficacy be reduced to the function of
recording speech (i.e., writing in the narrow sense), leaving out entirely
graphic systems or forms of writing that are not speech based, are not
concerned with either recording or substituting for speech, nor necessarily even to convey information but, instead, to paraphrase Verger, have
an effect or act. To quote Spivak again, "Western metaphysics opposes
the general principle of speech [in the sense that it stands for and sub-
sumes or makes invisible the nonverbal aspects of communication], on
the one hand, to writing in the narrowest sense [i.e., on forms of graphic
representation that record or substitute for speech] on the other" (Spivak
1993: 98). What is surprising is the tenacity of this Western metaphysical behemoth in the text of an author who nonetheless describes Yorùbá
religious culture with such apparent fidelity, sensitivity, authenticity,
and the insight born of long years of work and study.

Indigenous African Scripts and Graphic Systems

In at least some locations in West Africa it is clear that indigenous
graphic signs, ideograms, syllabaries, and alphabets have served as media for the transmission of religious knowledge. Dalby (1968) reviews
ten indigenous scripts from West Africa arising in modern times: five
from Liberia and Sierra Leone (the Vai [1833], Mende [1921], Kpelle
[1930s], Loma [1930s] and Bassa [1920s] scripts) varying from 30 characters with five tonal diacritics to 212 characters. These are syllabaries

for correspondence and record keeping, and they were vehicles for translations of the Christian Bible and Islamic Qur'an. The other scripts were from Cameroon and east Nigeria (Bamum [1903], Gabgam [1917 and based on the Bamum script] and Ibibio-Efik [1930]). Two others were from the Ivory Coast (Bete 1956), plus a syllabary from Surinam.

Dalby defines a script as a linear system of writing, recording the spoken sequence of a particular language. The genesis of such linear language-bound scripts of the Old World—the Chinese script and its derivatives being excepted—trace back to the Near East. The African inventors of the scripts had probably become aware of the concept of linear writing to record speech through exposure to the Roman alphabet (via the French, German, Dutch, and English) and the Arabic writing system imported with Islam via trade and warfare. We know that the inventors were literate in one or both of these systems and that they were not alone; they had contact with other individuals who were literate, too. In addition, the men who designed the Bassa and Bete scripts had considerable Western education. Therefore, the modern indigenous scripts need to be placed in the context of prolonged colonial and Islamic penetration into West Africa and the challenge and threat that traditional religious and social values represented by both Christianity and Islam.

Just as clearly as converts saw that God was revealing himself in the written word of the Bible and the Qur'an, it could not be denied that God had given the power of writing to other peoples with alien religions—people who had been able to exploit and conquer the Africans—while withholding the gift of writing from the African peoples themselves. Given this situation it is not surprising that, in their accounts of the origins of the indigenous scripts, their inventors so often describe how the scripts were revealed to them in dreams and visions and in confrontations with God. In areas of southern Nigeria where Catholic influence was stronger than that of the Muslims, the evolution of these inspired indigenous scripts is part of an interaction between traditional beliefs and the development of native churches.

Each of the areas where the scripts arose were areas of relatively intense missionary activity, and the Roman and Arabic scripts were not seen solely as a rational technology for recording speech but also within a larger religious context in which the Roman script was associated with the Bible and revealed religion and the Arabic script with orthodox Islamic teaching on one hand and the preparation of charms and talismans and the use of written Arabic formulae in magic and healing on the other.

Furthermore, in the African context even the indigenous alphabets and syllabaries interacted with an older body of pre-existing graphic symbolism and religious iconography. Some characters in the scripts may reflect or incorporate pre-existing graphic signs and symbols, none of which was intended to record or represent speech. Important repositories of non-linear graphic symbol systems: (bracketing any Egyptian influence for the moment) Bambara, Dogon, secret societies of the Cross River Delta of Nigeria from Calabar to Cameroon [Nsibidi]. These appear to be indigenous but perhaps abetted by Arabic and pre-Arabic influences from across the Sahara. The traditional indigenous use of these graphic symbols was frequently surrounded with secrecy, mystery, and magical or religious taboos. All of these media for the transmission of religious knowledge—oral, written, and nonlinear graphic symbolism—have existed in various complex and not always oppositional relationships for some time. African Islam provides some especially enlightening examples demonstrating this.

Education and Magic

Many Yorùbá Christians and Muslims still participate in their indigenous traditions to varying degrees, but the relationship of Islamic writing and Arabic to traditional religious transmission is entirely different from that of the Roman alphabet, Christianity, and English. Because of this we will pay much greater attention to the latter in succeeding sections of this essay, but it should be stated now that these differences are not related to an oral/written dichotomy since both Christianity and Islam are literate traditions; nor do they correlate in any obvious way with technical differences in the Roman and Arabic scripts as forms of writing. What we are concerned with here is to show that a variety of relationships exists empirically between orality and literacy above and beyond or in place of the kind of radical and antagonistic opposition that is so often assumed to exist by some scholars.

Orality and Literacy in Islamic Education in Africa

"The cultural idea of religious knowledge has remained remarkably constant over time throughout the regions of Islamic influence" (Eickelman 1978: 489). This is true even of areas as marginal to the world centers of

Islam as North and West Africa. The emphasis everywhere is on fixity
and memory with accurate memorization of the Qur'an in one or more
of the seven conventional recitation styles being the first step in the mastery of the Islamic religious sciences (489). "Normatively the emphasis in transmitting knowledge is conservational," and the "two features
consistently associated with Islamic education are its rigorous discipline
and its lack of explicit explanation of memorized material. Both of these
features are congruent with the essentially fixed concept of knowledge
that is at the base of Islamic education" (490, 493). These sciences are
thought to be transmitted down a quasi-genealogical chain of authority
descending from master to student to ensure that the knowledge of an
earlier generation is passed down intact (492).

Despite the fixity of Islamic knowledge and the emphases on discipline, memorization, conservation, and an unbroken line of transmission, there is still considerable variation throughout the Islamic world
as to what exact bodies of knowledge are to be included in the religious
sciences, and in some locations the content of the religious science instruction has been shown to have altered over time (see Eickelman 1978:
490). In other words, there is more variation in the content of what is
learned than there is in the principles guiding the way in which it is
learned. Eickelman points out another source of variation and its implicit
consequences. That is, that the cognitive style associated with Islamic
knowledge may be closely tied to popular understandings of Islam and
have important analogues in nonreligious spheres of knowledge. This
relationship between Islamic knowledge and popular understandings
affects the popular legitimacy of religious knowledge and its carriers
and may affect the pace and rate of change in Islamic education and
the ways in which changes are perceived (491). To illustrate the differences possible within a religious tradition that uses both oral and written
transmission we will use two examples: one from North Africa and one
from West Africa.

Dan Eickelman described the pedagogical methods of Islamic education that were in use in the 1920s and 1930s from historical records and
also from interviews with students who had experienced them. "Islamic
education as practiced in Morocco was in some ways intermediate between oral and written systems of transmission of knowledge. Its key
treatises existed in written form but were conveyed orally, to be written
down and memorized by students . . . No printed or manuscript copies
of Qur'an were used in the process of memorization." This was in part

because of a lack of printed or manuscript books and in part because of the cultural concept of learning implicit in Islamic education (Eickelman 1978: 487, 493). The material in their treatises was set out and learned as rhymed verse. The teacher recited the verses to be learned; students wrote them down in Arabic on their slates and practiced reciting them aloud for the remainder of the learning session. The next day they recited for the teacher the previous day's lesson as well as recent past lessons. If the recitation was correct, the teacher erased the old verse from the slate and gave the student a new one; if the recitation was not correct, the student continued to practice aloud until it was correct and could be erased (493). The Moroccan Muslim students that Eickelman interviewed insisted that although memorization of the Qur'an was their major form of learning, there was a complete absence of any devices or techniques to help them do it. Some students recalled visualizing the shapes of the calligraphic letters on their slates and could recall the circumstances under which they learned specific texts, but none of this was either taught or cultivated as an aid to memory. Nonetheless at least one psychological study has suggested that patterns of rhyme and intonation present in the verses may have served, unconsciously, as mnemonic markers (Wagner 1978). (Note: This is a rather arduous procedure, and Eickelman cites evidence suggesting that it represents an extreme even in the North African context. Working in this way a student in Morocco might spend six to eight years learning material that a student in Tunisia could learn in five.) A nearly opposite situation existed in at least some areas of West Africa.

Ronald Judy (1993) reports an interview that took place in the nineteenth century between Lamen Kabe, an African American slave who had been a Muslim scholar and teacher in West Africa before being forcibly imported to the United States, and an early ethnologist, Theodore Dwight. Kabe provided Dwight with a description of a West African mode of teaching Qur'anic Arabic that, at first, seems to fit what Westerners generally take to be the norm in such West African scenes of instruction. Certainly, principles and devices to aid the memory were emphasized to a vastly greater extent than what we have seen in the Moroccan system that Eickelman described, but the differences extend beyond that. What was practiced in Lamen Kabe's school was memorization by graphic reproduction rather than oral presentation. His pedagogical method was that the written word, and not the heard word, was what was memorized through recitation. The students were taught to be

·readers before anything else and, above all, readers who could decipher (Judy 1993: 173).

Arabic Writing and Magic in West Africa

More than Qur'an verses compose the religious sciences of Muslim clerics in West Africa. The Muslim cleric is also a medicine man who creates amulets, and the lore of amulet making is not a marginal study but an integral part of his training. The making of Islamic amulets and the practice of writing are so melded and intertwined that in the West African context the Arabic script cannot be looked at solely as a rational technology for recording speech; rather, it is caught up in the currents of divine power, magic, and religious values.

In their attempts to abolish sacrifices to the spirits, Muslims neither denied the existence of spirits nor attempted to placate them; instead, they offered the traditional believers protection against the spirits in the form of written amulets. Islamic amulets involved prayers to God and also occult knowledge. The Muslim cleric functioned as a medicine man whose magic was practiced from within the domain of Islam and obeyed its laws concerning the lawful and the forbidden. This required no change in the attitude toward magic on the part of unbelievers or converts; it simply introduced a new technology that could supplement or substitute for an old amulet a new one, distinguished from the old only in that it contained Arabic writing.

The amulets take two forms: In one form the passages are written on paper and worn on the body or placed on the animal or objects they are supposed to protect. In the second form, sometimes associated with healing, the passages are written on a slate and then washed off with water that is drunk or rubbed on the body. The written passages include Qur'anic verses, the names of angels and jinn, descriptions of the goal to be achieved by the amulet, a number of occult formulas, and sometimes the Islamic taboos the wearer must observe for the amulet to keep its power. People who also participate in the traditional religion may later add things to the amulet: roots, stones, or other empowered objects; indeed, beyond the use of a written paper there is little that distinguishes Islamic charms from the traditional African ones. Furthermore, according to Trimingham, the advent of the commercial mass production of printed as opposed to written amulets in the 1950s and the condemnation

of this trend by Islamic clergy eager to protect this portion of their liveli-
hood, brought to light two forces underlying the unique power that the
written amulets were thought to contain. One source of power derives
from the virtue of the Muslim cleric, a power obtained from sustained
contact with the supernatural and passed on to the amulet's wearer via
the amulet as a kind of sacred energetic contagion. The other, particularly ironic in the present context, concerned the ink used to print the
mass-produced amulets. This ink, the clerics objected, could not be sacred. It was powerless and profane because it was not prepared from
ingredients in a procedure that included the proper incantations. Behind
the efficacy of the written amulet lay the oral incantation that, rather
than standing against or separate from the written word, actually helped
compose it and constituted one source of its power. From the perspective
of the Yorùbá amulet wearer, the writing was valued as a new technology associated with Islam that could be harnessed to traditional ends, an
additional source of power to be added to the others. The writing was
valued, not because it was comprehensible but because it had been associated with a powerful person, not because it was understood but because its incomprehensibility was part of its magical power, not because
it was a rational technology but because it was thought to be a spiritually
powerful one (Trimingham 1959: 111–16). In the words of a Fulbe saying quoted by J. S. Trimingham, "Those who write are no better than
magicians" (113).

Nigeria

Writing and Christian Missionaries

No evidence of an ancient indigenous Yorùbá script has become known.
Despite contacts with Islam and African Muslims that predate the
nineteenth-century Islamic jihads, the Arabic writing system was not
adopted by Yorùbá before the holy wars and, even then, was not a medium of communication learned or used by Yorùbá who were not Muslim. While interaction between oral and written media may well have
accelerated during this century, it certainly extends back as far as the development of an orthography for writing Yorùbá. The earliest alphabetic
documents therefore had to follow the development of an orthography
derived from the Roman alphabet used by Christian missionaries who

compiled the first bilingual Yorùbá dictionaries. The first of these, a Yorùbá-English dictionary, was created by an African, Samuel Crowther (later Bishop Crowther) in 1843. The Anglican Church Missionary Society published a second edition, greatly altered and expanded, in 1852. This work remained the standard reference into the twentieth century, when it was supplemented by the work of other Yorùbá scholars, including Rev. E. J. Sowande's 1911 dictionary with the entries contributed by T. A. J. Ogunbiyi. The Church Missionary Society (CMS) let the book go out of print but eventually turned the texts over to Oxford University Press, which still publishes it. T. J. Bowen, who spent the years 1850 to 1856 in Yorùbá territories, published a Yorùbá-English dictionary in 1858 with an American publisher in New York. Twenty-seven years later, in 1885, Noel Baudin published a bilingual dictionary in Yorùbá and French (Dianteill 1997). Crowther, Bowen, Sowande, and Baudin were all Christian missionaries whose intent in creating their dictionaries was to allow French and English missionaries to communicate with and understand Yorùbá in order to more successfully evangelize the Yorùbá. This evangelizing communication was not solely oral and took a variety of forms.

As early as 1861 there were enough Yorùbá under Christian influence and able to read the new orthography that it made sense for the CMS branch in Abeokuta to publish a journal, *Iwe Irohin,* for them for the read (Lucas 1948: 420). This first generation of literate Yorùbá were both subjects and agents of the missionary effort. Many of them kept journals describing their experiences as converts and as missionaries. Some were employed as researchers, native ethnographers, to describe traditional beliefs and practices. As a result, texts in the archives of the Anglican Christian Missionary Society in England by Yorùbá converts who occasionally reverted after devoting considerable time to researching their own indigenous heritage and writing about it. This material is in Yorùbá, rather than English, and is of great importance. It shows the context in which the Yorùbá came to think of themselves as a distinctive people in the contexts of the politics of warfare among the various nineteenth-century city-states, encroaching colonialism, and the complex of Christian, Islamic, and traditional religious practices people had to negotiate. Recent work by J. D. Y. Peel, who has researched these archives from the direction of Christian conversion, could be looked at from other perspectives as well, for what they say about perceptions of traditional religion among the early generations of literate Yorùbá (Peel 2001).

A Split Pattern among Christian Converts

In the nineteenth century, the Yorùbá had developed a pattern in which a domestic realm of traditional religion could complement but be separate from the church or the mosque. This remained especially viable as long as the traditional religion remained strong. However, particularly in the late nineteenth century and the early twentieth century up to the 1920s, the balance began to shift, the traditional system began to wane and waver, and Christianity and Islam, albeit in different ways, seemed to be the future. Nevertheless, there was a countervailing tendency even among converted Christian Yorùbá who attempted to resuscitate the transmission of religion by working outside the normal channels of the traditional system and outside those controlled by the church and the colonial government. What we have here is a literate tradition of transmission springing from Yorùbá converts to Christianity who, in some but not all cases, were reverting or reconnecting in an intensive way with the traditional religion as adults, a process that occurs over and over again in succeeding generations, the process itself having a decisive impact on the literature that comes out as well as the context in which it evolves and the social forms in which it is transmitted.

One example of this is the Imolè Oluwa Institute. Rev. D. Onadele Epega founded the Imolè Oluwa Institute in 1904. The institute published books on òrìṣà religion and Ifá philosophy in Yorùbá and, most radically innovative, gave instruction in Ifá divination through correspondence courses. They also published works in English, most notably the *Mystery of the Yorùbá Gods* (D. Epega 1936). The institute still exists, as does their publication program. Rev. D. Onadele Epega was succeeded by his son Patriarch D. Olarimiwa Epega, author of an introductory text on Yorùbá religion, and then by his grandson Afolabi A. Epega, who continued to publish books under the Imolè Oluwa Institute imprint (A. Epega 1985) as well as in collaboration with other authors and other presses (Epega and Niemark 1995). What we have here is an intergenerational stream of literate transmission of Yorùbá religious knowledge going back almost one hundred years.

Other examples are Ijo Ọ̀rúnmìlà groups. G. E. Simpson, who was in turn conveying information given to him by Fela Sowande, mentions a Nigerian organization having this same name. The Ijo Ọ̀rúnmìlà Mimo and the organizations from which it had descended were made up of Yorùbá Christians who had turned away from Christianity and were attempting to reestablish direct contact with traditional Yorùbá religions. "In 1934, Mr. A. O. Oshiga, a former Christian, founded the Ijo Ọ̀rúnmìlà Adulawo. Ijo Ọ̀rúnmìlà Adulawo had hymnbooks, a prayer book, *and a collection of the stanzas of Ifá from which lessons were read and texts taken for sermons. All were part of a framework usually associated with Christian worship* . . . Ijo Ọ̀rúnmìlà, with its typical nativistic ideology, soon split with Ijo Ọ̀rúnmìlà Ato and Ijo Ọ̀rúnmìlà Mimo breaking away from the original body. With the subsequent separation of Ijo Ọ̀rúnmìlà Ilupesin from Ijo Ọ̀rúnmìlà Ato, there were four Ijo Ọ̀rúnmìlàs: the Aduwalo, the Ato, the Ilupesin, and the Mimo" (Simpson 1980: 148; my emphasis). The typical social organization for these groups was the church. The groups lasted at least into the late 1950s, but Simpson failed to find any trace of them in Ibadan or in the villages where he did fieldwork in 1964 (Simpson 1980: 149). Nevertheless, in her *Fundamentals of the Yorùbá Religion (Orisa Worship)*, Chief Fama, a Nigerian priestess now residing in the United States who was raised as a Christian, recounts joining the Ijo Ọ̀rúnmìlà Ato in Lagos in 1984 and writing for *Ọ̀rúnmìlà Magazine*, one of the group's publications (Fama 1993: xxiii–xxiv). She has since embarked on a publication program of her own in both Yorùbá and English (Fama 1993, 1994). Perhaps the Nigerian Ijo Ọ̀rúnmìlà Mimo also still exists. It should be noted that at least one, and possibly more, of the African American *babaláwos* in the American association using this name was initiated as an Ifá priest in Nigeria (Karade 1994, 1996). Both of these groups used hymnbooks and transcribed Ifá texts as integral parts of their worship and education.

In the film *Doctors of Nigeria,* there is a scene in which we encounter a Dr. Fagbenro, an elderly but still vital Yorùbá *babaláwo,* seated in front of a vast pile of tattered and disintegrating bound notebooks. These, he says, include the notebooks passed on to him from his father's practice as an herbalist and the ones he had compiled himself from the teaching of his own mentor in Ifá. This scene always leaves me with two questions. Is this the same Fagbenro (Fagbenro-Beyioke) who wrote *Ọ̀rúnmìlàism: The Basis of Jesusism* back in the 1940s? Moreover, how many more Fagbenros are there with how many more piles of notebooks moldering in their homes?

Cuban Santería

There are several overlapping streams of literacy paralleling Santería's oral tradition. These include libretas compiled by devotees for their own use, self-published books and pamphlets and lexicons meant to circulate within a restricted community of believers, manuals and other books composed by the priesthood for instructing each other, and other works sometimes targeted at a wider public. The bulk of the known texts date from the 1920s onward, with an especially noteworthy flowering occurring in the 1950s.

During the years in which Cuba was a society based on the labor of enslaved Africans, reading and writing were practices reserved only for certain groups. Yet from the beginning of the nineteenth century we find in Cuba blacks and free mulattos who not only could read and write but who also produced literature. Juan Francesco Manzano and Gabriel de la Concepcion Valdez (a.k.a. Placido) were prominent literary figures of the 1830s. Both were Afro-Cuban, and there were other writers as well. Cuba has long had a relatively high rate of literacy compared to other Latin American and Caribbean nations, even before the Castro regime took power. In 1953, for instance, 76 percent of the Cuban population could read and write. (In Havana the rate was somewhere between 90 and 98 per cent. In 1976, 99 percent of Cuban children could read, and in 1988, 98 percent of Cuban children between the ages of six and fourteen were literate.)

A Notable Early Figure: Jose Antonio Aponte

We know that as early as 1812 there was in Cuba at least one literate *santero,* Jose Antonio Aponte. Aponte was a free black of Yorùbá descent who worked as a carpenter and sculptor. Not only was he a priest of Shango, but he also directed an Afro-Cuban religious fraternity, the Cabildo de Santa Barbara, also known as the Cabildo Chango Tedun. This *cabildo* lasted about forty years. Aponte assumed leadership of the organization around 1810, and the *cabildo* met in his home. Aponte also belonged to a paramilitary organization, a civilian militia made up of *pardos* and *morenos* that probably formed the backbone of the rebellion he led in 1812, a multiethnic conspiracy uniting members of the Bibi, Congo, Mandingue, Carabali, and Macua ethnic groups in a battle for independence from Spain. The revolt was not successful, and when the police came to Aponte's home searching for "secret documents," they also inventoried the contents of his house and his library. So, here at the opening of Cuba's momentous nineteenth century we have a free black Lucumi who was a religious leader, revolutionary activist, and intellectual, and also evidence of the penetration of reading if not writing into the Afro-Cuban religious community.

Folletos, Libretas, and Manuals

Most likely, the roots of the literate transmission of Santería lie in texts that devotees and priests created for their own use. The oldest of the documents that Dianteill's research on this literature was able to locate in Cuba trace back to a text dating from before 1850 (Diantiell 1997). This is *Folleto para uso del Santero (Obba)*. Published in 1959, this work is presented as a faithful copy and first printed edition of a manuscript composed in 1836 by E. Navarro and R. Varela. According to Dianteill, internal evidence also converges to place the *Folleto*'s composition around or before 1850. Such *folletos* or notebooks were used as supports for memory and a means of recording ritual, linguistic, and mythological information during the extended process over which it was slowly observed, revealed, and taught. Notebooks like this were never the only means of recording or retaining religious knowledge; spatial concepts, ritual gestures, and patterns of physical responses also served as supports and embodiments of memory. Usage of the *libreta* (also a notebook) that the new Santería priest or priestess compiles during the year of initiation possibly extends back at least to the 1920s (Leon 1971: 145). But *libretas* may well have existed long before that, the texts surviving only as tattered manuscripts or notebooks relegated to the side rooms of experienced *santeras'* homes since the priests now know what they are doing and need not consult them anymore.

In other cases, the *libreta* or *folleto* could become in whole or in part the basis of a pamphlet or book to be used by people other than the compiler. In this case, its function was not solely mnemonic but didactic as well. In the twentieth century, the notebook became a manual, which could be used by a priest to instruct devotees or by extension for priests to instruct each other. The manuals that describe rites and sacrifices, transcribe the stories of the òrìṣà, and propose lists of religious vocabulary were circulated among adepts. The number of texts of this type explodes in the 1950s, in part because of technological improvements favoring greater and cheaper reproduction, diffusion, and distribution of the manuals.

The effect of these manuals on the transmission of religious tradition was as contradictory and manifold as the works themselves. The effect of manuals for divination was that certain specialists in effect fixed the meaning of divinatory signs, for anyone following their definitions would interpret the signs through the categories they had established. At the same time as these manuals preserved and promoted Yorùbá religious vocabulary, one never finds in these manuals the diacritical signs for indicating tones that are an indispensable part of Yorùbá orthography, something that in effect hastens the disintegration of the language as a living tongue while calcifying a distorted version of it as a sacred language. By this time European and American anthropological studies of African religions, and Yorùbá religion in particular, have begun to appear, not to mention the Cuban writings of Ortiz, Lachatañeré, and Cabrera. The texts of these manuals sometimes appropriate passages from the anthropological works that, then even more than now, were not widely diffused in Cuba and had been published in London, Paris, New York, or even Nigeria. This worked both ways, and Rómulo Lachatañeré even placed a publication of his own squarely in this tradition by putting the word "manual" in its title (Lachatañeré 2004 [1942]).

Although some of this material was oriented toward a general literate public, most of it was not. Santería was subject to repeated programs of suppression and persecution, and most of this literature was produced by believers for believers; some of it was even produced outside of Cuba, in Mexico, and whether produced in Cuba or outside, it often had to be circulated clandestinely. For example, Cuba drummer, priest, and diviner Nicolas Valentine Angarica's 1950s work *Manual del Orihate*, which can now be picked up in various photocopied editions in the occult sections of some Spanish-language book stores in the United States for twenty to thirty dollars today, used to be sold under the table in much seamier environments at four or five times that price in New York into the 1970s. This book, a manual of instruction, is clearly aimed at the priesthood, people who eventually might actually assume the position of *oba orihate*.

The United States: Taking the Òrìṣà Online

In the United States, the òrìṣà have begun to colonize cyberspace, and there are more than 160 Internet Web sites devoted to one aspect or

another of Yorùbá religion. The types of Web sites include personal
sites (featuring devotees in photographs with their altars); portals such
as Orishanet that link to a wealth of other sites; the organizational sites
of specific churches or associations of priests; the academic sites put up
by individual scholars with a research interest in the Yorùbá religion and
its New World relatives; library sites that are essentially organized online introductory bibliographies to Yorùbá religious studies; collection
or assemblage sites that seem to have a little bit of everything; and discussion or news groups and chat rooms built around exchanges between
any people who can access the site. Despite the presence of graphics and
even sound files on a few sites, overwhelmingly the experience of being
at these sites is that of reading what is there.

Stefania Capone has made an initial foray into this welter of activity and voices and makes some acute observations in her article "Les
Dieux sur le Net." She notes several distinctive types who repeatedly
present themselves in cyberspace and categorizes them variously as
Recruiters, Lost Souls, the Suspicious Ones, Cyber Elders, and Web
Bricoleurs. An additional group, which she does not designate as such,
I call Border-Crossers. These categories by no means exhaust the activity that appears on these Web sites, but the ones I discuss here point to
important aspects of the problems of religious transmission with which
we are concerned.

Recruiters, Lost Souls, and the Suspicious Ones

Recruiters are *santeros* seeking to gain money, new clients, and followers for their cult houses by using the Internet as a recruitment vehicle.
They may offer services as diviners and post a contact electronic mail
address in order to arrange for consultations. Lost Souls are devotees
who, for one reason or another, have become separated or estranged
from their cult houses and godparents. They now try to continue their apprenticeship or maintain a connection with the community of believers
by other means, including the Internet. The Suspicious Ones are devotees who may be in a cult house, but nonetheless they feel the need to
confirm everything they learn there with some other religious authority
figure. At some level, these devotees do not trust either the knowledge
or the good intentions of their *santero,* and in reaction they revert to the
Internet in search of a more authoritative and neutral figure.

The traces left by these figures on the Internet reflect some of the internal problems in the adaptation of the Yorùbá religion's social organization to the contemporary realities of the United States. The isolation of a number of potential initiates, the fragility of the bond between godchild and godparent, and the separation from cult house membership are patched over with a technological fix: Priests recruit a following and potential devotees find godparents over the Internet. Godchildren separated from their cult house or godparents because of geographic mobility, interpersonal tension or breakdown, or death find themselves with no ready substitute or structure to take them up and place them again, and so they try to gain it over the Internet. The tension between direct apprenticeship face to face with a human spiritual guide and the apprenticeship by means of reading either on the Internet or in books, the subject of the argument with which I opened this chapter, appears here in the guise of the Suspicious Ones, in its true guise—that is, as an issue of trust. The Internet becomes a way out for the isolated and distrustful to enter into contact with a trustworthy community of believers or at least a community in which one's vulnerability to ill will and exploitation is minimized and more under the person's immediate control. Fundamentally, what was at stake in that Internet argument was not about orality versus literacy; it was about the nature of the relationships between devotees and priests and the character of relationships within the community of believers.

Cyber Elders and Web Bricoleurs

Issues of identity can be contentious and ambiguous in cyberspace. In the cyberspace of the Internet what you write and how you present yourself is who you are and largely without reference to any other reality. This hermetic identity space can become insubstantial and miasmic, swiftly shifting and ungraspable. This characteristic of cyberspace gives rise to two other distinctive types in the world of Yorùbá religion that exists there: the Cyber Elder and the Web Bricoleur.

The Cyber Elder is someone who signs on a particular òrìṣà-oriented Web site and maintains a continuing connection with it by sending messages there on a regular basis. The character of their communications changes fairly rapidly over time, however. The Cyber Elder signs on the Internet site as a novice but rapidly comes to think he has accumulated esoteric and religious knowledge to the point that in less than a year he is all ready to give a course to a discussion group, assume the teacher role in a chat room, or give divination readings. The Cyber Elder's apprenticeship, initiations, and so on have taken place at an accelerated pace and in an unverifiable place offline and may never even be discussed or divulged. The Internet becomes a place where reputations can be made and unmade, for the most part in almost total anonymity. The Cyber Elder presents a rapid metamorphosis from novice to authority that is public, anonymous, and unverifiable all at once.

The Web Bricoleur is a product of different traditions who arranges them on the Net in a library or assemblage, yet may frequently appear on other sites. He presents a picture of constant wide-ranging motion across traditions. He has studied the writings of a Nigerian *babaláwo,* converses via the Internet with a Cuban *santero* or a Brazilian priest, and then terminates his journey with a Haitian *manbo* that he asks for counsel. Often, he presents a mixture of Yorùbá religion, Congolese-based *palo mayombe,* and Kardecan spiritualism. With the Web Bricoleur type, you know where they have been, but you do not know where they are coming from. Their religious identity is constituted as a swirl of activity, visits, and encounters without an identifiable anchor, center, or commitment.

Border-Crossers

In many ways the Internet presents a veritable supermarket of the spirits in which one may easily slip into a neighboring world by going to its electronic address. Frequently people do so with the dual intentions of picking up something to add to their shopping cart and establishing their right to exist in that other world by presenting their own discourse in it. The decentralized and open access nature of the Internet allows those who wish to cross the borders between the religious traditions in cyberspace easily, and in most cases they cannot be refused entry. Hence the Border-Crosser. The difference between the Border-Crosser and the Web Bricoleur is that the Border-Crosser does have a stable religious identity, whether it is Native American, Neo-Pagan, or Wiccan, or related to ancient Egyptian Religion. What they want to do is establish a relationship between their religious identity and Yorùbá religion and have this relationship recognized or debated in an òrìṣà-oriented area of cyberspace in the hopes that the connection will be recognized and legitimated. Border-Crossers have a central tradition around which they are accumulating pieces of other traditions as well as affiliations with kindred spirits often with the implicit assumption that the class, racial, and ethnic factors that often impede or separate these same groups in the relationships in physical communities can be avoided or overcome in the virtual communities opened up in cyberspace.

Ritual and theological information is available to anyone who can access the Internet regardless of who they are or to what religion they belong and they can do with that information what they will. Ritual chants or interpretations of the *odùs* need not be learned from or solely from the voice of the initiating master but can be learned from compact discs or books. This permits the appearance of a new type of practitioner: the autodidact who constructs his own religious and esoteric path by reading, assisting in conferences, presenting himself on the stages of the religion and evidently consulting the Internet.

Not only are the incessant search for ritual information and the distrust and suspicion that devotees sometimes present on the Net related to the decentralized nature of the Internet; in the United States the Yorùbá religion's social organization is decentralized too. And, especially when devotees and priests see the differences in opinion and ways of doing things among the different cult houses, some desire to establish a hierarchy of houses on the Net and some priests oblige by stomping for an orthodoxy or pontificating on the orthodox way of doing things. In the end, however, the Internet remains decentralized, and cyberspace devotees in effect prostrate themselves before the ritual names and electronic addresses on their screens and ask for blessings in the blue light of their monitors.

Bringing It All Back Home

For application to African tradition and Yorùbá religious tradition in particular, both sides of the orality/literacy opposition need to be redefined. The "oral" should be reconceived as the whole of immediate corporeal transmission, while literacy should include non-alphabetic systems and those not intended to represent speech or ideas, the noncorporeal, external aspect of a gradated continuum in which alphabetic writing interacts in various ways with speech and the body. Western concepts of orality and literacy should not be allowed to form artificial barriers to our understanding the multiple forms and complex interactions through which the transmission of Yorùbá religious traditions has taken place. In this chapter I have tried to show that in Yorùbá religion the interaction of mouth and pen is older and more intricate than many have thought.

From far-flung places, individuals and groups of believers are increasingly in contact with each other using all available media on a global scale. The various media of religious transmission are multiplying the numbers of òrìṣà worshippers and òrìṣà communities, but they are also multiplying the numbers of types of believers and communities and their relationships to each other. Ultimately, religious traditions are not only about religious ideas, beliefs, and practices. Just as importantly, they are about the formation and maintenance of the human relationships that assure continuity and organize themselves to keep the traditions alive.

References

Capone, Stefania. 1999. "Les Dieux sur le Net: L'essor des religions d'origine africaine aux Etats-Unis." *L'Homme* 151: 47–74.

Dalby, David. 1967. "A Survey of the Indigenous Scripts of Liberia and Sierre Leone: Vai, Mende, Loma, Kpelle and Bassa." *African Language Studies* 8: 1–51.

———. 1968. "The Indigenous Scripts of West Africa and Surinam: Their Inspiration and Design." *African Language Studies* 9: 156–97.

Dianteill, Ewan. 1997. "Contribution à l'histoire d'une tradition populaire: L'ecriture religieuse afro-cubaine." *Bastidiana* 19–20: 235–65.

Eickelman, Dale F. 1978. "The Art of Memory: Islamic Education and Its Social Reproduction." *Comparative Studies in Society and History* 20, no. 4: 485–516.

Epega, Afolabi A. 1985. *Obi: The Mystical Oracle of Ifa Divination*. Lagos: Imole Oluwa Institute, Ode Remo.

Epega, Afolabi A., and Phillip Niemark. 1995. *The Sacred Ifa Oracle*. San Francisco: HarperCollins.

Epega, D. Onadele. 1938. *The Mystery of the Yorùbá Gods*. Lagos: Imolè Oluwa Institute, Ode Remo.

Fama, Chief. 1993. *Fundamentals of the Yorùbá Religion (Orisa Worship)*. San Bernardino, CA: Ile Ọrúnmìlà.

———. 1994. *Sixteen Mythological Stories of Ifa (Ìtàn Ifa Meríndinlogun)* San Bernardino, CA: Ile Ọrúnmìlà

Judy, Ronald. 1993. *(Dis)forming the Canon: African-Arabic Slave Narratives and the Vernacular*. Minneapolis: University of Minnesota Press.

Karade, Baba Ifa. 1994. *The Handbook of Yorùbá Religious Concepts.* York Beach, ME: Samuel Weiser.

———. 1996. *Ojise, Messenger of the Yorùbá Tradition.* York Beach, ME: Samuel Weiser.

Lachatañeré, Rómulo. 2004 (1942). *Manual de Santería.* Havana: Editorial de Ciencias Sociales.

León, Argeliers. 1971. "Un caso de tradición oral escrita." *Islas* 39–40: 139–51.

Lucas, J. Olumide. 1948. *The Religion of the Yoruba.* Lagos: CMS Bookshop.

Ong, Walter. 1982. *Orality and Literacy: The Technologizing of the Word.* London: Methuen.

Peel, J. D. Y. 2001. *Religious Encounter and the Making of the Yoruba.* Bloomington: Indiana University Press.

Simpson, George E. 1980. *Yorùbá Religion and Medicine in Ibadan.* Ibadan: Ibadan University Press.

Spivak, Gayatri Chakravorty. 1993. *Outside the Teaching Machine.* London: Routledge.

Trimingham, J. S. 1959. *Islam in West Africa.* Oxford: Oxford University Press.

Verger, Pierre Fatumbi. 1995. *Ewe: The Uses of Plants in Yorùbá Society.* Sao Paolo: Odebrecht.

Wagner, Dan. 1978. "Memories of Morocco: The Influence of Age, Schooling and Environment on Memory." *Cognitive Psychology* 10: 1–28.

24

Òrìṣà Traditions and the Internet Diaspora

JOSEPH M. MURPHY

The phenomenal growth of Yorùbá traditions at the beginning of the new millennium has been accelerated by new media of transmission and new communities of veneration. New images of the òrìṣà and new patterns of devotion to them have been developing beyond any single person or house's ability to quantify or sanction them. Devotions to the òrìṣà have spread beyond the communities that maintained them in Africa, that rebuilt them in the diaspora, and that brought them into renaissance in the second half of the twentieth century. Although it has been long recognized that òrìṣà traditions have been formed in intercultural dialogues in Africa and the Americas, these innovations have come about through physical contact between individuals and communities. Òrìṣà traditions have been spread by massive migrations of Yorùbá men and women because of the Atlantic slave trade. During and after the suppression of the trade, free and indentured Yorùbá brought new òrìṣà traditions to the Americas, returnees brought innovations to Yorùbáland, and inter-American migration cross-fertilized existent traditions in the Yorùbá diaspora. Each development of òrìṣà traditions has been catalyzed by physical movements of people, who have learned traditions in one geographic area and brought them elsewhere, where others learned them with their own eyes, ears, and experience.

In the twentieth century, new transportation beyond sail and steam made intercultural travel quick and òrìṣà dialogues much more frequent and fecund. Individuals and communities regularly travel thousands of miles by air to receive instruction and initiations. Nigerian *babaláwo* visit New York, American devotees crisscross the Atlantic between Nigeria, Brazil, and the United States. Many ethic groups, individuals, and communities with no Yorùbá ancestry at all have embraced its traditions. This embrace, of course, has been going on from slavery times when Fon and Kongo men and women shared traditions in the holds of the ships, on the docks, and in the cane fields. Spanish and Portuguese masters and workers sought Yorùbá wisdom and received initiations. By the mid-twentieth century, Cuban immigrants taught Puerto Rican and African American seekers in New York and Caracas. Bahian *mães de santo* received godchildren from Buenos Aires and Amsterdam.

With the telecommunications revolution at the beginning of the new millennium, contact, dialogue, and innovation among òrìṣà communities can be carried out electronically and instantly. In the last decade of the twentieth century, the Internet began to become accessible to ordinary individuals without scientific training or institutional support. For the price of a used car, individuals could access a World Wide Web of digitized information, including text, images, and motion pictures. And with a couple of hours of instruction, an individual could produce his or her own body of information, a page in an electronic book whose size was expanding with explosive speed.

This essay offers a first step in recognizing the unfathomed influence of new telecommunications media on òrìṣà traditions—in particular, the impact of the ever-growing Internet. Òrìṣà traditions, like every other aspect of information transmission, have moved from local to global to virtual. And, as with all representations of culture, òrìṣà traditions have been shaped by the new media as much as the media has extended them. By adapting to the conventions of the Internet, and the cultural assumptions that underlie it, we find in the electronic spread of òrìṣà traditions implications for new iconographies, new theologies, new communities. We begin with a survey of different kinds of òrìṣà-related sites on the Internet and move to a speculative analysis of the implications for the globalization of òrìṣà traditions in the virtual communities of the Internet.

Kinds of Sites

Pages or sites devoted to information about the òrìṣà are likely uncountable as new ones appear daily and old ones lapse or are withdrawn. There are hundreds of well-produced sites exclusively concerned with the òrìṣà and likely thousands that mention them in some way. We might distinguish five kinds of òrìṣà sites currently posted on the Internet: organizational, individual, devotional, academic, and commercial. Naturally, there may be considerable overlap: many organizations may have retail outlets; devotees may be academics, and so forth.

Organizational òrìṣà sites usually reflect pre-existing òrìṣà communities or overarching associations of them. The frequently stated purpose of these sites is to provide information about òrìṣà religion, which is sanctioned by the authority of the institution. Many sites seek to correct misapprehensions about the religion on the part of the public. They counter public misinformation by emphasizing the antiquity of òrìṣà traditions, the reverence and sacred quality of their tenets, and the respect for life and community values among their practitioners. Many organizational sites offer services for members and the wider community including calendars of events, counseling, and consultative services. Prominent among these sites is that of the Church of Lukumi Babalu Aye of Hialeah, Florida.[1] This organization has taken the path of legally incorporating as a church and winning status as a religious organization through the American courts. The landmark 1993 unanimous decision by the U.S. Supreme Court to overturn the city of Hialeah's ban on "animal sacrifice" was fought by the church and has led to considerable respite in the legal harassment of òrìṣà devotees throughout the United States.

Another pre-eminent example of òrìṣà organizations on the Internet is the site of Ilé Axé Opô Afonjá, one of the most famous houses of òrìṣà religion in Salvador da Bahia, Brazil.[2] Opô Afonjá was founded in 1910 by a charismatic olòrìṣà Mãe Aninha dos Santos. Under the leadership of Mae Stella do Oxossi, the community has grown to encompass a school, a daycare center, craft workshops, a clinic, and a museum spread across a multi-acre campus in Bahia. Opô Afonjá counts among its members many of the city's politicians and artists and has initiates from all over the world. Its Web site, with texts in English as well as Portuguese, reflects this cosmopolitan quality. Like the Church of Lukumi Babalu Aye site, the page of Opô Afonjá offers information about òrìṣà traditions with a mind to correcting the inaccurate notions of outsiders.

It too details the services that the organization provides and offers a magnificent photographic tour of its museum, which houses precious artifacts from the rich history of Bahian òrìṣà traditions.

Several organizational òrìṣà sites derive less from the leadership of a single community but rather feature associations of òrìṣà houses. The Egbe Lukumi was founded in Miami by *olòrìṣà* from several houses and is "dedicated to foster brotherhood among the Lukumi community and promote the awareness of its values, principles, and traditions."[3] The Organization of Lukumi Unity maintains a discussion board where initiates and non-initiates can exchange information about the òrìṣà.[4]

The line between an organization and an individual on the Internet may be very fine. An individual *babaláwo,* Efunmoyiwa of Seattle, has created a site that is a kind of institution in itself. This popular page, "OrishaNet," boasts 135,000 contacts per month, "dedicated to being an accurate source of information on La Regla Lucumí for those learning the religion and other interested parties."[5] OrishaNet maintains an online religious goods store, features an òrìṣà art gallery, and provides basic and advanced information on òrìṣà practices. Like the Organization for Lukumi Unity, OrishaNet displays an active discussion board, which is greatly enriched by Efunmoyiwa's trenchant comments. This board is archived and provides a panoramic view of the concerns of òrìṣà devotees throughout the world.

An interesting site that is also concerned with accurate information about òrìṣà traditions is the online magazine *Ashé una revista especializada en Santería.*[6] This Spanish-language site originating from Venezuela contains bimonthly articles on òrìṣà traditions, interviews with prominent priests, poetry, and Yorùbá vocabulary. It features regular documentation of *patakis,* stories derived from Ifá and ẹẹrìndínlógún. *Ashé* also features numerous photographs, some of which are scanned from published texts, whereas others are original images of òrìṣà objects and ceremonies in Venezuela.

Several sites are devoted to individuals' self-presentation as òrìṣà priests and priestesses. Ricardo Obàtálá's site is both an online botanica ("Rick's Spiritual Supplies") and a visual display of Ricardo as a priest of Obatala in ceremonial clothes and before his home altar.[7] Olòrìṣà Sokulosomi presents herself in Yemaya's *traje de desayuno* dress before her òrìṣà in state. These sites do not appear to seek to instruct viewers so much as to act as markers of identity. They are spiritual self-portraits in which men and women affirm the centrality of the òrìṣà in their lives.

Devotional sites tend not to be interested in presenting the *olórìṣà* as the òrìṣà themselves. They function as virtual altars, holy sites as it were, through which to encounter the òrìṣà in beauty and devotion. Yemoja Nina's home page for Yemoja is a lovely example of a devotional site.[8] It offers cooling, marine images and poetry inspired by Nina's devotion to Yemoja. There are a series of links to other virtual shrines dedicated "with love" to the major òrìṣà that have been constructed by Yemoja Nina from downloaded images from other Internet sites. Chango's page, for example, sets a series of photos against a brilliant scarlet background. Around the text of an *orìkí* for Chango, there is arranged Carybé's image of Xango in Bahia as well as photos of fresh fruit and fried foods. The effect is to place the viewer before an altar, a spatial and visual respite from the hurried commerce of the Internet.

Amy Willard has constructed a cross-cultural site for the Ocean Mother that honors Yemoja along with other goddesses of the ocean. The viewer scrolls through multiple images of moonlit surf, interspersed with words of praise for the divinity.[9] Another site devoted to Yemoja offers ocean images and a well-known "Lady of the Sea" chromolithograph, requesting that viewers "meditate on this image and let her communicate with you."[10]

A site that seems to bring together many features of different categories is Martin Tsang's page for the òrìṣà Erinle.[11] As the importance of Erinle has been underrecognized in the Americas, Martin has dedicated himself to enlightening Web browsers about the importance of this òrìṣà by presenting extensive scholarly documentation of Erinle iconography and lore. The site functions both as an act of devotion and a scholarly resource. Martin has also been developing an online book-selling business at the site to underwrite his initiation in Erinle.

Martin's researched approach to òrìṣà studies is reflected in a number of academic sites constructed by professional scholars. Andrew Apter of the University of Chicago has embarked on an ambitious project of linking Yorùbá-related sites through his Yorùbá Ethnographic Archive.[12] Deborah Wyrick has organized a good deal of Vodou and òrìṣà studies in her online resource essay "Divine Transpositions: Recent Scholarship on Vodou and Santería Religious Art."[13] Yvonne Chireau of Swarthmore maintains a sweet site with numerous links to òrìṣà topics.[14] Mary Ann Clark maintains what is likely the most complete list of òrìṣà-related links that includes new groups and list groups as well as a listing of virtual altars.[15]

The final significant category of òrìṣà-related sites is the commercial group, where entrepreneurial *olòrìṣàs* and others sell items for òrìṣà ritual. These online businesses, like the persons at the other sites, may vary widely in their connection to the traditional communities of òrìṣà devotion. Many carry the name of the traditional Cuban store, *botanica,* recalling the "botanical" base of òrìṣà work. Like their physical counterparts, virtual botanicas vend herbs, foods, crockery, candles, images, books, and other items important to òrìṣà devotion. Botanica Yemaya y Chango is an actual botanica in Washington, D.C., and maintains a beautiful Web page that features a full array of the *soperas,* the chinaware bowls for the òrìṣà.[16] It also promotes consultations with *ẹẹrìndínlógún,* divination with sixteen cowries. Botanica La Esperanza offers a full line of òrìṣà products as well as spiritual readings with cards and weekly horoscopes.[17] The Island of Salvation Botanica in New Orleans flows with the city's reputation to sell art, candles, and supplies for Voodoo and Santería.[18] There is an interesting connection set between Brazil and Cuba at the Obiexu Botanica and Health Foods site.[19] A final vendor whose connection to the òrìṣà traditions, who will be worth speaking of later, is Branwen's Cauldron of Light, which refers to itself as "a unique source for personalized witchcraft, Wicca, pagan, Santería, occult and magickal spells and supplies."[20] In addition to offering items for sale, Branwen's Cauldron acts as, in their words, "a resource for witchcraft and Wicca information through the detailed instructions that accompany many of our products and through reader contributions to our pages."

These are just a few representative examples of the hundreds of Web sites concerning the òrìṣà. Each site displays, and at times merges, the concerns of institution and identity building, information dissemination, and commerce. Their number and exponential growth signal new trends in òrìṣà traditions, expansion beyond borders conceived in Africa or the African diaspora. In the remainder of this essay, I sketch two implications of this florescence of òrìṣà traditions into cyberspace: changes in the understanding of òrìṣà and changes in the individuals and communities devoted to them.

Implications

A survey of òrìṣà images on the net reveals a growing tendency to represent the òrìṣà anthropomorphically. While digital images of natural elements (ocean, river, lightning) may be found to represent the òrìṣà, there are numerous and growing portrait galleries of the òrìṣà in anthropomorphic form. One of the formative influences in this trend was the Bahian artist Carybé, who in a series of drawings in the 1940s and 1950s depicted the ceremonial life of his adopted city's òrìṣà centers. His drawings show the òrìṣà-in-manifestation, human devotees vested in the regalia of their patron òrìṣà.[21] His concern was to document òrìṣà regalia and show the dignity of divine devotion in the Candomblé. The influence of his work can be seen in many collections of òrìṣà portraits available to visitors to Bahia in popular prints and postcards.[22] Yet, what in Carybé's drawings were depictions of òrìṣà-in-manifestation seem to be taken by many online devotees as portraits of the òrìṣà themselves.

These anthropomorphic views of the òrìṣà, and their grouping into collections and galleries, are perfectly suited to reproduction on the Internet. Many artists have turned their hands to producing òrìṣà series, in which we see anthropomorphic images of the òrìṣà, independent of their human ceremonial context. These might be called "mythological" images of the òrìṣà: they exist as gods in sacred time, often in their natural elements, and in archetypal poses. These images are often thoughtfully conceived—they may be bold or lovely—yet they portray the òrìṣà abstracted from the devotional contexts that formerly manifested them.

A striking series of mythological portraits by Bahian artist Francisco Santos may be found at the OrishaNet site. The page offers thirteen thumbnail images, each of a different òrìṣà radiating cosmic power.[23] Kathleen Barrett has painted evocative, abstract yet anthropomorphic portraits of nine òrìṣà.[24] Silvia Schiffman shows them interacting according to their *pataki* stories.[25]

The Internet yields hundreds of these portraits. Through several months of persistent searches for images of the òrìṣà Òṣun, I found over thirty original anthropomorphic portraits of her. Beyond these mythological renderings, I found over twenty photos of dancers in Òṣun regalia and at least ten photos of Òṣun shrines. Equal numbers may be found for other popular òrìṣà such as Sango or Yemọja.

Although I think that most devotees are perfectly aware that these images are anthropomorphic renderings of invisible powers, I believe that the tendency to abstract them in this way shows a distance from the ceremonial context where the òrìṣà have traditionally "lived" and to re-envision them as "principles" of an ordered cosmos. Frequently òrìṣà are seen as personifications of departments of life: Òṣun as the goddess of "love"; Ṣàngó as the god of "justice." This abstraction and grouping into clusters, what David Brown has called the "pantheonization" of the òrìṣà, works them into models of divinity owing more to the Olympic order of Hesiod than the òrìṣà devotions of Africa.

Another context in which òrìṣà portraits are appearing is in galleries of goddesses. Artist Hrana Janto has painted anthropomorphic portraits of Yemọja, Oya, and Ọṣun placed alongside fifty-three other world goddesses such as Celtic Brigid and Hawaiian Pèlé.[26] The images are part of a divination system called "The Goddess Oracle: A Potent Tool for Healing and Wholeness through the Goddess and Ritual." Artist Sandra M. Stanton has produced lovely and iconographically informed portraits of Oya, Ọṣun, and Yemọja in her series devoted to "The Goddess in World Mythology."[27]

I believe this tendency to render the òrìṣà anthropomorphically represents a change in their mode of representation, with theological and social implications. In one case the òrìṣà are grouped in a pantheon, a fixed or limited number of archetypal departments of life. In the other, they are pictured as avatars of one single goddess. Either brings us to a different understanding of the òrìṣà than that of the "blood, stones, and herbs" that William Bascom used to distinguish what was essentially African in Afro-Cuban òrìṣà traditions (Bascom 1950). The anthropomorphic rendering of the òrìṣà is not an African tradition, nor does it appear to be part of older Brazilian or Cuban ones. The famous chromolithograph of the òrìṣà as the "Seven African Powers" appears to have arisen under the influence of Spiritism. Òrìṣà priest and scholar Ysamur Flores would remind us that the images of the Catholic saints have never been considered *fundamento,* fundamental and essential objects symbolic of the òrìṣà's presence.[28] These *fundamentos* are indeed the "stones and herbs" of Bascom's typology, and all other images are secondary and ephemeral.

Once again, I am not suggesting that Internet devotees of the òrìṣà cannot or do not make a distinction between the image of the òrìṣà and what the òrìṣà may be independent of the image. This is the false problem of "idolatry" whose only referent is to discredit the image making of others. What I do find significant is the reliance on anthropomorphic images without reference to "stones and herbs" so fundamental to traditional òrìṣà devotion.

The social implications of this new form of òrìṣà imaging abstracted from the ceremony point toward new forms of community and religion.

Devotions to the òrìṣà have moved well beyond the communities that have traditionally sanctioned them. Earlier models of the spread of òrìṣà traditions conceived diffusion from Yorùbáland to Brazil and Cuba and from Afro-Cubans to non-Afro-Cubans. The lines radiated along paths of migration of individuals and communities, the most dramatic being the Cuban migrations following the 1959 revolution and the Mariel boatlift of 1980. With the advent of easy access to the Internet, these lines are rebounding with electric speed. Individuals who have never met an *olòrìṣà* face-to-face are constructing identities as òrìṣà devotees and linking to Web sites to acquire and pass on information.

A further development lies in the fact that access to the Internet is easy only for those who have the technological education and financial security to make use of it. This includes millions of households, but excludes many millions as well. Web access requires literacy and access to a wired computer. It is no surprise that Web users tend to be affluent, educated, and white.[29] Although Latino and African American devotees maintain many of the sites mentioned above, it is likely that the creators of the majority of sites, and the majority of people accessing them, are white. This much studied "digital divide" indicates a new development of òrìṣà traditions, that the majority of their devotees, whatever their level of commitment, knowledge, or initiation, may be white Americans.

Although the sketch of òrìṣà sites above seeks to include organizational sites that spring out of actual òrìṣà communities, it may be that the majority of sites concerned with òrìṣà are maintained by white Americans who would identify themselves as pagan or devotees of the goddess. The most common context for discussion of Ọ̀ṣun or Yemọja was among other goddesses of the world, often with expressions of a faith that the òrìṣà were African names or avatars of a universal goddess who is also called Hathor or Artemis.

It is understandable that those devotees committed to the cultural specificity of the òrìṣà as well as the inviolability of initiation-based knowledge would be concerned with this pagan appropriation of the òrìṣà. Yet, the acephalous nature of the Internet defies any attempts at correction or sanction. A glance at the discussion boards of the organizational sites reveals a frustration on the part of officers of organizations with inaccuracies and presumptions on the part of pagan devotees of the òrìṣà. The organizational Web site may itself be at least partly a response to this acephalism by its construction of institutions or sanctioning bodies. The model for the institutionalization of òrìṣà devotion seems to be, if perhaps only by default, that of Christianity, where councils of bishops hammered out doctrine and orthopraxis. The conference where this essay was presented, the Yorùbá millennium conference, was more than once referred to by some of its participants as the òrìṣà version of the Council of Nicea.

The display of òrìṣà on the Internet raises major questions about owning, belonging to, and committing to òrìṣà traditions. What is authentic in òrìṣà devotion independent of traditional communities of initiation and supervision by elders? And given that the very existence of an òrìṣà tradition in the African diaspora is the result of a mortal struggle for survival and justice, who is entitled to appropriate the òrìṣà for his or her own personal devotion?

Finally, the proliferation of òrìṣà sites on the Internet raises questions about the nature of community and religion itself. Is a cyber community a "real" one? I have argued elsewhere that òrìṣà are "made" in the service of the individual to the community: that concentrated ritual actions, "services," empower the òrìṣà to work in the lives of their devotees (Murphy 1994). The òrìṣà "come down" to dance because the community works to invite them. Without this communal "work" (*ebo*) will the òrìṣà come?

Many devotions to the òrìṣà have always been carried out in private, heart-to-heart exchanges between human children and òrìṣà parents. There is some evidence that contact with Western values may have shifted the interpretation of òrìṣà devotion from an affair of the community to one of the individual. Sheila Walker in her comparative study of African and Afro-Brazilian spirit manifestation concluded that the relationship in Africa was largely seen as an interaction between the spirit and the community, while in Brazil it was often viewed in terms of personal experience (Walker 1972). This valuing of personal experience, even seeing it as the primary criterion of religion, has a strong history of development in the West. Jesus himself, in his critique of the Pharisees, takes pains to distinguish between an external (and hence communal) religion of the letter of the law and an internal (and hence personal) spirit. The European Reformation and Enlightenment reaffirmed the centrality of individual faith in judging spiritual authenticity. This rise of individualism is extended by technology. Machines have contributed to the atomization of the workforce so that every individual is an economic unit unto him or herself. Thus, class, status, political affiliation, and, as we are now witnessing, race or gender are seen as products of individual choice.

It is not surprising that in the economies of the new world order of the new millennium we find religious affiliation a matter of choice, a "spiritual supermarket" where consumers choose among competing products. Thus, the devotee is seen as free to choose his or her own deity and construct his or her own mélange of doctrine and obligation. The potential of the personal computer to provide innumerable choices and to exempt the individual from other webs of social connection or obligation pushes the individualization of spirituality further than it has ever been taken. Every individual can be a church.

At the same time, in this cyber world of endless religious choice, many people are seeking community through the electronic networks of bulletin boards, chat rooms, list-serves, e-groups, and other methods of electronic communication. Howard Rheingold, an early and enthusiastic member of Internet groups, coined the term "virtual community" to refer to "social aggregations that emerge from the Net when enough people carry on . . . public discussions long enough, with sufficient human feeling, to form webs of personal relationships in cyberspace" (Reingold 1993).

A relatively long-standing virtual òrìsà community is alt.religion. orisha, which states the following mission: "alt.religion.orisha is an unmoderated forum for the discussion of African-based and derived belief systems throughout the African diaspora. These belief systems fall into several main categories: We welcome all comers to this newsgroup; practitioners, researchers, students, and those simply seeking a better understanding of widely-practiced, but often misunderstood belief systems. We ask that all who subscribe, and post to this group, enter with respect, agree to disagree, and warmly welcome those seekers of information who may not adhere to the beliefs expressed in this newsgroup. In the spirit of the *orishas* and *loas,* we welcome you."

Within sites like this one may be found extraordinary documentation of the concerns of cyber-devotees of the òrìsà. Messages contain queries ranging from beginners asking about the very elements of the tradition (what happens in spirit possession?) to more advanced concerns about ritual practice and esoteric information. Anyone is free to ask and anyone is free to reply. There is a great deal of contestation about who is right and wrong, and there are irenic calls for tolerance and unity. Occasionally there are condemnations from fundamentalist Christians and spirited rejoinders pointing out the evils of Christianity's collusion with colonialism and oppression. People post prayers to the òrìṣà and thanksgiving notices for favors granted.

One may also find calls to create new cyber communities centering on a particular òrìṣà. Here is a notice worth quoting in full that seeks devotees to form a group devoted to the òrìṣà Ọ̀ṣùmàrè:

> We are forming a group dedicated to the Yorùbá and Arara divinity of the Rainbow. Our group consists of initiates of various traditions who are coming together in this new age of understanding to work together for the betterment of humankind. Most of our members are initiated into various traditions such as Wicca/European Witchcraft, African traditions such as Santería, Candomblé, Voudun, shamanic traditions, and of course, we are all spiritualists. We invite you to join our group and become part of our spiritual family. We provide instruction and initiations, which are necessary tools for spiritual development. We are of the old school, and believe that without initiation, one cannot competently work within a tradition. Our traditions are not mixed, but have been brought closer together for mutual understanding. Like the colors of the rainbow, each tradition maintains its integrity. BECOME A RAINBOW WARRIOR OR WARRIORESS.
>
> We invite all who are serious to contact us about becoming a part of our group. We do not discriminate with regard to age, race, or cultural background. We ask that you come with respect, for without respect for a tradition or its members, you do not have anything. May the blessings of our Gracious Goddess in all her infinite forms and the blessings of Her Consort be upon you! May the blessings of all the Orishas, Voduns, and Mpungos be upon you! May the blessings of all the spirits of Light be upon you![30]

Not the least of concerns is that expressed by neophytes who are seeking an actual community: the whereabouts of a reliable *olòrìṣà;* often they have stories of misgivings and mistrust of those met previously. There are many referrals with testimonials to compassionate and knowledgeable *olòrìṣà* and occasionally "flaming" denunciations of others. Here we may see the cyber community and the real community reflecting each other, as experience with one leads to experience with the other.

Still I would argue that the trend is toward atomizing the tradition rather than building strong communities, virtual or actual. The nature of the technology itself reinforces lone viewing at the screen; a PC is a personal computer. The images of the òrìṣà that we see on the Internet and the expressions of devotion to them are at a distance from the communities that sustained them and the communal work that manifested them. It is likely that there will always be communities of òrìṣà devotees bound by filial ties of face-to-face initiation, if only in reaction to the virtual worlds of the new millennium. Òrìṣà devotions have survived stunning blows to their communities of devotion and have emerged vital and intact. At the same time, alongside traditional houses of òrìṣà devotion, there will be rapid extensions of other kinds of òrìṣà veneration: individuals creating unmediated personal devotions with òrìṣà and invocation of òrìṣà as avatars of universal principles.

Devotion to the òrìṣà has undergone many transformations through the fiery furnace of enslavement and oppression. It is tempting to try to adjudicate authenticity in the contrast between the work of the traditional *ilé* and the devotions of the virtual world. The history of struggle and resistance on the part of the enslaved and colonized ancestors of the *ilé* gives moral authority to those who remember and invoke them. Too, the challenge of real communal life, the obligations and self-denials necessary for the success of any group, make communal òrìṣà devotions a hard-won achievement. But does anyone or any group own the òrìṣà? The òrìṣà are known to initiate the call to devotion, not their human devotees. The anthropomorphic portraits of Hrana Janto and Sandra Stanton are beautiful, informed, and sincere: "pure," if you will. Are these not òrìṣà devotions appropriate to new times and new peoples? The traditional Yorùbá are not slow to recognize the source of true òrìṣà devotion in the proverb "Ori ni olori òrìṣà" (The head is the greatest òrìṣà).[31]

Notes

This essay was written in 1999, and surely much has changed or developed in its subject matter since then, given the torrid pace of progress in cyberspace. Likewise, all Web pages cited in this paper were accessed in 1999. Updated Web sites are listed where available and the older Web sites may be accessible through cached documents or an archive such as the Internet Archive.

1. http://home.earthlink.net/~clba [page not found] http://www.church-of-the-lukumi.org

2. http://www.geocities.com/Athens/Acropolis/1322/

3. http://www.egbeLukumi.com [page not found]

4. http://home.ican.net/~vreznik/lukumi [page not found] http://www.lukumiunity.org

5. http://www.seanet.com/~efunmoyiwa/ [page not found] http://www.orishanet.org

6. http://ashe.com/ve/

7. http://members.aol.com/rickspirit/RicardoObatala.html [page not found]

8. http://members.tripod.com/~yemoja/index-t.html [page not found]

9. http://www.goddess2000.org/OceanMother.html [page not found]

10. http://www.angelfire.com/f13/YEMAYA/page4.html [page not found]

11. http://inle.freeserve.co.uk [page not found]

12. http://anthro.spc.uchicago.edu/~aapter/yea/ [page not found]

13. http://social.chass.ncsu.edu/jouvert/v3i12/VODOU.HTM

14. http://www.swarthmore.edu/Humanities/chirea1

15. http://sparta.rice.edu/~maryc/AfroCuban.html#News

16. http://www.yemaya-chango.com/ [page not found] http://www.botanicayemayachango.com

17. http://www.bonicaesperanza.com [page not found]

18. http://www.mindspring.com/~cfeldman/bot2.html [page not found] http://www.feyvodou.com/index1.htm

19. http://www.obiexu.com [page not found] http://members.aol.com/_121b_ZWOXgSzf8Ga2C9ONP5Vy/3GyDVGmETjf

20. http://branwenscauldron.com

21. www.ufba.br/~analucia/orixas [page not found] http://www.pitoresco.com.br/brasil/carybe.htm

22. www.mediascript.teak.fi/kirsi/Visual/orixat.html [page not found]

23. http://www.seanet.com/~efunmoyiwa/art.html [page not found] Are images available at http://www.orishanet.org?

24. http://www.ifafoundation.com/gallery.html [page not found]

25. www.admet.com/silvia/ [page not found] http://www.admnet.com/silvia/ARTIST.HTM

26. www.goddessoracle.com

27. www.goddessmyths.com

28. Personal communication, October 1995.

29. See "Closing the Digital Divide," National Telecommunications and Information Administration," U.S. Department of Commerce, http://www.ntia.doc.gov/ntiahome/fttn99/charts.html.

30. http://www.oxumare.freeservers.com

31. Thanks to Jacob Olupona for the text of this proverb and for much, much more.

References

Bascom, William R. 1950. "The Focus of Cuban Santería." *Southwestern Journal of Anthropology* 6, no. 1: 64–68.
Murphy, Joseph M. 1994. *Working the Spirit: Ceremonies of the African Diaspora*. Boston: Beacon Press.
Reingold, Howard. 1993. *The Virtual Community: Homesteading on the Electronic Frontier*. Reading, MA: Addison-Wesley.
Walker, Sheila. 1972. *Ceremonial Spirit Possession in Africa and Afro-America*. Leiden: Brill.

25

Gender, Politics, and Hybridism in the Transnationalization of Yorùbá Culture

RITA LAURA SEGATO,
TRANSLATED BY ERNESTO IGNACIO DE CARVALHO

Frequently, anthropological theories speak more about anthropologists than about their discipline

—Edmund Leach, "Virgin birth"

[A] knowledge of other cultures, societies, or religions comes about through an admixture of indirect evidence with the individual scholar's personal situation, which includes time, place, personal gifts, historical situation, as well as the overall political circumstances. What makes such knowledge accurate or inaccurate, bad, better, or worse, has to do mainly with the needs of the society in which that knowledge is produced.

—Edward W. Said, *Covering Islam*

Of course, the "I" who writes here must also be thought of as, itself, "enunciated." We all write and speak from a particular place and time, from a history and a culture, which is specific. What we say is always in context, positioned.

—Stuart Hall, "Cultural Identity and Diaspora"

The everyday paradox of third world social science is that we find these
theories, in spite of their inherent ignorance of "us," eminently useful
in understanding our societies . . . why cannot we, once again, return
the gaze?
—Dipesh Chakrabarty, *Provincializing Europe: Postcolonial Thought
and Historical Difference*

I bring together, in this analysis, three different scholarly discourses about
the gender ideas of Yorùbá civilization and, despite their differences, link
them to two historical moments, distant in time and circumstances, of the
expansion of that culture. I refer these three models to what I understand
as the gender factor in the diffusion of Yorùbá religious worldview. I
first describe synthetically those three academic discourses, showing
how, despite their differences, they strive with the available words to
describe, within highly complex ethnographies, the sophisticated and
peculiar conception of gender in the universe of Yorùbá culture. In doing
so, they offer three different models but concur to point to a shared perception: the high level of abstraction of Yorùbá gender construction in
relation to the anatomic signifiers; in other words, the absence of biological essentialism that such a system of thought presents. Next I analyze
how academic discourses are nationally and interestedly situated, and I
show that, quite independently, three authors, I among them, have placed
complex gender issues at the center of the discussion of Yorùbá worldview. Reviewing briefly our writings, I reveal how the position—ethnic
and national—from which scholars produce their academic models affects their formulations. Finally I briefly review my own ideas and argue
that the complexities of Yorùbá gender construction were central in the
process of diffusion of Yorùbá religion and its social context from Africa
to the New World initially and, later, from Brazil to other countries such
as Argentina and Uruguay, where there was no presence of them.

Three Anthropologists Speak about Gender in the Yorùbá Religious World

I address here three models of interpretation of the Yorùbá ideas about
gender, as expressed in religious themes and practices. J. Lorand Matory, in 1994, and Oyèrónké Oyewumi, in 1997, formulated two models concerning the Yorùbá of Nigeria. Both models were published by

the University of Minnesota Press. The third model derives from my own work about the Yorùbá religion in Brazil, published in Portuguese around a decade earlier, in 1986 (reprinted in 1989, 1995, and 2000 and published in English in 1997). Although my publication on the theme came out earlier, I start with the last to appear and finish with my own work, for the sake of clarity of the exposition.

Oyèrónké Oyewumi

Oyewumi, a Yorùbá herself, published *The Invention of Women: Making an African Sense of Western Gender Discourses* while she was an assistant professor at the University of California at Santa Barbara. Despite working in the same field, she did not refer there to Matory's work on a similar topic from his book of 1994. She referred only to his doctoral dissertation, presented in 1991, and by quoting him in two paragraphs, not exceeding the extension of one page.

For Oyewumi, "the assumption that a gender system existed in Ọ̀yọ́ society before Western colonization is yet another case of Western dominance in the documentation and interpretation of the world" (1997: 32). In her view, colonialism introduced the vocabulary and practices of gender in the Yorùbá religion, and Western scholarship—as well as Western feminism—misread the existence of gender in that culture: "the usual gloss of the Yorùbá categories *obìnrin* and *ọkùnrin* as 'female/woman' and 'male/man,' respectively, is a mistranslation . . . these categories are neither binarily opposed nor hierarchical" (1997: 32–33). This is so, in Oyewumi's interpretation, because, as she argues:

1. "There was no conception there of an original human type (man, generic) over which the other variety had to be measured (the feminine, particular). *Eniyan* (in Yorùbá) is the non-gender-specific word for humans" (different from [fe]male or [wo]man) (1997: 33).
2. "*Obìnrin* is not ranked in relation to *ọkùnrin* (both sharing the same neutral root, *rin*)" (ibid.).
3. They only apply to adults. Children are all *omode*. Male and female animals are named *akọ* and *abo*. Plants are *abo* when they germinate.

"Thus"—she says on page 33—"in this study, the basic terms *ọkùnrin* and *obìnrin* are best translated as referring to the anatomic male and anatomic female, respectively; they refer only to physiologically marked differences and do not have hierarchical connotations."

Oyewumi also speaks of "ana-sex": *ana-males* and *ana-females:* "to underscore the fact that in the Yorùbá world-sense it is possible to acknowledge these physiological distinctions without inherently projecting a hierarchy of the two social categories." "Unlike 'male' or 'female' in the West, the categories of *obìnrin* and *ọkùnrin* are primarily categories of anatomy, suggesting no underlying assumptions about the personalities or psychologies deriving from such. Because they are not elaborated in relation and opposition to each other, *they are not sexually dimorphic* and therefore are not gendered. In Old Ọ̀yọ́, they did not connote social ranking; nor did they express masculinity or femininity, because those categories did not exist in Yorùbá life or thought" (1997: 34; my emphasis).

Oyewumi asserts the absolute absence of a gender symbolic structure in Yorùbá traditional (precolonial) society. She has as the reference a very standard definition of gender *not* as "a property of an individual or a body in and of itself by itself" but as "a construction of two categories in hierarchical relation to each other [. . .] embedded in institutions" that, as such, orients expectations and orders all social processes (1997: 39). She states, once more, that such particular kind of ideological cell was absent among the precolonial Yorùbá.

Regarding the deities of the pantheon, Oyewumi speaks of three levels. At the first level is *"Olodumare* (God—the Supreme Being), that did not have a gender identity, and it is doubtful whether she (or he) was perceived anthropomorphically before the advent of Christianity and Islam in Yorùbáland" (1997: 140). To support this, sources are quoted showing how post-Christianization scholars depicted Olódùmarè with masculine attributes and called the deity "He," using the masculine third person, without any basis for doing so. However, Oyewumi gives no evidence of sources from which she could speak of this deity as not anthropomorphic or anthropomorphic but not gendered. A supreme god not anthropomorphic would be quite a rarity though.

At the second level of the pantheon of divinities, according to Oyewumi, there are the òrìṣàs, of whom it is said: "though there were *ana-male* and *ana-female* (meaning anatomically male and anatomically female) òrìṣà, as in other institutions, this distinction was inconsequential; therefore, it is best described as a distinction without difference." The author here supports her assertion by mentioning that some òrìṣà of different anatomical sex shared some qualities (the "rage" she says, of Ṣàngó and Oya), or that some changed their sex from one locality to another.

This, in fact, also happens in the New World, where deities have specific personalities that are grouped using a gender criterion, despite the similarities that may be present crossing the gender line. Here, too, gender changes with locality or time. Ṣàngó is syncretized with the images of Saint Barbara in Cuba and of Saint John in Brazil; Oya (Iansã) is said to have been male in the mythical past and turned female after becoming Ṣàngó's partner. Logunede, in Bahia, is male half the year, and male and female half the year. This, however, I believe, is not the evidence of a symbolic construction marked by the absence of gender in this culture, but, rather, a coded *commentary* that reveals a specific conception of gender, a statement about gender, and a political discourse phrased in gender terms.

Reading Oyewumi, one is led to wonder why, if anatomy meant nothing socially among the Yorùbá—as she states—the òrìṣàs, mythical entities, deities, free from human constraints, did have sexualized anatomy and behavior in their mythological representations. How could it be that such ideal anatomy of the gods of the pantheon, pure signifier, meant nothing at all for human affairs? In other words, why did the òrìṣàs *have,* in their mythical representation, a body marked by anatomical dimorphism and gender qualities if this did not bear, as Oyewumi indicates, any consequence on social relations, if this did not express anything relative to the imaginary of gender among human beings?

At the third level, she places the cult of the ancestors, "both male and female, venerated by members of each lineage and acknowledged yearly in the *Egúngún* masquerade. . . . The priesthood of various gods was open to both males and females. . . . Yorùbá religion, just like Yorùbá civic life, did not articulate gender as a category . . . The roles of the òrìṣà, priests and ancestors were not gender dependent" (1997: 140).

For Oyewumi, the dominant idiom in Yorùbá society was the idiom of *seniority*—relative to age. What really mattered—and matters—states the author, is whether the person is a child, an adult, or an elder: *omo* means child, offspring (1997: 40–41); only lately, after the nineteenth century, "*ọmọkùnrin* (boy) and *ọmọbìnrin* (girl) that have gained currency today indicate *ana-sex* for children" (41). They show that what is privileged socially is the youth of the child, not its sexed anatomy. Similarly, when calling an individual either *ìyá* (mother) or *bàbá* (father), or *obìnrin* (woman) or *okùnrin* (man), the important designation is their identity as adults, in age of reproduction. "The most important attribute these categories indicate is not gender; rather, it is expectations that persons of a certain age should have had children." *Ìyá* (mother) or *bàbá* (father) "are not just categories of parenthood. They are also categories of adulthood, since they are also used to refer to older people in general. More importantly, they are not binarily opposed and are not constructed in relation to each other" (41).

By this, the author emphasizes that the attribute of relative age and majority is more relevant, in vocatives as *ìyá* of *bàbá,* than the implications of gender that the words seem to indicate.

Therefore, clearly, for Oyewumi, seniority prevails over gender and can introduce inversions in the order of gender when looked from a Western gender frame. For example, an older or religiously invested *obìnrin* can be regarded as a father by an *okùnrin.* Oyewumi quotes from Johnson's (1921) observations on the relationship between the Òyó ruler and the official *obinrin* of the palace, who commands the worship to the spirits of the departed kings:

> The king looks upon her as his father, and addresses her as such. . . . He kneels in saluting her, and she also returns the salutation, kneeling, never reclining on her elbow as is the custom of the women in saluting their superiors. The king kneels for no one else but her, and prostrates himself before the god Şàngó, and before those possessed with the deity, calling them "father." (37–38)

As I show later, a structure strikingly similar to this can be found in the Şàngó cult of Recife, Brazil; however, my interpretation arises from a different model. In fact, in Brazil as well, depending on the seniority and gender of her òrìşà, a priestess can be regarded as a "father," and a wife can be said to be more "virile" than a husband. Moreover, still more revealing is the fact that the ritual greeting called *odobale* is removed from anatomy in a much more radical way than in the African Yorùbá world. According to Oyewumi, in the African *dobale* (1997: 36) the form of the bow performed depends upon the sex of the person who greets, and, in Brazil, it depends upon the sex of his or her òrìşà.

For Oyewumi: "the challenge that the Yorùbá conception presents is a social world based on social relations, not the body. It shows that it is possible to acknowledge the distinct reproductive roles for *obìnrin* and *okùnrin* without using them to create social ranking. In the Yorùbá cultural logic, biology is limited to issues like pregnancy that directly concern reproduction. . . . I have called this a distinction without social difference" (1997: 36). "The terms *obìnrin* and *ọkùnrin* merely indicate the physiological differences between the two anatomies as they have to do with procreation and intercourse . . . they do not refer to gender categories that connote social privileges and disadvantages. Also, they do not express sexual dimorphism because the distinction they indicate is specific to issues of reproduction" (34–35). "A superior is a superior regardless of body-type." "*Ori* [the head, the vital principle] has no gender" (38). We see here expressed an unusual meaning of dimorphism, as I ask myself: does she by the way imply that there are more than two morphological elements intervening in procreation?

Alternatively, what I suspect is that, detached from the body, gender names remain as an idiom of social relationships of some kind and organize at least some realms of interaction. But, for Oyewumi, on the contrary, only reproductive roles remain glued to, collapsed onto, and conflated to the body. Just to anticipate a part of my own argument, this seems to come close to the pivotal role for the division of ritual labor that members of the Nagô or the Ketu cult in Brazil attribute to anatomy. (Nagô and Ketu are names for Yorùbá religion in Recife and Bahia, respectively.) It is, precisely, ritual—and not copulative sexual—intercourse that reproduces the African religious lineages in Brazil, and the distribution of ritual gender roles is the only sphere of socioreligious life that follows the guidelines of sexual dimorphism, being strictly oriented by it. However, evidently, it is the symbolic aspect of that dimorphism, and not its biological dimension, that counts—since we are here in the realm of religious and philosophical reproduction of a spiritual, not biological or even racial Africa. Only when seen from this broader perspective given by the New World can we reach the hard core of what was already at stake there and understand the amount of conventional, uncritical thinking that is present under the apparent radicalism of Oyewumi's thesis.

If, on the one side, the reproduction and continuity of Africa in Brazil is processed through anatomically distributed ritual roles, this, on the other side, contrasts with all the other spheres—religious, social, psychic, affective, and sexual—of the religious life. Just to give an example, even reproduction, child upbringing, and domestic organization are conceived, in the environment of Afro-Brazilian cults, as detached from biology. Here, the family—and domestic—unit of the cult, the "family of saint" operative for all matters of life, is not based on shared biological substance but on initiation, which is to say, in the shared ritual substance (called *ase,* inoculated in the body during initiation by the initiate's "father of saints"). Sexual orientation and personality are freed from biological constraints as well. I could go on endlessly giving examples of a gender milieu that operates freely in relation to the biological and anatomical data, and where the Africa described by Oyewumi can be recognized vividly, but where gender terms—and, from a Western point of view, a subverted gender map—can be also recognized.

Moreover, Oyewumi incurs a number of contradictions. For example, while denying any gender connotation of the words *oko* and *aya,* she traces the equivalence of these terms with positions in the household. She says: "the translation of *aya* as 'wife' and *oko* as 'husband' imposes gender and sexual constructions that are not part of the Yorùbá conception" (1997: 44). She adds then: "*oko* and *aya* [were, respectively] owner/insider and non owner/outsider in relation to the *ilé* as a physical space and symbol of lineage (in reference to the virilocal practice established in the culture). This insider-outsider relationship *was ranked* with the insider being the privileged senior" (my emphasis). Thus, clearly and undeniably, gender terms are associated with status here. In a household, says Oyewumi, all the older members of the house, male and female, were considered *oko*—husband, elder—to the *aya*— newly arrived wife—even though she only had a marital sexual relation with her conjugal partner. It is also suggested that when this latter died, younger "anamales" of the house could claim sexual rights to her, "*since this was a heterosexual world*" (*sic,* my emphasis), and when a (senior) *oko* "anafemale" claimed inheritance rights to the widow, the sexual access was passed on to one of her "anamale" children.

Significantly, Oyewumi also lets us know that while men or women could be *oko* to other men and other women due to seniority, *anamales* could not be *aya* (wives) of either *anamales* or *anafemales.* They could only be *aya* to the òrìṣàs they worshiped and received in possession, this meaning that anatomical males did not cross the gender frontier downward in the social field. Definitely, among the precolonial Yorùbá, male anatomy was linked to a condition of status and prestige that did not combine with a wifely social role, except under the command of a supernatural entity. It surprises one that a point of such importance with all its consequences passes thoroughly unnoticed by the author. This, I believe, ends by putting a serious limitation to the efficacy of her model.

However, despite the ethnographic difficulties that Oyewumi's model seems unable to overcome, or, perhaps, precisely as a consequence of this, the author offers us a look into the complexities of gender among the Yorùbá, giving us a hint of the highly malleable nature of the system. This malleability in the Yorùbá universe played doubtlessly a crucial role in the relocation of the cosmology particular to this culture—and of the practices associated with it—in the New World, particularly in Brazil and, later, in the recent wave of expansion southward, into the new national territories of Argentina and Uruguay.

J. Lorand Matory

J. Lorand Matory published *Sex and the Empire That Is No More* in 1994, and at the time of the publication, he was assistant professor of anthropology and Afro-American Studies at Harvard University. His text also testifies to the existence of a complex gender construction in the traditional Ọ̀yọ́ (Yorùbá) world. He tried as well to express those complexities—which take gender schemes of Yorùbá cosmology and religious practices almost to a condition of ineffability—by formulating a model based on the idea of transvestitism. However, Matory states, "the women remain the paradigmatic image of married wifeliness not only in the òrìṣà religions but across the Yorùbá religious spectrum" (Matory 1994: 108).

In Matory's model, what he calls "sartorial iconography" and diacritical idiosyncratic ritual and work gestures mark what is womanly—women dressing or statuary, engravings, or figures of women "kneeling to offer service and sacrifice, carry head loads, and/or tie a baby to their back" (1994: 108). However, although they might be strictly dependent on these emblematic—and not anatomic—marks, the link with biological determinations is still established through women: "Women's marital and reproductive status directly affects their standing in every local religious organization. Menstruation compromises the participation of women of childbearing age" (107–8).

Transvestitism is, for Matory, the main "ironic" idiom of gender structures in Yorùbá society, which allows, for example, for people of the same sex to enter in a social relationship as *oko* and *obinrin* (with or without sexual implications). Still, the paradigmatic standing of the female body and its anatomic, postural, or sartorial attributes as signifier of a feminine relational position (though a male body can enter into that position as well) reveals the existence of a cognitive map built clearly in gender terms.

For Matory, this map is neither verbal nor nominated by means of lexical categories but is preferentially visual, scripted with icons, gestures, and visual marks. Oyewumi, on the other hand, denies the importance of visualizing among the Yorùbá and states the dominance of the audible. She also states, as I mentioned, that no words exist in the Yorùbá language for masculine and feminine as opposed positions or personalities (Oyewumi, 1997: 34) and that there exist words only for the relational positions of wife and husband (*oko* and *obinrin*). In Oyewumi's model one is left wondering about the raison d'être of verbal categories, statuary, carvings, and genderized costume, if none of them are meant to have any meaning in social life. In Matory's model, we are entitled to ask why the generalized practices of transvestitism if gender social hierarchies were meant to be left in their place, untouched, in the Yorùbá gender ideology.

Both authors, however, seem to agree about the existence of a Yorùbá model where gender follows a radically different scheme than in the West. But although in Oyewumi's text there is belligerency and the premise of the collision of mutually untranslatable civilizations, one of them defeated and colonized, remaining only as a sophisticated and pure civilization anti-paradigm, in Matory there is a "lesson" to bring back home, as I try to show.

It seems to me that the discourse I have presented so far, Oyewumi's discourse, has its own hybridity introduced in her enunciation by her privileged interlocutor: the West. By stating an ancient Africa free from gender hierarchy—and she is clear about this—she is upholding a pure, precolonial Africa and has the introduction of genderized social and cosmological relations as the index of a Westernized, impoverished Africa. Matory's text also has a shadowed interlocutor. While Oyewumi is an antagonist, Matory is a reformist. It seems to me that he is bringing home the idea of transvestitism and gender centrality to the polis, to his fellows, to his country. As I try to show, in his ethnography, he speaks on behalf of a hierarchic gender structure that can remain as an organizing principle of an also hierarchic society despite the fact that its dramatis personae change skins, cross-dress. His is a stable, not menacing, though transformative gender relational cell.

Ethnographers, as scholars in general, never cease to be politically oriented, oriented by interests and values, conveying a message to peers, bringing arguments home.

Matory shows us a world where transvestitism always leads to a hierarchical, genderized, asymmetric arrangement. "[B]oth male wives and female husbands are central actors in the Ọ̀yọ́-Yorùbá Kingdom and village," he says (1994: xii); "all women are husbands to somebody and simultaneously wives to multiple others" (2); male transvestism in Ọ̀yọ́-Yorùbá is *not* only an idiom of domination and *not* only the evidence of the independence of gender categories from biological sex but a practice that "transforms existing gender categories" (3). However, the fact is that, in Matory's model, the practice of transvestitism transforms gender categories in the narrow sense of universalizing their hierarchical structure onto the social field, projecting them well beyond the field of gender roles and sexuality, and, of course, freeing them from straightjacket biological constraints. In this sense, Matory takes from Marilyn Strathern the idea, formulated for societies of the Pacific, that "sexual/gender inequality is the irreducible 'idiom' in which even inequality between persons of the same sex and gender is understood" (176–77).

At the core of Matory's model, one finds the idea—common in the descriptions of trance experience in African religions on the Old Continent and in the New World diaspora—of possessed humans "mounted" by gods. Rather simplistic bedrock, indeed, for such a complex system of thought as the one with which he deals. He says: "the vocabulary and dress code of the possession religions . . . illuminates the structure of that relationship. Recent initiates of *Yemọja, Osun, Obatala,* and *Ṣàngó* . . . are known specifically as 'brides of the god.' They wear women clothes or attributes. And the god is said to mount those he possesses" (1994: 7). The devotees invoke the god as "husband" and "lord." "The concept of 'mounting' (*gígùn*) likens the priest (*ẹlẹ́gùn*) to a royal charger (*esin*) and to a royal wife (*ayaba*)" (135). In addition, pots and calabashes are icons of that hierarchical orderliness in patrilineal marriage.

Gender hierarchy does not mean superiority of one biological sex to another but asymmetry as expressed by the relationship of genders in marriage. "Upon marriage, a woman *becomes a wife* (*ìyáwó*) not only to the man she marries (*ọkọ gidi*) but to all of that man's male and female agnates and to the women who married him and his agnates before her arrival. Conversely, not only the man she married but also all his agnates are classified as her husbands (*oko*)" (Matory 1994: 105). What we see here is a description identical to the one offered by Oyewumi concerning the wife newly arrived at her new home after marriage. In one word, wife and bride, in this social language, mean junior, subordinate. Oyewumi observes this typical organization too, as I showed, but whereas she interprets it as the absence of gender, Matory understands it as the generalization of gender terms as a classifying system in the hierarchical social field.

Gender and sexuality become an idiom for the hierarchical transitions characteristic of traditional Yorùbá society. Perhaps the clearest expression of this arrangement is provided by the fact that, when the senior male possession priest (ẹlẹ́gùn) receives the òrìṣà in possession, he does it as the divinity's bride, "mounted" by the god as a sexual metaphor. Many believe that Ṣàngó's mount, that is, the priest in state of possession, can himself "mount," that is, perform sexual intercourse with a woman in the audience (Matory 1994: 170). So, what I want to highlight here is the fact that the same social actor is described as subordinated in one relationship and empowered in the other, female to one partner, male to the other. I had pointed at this language of circulation of gender positioning for Brazil, too, though based on different ethnographic materials. The idea persists. However, its impact and destination are not merely to organize social relationships and institute a hierarchy using the gender idiom but also a certain undermining of patriarchy's solid rock foundations too. In my analysis of the Brazilian material, the application of gender terms by cult people leads to the subversion of their usual application outside the environment of the religion. The aspects of the gender system that Matory calls "ironic" for the Yorùbá are the core of the gender Afro-Brazilian plot.

The Author's Ethnography

I use here as a basis my ethnography of the Nagô (Yorùbá) of Recife, which shows a gender order that remains recognizable as Candomblé in general for Brazil, notwithstanding regional differences in myth and ritual. The pantheon of the cult presents the appearance of a formally arranged family group at first sight. However, as soon as we scratch the surface we find a father—Orisanla (Obàtálá in Cuba)—a patriarch, who, despite his ultimately revengeful personality, is not the acting authority among the òrìṣàs, once he is slow, impassive, and weak. A

mother—Iemoja—who, despite her apparently polite and meek countenance, is false and treacherous "like the sea," they say, "[s]ince you see
the surface but never the depths." Echoes of an encoded memory of the
middle passage may be heard here, since this element of her personality
parallels the treason of the sea that separated the slaves from their motherland and at the same time continued to link them to it.

Iemoja is a mother who does not bring up her own children, leaving
them to be cared for by a foster mother—Osun, the goddess of fertility who is not the childbearer but the caretaker. In a coded form, we
find here the historical split between the white mother, lady of the Casa
Grande—the manor house of landlords—and the slave wet nurse. The
father—Orisanla—brings up very lovingly a daughter—Osun—his favorite, though born from his wife Iemoja's affair of infidelity with a
more powerful god, Òrúnmìlà.

There is also a wife—Iansan (Oya)—who is said to have been male
in earlier times and to be today more "virile" than her husband, Ṣàngó,
because she rules over the spirit of the dead, the *eguns,* very much feared
by Ṣàngó. When Iansan finally agrees to marry Ṣàngó, she puts as a
condition never to be obliged to cohabit with him, since she simply and
adamantly abhors Ṣàngó's preferred food, *àgbò,* ram. A hard-working
first-born son of the dynasty, Ogum had his throne usurped by his self-
indulgent and cunning younger brother, Ṣàngó, with the lenience of the
mother, Iemoja, who immediately realized the maneuver but did nothing
to avoid it because, as it is said, "she fears anarchy more than injustice."
All the while the father, Orisanla, observed, either unconcerned or im-
potent, the injustice that was taking place. This is a "kingdom" in which
the mother, and not the father, has the prerogative of crowning the new
king and controls officially all the matters of the state. Not to be left
ignored, at least two episodes of homosexual seduction between deities
are narrated to support the social practices and a way of life relying on
this mythology.

In sum, invoked and alluded to in ordinary conversation, an endless
series of inversions transforms this apparently conventional hierarchical mythology in an ironic discourse about Brazilian society, where not
merely biological determination is removed from its usual pivotal place
in ideology, but also patriarchy and hierarchy are undermined by everyday activities and references to myth. The patriarchal foundations of a
privatized "domestic" state are also questioned. A fundamental doubt
about the gender structures upon which the dominant social moral is

built is inoculated into the political system as a whole (see Segato 1995, 2005).

Gender and Society: From the Yorùbá World to the West

Inversely, in Yorùbáland, according to Matory, the system and its vo-cabulary are used to create a social regime marked by rigid hierarchical relative positions that cross the whole range of relationships—among humans and between humans and gods. Unfortunately, his work does not answer the central questions: how does this really affect gender and sexuality; what is the feedback between the social and the gender plan? The gender grammar is approached as the idiom of social hierarchies. The argument emphasizes that gender icons are designed fundamentally to express and keep in place social hierarchy. Despite what the author says, we find ourselves looking at a gendered system in which detaching gender from biological sex does not disrupt or undermine the gender regime but enshrines it as the paradigm of all relationships of authority in a world intensely shaped by hierarchies.

In the Yorùbá system, as Matory holds, gender exists through predi-cates, and those predicates are sociological, relational or, at most, theat-rical. The feminine, as Matory leads us to understand, is "bridely," and the masculine is not manly but "husbandly." Gender, once again, is a position in relation and not a biological essence (1994: 164). However, a rigid, heterosexual, hierarchical power and prestige matrix prevails in this "technical"—as Matory calls it—highly self-conscious, artificial, gender order. Distribution of rights and duties and the code of etiquette are marked by "gender," thus understood as the language of relative ranks. Mobile, relational positions are contained within a fixed insti-tutional paradigm. "Beyond affirming or undermining existing gender categories, this sacred cross-dressing finances transformations of gender that make it the densest of all local emblems of power (*ase*) and subjec-tivity" (175).

Here, the act of "mounting" sets the scene of asymmetry (sexually, ritually, and, as an allegory, socially). "Gender, then, is the idiom of relations between gods and priests, riders and horses, parents and chil-dren, seniors and juniors, kings and plebes" (Matory 1994: 177). Thus, "as a source of metaphoric predications on political hierarchy, economic privilege and personal health, gender ceases to be gender as we know it" (177–78). And the author wonders: "Does *cross-dressing* affirm or undermine hegemonic gender roles? What boundaries does the *cross dresser* cross?" (202).

I would say that he himself gives the evidences for the answer: no boundary is crossed. The fixed positions man/woman are substituted by the relational, mobile positions husband/wife at the core of the system. The husband/wife structure transverses the system organizing it hierarchically. Husband/wife turns into a permanent metaphor of the hierarchical religious polis. Thus, "sartorial and cephalic transvestitism" practiced in Ọ̀yọ́ Yorùbá is not seen by Matory as a "ritual inversion intent on manifesting the power of disorder. . . . Nor does it appear to undermine gendered power inequalities" (1994: 211). Rather, and clearly, Matory speaks of the conservation of an order by means of a secondary symbolization of that order, and transvestitism is taken then to the center of the institutional order as a structuring force in it. This in the precise sense that, in Matory's own words, "transvestitism is not a marginal phenomenon. It is a central one, once codified and disseminated by an imperial state and now answering to the deepest aspirations of hundreds of thousands of Nigerians, Beninois, and, as we shall see, Brazilians" (215).

While Oyewumi tells the West that gender did not exist among the precolonial Yorùbá, claiming therefore the difference of her own world and her own difference, the news brought home by Matory seems to be that transvestitism and the transposition of fixed gender schemes into different skins is as efficacious an idiom of hierarchical social organization as a gender tailored by biology. This is so because, as stated in Matory's model, what counts is the untouched hierarchical logic of the gender matrix, not the anatomies that embody it.

The Gender Principle in the Diffusion of Yorùbá Worldview

The complex gender system that these scholars try somehow to describe at work in the traditional Yorùbá religious polis was one of the pillars, I believe, of the solid expansion of Yorùbá religion and cosmology in Brazil, and from Brazil to other countries in present days. In fact, whatever was or is in Africa the precise organization of the system that the authors quoted tried to describe, it is evident to me that an extraordinary work of preservation took place in the New World. It was not merely the elementary idea that the deity "mounts" its *medium* or "horse," so widespread in the Afro-American world to indicate possession, that was preserved, but also, and very specially, the intricacies and abstractions of the social management of gender. That preservation work did not restrict itself exclusively to the formal, ritualistic, and liturgical aspects of the Yorùbá tradition in the New World that are unequivocally tied to the mode of sociability indicated by the authors for the African context, but it has widened and become more radical, affecting the aspects of the gender construction that are most ineffable.

In my writings, I use the image of an "Afro-Brazilian *codex*" in order to make reference to this permanent, hard core of an anti-essentialist posture that cuts across practice and knowledge of Candomblé culture (see Segato 1998). With the term "codex," I emphasize a redundancy, that is, the meaningful repetition of some motifs. These repeated motifs point to the existence of a fixed code at work behind the observable practices, an encrypted inscription in a hidden layer that manifests itself constantly, however, in open discourse—*mythological, social, sexual, and ritual*—at the Yorùbá religious enclaves in the New World.

Indeed, it was very moving for me to find these two books, published around ten years after my first essay on the topic appeared. Other scholars have called attention to the peculiarities of the gender systems of African American religions and the presence of homosexuals in them—in Brazil (Landes 1940, 1967; Ribeiro 1969; Fry 1977, 1986; Wafer 1991; and Birman 1995), as well as in Cuban Santería (Dianteill 2000) and Haitian Voodoo (Lescot and Magloire 2002). However, I claim that the gender system is a structuring and crucial factor in the continuity of the tradition, the very core of it, and not a superfluous or additional element that could be absent without affecting the culture, the worldview, and the Afro-American society around Candomblé. In other words, I deal with what could be called—not without a semantic margin of error—its homosexual and androgynous features, pointed out so many times as a recurrent element in the sociability and sexuality of the cults, not as a separate element but rather as a consequence of a particular construction of the gender system that is not merely a cult's associated attribute among many but constitutes a central and fundamental structure for understanding the universe of Candomblé.

Much has been said about the reasons why the Yorùbá civilization prevailed over other African cultures that arrived in the New World in forming a structured religion and its social world. Two aspects are usually pointed out as crucial: (1) the massive arrival of a Yorùbá contingent after intercontinental trade was officially over, and (2) the solid institutions of the Yorùbá empire in Africa. From what I have been able to observe in the African religious environments in Brazil and, during the last twenty years, about the recent southern expansion of these religions to the countries of the River Plate basin (see Segato 1991, 1996), I think it is possible to add a third and fundamental factor to those reasons, that is, the malleability of the gender system and, with it, the flexibility and anti-essentialism of family arrangements.

For the first wave, I would say—briefly, since I have written on it extensively elsewhere—that a non-essentialist use of gender and family terms found a fertile terrain in the Brazilian colonial environment. This was so because constituted couples and their offspring could not find stability as family groups and were often dispersed, demographic ratios between males and females were highly inadequate, and marriage between slaves was not enforced but hindered for a long time almost everywhere in the country (Segato 1996). Therefore, a construction of gender and a terminology for family organization that could be freed from conflation with biological determinants, anatomical signifiers, or fixed relationships was ideal for this setting. Moreover, in this new environment, the whole system came to affect sexuality too and did not merely operate as an idiom for relative social status, as described by Matory.

In the second wave, Afro-Brazilian religions of a Yorùbá base (such as the Batuque of Porto Alegre and the Candomblé of Bahia) expanded to Argentina and Uruguay. In these countries, as my interpretation goes (Segato 1991, 1996), they provided the demarcation of a space of difference and symbolic inscription for groups without free expression or visibility in the society. Among those minorities, the homosexual one, traditionally asphyxiated in Hispanic countries and left without room for self-representation and recognition, found its niche for expression.

The Yorùbá world restored itself in Brazil around the cult of the òrìṣàs as the ideal embodiment of personality types. Personality was the notion that remained when the local, lineage, and family constraints for worshiping particular òrìṣàs were lost because of the slave trade. Marriage and the paradigmatic couple *oko/obin* described by Matory were also lost, and the line of ancestry was transposed into a ritually consecrated nonbiological family. Genealogy ran through "mother" or "father of saint" to "children of saint" by means of initiation into the membership of the cult. *Ìyáwó*, for example, which means "wife" and, therefore, "wife of the òrìṣà," when referred to a priest in Yorùbáland, becomes understood, in the Brazilian environment, as "child of saint," and the "ìyáwó's coming-out" refers to the ceremonial presentation of the newly initiated "child" in the cult's society. The òrìṣàs remained divided by gender, what turned them, more clearly than ever, into a classification of personalities as masculine and feminine. In this truly gendered zodiac, a person with a female body can have a personality classified as male if the tutelary divinity is male. In this case it will be said that the person's "saint owner of the head is a male saint." And a person with a male body can be, in the same fashion, the "child" of a "female" òrìṣà.

It is personality, in this model, that is predicated by gender, and the ideal, paradigmatic anatomy of the òrìṣà functions as the signifier of this difference. However, androgyny and transits of gender were ever present, embodied in some òrìṣà myths. As I said, Logunede, in Bahia, is said to be male for six months and male and female for six months, and Oya is said to have been male in the past and become female presently, after her marriage with Ṣàngó, though still exhibiting a rather virile personality. A *continuum* is traced along the range of òrìṣàs in their quality as personalities, with the result that some female saints are said to be more virile than others and that there may be degrees of masculinity for "male saints," to the point that, regarding some particular trait of character, a female saint can be "more virile" or "more masculine" than a masculine saint.

The profession of priesthood presents an organization closer to Oyewumi's description. Though it may contemplate gender *ritual* roles that neatly follow the anatomical divide, it does not present any differentiation or specificity as regards social roles. Yorùbá organization in Brazil also presents similitude to Oyewumi's and Matory's descriptions of the house, the *agbo ile*, called now *ile*, or *terreiro*. This cult house where a "family of saint" dwells and performs its rituals is the sociopolitical religious unit, as in Africa the *agbo ile* is the sociopolitical cell of society. But, as I said, the family is constituted based on ritual ties consecrated by initiation and periodical renewal of this vow. The biological criterion of ancestry is then relegated to a secondary role. In this organization, the priest—or the priestess—is the sole leader of the domestic unit, but despite having his or her name marked by the gender difference—"father" or "mother" "of saint"—his or her religious office's rights and duties are not specified according to gender; that is to say that the social role of a "father" or a "mother" "of saints" is exactly the same, and therefore an androgynous role, not responding to any gender difference. Similarly, a "son" and a "daughter" "of saints," a "brother," and a "sister" have no specific social privileges or obligations following the gender divide.

The reproductive labor, then, is ritual reproductive labor, in the sense that there, finally, the counterpart of the specific *ritual tasks* of a "mother" or "father of saints" becomes necessary. It is the inarguably required ritual presence of both, with their roles rigidly given by gender anatomies, that allows for the reproduction of the religious lineage. It is in this aspect that I find the greatest similitude with the "absence of gender" that Oyewumi attributes to the precolonial tradition of the Yorùbá: the fact that sexual dimorphism is given relevance exclusively for its reproductive role, in this case a ritual reproductive role.

Seniority of biological age, as it was in Africa according to the authors I am quoting, also becomes in Brazil a nonbiological criterion: seniority derives from time as a member of the cult, age as an initiate, and not age from biological birth.

Finally, the anti-essentialism and the androgyny pervading the whole system have an impact on sexual practices as well, since they free sexuality from the ideology of anatomical constraints. It is in this sense that the Brazilian system seems more radical to me in the dissolution of the heterosexual and hierarchical ideological matrix, and more detached from Western symbolic structure.

From what I have said, a four-layer scheme can be recognized in the gender system found in Brazil: ritual roles (anatomically marked), social roles (androgynous), personality (psychic dimorphism independent from anatomical determinants), and sexual orientation (nomad) follow independent rules and are not tied together by a straightjacket that binds them to a specific correlation with the anatomical data as in the dominant ideology of the Western system. Their interplay allows for gender mobility and open roads to androgyny. The overall gender of a person, that is, of a "child of òrìṣà," is the outcome of an ever-transitional situation in the complex intersection of those four layers. Gender circulation, as well as biological indetermination, are inscribed once and again in the codex. Of course, following the advance of the state and capital colonization of the cult, this fluidity may be withdrawing.

However, it is important to warn that in the Candomblé world, different from what was pointed out by Oyewumi, gender terminology as well as the terms that denote different positions in the organization of a nuclear family, even though dislocated from biological determinism and the anatomical domain, have full validity. This validity refers not to their usual function of organizing the world in the fashion described by Matory, which is to say, as an idiom to assign, restate, and reproduce relative social ranks, but rather as a scheme permanently subverted by practice, eroded by mythological commentary, and used in such a way as to disorganize the hierarchies they carry. The use of gender terms and of family classification—in the pantheon as well as in the "family of saint"—constitutes an acknowledgment and formal acceptance of the hegemonic patriarchal landscape in force within the broader society, but transgressed and undermined by use.

We are hereby facing the case of the subaltern that replicates the language of the dominant but, in its use, shifts it, makes it worn out, destabilized, thus eroding the dominant-dominated dialect itself, black-white, Christian-Afro-Brazilian.

Here at work is what I have already described elsewhere as the peculiar "double-voicing," the duplicity of the Afro-Brazilian voice, using the Bakhtinian idea of the responsive and dialogical aspects of enunciation (Bakhtin 1981). I am referring here to the fact that, even in the repetition of the hegemonic and totalizing discourse of the dominant, the subaltern—in this case the Afro-Brazilian—by introducing the mark of his differentiated position in the terminology used, doubles his voice. The same enunciation manifests that he recognizes and yields to the presence of a circumscribing world hegemonized by the dominant patriarchal Western morality, but a sensible hearing reveals that such enunciation, in the way and the circumstances it is conveyed, carries a second voice. In other words, even though accepting the dominant lexicon for family and gender, a corrosive mark of doubt, of "bad practice," of insubordination, is inserted, transforming the outcome of discourse. In this sense, what the cult's insider says may come in a *split voice, double voice,* affirmative and negative, ironical (Segato 1996).

In the first voice, the image of the world comes out as a positive print; there is recognition of how things should be. In the veiled, second voice, made up of slidings and inversions of the terms by use, a diverging image of the surrounding world is revealed, at the same time that, through the use of the double-voicing effect with its clues, a sense of complicity is created among peer members.

The subject of whom I speak, therefore, does not see himself as a substantive other; he is not affirmative of his "other," "distinct" reality, nor does he respond in a reactive form to the dominant order (as it is the inversely obedient reaction of fundamentalists), nor confirm the validity of that order. But rather he distorts the patriarchal family by the mimicry of the narratives about the members of the pantheon. This generates what I have called, in a different context, a "progressive mimesis" (Segato 2001): he imitates the master by worshiping a Jesus-like Orisala and a Mary-like Iemoja, responds to his expectations, yields to the image that the dominant order assigns him, while inserting an element of parody that transforms obedience into disrespect. What he says is: "Such is the world, I recognize its existence and the fact that I must live *with* it; I am aware of my place and my ascribed *image* in that order, but by replicating it I only express that I acknowledge, not that I accept it." It is all about an imitation that implodes that which it imitates, as when a black person calls another "nigger": he is saying that he "knows," and that he mocks what he knows.

It was possibly Homi Bhabha who offered the most precise conceptual framework for us to grasp this type of strategy, to which he refers using the idea of hybridism. "Hybridism," for Bhabha, is a dynamic process, plentiful of the discursive tactics of destabilization as those I have just discussed. In Bhahba's sense, "hybrid" does not refer to quiet, mechanical mixtures of symbols brought together by the encounter between cultures, as those spoken in the texts about syncretism. Hybridity is not about the stabilized outcome of worlds' encounters and the *bricolage* formation of a new cultural reality by means of mixture. The notion of hybridism has the advantage of placing the hybrid subject in motion, showing him in his dissatisfaction, in his uneasiness within the signifiers that, however, he is obliged to use. It denotes a subject who carries the burden that weighs upon him, but does so introducing a twist in it, inoculating it with doubt, inscribing it with a mark of distrust, never fully obeying.

In his text "Remembering Fanon," with which Bhabha introduces the 1986 English edition of *Black Skin, White Mask* by re-inscribing Fanon in contemporary critical thought after a decade of oblivion, he formulates a notion of identity produced as an enunciation adequate to its addressee, that is to say, as a *sign for the other*. This notion of identity, inspired by Lacan ("the transformation produced on a subject when he incorporates an image"; Lacan 1977), is close to the Bakhtinian idea of responsiveness of speech mentioned above in the sense that the voice of the interlocutor is audible in the enunciation of the subject, thus producing the dialogic or polyphonic effect described by Bakhtin. In this way of understanding it, hybridism results from the ambivalence of subaltern discourse pressed by the expectations of the dominant discourse and its effort to adapt to such expectations while being *other to it*. The epicenter of hybrid discourse is, therefore, the ambivalence of the subject in the act of identifying and signifying itself to the dominant other, counting on the elements that dominant discourse places at hand. Ambivalence derives from smuggling into hegemonic discourse an index of difference by the subaltern subject when making use of it. For this concept, Bhabha also relies on his reading of psychoanalysis:

> There is an important difference between fetishism and hybridity. The fetish reacts to the change in the value of the phallus by fixing it as object *before* the *perception of difference,* an object that can metaphorically substitute for its presence while registering the difference. So long as it fulfils the fetishistic ritual, the object can look like anything (or nothing!). The hybrid object, on the other hand, retains the actual semblance of the authoritative symbol but revalues its presence by resisting it as the signifier of *Entstellung* [displacement, distortion, tergiversation, recognition]—after the intervention [and acknowledgement] of difference. (Bhabha 1994: 115; clarifications in brackets are mine)

In other words, while a fetish can be any object standing for (replacing) the signifier of power, hybrid discourse preserves the signifier of power but withdraws its value, still recognizing it ("after the intervention [and acknowledgement] of difference"). Emphasis is placed on the subject's internal dissatisfaction with the sign that the dominant discourse throws upon him, makes available to him for identification. The epicenter of the argument is not placed in the other as an interlocutor to whom I must oppose an image stating my diverging identity, but rather in the partial and ambivalent acceptance of his categories, including the one offered as a sign for identification, though never yielding to a totalized signification by it.

This seems to be the case when Afro-Brazilians replicate in sociability, social organization, and mythology the apparent terms of hegemonic gender matrix and patriarchal family, but do so by destabilizing these very signs in a way that articulates them in practice and in the daily use of myths. Under the well-kempt appearance that it is a religion as good as any other, a family as legitimate as any other, it operates a corrosion of those signs and slips them in the direction of the eroded and subverted to the point of turning them unrecognizable. It is due to this maneuver, as

I have stated before (1995), that this society's mythological narratives are narratives of "after the fall," of times following the *Atlantic passage,* belonging to *postcolonial* society. It knows its place, but it slips ironically outside it.

In this context, there is a divinity that epitomizes all that has been said. This is Exu, the gatekeeper. He is servant to the òrìṣàs, but a mighty servant, without whose collaboration no door is open—the way remains blocked, the interpersonal relationships are hindered. Exu, who would grow locally to the point of acquiring a cult of his own—the Exu cult, a branch of Umbanda in clear expansion—is the divinity that symbolizes this *progressive mimesis* consisting in the use of elements from the hegemonic moral environment without endorsing them. The new, transformed Exus of the Umbanda cult are represented as white, drink champagne, and dress with elegant tuxedos and cloaks. But they are whites from brothels, pimps, and inhabitants of "the night." Their elegance is itself the parody of real elegance, a subversion of good manners in the performance of their underworld duties, an inverted sign inscribing their marginal world.

Fields, Ethnographers, and Their Shadow Interlocutors

While writing on the Yorùbá and formulating their models, Oyèrónké Oyewumi and J. Lorand Matory are, in fact, internally in dialogue with their respective significant audiences, both Anglo-Saxon: she, as an irreducible antagonist; he, as I see him, instilled by a purpose of minimalist reform. One wants her old world back; the other is struggling to introduce the fragments, the spoils, of the old empire "that is no more" into the new empire, always anxious for self-completing annexations. Like them, to a certain degree, I do hide myself behind my "data," practicing ventriloquism with the native in order to deliver my message, which is, I believe, not entirely removed from theirs.

Why is Oyewumi so emphatic in her effort to deny the existence of a gender structure—from her point of view, a Western category—among the precolonial Yorùbá? Probably because her main interlocutor in discourse is still the West, to whom she puts her demands of recognition for her difference. Why does J. Lorand Matory's argument emphasize so much social transvestitism, disciplining to the most whatever other divergences the Yorùbá world may contain in relation to Western morality and the gender order, by means of translating it back to the tight heterosexual matrix of the dimorphic hierarchical map? It seems to me that the author's underlying subject is the claim for rights within—and not outside—set standards of imperial morality and well in accordance with the established order. This is the struggle of the "good citizen" who, despite some superfluous peculiarity that could be contained as a well digested layer of behavior—for example, in relation to sexual orientation—aspires to nothing more that an appropriate niche for himself just to fit in within the narrow and conservative limits established by dominant morality and in accordance with the canon of social and political organization.

Through ethnography, the first presents her field and praises it as an uncontaminated model to thus claim the recognition of her own radical otherness; while the second presents it as an argument for admission in a world that does not need to be transformed more than the strictly necessary just to incorporate a "sartorial" difference in it—using his own terms.

My discourse does not lack an addressee either, or perhaps has more than one. On the one hand, I tell those who contend in the political arena set by state institutional idioms that the African descendents in Brazil have an encoded, cryptic way to criticize and disrupt the patriarchal foundation of Brazilian institutions that prevail around them. But this way is not that of the antagonism of *political identities,* as the globalized West would expect, but rather a much more complex and ambivalent way. The African religious tradition installs itself in a niche within a dominant context initially colonial and later national. Its discourse is referred, responsive, and disruptive to the hegemonic values present in that context, by means of a hybrid undermining appropriation of its elements. There is, as I said, in that appropriation, the acknowledgment of the existence and dominance of a surrounding world, affirmed as other to the tradition. However, this is an otherness within which the tradition, in a very peculiar way, is a part. That other world was there, in power, when the cult was constituted, and continues to be there, with recognizable boundaries and exchanges across them. Because of that, the cult's way of being is marginal, its identity is a self-centered identity at the margins, and this is the source of its strength. Not as a substitutive other, but as a supplementary other, in the Derridean sense (Derrida 1976).

The "people of saint" do not seem to imagine themselves as constituting a separate world, but rather as an in-fold, a crease, in an already hegemonized world. Modern Brazilian history is represented, in the daily conversations that invoke the cult's mythology, as a landscape open to transits, there to be traversed, even, as I said, to be undermined by cunning misuse, but seldom as the result of autonomous political building or decision making on the part of the members of the tradition. The surrounding landscape is believed to have been already there, encountered at the moment of arrival. To be a "passer-by" of the national history, in transit, does not mean to be a protagonist of its events. This installs the ambivalence between feelings of being there without plainly belonging into it.

Once, a prestigious member of the tradition told me, "ours is never a *frontal, ostensive politics*" (Segato 2003). I read, in this statement, the acknowledgment, by a representative member of the community, that the Afro-Brazilian political discourse is always formulated in the mode of the vocal duplicity, in the sense that was examined above: while they uphold a formal family in the pantheon of gods, they subvert it with their informal narratives about the amoral behavior of its members and with the practices of cult's sociability—including here members' sexual practices. In the cult's ironic commentary the patriarchal and hierarchical frontispiece of the mythological pantheon reaches its reversal: By focusing on the irony of the cult's commentary on Brazilian patriarchal institutions, my interpretation seeks, unknowingly, to deepen this surreptitious erosion of the conventional gender system, but without clinging to any other hierarchic articulation that could replace the one I have just deconstructed. It seeks no alternative stabilized pattern or set of rules. It is neither done in the name of another order, nor in the name of an antagonist other. This seems to me as a more radical critical stand, and I believe to have found it in my field, as much as Oyewumi and Matory believe to have the answers for their respective quests in theirs.

> [T]he apprehension of a unified identity, integrated and dialectical, guides the Western way of thinking identity—the identity as an image that corresponds to its metaphoric, vertical, totemic, dimension. But identity is also displacement, given its metonymic dimension . . . because there is always something missing in the presupposition of the sign's totality. It is necessary to recover its performative, although elliptic, although undefined, dimension, beyond the kind of dialectic discourse that simply repeats the other in its negation. (Pechincha 2002: 199)

In this sense, among my shadow interlocutors are scholars and activists who, more than often, reduce the struggling for recognition of their own right to difference to mere *claims of admission* within the system, losing sight of the need to frame and question the system itself by means of, possibly, its undermining and disruptive misuse (Segato 1998, 1999). I engage critically against them and the reified notion of political identity with which they many times work—a notion that totalizes the subaltern condition, putting it in a reactive mirror position in relation to the dominant condition, inside a stagnant and anodyne paradigm of multiculturalism, with fixed places in a world map. The diffident, innocuous "diversity" of bourgeois multiculturalism opposes itself, in Homi Bhabha's formulation, to the constant destabilizing inscription of "difference" in hegemonic texts (Bhabha 1994: 34).

If Oyèrónké Oyewumi is the postcolonial antagonist, a nativist, someone who asserts the principles of her Old World as an entirely respectable Other in an uncontaminated condition, J. Lorand Matory brings home the idea of a society where transvestitism, an apparently moral heresy for the West, does not threaten the established order but, precisely on the contrary, can collaborate with power and be functional within hierarchical institutions. I speak on behalf of a tradition that runs besides and underneath the hegemonic voice of the Brazilian patriarchal Catholic state elites as a corrosive counter-discourse, an unpleasant supporting character, which, humorous and ironic, erodes, destabilizes, and deconstructs the lexicon of domination.

References

Bakhtin, Mikhail. 1981. *The Dialogic Imagination: Four Essays.* Trans. Caryl Emerson and Michael Holquist. Austin: University of Texas Press.

Bhabha, Homi K. 1986. "Remembering Fanon: Introduction." In *Black Skin, White Mask,* by Frantz Fanon, 7–16. London: Pluto Press.

———. 1994. *The Location of Culture.* London: Routledge.

Birman, Patrícia. 1995. *Fazer estilo criando gêneros.* Rio de Janeiro: UERJ/Relume Dumará.

Chakrabarty, Dipesh. 2000. *Provincializing Europe: Postcolonial Thought and Historical Difference.* Princeton: Princeton University Press.

Derrida, Jacques. 1976. *Of Grammatology.* Baltimore: Johns Hopkins University Press.

Dianteill, Erwan. 2000. *Des dieux et des signes: Initiation, écriture et divination dans les religions afro-cubaines.* Paris: Éditions de L'École de Hautes Études en Sciences Sociales.

Fry, Peter. 1977. "Mediunidade e sexualidade." *Religião e Sociedade* 1:105–23.

―――. 1986. "Male Homosexuality and Spirit Possession in Brazil." *Journal of Homosexuality* 11, no. 3–4: 137–53.

Hall, Stuart. 1996. "Cultural Identity and Diaspora." In *Contemporary Postcolonial Theory: A Reader,* ed. Padmini Mongia, 110–21. New York: Arnold.

Johnson, Samuel. 1921. *The History of the Yorùbás.* New York: Routledge and Kegan Paul.

Lacan, Jacques. 1977. *Écrits: A Selection.* New York: W. W. Norton.

Landes, Ruth. 1940. "A Cult Matriarchate and Male Homosexuality." *Journal of Abnormal and Social Psychology* 25, no. 3: 386–97.

―――. 1967. *A cidade das mulheres.* Rio de Janeiro: Civilização Brasileira.

Leach, Edmund R. 1966. "Virgin Birth." *Proceedings of the Royal Anthropological Institute.* London: Royal Anthropological Institute.

Lescot, Anne, and Laurence Magloire. 2002. *Des hommes et dieux.* Port-au Prince, Haiti: Video, color, 52 minutes.

Matory, J. Lorand. 1994. *Sex and the Empire That Is No More.* Minneapolis: University of Minnesota Press.

Oyewumi, Oyèrónké. 1997. *The Invention of Women: Making an African Sense of Western Gender Discourses.* Minneapolis: University of Minnesota Press.

Pechincha, Mônica Theresa Soares. 2002. "Uma antropologia sem outro: O Brasil no discurso da antropologia nacinoal." Ph.D. diss., Graduate Program in Anthropology, University of Brasília.

Ribeiro, René. 1969. "Personality and the Psychosexual Adjustment of Afro-Brazilian Cult Members." *Journal de la Societé des Américanistes* 58: 109–20.

Said, Edward W. 1997. *Covering Islam.* New York: Vintage Books.

Segato, Rita Laura. 1986. "Inventando a natureza: Famlia, sexo e gênero nos Xangôs de Recife." *Anuário Antropológico* 85 (Rio de Janeiro). Reprinted in *Candomblé: Religião do corpo e da alma,* ed. Rita Laura Segato and Carlos Eugênio Marcondes de Moura. São Paulo: Pallas, 2000.

―――. 1989. *Meu sinal está no teu corpo.* ed. Carlos Eugênio Marcondes de Moura. São Paulo: EDICON/EDUSP.

―――. 1991. "Uma vocação de minoria: A expansão dos cultos afro-brasileiros na Argentina como processo de re-etnização." *Dados–Revista de Ciências Sociais* 34, no. 2: 249–78.

―――. 1995. "Cidadania: Por que nao? Estado e sociedade no Brasil à luz de um discurso religioso afro-brasileiro." *Dados–Revista de Ciencias Sociais* 38, no. 3: 581–631.

―――. 1996. "Frontiers and Margins: The Untold Story of the Afro-Brazilian Religious Expansion to Argentina and Uruguay." *Critique of Anthropology* 16, no. 4: 343–59.

————. 1998. "The Color-Blind Subject of Myth; or, Where to Find Africa in the Nation." *Annual Review of Anthropology* 27:129–51.

————. 1999. "Identidades políticas/Alteridades históricas: Una crítica a las certezas del pluralismo global." *Anuário Antropológico* 97:161–96.

————. 2001. "Religião, vida carcerária e direitos humanos" In *Direitos humanos: Temas epPerspectivas,* ed. Regina Novaes. Rio de Janeiro: ABA/MAUAD/Fundação Ford.

————. 2003. "Candomblé and Catholicism: Coexistence and Discrepancy of Two Religious Repertoires." In *Religions in Transition: Mobility, Merging and Globalization in the Emergence of Contemporary Religious Adhesions,* ed. Jan-Ake Alvarsson and Rita Laura Segato, 264–76. Uppsala Studies in Cultural Anthropology 37. Uppsala, Sweden: Uppsala University Library.

————. 2005 (1995). *Santos e daimones: O politeísmo afrobBrasileiro e a tradição arquetipal.* Brasília: Editora da Universidade de Brasília.

Wafer, Jim. 1991. *The Taste of Blood: Spirit Possession in Brazilian Candomblé.* Philadelphia: University of Pennsylvania Press.

26

Is There Gender in
Yorùbá Culture?

J. LORAND MATORY

The title of this essay is one of two related questions that dominated debate at the 1999 conference that inspired this volume—"From Local to Global: Rethinking Yorùbá Religious Traditions for the Next Millennium." The answer to this first question—which is the main objective of this chapter—hinges on the definitions, methods, motives of the analyst, as well as the quality of his or her observations. The other, related question concerns who has the right to speak about and for the various religious traditions—such as West African òrìṣà-worship, Cuban Santería (or Ocha), Brazilian Candomblé, and Trinidadian Shango—with formative origins among the ancestors of today's Yorùbá people, and particularly among the ancestors of the Ọ̀yọ́-Yorùbá. Insiders and outsiders to any given local culture or tradition have qualitatively and quantitatively different knowledge of that culture or tradition. Also qualitatively and quantitatively different are the ways that insiders and outsiders are materially affected by the authoritative "truths" that the academy exports.

Therefore, what follows is also an intellectual history and an anthropology of scholarship. Such a study speaks not only to the changing assumptions behind the study of sex and gender but also to the changing

513

assumptions behind the term "culture" itself and the politics of its representation in a transnational world. Is the analysis of any given culture best monopolized by the people who grew up in it? What if they have long lived elsewhere or occupy a highly distinctive class position within that culture? Are the ideological and positional biases of natives (including the temptation of émigré natives to idealize the homeland) inherent obstacles to nonpartisan social analysis? Is the evidence that is available to non-natives quantitatively and qualitatively inferior, or simply different by virtue of the perspective and disciplinary framing from which it arises?

These questions necessarily arise in the comparison of two recently published books about the Ọ̀yọ́-Yorùbá people of Nigeria. Published three years apart by the University of Minnesota Press, both of these books examine the theme of gender and its relevance to the study of Ọ̀yọ́-Yorùbá history and society. Yet they reach opposite conclusions. My *Sex and the Empire That Is No More: Gender and the Politics of Metaphor in Ọ̀yọ́ Yorùbá Religion* (1994; also 2005b) and Oyeronkẹ Oyewumi's *The Invention of Women: Making an African Sense of Western Gender Discourses* (1997) have thus inspired the most vigorous controversy of the past half-century in Yorùbá studies.

Sex and the Empire That Is No More is based upon twelve months of field and archival research in Ìgbòho, a former capital of the Ọ̀yọ́ royal empire. It focuses on the priesthoods of Ṣàngó (an early Ọ̀yọ́ monarch now apotheosized as the god of thunder and lightning) and Yemọja (goddess of the River Ògùn and, in Ìgbòho, tutelary goddess of a chiefly dynasty in conflict with the Ọ̀yọ́ palace's local representative for sovereignty in the town). From September 1988 to August 1989, I lived day in and day out with the priests of these two gods and with the main partisans in this chieftaincy dispute. I also sought out—at the National Archives (housed at the University of Ìbàdàn) and at the Ọ̀yọ́ State Secretariat at Ìbàdàn—all of the documents available on the history of the town and on the decades of local political and judicial activity that led to the current standoff in local chieftaincy affairs.

Sex and the Empire interprets this field and archival research in the broader context of the available literature on Yorùbá history and culture and on the Yorùbá-Atlantic diaspora, as well as seven years of my own prior field research among practitioners of Afro-Cuban Ocha in the United States, eight months of field research among practitioners of Candomblé in Bahia, Brazil, a prior year of research, classroom study, and residence in Ìbàdàn (1982–83), and repeated, extensive interaction with the Muslims, Christians, and devotees of all the òrìṣà in Kétou (Benin Republic), Ọ̀yọ́ Town, Ìbàdàn, Òkè Ihò, Ìgbòho, Sakí, Ṣẹ̀pẹ̀tẹ̀rí, and other Ọ̀yọ́ North towns. I am acutely aware of both the similarities and the differences of history, worldview, and practice among these diverse locales, all the better to grasp what political interests and social history motivate interregional and intergroup divergences of ritual and mythic narrative and to grasp what shared vocabulary of action and performance enables these diverse assertions of sociopolitical interest.

Though published three years earlier and focused on gender in the same region, my *Sex and the Empire That Is No More* curiously receives no mention in Oyeronkẹ Oyewumi's *The Invention of Women: Making an African Sense of Western Gender Discourses.* Oyewumi chooses instead to refer her readers to my relatively inaccessible 1991 Ph.D. dissertation at the University of Chicago. Yet the differences between Oyewumi's dissertation and her book appear largely to be a response to the ethnographic and historical materials presented in both my dissertation and my book.

The Invention of Women critically re-examines the existing historical and ethnographic literatures based on Oyewumi's own lifelong sense of Yorùbá language and society. She rereads these literatures in the light of the highly novel hypothesis that gender did not exist in Yorùbá culture during what she represents as the unchanging period before "colonialism" and does not exist in the deep essence of present-day Yorùbá culture. Oyewumi dates "colonialism" variously—and confusingly— from the slave trade, from the beginning of the nineteenth century, and from European colonization, the last of which did not take place in Ọ̀yọ́ until the end of the nineteenth century. She does not claim to have conducted intensive research on any particular area of Yorùbá life but implies that her personal identity as a princess and her upbringing in the twentieth-century Ògbómọ̀ṣọ́ palace grant her superior insight into pre-nineteenth-century Ọ̀yọ́-Yorùbá culture and into the essence of twentieth-century Ọ̀yọ́-Yorùbá culture. She writes,

> I would assert that I am Yorùbá. I was born into a large family, and the comings and goings of my many relations constituted an important introduction into Yorùbá lifeways. In 1973, my father ascended the throne and became the *Ṣọ́ún* (monarch) of *Ògbómọ̀ṣọ́,* a major Ọ̀yọ́-Yorùbá polity of some historical significance. Since then and up to the present, *ààfin Ṣọ́ún* (the palace) has been the place I call home. Daily,

I have listened to the drummers and heard the *oríkì* (praise poetry) of my forebears recited as the royal mothers rendered the poems to family members as greetings as we passed through the *saarè*—the courtyard in which the departed monarchs are buried. Our ancestors are still very much with us.

.... All these happenings [in the palace] provided ample opportunity for me to observe and reflect on the personal and public aspects of living culture. (Oyewumi 1997: xvi)

Oyewumi's identity and upbringing are impressive. Yet, like any social scientist's autobiography, they help the reader to appreciate not only the potential empirical strengths but also the sociopolitical interests and the class-specific, region-specific, and network-specific experience and perspective from which she speaks. Thus, Carole Boyce Davies (2002) wonders whether so elite an observer as Oyewumi will automatically understand or represent the experience of non-elite women as they would. Mojiṣọla F. Tiamiyu (2000: 122) denies Oyewumi's assertion that her gender-free model of Yorùbá culture applies to all Yorùbá subgroups, such as the Èkìtì and the Òndó, with whom Tiamiyu—another Yorùbá woman—is familiar. Moreover, Oyewumi's argument and reporting of her sources reveal no evidence of participation in òrìṣà worship or long-term, intensive participant observation among any of the diverse categories of òrìṣà worshipers. Today, the vast majority of Ọyọ́-Yorùbá people and their monarchs are Muslim or Christian, while òrìṣà worshipers are a highly marginalized lot. Being an Ọyọ́-Yorùbá person—even a princess—guarantees no familiarity with their beliefs, practices, or daily experience.

The Matory-Oyewumi debate at the 1999 Florida International University conference inaugurated the most vigorous debate in Yorùbá studies since scholars in the 1960s and 1970s debated the relative importance of agnation and cognatic principles in Yorùbá kinship (see, for example, Eades 1980: 37–38). The debate over whether there is gender in Yorùbá culture holds considerably broader implications for worldwide scholarship and, despite its frequent testiness, bespeaks the academic health and importance of Yorùbá studies. Since 1999, this debate has inspired scores of public lectures, a 2002 African Studies Association roundtable, a dozen scholarly articles, the founding of an online journal, an edited volume, hundreds of citations, and at least one book primarily devoted to the topic.[1] This essay, then, examines the substance and the context of this debate, exploring the diverse definitions, methods, motives, and facts that appear to have motivated Oyewumi's and my opposite conclusions, as well as other scholars' responses to this debate. What scholarly traditions does this debate revise or amplify? How do the scholar's social origins affect the credibility and the social effects of his or her publications? In particular, what does this debate between an Òyó-Yorùbá princess and an African American—both scholars in the Western mold—teach us not only about Yorùbá society but also about the social dynamics of authoritative truth making in the academy?

Definitions

Like "kinship," "mental illness," "medicine," "physics," and so forth, the analytic rubric "gender" has undergone continual definitional revision, while the scholars who employ the term have debated and changed their minds over time about what aspects of it do and do not vary across time and space. An understanding of this debate about gender in Yorùbá culture also depends on a contextual understanding of such terms as *ìyáwó, oko, gùn,* "cross-dressing," "transvestism," and "homosexuality."

"Gender" is not a theory or a general premise about how everything in all societies works at all times. Rather, it is the descriptive rubric for an aspect of society—that is, the learned ways in which reproductive roles are assigned and meaningfully interpreted—an aspect of society that was once assumed to be merely natural (e.g., Rubin 1975). Before "gender" became a named line of questioning it had been easier to overlook the fact that people with different biological and socially assigned roles in reproduction often have commensurately different roles in and perspectives on the rest of their social lives and are unequally willing or able to talk to researchers and reporters (Ardener 1975). As a research agenda, "gender" implies that there is nothing merely natural about those roles and perspectives and that we must ask where and how they matter.

Influential gender scholars have repeatedly and emphatically denied that any given set of biological categories—such as "male" vs. "female"—and any given choice of the distinguishing features—such as X and Y chromosomes, external genitalia, mammary size, role in coitus, or fertility—is culturally and historically universal in its salience (e.g., Ortner and Whitehead 1981: 1; Matory 1994, 2005a: ix–xiv). Even scholars who still assumed that there was something natural about the "male"/"female" contrast have argued that gender categories "are not reducible to, or derivative of natural, biological facts. They vary from one language to another, one culture to another, in the way in which they order experience and action" (Shapiro 1981: 449).

Not all gender theorists regard gender categories as binary or dichotomous. A sizable literature has discussed cross-gender behaviors and social roles, third genders, gendered roles in social reproduction such as "husbands" and "wives" (whose local counterparts in sub-Saharan Africa often encompass members of both sexes), and the use of male-female difference in the metaphoric construction of same-sex relationships (Trexler 1995; Whitehead 1981; Amadiume 1987; Matory 1994, 1988; for a further listing, see Matory 1994: 1–3, 180–83).

Nor does the term "gender" require its users to believe that all women in the world, or all women in any particular society, think alike and have the same interests. The population describable as "women," for example, is regularly subdivided and cross-cut by identities referent to race, ethnicity, citizenship, class, sexual orientation, marital status, age, kinship, parenthood status, and so forth (e.g., Moraga and Anzaldúa 1983; Butler 1990: 3; Behar 1995; hooks 1981; Collins 1989).

Nor does the term "gender" require the premise of universal male dominance or even universal sexual asymmetry. Most authors in gender studies do report the universality of male dominance or male bias among historically recorded human societies (e.g., Rubin 1975; Rosaldo and Lamphere 1974; Ortner and Whitehead 1991), but many other authors contest this assumption (e.g., Mead 1928, 1963; Rogers 1975; Sacks 1976, 1979; Leacock 1978; Schlegel 1977; Caulfield 1981; Nzegwu 2001). Moreover, the use of the term "gender" does not imply that gender is the *only* form of social differentiation or even the *preeminent* one (Yanagisako and Collier 1987: 7).

Thus, positions in the debate over the degree of biological determinism, the salience of binarism, the isomorphism of all gender with reproductive dimorphism, the relative salience of inter- and intrasexual social difference, and the universality of male dominance and sexual asymmetry do not constitute the *definition* of "gender." Instead, these questions constitute the diverse research agendas inspired by "gender"—the set of learned social categories, moral judgments, rights, constraints, social processes, normative behaviors, symbolism, and metaphors that, to quote Judith Shapiro, "have some connection to sex differences" (1981: 449).

Matory's Definitions

My *Sex and the Empire* and Oyewumi's *The Invention of Women* are both deeply engaged with the tradition of cross-cultural gender studies and debate, but in different ways. Whereas I embrace and attempt to expand this tradition, Oyewumi critiques and ultimately dismisses it.

I observe that Ọ̀yọ́-Yorùbá life is full of gender-related vocabulary, practices, social processes, iconography, and moral expectations that differ from those of most English-speaking North Americans. Based upon that understanding, I detect in many Ọ̀yọ́-Yorùbá historical narratives, sacred icons, and ritual practices symbolically transformed citations of daily forms of heterosexual marriage, female dress, and female head-bearing. Yet Ọ̀yọ́-Yorùbá narratives, icons, and ritual practices also cite and validate particular standards of parent-child relations, master-slave relations, blood kinship relations, equestrianism, relations of containment, relations of economic stratification, and relations of imperial subjection. *Sex and the Empire* describes not only the historical subcultures in which these gendered and nongendered arrangements have mattered but also the ways in which those arrangements vary amid the religious pluralism of Ọ̀yọ́ North and have changed over time, during the rise and fall of the Ọ̀yọ́ royal empire, the rise of the nineteenth-century military republics of Ìbàdàn and Ìjàyè, British indirect rule, and postcolonial republicanism.

I argue that the shrine iconography, the initiations, and the spirit possession performances of the Ṣàngó and Yemọja priesthoods of Ọ̀yọ́ North employ representations of these gendered and nongendered arrangements and combine those representations in powerful mixed metaphors, in a way that makes the priests' ritual assertions about the proper order of authority in society seem inevitable and inexorable to the people seeking the gods' help. In exchange for obedience to these metaphoric ritual prescriptions of social order, supplicants are promised, above all, uterine fertility. In my observation, gendered terms and symbols are—*pars pro toto*—the most prominent public representations of the complex gendered and nongendered arrangements that underlie their meaning.

So, for example, initiates of the possession priesthood are called *ìyáwó,* or "brides," of the gods, whether those initiates are male or female. I regard the term ìyáwó as gendered because, aside from the male brides of the god, all brides in Ọ̀yọ́-Yorùbá society are female. Gender is not *all* that is denoted by the term ìyáwó; it also refers to hierarchies of relative seniority in the affinal home. Hence, senior members of a household paradigmatically address *junior* wives by this term. Nonetheless, ìyáwó may denote *any* woman who is married to the speaker or to the speaker's male and female agnates. In Yorùbá language, the term ọkọ, which Yorùbá English speakers translate as "husband," refers not just to the bride's connubial partner and paradigm of the relationship—the ọkọ gidi—but also to his male and female relatives. The term ọkọ, however, *is* gendered: it differs in meaning from the term *ana,* or "in-law," in that nonpriestly men have *ana,* but not ọkọ. In the world beyond the possession religions, only a woman can have ọkọ, and a man cannot be an ìyáwó. Nor can a man have a male ìyáwó. A married woman is both an ìyáwó to a certain group of males and females and an ọkọ to a specific group of women. Whether a woman is, at the moment, an ọkọ or an ìyáwó is relative to the reference group. On the other hand, no man experiences this situational relativity of marital status in relation to human interlocutors. Thus, I describe ọkọ and ìyáwó as categories of *relational* gender, structured by the gendered conventions of marriage.

Although the ọkọ-ìyáwó relationship is not isomorphic with the man-woman distinction, the first pair is clearly related to the second. First, except for the male possession priest, all ìyáwó are female. Second, the paradigmatic exemplar of the husband category, and the indispensable linchpin in the relationship between an ìyáwó and her multiple ọkọ, is invariably a man. Third, the gifts of cash and kind that legitimize a marriage—owó orí ìyáwó, or bridewealth—always flow asymmetrically from the male spouse's house to the female spouse's house. Fourth, it is conventionally the female spouse who moves to the male spouse's family home, and not vice-versa. In her affinal home, she automatically becomes junior and therefore subordinate to every co-resident who was born before she married in. This constitutes a loss of status in the primary residence that men do not conventionally suffer. Moreover, marriage in Ìgbòho does entail some loss of rights in the wife's natal home. The moral opprobrium heaped upon ọmọ oṣú, or ilémoṣú—that is, estranged wives and widows who return to reside or consume resources in their natal homes—strongly suggests that women do not retain the same moral rights in their natal homes as do their brothers (see also Cornwall 2002). The ọkọ-ìyáwó relationship is therefore not reducible to the anatomical contrast between men and women. Yet, clearly, the *ọkọ-ìyáwó* relationship is deeply marked by gender—in linguistic principle, moral expectation, social process, and demographic fact.

I argue that the male wives of the possession priesthood dress like women because the paradigm case of the "wife" is clearly a woman. The presence of a gendered metaphor is also evident in the fact that even male initiates wear a style and combination of clothing—including *ìró* (wrap skirts), *bùbá* (blouses), *ọ̀já* (baby-carrying slings)—that are worn conventionally by almost all women and by no other class of men. In the Ọ̀yọ́ North towns where I conducted my research, the most important ritual duty of a bride on her wedding night is to carry a pot of water on her head into the affinal house. This act is understood to demonstrate the social fact that she owes labor to her affines and to highlight the most onerous and symbolically important subset of that labor—the head-bearing of water for household use. In the towns where I conducted my research, children too are responsible for the head-bearing of water and other loads, but boys endeavor, as soon as their arms are strong enough, to avoid bearing anything on their heads. Head-bearing becomes, for them, a shameful act, and adult men avoid it entirely. Girls and women express no such shame and attempt no such avoidance. Thus, the concept of gender also helps us to understand the social references behind the ritually central head-bearing of pots full of iconic substances in the òrìṣà possession religions. In my observations among the Ọ̀yọ́-Yorùbá, Ṣàngó possession priests are the only adult men who are ever seen carrying pots on their heads. In Ìgbòho, where most of my West African research took place, bar keeping and strip weaving were exclusively female vocations, except for the one male Ṣàngó possession priest who kept a bar and the one male Ṣàngó possession priest who wove cloth. Senior male priests also braid their hair in a manner that is sometimes expressly compared to a woman's bridal coiffure, and they are the only males in Ìgbòho who braid their hair at all. Thus, in Ọ̀yọ́ North, male possession priests build much of their ritual and nonritual lives around a gendered metaphor.

The term *gùn* ("to mount") also condenses a number of literally and symbolically gendered phenomena. The term *gùn* denotes not only what a god does to a priest in possession but also what a rider does to a horse and what a male animal or brutish person does sexually to his female partner. It is no surprise, then, that mature possession priests are called not only "mounted ones" (*ẹlẹ́gùn*) but also "horses of the gods" (*ẹṣin* òrìṣà). Ọ̀yọ́-Yorùbá sacred arts—which, contrary to Oyewumi's argument, are highly visual and socially significant—suggest that horseback riding is a gendered activity. The two most common visual themes in wooden shrine sculpture are men on horseback (equestrian images of women are extremely rare [e.g., Fagg and Pemberton: esp.126]) and kneeling women (often bearing children on their backs and vessels on their heads or in their hands). The sacred myths of virtually every goddess—and of no male god that I know of—also include accounts of the pots or expressly pot-like breasts with which the goddess fled from her estranged male husband. In Ìgbòho, even the àkúdàáyà tales of the dead describe the spirits of dead women walking away with head-borne pots and baskets. No such vessels appear in the akudaaya tales about men. Amid this proliferation of gendered signs in Ọ̀yọ́ possession terminology, sacred mythology, secular storytelling, ritual, and iconography, it requires no great leap of imagination to grasp the notion that the verbal symbolism of *sexual congress* and *sexual domination* implicit in the term gùn also illuminates the symbolically sexual, gendered, and hierarchical nature of the "marriage" between Ṣàngó and his bride.

Oyewumi and some other scholars have contested my view that sexual intercourse—*gígùn*—is one dimension of the gendered metaphors illuminating spirit possession in the Yemọja and Ṣàngó priesthoods (Oyewumi 1997: 117; Abimbọla in Matory 1991: 117; Olajubu 2003: 114). In a July 2006 personal communication, Mọlara Ogundipẹ argued that sexual references by a priest would be undignified and are therefore unlikely to be implied by the term gùn in religious contexts. I must give careful thought to this objection, because, at this point, I find it perplexing. At least nowadays, these priesthoods—and most others throughout Yorùbáland—are devoted above all to facilitating sexual reproduction. This function may have grown, in colonial and postcolonial times, relative to the priesthood's state administrative functions, but it can hardly be regarded as a new function. Why would such religions avoid references to sexual intercourse? On the contrary, in my year of participant observation among the priests of Yemọja and Ṣàngó, I was party to numerous prayers, praise poems, double entendres, jokes, and conversations about sex, and I witnessed many a ribald dance by the Ṣàngó possession priests. Indeed, at one leisurely gathering of the priests, an elderly possession priestess of Ṣàngó grabbed at my crotch and jokingly proposed marriage. The fifteen or so Ṣàngó priests present laughed happily and congratulated me on my good fortune. The Ṣàngó and Yemọja priests I know are socially responsible, respectable, and reasonable people. Following their own joy and realism about life, they sometimes joke and sometimes entertain serious conversations about sex, in ritual and nonritual contexts.

I must consider multiple explanations for the resistance of some Yorùbá scholars to the discussion of sexuality and its symbolism in the Yorùbá possession religions. First, it is possible that few of these scholars have spent much relaxed time with òrìṣà possession priests, who generally belong to a social class and age rank quite different from those of my scholarly colleagues. In my experience, Yorùbá peers who are close to each other discuss sex quite openly, but such conversations are virtually prohibited across generations. I also suspect that conversations between unschooled, older priests and schooled, younger scholars— especially ones who are daughters of the reigning monarch—would be constrained by courtly displays of formality and mutual respect. Certain matters would be especially difficult to discuss or ask about (see also Olajubu 2003: 18). As a young foreigner who, laughably, sometimes carried things on his head and yet displayed obvious respect for their religion—while most educated Yorùbá people treat it with contempt or fear—I might have inspired some level of confidence, or at least generated the feeling that they need not care about my potential disapproval.

Abimbọla's view that I exaggerate the gender implications of òrìṣà possession also demands acknowledgment and respect. He emphasizes the fact that the admittedly gendered term *ìyáwó* is applied to the priests but temporarily, and not throughout their lives. He says that the term *gùn,* while applied throughout the priest's life, has bestial or brutish implications, which make it inappropriate. I, on the other hand, regard this implication as consistent with the violence that worshipers and priests indeed ideally attribute to Ṣàngó and his possession episodes (see Matory 1991: 538).[2] Abimbọla speaks with the authority of the Àwíṣẹ, or spokesperson, of the Ifá priesthood in Ifẹ and as the son of a late Aṣípadẹ, or chief priest of Ògún, in Ọ̀yọ́ town. These factors make his opinion invaluable but also demonstrate a gendered difference of perspective. Both the priesthood for which he speaks and the one that he came to know through his father are—quite unlike the Yemọja and Ṣàngó priesthoods of the Ọ̀yọ́-Yorùbá—almost entirely male, non-possession-related, and virtually devoid of the vocabulary and symbols of marriage, mounting, and horsemanship that characterize the òrìṣà spirit possession religions. Far from dismissing Abimbọla's point, however, I take it as a demonstration of the diversity of gender concepts within Yorùbá culture and of the fact that, even within the heart of the òrìṣà religions, the same sacred signs are available for diverse and interested readings.

Okome implicitly faults me for using the terms "cross-dressing" and "transvestitism" in reference to Yorùbá possession priests when I would not, in her opinion, describe Roman Catholic priests in those same terms: "if we contrast the cross[-]dressing claim with the fact that when Catholic and [P]rotestant priests become brides of Christ at the final moment of their initiation, and are given rings to symbolize this relationship, it is not cast as transvestitism. Why then use such characterization to describe Yorùbá ritual?" (Okome 2001: 12; also Oyewumi 1997: 118).

The fact is that I *would* use those terms if there were evidence that male Christian priests wore clothing that is otherwise associated only or chiefly with women, but the garb of male Christian priests does not generally resemble or share the names of any women's clothes that I know of in the societies where the priests wear those clothes. Nor are my Christian informants aware of the practice of male Catholic or Protestant priests' wearing wedding bands or being described "at the final moment of their initiation" as "brides of Christ." However, the initiation of *nuns* in some orders did, in the past, involve this parlance and practice of ring wearing (e.g., Father George Saltzman, St. Paul's Roman Catholic Church, Cambridge, Massachusetts, personal communication, July 11, 2006). Okome's assertions about Christian priestly dress and epithets deserves further research, but neither those assertions nor her speculations about the terms I would use in the description of a phenomenon on which I profess no expertise is a good reason to avoid so clearly substantiated and carefully contextualized a description of male Ṣàngó priests.

We cannot discount the possibility that the responses of Abimbọla and other scholars to my observations about sexual symbolism in òrìṣà religion are partly defensive reactions to (1) *Christian* notions that sexuality is not respectable in a religion (celibacy being especially respectable in Pauline Christianity) and (2) the white racist notion that non-whites are profligate and therefore uncivilized and unworthy of equal rights. Such Western prejudices might shape what Abimbọla is willing to say as the foremost spokesperson of these traditions in the West, and what Yorùbá-diaspora scholars are willing to say as de facto representatives and members of a stigmatized continent-of-origin group in the United States—that is, Africans.

That being said, my own perspective is no more objective than theirs, and I could be wrong, though my moral premise be right. I have little respect for the sexual puritanism and homophobia of the Abrahamic religions, and my respect for non-Abrahamic religious traditions could never hinge upon either. This particular detail of my argument—that sexual intercourse is among the aspects of the gendered metaphor that structures Ọ̀yọ́-Yorùbá spirit possession—just might not apply to any Ọ̀yọ́-Yorùbá possession priest's demonstrably conscious or unconscious experience of possession or to any nonpriest's perception of it. The main proof that I rely upon is the uncontestedly multiple meanings of *gùn* ("to mount"), the priests' *choice* to use this term (rather than other terms), and the contextual backdrop of vivid and continual references to male-female difference, sexual reproduction, marriage, and other forms of intergender merger, or *religio* (from the Latin for "binding together again"), that numerous other scholars of these traditions have also documented.

I report that the word that all local parties use for possession by Ṣàngó has, in daily language, sexual intercourse as one of its referents. It is a fair question to ask if or when any given priest thinks about this homonymy in reflecting upon and acting out his or her relationship to the god. It is fair to ask what *aspects* of the acts of sexual intercourse called *gígùn* are thus identified as characteristics of the god-priest relationship. Domination? Fecundity? Physical superposition (i.e., the god's being on top of the priest)? Interiority (i.e., the god's being inside of the priest)? The combination of force and cooperation with potential pleasure and potential pain? Post-interactional exhaustion? I cannot specify or generalize. Sacred symbols do not, as Victor Turner (1967) pointed out, always work at a conscious level, possess a single, settled meaning, reveal all of their implications at once, or have the same meaning under all circumstances for all people.

American English includes similarly latent metaphors. For example, the components of an electrical plug can be described as "male" and "female." An inexperienced person can be described as a "virgin" to some nonsexual activity, and upon his first experience, it can be said that he has "lost his cherry." Sexual intercourse is so important and widely known a feature of human social life that it is frequently employed as a metaphor to describe less familiar or less concrete experiences (see Fernandez 1986). To give another example, in white American youth dialect, a young man in trouble might exclaim, "I'm really fucked now!" or, "The boss really stuck it to me!" The metaphor of intercourse, as it is interpreted in this subculture, is thus used to visualize the subordinated or diminished status of the victim. The young speaker would likely find it shocking to be accused of imagining himself being "symbolically if not actually" (see Oyewumi 1997: 117) penetrated by his boss. Nonetheless, the meaning of the young man's speech would be incomprehensible without a consideration of the literal meaning of "to fuck," as well as the local conceptions of male and female honor and the local understandings of the power hierarchy implicit in acts of sexual intercourse.

Inattentive to such meanings and pragmatics of metaphor, Oyewumi and some other Yorùbá scholars have explicitly (Oyewumi 1997: 117) or implicitly (Olajubu 2003: 14) accused me of attributing "homosexuality" to West African male Ṣàngó priests. To such critics, I recommend a more careful and firsthand reading of my work. It would require some mischievous intent to conclude from my locally based semiotic analysis, as does Oyewumi (1997: 117), that I am describing Ṣàngó priests as "drag queens" or as practitioners of "symbolic if not actual homosexuality."

In fact, I have never said or believed that the West African "cross-dressing," or "transvestite," priests were or are in any sense homosexual (Matory 1994: 208, 1991: 22, 520–21, 538 for relevant passages), and Oyewumi avoids all direct quotation of my work, which at least would have guaranteed some fidelity to what I had actually said. I wrote explicitly that, in Ìgbòho, male Ṣàngó priests "regularly have multiple wives and children, and no one even seems to wonder if they engage in sex with other men" (1994: 208). The terms "transvestism" and "cross-dressing" do not denote any particular sexual object choice, or even imply it to the serious scholar of gender. Nor is homosexuality implied by the verbal analogy among possession, horsemanship, and sexual intercourse that I observe in the term gùn—which, beyond any dispute, refers to all three actions.

An analogy might clarify the nature of Oyewumi's rhetorical strategy. I sometimes call my wife Bunmi iyùn mi (thus comparing her metaphorically to a rare and precious stone bead) and òdòdóo mi (comparing her metaphorically to a flower). A person intent on distorting my meaning and undermining my marriage might spread the rumor that I called my wife an "ornament" or a "symbolic if not actual plant reproductive organ and a piece of agricultural produce." Similarly, Oyewumi's gloss of my argument is no more logical or true than it would have been to say that I had called the priests "broncos" and accused them of practicing "symbolic if not actual rodeo." But such a slam would not have carried the same homophobic appeal. In sum, *Sex and the Empire That Is No More* has nothing to do with the sexual object choice or orientation of Nigerian òrìṣà priests; it concerns the history, metaphorical representation, and sociopolitical entailments of the priests' symbolic if not actual *marriage* to the gods.

Only in her own introduction of the term "drag queens" into her gloss of my argument does Oyewumi find evidence that I introduce "homosexuality into Yorùbá discourse," which is, in her view, "nothing but an imposition of yet another foreign model" (Oyewumi 1997: 117). Yet it must be noted that the exclusion of same-sex intercourse from Oyewumi's "Yorùbá conception" is prima facie evidence that conceptions of male and female anatomy are, contrary to her own argument, significant beyond the act of procreation: people's nonreproductive sexual partnerships and behavior are, in Oyewumi's "Yorùbá conception," limited by their own sex-specific anatomies and by those of their partners.

What I *do* argue is that the culture-specific and cult-specific gender symbolism of the Ọ̀yọ́-Yorùbá possession religions has, in *Brazil,* been "reinterpreted" in the light of the culture-specific constructions of sociosexual roles in *Brazil,* a country whose gender conceptions not only differ from Nigeria's but also belie the internal homogeneity that Oyewumi attributes to "the West." On the one hand, English-speaking North Americans tend to distinguish sharply between those men who engage in sex with other men ("homosexuals") and those who do not ("heterosexuals"). On the other hand, like many Mediterranean peoples and pre-Columbian Americans, Brazilians are far more likely to distinguish men who penetrate others during sexual intercourse (*homens,* or "[real] men") from those who are penetrated (*bichas, viados,* or, in Candomblé language, *adés*).[3] Even when the Brazilians I know use the term *homossexual* ("homosexual"), most are referring only to the party in sexual intercourse who is assumed to be habitually penetrated, or "passive." Of course, the real behavior of both *homens* and *bichas,* or *adés,* is regularly more varied than what is stereotypically attributed to them, and the normative assumption that the "active" party is dominant in the sexual act and in nonsexual dimensions of the social relationship is often more fantasy than material reality. However, local ideological assumptions and expectations tend to link habitual male "passivity" in sexual intercourse with transvestism, feminine gestures, feminine occupations, and the social subordination of the penetrated party.

Ever since the 1930s, scholars have documented the presumption among Candomblé insiders that most male possession priests of the Brazilian *orixás* are *adés*. Yet I am the first scholar to introduce West African cultural history as part of the explanation. The enormous influx of Ọ̀yọ́ captives into Bahia, Brazil, in the first half of the nineteenth century constituted the foremost influence on the Candomblé religion today and helps us to make sense of the syncretic logic implicit in the following words of journalist and long-term Brazilian Candomblé affiliate Édison Carneiro:

> Sometimes they call a priestess the *wife* of the god, and sometimes she is his *horse*. The god gives advice and places demands, but often he just *mounts* and plays.
>
> So you can see why the priestesses develop great influence among the people. They are the pathway to the gods. But no *upright man* will allow himself to be *ridden* by a god, unless he does not care about *losing his manhood* . . .
>
> Now here's the loophole. Some men do *let themselves be ridden*, and they become priests with the women; but they are known to be *homosexuals*. In the temple they *put on skirts and mannerisms of the women*. . . . Sometimes *they are much better-looking than the women*. (In Landes 1947: 37; emphasis added)

In sum, the West African men who are regularly "mounted" spiritually by the gods have a great deal in common (sartorially, professionally, and symbolically, though not necessarily sexually) with the Brazilian *bicha* or *adé* category. Yet the comparison in no way relies on the premise that these two Ọ̀yọ́-influenced traditions are identical, or that "homosexuality" is an accurate description of the social and sacred practices in either place. I am not reliably aware of any widely known or religiously acknowledged category of male-male sexual relationship among West African Yorùbá people. Therefore, I refer to or imply the existence of no such category or behavior in my discussion of the West African priesthood. Moreover, in Bahia, male-male intercourse is construed not in terms of the identical sexual anatomy of the participants—as the term "homosexual" suggests—but in terms of the putatively dissimilar and hierarchically arrayed, non-anatomical *social* personalities of the partners. In neither case does my native, English-speaking North American concept of "homosexuality" seem the best description of the local logic of sociosexual classification or of what those sociosexual classifications, as metaphors, imply about the relationship between the possession priest and his or her god.

Imagine my surprise, then, when I made the acquaintance of a highly respected Yorùbá art historian from Ọ̀yọ́, whose extended family includes many Ṣàngó priests in that West African cultural capital. During his time among òrìṣà-worshipers in the United States, this scholar, too, became aware of the importance of men who love men in the New World priesthoods. Without having read my work, he had concluded that male-male sexual conduct among New World priests was a *continuation* rather than a mere reinterpretation of the West African religious traditions. He told me that, on two occasions between 1968 and 1973, he witnessed possessed male Ṣàngó priests anally penetrating unpossessed male priests in an Ọ̀yọ́ shrine. He does not know, however, if this practice was widespread or whether it represented a tradition or norm. Nor do I. As yet, I would extend my case no further based upon this unique testimony, which the original observer has shared with me privately but has himself hesitated to publish.

I cannot say whether male Ṣàngó priests experience anything akin to a "homosexual relationship" or a "sexual drive" in relationship to Ṣàngó (see Olajubu 2003: 14, 114). That is why I did not say so. I have, however, met Yorùbá men who love men in both Lagos and London, some of whom wear Yorùbá women's clothing, and several Yorùbá women I know have spoken to me vividly of the "lesbian" relationships they witnessed in boarding schools. These phenomena do not fall within my expertise, but they do lead me to conclude that a society as populous and complex as West African Yorùbá society is far more internally heterogeneous in its ways of thinking and acting about gender and sexuality than phrases like "the Yorùbá conception" (Oyewumi 1997) will allow us to recognize.

Given Oyewumi's sensational gloss of my argument, I must summarize here what I believe to be the analytic implications of the Nigerian Ọ̀yọ́-Yorùbá case. Strathern (1987: 6–7) argued that in Pacific societies, sexual/gender inequality is the irreducible "idiom" in which even inequality between persons of the same sex and gender is understood. Yet, like some other gender scholars, Strathern implies that the gender difference between biological men and women is simply given and is therefore not constructed, historically or logically, under the influence of nonsexual axes of inequality. On the contrary, I argue that, in the

Ọ̀yọ́-Yorùbá case, the creation and inscription of gender are themselves extensive projects in social coordination and are influenced by nongendered conceptions and metaphorical ritual operations. "Gender" in this case refers only indirectly to the anatomical or reproductive role contrasts between "man" and "woman," or ọkùnrin and obìnrin. The West African possession priests use gendered words, clothing, and ritual to present their relationship to the gods not as analogous to the relationship between anatomical women and men but as analogous to the highly socially conditioned relationship between wives, who are almost always female, and their earthly husbands.

I argue, furthermore that such ritual "arguments by analogy" (see also Fernandez 1986) are subject to enactment and resistance by parties with diverse interests. Thus, not only individual gender transformation but also changes in collective conceptions of gender are *negotiated* according to resolutions of the divergent political interests of royals and commoners, the rulers and the ruled, the urban and the rural. Gender concepts are subject to influence from various non-gender-based realms of ideological and social production, just as gender concepts influence them. Thus, I do not argue that initiation and possession by the god Ṣàngó is all about gender. I simply argue that the symbolism of marriage is the primary way of naming and forming a sacred relationship— between god and priest—that is also illuminated and shaped by symbols of parent-child relations, master-slave relations, "blood" kinship relations, relations of containment, relations of economic stratification, and relations of imperial subjection (see Matory 1994: 170–215; 2005: 179–225).

Nor do I take the compacting of multiple metaphors of relationship into the gendered signs on the body of the Ṣàngó priest as a representation of a gender conception shared by *all* Yorùbá people. Instead, I identify it as a ritual assertion of power designed strategically by the Ọ̀yọ́ palace in its project of eighteenth- and early nineteenth-century rule, a brand of ritual assertion that has remained useful to and adaptable by a certain subset of the Ọ̀yọ́-Yorùbá population—that is, the possession priests, as well as the monarchs, the chiefs, and the worshipers who call upon the priests for help. I observe a very different set of assumptions about gender roles—and about which ones should serve as the primary model of god-priest relations—in the Ọ̀yọ́ Yorùbá worship of, for example, Ògún and Ifá. In Ọ̀yọ́ North, the priesthoods of Ògún and Ifá, unlike the predominantly female priesthoods of the other òrìṣà, are almost exclusively male, do not cross-dress, are not called "wives" of the god, and are not "mounted" (or possessed) by the god (Matory 1994: 1–25, 133–35, 229–30; 2005: 1–27, 140–42, 240).[4]

I embrace the "gender" rubric as the foundation of my observation not only that Yorùbá gender constructs are different from Anglo-American ones but also that gender constructions in Yorùbáland, like those in the West, are multiple, varied, and subject to debate, transformation, and strategic manipulation—often through metaphor. Gender constructions are available for use as models for or paradigms of the relationship between in-laws, gods and their worshipers, and monarchs and their delegates, although the partners in these relationships are often of the same real or imagined anatomical sex.

Oyewumi's Definitions

Though also immersed in the scholarship on gender, Oyewumi distances herself from that intellectual legacy in highly critical terms. Indeed, despite having borrowed insights from influential Western scholars who articulate analytic premises identical to her own (such as Collier and Yanagisako 1987 and Butler 1990), Oyewumi seems to argue that all Westerners—including scholars—have always believed in one specific and extreme set of hypotheses, so much so that these hypotheses are taken to define the term "gender" itself.

For example, Oyewumi's definition of "gender" severely modifies that of Lorber (1994: 1), while merely appearing to quote it:

> Gender is a construction of two categories in a hierarchical relation to each other; and it is embedded in institutions. Gender is best understood as "an institution that establishes patterns of expectations for individuals [based on body type], orders the social processes of everyday life, and is built into major social organizations of society, such as the economy, ideology, the family and politics." (Oyewumi 1997: 39)

Whereas the internal quote derives from Lorber, the prefatory sentence and the bracketed amendment come from Oyewumi.

Astonishingly, all of the ways in which Oyewumi frames and amends the quote with her own glosses precisely *contradict* what Lorber herself said in the rest of her book. Lorber argues specifically that gender is *not* necessarily hierarchical, *not* binary or dichotomous, and *not* wedded—outside of specific historical and cultural circumstances—to anatomy.

Lorber writes, "gender is not synonymous with patriarchy or men's domination of women. *Gender* is a more general term encompassing all social relations that separate people into differentiated gender statuses" (Lorber 1994: 3). Citing her agreement with black feminists and "cultural feminists" since the 1960s, Lorber expressly denies "a binary opposition of women and men" and challenges "the concept that gender categories are dual and oppositional" (4). Lorber denies that "gender inequality is ultimately based on procreative differences" (6). Oyewumi's entire theoretical argument rests, without citation, on Lorber's own gender-based point that "where women and men are different but not unequal, women's birth giving is not a source of subordination" (6).

Indeed, Oyewumi borrows, uncited, some of the most insightful and influential scholarly arguments of the past forty years and then, with considerable exaggeration, proclaims the Yorùbá the perfect example. In order to highlight her point, "the West"—including the Western scholars who first articulated Oyewumi's theoretical premises—is depicted as the cartoonish opposite of an almost equally cartoonish "Yorùbá conception."

Oyewumi's opening proof that "the West" has gender and that "Yorùbá culture" lacks it (Oyewumi 1997: ix–xxi; 1–17) requires us to accept (1) that the term "gender" denotes the allegedly "Western" notion that every aspect of an anatomical female's life is determined by her anatomy, (2) that no cross-cutting identity or category of social belonging (such as kinship, age, parenthood, or marital status) shapes any anatomical female's social role or status, (3) that every anatomical female is always socially inferior to every anatomical male, (4) that an anatomical female may perform no roles that anatomical males also perform, (5) that no woman can ever rise within the system, and (6) that the gender categories are determined entirely by the referent's visible or chromosomal biology. Moreover, despite her citation of several scholarly works that discuss third genders or relational gender (Amadiume 1987; Lorber 1994; Matory 1991, see also 1994 and 2005), she argues (7) that the analytic term "gender" always imposes an anatomically based binary or dichotomy upon its referents. In sum, Oyewumi's definition of the term "gender" is a straw person unprecedented in any scholarly work or in the thinking of any "Western" person I know.

Yet, on the basis of the inapplicability of this extreme definition to any aspect of what she calls "the Yorùbá conception," she concludes that there is no "gender" whatsoever in authentic Yorùbá culture. Writes

Oyewumi, "Yorùbá is a non-gender-specific language" (1997: 158), which she takes as evidence that "gender was not an organizing principle in Yorùbá society prior to colonization by the West" (31) and that "Yorùbá society did not make gender distinctions and instead made age distinctions" (157). People's anatomical sex "did not privilege them to any social positions and similarly did not jeopardize their access" (78). And her claims are not limited to the distant past. "In Yorùbá society," she declares, the physical differences between men and women "count only in regard to procreation, where they must" (12); "those differences are not codified [in the Yorùbá lexicon] because they do not have much social significance and so do not project onto the social realm" (42).

Contrary to summaries of her argument that I have heard from her defenders—at the FIU conference and in the hallway outside the 2002 African Studies Association Roundtable devoted to assessing the book and its impact—Oyewumi is *not* arguing that Yorùbá gender works *differently* from Western gender or that Yorùbá gender is more *flexible* than Western gender. She argues point-blank that gender characterizes the West and its thought, and that gender is absent from both the precolonial Yorùbá past and from the essence of present-day Yorùbá culture and society. It follows from this definitional premise that, as soon as Yorùbá people can extricate English influences from their thought and language, anatomical females will cease to be a population class tending to share any experience (besides the bare biological facts of their physical role in intercourse and birth) that distinguishes them from anatomical males, and all forms of social convention and practice that confer advantages upon anatomical maleness will disappear.

Methods

The centerpiece of value-neutral, comparative, and cross-cultural research in the academy is sociocultural anthropology. The anthropological tradition of ethnography begins with the assumption that human lifeways vary across time and space, but that a population united by longtime interaction—on the same area of land or around the same long-distance projects—tends to develop conventions of meaning and conduct that differ in their content and overall shape from those of other populations. Ethnographers, who write comparatively about any given people's culture, begin with the indispensable task of learning the people's language and thus grasping how that population understands the shape and work-ings of the world. The awareness that the words of one language seldom translate perfectly into other languages is well understood. Thus, simple, readable glosses—such as "husband" and "wife"—are regarded as a necessary evil, which must always be accompanied by the culturally sensitive explanation of the indigenous concepts to which those glosses refer.

The best of ethnographers will also document the *diversity* of local sociopolitical interests and the diversity of their worldviews. Yet a good ethnographer still does not rely solely upon what people *say* about them-selves or about anything else. He or she also watches what the people *do* and records *patterns* of their social interaction—even the patterns that most of those people may take for granted, ignore, or suppress discus-sion of because they violate the dominant public sense of what is good and right or normal. Of recent, the use of archives has become standard in the ethnographic project of determining how apparently primordial ideologies and patterns of conduct came about historically and through the workings of human effort, rivalry, and strategy.

The Africanist ethnography in the 1970s had put to rest any lingering supposition that the gender roles and gendered social arrangements of African societies duplicated those in the West, and had established the heterogeneity of gendered social arrangements across African societies as well. Opportunities for female agency were not everywhere the same, and one could no longer posit that African women suffered dispropor-tionately in the comparison with Western women (e.g., Hafkin and Bay 1976). At the same time, anthropologists were outgrowing the notorious "ethnographic present," which represented colonized societies as though they had never been touched by a history of both precolonial and colonial change. By the mid-1980s, anthropologists had increasingly recognized that African societies were as inherently dynamic as European ones and that colonialism itself was but one among the historical transformations that had shaped African life and that deserved documentation.

Matory's Methods

Sex and the Empire builds upon the standard methods of sociocultural anthropology, grounding its interpretation, to an innovative degree, in (1) the assumption of ongoing historical change and (2) the sense that the personal agency of many powerful actors expresses and is shaped by a culture-specific logic of personhood and history. In sum, I wanted to *historicize* Yorùbá religion, which most previous scholars had represented frozen in the "ethnographic present"—as though Yorùbá religion had remained static throughout the precolonial period and as though colonial and postcolonial changes were uniquely inorganic and therefore unworthy of study. I endeavored to revise the view—common in studies of diasporas and homelands, Yorùbá and non-Yorùbá alike—that a people's religion represents that people's timeless essence. Religions are as historical and as dynamic as any other aspect of a people's history, and all of these aspects of life change in dialogue with each other. Also innovatively, I sought to describe Yorùbá cultural history in terms of the tropes of personhood and agency that I heard vocalized in indigenous narratives and saw mimed in òrìṣà worship. Thus, the distinctive watchword of my own method is "icono-praxis."

The versions of myth and history recounted within Ìgbòho and across the territory of the Ọ̀yọ́-Yorùbá vary greatly, as do the religions practiced and the gods worshiped. I interpret this variation—and the rival political positions it represents—in the light of the ritual iconography shared among Ọ̀yọ́-Yorùbá religion, Brazilian Candomblé, and Cuban Ocha. That is, amid the enormous doctrinal variation among these sub-Yorùbá and Yorùbá-diaspora traditions, I also noticed elements of ritual iconography that virtually all of the òrìṣà-based religions of the African diaspora share with the Ọ̀yọ́-Yorùbá possession religions—an emphasis on marriage, on "mounting" (with its homologous spiritual, equestrian, and sexual implications), and on vessels that contain objects and substances iconic of the gods (Matory 1986, 1994, 2005b). While resting on the heads of priests or on altars, filled vessels mime the forms of power and agency that can be made to repose in or depart from the vessel-like heads, breasts, and wombs of possession priests and other important actors. Ritual and narrative references to marriage, horsemanship, sexual intercourse, sexual betrayal, and vessels are interpreted as metaphors that stipulate the essential or proper character of the nonmarital, nonequestrian, nonsexual and non-vessel-related relationships upon which the ritual experts and narrators wish to act.

An enormous variety of conflicting assertions in the competition among royal authorities is debated through verbal narratives and ritual performances that take these iconographic themes for granted. I assume that rituals and narratives borrow daily verbal and iconic forms because these daily forms embody powerful and widely shared assumptions, which, when arranged and displayed in new persuasive combinations, can re-arrange social relations in ways favorable to the political interests of those actors who invented or, through history, continually adapted and reinvented these rituals and narratives. All parties' interests, understandings, and actions shape and are shaped by such a genealogy of "icono-praxis" and by its rivalry with other equally ideologically tendentious and conflict-driven genealogies of icono-praxis, such as the anvil-, iron-, gun-, hunting- and male camaraderie–based icono-praxis of Ògún worship among the Ọ̀yọ́-Yorùbá. The contrasting gendered logics of today's Ṣàngó and Ògún cults are employed to illuminate past changes in the Ọ̀yọ́ polity and religion. Conversely, past changes in the Ọ̀yọ́ politics and ritual are used to illuminate the thematic preoccupations of contemporary Yorùbá historians, as well as the contrasting projects best served by these two ritual formations today.

From 1988 to 1989, I listened closely to the oral histories and tendentious etymologies that the people of Ìgbòho recounted to justify their rival positions in the local struggle for power between Muslims and non-Muslims, between rival factions of the priesthood of the goddess Yemọja, between husbands and wives, and between partisans in the town's ongoing "chieftaincy tussle." I also had the benefit of access to the court records of a major public inquiry into that tussle. In all of the written and oral accounts that I encountered, otherwise self-explanatory military victories, defeats, and changes of political regime are punctuated with unexpected details of marital loyalty or betrayal, surprising sexual acts, and the head-bearing or destruction of vessels—none of whose relevance was obvious from the standpoint of my own indigenous hermeneutics of history. Key to my understanding of those signs was their side-by-side appearance in both nineteenth- and twentieth-century historical narrations and the late twentieth-century rituals of marriage, burial, òrìṣà spirit possession, and, reputedly, money-making magic.

Unlike many prior studies of such indigenous African priesthoods, *Sex and the Empire* is set in real time and in the real-world context—recognizing not only the circum-Atlantic growth of òrìṣà religion and ongoing local chieftaincy disputes, but also four centuries of Islamic influence, nineteenth-century warfare, British colonialism, and Christian and Muslim dominance in the postcolonial Federal Republic of Nigeria. European colonialists were not the original arbiters of culture change among the Yorùbá and their ancestors. Nor were the Europeans *omnipotent* agents of change. Another aspect of this real-world context is the reality that Yorùbá priests have, over the past century and a half, been talking across religions, national boundaries, and oceans (see Matory 2005a, 2005b, 1994). For a century, priests, nationalist activists, politicians, and scholars have also collaborated in selectively canonizing and therefore reshaping òrìṣà worship—all amid a circum-Atlantic circulation of ideas among Nigeria, Benin Republic, Brazil, Cuba, Trinidad, and the United States.

I do not assume that there was some primordial period in which the Yorùbá or their ancestors were a single, bounded collective isolate—by virtue of language, culture, or conduct—sheltered from interregional streams of marriage, migration, commerce, and communication of ideas by itinerant hunters, soldiers, priests, traders, pilgrims, slaves, and wives. There is neither archaeological nor linguistic evidence of such a period of Yorùbá isolation, making overly confident speculations about a prehistoric and transhistorical Yorùbá essence little more than a fiction in the service of colonial indirect rule or xenophobic nationalism. Oyewumi has unwittingly borrowed a very un-African model of cultural history long after all but the most politically conservative and xenophobic of Western thinkers have renounced it as an accurate model of their own cultural history (see, e.g., Bernal 1987; Levine 1996).

Oyewumi's Methods

Oyewumi has set out for herself a method that is, at once, historical and profoundly ahistorical. She uses the lexicon of the colonial and postcolonial Yorùbá language to infer the nature of precolonial gender arrangements. Her basic technique is to locate genderless aspects of Yorùbá language and remove them so far from the existing oral historical, historiographic, and ethnographic context that they appear to give evidence of a prehistoric Yorùbá past and of a present, ahistorical Yorùbá essence. Beginning with her unusual definition of "gender" and an empirically inaccurate assessment of "Western" social life, she seeks to prove that all gender and all male bias in Yorùbá society today originated from a single, foreign source—European colonialism. According to Oyewumi, in precolonial Yorùbá society and its deep present-day essence, family membership differentiates people, but the *only* value according to which one person outranks another in authentically Yorùbá society is chronological seniority.

The result is an argument far more extreme than her supporters attribute to her. Although many scholars have acknowledged that Yorùbá women as a class enjoy enormous *power and a high status*—owing to respect for *motherhood,* the "flexibility" of Yorùbá gender categories, and/or the valorization of the *complementarity* between men's and women's duties—Oyewumi *alone* claims that there is *no* difference between the normative social roles of men and women or between men's and women's de jure or de facto opportunities in Yorùbá society. Oyewumi is *not* saying that seniority is *more important than* gender hierarchy and yet *overlaps* with it (in that women tend to marry men older than themselves and only women lose decades of seniority in relation to their co-residents upon marriage). She is *not* saying that Western influence *amplified* the importance of gender and *increased* sexual asymmetry in Yorùbá society. *Nor* is she saying that the culture-specific gender order of Yorùbá society *converged* with the culture-specific gender order of Western society to form a hybrid order that *changed* the opportunities available to and constraints imposed upon men and women. These are the sort of arguments that have been trained by a century of careful ethnographic, archival, and statistical scholarship on societies at the crossroads and by nearly eight decades of scholarship on gender.

Because there are literally no written sources about the "precolonial" period to which she refers, Oyewumi relies for evidence upon those cherry-picked aspects of present-day Ọ̀yọ́-Yorùbá language and, occasionally, aspects of social convention that, she says, do not encode gender. Oyewumi cites the extensive gender coding of pronouns, names, kinship terms, and occupational terms in English, alongside numerous Yorùbá pronouns, kinship terms, and occupational terms that, in her opinion, do not encode gender—such as *òun* ("she/he"), *ọmọ* ("child"), *ẹ̀gbọ́n* ("senior sibling or cousin"), *ọba* ("monarch"), *Ìyá Olónje* ("Food Vendor" [lit., "Senior-Female Owner-of-Food"]), and *Bàbá Aláṣọ*] ("Cloth-Seller" or "Weaver" [lit., "Senior-Male Owner-of-Cloth"]).

Oyewumi deserves credit for reminding me and others that *ọba* does not specify the gender of the titleholder. Ever since her reminder, I have taken care to translate the term as "monarch," rather than "king" or "queen." However, Oyewumi surely exceeds logic and the facts of comparable cases (where the efficacy of her deductive method cannot be demonstrated) when she claims that the gender-neutrality of the term *ọba* implies that men and women had, until the colonial period, equal access to this office and that Yorùbá oral historians would have forgotten the sex of past monarchs. Given the importance of patriliny in

Ọ̀yọ́-Yorùbá kinship, the difference between having one's mother on the throne and having one's father on the throne is the difference between being ineligible and being eligible for the throne. The difference would matter to every member of the royal family and to the loyalists of every potential heir to the throne. This is far more than a "distinction without a difference," to borrow Oyewumi's parlance.

The selectiveness of Oyewumi's evidence in the pursuit of a fore-gone conclusion is evident when one considers the many gender-neutral English terms for heads of state as a comparison case. For example, the terms "head of state," "chief executive," "ruler," "prime minister," "president," "monarch," and "sovereign" would hardly count as evidence that men and women are even nearly equally represented in these offices—even in the distant past of the Anglophone West. Nor does the availability, in English, of gender-specific words like "kinglist" mean that, in the distant past of England, no woman ever became a monarch.

Oyewumi takes pains, then, to explain away or conceal the gender coding that actually does appear in much Yorùbá terminology and so-cial practice. For example, there are clearly words in Yorùbá for "male" (*akọ*), "female" (*abo*), "man" (*ọkùnrin*), and "woman" (*obìnrin*). The terms of address and reference for parents, senior relatives, senior strang-ers, and people of almost every occupation indicate the referent's gen-der—as in *Bàbá Ayọ̀* (the teknonymic "Father of Ayọ̀"), *Bàbá Ẹléran* ("butcher"), and *Ìyáa mi* ("Mommy").

Most professions in Yorùbáland have long had vastly more of one sex than another practicing them, and virtually all social clubs (*ẹgbẹ́*) are segregated according to sex. Certain Yorùbá religious and political titles are strongly gender-marked, despite their infrequent adoption by a person of the other sex, such as *babaláwo* (a type of divination priest [lit., "senior male-who-owns-the-mystery"]), *baálẹ̀* (nonroyal quarter or town chief [lit., "father of the land"]), *ìyálé* (eldest wife of the house [lit., "mother of the house"]), and *baálé* (head of residential compound [lit., "father of the house"]). It should be noted that *baálé* and *ìyálé* are *etymologically* distinguished from each other *only* by the gender of the referent. Yet, *in real social life* the persons described as "fathers of the house" rank far higher in the house than do the people called "mothers of the house." On the other hand, one of the most important chieftaincies of the nineteenth century was that of the *ìyálóde* (the chief of the market [lit., "mother-who-owns-the-outside"]), and, as far as I know, this title has never been held by a man.[5] Moreover, the fact that there are a few female *baálè*, or "village chiefs," near Oyewumi's hometown should not allow us to overlook the male gendering of power that the term implies, especially if Oyewumi intends to be true to her hypothesis that vocabulary reveals the culture-specific ideology underlying statistics of otherwise unclear implications. In this case, contrary to her general deductive argument, Oyewumi chooses to privilege the statistic of the exception over the linguistically implicit ideology of male dominance (see Oyewumi 1997: 41, 49, 75, 77).

This is a society in which men and women have long worn markedly different styles of clothing, a wife is regularly expected to supply her husband with cooked food (and not vice-versa), almost all professional cooks (except in European-style establishments) are women, and the social norms of legitimate reproduction differentially affect the experience of anatomical males and females throughout the life cycle—in ways ranging from infant clitoridectomy to earlier marriage for women than for men, bridewealth and its asymmetrical implications for female fidelity and obedience, polygyny (and the unthinkability of polyandry), viri-patrilocal postmarital residence, the levirate, and the normatively different roles of mothers and fathers in childcare. Oyewumi even makes the credible claim that motherhood is the most honored of Yorùbá institutions, but given her unusual definition of "gender," this observation is taken to illustrate the absence of gender in Yorùbá society (1997: 75). The author also claims that polygyny is frequently initiated by the existing wife, that male interests are not supreme in polygynous marriages, that married women's sexual dalliances are tacitly accepted, and that husbands have no rights over the wife's labor. These indications of wifely "agency," alongside Oyewumi's argument that polygyny entails male self-discipline and deprivation, are taken to prove that polygyny is "ungendered" (61–62).

Most of these reports are inconsistent with my observations in Òyó North, Ìbàdàn, and Lagos over the past quarter century and with others' observations during the past two centuries. Even if they were true, however, the claim that they prove an absence of gender in Yorùbá culture follows more from Oyewumi's shifting, idiosyncratic definition of "gender" than from a careful assessment of the Yorùbá lexicon or the empirical data on Yorùbá marriage. Oyewumi's conclusions also reflect a distortion of what has been described in terms of "gender" in Western marriage and social life, and of how "gender" has been used to illuminate other non-"Western" social arrangements as well.

Oyewumi's reliance on lexicon-based deductions, to the near-exclusion of other evidence, can result in terrible empirical errors. For example, the *levirate* (or "widow inheritance") is no longer commonly practiced in Yorùbáland, but the archival records of the Customary Courts during the early colonial period demonstrate, contrary to Oyewumi's claim, that it was often practiced without the widow's consent (pace Oyewumi 1997: 45, 53, 62). Records from just before the actual colonization of the Ọ̀yọ́ kingdom indicate that female adultery was often severely punished by indigenous authorities, and women were sometimes forced, on threat of violence, to remain in marriages that they wished to leave (Matory 1994: 28–44). The colonial codification of the legal terms of women's release from marriage enabled many women to act upon dissatisfactions that Oyewumi has declared foreign to "the Yorùbá conception" (see, e.g., Denzer 1994). Oyewumi fails to produce any documentation of her claims that Yorùbá marriage does not and did not, throughout its documented or inferable history, entail systematically different social experiences for the male and female partners. The statistical and ideological norm that a wife moves to her husband's natal household and enters as a subordinate to every person previously born to or married into that household is a structural disadvantage that affects almost all women in this society *because* they are women and not men. These facts are not easily dismissed. It is not that Oyewumi has examined alternative sources of information—such as archives and statistics—and found evidence of their inaccuracy. Rather, she has simply decided to ignore them.

Oyewumi focuses great attention upon lexical evidence because any claim that present-day Yorùbá culture fails to distinguish men from women, or offers them equal access and privileges to the same important social options, is manifestly false. Any such claim about the documented precolonial, nineteenth-century antecedents of this culture would be just as manifestly false. Hence, Oyewumi claims that her analysis reconstructs the *real* Yorùbá culture, which preceded colonization, the nineteenth century, and/or the slave trade, a period to which we have hardly any documentary access. The earliest document the author consults is dated 1829, long after the slave trade had begun to affect the Ọ̀yọ́-Yorùbá, and the author elides all historical periods that preceded the elastic period that she calls "colonialism" into a single "authentic" prototype, which she believes remains evident and selectively alive only in those aspects of present-day Yorùbá parlance that do not mark gender.

When evidently old gender-marked aspects of Yorùbá language are addressed at all, they are excused by various means. For example, *bàbá* ("father" or "senior man") and *ìyá* ("mother" or "senior woman") are said to indicate *not only* anatomical sex but *also* adulthood; therefore, they are not gendered, argues Oyewumi. Does it follow, then, that the terms "man" and "woman" in English are not gendered? They too indicate not only anatomical sex but also adulthood. In English, "mother" and "father" indicate not only anatomy but, more importantly, social responsibility for the children. Do those terms then cease to be gendered? Oyewumi argues that the term for *ìyáwó* ("bride" or "wife") is ungendered because it refers to both the female brides of worldly husbands and possession priests regardless of sex. Does the fact that the church is called the "bride of Christ" in English then imply that the English term "bride" is also ungendered? Is the church not made up of males and females? The fact that a fruitful year is called a "female year" (*abo òdun*) is said not to indicate any Yorùbá conception of gender because, Oyewumi reports falsely, no one speaks of its opposite as a "male year" (*ako òdun*) (Oyewumi 1997: 33).[6] Even if the statement were true, its logic would imply that the term "phallic symbol" in English is ungendered because there is no commonplace word for its feminine opposite.

Moreover, in English, as in Yorùbá, one could recite an endless list of gender-free references to people without ever proving that the language or the culture is or once was gender-free. Could one reliably infer from the gender-neutral English terms "I," "you," "we," "they," "parent," "cousin," "sibling," "child," and "president" that Anglo-Saxon or Western language and culture are in their essence or once were free of gender and of gender hierarchy? I think not. But this is the logic of Oyewumi's linguistic argument that Yorùbá culture, in its deep past and in its present essence, is completely without gender. The weakness of this logic is evident if we imagine the linguistic future of today's social arrangements. For example, certain weighty moral judgments (such as the opprobrium directed toward *omo osú* in Ìgbòho) and structurally important demographic facts (such as the huge gender imbalance in most Yorùbá occupations and in childcare roles) are not inscribed in the present-day lexicon of Yorùbá, and they will be invisible to future students of gender history among the Yorùbá if those students rely on mere word lists as evidence for the way that Yorùbá people live today. The fact is that Oyewumi's deduction that relative gender neutrality in the lexicon of a language reveals a distant past of gender neutrality in social organization cannot be demonstrated in any other case—whether in the nearby and historically connected cultures of West Africa or in the distant case of China, where pronouns are also gender-neutral and written documents from the precolonial past could easily have been used to prove the principle, if it were true.

Oyewumi's translations are sometimes highly misleading. For example, she mistranslates *ayaba* as "palace mothers," when it clearly means "wife/wives of the monarch" (1997: 49). Oyewumi apparently intends to emphasize these women's dignity and authority, since calling them "wives" (*aya*) would, instead, emphasize their subordination to their *ọkọ* ("husband")—in this case the almost always male *ọba* ("monarch") of the Ọ̀yọ́ palace. But Oyewumi's mistranslation does less to prove the *ayaba's* authority than to distort the gendered marital logic that confers their great authority upon these "wives." Oyewumi also conceals the gendered polygynous and sexually asymmetrical context of its exercise. Many of the women called *ayaba* in the Ọ̀yọ́ palace historically exercised enormous power, but because they were nonroyal outsiders marrying into the palace, their sole source of authority and legitimacy lay in their having married a male monarch or the male predecessor of a female monarch. Their authority in the palace hierarchy does and did not derive from their motherhood but from their wifeliness. Like palace slaves in many other kingdoms across the globe, their virtue as powerful delegates of the monarch's authority lay precisely in the fact that—unlike the monarch's siblings, cousins, and children—the *ayaba* possessed no legitimacy to usurp the throne. In fact, their de facto power as mothers of future monarchs was a *threat* to the legitimate order of palace life. According to Johnson, the mother of the ascending monarch was conventionally put to death, on the grounds that the reigning monarch must be supreme in the land and owe obedience to no one (Johnson 1921: 63; Matory 1994: 8–13; 2005: 8–13).

At the 1999 FIU conference, Oyewumi's conference paper underlined the importance of careful translation and later inspired the consensus that Yorùbá concepts are most accurately conveyed in the Yorùbá language. Later, a senior Yorùbá scholar consented to deliver the remainder of his lecture on the Ifá priesthood in Yorùbá, and Oyewumi asked to be the translator. Yet, when the scholar spoke of the important assistance rendered to a *babaláwo* divination priest by *àwọn ìyáwó ẹ̀* ("his [the *babaláwo's*] *wives*"), Oyewumi translated the phrase as "his [the *babaláwo's*] *wife*." Spontaneous translation is not easy, but given the centrality of the theme of gender and the importance, for Western audiences, of polygyny as an indicator of sexual asymmetry in other societies, it is surprising that Oyewumi would overlook the conspicuous plural-marking term *àwọn* in this senior scholar's statement. Oyewumi's mistranslation, in violation of her own clarion call for careful translation, appears strategic. It also further clarifies the weakness of her linguistic method of inference about the Yorùbá past. Yorùbá grammar does not automatically mark number any more than it marks gender. Yet, in social context, number is often highly relevant—as in the difference between one sack of cowries and fifty. Like gender, number can be neglected or it can be marked, and *is* marked on the frequent occasions when it matters. Thus, when the senior scholar took pains to include the plural marker *àwọn* in his description—though nothing in the Yorùbá lexicon or syntax required him to do so—he indicated clearly that polygyny is what he had in mind as the context of the *babaláwo*'s practice. When I volunteered a correction from the audience, Oyewumi replied angrily, "It doesn't matter!" I was left wondering what principles of truth and accuracy *do* matter to Oyewumi.

Oyewumi's linguistic method simply does not stand up to sustained ethnographic investigation, as is demonstrated by the work of numerous Yorùbá scholars who intensively study the ancient palaces and priesthoods from which Oyewumi selectively draws real-world facts to support her lexicon-based inferences. For example, Olupọna (1997) demonstrates that the Òndó political structure includes a category of obligatorily male chiefs and a category of obligatorily female chiefs, and that the foundation of both categories is attributed to the action of the town's founding *ọba*. The fact that this *ọba* was female is an important element of palace oral histories and lies at the heart of official explanations for what Olupọna describes as the kingdom's "dual-sex political system"—a common West African political form (Olupọna 1997: 318; see also Nzegwu 2001; Okonjo 1976).

Renowned expert on the visual arts in Ṣàngó worship Babatunde Lawal verifies the terms and principles of my 1988, 1991, and 1994 argument about the metaphoric meaning of possession priests' titles, hairstyles, and attire. He shows that the even male priests bear female-coded titles, clothing, and hairstyles in order, metaphorically, to symbolize their likeness to female wives. Lawal shows that "cross-dressing" certainly has multiple and overlapping meanings in Yorùbá culture, and that nothing about the term is inherently nonsensical or inapplicable to Yorùbá cultural phenomena (2001: 7–8).

According to Abimbọla, a world-renowned *babaláwo,* Ifá represents only women as capable of being an *àjẹ́,* which he defines as "a blood-sucking, wicked, dreadful cannibal who transforms herself into a bird at night and flies to distant places, to hold nocturnal meetings with her fellow witches who belong to a society that excludes all men" (Abimbọla 1997: 403). On the one hand, Ifá credits women uniquely with the marvelous capacity to bear children and to be loyal wives. On the other hand, it represents women as deceitful (Abimbọla 1997: 408–9). Abimbọla summarizes, "These few examples of women in the Ifá literary corpus clearly demonstrate the ambivalent attitudes of Yorùbá men to women and the powers women possess. There is a love-hate relationship in the attitude of Yorùbá men to women" (411).

One of the pillars of Oyewumi's argument is that whereas Western culture is "visual" and judges people according to their bodies, Yorùbá culture is "aural" and judges people only according to the words they use or the words that are used about them. This claim ignores, among other things, the highly visual use of facial scarification to identify group membership in Yorùbáland (e.g., Daramọla and Jeje 1975; Abraham 1962), as well as the extraordinarily elaborate depiction of the human body in Yorùbá sculpture, in which breasts, kneeling, and the bearing of children on the back are crucial visual and bodily symbols of *distinctively* female forms of social subordination, power, and nurturance. In Ọ̀yọ́-Yorùbá sculpture, women's bodies are rarely shown on horseback, the men on horseback regularly feature gender-accentuating beards, and men are never shown backing babies.

Contrary to Oyewumi's linguistic inference, it is highly doubtful that the gendered elements of the Òǹdó "dual-sex" political system described by Olupọna, of the "cross-dressing" that Lawal identifies in Ṣàngó worship, of men's ambivalence to women that Abimbọla identifies in the Ifá literary corpus, and of gendered iconography in sacred sculpture were imposed upon Yorùbá culture in the colonial period by "the West."

Oyewumi suggests that Yorùbá scholars who disagree with her do so because they are mentally colonized by English language and English concepts, and that foreign scholars who disagree with her do so because of their linguistic incompetence in Yorùbá. Oyewumi's own unique breakthrough is attributed to her upbringing in the palace (see, e.g., Oyewumi 1997: xvi; 17–30). Hence the credibility of Oyewumi's argument rests not on evidence or on tested principles of historical and scientific inference, but on autobiographical claims of authority, tendentious glosses and mistranslations, and the *hope* that Yorùbá exceptionalism provides to feminists and to people in the African diaspora who recognize in Oyewumi's "Yorùbá conception" a potential source of dignity for subaltern ethnic groups, races, or sexual identities.[7]

Oyewumi's book has received its heartiest published accolades from scholars who know little about Africa or its diaspora (e.g., Ficek 2006; Chaudhuri 2001; see also Matory 2004: 37 on the Sex and Gender Section of the American Sociological Association). They are impressed by Oyewumi's claim to have unveiled a society that proves the reality of what, in truth, more than a few gender scholars (e.g., Yanagisako and Collier 1987; Lorber 1994) had imagined as the most extreme of possibilities—a society completely free of sexism, where male-female anatomical difference makes no social difference at all. On the other hand, not a single Africanist has come out in writing to support this representation of Yorùbá society, though several have—in the wake of Oyewumi's publication (and usually in publications edited by Oyewumi herself)—sought to reinforce the more moderate and well-established ideas that (1) African women occupy many highly esteemed social roles in their societies, and that (2) precolonial African gender systems often differ radically from Western ones (e.g., Adeekọ 2005; Okome 2001; Nzegwu 2001; Oyewumi 2005).

Motives

Rita Laura Segato, who attended the 1999 FIU conference, observes that scholars use social analysis to "ventriloquize" hidden political agendas (Segato 2003: 19). It is a condition of our shared humanity that Oyewumi and I share certain motives and diverge radically on others. We are equally invested in the premise that Western ethnocentrism and racism generate inadequate thinking about both the West and the rest, and that ethnocentric assumptions about other cultures generate misunderstanding and often facilitate oppression. We are also equally aware of unfair stigma that attaches particularly to blackness, Africanness, and femaleness in U.S. society, and both of us see the liberatory value in changing the minds of the oppressors and of the oppressed. Though we share the same desire for equality of opportunity across races and genders (she is less liberal about sexual orientation), we appear to understand the nature of oppression and, therefore, the possible means of liberation in very different terms. Whereas I view the operation of social hierarchy within any given society as complex, multi-axial, negotiated, and crisscrossed by multiple channels that are not equally visible to people in every class position, Oyewumi views social hierarchy as simple, mono-axial, fixed, and equally self-evident to everyone native to a given society. Moreover, whereas Oyewumi bets on the efficacy of supra-empirical clarity and of dichotomizing battle lines, I bet on respect for the complexity and intelligence of the people I study and of the people who I hope will, as a result of reading my analyses, better appreciate the complexity and humanity of black people and women in general. To me, it is equally unproductive to represent the oppressed as angels or as devils.

Matory's Motives

In *Sex and the Empire,* I seek to show that Yorùbá people, who are such important players in the creation of African-diaspora culture, are real-live, multidimensional, historical human beings, not cardboard cut-out mascots of white supremacy or Black Nationalism. To my mind, the image of an unchanging, innocent, and isolated Africa, where no one faced ambiguity or made choices, is both untrue and insulting. As a child of racist America, I have found much liberation in my experience of Nigeria, where my chocolate skin qualifies me as a human being, not as an exceptional being whose humanity and complexity require proof. As a child of the feminist movement as well, I looked kindly, from my first moments in southern Nigeria, upon evidence of women's power and symbolic importance, which are equally important in African American culture. But I was not naive to the differences between these two black cultures or to the internal complexity and ambiguity of each. Indeed, it was the complexity of racial and gender hardship in the Americas and of gender hardship all around the Atlantic perimeter that, to me, made the triumph of many black women so heroic and worthy of study. These facts are what, to my mind, make the study of straight, white, Christian or Muslim men so much less interesting.

Nonetheless, understanding the travails of less powerful populations requires us simultaneously to grasp the cultural meanings, logical principles, and sociopolitical structures that have conferred disproportionate advantage upon other populations. Having come of age in a racially de-segregated but not-yet-integrated United States, I was keenly aware of how dominant populations—even in the absence of any explicit rules (or racially coded pronouns)—can both benefit from and deny the existence of structural bias against other populations. For example, by the time of my first year in Nigeria, virtually every American law that named whites as a privileged social category or named blacks as an encumbered one had been rescinded. Moreover, whites had begun a trend toward calling themselves "Irish," "Polish," "Italian," and so forth in order to avoid calling themselves "white," thus rendering inaudible the benefits that continued to accrue to their phenotypical whiteness (Alba 1990). Yet invisible and inaudible structural distinctions often have the most palpable effects.

I had been attracted to Yorùbáland not only because it provided evidence nonpareil of the African diaspora's enduring cultural connection to Africa but also because the reputed power, dignity, and perhaps even equality of Yorùbá women to men gave evidence of that cultural connection. The mighty goddess Yemoja and her New World avatars—the Brazilian Iemanjá and the Cuban Yemayá—attracted me long before Şàngó, Xangô, and Changó demanded my attention. Upon my first sojourn in Yorùbáland, I was not disappointed. At Ìbàdàn's Institute of African Studies, I met no scholar more respected and formidable than Bọlanlẹ Awe. I confronted the power of market women and their daughters everyday. More often than not, I had to capitulate. Even more than in the United States, I noticed, men were far more likely than women to possess and publicly display their multiple sexual or marital partners, and, particularly in the context of polygyny, people tended to feel much more warmly toward their mothers than toward their fathers. When I traveled to a town or a compound to meet the priests, most of whom were female, the person to whom I was always sent to ask first for approval was a male *baálé, baálẹ̀, olóyè, ọba,* or *olórí ẹlẹ́gùn.* What I ultimately saw was a setting where many women had significant dignity, power, and power over me, but I did not see a gender-free idyll. Nor was it possible for me to imagine that Yorùbá culture had ever been gender-free.

I was fascinated by the cultural logics and social conventions that so empowered some Yorùbá women, but, after years of intensive co-residence, I find it difficult to ignore the ways in which some highly gendered logics—such as wifeliness—could empower some men and women, while disempowering many more women. It was impossible, in

Ìgbòho, not to notice how the entrepreneurial success of the visiting and more Westernized Ìjèbú-Yorùbá women yam traders contrasted with the poverty and political marginality of the local Òyó-Yorùbá women. Moreover, the most dissatisfied people I met in the town were the *ìyáwó* ("wives") of overbearing *omo osú* (adult divorcées and widows who have returned to their natal home), and no class of people was more resented by men and other women than were the *omo osú*. I met no men who faced similar levels of dissatisfaction or hostility in their residential homes—a fact that I could only attribute to the different structural norms of men's and women's lives in Ìgbòho. My sympathy for and admiration of Yorùbá women coincides with my sympathy for and admiration of black people generally, gay people generally, and poor people generally. Yet my sympathy does not rest on the assumption that such groups are powerless, or that people of these categories do not find ways of oppressing or exploiting other people when they have a chance. Nothing in my experience of Nigerian society could convince me that contemporary Yorùbá people are hapless dupes of mental colonization by "the West," or that such an assumption is an effective first step toward the empowerment of Yorùbá people, black people, gay people, or poor people.

In pursuit of my motives, Segato (2003) summarizes my argument as follows: that the structure of gender in and around the Òyó-Yorùbá possession religions allows many women to achieve power, despite the enduring androcentric bias of the system. She reads this argument as an appeal to majority groups not to discriminate against minority groups, because admitting them to the system does not really, in the end, undermine the system. Though this implication was not my conscious intention, I tend to believe that it is true—and far too unfair for me ever to endorse it as a sufficient program of social change.

Oyewumi's Motives

Oyewumi shares her motives with at least two major traditions of feminist writing and another major tradition of African nationalist writing. The first is the tradition of seeking in the distant past or in faraway places role models of matriarchy or gender equality. Each example asserted or discovered is taken as further proof that the sexual asymmetry plaguing the nearby and present-day societies with which we are familiar is neither natural nor universal or, therefore, inevitable and immutable. Oyewumi is the most extreme partisan of this motive that I have yet read. She is the first scholar to deny not only the phenomenon of sexual asymmetry but also the salience of male-female diversity at any moment in the social process other than copulation and parturition.

Oyewumi also extends the worthy tradition of assertions by feminists of color that their interests have been overlooked by a white, middle-class-dominated feminist movement that once presumed to speak for all women (Amadiume 1987: 1–10; Nzegwu 2001; Moraga and Anzaldúa 1983; Davis 1985; hooks 1981; Collins 1989). Two decades of scholarship and literature by feminists of color has demonstrated beyond doubt the impossibility of the demand that women of color forget about the array of hierarchical social differences beyond gender that privilege some women and marginalize others—such as race, class, sexual orientation, educational level, and nationality. Contrary to Oyewumi's critique of feminist scholarship, there is hardly a white feminist scholar writing today who has not recognized the importance of this critique.

In overlapping ways, Oyewumi and I recognize that people like us are stigmatized and marginalized according to multiple indices of social difference in the West. However, our responses to this problem differ. My response is to recognize the complex internal and externally imposed realities that stigmatized or marginalized people must understand in order to overcome those realities. Oyewumi's response, on the other hand, is to deny that there was ever any internal problem or complexity.

It is important for women, women of color, and Yorùbá women—not to mention Western people, Americans, African Americans, African American women, *santeros, candomblecistas,* Ṣàngó worshipers, Nigerian Christians, Yorùbá people, and so forth—to "speak for themselves," to borrow Marta Moreno Vega's statement at the FIU conference. However, such groupings so easily become an artifact of the leadership strategies of the people who manage to position themselves as spokespeople and who then subject dissenting subgroups of the spoken-for to insinuation, ridicule, defamation, misrepresentation, and worse. One Yorùbá woman or even a committee of Yorùbá women does not instinctually speak for every subset and cross-cutting subcategory of Yorùbá women, any more than one white woman or committee of white women can speak instinctually for every kind of woman. And the classification of whole areas of discussion as foreign—as Oyewumi has branded "gender"—entails the risk of silencing those subsets of Yorùbá women and men who recognize previously unnamed or unquestioned dimensions of their experience through it.

Oyewumi's argument shares the motives of a major tradition in Black Nationalist activism and scholarship as well, a tradition that seeks liberation from the European definitions and standards that are inherently biased against the interests, values, and realities of Africans and black people generally. However, some strategies in this tradition, such as Senghor's Négritude, much of Afrocentrism, and the "acting white" phenomenon (e.g., Fordham and Ogbu 1986),[8] imprison black people within an inverted mirror of those very European standards, and the inversion makes those inverted definitions and standards no less confining and no less capable of blinding us to our own complex realities. Declaring ourselves inaccessible to the analytical tools generated by cross-cultural analysis—rather than refining those tools and contributing new ones— further marginalizes Africa and subjects us to the Mobutus of the world, who, in the name of African distinctiveness, would kill Africa's greatest virtues—diversity, open-mindedness, and democracy.

What Is at Stake in This Debate?

Two fundamental issues seem to be at stake in this debate. First, what, in truth, is the usefulness of the gender concept in the scholarly analysis of Yorùbá history and social life? Second, which answers are most liberating to women and dignifying to women and to the other disempowered populations that crosscut this gender category, such as Yorùbá people and black people generally?

At a rational level, it is entirely reasonable to ask whether the axes of social differentiation and hierarchy that shape one society, or even most societies, also shape any given society. It is reasonable to ask whether male-female anatomical difference corresponds to any difference of normative social role or opportunity in that society. It is reasonable to ask which differences of reproduction-related anatomy are construed as indexing salient social categories, as well as what anatomical, sartorial, behavioral, or age-related variations exempt some people from these particular social categories. It is even reasonable to ask if there are some societies where anatomical differences correspond to *no* expected or statistically demonstrable differentiation between the roles of males and females—or of any other visibly distinct bodies—in childcare, clothing, subdialect, occupation, access to any given political office or to political offices in general, and so forth.

Even if one can conceive of a culture in which the anatomical differences between males and females—or any other bodies—are never interpreted as reasons for or symbols of noncoital or nonparturitional social role differences, Yorùbá culture is *not* such a culture. No definition and no analytical method could change that fact, though certain motives could lead a partisan actor to conceal it. However, such motives are not, to my mind, inauthentic or foreign to Yorùbá culture. Within the heart of any culture, any given actor will find it advantageous to emphasize some principles, rules, and precedents over others. A culture is not some perfectly unchanging, essential, or internally consistent set of rules that people simply "follow" until they are colonized. Culture is that aspect of collective social life in which the legitimacy and efficacy of our actions flow from references to an often-conflicting set of available precedents. In Yorùbá society, actors continually select and reframe legitimizing precedents from near and far, and have done so as long as the Yorùbá have been studied.

The second fundamental issue in the Matory-Oyewumi debate concerns which analysis will be the most liberating to the marginalized and stigmatized. At the end of this debate, what allies do we stand to gain or lose in the struggle for fairness to all? If Oyewumi wins, will Yorùbá men feel exonerated of sexism (Ogundipẹ 2002)?[9] Will they feel let off the hook? Will Yorùbá men and women be persuaded that the intrafamilial tensions inherent in polygyny—as well as the gender hierarchy induced by wives' competition for their husbands' resources and affection—are mere figments of their colonized imaginations?[10] Will women be further persuaded that the heartless exploitation of the junior domestic workers called ọmọ odo is consistent with the exclusive value placed on "seniority" in Oyewumi's "Yorùbá conception" and therefore a justifiable reward of restoring Yorùbá cultural authenticity? Will critics skulk in fear of betraying Yorùbá nationalism, or of being told, "It's a Yorùbá thing; you wouldn't understand"?

Let us also suppose that the credulous feminist scholars who once believed that Africa was women's hell now believe that Africa is women's heaven. Will they have understood better, or become better allies in the struggle against the truly complex forms of inequality and exploitation that afflict Africa and the West? For example, would they be right to discourage development agencies from funding programs targeted at un-Westernized rural Yorùbá women as a class, or from scrutinizing programs that do not consider their potentially differential effects on the lives of un-Westernized rural Yorùbá men and women, under the pretense that authentic Yorùbá people have no gender in the first place? Let us also suppose that many feminist and nonfeminist scholars will read Oyewumi's work carefully and, drawn by this complex and beautiful culture, will undertake archival and ethnographic research in Yorùbáland on their own. Will they emerge with a greater respect for the scholarship of people like us?

Notes

1. The roundtable featured formal remarks by Mọlara Ogundipẹ, Niara Sudarkasa, Carole Boyce Davies, Titilayọ Ufomata, J. Lorand Matory, and Desirée Lewis. For other critiques, see, for example, Afọnja 2005 and Bakare-Yusuf.

2. Their devotees often identify outrageous, antisocial actions as evidence of the gods' indefatigable power and impunity in defense of their followers (Barber 1981: 735, 743, n. 23).

3. *Adé* in Portuguese orthography has an open "e" sound, as in the English word "pet," and should not be confused with the Yorùbá term for "crown."

4. See also Peel (2002) on the gender imbalance among the nineteenth-century devotees of Ifá, who were predominantly male, and of the other òrìṣà, who were predominantly female.

5. Oyewumi argues that the *ìyálóde* title originated in the nineteenth century and was a product of Ìbàdàn influence (1997: 108). Oyewumi does not mention that Ibadan is the largest and one of the most important Ọyọ́-Yorùbá polities— far more populous and historically important than Ògbómọ̀ṣọ́. Nor does she demonstrate the sense in which the gender-specificity of the *ìyálóde* title results from foreign or Western influence or is foreign to "the Yorùbá conception." She also argues that, because not all women fell under the authority of the *ìyálóde* and the *ìyálóde* governed affairs beyond the affairs of women, the title is not gendered. I fail to see how this cascade of evidence proves that a title reserved for women escapes analysis in terms of gender. Moreover, the fact is that, in some Yorùbá towns, the *ìyálóde* did indeed govern the affairs of all women or of women as a class (Denzer 1994; also Olupọna 2005).

6. Consider also the Yorùbá proverb *Pẹ̀lẹ́ l'ábo; pẹ̀lẹ́ l'ákọ* ("Even in expressing sympathy, there's a nice [lit. 'female'] way and a mean, ornery [lit., 'male'] way"). In both verbal expressions, the contrast between male and female has a moral valence easily recognized by most Yorùbá people.

7. See also Case (2002), Clark (2001), Cooper (2004), and Customer reviews of *The Invention of Women* (2006). These are among the African American and Caribbean scholars who find in Oyewumi's work inspiration to appreciate female sexual freedom and resistance to racism.

8. Fordham and Ogbu (1986) were the first in a series of researchers who have reported, among young African Americans, a tendency to identify school achievement and related forms of social conformity as "acting white" and, therefore, as a betrayal of their race, thus discouraging their peers from efforts at academic success.

9. Ogunpidẹ specifies that the argument appears to exonerate Yorùbá men of "*male* sexism," since female sexism also exists.

10. Consider the contrary hypothesis that such tensions and hierarchy are quite old in Yorùbá society. A widespread myth reports that another of Ṣàngó's wives—either Ọya or Oṣun—tricked Ọbà into slicing off her ear, under the pretense that human ear was Ṣàngó's favorite food.

References

Abimbọla, Wande. 1997. "Images of Women in the Ifa Literary Corpus." In *Queens, Queen Mothers, Priestesses, and Power,* ed. Flora E. S. Kaplan, 401–14. New York: New York Academy of Sciences.

Abraham, R. C. 1962. *Dictionary of Modern Yorùbá.* London: Hodder and Stoughton.

Adeekọ, Adeleke. 2005. "Ko Sohun Mbe ti o Nitan (Nothing Is That Lacks a [Hi]story): On Oyeronkẹ Oyewumi's *The Invention of Women.*" In *African Gender Studies: A Reader,* ed. Oyeronkẹ Oyewumi, 121–26. New York: Palgrave Macmillan.

Afọnja, Simi. 2005. "Gender and Feminism in African Development Discourse." Unpublished paper prepared at the Institute for Advanced Study, Indiana University, Bloomington, October/November.

Alba, Richard D. 1990. *Ethnic Identity: The Transformation of White America.* New Haven: Yale University Press.

Amadiume, Ifi. 1987. *Male Daughters, Female Husbands: Gender and Sex in an African Society.* London: Zed Books.

Ardener, Edwin. 1975 (1972). "Belief and the Problem of Women." In *Perceiving Women,* ed. Shirley Ardener, 1–18. New York: John Wiley and Sons.

Bakare-Yusuf, Bibi. N.d. "'Yorùbá's Don't Do Gender': A Critical Review of Oyeronkẹ Oyewumi's *The Invention of Women: Making an African Sense of Western Gender Discourses.*" www.codesria.org/Links/conferences/gender/BAKERE%_YUSUF.pdf. Accessed 23 April 2007.

Barber, Karin. 1981. "How Man Makes God in West Africa: Yoruba Attitudes towards the Orisa." *Africa* 51, no. 3: 724–45.

Behar, Ruth. 1995. "Introduction: Out of Exile." In *Women Writing Culture,* ed.

Ruth Behar and Deborah A. Gordon, 1–29. Berkeley: University of California Press.

Bernal, Martin. 1987. *Black Athena: The Afro-Asiatic Roots of Classical Civilization.* New Brunswick, NJ: Rutgers University Press.

Butler, Judith. 1990. *Gender Trouble: Feminism and the Subversion of Identity.* New York: Routledge.

Case, Menoukha. 2002. "Disciplining Possession/s." In "The Forum." *Critical Sense* 11, no. 1 (Fall): 138–45.

Caulfield, Mina Davis. 1981. "Equality, Sex, and Mode of Production." In *Social Inequality,* ed. Gerald Berreman, 201–19. New York: Academic Press.

Chaudhuri, Nupur. 2001. Review of *The Invention of Women: Making an African Sense of Western Gender Discourse,* and *For Women and the Nation: Funmilayọ Ransome-Kuti of Nigeria,* and *Dislocating Cultures: Third World Feminism and the Politics of Knowledge. NWSA Journal* 13, no.1: 172–76.

Clark, Mary Ann. 2001. "When Men Are Wives and Women Are Kings: Using Santeria Ritual Practice to Deconstruct Notions of Gender." Lecture summary, American Academy of Religion's Online Program Session—Unicode. Accessed June 30, 2006, from http: //aarweb.org/annualmeet/ 2001/pbook/abstract-unicode.asp?ANum=A144.

Collins, Patricia Hill. 1989. "The Social Construction of Black Feminist Thought." *Signs* 14: 745–73.

Cooper, Carolyn. 2004. *Sound Clash: Jamaican Dancehall Culture at Large.* New York: Palgrave Macmillan.

Cornwall, Andrea. 2002. "Spending Power: Love, Money, and the Reconfiguration of Gender Relations in Ado-Odo, Southwestern, Nigeria." *American Ethnologist* 29, no.4: 963–80.

Customer reviews of *The Invention of Women,* by Oyeronkẹ Oyewumi. 2006. Amazon.com. www.amazon.com/gp/product/0816624410/104–5231999 –0245. Accessed June 18, 2006.

Daramọla, Olu, and Adebayọ Jeje. 1975 (1967). *Awọn Aṣa ati Oriṣa Ilẹ Yoruba.* Ibadan: Onibọn-Oje Press.

Davies, Carole Boyce. 2002. "A View from the Palace." Lecture presented at Roundtable: The Invention of Women—Theorizing African Women and Gender Now and into the Future. African Studies Association, Washington, DC, December 6.

Davis, Angela. 1985. "Sex-Egypt." In *Women: A World Report,* ed. Anita Desai, Toril Brekke, et al., 325–48. London: Methuen.

Denzer, LaRay. 1994. "Yorùbá Women: A Historiographical Study." *International Journal of African Historical Studies* 27, no. 1: 1–39.

Eades, J. S. 1980. *Changing Cultures: The Yorùbá Today.* Cambridge: Cambridge University Press.

Fagg, William, and John Pemberton, III. 1982. *Yorùbá Sculpture of West Africa,* ed. Bryce Holcombe. New York: Alfred A. Knopf.

Fernandez, James W. 1986. *Persuasions and Performances: The Play of Tropes in Culture.* Bloomington: Indiana University Press.

Ficek, Douglas. 2006 "Distinction without Difference." Review essay of *The Invention of Women,* by Oyeronkę Oyewumi. *Philosophy and Social Criticism* 32, no. 4: 543–49.

Fordham, Signithia, and John U. Ogbu. 1986. "Black Students' School Success: Coping with the 'Burden of "Acting White."'" *Urban Review* 18, no. 3: 176–206.

Hafkin, Nancy J., and Edna G. Bay, eds. 1976. *Women in Africa: Studies in Social Change.* Stanford, CA: Stanford University Press.

hooks, bell. 1981. *Ain't I a Woman: Black Women and Feminism.* Boston: South End Press.

Johnson, Samuel. 1921. *The History of the Yorùbás.* Lagos: CSS Bookshops.

Landes 1947.

Lawal, Babatunde. 2001. "Oriloniṣe: The Hermeneutics of the Head and Hairstyles among the Yorùbá." *Tribal Arts* 8: 2.

Leacock, Eleanor. 1978. "Women's Status in Egalitarian Society: Implications for Social Evolution." *Current Anthropology* 19, no. 2: 247–75.

Levine, Lawrence W. 1996. *The Opening of the American Mind: Canons, Culture, and History.* Boston: Beacon Press.

Lorber, Judith. 1994. *Paradoxes of Gender.* New Haven: Yale University Press.

Matory, J. Lorand. 1986. "Vessels of Power: The Dialectical Symbolism of Power in Yorùbá Religion and Polity." Master's thesis, University of Chicago.

———. 1988. "Homens montados: Homossexualidade e simbolismo da possessão nas religiões afro-brasileiras." In *Escravidão e Invenção da Liberdade,* ed. João José Reis, 215–31. São Paulo: Editôra Brasiliense.

———. 1991. "Sex and the Empire That Is No More: A Ritual History of Women's Power among the Ọ̀yọ́-Yorùbá." Ph.D. diss., University of Chicago.

———. 1994. *Sex and the Empire That Is No More: Gender and the Politics of Metaphor in Ọ̀yọ́ Yorùbá Religion.* Minneapolis: University of Minnesota Press.

———. 2004. "Gendered Agendas: The Secrets Scholars Keep about Yorùbá-Atlantic Religions." In *Dialogues of Dispersal,* ed. Sandra Gunning, Tera W. Hunter, and Michele Mitchell, 13–43. Malden, MA: Blackwell.

———. 2005a. *Black Atlantic Religion: Tradition, Transnationalism, and Ma-*

triarchy in the Afro-Brazilian Candomblé. Princeton: Princeton University Press.

———. 2005b. *Sex and the Empire That Is No More: Gender and the Politics of Metaphor in Oyo Yorùbá Religion.* New York: Berghahn.

Mead, Margaret. 1928. *Coming of Age in Samoa.* New York: William Morrow.

———. 1963 (1935). *Sex and Temperament in Three Primitive Societies.* New York: Morrow Quill.

Moraga, Cherríe, and Gloria Anzaldúa, eds. 1983. *This Bridge Called My Back: Writings by Radical Women of Color.* New York: Kitchen Table, Women of Color Press.

Nzegwu, Nkiru. 2001. "Gender Equality in a Dual-Sex System: The Case of Onitsha." *JENDA: A Journal of Culture and African Women Studies* 1, no. 1 (online). http://www.jendajournal.com/vol1.1/nzegwu.html. Accessed 24 April 2007.

Ogundipẹ, Mọlara. 2002. "The Invention of Women: Theorizing African Women and Gender. Now and Into the Future." Lecture presented at Roundtable: The Invention of Women—Theorizing African Women and Gender Now and into the Future. African Studies Association, Washington, DC, December 6.

Okome, Mojubaolu Olufunkẹ. 2001. "African Women and Power: Reflections on the Perils of Unwarranted Cosmopolitanism." *JENDA: A Journal of Culture and African Women Studies* 1, no. 1 (online). http://www.jendajournal .com/vol1.1/okome.html. Accessed 24 April 2007.

Okonjo, Kamene. 1976. "The Dual-Sex Political System in Operation: Igbo Women and Community Politics in Midwestern Nigeria." In *Women in Africa: Studies in Social and Economic Change,* ed. Nancy J. Hafkin and Edna G. Bay, 45–58. Stanford, CA: Stanford University Press.

Olajubu, Oyeronkẹ. 2003. *Women in the Yorùbá Religious Sphere.* Albany: State University of New York Press.

Olupọna, Jacob. 2005. "Imagining the Goddess: Gender in Yorùbá Religious Traditions and Modernity." *Dialogue and Alliance* 18, no. 1: 71–86.

Ortner, Sherry B., and Harriet Whitehead. 1991 (1981). "Introduction: Accounting for Sexual Meanings." In *Sexual Meanings: The Cultural Construction of Gender and Sexuality,* ed. Sherry B. Ortner and Harriet Whitehead, 1–27. New York: Cambridge University Press.

Oyewumi, Oyeronkẹ. 1997. *The Invention of Women: Making an African Sense of Western Gender Discourses.* Minneapolis: University of Minnesota Press.

———, ed. 2005. *African Gender Studies: A Reader.* New York: Palgrave Macmillan.

Peel, J. D. Y. 2002. "Gender in Yorùbá Religious Change." *Journal of Religion in Africa* 32, no. 2: 136–66.

Rogers, Susan Carol. 1975. "Female Forms of Power and the Myth of Male Dominance: A Model of Female/Male Interaction in Peasant Society." *American Ethnologist* 2, no. 4: 727–56.

Rosaldo, Michelle Zimbalist, and Louise Lamphere. 1974. Introduction to *Women, Culture and Society,* ed. Michelle Zimbalist Rosaldo and Louise Lamphere, 1–15. Stanford, CA: Stanford University Press.

Rubin, Gayle. 1975. "The Traffic in Women: Notes on the Political Economy of Sex." In *Toward an Anthropology of Women,* ed. Rayna R. Reiter, 157–210. New York: Monthly Review Press.

Sacks, Karen. 1976. "State Bias and Women's Status." *American Anthropologist* 78, no. 3: 565–69.

———. 1979. *Sisters and Wives: The Past and Future of Sexual Equality.* Westport, CT: Greenwood.

Schlegel, Alice. 1977. "Toward a Theory of Sexual Stratification." In *Sexual Stratification: A Cross-cultural View,* ed. Alice Schlegel, 1–40. New York: Columbia University Press.

Segato, Rita. 2003. "Género, política e hibridismo en la transnacionalización de la cultural Yorùbá." *Estudos Afro-Asiáticos* 25, no. 2: 333–63.

Shapiro, Judith. 1981. "Anthropology and the Study of Gender." *Soundings* 64, no. 4: 446–65.

Strathern, Marilyn. 1987. Introduction to *Dealing with Inequality: Analysing Gender Relations in Melanesia and Beyond,* ed. Marilyn Strathern, 1–32. Cambridge: Cambridge University Press.

Tiamiyu, Mojişǫla F. 2000. Review of *The Invention of Women* by Oyeronkę Oyewumi. *International Journal of African Studies* 2, no. 1: 121–24.

Trexler, Richard C. 1995. *Sex and Conquest: Gendered Violence, Political Order, and the European Conquest of the Americas.* Ithaca, NY: Cornell University Press.

Turner, Victor. 1967. *The Forest of Symbols.* Ithaca, NY: Cornell University Press.

Whitehead, Harriet. 1981. "The Bow and the Burden Strap: A New Look at Institutionalized Homosexuality in Native North America." In *Sexual Meanings: The Cultural Construction of Gender and Sexuality,* ed. Sherry B. Ortner and Harriet Whitehead, 80–115. Cambridge: Cambridge University Press.

Yanagisako, Sylvia Junko, and Jane Fishburne Collier. 1987. "Toward a Unified Analysis of Gender and Kinship." In *Gender and Kinship: Essays toward a Unified Analysis,* ed. Jane Fishburne Collier and Sylvia Junko Yanagisako, 14–50. Stanford, CA: Stanford University Press.

Postscript

JOHN PEMBERTON III

For a volume of essays by distinguished scholars from Africa and the Americas, this is a most unusual "Postscript." Indeed, my participation in the conference in Miami in 1999 was a bit unusual. Professor Jacob Olupona called me some months in advance of the gathering to ask me to reserve the dates of the conference on my calendar, since he wished me to attend. In fact, I was out of the country when he reached me. The subject of the conference was of great interest to me, but it was not at all clear whether I was being asked to prepare a paper or simply attend. It did not help to hear him say that he wanted me to speak, but I need not prepare a paper.

In the weeks that followed, I was informed that he wished to have me attend so that my "contributions to the study of Yorùbá religion and art could be recognized." I was incredulous. I could think of many other scholars who deserved such recognition far more than I. Attempts to dissuade him were fruitless and bordered on being rude. But what was I to say? He finally suggested that I address issues in the future study of Yorùbá religion. As it turned out, when it was time for me to speak, the evening session had run so far overtime that I decided to set aside my prepared remarks and respond to Olupona's and Rowland Abiodun's introductions with a brief personal statement of my own intellectual and spiritual sojourn in Yorùbá studies and in the process recognize those who had so generously encouraged and supported my inquiries. The moment was saved, at least for me, when, as I finished, the drums of Olatunji sounded, and the entire gathering began to dance.

Professor Olupona asked me to permit him to use those highly personal remarks as a postscript to this volume of essays. I do so with appreciation and some reluctance. Hence, this is not a critical response to the papers presented at the conference or those published in this volume, although my comments at the time were aware of those who had spoken and, at times, the intense, even heated, debate of some of the sessions. In recent months, Professor Olupona has kindly permitted me to read the papers prepared for this volume. Insofar as I address the question of the future of the study of Yorùbá religion, I do so as a gloss on what the conferees have presented in their papers. For in their studies one discerns the rich complexity, insight, and importance of what is now happening in the study of Yorùbá religion. It is clear that òrìṣà worship has taken its place among the world religions, and it has to come to grips with all the questions that such a status asks of its devotees.

A Personal Sojourn

In 1970, I visited West Africa for the first time. The trip was the result of having served on a committee to determine whether Amherst College should make an appointment in the discipline of anthropology. I read extensively in the literature and found anthropological studies of African peoples by British and French scholars especially interesting. In the process, I began to ask what anthropology might contribute to my studies in medieval and Reformation history. I was to discover the following year that Peter Brown, a scholar of late Roman antiquity at All Souls College in Oxford, was asking the same question. At the time, I was fascinated by Victor Turner's new book, *The Ritual Process* (1969), which E. E. Evans-Pritchard was to dismiss as illustrative of what happens when an anthropologist becomes a convert to Roman Catholicism (an odd criticism from one who was himself a Roman Catholic). I read with interest Evans-Pritchard's *Witchcraft, Oracles, and Magic among the Azande* (1968), as well as Godfrey Lienhardt's *Divinity and Experience: The Religion of the Dinka* (1961). However, what captured my attention was the sculptural art of Africa's peoples, especially the remarkable artistry of the Yorùbá people, their superb Ife terra cotta and bronze sculptures. I read Frank Willett's *Ife in the History of West African Sculpture* (1967) and had the good fortune of meeting Fr. Kevin Carroll, whose book, *Yorùbá Religious Carving* (1966), introduced me to the artistry of contemporary Yorùbá carvers. Fr. Carroll's admiration for and close working relationship with the master carvers Areogun of Osi-Ilorin and Bamgboye of Odo-Owa also raised the question for me of the relationship between Christian missions and Yorùbá religious thought and practices.

While a visiting fellow at Oxford's Institute of Social Anthropology in 1970–71, I made two trips to Nigeria. Little did I realize that this year of intellectual play would lead to a significant change in my professional and personal life. While visiting the Institute of African Studies at the University of Ibadan in the summer of 1970, I inquired about the carver of the veranda posts at the entry to the institute and was informed that they were the work of Lamidi Fakeye. I found Fakeye in the Makola section of Ibadan and asked him to carve a sculpture depicting an Ifá divination priest similar to one that he had carved for Robert Armstrong, who at the time was director of the institute. He agreed, and I spent parts of two or three days each week for several weeks taking photographs and enjoying conversations with Lamidi about carvers in the Igbomina and Ekiti areas. On one occasion he invited me to go with him to his hometown, Ila-Orangun, and to drive further east to Ekiti to meet "the last of the great carvers," Bamgboye of Odo-Owa, and Bamidele, son of the famous Areogun of Osi-Ilorin. It was a remarkable trip. Bamgboye was a tall and dignified man in his late seventies and still carving with extraordinary skill. When he died a few years later, his *oríkì* concluded with the fitting tribute to his genius as a carver.

> The elephant has fled in the face of the hunter.
> The mighty one has fallen in the forest and can no longer rise.
> The elephant has fallen; the elephant is gone.
> The elephant has fallen; the elephant is gone.
> Ajanaku the mighty one has fallen and can no longer rise.
> Ajanaku has fallen and cannot climb the mountain.
> Our father has indeed departed.
> Well done, son of Olora, who walks majestically.

I had never traveled *waka-waka* roads, eaten so much *iyan,* been so hospitably received as a foreigner, seen torch-lit markets, or sat in the courtyard of a palace sipping beer while listening to an *ǫba* resolve a conflict among several junior chiefs. I also heard the sharp staccato sounds of *bàtá* drums, saw people dancing in procession for òrìṣà Shango, and was admitted to shrines for deities utterly foreign to my experience. I was fascinated, overwhelmed, charmed, and felt the weight of my ignorance.

One morning, while at the University of Ibadan, I asked a young man if I might join him for breakfast. All other tables at the Staff Club were filled, and he was alone. He introduced himself, and to my delight, I was seated with Wande Abimbola, whose two-volume doctoral thesis on Ifá divination I had been reading at the institute's library. It was a chance meeting that would lead to a long-term friendship and to Wande's repeated visits to Amherst College. In 1981, he became the first Henry Luce Professor of Comparative Religious Ethics at the college. The peripatetic Abimbola would give Luce a new spelling, but his year at Amherst would lay the foundation for significant developments in African studies at the college and in the Five College area. I recall the perplexity of faculty in the Department of Religion at Ife, which was largely made up of Christian theologians and Islamic scholars, when they learned of the invitation. Why Abimbola? He was not a professor of religion. True, but he was learned in Ifá, which is at the heart of Yorùbá religious thought and practice. He was a *babaláwo,* a priest of Ifá, and he had the capacity to articulate with clarity the Odù of Ifá.

Upon returning home, I soon realized that I wanted to return to Ila, a small town of dusty, red, laterite streets, having nothing to charm the tourist, but providing entree to a culture from which I believed I had much to learn. Hence, I returned in 1972, 1974, 1976, and 1981, each trip being the last, as I would tell my wife, but each trip opening up new areas of inquiry.

On the flight home in 1974, I was reading Norman O. Brown's study of a Greek god, *Hermes, the Thief: The Evolution of a Myth* (1969). I began to think of the shrines for Èṣù that I saw everywhere in Ila: at entrances to compounds and the *ǫba's* palace; at crossroads and the town gates; and the wonderfully impressive shrine for Èṣù in Elemukan's compound. I was intrigued and puzzled by the reputation of this òrìṣà who was referred to as "the trickster" by folklorists, "the devil" by Christians, and "the messenger, the bearer of sacrifices" by his devotees. I recalled having read Wole Soyinka's early essay, "The Fourth Stage," in which he had employed the concept of tragedy and images from ancient Greek plays to reflect upon the figures of Ògún and Ọbàtálá in contemporary Yorùbá thought. "Ògún the first actor," he wrote, "first suffering deity, first creative energy, the first darer and conqueror of transition." In his splendid preface to this volume, Soyinka continues to move with grace and insight across cultures, revealing shared human concerns—the universality of human suffering and the quest for meaning—and reveals how understanding the power of images from one culture can inform our understanding of the expressive images of another.

When I returned home, I wrote an essay on Èṣù, "the trickster figure," as I then unfortunately referred to the òrìṣà who is the guardian of the ritual way. I sent a copy of the paper, along with photographs, to Robert Farris Thompson at Yale. He quickly responded, recommending that I forward it to *African Arts*. To my amazement they published it (1975). A few months later, I was going to a rather formal dinner party at a friend's home in Cambridge. Olúfémi Richards had suggested that I drop by at a gathering at Harvard of persons interested in African art. Arriving at the time for libations and not dressed in a Peace Corps dashiki, I was directed to another gathering across the hall. When I introduced myself, I was invited to join the African contingent. In some respects, it was like stepping back into Ila—such generosity was in their welcome. I was pleased by the comments about the essay on Èṣù, but it was clear that I was an unknown and posed a dilemma. After all, I had not been trained in graduate programs in African studies. I disclaimed any credentials as an Africanist, but someone said: "Look here. We are such a small group, and there is very little work being done in the study of religion; we need all the help we can get." Hence, I was to be included, if I so chose. Wande Abimbola was to tell me later that whatever success I had had in my research was because of the fact that I had made my first sacrifice to Èṣù!

My attention had turned to the pantheon of the òrìṣà in Ila and neighboring communities, their overwhelming number and diversity manifest on shrines and in sculptural form, as well as in festivals and *oríkì*. I was intrigued by the variation in their configuration and importance among persons, families, compounds, and towns. In 1976, I was invited by the American Academy of Religion to give the first plenary session address on African religion. Like it or not, I was an Africanist; and I liked it very much. I recall with pleasure and appreciation Karen Brown speaking to me following my address about the relevance of my analysis of the pantheon of the òrìṣà to her work in Haiti. Years later, she would make famous the Haitian priestess Mama Lola, providing us with a penetrating insight into the spirituality of Haitian Vodou.

Throughout the first decade of my research, I would have achieved little if it had not been for the interest and support of Ọba William Adetona Ayeni, Orangun-Ila. For years he had the only gasoline-powered generator in Ila and, hence, the only cool beer. We spent many hours in relaxed conversation about my work and his role as ọba. He had ascended the throne in 1967, three years before my first visit to Ila. It was through him that I met Chiefs Obala, Obale, Elemona, Odoode, and a host of others who opened their homes and their lives to me over the years. A few months before the conference on "Orisha Devotion as World Religion" convened, a friend sent an e-mail message that simply said: "His Highness has joined the ancestors." I had lost a great friend, indeed a parent, and I knew that a chapter in my life was closed. I would not return again to Ila-Orangun.

Over the years and in varying contexts I met many persons who significantly influenced my research and my life. As I watched her interview and tape-record elders in Ila, Deirdre Lapin introduced me to the importance and role of ìtàn and oríkì as forms of historical consciousness and expressions of family, community, and personal identity. With Margaret and Henry Drewal, I was introduced to the distinctive culture of the Ijebu Yorùbá and furthered my understanding of the phenomenon of the masquerade as we photographed and taped the Agemo Festival in 1982 and 1986. Conversations with Oyin Ogunba in Ife and Ijebode about Agemo were invaluable. I took issue with his model of the theater for analyzing rituals and festivals, but he never ceased to be generous with his extensive knowledge of Odun Agemo. I met Karin Barber, whose splendid essay "How Man Makes Gods in West Africa: Attitudes towards the *Orisa*" (1981) took a very different approach, more in the tradition of Durkheim's study of religion than the one I developed in my earlier essay, "A Cluster of Sacred Symbols: Orisha Worship among the Igbomina Yorùbá of Ila-Orangun" (1977), which was influenced by reading Max Weber and Clifford Geertz and their emphasis upon the inextricable relationship between religion and culture with respect to human suffering and the quest for meaning. The two approaches are not mutually exclusive as long as one does not subsume forms of religious expression within a priority given to social systems or assume that one's study of the religious life of a people at a particular time and place speaks for the whole of Yorùbáland—one of the problems from which E. B. Id-owu's book, *Olodumare: God in Yorùbá Belief* (1962), suffers. A number of essays in this volume are acutely aware of the ways in which Yorùbá religious patterns of belief and ritual behavior are adapted to new histori-cal and cultural circumstances; and Olabiyi Yai's insightful essay shows how the process of globalization has been an ongoing phenomenon in Yorùbá culture for centuries prior to the shocking "second phase" cre-ated by the transatlantic slave trade and the subsequent development of distinctive forms of òrìṣà worship in the new and diverse cultural con-texts of Brazil, Cuba, Haiti, and the United States.

To be sure, studies of Yorùbá religious thought and practice in par-ticular times and places, such as those that Barber and I have pursued, are essential to our understanding of Yorùbá religion. However, one must hesitate in using the term "Yorùbá religion," since it suggests a singular phenomenon. Yorùbá culture in West Africa and its numerous forms of religious thought and practice and artistic styles have varied from region to region, as well as over time. Yorùbá culture has been aptly described as a river never at rest. In the pantheons of the òrìṣà (and I deliberately use the plural "pantheons") Ògún is the principal deity in Ila-Orangun, Òṣun in Oshogbo, Osi in Ife Ijumu, Ṣàngó in Ọ̀yọ́, Odùduwà in Ilé-Ifè. To be sure, these deities have their shrines and festivals in almost every town and region, but their relative importance in the configuration of local pantheons changes in relationship to local histories shaped by the experience of a region, a town, a lineage group, and the life of an indi-vidual. In West Africa the extent of the worship of òrìṣà Shango seems to correspond to the boundaries of the Old Ọ̀yọ́ Empire, and one does not find the carvings for Ibeji in Owo and Ijumu, areas that were beyond the reach of Old Ọ̀yọ́, although over time persons have carried the wor-ship and shrine sculptures of Ṣàngó and Ibeji into these areas. And then there is the host of deities and other spiritual powers that appear to be purely local, associated with rivers, streams, hills, and forests—each with his or her own name (or names) and places of ritual activity. Some are widely known, others are not; some are worshiped for centuries, others soon forgotten. In every culture gods are born, transformed, and even die.

Festivals for the ancestors, Odun Egúngún, appear throughout Yorùbáland, rich in the variety of masquerades and rites. Odun Epa and Elefon, however, are found only in the Ekiti and Igbomina areas; the spectacle of Gèlèdé is celebrated solely among the Egba, Egbado, and

Ketu peoples; and Odun Agemo in the towns and villages surrounding Ijebode. Every town has its own festival calendar, the times determined by local histories, as well as the cycle of agricultural seasons.

But to return to the personal narrative. When I first met Jacob Olupona in the mid-1970s, he was in the Religion Department of the University of Ife feeling somewhat alone in his interests in Yorùbá religious studies and his work on the festivals of kingship in the Ondo area. I was impressed by his research program and would eventually follow his lead in focusing on the role of the oba in Ila's festival cycle. It was a selfish privilege to be able to arrange a Copeland Fellowship at Amherst College for him; he is well remembered for his contribution to increasing interest in African Studies at the college. In the late 1970s, Henry Drewal introduced me to Rowland Abiodun. Little did I know at the time that Rowland would become a member of the Amherst College faculty in the Department of Fine Arts and Black Studies and would become only the third person in my forty years at the college who, as a visiting professor, was appointed directly to a full professorship with tenure. His contributions to the college and African Studies in the Five Colleges have been incomparable. More importantly, he is a distinguished scholar on Yorùbá art and aesthetics whose essays have richly informed my understanding of Yorùbá religion and ritual artifacts.

In 1979, I met William Fagg. It took awhile to learn how to hear and understand Bill's distinctive manner of speech, but once achieved, he was an extraordinary repository of information and generous to a fault. Through his many essays, written with impeccable style, and in conversations, while collaborating on the catalogue *Yorùbá Sculpture of West Africa* (1982), Bill trained my eye so that I was no longer looking "through my nose," to borrow a Yorùbá phrase, in seeing and thinking about Yorùbá sculptural form.

There are a host of others whom I should mention: John Picton, whose painstaking research on the carvers in northern Ekiti in many ways became a model for my studies of the carving traditions and shrine sculpture in the Igbomina area; so, too, Ulli Beier and his wonderful monographs on the shrines of Ilobu; and Susan Vogel, who produced the finest series of exhibitions and catalogues in her ten years as director of the Center for African Art than all the rest of the catalogues published elsewhere in the same period. It was Susan who encouraged and supported the idea that Henry Drewal and I prepare a major exhibition of Yorùbá art and invite Rowland Abiodun to co-author the catalogue

Yorùbá: Nine Centuries of African Art and Thought (1989). After years of collaborative research in Ijebode and our investigations of public and private collections in Europe and the United States, as well as our individual research programs, we were suddenly to discover that Nigeria's museums would not lend the crucial artworks from Ife and Esie necessary for the exhibition. It was clear from my conversations with Ade Obayerni, who was director general of museums and monuments, that he was sympathetic to our request, but his authority had been limited by a new Commission on Antiquities at the time of his appointment. Not even the Ife terra cottas from Obafemi Awolowo University's collections would be given permission to leave Nigeria. I despaired at the thought of having to tell Hank and Susan of this turn of events. It was the summer of 1988, and the exhibition was scheduled for the fall of 1989. Several months later I received a cable from Wande Abimbola. It simply read: "Come immediately to sign papers." There were three weeks of classes to be completed, but colleagues took over, and I flew to Lagos. I met Ade and Wande in the offices of the director general, and we came to an agreement on seventeen pieces that I would convey to New York. Ade then took me to visit his home in an area beyond northern Ekiti, now in Kogi State. The town was Iffe Ijumu (pronounced Uffe Ijumu). He delighted in saying that he was borderland Yorùbá, that he came from an area that was not to be identified with Ilé-Ifè or Ọ̀yọ́ or Owo. As I quickly discovered, it was a different religio-cultural world with its distinctive òrìṣà traditions, although Ṣàngó and Ọ̀ṣun devotees and their shrines were to be found.

Ade Obayemi was an archaeologist and a historian committed to the collection of oral histories in his home area. He held a professorship at Ilorin University. And even while he was in the office of director general, he was training school teachers and students in the art of collecting oral materials, engaging them in a new appreciation for a cultural heritage that was rapidly being lost to the inroads of Christian missionary schools and forms of popular culture imported from other parts of Nigeria. He hoped to found an institute in his village for Nigerian scholars and others from abroad to meet and pursue their studies. Alas, he died an untimely death, and his vision for the study of Ijumu history and culture waits for someone to build upon the foundation that he laid.

There is a final moment in my sojourn that I would like to share. In the late 1980s, I stopped at Obafemi Awolowo University on my way to Ila. As I was crossing the campus, a young man hailed me: "Are you

Professor Pemberton? I am Funso Afolayan, a graduate student in history. I heard that there was an *oyibo* writing on Igbomina religion and art. I didn't believe it. I read your essays." And then he said with a clear and disarming tone of surprise in his voice: "They are good!" For me this was the ultimate compliment. He asked me to read his master's thesis on Igbomina history during the colonial period and wanted to share his current research on gathering oral histories in the Igbomina area. We talked for an hour or more. I read his thesis, and we talked again and again. We agreed to pursue collaborative studies in Ila and neighboring towns in the year to come, since he had not pursued research in Ila, and I had done little work in the surrounding towns and villages. He, too, came as a Copeland Fellow to Amherst College, and there we worked on the first draft of *Yorùbá Sacred Kingship: "A Power Like That of the Gods"* (1996). The model that J. D. Y. Peel provided us in his splendid study *Ijeshas and Nigerians: The Incorporation of a Yorùbá Kingdom, 1890s–1970s* (1983) was a challenge and an inspiration. Ade Obayemi was wonderfully helpful in reading and commenting on early drafts, and it was Ade who carried a copy of the book to Ila and presented it to the Orangun-Ila for us.

While working with Afolayan, I became acutely aware of Ila's history as one of constant change preserved in a people's collective memory by palace historians and elders of individual lineage groups in the telling of *orile* and *ìtàn:* conflicts at the time of the founding of the town, which come again to the fore when an *ọba* must be chosen (as is now happening once again in Ila); disputes among lineage groups over land and chieftaincy titles; and scars left by the Ibadan/Ilorin war when Ila was ravaged and for a period abandoned. I was also made aware of the complexity of the history of each house or compound (*ilé*) composed of the descendants of the founders but also of subgroups with their own histories—some claiming origins in Ilé-Ifè or Old Ọ̀yọ́, even Esie; others acknowledging that they were of immigrant origin, their forefathers refugees from neighboring towns during the nineteenth-century war, or that the family was a spinoff of an older house where limited space or family conflicts had led them to found a new house and their own lineage identity. With historical and social change, came changes in òrìṣà worship, for deities with their myths, rituals, and ritual artifacts move with people—whole families and also individuals—and undergo transformation (reinterpretation) over time. In reading many of the essays in the present volume, I was made aware of similar patterns of change and the extraordinary and imaginative adaptation of Yorùbá peoples, not only in West Africa but also in Brazil, Cuba, Haiti, and the United States. And, I believe, this capacity for imaginative adaptation and the enlarging of one's vision is a gift given by the òrìṣà. As creative powers, they will not be limited by the human propensity to reification, to render them idealized abstractions or fixed in their identity.

Reflecting on my sojourn from 1970 to 1992 in Nigeria (a continuing sojourn to this day), the title the master carver Bamgboye of Odo-Owa gave to one of his great Epa masks comes to mind: "No One Thinks Alone." Such has been my experience. I began my sojourn as a visitor, then became an observer, then a participant-observer, and throughout welcomed as a friend. In the course of the conference in Miami, there was repeated reference to the question of the relationship between scholarship and participation in the religious life of a people. My own experience has not been one that has suffered such a dichotomy.

In my early visits to Ila, I lived in Iren's House, the home of the Fadeyi family. There was a shrine for òrìṣà Osanyin that was cared for by the surviving wife of the elder Fadeyi, who had been a famous herbalist. The family, however, had become Christian at their father's request, since he saw the mission schools as the wave of the future. Hence, the seven sons were all members of Christian churches—Anglican, Baptist, and Mustard Seed Apostolic. I was in Ila to study òrìṣà worship and, therefore, did not attend services at St. Matthew's Anglican Church for fear that it would somehow compromise my access to the òrìṣà worshipers. Finally, my host insisted that I attend Sunday service with him. It was their Thanksgiving, or New Yam Festival. I did not wish to be rude, but I was concerned about my research. At St. Matthew's I was put on display in the choir and soon became fascinated with their celebration of the Anglican liturgy with which I was quite familiar. Then, a choirboy nudged me to look in the direction of the altar. The Orangun was bidding me to come and stand next to him. I did so and knelt with him and several chiefs before the altar, where new yams were stacked. We made our offerings and rose, and then he said: "Today, Professor, I dance with my people. Dance!" The drums sounded, and I did my best to follow in his steps, to the amusement of the congregation. Rather than alienating me from the òrìṣà worshipers, word spread that I had danced with the Ọba, and now they knew what they had long suspected. I was a Christian, as well as a scholar, and they opened their doors and their lives in appreciation for my respect for and interest in their religious life.

In the course of my studies, I was invited to witness Ifá divination rites for persons and families struggling to discern the causes of their suffering and desiring to know how to cope. With permission, I photographed and tape-recorded the rituals. Over time, I found myself identifying with the needs and hopes of the suppliants. I understood and shared their human concerns. There were moments when the Ifá priest touched my forehead, as he touched the foreheads of all present, with the offerings for òrìṣà Ọ̀rúnmìlà, the god of wisdom, who was present at Creation and knows the *orí inú,* the inner head or prenatal destiny, of each of us. Friendship and research became inextricably related. I realized that I was thinking about various matters in terms of Ògún, Ọ̀ṣun, Ṣàngó, and other òrìṣà. They not only made sense and had become intelligible, but they also aided me in making sense of my life. And then they appeared in my dreams. In Plato's definition of religion, I was "attending to the gods." Or, was it that the òrìṣà were attending to me? I did not seek to become an initiate, although it was suggested on more than one occasion. I had a fairly clear sense of my own *orí inú* and my baptism. My relationship with the òrìṣà and their devotees would be that of a respectful dialogue.

In light of this intellectual and spiritual sojourn, I listened with care to persons at the conference (and traces may be seen in a few of the papers in this volume) who were concerned with "authenticity" and "accuracy" in the transmission of Odu Ifá and rituals for the òrìṣà. There seemed to be a desire for orthodoxy and ortho-practice, for true "beliefs" and correctness in the performance of "traditional" rituals. Every world religion faces such concerns. When a religion moves beyond geographical and cultural borders within which it had its origin, there can be a growing uncertainty among devotees about how its worldview is to be articulated in new lands and under new conditions, especially when the circumstances are brutally hostile, as in forced displacement and slavery, but also when confronted by alternative worldviews and ritual practices that at times speak meaningfully. In contrast to orthodoxy, another response is a plethora of adaptations to new circumstances, the emergence of sectarianism, groups loosely related and often in conflict with one another, especially when issues of race intrude. It is clear that both types of responses are evident in the current situation of òrìṣà worship in West Africa and the diaspora today. And that is why this present volume is so very important. It lays the groundwork for a continuing study of òrìṣà worship as an authentic world religion.

References

Barber, Karin. 1981. "How Man Makes Gods in West Africa: Yorùbá Attitudes towards the Orisa." *Africa* 51, no. 3: 724–45.

Brown, Norman O. 1969. *Hermes, the Thief: The Evolution of a Myth*. New York: Vintage.

Carroll, Kevin. 1966. *Yorùbá Religious Carving: Pagan and Christian Sculpture in Nigeria and Dahomey*. New York: Praeger.

Drewall, Henry John, John Pemberton III, Rowland Abiodun, and Allen Wardwell, eds. 1989. *Yorùbá: Nine Centuries of African Art and Thought*. New York: Center for African Art in Association with H. N. Abrams.

Evans-Pritchard, E. E. 1968. *Witchcraft, Oracles, and Magic among the Azande*. Oxford: Oxford University Press.

Fagg, William, and John Pemberton. 1982. *Yorùbá Sculpture of West Africa*. New York: Alfred A. Knopf.

Idowu, E. B. 1962. *Olodumare: God in Yorùbá Belief*. London: Longman.

Lienhardt, Godfrey. 1961. *Divinity and Experience: The Religion of the Dinka*. Oxford: Oxford University Press.

Peel, J. D. Y. 1983. *Ijeshas and Nigerians: The Incorporation of a Yorùbá Kingdom, 1890s–1970s*. Cambridge: Cambridge University Press.

Pemberton, John, III. 1977. "A Cluster of Sacred Symbols: Orisha Worship among the Igbomina Yorùbá of Ila-Orangun." *History of Religions* 17, no. 3: 1–28.

Pemberton, John, III, and Funso Afolayan. 1996. *Yorùbá Sacred Kingship: "A Power Like That of the Gods."* Washington, DC: Smithsonian Institution Press.

Soyinka, Wole. 1976. "The Fourth Stage." In *Myth, Literature and the African World*. New York: Cambridge University Press.

Turner, Victor. 1969. *The Ritual Process: Structure and Anti-structure*. New York: Aldine.

Willett, Frank. 1967. *Ife in the History of West African Sculpture*. London: Thames and Hudson.

Glossary

Yorùbá, Spanish, and Portuguese

abagbon   warrior
abo   female
abòrìṣà   one who propitiates or worships *òrìṣà*
adé   crown
adé babaláwo   Ifá priest's crown
àdúrà   prayer
agbádá   traditional shirt
agbè   drum or gourd
àgbò   ram, Ṣàngó's preferred food
agere-Ifá   bowl, symbolic temple of Ọ̀rúnmìlà
agogo   iron bells for percussion (Brazil)
àjẹ́   witch
a-jẹ́-ju-oògùn   culmination of medicine
akọ   male
àkúnlẹ̀gbà   received kneeling down
Àkúnlèbọ   those-who-must-be-worshiped-kneeling-down, deities
Aláàfin   the king of Ọ̀yọ́ City
alabe   one who directs *candomblé*
alabe or iyatabexé, iyatabeshe   soloist singer
Aládurà   *ala-* (owner of) + *àdúrà* (prayer)
alábàágbé   sojourner, refugee
àlọ   folktales, stories
alujá   quick sounding, characteristics of war
apènà   leader of Oshugbo secret society
àpò Ifá   beaded bag of Ifá priest
àpò jèrùgbé   Ifá priest's shoulder bag

573

arere or ilarere   cowries
àrokò   sculpture, dance, drama, song, chanting poetry
arota   slave
àṣẹ (aché, ashe, axexê)   power, catalytic life force of all things, vital force
atabaques- drums (Brazil)
ayé   the realm of phenomena, this world
awo   secret, deep, and esoteric nature of the *ikin*
àwọn ẹlẹyẹ   malevolent powers
axexê (àjèjé, àsèsè)   funeral rites (Brazil)
àyájọ́   incantation
àyànmọ́   that-which-is-affixed-to-one
ayé   realm of human experience phenomena
baálé   head of residential compound
bàbá   father
babalao   Ifá priest
babaláwo   Ifá priest, literally "father of secrets"
babátúndé   "father-comes-back"
barracão   a large, central temple room (Brazil)
bàtá   drum
bàtácotos   war drums
bembes   communal drum ceremony
bọ   propitiate, sacrifice to, cultivate, serve
Cabildo   African ethnic gild, association (Cuba)
candomblé, xangô, tambor-de-mina, batuque   religious traditions, sacred
   texts in Yorùbá language preserved in Brazil
Candomblé religious community   Nago, Xangô, Ketu, Ijesha (Brazil)
chekere or sekeres   Afro-Cuban musical instrument
dùndún   the Yorùbá talking drum
ẹbí   kinship
ẹbọ, ebó   sacrifice (Cuba, Brazil)
èdè   language or speech
ẹdùn   New Stone Age axe
ẹdun-àràá   thunderstone to earth
eégun (egun, égún)   ancestor spirit
ẹfun   white chalk, sacred symbol
ẹgbẹ́   social club, heavenly society
ègbọ́n   senior sibling or cousin
egun, égún   the spirit
egúngún   ancestral masquerade or festival
egúnngún   ancestor (Brazil)
ègúsí   food from seeds of melon
èjìogbè   the odù-Ifá chapter of Ifá literary corpus

Ẹ káàbọ̀ "you are welcome"

ekpebi room for installation

ẹlẹ́gùn senior male possession priest

erelú female officeholder

ẹẹ́rìndínlógún cowry divination

ẹsẹ parable or verse; the most important part of Ifá divination, chanted by the priests

èsìn, èsìn worship, observance

ẹwà beauty, beautiful

ẹyẹ-ilé (pronounced ẹyẹlé) bird of the home

ẹyẹkàn sacred pigeon, the lone or one bird

ẹyẹlé bird or birds

filà flashy traditional Yorùbá hat

gígùn sexual intercourse

gún to straighten, settle, or resolve

gùn to mount, possession, horsemanship

ibá greeting, salutation

ibiga slave

idejo landowning

ìgbàgbọ́ belief

Ìgbò ethnic group or language in Nigeria

Ìgbòho Yorùbá town near Ọ̀yọ́

ìjálá poetic chants of hunters for Ògún

Ìjẹbú subgroup of Yorùbá people

Ijesha and Ketu Yorùbá Nations in Bahia, Brazil

ikanse salute to a ruler

ikin the sixteen oil-palm nuts of Ifá divination, oil-palm nuts of shiny black patina

ìkólàbá Ifá Ifá priest's shoulder piece

ìkúnlẹ̀-abiyamọ the-kneeling-of-the-pains-at-childbirth

ìkúnpá Ifá the Ifá priest's armband

ìkùtè-Ifá the Ifá priest's scepter

ilarere, arere cowries

ilé home, lineage compound

ilẹ̀ earth

Ilé-Ifè, Ifè sacred ancestral home of the Yorùbá

ìmọ̀ knowledge

ìre prayer

ìrọ́kẹ́ divining tapper to invoke Ọ̀rúnmìlà

ìrókò-tree African teak (*Chlorophora Excelsa, Ficus Doliaria*) (Brazil); deity

ìrùkẹ̀rẹ̀ Ifá beaded horsetail flywhisk of priests

ìsìn   worship
ìtàn   narrative, history
ìta-ọ̀run   the spiritual realm, otherworldly space
ìwà   character
ìwúyè   installation ritual
ìyá   mother
ìyálé   eldest wife of the house
iyalòrìṣà, iyalorichas, iyálòrìsà   priestess of an òrìṣà
ìyáwó   bride, wife
ìyẹ̀rosùn   cam wood dust
jihad   to exert utmost effort, strive, struggle (Islam)
jogo de búzios   oracle of sixteen cowries (Brazil)
kele   dazzling beads worn by disciples of Ọya
Ketu and Ijesha   Yorùbá Nations in Bahia, Brazil
kúkúṅdùkú   sweet potato
lábá   leather bag, pouch, or wallet
lucumí, lukumi (orú, Cuba)   Yorùbá culture/religion in Cuba
Lukumí (Lucumí)   Òrìṣà religion in Cuba and among Cuban exiles
màrìwò   palm leaves
meridilogun   cowry shells
Nago   name of the Yorùbá in Recife, Brazil
ní òrìṣà   to have *òrìṣà*
ọba, or Ọba   monarch or paramount ruler, king
òbàrà Ofún   epic poetry of Ifá divination
obì   divinatory system
obi abata   kola nut
obìnrin   woman
òdìgbe Ifá   the casket for Ifá
odobale   ritual greeting
odù   sacred Ifá verses, shrine
Odù-Ifá   chapter of Ifá literary corpus
òfò   curse, chants directed toward herbs
ofu   medicines
ogalade   priestly class of chiefs
Ogane   ancient ruler
ọgbọ́n   wisdom
ògẹ́gẹ́-a- gbáyé-gún   perfection, primeval order regulative principle of the universe
òjíṣẹ́   one who delivers or executes a commission
ọjọ ìṣéde   day of curfew
ọkọ   husband
ọkọ gidi   male and female relatives of the husband

ọkùnrin   man

Olohoun   a name for the Supreme Creator God in Vodou (more commonly Boudye)

olórìṣà, oloricha   *òrìṣà* guide or trainer

olóyè   chiefs, titled heads of chieftaincy

ọmọ   child

omobinrin   girl

ọmọkùnrin   boy

ọmọye   members of chieftaincy family

oògùn   medicine

ọ̀pá   staff or scepter

ọ̀pá Ifá   staff of Ifá

ọ̀pá odiyon   staff

ọ̀pá ọ̀rẹ̀rẹ̀, ọ̀pá ọ̀ṣoòrò, osùn babaláwo   iron staff that can be carried by *babaláwo*

ọ̀pẹ̀lẹ̀   divining chain

ọpọ́n   divining tray, to honor Ifá

ọpọ́n Ifá   divining tray of Ifá

Ọ̀rànmíyàn   son of Odùduwà

orí   inner spiritual head or destiny, one's past, present, and future

orí inú   the inner head

oríkì   citation poetry, praise songs, or chants

orí òde   the visible head or skull

òrìṣà, òrìshà, oricha, orisa, ocha, orixá (òrìshàs, pl.)   deity

Òrìṣà, Santería, Lucumí, Lukumi of the Yorùbá   Ocha, Yorùbá religion in Cuba

orísùn   progenitor

ọ̀rọ̀   embodiment of wisdom, knowledge, and understanding

orò ìdílé   lineage tradition or ritual, roots reading

ọ̀run   otherworld, metaphysical realm of spirits

osega   ceremonious meeting of Lagos chiefs

òwe   proverbs, the language of communication, metaphor

òye   understanding

Ọ̀yọ́   Yorùbá town

Ọ̀yọ́túnjí   African American Yorùbá community in South Carolina

pa ìtàn   narratives, shed light on human existence

Regla de Ocha   Rite of the Òrìshà, Òrìshà System (Cuba, Miami, New York)

Santería, la Santería, La Regla de Ocha, Yorùbá   based religion, the worship of African gods (òrìṣàs) under the appearance of Catholic Saints (Cuba, Miami, New York)

santo/a   saint, Yorùbá òrìṣà (Cuba, Hispanic America)

ṣ́ẹ́ẹ́rẹ́, sheres   gourd rattle
shire   sequence of songs, Brazil
shirk   associating other deities with God
Vodou   African-derived religion originating in Haiti
Vodouisants   practitioners of Vodou (Haiti)
wala   slate of a Muslim student
waqa   songs of Islamic Yorùbá
Xangô   Yorùbá group or language (Candomblé, Nago, Ketu, Ijesha [Brazil])
xangô, Ṣàngó, Chango   name of òrìṣà of lightning, or of Yorùbá religion in Trinidad (Shango)
Xirê   xirê memorial rites
Yéyé   the Good Mother
Yorùbá   ethnic group or language (Nigeria) (Candomblé, Nago, Xangô, Ketu, Ijesha [Brazil])

Yorùbá Deities, the Òrìṣà

Aganju   òrìṣà deity, Cuban
Àjàlá   the great molder of orí
Ayélála   a deity of the river
Changó   Ṣàngó, God of Thunder
Èlà   explicatory principle in the Ifá divination
Elegba (Elegbàrá)   Yorùbá deity, also called Èṣù
Elegua or Eleggua   Cuban òrìṣà of the Crossroads
Èṣù (Eshu)   broker between malevolent and benevolent powers
Èṣù-Elegba or Oṣetura
Hòò-rò (Òrò)   Òrò descended to earth and became Èlà
Ifá   deity of divination, wisdom, and the divination process
Ìrókò   deity of the giant African teak Ìrókò-Tree
Ìwà   beloved wife of Òrúnmìlà, signifies character
Logunede   god/goddess in Bahia, Brazil
Mọrèmi   legendary hero, woman of Ifè
Ọbàtálá or Òrìṣà   god of human creation, known as Òrìṣà-Ńlá and Òrìṣà-Àlà
Obàtálá Yeza   Cuban Yorùbá òrìṣà of creation
Ochún   Òṣun, goddess of the great source
Odù   wife of Òrúnmìlà
Odùduwà   legendary Father of the Yorùbá
Ògún   deity of hunting, iron-working, and warfare
Olódùmarè (Ododuwa in Benin)   Supreme Being, Prime Mover

Olókun Sèníadé   God the Creator

Olórun   the Supreme God (Brazil)

Orí   deity of the inner head

Òrìṣà-Ńlá   Supreme òrìṣà or Ultimate Godhead, also known as Olódùmarè

Òrìṣà-Oko   god of agricultural prosperity

Òrúnmìlà   patron deity or Ifá, father of secrets

Òsanyìn   deity of herbs and medicine

Oṣẹtura or Èṣù-Elegba   Ifá verse symbol of Èṣù

Òshùnmarè or Osumare

Òṣun (Oshun, Òshún, Ochún)   mother of Èṣù, the power of our mothers, great source, pathway to destiny, goddess of Òṣun River

Oya   goddess of wind and tempest, wife of Ṣàngó

Ṣàngó (Sàngó, Shangó, xangô, Xango)   god of thunder and lightning, healer

Yemayá (Yemọja)   a river goddess

Yemọja   goddess of sweet waters (Nigeria); goddess of the sea (Brazil)

Yemòó   wife of Obàtálá

Contributors

ROWLAND ABIODUN is John C. Newton Professor of Fine Arts and Black Studies at Amherst College. He is the author of *"What Follows Six Is More Than Seven": Understanding African Art,* for the London British Museum Department of Ethnography (1995). He coauthored *Yorùbá: Nine Centuries of African Art and Thought* (1989) and *Yorùbá Art and Aesthetics* (1991) and coedited *The Yorùbá Artist: New Theoretical Perspectives on Africa* (1994). He is also coauthor of *Cloth Only Wears to Shreds: Yoruba Textiles and Photographs from the Beier Collection* (2004).

CORNELIUS O. ADEPEGBA (d. 2003) received his Ph.D. in 1976 in art history at Indiana University. He was the director of the Institute of African Studies and Research Professor of Art History at the University of Ibadan, Nigeria. In 1995 he published two books: *A Comparative Study of the Fulani and the Moroccan Decorative Arts: Another Look at the Historical Study of African Material Culture* and *Nigerian Art: Its Traditions and Modern Tendencies.* Adepegba was also author of *Decorative Arts of the Fulani Nomads* (1986) and *Yorùbá Metal Sculpture* (1991) and editor of *Osogbo: Model of Growing African Towns* (1995).

AFE ADOGAME received his Ph.D. (history of religions) from the University of Bayreuth, Germany. He teaches world Christianity/religious studies at the University of Edinburgh, UK. His teaching and research expertise include African indigenous churches; African diasporic religions; religion, migration, and globalization; and African new religious movements. He is the author of *Celestial Church of Christ: The Politics of Cultural Identity in a West African Prophetic-Charismatic Movement* (1999). He is the coauthor of *European Traditions of the Study of Religion in Africa* (with F. Ludwig, 2004) and *Religion in the Context of African Migration* (with C. Weisskoeppel, 2005).

DIEDRE L. BADEJO (Ph.D., UCLA) is Professor of African World Literatures and Cultural Histories, formerly the chair of the Department of Pan-African Studies, and currently associate dean of curriculum in the College of Arts and Sciences at Kent State University, Ohio. Some of her recent works include *Òsun Sèègèsí: The Elegant Deity of Wealth, Power, and Femininity* (1996); "Authority and Discourse in Orin Òdun Òsun," in *Òsun across the Waters: A Yorùbá Goddess in Africa and the Diaspora* (2001); "Womenfolks: Race, Class, and Gender in Works by Zora Neale Hurston and Toni Morrison," in *Black Identity in the Twentieth Century: Expression of the US and UK African Diaspora* (2002); and "Methodologies in Yoruba Oral Historiography and Aesthetics," in *Writing African History* (2005). She is a contributing editor for *Women Writing Africa: West Africa and the Sahel* (2005).

SANDRA T. BARNES is Professor of Anthropology at the University of Pennsylvania, past president of the African Studies Association, and founding director of Penn's African Studies Center. She has written and edited numerous works, including *Africa's Ogun: Old World and New* (1989) and *Patrons and Power: Creating a Political Community in Metropolitan Lagos* (1986), which received the Amaury Talbot Prize for best book on Africa. She has held several national fellowships, sat on the boards of directors of the American Council of Learned Societies, African Studies Association, Stanford Humanities Center, and Foundation for the Advancement of International Medical Education and Research. Her current research focuses on West Africa: precolonial social and cultural life along the Guinea Coast, postcolonial popular culture, and U.S. policy in Africa's oil-producing states.

GEORGE EDWARD BRANDON received his Ph.D. in anthropology from Rutgers University and is Associate Medical Professor of Behavioral Medicine at the Sophie Davis School of Biomedical Education of the City University of New York, as well as an adjunct associate professor in the Biomedical Engineering Department of the Andrew Grove School of Engineering of the City College of New York. He has received fellowships from the National Endowment for the Humanities, the National Science Foundation, and the National Endowment for the Arts. His works include *Santeria from Africa to the New World: The Dead Sell Memories* (1993); *Light from the Forest: How Santeria Heals through Plants* (1991); "Ochun in the Bronx," in *Òsun across the Waters: A Yorùbá Goddess in Africa and the Americas* (2001); and "Getting into the Spirit: An Ethnographic Profile of African-American Spiritual Healers," in *Portraits of Culture* (1994).

KAMARI MAXINE CLARKE (Ph.D. 1997, University of California, Santa Cruz) is Professor of Anthropology at Yale University and a senior research scientist at the Yale Law School. Over the years, Clarke's research has ranged from studies of social and religious movements in the United States and West Africa to related transnational legal movements to inquiries into the cultural politics of power and justice in the burgeoning realm of international tribunals. She is the author of *Mapping Yorùbá Networks: Power and Agency in the Making of Transnational Networks* (2004), *Globalization and Race: Transformations in the Cultural Politics of Blackness* (2006), and a book on emergent international human rights regimes as it relates to competing religious and ethnic politics of justice in local and transnational contexts to be published by Cambridge University Press in 2008.

H. O. DANMOLÉ is a professor in the Department of History at the University of Ilorin, Nigeria. He is the coeditor of *Contemporary Issues in Nigerian Affairs* (1995). A leading expert on Islam in West Africa, he has written many articles, including "The Spread of Islam in Ilorin Emirate in the Nineteenth Century," in *History in* Africa (1981); "Religion and Politics in Colonial Nigeria: The Case of Ilorin," in *Journal of Religious History* (1990); "The Documentation of Ilorin," in *History in Africa* (1993); and "A Visionary of the Lagos Muslim Community: Mustapha Adamu Animashaun, 1885–1968," in *Lagos Historical Review* (2005).

JOSÉ JORGE DE CARVALHO is Professor of Anthropology at the University of Brasília. Formerly he was a visiting professor at Rice University, Rockefeller Scholar at the University of Florida, Gainesville, and Tinker Professor at the University of Wisconsin–Madison. He is author of *Shango Cults in Recife, Brazil* (with Rita Segato, 1992); *Cantos Sagrados do Xangô do Recife* (1993); *Mutus Liber: O Livro Mudo da Alquimia* (1995); *O Quilombo do Rio das Rãs* (1996); *Rumi: Poemas Místicos* (1996); *Os Melhores Poemas de Amor da Sabedoria Religiosa de Todos os Tempos* (2001); *Inclusão Etnica e racial no Brasil* (2005); *Las Culturas Afroamericanas en Iberoamérica* (2005); and *Yoruba Mythopoetics in Brazil* (forthcoming).

IKULOMI DJISOVI EASON (d. 2005) received his Ph.D. in American Culture Studies from Bowling Green State University, Ohio, where he was a professor of African Studies, director of the Educational Transformative Cultural Arts Program, and coordinator of the Dr. Babatunde Olatunji Drum Circle for World Peace. Specializing in Ifá/Fa traditions among the Yorùbá, Fon, and African Americans, he focused on diaspora religions, Ifá culture and festivals, Ilé-Ifè, Nigeria, and the Òyọ́túnjí African Village Project in Sheldon, South Carolina. Dr. Eason was a member of the Society for the Study of Black Religion, American Culture Studies Association, and Africana Faculty and Staff Caucus; a priest of Hevioso affiliated with the Òyọ́túnjí African Village and Ilé-Ifè, Nigeria's Egúngún Society, and Chief Atokun Eegun.

BARRY HALLEN is Professor of Philosophy and the chair of the Department of Philosophy and Religion at Morehouse College. He is a fellow of the W. E. B. Du Bois Institute for African and African American Research at Harvard University. His latest book, *African Philosophy: The Analytic Approach,* was published in 2006.

TRACEY E. HUCKS is Associate Professor of Religion at Haverford College. She is the author of several articles on the history of African-derived traditions in North America and the Caribbean. Her forthcoming book, *Approaching the African God,* examines the history of Yorùbá practice among African Americans in the United States. Her current research involves the study of African-derived traditions in the Republic of Trinidad and Tobago.

LAËNNEC HURBON holds a doctorate in sociology from the Sorbonne and a doctorate in theology from the Institut Catholique de Paris and is a graduate of l'Ecole des Hautes Etudes. He is the director of research at the Centre de Récherche Scientifique in Paris and a professor at Quisqueya University, Port-au-Prince, Haiti. He has published many books on the themes of religion, culture, and politics in Haiti and the Caribbean, including *Les mystères du Vaudou* (English ed., *Voodoo: Search for the Spirit,* 1993); *Pour une sociologie d'Haïti au XXIe siècle: La démocratie introuvable* (2001); *Religions et lien social: L'Eglise et l'Etat moderne en Haiti* (2004); and, most recently, *Voodoo* (2005).

FLORA *EDOUWAYE* S. KAPLAN is Professor Emerita in the Faculty of Arts and Science and the founding director of the graduate Museum Studies Program at New York University. She received a Ph.D. (cultural anthropology) from the Graduate Center of the City University of New York and a master's degree (archaeology) from Columbia University. A former Fulbright Professor (University of Benin, 1983–85), she publishes widely on Benin, religion, politics, and musology: *Museums and the Making of "Ourselves": The Role of Objects in National Identity* (1994) and *Queens, Queen Mothers, Priestesses, and Power: Case Studies in African Gender* (1998). *Benin Art and Culture* is forthcoming. His Royal Highness, Oba Erediauwa of Benin, in 1991, named her *Edouwaye* (meanings: "There is spiritual wealth in Benin," and "You have come home to Benin"); she was the first woman scholar honored with an equivalent Edo chieftaincy title.

J. LORAND MATORY (Ph.D., University of Chicago) is Professor of Anthropology and of African and African American Studies at Harvard University. His numerous works concern the cultural links between Africa and the Americas, as well as ethnic diversity in the black population of the United States. He studies Brazil, West African Yorùbá civilization, and Latin American religions rooted in Africa: Haitian "Vodou," Brazilian Candomblé, and Cuban Ocha, some of which have deeply penetrated U.S. urban landscapes. His work *Sex and the Empire That Is No More* (1994) concerns male wives and female husbands in Yorùbá religion and politics. His *Black Atlantic Religion: Tradition, Transnationalism, and Matriarchy in the Afro-Brazilian Candomblé* appeared in 2005 and won the Herskovits Award of the African Studies Association for the best book of the year.

JOSEPH M. MURPHY is a professor in the Theology Department at Georgetown University and teaches courses in comparative religion and religions of the African diaspora. He received his Ph.D. from Temple University and is the author of *Santería: An African Religion in America* (1988) and *Working the Spirit: Ceremonies of the African Diaspora* (1994). With Mei-Mei Sanford, he edited the volume *Òsun across the Waters: A Yorùbá Goddess in Africa and the Americas* (2001).

JACOB K. OLUPONA (Ph.D., Boston University) is Professor of African Religious Traditions at Harvard Divinity School and Professor of African American Studies in the Faculty of Arts and Sciences at Harvard University. He is the author of *Kingship, Religion, and Rituals in a Nigerian Community: A Phenomenological Study of the Ondo Yorùbá Festivals* (1991). His edited volumes include *African Spirituality: Forms, Meanings, and Expressions* (2000) and *Beyond Primitivism: Indigenous Religious Traditions and Modernity* (2004). He has organized conferences including "Beyond 'Primitivism': Indigenous Religious Traditions and Modernity" and "The Globalization of Yorùbá Religious Culture." In 2002, the University of Edinburgh, Scotland, awarded him an honorary Doctorate of Divinity.

ọLÁSOPÉ O. OYÈLÁRÀN received an A.B. in classics at Haverford College and a Ph.D. in linguistics at Stanford University. He is a visiting professor in the College of Arts and Sciences and the director of international studies in the Diether Haenicke Institute for Global Education, Western Michigan University, Kalamazoo, Michigan. He served as an associate professor in the Department of English and Foreign Languages and the director of the Office of International Programs at Winston-Salem State University, North Carolina. He established the Department of African Languages and Literature at the University of Ife, Ilé-Ifè (1975). In 1996 he was honored as Curator of the African American Arts and Culture for contributing to the National Black Theatre Festival. He is widely published.

JOHN PEMBERTON III is Crosby Professor of Religion, Emeritus, Amherst College. From 1970 to 1992 he pursued research on Yorùbá religion and art in Nigeria. Among his collaborative writings are *Yorùbá Sculpture of West Africa* (with William Fagg, 1982) and *Yorùbá: Nine Centuries of African Art and Thought* (with Henry J. Drewal and Rowland Abiodun, 1989). With Funso Afolayan he produced *Yorùbá Sacred Kingship: "A Power Like That of the Gods"* (1996). He edited the volume *Insight and Artistry in African Divination* (2000).

JOSÉ FLÁVIO PESSOA DE BARROS is Professor of Social Anthropology and the director of the Program for Religious Studies and Research at Universidade do Estado do Rio de Janeiro, Brazil. He has taught at Université de Paris and the University of Warsaw. In thirty years of researching Afro-Brazilian religions, Pessoa de Barros has authored dozens of articles and seven books, including *O Segredo das Folhas: Sistema de Classificação de Vegetais no Candomblé Jêje-Nagô do Brasil* (1993); *Uma introdução à música sacra afro-brasileira* (2002); *Na Minha Casa: Preces e Orações aos Orixás e Ancestrais* (2003); and *O Banquete do Rei: Olubajé* (2005).

REGINALDO PRANDI (Ph.D., sociology) is Professor of Sociology at the University of São Paulo, Brazil. Among his many publications on Afro-Brazilian religions are *Mitologia dos Orixás* (2000); *Encantaria Brasileira* (2001); *Os Príncipes do Destino* (2001); *Ifá, o Adivinho* (2002); *Xangô, o Trovão* (2003); *Minha Querida Assombração* (2004); *Oxumarê, o Arco-Íris* (2005); *Segredos Guardados: Orixás na Alma Brasileira* (2005); and *Morte nos Búzios* (2006).

TERRY REY (Ph.D., Temple University) is Associate Professor of Religion at Temple University. Formerly Professeur de Sociologie des Religions at l'Université d'Etat d'Haïti, he is author of *Our Lady of Class Struggle: The Cult of the Virgin Mary in Haiti* (1999), *Bourdieu on Religion* (2007), and numerous scholarly articles on religion in Haiti and the Congo.

MERCEDES CROS SANDOVAL is Professor Emerita of Social Sciences (Miami-Dade College) and an adjunct assistant professor of the Department of Psychiatry, School of Medicine (University of Miami). She has a doctorate in social sciences (University of Havana), a master's degree in anthropology (Florida State University), and a Ph.D. in cultural history of the Americas (University of Madrid), and is author of *La Religion Afrocubana* (1975), *Mariel and Cuban National Identity* (1985), and *Worldview, the Orichas and Santería: Africa to Cuba and Beyond* (2007).

RITA LAURA SEGATO received her Ph.D. from the Queen's University of Belfast. She is a professor in the Department of Anthropology, University of Brasília, and a researcher of the National Council of Scientific and Technological Research. Her books include *Shango Cult in Recife, Brazil* (1992, in collaboration with José Jorge de Carvalho); *Santos e Daimones: O Politeísmo Afro-*

Brasileiro e a Tradição Arquetipal (1995, 2005); *Las Estructuras Elementales de la Violencia: Ensayos sobre género entre la Antropología, el Psicoanálisis y los Derechos Humanos* (2003); and *La nación y sus otros: Raza, etnicidad y diversidad religiosa en tiempos de política de la identidad* (2006). She has also coedited *Religions in Transition: Mobility, Merging and Globalization in the Emergence of Contemporary Religious Adhesions* (2003) and has published several articles in Brazil and abroad on Afro-Brazilian religions, gender, and society.

REV. JUAN J. SOSA, M.Div. (1972), M.Th. (1973), M.A. (social science, 1981), is a Catholic priest in the Archdiocese of Miami. The pastor of St. Catherine of Siena Catholic Church, Fr. Sosa was the executive director of the Ministry of Worship and Spiritual Life for the archdiocese from 1984 to 2001; he is presently the chair of its Committee on Popular Piety. Since 1979 Fr. Sosa has been a senior lecturer at Miami's St. John Vianney College Seminary and St. Vincent de Paul Regional Seminary in Boynton Beach. Researching and reflecting on Santería for three decades, he has written *Sectas, cultos, y syncretismos* (1999) and many articles on Catholic worship, popular piety, and religious syncretisms.

WOLE SOYINKA received the Nobel Laureate in Literature in 1986. Soyinka studied at University College, Ibadan, and received his Ph.D. from the University of Leeds, England. As a playwright, poet, novelist, and social critic, he has produced many works including a lyrical satire showing that even with the end of colonialism, the celebration of Nigeria's independence in 1960 was no halcyon age: *A Dance of the Forests* (1963). During long periods in exile and prison for his criticism of the government, he risked his life advocating human rights and justice. He described two years of solitary confinement in *The Man Died: Prison Notes of Wole Soyinka* (1972). One of his most popular plays is *The Lion and the Jewel* (1963). His works include *The Open Sores of a Continent: A Personal Narrative of the Nigerian Crisis* (1996); *The Burden of Memory, the Muse of Forgiveness* (1999); and *You Must Set Forth at Dawn: A Memoir* (2006).

OLUFEMI TAIWO is the director of the Global African Studies Program and Professor of Philosophy and Global African Studies at Seattle University in Seattle, Washington. He was a Ford Foundation Visiting Postdoctoral Research and Teaching Fellow at the Carter G. Woodson Institute for Afro-American and African Studies, University of Virginia. He was Visiting Distinguished Minority Scholar, University of Wisconsin–Eau Claire, and a visiting professor at the Institut für Afrikastudien, Universität Bayreuth, Germany. He is the author of *Legal Naturalism: A Marxist Theory of Law* (1996).

MARTA MORENO VEGA (Ph.D., Temple University) is Adjunct Professor of Afro-Caribbean Religions and Afro-Latinos at Hunter College, City University of New York. An expert on Yorùbá belief systems of the African diaspora, she has organized conferences in Ilé-Ifè, Nigeria; Salvador de Bahia, Brazil; and New York City. She was initiated in Havana into La Regla de Ocha as an *omo Obàtálá,* and she is the author of *The Altar of My Soul: The Living Traditions of Santería* (2000) and *When the Spirits Dance Mambo: Growing Up Nuyorican in El Barrio* (2004). Dr. Moreno Vega is founder and president of the Caribbean Cultural Center African Diaspora Institute (CCCADI) and cofounder of the Global Afro Latino and Caribbean Initiative, a program of CCCADI and Hunter College. She is the executive producer of *When the Spirits Dance Mambo,* a documentary on African Cuban belief systems filmed in Cuba.

OLABIYI BABALOLA YAI is a professor of Yorùbá studies. He was the chair of the Department of African and Asian Languages and Literatures, University of Florida, Gainesville. He received his education with the elders of Ilé-Sabé, capital of the ancient Yorùbá Kingdom of Sabé, and at the Sorbonne. He has held teaching and research positions in various universities, including Ibadan, Ifè (Nigeria), Bahia (Brazil), and Kokugakuin (Japan), and has published on Yorùbá and Fon cultures. He is currently the ambassador of the Republic of Benin to the United Nations Educational, Scientific, and Cultural Organization (UNESCO).

Index

589